Adaptations of Shakespeare

D0073899

Shakespeare's plays have been adapted or rewritten in various, often surprising, ways since the seventeenth century. This groundbreaking anthology brings together twelve theatrical adaptations of Shakespeare's work from around the world and across the centuries. The plays include:

- *The Woman's Prize; or The Tamer Tamed* John Fletcher
- *The History of King Lear* Nahum Tate
- *King Stephen: A Dramatic Fragment* John Keats
- *The Public (El público)* Federico García Lorca
- *The Resistible Rise of Arturo Ui* Bertolt Brecht
- *uMabatha* Welcome Msomi
- *Measure for Measure* Charles Marowitz
- *Hamletmachine* Heiner Müller
- *Lear's Daughters* The Women's Theatre Group and Elaine Feinstein
- *Desdemona: A Play About a Handkerchief* Paula Vogel
- *This Island's Mine* Philip Osment
- *Harlem Duet* Djanet Sears

Each play is introduced by a concise, informative introduction with suggestions for further reading. The collection is prefaced by a detailed General Introduction, which offers an invaluable examination of issues related to theatrical adaptation and the rewriting of Shakespeare. The editors conclude with a section on further adaptations of interest.

Adaptations of Shakespeare is the essential guide to an increasingly important area of study.

Daniel Fischlin is Associate Professor in the School of Literatures and Performance Studies in English, University of Guelph, Canada. He is the author of *In Small Proportions: A Poetics of the English Ayre, 1596–1622* (Wayne State University Press: 1998). **Mark Fortier** is Associate Professor in the English Department at the University of Winnipeg, Canada. He is the author of *Theory/Theatre: An Introduction* (Routledge: 1997).

Adaptations of Shakespeare

A critical anthology of plays from the seventeenth century to the present

Edited by

Daniel Fischlin and Mark Fortier

 Routledge
Taylor & Francis Group

LONDON AND NEW YORK

First published 2000 by Routledge
2 Park Square, Milton Park, Abingdon, Oxon, OX14 4RN
Simultaneously published in the USA and Canada
by Routledge
270 Madison Ave, New York, NY 10016

Reprinted 2005, 2008 (twice) and 2009

Routledge is an imprint of the Taylor & Francis Group, an informa business

© 2000 Edited by Daniel Fischlin and Mark Fortier
Typeset in Veljovic by Keystroke Ltd, Jacaranda Lodge, Wolverhampton
Printed and bound in Great Britain by TJ International Ltd, Padstow, Cornwall

British Library Cataloguing in Publication Data
A catalogue record for this book is available from the British Library

Library of Congress Cataloging in Publication Data
Adaptations of Shakespeare : a critical anthology of plays from the seventeenth century
to the present / edited by Daniel Fischlin and Mark Fortier.
    p.   cm.
    Contents: The woman's prize, or, The tamer tamed / John Fletcher – The history of
King Lear / Nahum Tate – King Stephen / John Keats – The public / Federico García
Lorca – The resistible rise of Arturo Ui / Bertolt Brecht – Umabatha / Welcome Msomi
– Measure for measure / Charles Marowitz – Hameltmachine / Heiner Müller – Lear's
daughters / The Women's Theatre Group and Elaine Feinstein – Desdemona / Paula
Vogel – This island's mine / Philip Osment – Harlem duet / Djanet Sears.
    ISBN 0-415-19893-3 (hardback) – ISBN 0-415-19894-1 (pbk.)
    1. Shakespeare, William, 1564–1616—Adaptations. 2. English Drama—Adaptations. I.
Fischlin, Daniel. II. Fortier, Mark, 1953–
    PR2877.A33 2000
    808.82—dc21   99–054842

ISBN 10: 0-415-19893-3 (hbk)
ISBN 10: 0-415-19894-1 (pbk)
ISBN 13: 978-0-415-19893-6 (hbk)
ISBN 13: 978-0-415-19894-3 (pbk)

Contents

Acknowledgements

in memoriam, Jerry Rubio

We are indebted to numerous colleagues and friends who fed us with their knowledge, scepticism, and perspicacity over the years it took to assemble this anthology. Ian Sowton and Skip Shand were wonderful mentors during the prehistory of this book. Jerry Rubio provided a constant flow of Shakespeareana, from the popular press through to children's adaptations. Ann Wilson and Alan Filewod provided their respective expertise on feminist and African theatre. Ric Knowles was immensely helpful as we set about producing an extensive list of little-known as well as more familiar adaptations. Michael Keefer gave generously of his critical acumen in numerous exchanges. Martha J. Nandorfy lent her knowledge on Lorca, as did Nigel Dennis, Andrew Anderson, and Paul Julian Smith. Jennifer Ailles, who worked as an undergraduate research assistant on the project, was indispensable; her work on playlists, bibliographies, glosses, and sundry other items smoothed the many technical and conceptual difficulties this book presented. Harry Lane spotted a number of inconsistencies early on and helped shape the pedagogical framework, not to mention the many difficult decisions we had to make as we tried to stay true to what we originally imagined for the book. Talia Rodgers and Liz Brown have been diligent and helpful editors. Personal thanks go to Debra Miller for her careful and caring attendance on the project.

Thanks go, too, to the many students in Shakespeare classes we both have taught over the years – this book is in many ways a response to their (and our) attempts to address Shakespeare in the here and now of the classroom. And, it should be added, this book has come about because many of those students responded so positively to course work that took them out of the established canon of Shakespeare studies. The readers for Routledge, including Nigel Wheale, Barbara Hodgdon, and one reader who wished to remain anonymous, were extremely generous in their suggestions and, we hope, have helped make this the kind of book they thought worth producing. A production of *Hamletmachine* at the University College Playhouse, University of Toronto, in 1987, provided one of the first and strongest impetuses for this project. We wish to thank those who provided us with illustrations. Finally, to the living dramatists who generously contributed, or were willing to contribute, their work to what would have been an impossible project without their good will, we extend our most sincere appreciation. We hope that readers will come to this book and be struck by the ongoing importance of the theatre as a space for communicating and questioning the shapes we give our lives via the transformations and adaptations we all necessarily live.

General Introduction

As long as there have been plays by Shakespeare, there have been adaptations of those plays. For almost four hundred years, playwrights have been taking Shakespeare's works and remaking them, in an overwhelming variety of ways, for the stage. In fact, Shakespeare himself was an adapter, taking existing materials from various sources and crafting them into 'new' artistic creations. However, much of the long history of appreciating and thinking about Shakespeare has stressed his unsurpassed originality, the sanctity of his texts, and the cultural taboo on presuming to alter them. This view is, nevertheless, beginning to change. As critical theory has taken hold in academic institutions, students and scholars have become increasingly interested in such issues as text and source, text and context, authorship, originality, interpretation, and the production of meaning. These interests have allowed what has always been true to come into sharper focus: that Shakespeare's works have, from their inception, been both the product and the source of an ongoing explosion of re-creation. This book offers an introduction to the long history of theatrical adaptation of Shakespeare's plays for students and others interested in literary, cultural, and theatrical activity. It offers a sample of that history and illustrates the way in which the rewriting of Shakespeare can be seen as a key location for the exploration of culture and its transmission.

We have chosen works that adapt a spectrum of Shakespeare's genres and plays. There are adaptations of tragedy, comedy, history, romance, and problem plays. In terms of specific plays, the adaptations rewrite *The Taming of the Shrew*, *King Lear*, *Romeo and Juliet*, *Richard III*, *Measure for Measure*, *Hamlet*, *Othello*, *Macbeth*, and *The Tempest*. *Othello* and *King Lear* are represented in more than one adaptation. This is because these plays, along with *Hamlet*, *Macbeth*, *Romeo and Juliet* and *The Tempest*, are ones which, for whatever reasons (prominence, contemporary relevance, controversy, historical taste and circumstance, and so forth), have inspired a large number of adaptations.

We have also brought together plays with a range of approaches to adapting Shakespeare. Some wander from Shakespeare's genres while others adhere to the original models; some replace Shakespeare's language; others parody it; others stick close to it; some do all at once. These plays invoke very different stage conventions, from Renaissance and Restoration to the epic theatre of Brecht and the postmodernism of Müller (there is more on such terms in the introductions to specific plays). The cultural politics of these plays are varied (feminist; materialist/marxist; post-colonial; queer), and we have also sought to include representative writers: male, female, gay, straight, white, and of colour. The writers here also represent six countries (Britain, Spain, Germany, the United States, Canada, and South Africa) on three continents (Europe, North America, and Africa).

We have included a broad historical chronology of works, from Shakespeare's own time to the present. The first play, John Fletcher's *The Woman's Prize*, a sequel to *The Taming of the Shrew*, comes from one of Shakespeare's contemporaries – indeed, from one of his collaborators – and from a time when artistic borrowing was unimpeded by copyright law or constraining notions of authorship. The next play, Nahum Tate's *History of King Lear*, is a Restoration adaptation, Shakespeare 'made fit' as Sandra Clark's recent anthology has it. The Restoration was an early highpoint in the adaptation of Shakespeare, a period in which modifying Shakespeare's language, story, and staging became commonplace, in which, paradoxically, respect was shown for Shakespeare precisely by rewriting him. The nineteenth century is represented by

1

John Keats's *King Stephen*, a moment when a major poet attempts to follow in the footsteps of Shakespeare. The first half of the twentieth century is represented here by the work of two modernist giants, Federico García Lorca's *The Public*, an adaptation of *Romeo and Juliet*, and Bertolt Brecht's *The Resistible Rise of Arturo Ui*, an adaptation of *Richard III*. Here we see the very different kinds of liberties that a modernist aesthetic allows playwrights to take with Shakespeare's work. The twentieth century, especially its second half, has been, like the Restoration, a highpoint in the theatrical adaptation of Shakespeare, and the majority of the plays in this anthology are from this period: Heiner Müller's poetic, postmodern, and caustic *Hamletmachine*; Charles Marowitz's rendition of *Measure for Measure* as oppressive nightmare; the collective feminist adaptation *Lear's Daughters*; Welcome Msomi's colourful and ritualized *uMabatha*, an African adaptation of *Macbeth*; Paula Vogel's lewd and surprising *Desdemona*, an adaptation of *Othello*; Philip Osment's *This Island's Mine*, which brings the colonial history of *The Tempest* back to contemporary, post-colonial, gay Britain; Djanet Sears's *Harlem Duet*, which tells the story of Othello in historical and contemporary black New York. These plays feature a dizzying arsenal of approaches to adapting Shakespeare.

For each play in the anthology we have provided an introduction and a select bibliography, with a small number of particularly accessible titles asterisked (*). Each introduction includes basic biographical information, performance history, a discussion of the adaptation's striking qualities as well as its relationship to the play which it adapts. Lists of characters have been provided when appropriate and informative. In the case of *The Woman's Prize*, where the language is less accessible to the contemporary reader, we have included a basic glossary of early modern terms.

This is an anthology of *theatrical* adaptations of Shakespeare, of play texts intended (with the possible exception of Keats's *King Stephen*) to be mounted on stage. This focus has meant, first off, that a wide range of adaptations in other media has been excluded. There are no prose narrative adaptations, poems, works of fine art, comic books, opera libretti, or film scripts. The cultural adaptation of Shakespeare takes place in all these media, and theatrical adaptation must be seen as part of this bigger picture. We have, however, chosen to introduce one field more carefully than many fields haphazardly. Moreover, as theatrical adaptations, these plays are meant not just to be words on the page but to be performed. To understand these works, therefore, demands an engagement with the realities of theatre and performance and the way in which these affect specifically theatrical modes of meaning and interpretation (see, for example, Carlson 1996). Nevertheless, we have sought out play texts that are interesting on the page as well as on the stage. All of the plays are, we hope, accessible, if not without controversy, to non-specialist readers.

Consideration of the plays collected here raises many questions about adaptation. In the remainder of this introduction, we set out some of the key ideas in the current intellectual and artistic understanding of the concept of adaptation. In the first section, 'Towards a Theory of Theatrical Adaptation,' we position adaptation in the theoretical discussion of cultural re-creation, exploring such ideas as intertextuality, cultural politics, canon formation, the relations between literature and theatre, and the interplay between artistic activity and its critique. Next, in the section entitled 'Virtual Shakespeares,' we explore the complex place of Shakespeare in cultural creation: as an adapter, as an international tradition, and as an industry with interests in many different media. In this way, we hope to equip readers with the ideas necessary to place adaptations of Shakespeare in the fullest possible cultural context. We hope to reveal the limitations of a naive belief in an ahistorical and unalterable Shakespeare, and to guide readers to a fuller appreciation of the plays we have gathered together.

1 Towards a theory of theatrical adaptation

> Perhaps the desire to write is the desire to launch things that come back to you as much as possible in as many forms as possible. That is, it is the desire to perfect a program or a matrix having the greatest potential, variability, undecidability, plurivocality, et cetera, so that each time something returns it will be as different as possible.
>
> (Derrida 1985: 157–158)

The problem of naming

Adaptation is not the right name for the work represented in this anthology, because there is no right name. There are only labels with more or less currency, connection to history, and connotations both helpful and misleading. Critic Laura Rosenthal notes that in the eighteenth century plays that reworked pieces by Shakespeare were called 'alterations' or 'imitations' (323); in a current electronic Shakespeare discussion group they are called 'spinoffs'; Denis Salter, writing of contemporary foreign-language works, borrows fellow critic Michel Garneau's term 'tradaptations' (1996a: 123). Each term is suggestive and captures an aspect of the field; none, however, is wide enough to be a general label. The eighteenth-century terms are historically limited; 'spinoff' connotes Hollywood movies and network television in a way misleading in cases less oriented to the mass media; 'tradaptation' implies a change from one language to another.

In her classic book on reworkings of Shakespeare, *Modern Shakespeare Offshoots*, Ruby Cohn provides an alphabetical list of labels, from 'abridgement' to 'version,' but settles on the umbrella term 'offshoot,' with subcategories 'reduction/emendation,' 'adaptation,' and 'transformation' (3–4). 'Offshoot,' she writes, is 'a looser and more neutral word,' but undercuts this idea by adding 'I should like to indicate how far the shoots grow from the Shakespearean stem.' This hardly seems to valorize mere offshoots. Thus her foreword begins: 'It is easy to predict a conclusion to this book: Shakespeare offshoots are not Shakespeare. Or, a little less tersely, no modern Shakespeare offshoot has improved upon the original' (vii). Must this necessarily be true? What would we call a play which, by whatever judgement, did succeed in bettering the Shakespearean original? What do we call Shakespeare's plays themselves? Is his *Henry V* an offshoot of its anonymous source, *The Famous Victories*? As an offshoot has it not improved upon the original? If we think outside the distortion caused by the high regard in which our culture has held Shakespeare's plays, it becomes clear there is no necessary relation of value between original and adaptation. Johann Wolfgang Goethe's *Faust* is not necessarily inferior to prior treatments of the story, for example.

While 'offshoot' is loaded with limiting value-laden connotations, Cohn's categorizations are ultimately untenable. 'Reduction/emendation' includes any production in which lines are cut and words altered, making almost any production of any play a reduction/emendation. Cohn's primary concern is with what she calls 'adaptation' and 'transformation.' Adaptation, in her terminology, is limited to plays that include 'substantial cuts of scenes, speeches, and speech assignments; much alteration of language; and at least one and usually several important (or scene-length) additions.' She adds, '*Additions* are crucial in distinguishing reduction/emendation from adaptation.' Transformation is characterized by 'invention': 'characters are often simplified or trundled through new events, with the [original] ending scrapped' (3–4). These distinctions, however, are undone by a work such as Charles Marowitz's *Measure for Measure*. Marowitz uses no lines not in Shakespeare's original and proceeds solely by cutting, rearranging, and reassigning. There are none of the additions crucial to Cohn's category of adaptation. Nonetheless, the characters are simplified, trundled through new events, and the original ending is scrapped. If anything, what we have here is, by Cohn's definitions, a reduction/transformation and it becomes apparent that any attempt to classify the possibilities of rewriting too narrowly will run up against many such anomalies.

A current label for the type of play in this anthology might be 'appropriation.' This word suggests a hostile takeover, a seizure of authority over the original in a way that appeals to contemporary sensibilities steeped in a politicized understanding of culture. It is not certain that this label does justice to other, more respectful, aspects of the practice we are examining. Moreover, appropriation can take place without altering the original in itself – a sonnet quoted in full on a Valentine's Day card, for instance. As such, appropriation is not the idea we need.

For lack of a better term, therefore, we fall back on adaptation. But adaptation has some unfortunate insinuations. In as much as it echoes natural adaptation and a residual myth of progress, the word adaptation implies that adaptations are better than originals, which is no more tenable as a general principle than its opposite would be. On the other hand, adaptation comes from a Latin word meaning to fit to a new context, and recontextualization is an important aspect of the process that leads, for instance, to rewrites of *Othello* by black writers and women writers. Adaptation implies a process rather than a beginning or an end, and as ongoing objects of adaptation all Shakespeare's plays remain in process. Finally, to fall back on adaptation as the working label is to take advantage of its general currency. It is the word in most common usage and therefore capable of minimizing confusion. Adaptation is the term used, for instance, by Laura Rosenthal in her discussion of eighteenth-century plays. Similarly, Sandra Clark's recent edition of Restoration plays based on Shakespeare is subtitled 'Restoration Adaptations.' Even a neologism like 'tradaptations' depends for its effect upon the general currency of adaptation as a label.

What does adaptation imply, however unsatisfactorily, in this context? Adaptation as a concept can expand or contract. Writ large, adaptation includes almost any act of alteration performed upon specific cultural works of the past and dovetails with a general process of cultural re-creation. More narrowly, its focus in this anthology is on works which, through verbal and theatrical devices, radically alter the shape and significance of another work so as to invoke that work and yet be different from it – so that any adaptation is, and is not, Shakespeare.

Adaptation and contemporary cultural theory

Although Shakespeare himself produced theatrical adaptations and despite his place at the centre of the canon of English literature, theatrical adaptation has remained a relatively marginalized and under-theorized activity. When it has been the object of consideration, it has often been judged and understood in opposition to a criterion of 'originality' – often, paradoxically, to the assumed originality of Shakespeare. Moreover, adaptation has been found lacking in 'fidelity' to the original work of whichever canonical figure is being adapted. Critical understanding, in these instances, remains bound by the concept of authorship, supported by such notions as originality in creation and fidelity in interpretation, in other words by what scholars Martha Woodmansee and Peter Jaszi call, in the context of copyright law, 'the continuing power of [the] misrepresentation of a collaborative process as a solitary, originary one' (4).

Such a set of values is at work in film critic Richard Schickel's 1985 appraisal in *Time* magazine of Akira Kurasawa's *Ran*, a cinematic adaptation of *King Lear*. Schickel writes: 'Indeed in *Ran* . . . we venture into a territory where the very word adaptation distorts and diminishes both intention and accomplishment' (quoted in Rosenthal: 335). As Rosenthal comments on this passage: 'The reviewer recognizes that to call it an adaptation diminishes it, for in a culture of literary property, originality becomes a primary value in art' (335). In other words, if *Ran* is an adaptation, it cannot be the masterpiece we take it to be.

The idea of originality, however, posits an independence where none exists – or where only a limited invention is possible. Shakespeare in his own work was not original in the way these judgements seem to presume. Any number of contemporary theoretical concepts are concerned with the activity of reworking already-existing cultural material; in fact, such concepts imply that reworking material is to some extent the only kind of cultural activity there is. From such a perspective, originality and fidelity become largely spurious ideas. Theatrical adaptation can be retheorized as a specific form of the cultural reworking taken to be basic to cultural production in general.

The concept of intertextuality, for example, developed in France by Roland Barthes and Julia Kristeva, suggests that all writing, like all cultural production, is an interweaving of already-existing cultural material. In myriad ways, we draw upon what has come before us and exists around us in anything we create. Barthes writes: 'any text is an intertext; other texts are present in it . . . the texts of the previous and surrounding culture . . . Intertextuality [is] the condition of any text whatsoever.' Other cultural texts are present not only as acknowledged sources or influences but also as 'a general field of anonymous formulae whose origin can scarcely ever be located; of unconscious or automatic quotations' (1981: 39). Intertextuality implies that all creation is social creation, all production always reproduction: everything we think, say, or do relies upon ideas, words, and cultural norms that pre-exist us. This links to Antoine Compagnon's theory of citation. According to Compagnon, citation, which may at first seem only 'a peripheral characteristic of reading and writing,' when liberated from its 'narrow definition associated with quotation marks,' takes up its place at the heart of a theory of reading, writing, and textuality (11–12, our translation). 'All enunciation is repetition,' and, 'We do nothing but gloss each other.' Put another way, all writing is second-hand.

Intertextuality and citation suggest a generalized borrowing and rewriting of existing cultural material, more or less explicit, deliberate, or conscious, as the origin and limit of cultural activity. Seen in this light, a work of adaptation such as Heiner Müller's *Hamletmachine*, centred on Shakespeare's *Hamlet* yet quoting from a wide variety of other cultural material, is not a marginal and valueless exercise. Such an adaptation is, rather, an act touching on the very nature of cultural production as a remaking of existing material. If it is particularly striking, it is only because it is so rich in its borrowing.

Contemporary theory provides a related perspective when it looks not at the borrowing that happens in the creation of new works but at what happens to such works once they have been written. French philosopher Jacques Derrida, for example, sees 'iterability' or 'recontextualization' as the inevitable condition of texts in history. By this he means that every act of writing, of meaning, all motivated human endeavour, loses its original context, which cannot entirely enclose it, and plays itself out in a potential infinity of new contexts, in which the significance of the writing will inevitably be different – again and again – from what it was (see Derrida 1988). When we recontextualize, we inevitably rework and alter, even if we are trying to be faithful to our sense of the original. Reception and reader-response theories also stress how the meaning of texts from the past is changed by their appearance in new conditions. In this light, critic Graham Holderness writes, 'Shakespeare is, here, now, always, what is currently being made of him' (xvi).

In this theorization of the making and remaking of cultural work, certain activities directly concerned with rewriting and recontextualization have entered into renewed theoretical prominence. Translation and parody, for example, have been subject to extensive reconsideration. The understanding of translation moves from that of a faithful transformation of an original work to the processing, with inevitable critical differences, of a source text that is itself already a rewriting of prior cultural material (Steiner 1992: xii; Lefevere: 222; Hermans 14, 11). Theorist Linda Hutcheon rejects the narrow definition of parody, that it is reworking done 'with comic effect' (20), and argues for a more open 'repetition with critical difference' (25). Parody moves from a somewhat marginal and specific practice to one almost without limits. Adaptation, like translation and parody, is part of a generalized cultural activity that posits reworking in new contexts as more characteristic of cultural development than are originality in creation and fidelity in interpretation.

This might lead one to conclude, with Derrida, that 'the desire to write is the desire to launch things that come back to you as much as possible in as many forms as possible.' The problem is that cultural forces stand in the way of such a desire. Foremost are notions attached to the author and authorship: proprietary, moral, and restrictive legal rights over texts, intentions, and interpretations. For French historian Michel Foucault (in 'What Is an Author?') the author is not a person but 'a certain functional principle by which, in our culture, one limits, excludes, and chooses' (1979: 159). The principle of the author allows only a limited set of acceptable works and ideas to flourish: 'great books' by 'great authors' flourish; anonymous or collective writing or works by those considered inconsequential are ignored. The 'author-function' is a historically specific development, which changes over time in as much as 'The modes of circulation, valorization, attribution, and appropriation of discourses vary with each culture and are modified within each' (158). Foucault foresees a world in which the author-function will disappear, although he sees it replaced by another as yet unformulated 'system of constraint' (160). Roland Barthes, on the other hand, argues that the death of the author liberates practices and options of remaking available to the reader (Barthes 1988: 143) and the adapter.

The politics of adaptation

Contemporary theory often employs a strategic or political understanding of culture. Works of culture are seen to engage with all the broad political concerns of the world at large: race, empire, gender, economics, and so forth. In this light, adaptation is understandable in the same terms André Lefevere applies to rewriting and recontextualization in general: 'Works of literature exist to be made use of in one way or another' (217), and, 'Rewriting, then, in all its forms, can be seen as a weapon in the struggle for supremacy between various ideologies, various poetics. It should be analyzed and studied that way' (234). Furthermore, a theory of adaptation, like a theory of translation, turns to a 'functional view' of cultural and political practice: 'all translation implies a degree of manipulation of the source text for a certain purpose' (Hermans 1983: 11). Adaptations, therefore, often attempt to recontextualize Shakespeare politically. Philip Osment, for instance, repositions *The Tempest* in relation to current post-colonial concerns, while *Lear's Daughters*, by the Women's Theatre Group and Elaine Feinstein, and Paula Vogel's *Desdemona* reconfigure the gender politics of Shakespearean tragedy – the latter by rejecting the role of 'faithful wife,' which makes Desdemona, under patriarchy, a spotless and sympathetic victim.

Any cultural work, including any theatrical adaptation, has to be studied in its specifics to see how political issues play out within, and are

5

affected by, that work. Moreover, any work of culture has a history in which its political import is repeatedly transformed. *Hamletmachine*, for instance, has gone from being a banned work questioning socialism from within in the former East Germany to the North American aestheticism of Robert Wilson to return to Germany after the fall of the Eastern Bloc as part of a seven-and-a-half-hour *Hamlet* in which 'Fortinbras, wearing a business suit and a gold mask, a star warrior of capitalism, takes over' (Höfele 1992: 84–85). Context is crucial when we study the political significance of art.

To understand the cultural politics of adaptation, we must also examine how adaptation takes place within a certain structured relationship to such institutional (and politically significant) notions as the author and the canon, a broadly accepted group of works that is a consensual (though not uncontested) site of foregrounded study within the academy. Adaptation is not a simple rejection of these notions, but rather an ongoing engagement with them. French philosopher Gilles Deleuze, in his discussion of the Italian director Carmelo Bene's radical, avant-garde adaptation of *Richard III*, notes that Bene's adaptation does everything possible to disrupt and do away with Shakespeare's status as major author in a major literature, fragmenting and distorting plot, character, language, and gesture beyond recognition. For Deleuze and Bene, the major author is the despotic ego, the man of the state, the king, the ruling 'majority.' To disrupt the work of the major author is, therefore, to disrupt the basis of the state and its rulers. There are reasons to be skeptical of such claims. According to Lefevere, in all forms of rewriting the author is decentered and enters into play with rewriters (220): Shakespeare the major author becomes one agent among others. Sometimes, however, those who adapt Shakespeare admire the original, are interested in a kind of collaboration with Shakespeare, or make use of Shakespeare's status to authorize their own work. John Keats in *King Stephen*, for instance, approaches Shakespeare with less than a hostile or subversive attitude. The author, it was noted earlier, is a restrictive principle at odds with rewriting and adaptation, but this is not the whole story. Shakespeare is adapted in large part simply because he is a major author, and if the author function were completely dead it would likely mean the end of the kind of rewriting anthologized in this book. Thus, as in translation, parody, and citation, rather than the rejection of the author function, there is

ambivalent support for it, or an attempt to reinscribe it otherwise.

In literary, dramatic, and other cultural spheres, the struggle for new directions is often fought out over the canon. The practices of rewriting that we have examined take up a complex and ambivalent relation to the canon, as they do to the question of the author. Once again, adapters of Shakespeare undertake a number of responses to Shakespeare's canonical status: some seek to supplant or overthrow; others borrow from Shakespeare's status to give resonance to their own efforts. If adaptations of Shakespeare somehow reinforce Shakespeare's position in the canon, however, it is a different Shakespeare that is at work; and if Philip Osment and Paula Vogel have their names inscribed alongside or over the name of Shakespeare, the canon, like 'Shakespeare,' becomes something different from what it was.

How these relations play themselves out can only be observed in the details of history. Rosenthal observes that when Shakespeare used already-written texts to compose his own, he had no concern for attribution; 'For Shakespeare, the story of Lear had no particular owner or specific textual origin,' while for those who have since adapted Shakespeare, 'Writing King Lear has necessarily become an engagement with Shakespeare' (324–325). After the Restoration in 1660, Shakespeare was given a moral, if not a legal, claim to proprietary originality, although Restoration adapters routinely replaced Shakespeare's texts with their own versions. To show the complexities in our own era, when the American Repertory Theatre attempted to adapt Samuel Beckett's *Endgame*, they ran up against a living author's legal power to invoke copyright law in such a way as to prohibit the work of adaptation (Rabkin: 142–159). Long dead, Shakespeare lies outside copyright protection, but a moral right is still invoked by conservative critics on his behalf. Thus the Toronto *Globe & Mail*, in an editorial condemning what it characterized as 'Troilus and Cressida in spacesuits,' concluded, 'If you tried it on a modern playwright he'd sue your pants off' (D6). But the editorial writer can only rage in vain, because, ironically, it is the adapter who is now protected by copyright, free to do whatever he or she desires to Shakespeare's plays. This means adapters can withhold permission to produce or republish their adaptations and can, if they wish, fall back on their legal status as authors and prohibit adaptations of their adaptations.

Analyzing a specific form of rewriting, Linda Hutcheon sees at the heart of parody a paradox:

'The dual drives of conservative and revolutionary forces that are inherent in its nature as authorized transgression' (26). Therefore 'parody can be a revolutionary position; the point is that it *need* not be' (75). The same is true of adaptation. The task of a careful reader is to see exactly how an adaptation functions in any particular situation, and what effects it has or may have on the literary politics of author and canon, as well as on larger social and political questions.

Literature and theatre

The focus of this introduction and anthology is not just adaptation but theatrical adaptation. However, working across media and genres is an important part of the big picture of borrowing and recontextualizing. Furthermore, it is nothing new but rather the ongoing development of a history that includes Shakespeare's own adaptations from poetry, fiction, and history-writing, as well as from works of theatre.

Within the limits of theatrical adaptation, a degree of emphasis is due to the drama text: much of the work of adaptation is done by rewriting or rearranging the words of previous texts. However, they remain texts for the stage. Nahum Tate's *King Lear* first came to life on a Restoration stage markedly different from the early modern varieties available to Shakespeare himself. A text such as Lorca's *The Public* is a striking verbal creation; yet, it is a play text open to a wide range of styles of staging, each of which will produce a very different version of the play. Finally, in the work of the French Canadian Robert Lepage, adaptation works not so much by rewriting Shakespeare's language – the verbal text of his *Elsinore* is little more than a heavily edited version of *Hamlet* – but by radical acts of technological restaging, allowing, for example, Lepage to alter his voice electronically so that he can perform all the characters in the play. To understand the process of adaptation in these cases it is necessary to see it as often largely, sometimes solely, a theatrical practice.

The theories we have been discussing open up to include theatrical and nonverbal aspects of cultural renewal. For instance, intertextuality and citation need not be limited to verbal activity. Kristeva defines intertextuality as follows: 'The term . . . denotes this transposition of one (or several) sign systems into another . . . every signifying practice is a field of transpositions of various signifying systems' (59–60). The Indo-American theorist Gayatri Chakravorty Spivak defines textuality as a 'network of politics–history–society–sexuality' (121). Theatrical adaptation is an intertextual apparatus, a system of relations and citations not only between verbal texts, but between singing and speaking bodies, lights, sounds, movements, and all other cultural elements at work in theatrical production.

Given the complexity that recontextualization brings into play, it is not surprising to read critic James Bulman writing of 'the radical contingency of performance – the unpredictable, often playful intersection of history, material conditions, social contexts, and reception that destabilizes Shakespeare and makes theatrical meaning a participatory act' (1). In the same volume Laurie Osborne writes: 'The productions of Shakespeare's plays reveal the flaw in imagining a fixed and immutable canon of his work, since every presentation . . . represents a version of the play, not the play itself' (170). The complexity of theatrical recontextualization is recognized by theorist Susan Bassnett-McGuire in her discussion of translation and theatre:

> the written text is one code, one system in a complex set of codes that interact together in performance. The translator therefore has to work on a text that is, as Anne Ubersfeld defines it, *troué*, not complete in itself. And in creating a text for performance in the TL [target language], the translator necessarily encounters an entirely different set of constraints in terms of TL conventions of stage production.
>
> (1983: 94)

In this context, every drama text is an incomplete entity that must be 'translated' by being put on stage. Adaptation is, therefore, only an extreme version of the reworking that takes place in any theatrical production. Theatre does things to the drama text that cannot be justified as acts of fidelity, and yet are necessary for any production to take place. For example, Isabella's reaction to the Duke's two proposals at the end of *Measure for Measure* must be staged in some way, although the text itself gives no indication as to what this reaction should be. Theatre is always a form of reworking, in a sense the first step toward adaptation.

Theatrical production also complicates notions of the author. Not only are there relations between the first writer and the adapter but between those who put words on the page and all others involved in a theatrical event. Theatre theorist Gerald Rabkin traces the plural 'authorship' of the theatrical performance: from author to director to performer to audience and critics: 'we have in theatre two sets of readers – the theatre artists who traditionally "read," interpret, the written text, and the audience who read the new theatrical text' (159). In *Hamletmachine* there is a moment when the picture of the author is ripped in half. Is this author Shakespeare? Is it Müller? Or is it any force which attempts to exert singular control over cultural production?

Adaptation, interpretation, and critique

At the beginning of this section, theatrical adaptation was labelled a 'genre,' an activity distinct enough to be taken as a specific mode of cultural labour. Within specific adaptations, adapters from Tate to Marowitz have altered the generic conventions and outcomes of Shakespeare's plays. The generic overlapping in theatrical adaptation can, however, be even more complicated. Ann-Marie MacDonald's theatrical adaptation of two Shakespearean tragedies, *Goodnight Desdemona*, was originally labelled 'a comical Shakespearean romance,' indicating the complex genrebending this adaptation involved. MacDonald employs Shakespearean comic devices of mistaken identity and cross-dressing to open a new space of possibility and sexuality for her female characters. Ultimately, the play moves beyond comedy to embrace romance, Shakespeare's late genre, with its interest in redemption and reconciliation, between the play's women characters and between MacDonald and Shakespeare.

A common generic mixing that goes on in theatrical adaptation in an especially marked way is the interplay between creation and criticism. Every act of interpretation, every theatrical production implies a critical reading, but adaptation features a specific and explicit form of criticism: a marked change from Shakespeare's original cannot help but indicate a critical difference. In addition, adaptation can also meld with theory. Sometimes the theoretical side of adaptation is more implicit than explicit, and there is no need to think that the work of adapters is always or often informed by the theoretical concerns we have been raising. But sometimes they are. Charles Marowitz brings to his plays extensive discussion of his critical relationship to Shakespeare. Carmelo Bene's *Richard III* is coupled in publication with Gilles Deleuze's theoretical analysis of the play, so that theatre and theory

work as 'superimpositions,' the one upon the other, to create a new double vision. Herbert Blau's *Elsinore* is called 'an Analytic scenario.' The plays anthologized here, therefore, are not just objects for critical and theoretical understanding but works that imply, undertake, or inform criticism and theory.

2 *Virtual Shakespeares*

> The story goes that, before or after [Shakespeare] died, he found himself before God and he said: 'I, who have been so many men in vain, want to be one man: myself.' The voice of God replied from a whirlwind: 'Neither am I one self; I dreamed the world as you dreamed your work, my Shakespeare, and among the shapes of my dream are you, who, like me, are many persons – and none.'
>
> (Borges 1964: 47)

Source and adaptation

Looming over a literary landscape dotted with lesser icons is Shakespeare, whom the South American writer Jorge Luis Borges in the above epigraph imagines in conversation with God. In Borges's story, Shakespeare laments his Godlike status as both 'many' and 'none.' The passage mythifies and consolidates Shakespeare's elevated status in the canon. But the Borges passage also points to a fundamental paradox at the heart of this anthology's examination of subsequent adaptations of Shakespearean 'originals.' Shakespeare's exalted canonical status is a function of his unique creative abilities as a writer, but this status derives from his ability to assimilate the texts of many others into his work. Adaptation is central to Shakespeare's work and to his continuing cultural presence: Shakespeare adapted source texts and now his 'adaptations' are adapted in an enormous range of cultural contexts.

Shakespeare, for better or for worse, has long been what Lawrence Levine calls a 'cultural deity' (Levine 1988: 53), one of the privileged sites around which Western culture has struggled to authenticate and sustain itself. Evidence of this struggle is as much to be found in critical studies that attribute to Shakespeare the invention of 'poetic subjectivity' or, more egregiously, the 'human' (see, for instance, Joel Fineman and Harold Bloom) as it is to be found in the astonishing range of performance and textual contexts affiliated with the Shakespeare effect. In the United States, on the occasion of the three-hundredth anniversary of Shakespeare's death in 1916, 'a ten-day run of an extravaganza entitled *Caliban by the Yellow Sands*, written by the poet Percy MacKaye, and performed by a cast of over 1,500 actors, singers, and dancers' attracted an enormous audience of 135,000 people (Levine: 80). By the end of the century, a survey of 'the most influential figures of the past 1,000 years' had Shakespeare ranked alongside Karl Marx as number four on the list of 'the chosen 100,' sandwiched among the likes of Einstein, Luther, Newton, Hitler, and Columbus (Alaton: D1).

The critic Barbara Hodgdon asserts that 'what "Shakespeare," and especially performed Shakespeare, is now caught up in is an attempt to incorporate the global array that forms the imaginative landscape of contemporary cultural life and includes crossings, graftings, and modes of articulation between high- and low-culture media as well as among nations' (190). More than a figure of literary history or a cultural obsession, Shakespeare defies any attempt at easy definition as cultural practice, embodiment of a national literary tradition, or sign of the ultimate form of literary achievement. Rather, Shakespeare, perhaps one of the most inventive and prolific of literary and theatrical adapters himself, has become a complex network of discursive, cultural, and historical practices, not all necessarily literary. These practices are associated, negotiated, and mediated by Shakespeare's virtual cultural presence, whether as literary figure or as sublime touchstone against which cultural identity is measured, however problematically.

Conventionally situated at the epicentre of the English literary tradition and viewed as an 'original genius,' Shakespeare's writing practice was based on borrowing from earlier materials. As critic and editor Gary Taylor succinctly puts it in a discussion of the debate over the supposedly original nature of Shakespeare's genius, 'Shakespeare, of course, was as guilty of theft . . . as any author . . . Shakespeare stole with a clear conscience. He copied plots, characters, speeches, images, and aphorisms from classical authors and from his own contemporaries, without acknowledgment' (140–141; see also J. M. Robertson 1909, rpt. 1969: 290–291). A brief survey of Shakespeare's plays in various genres reveals the degree to which they echo, invoke, or comment on source material. *Hamlet*, for instance, has close connections to Thomas Kyd's *The Spanish Tragedy* and to a lost play known as the *Ur-Hamlet*, 'written either by Kyd or by an imitator of Kyd' (Bullough, vol. 7: 16); *Othello* derives from

Cinthio's *Gli Hecatommithi* (1566), a framed series of tales like Boccaccio's *Decameron* (itself a source for the Posthumus–Imogen plot in *Cymbeline*), with another probable source being Richard Knolles's *The General Historie of the Turkes* (1603); *The Comedy of Errors* is based on Plautus's *Menaechmi* and lines from John Gower's *Confessio Amantis*; and Shakespeare's so-called Roman plays, *Julius Caesar*, *Antony and Cleopatra*, and *Coriolanus*, though derived primarily from Plutarch's *The Lives of the Noble Grecians and Romanes*, translated by Sir Thomas North (1579), also show evidence of a wide range of influences. Despite this, Taylor notes that in the eighteenth century 'The proprietorial concept of authorial copyright, the criminalization of literary expropriation, the entrepreneurial cult of originality – all were harnessed, like so much else, to the bandwagon of Shakespeare's reputation' (1989: 141).

Taylor leaves out the crucial information that Shakespeare's borrowings were typical of Renaissance compositional practice, which was based on a mastery of imitation: 'One learned to write by imitating the "best" authors, that is the most admired classical writers' (Martindale 1994: 10, 12). Geoffrey Bullough asserts, in the preface to his multi-volume *Narrative and Dramatic Sources of Shakespeare*, that 'Without a knowledge of the material available to him neither his debts nor the transcendent scope of his creative energy can be assessed' (vol. 1: xii). The range and depth of source appropriations gathered by Bullough are staggering, and denote the degree to which Shakespeare's own texts were thoroughly implicated in a long tradition of Western writing practices. The anthology is arranged by categories: direct source, analogue, translation, possible source, and probable source. Scholars other than Bullough have produced a variety of books that examine various sources in different genres for Shakespearean drama. These sources include classical Greek and Latin authors, such as Seneca, Ovid, and Plutarch (see, among others, Bate, Jepsen, Lynch, Miola [1992], Shackford, Skeat, and Spencer); English authors such as Chaucer, Holinshed, and Spenser (see Donaldson, Potts, and Thompson); continental influences such as Montaigne (see Coffin); and forms of plot motif and popular tales (see Scragg).

While Ovid, Plutarch, and Holinshed seem crucial to understanding Shakespeare's relations with antecedent literary practices, Russ McDonald argues that it is essential 'to expand our definition of *source*, to look beyond the indisputable originals of the plays into less obviously influential books and especially into non-canonical forms of writing such as pamphlets and ballads' (101). We must, for instance, consider the contexts of Elizabethan and Jacobean popular culture.

The notion of authorial originality and authenticity, so clearly at stake in discussions of Shakespeare, compels an examination of what it means to have a relation with a source text, and poses the question of what precisely constitutes a source. Robert Miola argues that

> The variety of substitutes for 'source' in our current critical lexicon suggests this range of possibilities: deep source, resource, influence, confluence, tradition, heritage, origin, antecedent, precursor, background, milieu, subtext, context, intertext, affinity, analogue. The word 'source' can now signify a multitude of possible relations with a text, ranging from direct contact to indirect absorption.
>
> (1992: 7; see also Miola 1988)

Whether the source materials are manipulated by an author to achieve a specific outcome, or whether the source texts have a generic quality that produces particular results, the point remains that sources lead to adaptation, that is, to (inter)textual choices that produce new narrative and performative effects. Moreover, it is worth remembering that the term 'source' itself is potentially misleading insofar as it is thought to refer to (or to imply) an authentic point of origin. In using source materials, Shakespeare frequently relied on translations, or even on translations of translations, as well as on historical sources, like Holinshed, or on sources themselves derived from other source materials. Any attempt to peg the 'source' as authentic or original needs to be carefully evaluated when thinking through Shakespeare's use of a particular text as a springboard for his texts (or indeed when thinking of the use of Shakespeare as a source by adapters of his plays).

An analysis of source materials allows readers to achieve no small degree of insight into Shakespeare's own adaptive writing practices. For instance, readers aware that the Pyramus and Thisbe episode from *A Midsummer Night's Dream* is based on the Arthur Golding translation (1567) of Ovid's *Metamorphoses*, will realize that Shakespeare derived some of the comic energy for the scene from the bathetic lines that describe Pyramus's suicide in the source: 'The blood did spin on hie / As when a Conduite pipe is crackt,

the water bursting out / Doth shote itselfe a great way off and pierce the Ayre about' (Bullough, vol. 1: 407). Similarly, the characterization of Macbeth as a tragic figure held in the throes of the malevolent energies of the Weird Sisters and of Lady Macbeth, gains its energy directly from Raphael Holinshed's description, in *The Chronicles of England, Scotland, and Ireland* (1577), of Macbeth's motivations: 'The woords of the three weird sisters also (of whom before ye haue heard) greatlie incouraged him herevnto [the crown], but speciallie his wife lay sore vpon him to attempt the thing, as she that was verie ambitious, burning in vnquenchable desire to beare the name of a queene' (Boswell-Stone: 25). In both cases, adaptation of a source produces both obvious and more nuanced effects, whether allowing for the hint of parody in *A Midsummer Night's Dream* or describing the complex relations among the desire for power, erotic appetite, and the influence of women in *Macbeth*.

In some cases, what the source text clearly leaves out, becomes an opportunity for adaptation, in the form of an active insertion that dramatically refigures the source. A striking example of this occurs in Shakespeare's version of *Coriolanus*. In Thomas North's translation, Coriolanus, now in exile from Rome, encounters his arch-rival Tullus Aufidius in Antium and makes a speech saying he will join with Aufidius to defeat Rome. The North version of the scene ends with Tullus, 'a marvelous glad man . . . taking [Coriolanus] by the hand' and welcoming him, 'entertain[ing] him in the honorablest manner he could, talking with him in no other matters at that present: but within a fewe dayes after, they fell to consultation together, in what sorte they should beginne their warres [against Rome]' (Plutarch: 203).

Shakespeare rewrites the source text, converting a fairly neutral scene that reconciles enemies into a charged depiction of homoerotic passion and sensuality. Aufidius, after the speech made by Coriolanus, states, in the Shakespeare version: 'Know thou first, / I lov'd the maid I married; never man / Sigh'd truer breath; but that I see thee here, / Thou noble thing, more dances my rapt heart / Than when I first my wedded mistress saw / Bestride my threshold' (4.5.113–118; all Shakespeare quotations are from Evans's *The Riverside Shakespeare*). The fifth scene of Shakespeare's fourth act of Coriolanus is riddled with erotic language ('We have been down together in my sleep, / Unbuckling helms, fisting each other's throat, / And wak'd half-dead with nothing'). One of Aufidius's servingmen observes that 'Here's a strange alteration!' (4.5.148), as if to draw attention not only to the change in relations between the two men (from antagonists to lovers), but also to Shakespeare's emphatic alteration of the source text itself. Here, the adaptation of the 'original' produces a novel scene that ends with the cynical observation that peace 'makes men hate one another' (4.5.230), as if to suggest that war breeds homoerotic love. In this case, Shakespeare's adaptation of a source text does not involve imitation, though it does depend on the 'picturing' of a possibility implicit in the original. Adaptations of Shakespeare which examine the possible lives of Shakespeare's minor characters, for example, function in the same way.

One point here is that Shakespeare's intervention in the story of Coriolanus is no passive act of interpretation, but rather has material consequences that are highly suggestive for those involved in staging Shakespeare's version. Textual alteration of a source has significance for how the material bodies of actors playing these roles address the issues implicit in the changes made by Shakespeare.

Shakespeare, nation, difference

Some years ago, Allardyce Nicoll, speaking on the importance of Shakespeare in the English national imaginary, proclaimed Shakespeare a 'figure so colossal that he forms a kind of touchstone to any particular period, and we could almost write a history of English thought from 1623 to 1921 by studying alone the attitude displayed towards him by succeeding poets and critics' (6). There is a disturbing truth to Nicoll's observation, if only for the way it puts into play what is at stake in subsequent adaptations of Shakespearean texts in English culture. In this view, which is most emphatically not the only view, Shakespeare is the ultimate guarantor of greatness and aesthetic value, the backdrop against which 'English thought' is diffused through his intertextual influence on subsequent writers. Critic Michael Dobson suggests that 'Shakespeare has been as normatively constitutive of British national identity as the drinking of afternoon tea' (7). Since that national identity is so clearly linked with colonial and imperial imperatives, Shakespeare functions as a relay by which an essential Englishness is disseminated. Shakespeare, as a sign of imperial culture, is instrumental in glossing over cultural difference, even as his use in colonial contexts paradoxically promotes a recognition that there are differences to be glossed over.

Adaptation as a stage and textual practice, then, is tied to the business of producing nation.

National identity is a function of the production of cultural homogeneity in the name of difference: those of a nationality think of themselves as being like each other and different from everyone else. Shakespearean adaptation produces a similar structure insofar as it relies on the consensual acceptance of Shakespeare as a guarantor of cultural value (an author who adapts Shakespeare participates in the aura of 'greatness' associated with Shakespearean creation), even as the adapter produces changes to the Shakespearean source as a way of asserting an independent authorial identity. And authorial identity can be significantly linked to the creation and sustenance of national identity. Theatre theorist Martin Esslin argues, for example, that 'In many Eastern European countries . . . the national literature, and therefore national consciousness itself, had crystallized around translations of Shakespeare. Only after a language had passed the test of being able to accommodate the form and content of the greatest drama (and Shakespeare is seen as that) could it lay claim, in the eyes of the people concerned, to be regarded as a vehicle for the highest flights of thought and poetic expression' (xii).

Adaptation, like the vexed issue of translation discussed earlier in this introduction, is one such form of accommodation that leads to authoritative national self-expression. In relation to English national self-interest, particularly evident in colonial and post-colonial discourses,

> The Shakespeare 'industry' – as it impacts on the educational systems, the critical discourses, and the theatrical culture of a society – often operates in ways that sustain ideas, values, and even epistemologies which are foreign to the receivers and therefore of limited relevance, except in maintaining the interests of imperialism.
> (Gilbert and Tompkins 1996: 19)

(For Shakespeare and post-colonialism, see also Cartelli 1999 and Loomba and Orkin.) But other national traditions have laid claim to Shakespeare in the name of their own cultural difference, in order to bolster identity formations that gain from the authority of his name. Ron Engle, for instance, argues that 'Shakespeare is a German tradition and no respectable theatre company in Germany would go more than a season without mounting a new Shakespeare production' (93; see also Williams, Hortmann and Hamburger, and Guntner and McLean). The Polish critic Andrzej Zurowski, in a similar mode, writes that 'The Polish people talk through Shakespeare about their own politics, history, power structures, jobs, orders, and disorders. . . . His plays have been the mirror of our times; and through them we have seen the artistic, but not simply artistic, transformation of our history' (169–170). Not only does Shakespeare mirror Polish national history, in this startling proposition, he transforms it through the very act of being appropriated to a Polish context.

As concerns South Africa, Martin Orkin writes that

> Shakespeare has been primarily appropriated by most amongst the English-speaking educated members of the ruling classes as a means of evidencing their affiliations with the imperial and colonial centres. Possession and knowledge of Shakespeare texts become evidence of empower-ment, enabling these members of the ruling classes to construct themselves as both affiliates of the metropolis and as superior to the subordinate classes. . . . Shakespeare has thus become for members of the educated ruling classes one signifier of 'civilisation,' astoundingly that is, it should never be forgotten, in South Africa one signifier for white apartheid 'civilisation.' The web of such a use of Shakespeare spins not only through institutions of education, the media, establishment theatre, public cultural bodies, but even into the thinking of some of the country's large conglomerates of capital.
>
> (1991: 235)

David Johnson's discussion of Shakespeare and apartheid in the South Africa of the 1950s affirms that Shakespeare is 'an emblem of English culture, symbolizing a contradictory cluster of values that, on the one hand, purport to be entirely opposed to apartheid, and, on the other, fit quite comfortably within the apartheid education system' (173). For Johnson 'The challenge then is to resist the reflex of installing the products of Western cultural projects – including the 'radical Shakespeare' [associated with European and American materialist criticism] – as *automatically* having the same political meaning and resonance in neo-colonial contexts' (185). What is progressive in Europe is not necessarily progressive elsewhere.

The availability of Shakespeare for a variety of political positionings always makes the incursion of Shakespeare into a cultural space such as that of South Africa a problem, even when Shakespeare is figured as sympathetic to the politics of freedom from oppression. Johnson's argument hints at

Shakespeare as always already complicit with forces that do not value cultural difference, thus making even radical Shakespeare potentially complicit with, in this case, neo-colonialism. Such a position can lead to contradictory positionings, as it does in the case of South African Bloke Modisane's autobiography, *Blame Me on History*, which uses 'the words of Shakespeare's characters in order to explain his own psychological processes, and especially in order to justify his often angry responses to the injustices he sees around him' (175–176). For Johnson, Modisane sees 'Shakespeare as a possession of the West,' which he nonetheless appropriates 'in order to explain the violent world of Sophiatown to his readers' (176). Despite his seeming complicity, in other words, Shakespeare has his highly ambivalent uses in articulating resistance and difference. Clearly, complicity with oppression is part of the way in which Shakespeare has been adapted to colonial and neo-colonial contexts. But such complicity is never necessarily the whole story, as Modisane's example hints. Simplistic assumptions about the place of Shakespeare in relation to cultures of resistance or complicity are to be avoided, if only because they reproduce the reductive hegemonies (cultural practices and beliefs that dominate in any particular society) they are seeking to overturn or sustain.

A striking example of this cultural dissonance embodied in the interpretative struggle to open up Shakespeare occurred in the 1980s, when American anthropologist Laura Bohannan left Oxford for a field trip to West Africa. An English friend gave her a copy of *Hamlet* saying 'You Americans . . . often have difficulty with Shakespeare. He was, after all, a very English poet, and one can easily misinterpret the universal by understanding the particular' (Bohannan: 86). On the one hand, *Hamlet* will be, in Bohannan's understanding, a reminder of her own colonial relation to English culture, and, on the other, a talisman of Western culture, to ward off the sense of cultural isolation she is sure to experience in a remote part of Africa. When asked by the elders of the tribe to tell the story of Hamlet, which she does hesitantly, expecting the cultural gaps to be too wide for the story to translate, let alone be understood, Bohannan begins:

> 'Not yesterday, not yesterday, but long ago, a thing occurred. One night three men were keeping watch outside the homestead of the great chief, when suddenly they saw the former chief approach them.'

'Why was he no longer their chief?'

'He was dead,' I explained. 'That is why they were troubled and afraid when they saw him.'

'Impossible,' began one of the elders, handing his pipe on to his neighbor, who interrupted, 'Of course it wasn't the dead chief. It was an omen sent by a witch. Go on.'

(1988: 88)

Bohannan concludes her attempt at storytelling, in which she is interrupted numerous times by the elders who see she doesn't really understand the story, with one of the elders telling her 'That was a very good story and you told it with very few mistakes. . . . Sometime . . . you must tell us some more stories of your country. We, who are elders, will instruct you in their true meaning, so that when you return to your own land your elders will see that you have not been sitting in the bush, but among those who know things and who have taught you wisdom' (95). The story is a handy parable that inverts stereotypes about the transmission of cultural narratives from supposedly civilized culture to a primitive culture that is anything but.

In the Indian colonial context, Gauri Viswanathan argues that Shakespeare and other canonical figures from English literature were used to supplant a native tradition because 'Indian defects of character could be traced to ancient Indian literature' (87). The moral imperative aligned with the colonial mission required that such defects be undone through exposure to the salutary values embodied in canonical English literature. For critic Harish Trivedi 'Shakespeare's status, popularity and dissemination in the post-colonial India of today, nearly half a century after Independence, is determined to a large extent by a nonliterary factor, just as it was in colonial India. Then it was Empire; now it is ELT (English Language Teaching), or the hegemony of English as the pre-eminent international language' (20). In this view, Shakespeare's literariness is at the service of other agendas having to do with globalization and the linguistic imperialism of English.

Critic Jyotsna Singh, in a discussion of Shakespeare and the civilizing mission of British imperial culture, notes that the interculturalism with which Shakespeare is associated in India leads to a process in which 'native cultural forms often undergo a complex process of *transculturation*' (148). Singh argues that on the 'Indian stage, multi-lingual hybrid Shakespearean productions have consistently countered the

univocal authority of the colonial book' thus 'enabl[ing] native directors to re-discover indigenous cultural forms via the revered Shakespearean canon.' Even as the Shakespeare effect becomes an instrument of colonial hegemony, it also facilitates a form of transcultural exchange that produces a new literary and performative hybrid.

Nor are such hybrids uncontested sites of cultural harmony, as Suresh Awasthi shows in an analysis of an adaptation of *King Lear* to the Indian performance tradition of *kathakali*. *Kathakali* is an epic, classical dance form of 'strictly non-verbal theatre' based on the 'practice of *monodharma*, or intuitive improvisation' using playscripts whose performance depends on a process of 'elaboration and embellishment' (172–173). The *kathakali* tradition excludes many theatrical conventions common to Western audiences, including rehearsals, organized companies, and the use of words by the actors (the singing of the text is accomplished by two reciters). Awasthi calls *kathakali* a 'theatre of performance text' (175), which depends for its reception upon an audience that has received an 'aesthetic initiation' (176) into the form. The attempt, by an international co-production involving the Australian playwright–director David McRuvie and the French actress–dancer Annette Leday, to adapt *King Lear* to the highly evolved formal traditions of *kathakali* failed, in Awasthi's terms, because the cultural specificity of the form prohibited assimilating an unfamiliar text like *King Lear* into an Indian context. As Awasthi explains, performance traditions are so powerful in *kathakali* that 'performers are no more interested in telling new stories than the spectators in going to a performance to see them: they go to see how familiar stories will be told and performed . . . . And this familiarity of initiated spectators with the performance conventions, signs, and codes generates communication with the performers' (177).

The ostensible failure of the westernized *kathakali* production takes its place in a long line of similar hybrid theatrical experiments that were far from satisfying in 'forms like Noh, Kabuki, and the Peking Opera.' Awasthi does not exclude the possibility of success in such intercultural experiments, arguing that success depends 'upon a creative utilization and merger of two performance cultures' such as that found in B. V. Karanth's production of *Macbeth*, which used a 'new Hindi verse translation' as well as 'stylized movements by the actors and costumes inspired by Indian and Indonesian traditions' (178). But it must be remembered that what Awasthi sees as a failure represents only one side of the ongoing critical debate about the experiment. Theatre scholar Phillip Zarrilli concludes that 'Kathakali King Lear was an intercultural project that did not impose meaning. With its collaborative process of creation and its respect for the kathakali aesthetic, it "allow[ed] meaning to arise from the material"' (36). If part of the meaning of intercultural juxtapositions is to expose the tension 'between a simplified Western narrative played in a fully codified theatrical and choreographic reelaboration of that narrative' (36), then adaptation serves a particularly useful function in representing difference as a tradeoff between the exotic and the familiar.

Moreover, Shakespearean adaptations in inter- and transcultural contexts point to differences that even the weight of Shakespearean authority cannot necessarily overcome. In some theatrical and cultural traditions such authority remains meaningless when understood in light of a performance tradition with particular aesthetic demands and deep-rooted historical conventions and expectations. Adaptations that attempt to penetrate such traditional forms of theatre as kathakali through the notion that Shakespeare is always 'other,' always open and appropriatable to all forms of cultural difference, merely repeat the vexed notion of Shakespeare's universality while reminding us that such a universality is as much a cultural construction as anything. Intercultural adaptations destabilize any reductive notion of Shakespeare's ability to transcend difference.

Critic Hsiao Yang Zhang states, with regard to Shakespeare and Chinese theatre, that 'The interaction between Shakespeare and traditional Chinese drama reflects the nature of the exchange between Western and Asian theater in the twentieth century and forms a substantial part of the tendency towards the interculturalism of the postmodern theater' (14; on Shakespeare in relation to Eastern culture see also Pronko, Kim, Bradshaw and Kishi, Sasayama et al., Brown). For Zhang, not only does 'realism-oriented Western theater [show] an interest in the "distancing sense" and stylized techniques of Asian theater, while the nonrealistic Far Eastern theater tries to imitate the naturalistic dramatic techniques of Western theater,' but the 'interaction between Shakespeare and Chinese culture . . . represents in microcosm the relationship between Western and Chinese cultures' (14). According to Zhang, 'from Shakespeare's plays the Chinese see the

celebration of individuality, the awakening of self-consciousness and competitive individualism, a moral principle against obscurantism, and the concepts of freedom, equality, and universal love . . . all of these qualities function as the basic ideology and values for a prosperous bourgeois society or a democratic industrialized country' (242). Shakespeare, in this critical view, is an emblem of freedom and humanism in the face of a totalitarian state addressing the pressures to democratize.

This reading of Shakespeare reminds us that the reception of Shakespeare, and the very contexts that produce culturally specific readings of Shakespeare, are adaptations – structures that make Shakespeare 'fit' a particular ideology, culture, historical moment, and so forth. A Western materialist critic reading Zhang's sense of Shakespeare as a proponent of freedom and universal love might well have trouble reconciling such a view to his or her own sense of Shakespeare's complicity with hegemonic state structures. This is the case with critic Terence Hawkes's sense of Hamlet as a play that 'becomes part of a means of first formulating and then validating important power relationships' (4). Validation is precisely what occured when the American Secretary of State George Schultz proclaimed, 'in respect to America's policy towards Nicaragua, that America will not become "the Hamlet of nations,"' meaning that the US foreign policy will not become 'a character who (with fatal consequences) "could not make up his mind"' (Cartelli: 99). Such a reading confirms Hawkes's materialist analysis of Hamlet as serving to reinforce relationships of power that weaken notions of social justice and democratic government. Or, as is the case with Michael Bristol, a Western critic may find in Zhang's reading a confirmation of ideologies linked with Western democratic values. Bristol's reading of Hamlet, for instance, argues that 'Hamlet struggles towards an important historical revision of the experience of self in terms of critical self-reflection, deliberative competence, and a strong sense of political vocation that will be fundamental for the possibility of modern liberal democracy' (1996: 224).

Our point here is that Shakespeare, as he is adapted in particular readings, is used to produce vastly different ideological positions. And adaptation, whether as a function of reading reception, theatrical reinscription, or pop-cultural transmission, appropriates Shakespeare's culturally dominant position to perform a wide range of contradictory ideological functions. Li notes as much in an evaluation of Chinese Shakespearean reception:

> Shakespeare's plays were the best choice for Chinese intellectuals since they could be accepted by both parties – the authorities and the artists. Shakespeare happened to be one of the favorite writers of both Marx and Engels, and their quotations are often cited in critical articles in China to justify his image as a giant of the humanistic Renaissance outlook. His special status explains why even during the Cultural Revolution, when Shakespeare was banned together with other foreign writers, nobody dared use him as a specific target for attack. The fact that there is no explicit political message in his plays has lent them the quality of neutrality which can accept light of any color and then be transformed.
>
> (1995: 75)

A good example of adaptation in the service of American nationalism occurs in Charlotte Barnes's *The Forest Princess; or, Two Centuries Ago*, premiered in 1844 in Liverpool, then in 1848 in Philadelphia. The play adapts to an American context, via the story of Pocahontas and her friendship with Captain John Smith in the early days of the Virginia colony, Shakespeare's *The Tempest*. In so doing, Barnes creates a sentimentalized notion of American national identity by imagining Pocahontas as a symbolic bridge between native and colonial cultures, thus linking Shakespeare *and* American indigenous culture (Loeffelholz: 59). In her analysis of the filiations between *The Tempest* and *The Forest Princess*, Mary Loeffelholz argues that Barnes was writing at a time

> when Shakespeare as an ideological property was undergoing a complex conversion in the United States – from pre-Revolutionary Tory to something like an American national romantic. . . . In Barnes's rewriting of *The Tempest*, the characters of Shakespeare's play and the contemporary figure of the vanishing American Indian collaborate in the expression of American post-Revolutionary 'national character.'
>
> (1990: 58–59)

Barnes, according to Loeffelholz, 'revises *The Tempest* from a point of view that is both nationalistic and Anglocentric, so that *The Forest Princess* uses the story of Pocahontas and the

subtext of *The Tempest* to ratify the central and abiding importance of English culture for American nationalism' (70).

In adapting Shakespeare's New World play to the demands of nineteenth-century American colonial imperatives, and in doing so in a way that uniquely empowers a female character, Barnes's play demonstrates the power of the symbolic capital, the commodity that is (and was) Shakespeare, as she shaped that capital to her own uses. Shakepearean adaptation in this instance reconciles, however illusorily, the anomalies of what Benedict Anderson has called 'imagined communities,' whether native, English, or American. Whatever those seemingly (and strategically) fixed categories may ultimately mean, Barnes addresses a world absurd enough to produce a statute that stated 'persons who have one-sixteenth or less of the blood of the American Indian and have now other non-Caucasic [sic] blood shall be deemed to be white persons,' a part of the Virginia Code which sought 'to recognize as an integral and honored part of the white race the descendants of John Rolfe and Pocahontas' (cited by Loeffelholz: 73).

The reconciliatory work of the Virginia Code is implicit in Barnes, with Shakespeare as the lynch-pin on which racial interbreeding becomes permissible for the sake of building a coherent national identity that is racially 'white.' Not surprisingly, the fear of what miscegenation could mean to civil culture had already been prefigured in *The Tempest* at the crucial point where Caliban speaks of 'peopl[ing] . . . / This isle with Calibans' through the (potentially) nation-building gesture of raping Miranda (1.2.344–351). In Barnes, the violence of that gesture is subsumed in the courtly romance of Pocahontas's and John Rolfe's marriage. Their union reinforces the myth of a symbolic, mutual consent between opposed powers, even as it obliterates the memory of the 'Trail of Tears,' the 'mass forced removals of American Indians from the eastern United States [that] had begun in the 1830s [enshrined in the law of the land by the Indian Removal Bill of 1830] and were still proceeding, against the few remaining southeastern pockets of Indian settlement, in the 1840s' (Loeffelholz: 59).

Here the work of Shakespearean adaptation shapes the way in which literary culture participates in the construction of a seemingly palatable (commodifiable) narrative that is also a form of sentimental, historical amnesia. Shakespeare, in this context, becomes the nexus for an American identity formation that seeks to reconcile American civil and literary culture with the barbarity of its colonial practices. Shakespeare's presence guarantees that Shakespearean and American notions of value, authority, and ultimately power are solidly aligned, *virtually* coincident with each other (for further discussion of Shakespeare in relation to America, see, among others, Burt, Bristol 1990, Dunn, and Levine).

To return full circle to Britain, it is not accidental that, at a time when England is experiencing an intensification of the effects of multi- and transcultural influence, there is a concerted effort to restore the original site of Shakespeare's Globe to its former, authentic glory. The gesture, however unintentional, addresses the degree to which Shakespeare's canonical power is in alignment with a coherent national imaginary, a bulwark against the invasive otherness threatening to undermine the very Englishness he represents. Not all subscribe to such a project. Critic Nigel Wheale's 'Introduction' to a book on the changing use of Shakespeare in the British curriculum observes that

> The appeal to canonical texts which will revive the nation through the power of their language is an ignorant fundamentalism. While competing nationalisms re-emerge in our period as a consequence of the collapse of 'superpower' hegemonies, the British Isles must also carefully define their identity, and the educational curriculum plays a crucial role here. Shakespeare is not now just a quaint icon of Englishness, but a world text.
>
> (1991: 26)

In this view, the Shakespearean 'world text,' which in our understanding includes all the various forms of Shakespearean adaptation, suggests the limitations of the British nationalism traditionally associated with Shakespeare. Even as Shakespeare is used to produce coherent visions of national, ideological, and cultural affiliation, the vulnerability of such visions to forces of change is exposed by the way Shakespeare is inevitably altered by new circumstances.

Commodification and the Shakespearean sublime

Here, in the rewriting of Shakespeare around the world, is the Shakespeare myth at work, the virtual Shakespeare: a colossus, within whom all history congeals and against whom the imaginary essence of a nation, its 'thought,' is to be

measured. Thus, 'virtual Shakespeare,' as we intend it, has an etymological link to the Latin *virtus*, suggestive of masculine strength, courage, moral worth, power, efficacy and to the Italian derivative *virtuoso*, meaning someone with exceptional skills, merits, talents. Virtual, too, as linked with 'virtue,' especially in relation to the latter's usage in Shakespeare to signify, among others, 'moral goodness,' 'power, efficacy,' and 'the very substance, essence' (see Schmidt, vol. 2: 1320–1321). But virtual also implies, in its contemporary sense, a form of illusive presence, a recognition that the 'real' or the 'original' is transformed by the media that determine the shapeshifting forms of all cultural making.

The Shakespeare industry, all those elements of economic and cultural production that support and profit from traffic in virtual Shakespeares, has a powerful investment in Shakespeare's continuing presence, itself a function of methodologies of recuperation, authenticity, reproduction, and, perhaps least evidently, adaptation. Shakespeare as a cultural phenomenon is equally at home as an image on British bank cards (smiling benignly in hologram at the monetary practices of late capitalism) and on grunge T-shirts or Charlie the Tuna commercials as on the main stage of classical repertory companies. Following Marx, Richard Halpern states that the 'value of a commodity is the amount of labor expended to produce it; this is the commodity's invisible, "spiritual" being' (12). In this formulation, the value of the Shakespearean commodity comes of a presence that graces, by association, the cultural artefacts produced in Shakespeare's wake. A Shakespearean commodity, therefore, carries not only its inherent value as a work in its own right but also the value significantly redoubled through association with the massive expenditure of energy and labour in the name of the Shakespeare biz.

The Shakespeare industry and its adaptations have a long history in many media. Beginning with theatre, the significance of radical adaptive practices related to Shakespeare has been noted by Jean I. Marsden, who, in a brief synopsis of Restoration and eighteenth-century adaptations of Shakespeare, sets the context in hyperbolic terms:

> The Restoration and eighteenth century produced one of the most subversive acts in literary history – the rewriting and restructuring of Shakespeare's plays. We have all heard of Nahum Tate's 'audacious' adaptation of *King Lear* with its resoundingly happy ending, but Tate was only one

of a score of playwrights who adapted Shakespeare's plays. Between 1660 and 1777, more than fifty adaptations appeared in print and on the stage, works in which playwrights augmented, substantially cut, or completely rewrote the original plays. The plays were staged with new scenes, new endings, and, underlying all this novelty, new words.

(1995: 1)

Marsden goes on to note the 'conservative politics of most of the adaptations, where instability becomes an ideological evil' (15), thus making the point that even radical revisions have often served to perpetuate a notion of theatrical stability with which the Shakespearean text is frequently wholly incompatible. That incompatibility is a function of numerous factors – the editorial problems that arise from Shakespeare's indifference to the publication of his plays; the difficulties of interpreting texts as dense and playful as Shakespeare's; the loss with time of performance practices that were so different from our own; and so forth.

Interestingly, no matter what the degree to which an adaptation attempts to remain faithful to the original, it is always in some sense a distortion of its source. More recent playwrights, for instance, have written alternative plots or intercut the staging of a Shakespeare play with another plot. They have also written texts that precede or follow the Shakespearean source: Djanet Sears's blues version of Othello, *Harlem Duet*, shows Othello with a first wife and serves as a prelude to Shakespeare's *Othello*. Shakespearean adaptation in this mode is not about faithful adherence to the narrative or performative conventions of traditional Shakespeare, but about the degree to which the playwright can transform that material and reshape conventions in such a way as to expose the orthodoxies that support the tradition. When successful, such a reshaping puts the enormous cultural power of Shakespeare to work in a way that undermines the way in which that power conventionally operates.

Adaptation as a material, performance practice can involve both radical rewritings, and a range of directorial and theatrical practices, from the omission or addition of passages (or even scenes) to suit a particular director's requirements to the creation of a material practice that takes into account the public demand for spectacle, one that places Shakespeare in direct competition with the rock concert, sporting event, or cinematic blockbuster. The notion of adaptation (from the

Latin *adaptare*, to fit, to make suitable) implies a way of making Shakespeare fit a particular historical moment or social requirement. One of the other ways in which Shakespeare is made fit is through criticism, itself a form of adaptive undertaking by virtue of its intertextual dependence on a source text. A related area that concerns adaptive practice has to do with how editorial practices that seek to stabilize or destabilize texts literally adapt Shakespeare, making him conform to a particular editorial vision.

If Shakespeare can be associated with the explicit techniques of colonization exerted upon cultural difference, he can also be associated with the processes by which those in the West (let us not forget, also the product of powerful colonial forces) internalize the lessons of identity. Shakespeare's reception, his role in teaching from early childhood on, reinforces his own sublime status in the act of establishing shared values while consolidating the very means by which those values are disseminated.

In the primary education system at Hamlet Public School in Stratford, Ontario, for instance, bardolatry serves a specific function related to instruction in conventional reading practices. Teacher Lois Burdett, recipient of numerous awards and subsidies from the Bank of Montreal and Petro Canada, uses adaptations such as her *Twelfth Night for Kids*, the first instalment in a series entitled 'Shakespeare Can Be Fun!', co-authored with Christine Coburn, to introduce children to Shakespeare and Shakespearean intepretative practices. The series title suggests that Shakespeare can be painful and difficult and thus in need of redemption by adapters (who in this case are pedagogues intent on finding the 'fun' in Shakespeare), while also assuming that Shakespeare for kids is necessarily a good thing. Reviewer Philippa Sheppard points to the trouble she has with 'the attempt to keep everything bright and cheerful for the sake of her youthful readership' (54). Such a reading strategy has direct precedents in Charles and Mary Lamb's *Tales from Shakespeare*, as well as in Henrietta Maria Bowdler's *The Family Shakespeare*, both published in 1807. The adaptive strategies deployed in these works involved transforming the Shakespearean original to 'make Shakespeare safe for young women, by removing from his works anything to which a young woman should not be exposed' (Taylor: 207). A good example of this occurs in the Lambs' opening to *A Midsummer Night's Dream*, whose plot is premised, in the original, on Egeus's legal right to have his daughter, Hermia, put to death for her failure to marry the man of his choice. In the Shakespearean original no context is provided that might allow us to come to grips with this law, thus adding considerably to the contrast between the play's comic proceedings and the absurd and cruel patriarchal formations that underlie those proceedings. The Lambs, in contrast, add a qualification: 'but as fathers do not often desire the death of their own daughters, even though they do happen to prove a little refractory, this law was seldom or never put in execution, though perhaps the ladies of that city were not unfrequently threatened by their parents with the terror of it' (19). Even as the Lambs soften and explain this opaque and harsh Shakespearean element, the death threat remains as a useful tool in controlling daughters' behaviour.

Sustaining good cheer among children or reinforcing domestic, moral values, regardless of the content of the texts to which they are exposed, produces a certain kind of reader and political subject, one shielded by the veneer of good cheer or moral purity from the realities of the human condition. Shakespeare here serves as protection from the possibility of reading the world in terms of its less-than-ideal circumstances. Or, as Charles Marowitz puts the problem, in typically blunt fashion:

> I have to confess that some of the most contemptible people I have ever known have loved Shakespeare, and I have found them very hard to take. It is like sharing your bed with bigots, junkies and bores. For many of them, Shakespeare was a confirmation of their world-view. The Christian Universe was memorialised in his work and, from his sentiments, they would easily justify their bourgeois smugness, their conventionality and their pompous morality. For them, it was as if Shakespeare wrote only so that they could quote his aphorisms on their calendars.
>
> (1991: 17)

Shakespeare has provided the cultural capital for a wide range of adaptive practices, from operatic rewrites by nineteenth-century composers such as Verdi, to a gamut of cinema: film versions of Shakespeare's plays, such as Kenneth Branagh's Tsarist *Hamlet* and Ian McKellen's totalitarian *Richard III*, or a series of versions of *Romeo and Juliet* redone to suit the style and sensibility of new generations of consumers; films of theatrical adaptations of Shakespeare, such as Stoppard's *Rosencrantz and Guildenstern Are Dead*; new

adaptations for film, such as the recent adaptation of *The Taming of the Shrew, 10 Things I Hate about You* (on visual Shakespeares, see Davies and Wells, Kennedy 1996, Boose and Burt, Burt, and Anderegg). Pop-culture adaptations are not necessarily unsophisticated creations. Neil Gaiman's graphic novel version of *The Tempest*, for instance, attributes Shakespeare's uncanny ability with story and language to a Faustian deal made with Dream. In the final frame, Dream states that 'I am Prince of stories, Will; but I have no stories of my own. Nor shall I ever' (Gaiman and Vess 1996: 36). Gaiman's pop-culture version of Shakespeare understands perfectly well that narratives like *The Tempest* are an amalgam of multiple sources. For instance, Shakespeare, in Gaiman's version, states that 'I took the inspiration for it [*The Tempest*] from the wreck of the Sea-Venture in the Bermudas last year. The story is merely the sort of fairy story all parents tell to amuse their children. . . . There is some of *me* in it. Some of Judith. Things I saw. Things I thought. I stole a speech from one of Montaigne's essays, and closed with an unequivocally cheap and happy ending' (35).

The Gaiman text troubles Shakespeare's narrative authenticity while deploying a sophisticated understanding of how to receive Shakespearean narrative. But it does so by also pointing to Shakespeare's own adaptive processes ('I stole a speech') as a conflation of multiple source texts (shipwrecks, fairy tales told by parents, Montaigne's essays, and so forth) and authorial inspiration. Gaiman's reading of Shakespearean authenticity is quite different from Leon Garfield's, who in the introduction to an illustrated abridgement of *The Tempest* that was also shown on HBO (Home Box Office) as an animated film for children in the series *Shakespeare: The Animated Tales*, states that, apart from 'the account of a shipwreck on the island of Bermuda . . . [*The Tempest*] owes little to any known source. Its magic is all Shakespeare's own' (Garfield: n.p.). Gaiman's and Garfield's positions neatly summarize the critical extremes related to how best to receive Shakespeare: as either someone working in and with a culture or as an original and unfettered genius.

Adaptation involves the interpenetration of contemporary circumstances and contingencies with earlier histories and values that may well be at odds with the contemporary moment. In this regard, Zurowski argues that 'Shakespeare has sometimes been our contemporary and could be so in the future, but only on condition that he is translated into the questions of our time and takes on the colour of our historical personality' (Zurowski *et al.* in Elsom 1989: 169). Many of the plays included in this anthology point to the troubled business of making Shakespeare suitable to a particular moment that contests the traditions of value by which Shakespeare has commonly been appropriated and commodified. Marowitz asserts in this regard that

> The question is not, as it is so often put, what is wrong with Shakespeare that we have to meddle with his works, but what is wrong with us that we are content to endure the diminishing returns of conventional dramatic reiteration; that we are prepared to go to the theatre and pretend that what dulls our minds and comforts our world-view is, by dint of such reassurances, culturally uplifting; not to realise that there is nothing so insidious as art that perpetuates the illusion that some kind of eternal truth is enshrined in a time–space contin-uum called a 'classic'; not to challenge the notion that its theatrical performance is *automatically* an experience because our presumption of a play's worth guarantees us that experience.
>
> (1978: 25)

Marowitz's own radical adaptive strategies are a potent reminder that adaptation is a form of reception, one with the potential to disrupt the workings of conventional theatrical expectations, while undoing the sublime, 'eternal truth' of the classic that consolidates cultural self-esteem. In this guise, adaptation as reception is as much a poetics of performative presence as it is a textual revisioning that marks how the living speak to (and for) the dead.

Conclusion: Shakespeare ongoing

> 'Every page is a paper mirror. You bend over it and look at yourself. Water likewise gives back our image; but what image has ever been able to hold the river?' he replied.
>
> (Jabès: 66)

There is no end to the ongoing adaptation of Shakespeare. Since the contract for this book was signed, many new examples have already appeared. The 1998 fringe festival theatre circuit in Canada, for example, featured *Fortinbras*, a sequel to *Hamlet* by Lee Blessing, *A Midsummer Night's Fever*!, a '70's Musical' by Leith Clark, and from Britain, Screwed and Clued's *Shooting Up Shakespeare*, another take on *A Midsummer Night's*

Dream. On video, one can now see Lloyd Kaufman's *Tromeo and Juliet*, 'the movie,' as the publicity blurb has it, 'with all the car crashes, kinky sex, and body piercing that Shakespeare always wanted but never had.' On a different note, *Love's Fire* is a 1998 collection of plays inspired by Shakespeare's sonnets from such prominent American playwrights as Eric Bogosian, Tony Kushner, Ntozake Shange, and Wendy Wasserstein. Finally, Shakespeare himself, that somewhat dowdy, bald man in the Droeshout portrait, has become, in the film *Shakespeare in Love*, a dashing member of the Generation X of the late sixteenth century. We have found in putting together this anthology that it is impossible to keep on top of the vast range of Shakespearean adaptations either already existing or coming into existence. What we offer, therefore, is an introductory volume, a sampler of various approaches to adapting Shakespeare for the theatre.

Denis Salter, in a special issue of *Essays in Theatre* he edited, calls for 'an anthology of worldwide, postcolonially-inspired (and often, as well, feminist- and queer-inflected) revisions and contestations of Shakespeare.' He also calls for an 'anthology of postcolonial adaptations and complete reworkings of Shakespeare undertaken by those contemporary playwrights . . . who have had the courage to interrogate their own imperialist legacy' (1996b: 8). Though both of Salter's suggestions are exciting, there is to date no anthology of Shakespearean adaptations that meets the criteria of historical, national and linguistic, and ideological breadth. We have therefore opted for a broader route involving a selection of plays from a range of historical moments, with a clear emphasis on more recent works, suited to a range of different teaching interests.

It would be naive to suggest that a volume such as this one does not play some role in canon formation or can escape contributing to the standardization of certain texts. In this light, we would ask that readers consider the texts we have chosen as an opening onto the possibilities of adaptation, not only in relation to Shakespeare as the centre of this particular web of textualities, but in relation to other writers who have come to wield canonical influence.

We hope to have presented an anthology engaging and useful in itself and yet a book that – through introductions, suggestions for further reading, and bibliographies – helps map and make accessible a much wider field of study. We will be happy to see other volumes take up and expand upon what *Adaptations of Shakespeare* has begun. Like Jabès's vision of the page as a mirror of ever-changing reflections, this anthology brings together some of the images that emerge from adaptations of the Shakespearean page, while recognizing that those images will always fail to contain their source and its continuing flow.

Select bibliography

Alaton, S. (1999) 'The Millennium 100: Our Readers' Choice: Einstein,' *Globe and Mail* (2 January): D1.

Anderegg, M. (1999) *Orson Welles, Shakespeare, and Popular Culture*, New York: Columbia University Press.

Anders, H. R. D. (1904; rpt. 1965) *Shakespeare's Books: A Dissertation on Shakespeare's Reading and the Immediate Sources of his Works*, New York: AMS Press.

Anderson, B. (1991) *Imagined Communities: Reflections on the Origin and Spread of Nationalism*, London: Verso.

Awasthi, S. (1993) 'The Intercultural Experience and the Kathakali "King Lear,"' *Asian Theatre Review* 9,34: 172–78.

Barnes, C. (1848) *The Forest Princess*, in *Plays, Prose and Poetry*, Philadelphia: E. H. Butler: 145–270.

Barthes, R. (1981) 'Theory of the Text,' in R. Young (ed.) *Untying the Text: A Post-Structuralist Reader*, Boston: Routledge & Kegan Paul.

— (1988) 'The Death of the Author,' in D. Lodge (ed.) *Modern Criticism and Theory: A Reader*, London: Longman.

Bassnett-McGuire, S. (1983) 'Ways through the Labyrinth: Strategies and Methods for Translating Theatre Texts,' in T. Hermans (ed.) *The Manipulation of Literature: Studies in Literary Translation*, London: Croom Helm.

Bate, J. (1994) *Shakespeare and Ovid*, Oxford: Clarendon Press.

Bene, C., and Deleuze, G. (1979) *Superpositions*, Paris: Les Éditions de Minuit.

Blau, H. (1981) *Elsinore: An Analytic Scenario, Cream City Review* 6,2: 57–99.

—— (n.d.) *Crooked Eclipses*, unpublished play.

Bloom, H. (1998) *Shakespeare: The Invention of the Human*, New York: Riverhead Books.

Bohannan, L. (1988) 'Shakespeare in the Bush,' in J. B. Cole (ed.) *Anthropology for the Nineties: Introductory Readings*, New York: Free Press: 86–95.

Boose, L. E., and Burt, R. (eds) (1997) *Shakespeare, the Movie*, London: Routledge.

Borges, J. L. (1964) 'Everything and Nothing,' in *Dreamtigers*, Austin: University of Texas Press: 46–47.

Boswell-Stone, W. G. (ed.) (1966) *Shakespeare's Holinshed: The Chronicle and the Historical Plays Compared*, New York: Benjamin Blom.

Bradshaw, G., and T. Kishi (eds) (1999) *Shakespeare in Japan*, London: Athlone.

Bristol, M. (1990) *Shakespeare's America, America's Shakespeare*, London: Routledge.

— (1996) *Big-Time Shakespeare*, London: Routledge.

Brown, J. R. (1999) *New Sites for Shakespeare: Theatre, the Audience, and Asia*, London: Routledge.

Bullough G. (1957–1975) *Narrative and Dramatic Sources of Shakespeare*, 8 vols, London: Routledge & Kegan Paul.

Bulman, J. C. (ed.) (1996) *Shakespeare, Theory, and Performance*, London: Routledge.

Burt, R. (1998) *Unspeakable ShaXXXspeares: Queer Theory and American Kiddie Culture*, New York: St. Martin's Press.

Carlson, M. (1996) *Performance: A Critical Introduction*, London: Routledge.

Cartelli, T. (1990) 'Prospero in Africa: The Tempest as Colonialist Text and Pretext,' in J. E. Howard and M. F. O'Connor (eds) *Shakespeare Reproduced: The Text in History and Ideology*, New York: Routledge: 99–115.

— (1999) *Repositioning Shakespeare: National Formations, Postcolonial Appropriations*, London: Routledge.

Clark, S. (ed.) (1997) *Shakespeare Made Fit: Restoration Adaptations of Shakespeare*, London: J. M. Dent.

Coffin, G. C. (1925; rpt. 1968) *Shakespeare's Debt to Montaigne*, New York: Phaeton Press.

Cohn, R. (1976) *Modern Shakespeare Offshoots*, Princeton: Princeton University Press.

Compagnon, A. (1979) *La Seconde Main ou le travail de la citation*, Paris: Éditions de Seuil.

Davies, A., and Wells, S. (eds) (1995) *Shakespeare and the Moving Image: The Plays on Film and Television*, Cambridge: Cambridge University Press.

Derrida, J. (1985) *The Ear of the Other: Otobiography, Transference, Translation*, New York: Schocken Books.

— (1988) *Limited Inc.*, Evanston, Illinois: Northwestern University Press.

Dobson, M. (1992) *The Making of the National Poet: Shakespeare, Adaptation and Authorship, 1660–1769*, Oxford: Oxford University Press.

Donaldson, E.T. (1985) *The Swan at the Well: Shakespeare Reading Chaucer*, New Haven: Yale University Press.

Engle, R. (1993) 'Audience, Style, and Language in the Shakespeare of Peter Zadek,' in D. Kennedy (ed.) *Foreign Shakespeare: Contemporary Performance*, Cambridge: Cambridge University Press: 93–105.

Esslin, M. (1974) 'Introduction,' in J. Kott, *Shakespeare our Contemporary*, New York: Norton: xi–xxi.

Evans, G. B. (ed.) (1974) *The Riverside Shakespeare*, Boston: Houghton Mifflin.

Fineman, J. (1986) *Shakespeare's Perjured Eye: The Invention of Poetic Subjectivity in the Sonnets*, Berkeley: University of California Press.

Foucault, M. (1979) 'What Is an Author?' in J. Harrari (ed.) *Textual Strategies: Perspectives in Post-Structuralist Criticism*, Ithaca: Cornell University Press.

— (1980) *Power/Knowledge: Selected Interviews and Other Writings 1972–1977*, New York: Pantheon.

Gaiman, N., and Vess, C. (1996) 'The Tempest,' *The Sandman* 75, DC Vertigo.

Gilbert, H., and Tompkins, J. (1996) *Post-Colonial Drama: Theory, Practice, Politics*, London: Routledge.

Grady, H. (1991) *The Modernist Shakespeare: Critical Texts in a Material World*, Oxford: Clarendon Press.

Graham, J. F. (1985) *Difference in Translation*, Ithaca: Cornell University Press.

Guntner, J. L., and McLean, A. M. (eds) (1997) *Redefining Shakespeare: Literary Theory and Theater Practice in the German Democratic Republic*, Newark: University of Delaware Press.

Halpern, R. (1997) *Shakespeare Among the Moderns*, Ithaca: Cornell University Press.

Hawkes, T. (1992) *Meaning by Shakespeare*, London: Routledge.

Hermans, T. (ed.) (1983) *The Manipulation of Literature: Studies in Literary Translation*, London: Croom Helm.

Hodgdon, B. (1998) *The Shakespeare Trade: Performances and Appropriations*, Philadelphia: University of Pennsylvania Press.

Höfele, A. (1992) 'A Theater of Exhaustion? "*Posthistoire*" in Recent German Shakespeare Productions,' *Shakespeare Quarterly* 43,1: 80–86.

Holderness, G. (1988) *The Shakespeare Myth*, Manchester: Manchester University Press.

— and Loughrey, B. (1991) 'Shakespearean Features,' in J. I. Marsden (ed.) *The Appropriation of Shakespeare: Post-Renaissance Reconstructions of the Works and the Myth*, New York: St. Martin's Press: 183–201.

Hortmann, W., and Hamburger, M. (1998) *Shakespeare on the German Stage: The Twentieth Century*, Cambridge: Cambridge University Press.

Hutcheon, L. (1985) *A Theory of Parody: The Teaching of Twentieth-Century Art Forms*, New York: Methuen.

Jabès, E. (1990) *The Book of Resemblances*, Hanover: Wesleyan University Press.

Jepsen, L. (1971) *Ethical Aspects of Tragedy: A Comparison of Certain Tragedies by Aeschylus, Sophocles, Euripides, Seneca, and Shakespeare*, New York: AMS Press.

Johnson, D. (1996) *Shakespeare and South Africa*, Oxford: Clarendon Press.

Kennedy, D. (1993) 'Introduction,' in *Foreign Shakespeare: Contemporary Performance*, Cambridge: Cambridge University Press: 1–18.

— (1996) *Looking at Shakespeare: A Visual History of Twentieth-Century Performance*, Cambridge: Cambridge University Press.

Kim, J. (1994) *Bi-Cultural Essays on Shakespeare*, Cambridge: D. S. Brewer.

— (1995) 'Shakespeare in a Korean Cultural Context,' *Asian Theatre Journal* 12,1: 37–49.

Kristeva, J. (1984) *Revolution in Poetic Language*, New York: Columbia University Press.

Lamb, C., and Lamb, M. (1950) *Tales From Shakespeare*, New York: Macmillan.

Lefevere, A. (1983) 'Why Waste Our Time on Rewrites? The Trouble with Interpretation and the Role of Rewriting in an Alternative Paradigm,' in T. Hermans (ed.) *The Manipulation of Literature: Studies in Literary Translation*, London: Croom Helm.

Levine, L. W. (1988) *Highbrow/Lowbrow: The Emergence of Cultural Hierarchy in America*, Cambridge, Massachusetts: Harvard University Press.

Li, R. (1995) 'The Bard in the Middle Kingdom,' *Asian Theatre Journal* 12,1: 50–84.

Loeffelholz, M. (1990) 'Miranda in the New World: The *Tempest* and Charlotte Barnes's *The Forest Princess*,' in M. Novy (ed.) *Women's Re-Visions of Shakespeare: On the Responses of Dickinson, Woolf, Rich, H.D., George Eliot, and Others*, Urbana: University of Illinois Press: 58–75.

Loomba, A., and Orkin, M. (eds) (1998) *Post-Colonial Shakespeares*, London: Routledge.

Love's Fire: Seven New Plays Inspired by Seven Shakespearean Sonnets (1998) New York: William Morrow.

Lynch, S. J. (1998) *Shakespearean Intertextuality: Studies in Selected Sources and Plays*, Westport: Greenwood Press.

MacDonald, A.-M. (1990) *Goodnight Desdemona (Good Morning Juliet)*, Toronto: Coach House Press.

MacKaye, P. (1916) *Caliban by the Yellow Sands*, Garden City, NY: Doubleday.

Marowitz, C. (1978) *The Marowitz Shakespeare*, London: Marion Boyars.

— (1991) *Recycling Shakespeare*, New York: Applause.

Marsden, J. I. (ed.) (1991) *The Appropriation of Shakespeare: Post-Renaissance Reconstructions of the Works and the Myth*, New York: St. Martin's Press.

— (1995) *The Re-Imagined Text: Shakespeare, Adaptation, and Eighteenth-Century Literary Theory*, Lexington: University Press of Kentucky.

Martindale, C., and Martindale, M. (1994) *Shakespeare and the Uses of Antiquity*, London: Routledge.

McDonald, R. (1996) '"I Loved My Books": Shakespeare's Reading,' in *The Bedford Companion to Shakespeare: An Introduction with Documents*, New York: St. Martin's Press: 100–117.

Miola, R. S. (1988) 'Shakespeare and his Sources,' *Shakespeare Survey* 40: 69–76.

— (1992) *Shakespeare and Classical Tragedy: The Influence of Seneca*, Oxford: Clarendon Press.

Modisane, B. (1963) *Blame Me on History*, London: Thames & Hudson.

Muir, K. (1977) *The Sources of Shakespeare's Plays*, London: Methuen.

Nicoll, A. (1922) *Dryden as an Adapter of Shakespeare*, London: Oxford University Press.

Orkin, M. (1991) *Drama and the South African State*, Manchester: Manchester University Press.

Osborne, L.E. (1996) 'Rethinking the Performance Editions: Theatrical and Textual Productions of Shakespeare,' in J. C. Bulman (ed.) *Shakespeare, Theory, and Performance*, London: Routledge.

Plutarch. (1928) *The Lives of the Noble Grecians and Romanes*, Oxford: Basil Blackwell.

Potter, L.R. (1995) 'Shakespeare's "Sisters": Desdemona, Juliet, and Constance Ledbelly in *Goodnight Desdemona (Good Morning Juliet)*,' *Modern Drama* 38,3: 362–377.

Potts, A. F. (1969) *Shakespeare and The Faerie Queene*, New York: Greenwood Press.

Pronko, L. C. (1967) *Theater East and West: Perspectives Toward a Total Theater*, Berkeley: University of California Press.

Rabkin, G. (1985) 'Is There a Text on this Stage?' *Performing Arts Journal* 9,2–3: 142–159.

Renan, E. (1911) *Caliban*, Queensborough, NY: Marion Press.

Rose, M. A. (1979) *Parody/Meta-fiction: An Analysis of Parody as a Critical Mirror to the Writing and Reception of Fiction*, London: Croom Helm.

Robertson, J. M. (1909; rpt. 1969) *Montaigne and Shakespeare and Other Essays on Cognate Questions*, New York: Burt Franklin.

Rosenthal, L. J. (1996) '(Re)Writing Lear: Literary Property and Dramatic Authorship,' in J. Brewer and S. Staves (eds) *Early Modern Conceptions of Property*, London: Routledge: 323–338.

Salter, D. (1996a) 'Acting Shakespeare in Postcolonial Space,' in J. C. Bulman (ed.) *Shakespeare, Theory, and Performance*, London: Routledge.

— (1996b) 'Introduction: The End(s) of Shakespeare?' *Essays in Theatre* 15,1: 3–14.

Sasayama, T., Mulryne, J. R. and Shewring, M. (eds) (1999) *Shakespeare and the Japanese Stage*, Cambridge: Cambridge University Press.

Schmidt, A. (ed.) (1971) *Shakespeare Lexicon and Quotation Dictionary*, 2 vols, New York: Dover.

Scott, M. (1989) *Shakespeare and the Modern Dramatist*, New York: St. Martin's Press.

Scragg, L. (1992) *Shakespeare's Mouldy Tales: Recurrent Plot Motifs in Shakespearian Drama*, London: Longman.

— (1996) *Shakespeare's Alternative Tales*, London: Longman.

Shackford, M. H. (1929) *Plutarch in Renaissance England with Special Reference to Shakespeare*, n.p.

Sheppard, P. (1996) 'Bardolatry for Beginners,' *Quill & Quire* (June): 53–54.

Singh, J. G. (1996) *Colonial Narratives/Cultural Dialogues: Discoveries of India in the Language of Colonialism*, London: Routledge.

Skeat, W. W. (1975) *Shakespeare's Plutarch*, New York: AMS Press.

Spencer, C. (ed.) (1965) *Five Restoration Adaptations of Shakespeare*, Urbana: University of Illinois Press.

Spencer, T. J. B. (ed.) (1968) *Shakespeare's Plutarch*, London: Penguin.

Spivak, G. C. (1987) *In Other Worlds: Essays in Cultural Politics*, New York: Methuen.

Steiner, G. (1992) *After Babel: Aspects of Language and Translation*, 2d edn, Oxford: Oxford University Press.

— (1998) 'Theirs By Right, Ours By Mistake? Germany's Possessive Love Affair With Shakespeare,' *Times Literary Supplement* (2 October): 23.

Stoppard, T. (1967) *Rosencrantz and Guildenstern Are Dead*, New York: Grove.

Summers, M. (ed.) (1966) *Shakespeare Adaptations*, New York: Haskell House.

Taylor, G. (1989) *Reinventing Shakespeare: A Cultural History from the Restoration to the Present*, New York: Weidenfeld & Nicolson.

Thompson, A. (1978) *Shakespeare's Chaucer: A Study in Literary Origins*, New York: Barnes & Noble.

Trivedi, H. (1995) *Colonial Transactions: English Literature and India*, Manchester: Manchester University Press.

'Troilus and Cressida in Spacesuits' (1988) Toronto *Globe & Mail* (9 April): D6.

Viswanathan, G. (1989) *Masks of Conquest: Literary Study and British Rule in India*, New York: Columbia University Press.

Wheale, N. (1991) 'Introduction,' in L. Aers and N. Wheale (eds) *Shakespeare in the Changing Curriculum*, London: Routledge: 1–29.

Williams, S. (ed.) (1990) *Shakespeare on the German Stage*, vol. 1, Cambridge: Cambridge University Press.

Wilson, A. (1992) 'Critical Revisions: Ann-Marie MacDonald's *Goodnight Desdemona (Good Morning Juliet)*,' in R. Much (ed.) *Women on the Canadian Stage: The Legacy of Hrotsvit*, Winnipeg: Blizzard: 1–12.

Woodmansee, M., and Jaszi, P. (eds) (1994) *The Construction of Authorship: Textual Appropriation in Law and Literature*, Durham, North Carolina: Duke University Press.

Zarrilli, P. B. (1992) 'For Whom Is the King a King? Issues of Intercultural Production, Perception, and Reception in a *Kathakali King Lear*,' in J. G. Reinelt and J. R. Roach (eds) *Critical Theory and Performance*, Ann Arbor: University of Michigan Press: 16–40.

Zhang, H. Y. (1996) *Shakespeare in China: A Comparative Study of Two Traditions and Cultures*, Newark: University of Delaware Press.

Zurowski, A. *et al.* (1989) 'Should Shakespeare Be Buried or Born Again,' in J. Elsom (ed.) *Is Shakespeare Still Our Contemporary*, New York: Routledge: 169–182.

The Woman's Prize; or the Tamer Tamed

John Fletcher

Introduction

John Fletcher was born in Sussex in 1579. His father was the future bishop of London, and Fletcher was educated at Cambridge starting in 1591. Around 1606 he began to work in the theatre in London, most famously in collaboration with Francis Beaumont on such plays as *The Maid's Tragedy* and the tragicomedy *Philaster*. Fletcher also collaborated with other dramatists, such as Philip Massinger, and wrote plays on his own. *The Woman's Prize* is Fletcher's work alone and most likely dates from 1611. Around 1612 Fletcher began collaborating with Shakespeare, who was near the end of his career: on the lost play *Cardenio*, on *The Two Noble Kinsmen*, and probably on *Henry VIII*. After Shakespeare's retirement, Fletcher succeeded him as the principal playwright for the King's Men, the foremost theatre company of the period. Fletcher has the distinction, therefore, of being Shakespeare's adapter, collaborator, and successor. The complexities of influence and exchange between the two men are discussed at length by Christopher Leech (144–168), who concludes: 'Our image of Shakespeare will be truer if we do not put out of our minds the closeness of his relationship with Fletcher in the last years of his working life.' Fletcher died in 1625.

The Woman's Prize is a sequel to Shakespeare's *The Taming of the Shrew* – Charles Squier calls it a 'spinoff' (120). Petruchio and Katherine's marriage was stormy and she is now dead. Petruchio marries Maria, a young woman who sets out to avoid the patriarchal domination and cruelty for which Petruchio has become famous. Fletcher's play concerns her successful struggle to tame Petruchio and his ongoing exasperation at her actions. *The Woman's Prize* is set not in Padua but in London, and other than a few familiar names there is little direct detail or circumstance taken from Shakespeare. Molly Easo Smith, however, writes of 'Fletcher's pervasive commentary on Shakespeare' and asserts, 'characters and situations in *The Woman's Prize* seem closely modelled on *The Shrew*, and Fletcher's calculated intertextual glance comments [on], rewrites, and undermines the ideological assumptions in Shakespeare's play' (39). One of the revampings that has been noted is Fletcher's borrowing of female solidarity from Aristophanes' *Lysistrata* (Ferguson: 12–13): in *The Woman's Prize*, too, women band together in refusing sexual relations with men in order to make the men submit to their agenda. The women in *The Taming of the Shrew* – especially Katherine – are much more isolated from each other than they are in Fletcher's sequel. In obvious ways, therefore, Fletcher's play presents itself in relation to Shakespeare's as its reversal or opposite, with the triumph of its women over its men.

The Taming of the Shrew and *The Woman's Prize* were presented together in remountings before the court of Charles I in 1633. At this time, *The Woman's Prize* initially ran afoul of the Master of the Revels, in his capacity as censor, for its 'oaths, prophaness, and ribaldrye' (Ferguson: 22); at court, however, Shakespeare's play was 'liked,' while Fletcher's was 'very well liked' (Marcus: 199–200).

Readings of the sexual politics of *The Taming of the Shrew* tend to fall into three categories: those that defend the work's apparent sexism as benign or healthy (a view that has become progressively rarer in academic scholarship); those that condemn the work's apparent sexism and misogyny; those that find in the play elements that, at least in part, call into question or undermine the apparent sexism. There is, similarly, no consensus about *The Woman's Prize*. Some critics find the sexual politics obviously more balanced and egalitarian than in

Shakespeare's play. This is how Smith reads *The Woman's Prize*. Leech writes that the 'insistence that encounters between men and women should be on equal terms is basic in Fletcher's dramas' (52); Gordon McMullan sees the play enacting a reconciliation of men and women, but under the guidance of a woman (176). Ferguson sees the brazen bawdiness of the women in the play in positive terms:

> The women are seeking equality and are fighting a man's world; in order to win they must assume their equality and fight force with force. As they see their cause, they can no longer be merely objects to be pursued or pawns to be captured; they must assert their rights and bring the men to a recognition of those rights; thus the action, language, and wit of the men is met with similar action, language, and wit by the women.
>
> (1966: 15–16)

Sandra Clark has a less upbeat reading of the play: she notes, for instance, that much more time is spent on the articulation of male grievance in Fletcher's play than was given to female grievance in Shakespeare's (97), and points to 'the play's general discourse of misogyny, which emphasises the monstrousness of female sexuality' (99). Moreover, Squier writes, in response to the boisterousness of the city and country wives in *The Woman's Prize*:

> These harridans serve to counterbalance any view that Fletcher was greatly serious about the rights of women, as does his romantic subplot in which Livia, a romantic heroine, joins the rebel ladies only to save herself from marriage to old Moroso and to trick him and her father into consenting to her marriage with her true love. Petruchio is tamed, but the social fabric is hardly threatened; and no opportunity for traditional antifeminine rant and roaring is lost. The battle of the sexes in *The Woman's Prize* is ultimately a draw.
>
> (1986: 121)

A draw, however, may very well be a preferable outcome for women than that presented in *The Taming of the Shrew*. Kathleen McLuskie sees whatever equality develops in Fletcher's play in economic terms: 'the play presents sexual relations less as a reversal of male supremacy than as a kind of bargaining, a negotiation of terms in the free market,' and the 'dangerous aspect for men in this world is that the free market is equally available to women' (215, 217). Moreover, Leech writes that Fletcher 'was no serious defender of women's rights, but rather a man who took some interest and pleasure in watching a fight between well-matched opponents' (53). At any rate, *The Woman's Prize* reveals that adaptations and rewritings of Shakespeare have a long history, going back to the lifetime of Shakespeare himself.

A glossary of seventeenth-century terms and phrases has been placed at the end of the play.

Select bibliography

Entries marked * are particularly accessible.

Clark, S. (1994) *The Plays of Beaumont and Fletcher: Sexual Themes and Dramatic Representation*, Hemel Hempstead, Hertfordshire: Harvester Wheatsheaf.

Ferguson, G. B. (ed.) (1966) *The Woman's Prize or The Tamer Tamed: A Critical Edition*, The Hague: Mouton.

*Finkelpearl, P. J. (1990) *Court and Country Politics in the Plays of Beaumont and Fletcher*, Princeton: Princeton University Press.

Leech, C. (1962) *The John Fletcher Plays*, London: Chatto & Windus.

McKeithan, D. M. (1970) *The Debt to Shakespeare in the Beaumont-and-Fletcher Plays*, New York: AMS.

McLuskie, K. (1989) *Renaissance Dramatists*, Atlantic Highlands, New Jersey: Humanities Press International.

*McMullan, G. (1994) *The Politics of Unease in the Plays of John Fletcher*, Amherst: University of Massachusetts Press.

Marcus, L. (1992) 'The Shakespearean Editor as Shrew-Tamer,' *English Literary Renaissance* 22,2: 177–200.

*Smith, M. E. (1995) 'John Fletcher's Response to the Gender Debate: *The Woman's Prize* and *The Taming of the Shrew*,' *Papers on Language and Literature* 31,1: 38–60.

Sprague, A. C. (1926) *Beaumont and Fletcher on the Restoration Stage*, Cambridge, Massachusetts: Harvard University Press.

Squier, C. L. (1986) *John Fletcher*, Boston: Twayne Publishers.

The Woman's Prize; or The Tamer Tamed _____

John Fletcher

Characters

MOROSO, an old rich doating citizen, suitor to LIVIA

SOPHOCLES, } two gentlemen, friends to PETRUCHIO
TRANIO,

PETRUCHIO, an Italian gentleman, husband to MARIA

ROWLAND, a young gentleman, in love with LIVIA

PETRONIUS, father to MARIA and LIVIA

JAQUES } two witty servants to PETRUCHIO
PEDRO

DOCTOR

APOTHECARY

WATCHMEN

PORTERS

MARIA, a chaste witty lady, } the two masculine
LIVIA, mistress to ROWLAND } daughters of PETRONIUS

BIANCA, their cousin, and commander-in-chief

CITY WIVES } who come to the relief of
COUNTRY WIVES } the ladies, of which two were drunk

MAIDS

Scene: LONDON

Prologue

LADIES, to you, in whose defence and right
Fletcher's brave muse prepared herself to fight
A battle without blood, ('twas well fought too;
The victory's yours, though got with much ado,)
We do present this Comedy; in which
A rivulet of pure wit flows, strong and rich
In fancy, language, and all parts that may
Add grace and ornament to a merry play:
Which this may prove! Yet not to go too far
In promises from this our female war,
We do entreat the angry men would not
Expect the mazes of a subtle plot,
Set speeches, high expressions, and, what's worse
In a true Comedy, politic discourse.
The end we aim at, is to make you sport;
Yet neither gall the city nor the court.
Hear, and observe his comic strain, and when
Ye are sick of melancholy, see't again.
'Tis no dear physic, since 'twill quit the cost,
Or his intentions, with our pains, are lost.

Act I

Scene 1

A hall in the house of PETRUCHIO.

> (*Enter* MOROSO, SOPHOCLES, *and* TRANIO, *with* ROSEMARY, *as from a wedding.*)

MOROSO God give 'em joy!
TRANIO Amen!
SOPHOCLES Amen, say I too!
    The pudding's now i' the proof. Alas, poor wench,
    Through what a mine of patience must thou work,
    Ere thou know'st good hour more!
TRANIO 'Tis too true: Certain,
    Methinks her father has dealt harshly with her,
    Exceeding harshly, and not like a father,
    To match her to this dragon: I protest
    I pity the poor gentlewoman.
MOROSO Methinks now,
    He's not so terrible as people think him.
SOPHOCLES (*to* TRANIO) This old thief flatters, out of mere devotion,
    To please the father for his second daughter.
TRANIO But shall he have her?

SOPHOCLES Yes, when I have Rome;
  And yet the father's for him.
MOROSO I'll asssure you,
  I hold him a good man.
SOPHOCLES Yes, sure, a wealthy;
  But whether a good woman's man is doubtful.
TRANIO 'Would 'twere no worse!
MOROSO What though his other wife,
  Out of her most abundant soberness,
  Out of her daily hue and cries upon him,
  (For sure she was a rebel) turn'd his temper,
  And forced him blow as high as she; does't
    follow
  He must retain that long-since-buried tempest,
  To this soft maid?
SOPHOCLES I fear it.
TRANIO So do I too;
  And so far, that if God had made me woman,
  And his wife that must be –
MOROSO What would you do, sir?
TRANIO I would learn to eat coals with an angry
    cat,
  And spit fire at him; I would, to prevent him,
  Do all the ramping roaring tricks, a whore
  Being drunk, and tumbling ripe, would tremble
    at:
  There is no safety else, nor moral wisdom,
  To be a wife, and his.
SOPHOCLES So I should think too.
TRANIO For yet the bare remembrance of his first
    wife
  (I tell you on my knowledge, and a truth too)
  Will make him start in's sleep, and very often
  Cry out for cudgels, colestaves, any thing;
  Hiding his breeches, out of fear her ghost
  Should walk, and wear 'em yet. Since his first
    marriage,
  He is no more the still Petruchio,
  Than I am Babylon.
SOPHOCLES He's a good fellow,
  And on my word I love him; but to think
  A fit match for this tender soul –
TRANIO His very frown, if she but say her prayers
  Louder than men talk treason, makes him
    tinder;
  The motion of a dial, when he's testy,
  Is the same trouble to him as a water-work;
  She must do nothing of herself, not eat,
  Drink, say, 'Sir, how do you?' make her ready,
    unready,
  Unless he bid her.
SOPHOCLES He will bury her,
  Ten pounds to twenty shillings, within these
    three weeks.
TRANIO I'll be your half.

(*Enter* JAQUES, *with a pot of wine.*)

MOROSO He loves her most extremely,
  And so long 'twill be honey-moon. – Now,
    Jaques!
  You are a busy man, I am sure.
JAQUES Yes, certain;
  This old sport must have eggs, –
SOPHOCLES Not yet this ten days.
JAQUES Sweet gentlemen, with muskadel.
TRANIO That's right, sir.
MOROSO This fellow broods his master. – Speed
    you, Jaques!
SOPHOCLES We shall be for you presently.
JAQUES Your worships
  Shall have it rich and neat; and, o' my
    conscience,
  As welcome as our Lady-day. Oh, my old sir,
  When shall we see your worship run at
    ring?
  That hour, a standing were worth money.
MOROSO So, sir!
JAQUES Upon my little honesty, your mistress,
  If I have any speculation,
  Must think this single thrumming of a fiddle,
  Without a bow, but even poor sport.
MOROSO You're merry.
JAQUES 'Would I were wise too! So, God bless
    your worship!   (*Exit.*)
TRANIO The fellow tells you true.
SOPHOCLES When is the day, man?
  Come, come; you'll steal a marriage.
MOROSO Nay, believe me:
  But when her father pleases, I am ready,
  And all my friends shall know it.
TRANIO Why not now?
  One charge had served for both.
MOROSO There's reason in't.
SOPHOCLES Call'd Rowland.
MOROSO Will you walk?
  They'll think we are lost: Come, gentlemen!
                                           (*Exit.*)

TRANIO You have wiped him now.
SOPHOCLES So will he ne'er the wench, I hope.
TRANIO I wish it.   (*Exeunt.*)

Scene 2

An apartment in the same.

(*Enter* ROWLAND *and* LIVIA.)

ROWLAND Now, Livia, if you'll go away to-night,
  If your affections be not made of words –
LIVIA I love you, and you know how dearly,
    Rowland:
  (Is there none near us?) My affections ever

Have been your servants; with what superstition
    I have ever sainted you –
ROWLAND Why, then take this way.
LIVIA 'Twill be a childish, and a less prosperous
    course
    Than his that knows not care; why should we do
    Our honest and our hearty love such wrong,
    To over-run our fortunes?
ROWLAND Then you flatter!
LIVIA Alas! you know I cannot.
ROWLAND What hope's left else
    But flying, to enjoy ye?
LIVIA None, so far.
    For let it be admitted, we have time,
    And all things now in other expectation,
    My father's bent against us; what but ruin,
    Can such a bye-way bring us? If your fears
    Would let you look with my eyes, I would shew
      you,
    And certain, how our staying here would win us
    A course, though somewhat longer, yet far
      surer.
ROWLAND And then Moroso has ye.
LIVIA No such matter:
    For hold this certain; begging, stealing, whoring,
    Selling (which is a sin unpardonable)
    Of counterfeit cods, or musty English crocus,
    Switches, or stones for th' tooth-ach, sooner
      finds me,
    Than that drawn fox Moroso.
ROWLAND But his money;
    If wealth may win you –
LIVIA If a hog may be
    High-priest among the Jews! His money,
      Rowland?
    Oh, Love forgive me! What faith hast thou!
    Why, can his money kiss me –
ROWLAND Yes.
LIVIA Behind,
    Laced out upon a petticoat. – Or grasp me,
    While I cry, oh, good thank you! (O my troth,
    Thou makest me merry with thy fear!) or lie
      with me
    As you may do? Alas, what fools you men are!
    His mouldy money? Half a dozen riders,
    That cannot sit, but stampt fast to their saddles?
    No, Rowland, no man shall make use of me;
    My beauty was born free, and free I'll give it
    To him that loves, not buys me. You yet doubt
      me?
ROWLAND I cannot say I doubt you.
LIVIA Go thy ways;
    Thou art the prettiest puling piece of passion –
    I' faith, I will not fail thee.
ROWLAND I had rather –

LIVIA Pr'ythee, believe me! If I do not carry it,
    For both our goods –
ROWLAND But –
LIVIA What *but?*
ROWLAND I would tell you.
LIVIA I know all you can tell me: All's but this;
    You would have me, and lie with me: is't not so?
ROWLAND Yes.
LIVIA Why, you shall; will that content you? Go.
ROWLAND I am very loth to go.

(Enter BIANCA *and* MARIA *conversing
in the back-ground.)*

LIVIA Now, o' my conscience,
    Thou art an honest fellow! Here's my sister!
    Go, pr'ythee go! this kiss, and credit me,
    Ere I am three nights older, I am for thee:
    You shall hear what I do. Farewell!
ROWLAND Farewell!   *(Exit.)*
LIVIA Alas, poor fool, how it looks!
    It would even hang itself, should I but cross it.
    For pure love to the matter, I must hatch it.
BIANCA Nay, never look for merry hour, Maria,
    If now you make it not: Let not your blushes,
    Your modesty, and tenderness of spirit,
    Make you continual anvil to his anger!
    Believe me, since his first wife set him going,
    Nothing can bind his rage: Take your own
      council;
    You shall not say that I persuaded you.
    But if you suffer him –
MARIA Stay! shall I do it?
BIANCA Have you a stomach to't?
MARIA I never shew'd it.
BIANCA 'Twill shew the rarer and the stronger in
    you.
    But do not say I urged you.
MARIA I am perfect.
    Like Curtius, to redeem my country, have I
      leap'd
    Into this gulph of marriage; and I'll do it.
    Farewell, all poorer thoughts, but spite and
      anger,
    Till I have wrought a miracle! – Now, cousin,
    I am no more the gentle, tame Maria:
    Mistake me not; I have a new soul in me,
    Made of a north-wind, nothing but tempest;
    And, like a tempest, shall it make all ruins,
    Till I have run my will out!
BIANCA This is brave now,
    If you continue it: But, your own will lead you!
MARIA Adieu, all tenderness! I dare continue.
    Maids that are made of fears, and modest
      blushes,
    View me, and love example!

BIANCA Here's your sister.

MARIA Here's the brave old man's love –

BIANCA That loves the young man.

MARIA Ay, and hold thee there, wench! What a
  grief of heart is't,
  When Paphos' revels should up-rouse old Night,
  To sweat against a cork, to lie and tell
  The clock o' th' lungs, to rise sport-starved!

LIVIA Dear sister,
  Where have you been, you talk thus?

MARIA Why at church, wench;
  Where I am tied to talk thus: I'm a wife now.

LIVIA It seems so, and a modest!

MARIA You're an ass!
  When thou art married once, thy modesty
  Will never buy thee pins.

LIVIA 'Bless me!

MARIA From what?

BIANCA From such a tame fool as our cousin
  Livia!

LIVIA You are not mad?

MARIA Yes, wench, and so must you be,
  Or none of our acquaintance, (mark me, Livia,)
  Or indeed fit for our sex. 'Tis bed-time:
  Pardon me, yellow Hymen, that I mean
  Thine offerings to protract, or to keep fasting
  My valiant bridegroom!

LIVIA Whither will this woman?

BIANCA You may perceive her end.

LIVIA Or rather fear it.

MARIA Dare you be partner in't?

LIVIA Leave it, Maria!
  (I fear I have mark'd too much) for goodness
    leave it!
  Devest you with obedient hands; to bed!

MARIA To bed? No, Livia; there are comets hang
  Prodigious over that yet; there's a fellow
  Must yet, before I know that heat – (ne'er start,
    wench,)
  Be made a man, for yet he is a monster;
  Here must his head be, Livia.

LIVIA Never hope it:
  'Tis as easy with a sieve to scoop the ocean, as
  To tame Petruchio.

MARIA Stay! – Lucina, hear me!
  Never unlock the treasure of my womb,
  For human fruit to make it capable;
  Nor never with thy secret hand make brief
  A mother's labour to me; if I do
  Give way unto my married husband's will,
  Or be a wife in anything but hopes,
  Till I have made him easy as a child,
  And tame as fear! He shall not win a smile,
  Or a pleased look, from this austerity,
  Though it would pull another jointure from him,

And make him ev'ry day another man.
  And when I kiss him, till I have my will,
  May I be barren of delights, and know
  Only what pleasures are in dreams and guesses!

LIVIA A strange exordium!

BIANCA All the several wrongs
  Done by imperious husbands to their wives
  These thousand years and upwards, strengthen
    thee!
  Thou hast a brave cause.

MARIA And I'll do it bravely,
  Or may I knit my life out ever after!

LIVIA In what part of the world got she this spirit?
  Yet pray, Maria, look before you, truly!
  Besides the disobedience of a wife,
  (Which you will find a heavy imputation,
  Which yet I cannot think your own) it shews
  So distant from your sweetness –

MARIA 'Tis, I swear.

LIVIA Weigh but the person, and the hopes you
    have
  To work this desperate cure!

MARIA A weaker subject
  Would shame the end I aim at. Disobedience?
  You talk too tamely: by the faith I have
  In mine own noble will, that childish woman
  That lives a prisoner to her husband's pleasure,
  Has lost her making, and becomes a beast,
  Created for his use, not fellowship!

LIVIA His first wife said as much.

MARIA She was a fool,
  And took a scurvy course: Let her be named
  'Mongst those that wish for things, but dare not
    do 'em;
  I have a new dance for him.

LIVIA Are you of this faith?

BIANCA Yes, truly; and will die in't.

LIVIA Why then, let's all wear breeches!

MARIA Now thou comest near the nature of a
    woman:
  Hang these tame-hearted eyasses, that no
    sooner
  See the lure out, and hear their husband's holla,
  But cry like kites upon 'em: The free haggard
  (Which is that woman that hath wing, and
    knows it,
  Spirit and plume) will make an hundred checks,
  To shew her freedom, sail in every air,
  And look out every pleasure, not regarding
  Lure nor quarry till her pitch command
  What she desires; making her founder'd keeper
  Be glad to fling out trains, and golden ones,
  To take her down again.

LIVIA You're learned, sister;
  Yet I say still, take heed!

MARIA A witty saying!
   I'll tell thee, Livia; had this fellow tired
   As many wives as horses under him,
   With spurring of their patience; had he got
   A patent, with an office to reclaim us,
   Confirm'd by parliament; had he all the malice
   And subtilty of devils, or of us,
   Or anything that's worse than both –
LIVIA Hey, hey, boys! this is excellent!
MARIA Or could he
   Cast his wives new again, like bells, to make 'em
   Sound to his will; or had the fearful name
   Of the first breaker of wild women; yet,
   Yet would I undertake this man, thus single;
   And, spite of all the freedom he has reach'd to,
   Turn him and bend him as I list, and mould him
   Into a babe again, that aged women,
   Wanting both teeth and spleen, may master
     him.
BIANCA Thou wilt be chronicled.
MARIA That's all I aim at.
LIVIA I must confess I do with all my heart
   Hate an imperious husband, and in time
   Might be so wrought upon –
BIANCA To make him cuckold?
MARIA If he deserve it.
LIVIA Then I'll leave ye, ladies.
BIANCA Thou hast not so much noble anger in
   thee.
MARIA Go sleep, go sleep! What we intend to do
   Lies not for such starved souls as thou hast,
     Livia.
LIVIA Good night! The bridegroom will be with
   you presently.
MARIA That's more than you know.
LIVIA If you work upon him
   As you have promised, you may give example,
   Which no doubt will be follow'd.
MARIA So!
BIANCA Good night!
   We'll trouble you no further.
MARIA If you intend no good, pray do no harm!
LIVIA None, but pray for you!   (Exit.)
BIANCA Cheer, wench!
MARIA Now, Bianca,
   Those wits we have, let's wind them to the
     height!
   My rest is up, wench, and I pull for that
   Will make me ever famous. They that lay
   Foundations are half-builders, all men say.

       (Enter JAQUES.)

JAQUES My master, forsooth –
MARIA Oh, how does thy master?
   Pr'ythee commend me to him.

JAQUES How is this? –
   My master stays, forsooth –
MARIA Why, let him stay!
   Who hinders him, forsooth?
JAQUES The revel's ended now, –
   To visit you.
MARIA I am not sick.
JAQUES I mean
   To see his chamber, forsooth.
MARIA Am I his groom?
   Where lay he last night, forsooth?
JAQUES In the low matted parlour.
MARIA There lies his way, by the long gallery.
JAQUES I mean your chamber. You are very
     merry, mistress.
MARIA 'Tis a good sign I am sound-hearted,
     Jaques.
   But, if you'll know where I lie, follow me;
   And what thou seest, deliver to thy master.
BIANCA Do, gentle Jaques.   (Exeunt.)
JAQUES Ha! is the wind in that door?
   By'r lady, we shall have foul weather then!
   I do not like the shuffling of these women;
   They are mad beasts, when they knock their
     heads together:
   I have observed them all this day, their whispers
   One in another's ear; their signs and pinches,
   And breaking often into violent laughters,
   As if the end they purposed were their own.
   Call you this weddings? Sure this is a knavery,
   A very trick, and dainty knavery;
   Marvellous finely carried, that's the comfort.
   What would these women do in ways of
     honour,
   That are such masters this way? Well, my sir
   Has been as good at finding out these toys,
   As any living; if he lose it now,
   At his own peril be it! I must follow.   (Exit.)

Scene 3

A court before the house of PETRUCHIO.

    (Enter SERVANTS *with lights*, PETRUCHIO,
      PETRONIUS, MOROSO, TRANIO,
        and SOPHOCLES.)

PETRUCHIO You that are married, gentlemen,
   have at ye,
   For a round wager now!
SOPHOCLES Of this night's stage?
PETRUCHIO Yes.
SOPHOCLES I am your first man: A pair of gloves
   Of twenty shillings.
PETRUCHIO Done! Who takes me up next?
   I am for all bets.

MOROSO Well, lusty Lawrence, were but my night now,
  Old as I am, I would make you clap on spurs,
  But I would reach you, and bring you to your trot too;
  I would, gallants.
PETRUCHIO Well said, Good-will; but where's the staff, boy, ha?
  Old father Time, your hour-glass is empty.
TRANIO A good tough train would break thee all to pieces;
  Thou hast not breath enough to say thy prayers.
PETRONIUS See how these boys despise us! – Will you to bed, son?
  This pride will have a fall.
PETRUCHIO Upon your daughter;
  But I shall rise again, if there be truth
  In eggs, and butter'd parsnips.
PETRONIUS Will you to bed, son, and leave talking?
  To-morrow morning we shall have you look,
  For all your great words, like St. George at Kingston,
  Running a foot-back from the furious dragon,
  That with her angry tail belabours him
  For being lazy.
TRANIO His courage quench'd, and so far quench'd –
PETRUCHIO 'Tis well, sir.
  What then?
SOPHOCLES Fly, fly, quoth then the fearful dwarf;
  Here is no place for living man.
PETRUCHIO Well, my masters,
  If I do sink under my business, as I find
  'Tis very possible, I am not the first
  That has miscarried so; that is my comfort;
  What may be done without impeach or waste,
  I can and will do.

(*Enter* JAQUES.)

How now! Is my fair bride a-bed?
JAQUES No truly, sir.
PETRONIUS Not a-bed yet? Body o' me, we'll up
  And rifle her! Here's a coil with a maidenhead!
  'Tis not entailed, is it?
PETRUCHIO If it be,
  I'll try all the law i' th' land, but I'll cut it off.
  Let's up, let's up; come!
JAQUES That you cannot neither.
PETRUCHIO Why?
JAQUES Unless
  You will drop thro' the chimney like a daw,
  Or force a breach i' th' windows; you may untile
  The house, 'tis possible.
PETRUCHIO What dost thou mean?

JAQUES A moral, sir; the ballad will express it:
    The wind and the rain
    Has turn'd you back again,
  And you cannot be lodged there.

  The truth is, all the doors are barricadoed;
  Not a cat-hole, but holds a murderer in't:
  She's victuall'd for this month.
PETRUCHIO Art not thou drunk?
SOPHOCLES He's drunk, he's drunk! Come, come; let's up.
JAQUES Yes, yes,
  I am drunk! Ye may go up, ye may, gentlemen;
  But take heed to your heads: I say no more.
SOPHOCLES I'll try that.   (*Exit*.)
PETRONIUS How dost thou say? the door fast lock'd, fellow?
JAQUES Yes, truly, sir, 'tis lock'd, and guarded too;
  And two as desperate tongues planted behind it,
  As e'er yet batter'd: They stand upon their honours,
  And will not give up without strange composition,
  I will assure you; marching away with
  Their pieces cock'd, and bullets in their mouths,
  Will not satisfy them.
PETRUCHIO How's this? how's this?
  They are? Is there another with her?
JAQUES Yes, marry is there, and an engineer.
MOROSO Who's that, for Heaven's sake?
JAQUES Colonel Bianca; she commands the works;
  Spinola's but a ditcher to her. There's a half-moon!
  I'm but a poor man, but if you'll give me leave,
  I'll venture a year's wages, draw all your force before it,
  And mount your ablest piece of battery,
  You shall not enter it these three nights yet.

(*Enter* SOPHOCLES.)

PETRUCHIO I should laugh at that, good Jaques.
SOPHOCLES Beat back again!
  She's fortified for ever.
JAQUES Am I drunk now, sir?
SOPHOCLES He that dares most, go up now, and be cool'd.
  I have 'scaped a pretty scouring.
PETRUCHIO What, are they mad? have we another bedlam?
  They do not talk, I hope?
SOPHOCLES Oh, terribly,
  Extremely fearful; the noise at London Bridge
  Is nothing near her.
PETRUCHIO How got she tongue?

SOPHOCLES As you got tail; she was born to't.
PETRUCHIO Lock'd out a-doors, and on my
    wedding-night?
  Nay, an I suffer this, I may go graze.
  Come, gentlemen, I'll batter. Are these virtues?
SOPHOCLES Do, and be beaten off with shame, as
    I was:
  I went up, came to th' door, knock'd, nobody
    answer'd;
  Knock'd louder, yet heard nothing; would have
    broke in
  By force; when suddenly a water-work
  Flew from the window with such violence,
  That, had I not duck'd quickly like a friar,
  Cætera quis nescit?
  The chamber's nothing but a mere Ostend;
  In every window pewter cannons mounted,
  You'll quickly find with what they are charged,
    sir.
PETRUCHIO Why then, *tantara* for us!
SOPHOCLES And all the lower works lined sure
    with small shot,
  Long tongues with firelocks, that at twelve-score
    blank
  Hit to the heart. Now, an ye dare go up –

(*Enter* MARIA *and* BIANCA *above.*)

MOROSO The window opens! Beat a parley first.
  I am so much amazed, my very hair stands.
PETRONIUS Why, how now, daughter? What,
    intrench'd?
MARIA A little guarded for my safety, sir.
PETRUCHIO For your safety, sweetheart? Why,
    who offends you?
  I come not to use violence.
MARIA I think
  You cannot, sir; I am better fortified.
PETRUCHIO I know your end; you would fain
    reprieve your maidenhead
  A night, or two.
MARIA Yes, or ten, or twenty,
  Or say an hundred; or, indeed, till I list lie with
    you.
SOPHOCLES That's a shrewd saying! From this
    present hour
  I never will believe a silent woman;
  When they break out they are bonfires.
PETRONIUS Till you list lie with him? Why, who
    are you, madam?
BIANCA That trim gentleman's wife, sir.
PETRUCHIO 'Cry you mercy! do you command
    too?
MARIA Yes, marry does she, and in chief.
BIANCA I do command, and you shall go without
  (I mean your wife,) for this night.

MARIA And for the next too, wench; and so as't
    follows.
PETRONIUS Thou wilt not, wilt 'a?
MARIA Yes, indeed, dear father;
  And till he seal to what I shall set down,
  For anything I know, for ever.
SOPHOCLES Indeed these are bugs-words.
TRANIO You hear, sir, she can talk, God be
    thanked!
PETRUCHIO I would I heard it not, sir!
SOPHOCLES I find that all the pity bestow'd upon
    this woman
  Makes but an anagram of an ill wife,
  For she was never virtuous.
PETRUCHIO You'll let me in, I hope, for all this
    jesting?
MARIA Hope still, sir.
PETRONIUS You will come down, I am sure.
MARIA I am sure I will not.
PETRONIUS I'll fetch you then.
BIANCA The power of the whole county cannot,
    sir,
  Unless we please to yield; which yet I think
  We shall not: Charge when you please, you shall
  Hear quickly from us.
MOROSO Heaven bless me from
  A chicken of thy hatching! Is this wiving?
PETRUCHIO Pr'ythee, Maria, tell me what's the
    reason,
  And do it freely, you deal thus strangely with
    me?
  You were not forced to marry: your consent
  Went equally with mine, if not before it:
  I hope you do not doubt I want that mettle
  A man should have, to keep a woman waking;
  I would be sorry to be such a saint yet:
  My person, as it is not excellent,
  So 'tis not old, nor lame, nor weak with physic,
  But well enough to please an honest woman,
  That keeps her house, and loves her husband.
MARIA 'Tis so.
PETRUCHIO My means and my conditions are no
    shamers
  Of him that owes 'em, (all the world knows
    that,)
  And my friends no reliers on my fortunes.
MARIA
  All this I believe, and none of all these parcels
  I dare except against; nay more, so far
  I am from making these the ends I aim at,
  These idle outward things, these women's fears,
  That were I yet unmarried, free to chuse
  Through all the tribes of man, I would take
    Petruchio
  In's shirt, with one ten groats to pay the priest,

Before the best man living, or the ablest
That e'er leap'd out of Lancashire: and they are
right ones.
PETRONIUS Why do you play the fool then, and
stand prating
Out of the window, like a broken miller?
PETRUCHIO If you will have me credit you,
Maria,
Come down, and let your love confirm it.
MARIA Stay
There, sir; that bargain's yet to make.
BIANCA Play sure, wench!
The pack's in thine own hand.
SOPHOCLES Let me die lousy,
If these two wenches be not brewing knavery
To stock a kingdom!
PETRUCHIO Why, this is a riddle;
'I love you, and I love you not.'
MARIA It is so;
And till your own experience do untie it,
This distance I must keep.
PETRUCHIO If you talk more,
I am angry, very angry!
MARIA I am glad on't, and I will talk.
PETRUCHIO Pr'ythee, peace!
Let me not think thou'rt mad. I tell thee,
woman,
If thou goest forward, I am still Petruchio.
MARIA And I am worse, a woman that can fear
Neither Petruchio Furius, nor his fame,
Nor anything that tends to our allegiance:
There's a short method for you: now you know
me.
PETRUCHIO If you can carry't so, 'tis very well.
BIANCA No, you shall carry it, sir.
PETRUCHIO Peace, gentle low-bell!
PETRONIUS Use no more words, but come down
instantly;
I charge thee, by the duty of a child!
PETRUCHIO Pr'ythee come, Maria! I forgive all.
MARIA Stay there! That duty, that you charge me
by,
(If you consider truly what you say,)
Is now another man's; you gave't away
I' th' church, if you remember, to my husband;
So all you can exact now, is no more
But only a due reverence to your person,
Which thus I pay: Your blessing, and I am gone
To bed for this night.
PETRONIUS This is monstrous!
That blessing that St. Dunstan gave the devil,
If I were near thee, I would give thee, whore;
Pull thee down by th' nose!
BIANCA Saints should not rave, sir:
A little rhubarb now were excellent.

PETRUCHIO Then, by that duty you owe to me,
Maria,
Open the door, and be obedient!
I am quiet yet.
MARIA I do confess that duty:
Make your best on't.
PETRUCHIO Why, give me leave, I will.
BIANCA Sir, there's no learning
An old stiff jade to trot; you know the moral.
MARIA Yet, as I take it, sir, I owe no more
Than you owe back again.
PETRUCHIO You will not article?
All I owe, presently – let me but up – I'll pay.
MARIA You are too hot, and such prove jades at
length.
You do confess a duty, or respect to me from
you again,
That's very near, or full the same with mine?
PETRUCHIO Yes.
MARIA Then, by that duty, or respect, or what
You please to have it, go to bed and leave me,
And trouble me no longer with your fooling;
For know, I am not for you.
PETRUCHIO Well, what remedy? (*To his friends.*)
PETRONIUS A fine smart cudgel. – Oh, that I were
near thee!
BIANCA If you had teeth now, what a case were
we in!
MOROSO These are the most authentic rebels,
next
Tyrone, I ever read of.
MARIA A week hence, or a fortnight, as you bear
you,
And as I find my will observed, I may,
With intercession of some friends, be brought
May be to kiss you; and so quarterly
To pay a little rent by composition.
You understand me?
SOPHOCLES Thou, boy, thou!
PETRUCHIO Well.
There are more maids than Maudlin; that's my
comfort.
MARIA Yes; and more men than Michael.
PETRUCHIO I must not
To bed with this stomach, and no meat, lady.
MARIA Feed where you will, so it be sound and
wholesome;
Else, live at livery, for I'll none with you.
BIANCA You had best back one o' th' dairy maids;
they'll carry:
But take heed to your girths, you'll get a bruise
else.
PETRUCHIO Now, if thou wouldst come down,
and tender me
All the delights due to a marriage-bed;

Study such kisses as would melt a man;
And turn thyself into a thousand figures,
To add new flames unto me; I would stand
Thus heavy, thus regardless, thus despising
Thee, and thy best allurings: All the beauty
That's laid upon your bodies, mark me well,
(For without doubt your minds are miserable,
You have no masks for them,) all this rare
    beauty,
Lay but the painter and the silk-worm by,
The doctor with his diets, and the tailor,
And you appear like flea'd cats; not so
    handsome.

MARIA And we appear, like her that sent us
    hither,
That only excellent and beauteous Nature,
Truly ourselves, for men to wonder at,
But too divine to handle: We are gold,
In our own natures pure; but when we suffer
The husband's stamp upon us, then allays,
And base ones, of you men, are mingled with us,
And make us blush like copper!

PETRUCHIO Then, and never
Till then, are women to be spoken of;
For till that time you have no souls, I take it.
Good night! – Come, gentlemen! I'll fast for this
    night;
But, by this hand – Well, I shall come up yet?

MARIA No.

PETRUCHIO There will I watch thee like a
    wither'd jury;
Thou shalt neither have meat, fire, nor candle,
Nor anything that's easy. Do you rebel so soon?
Yet take mercy.

BIANCA Put up your pipes; to bed, sir! I'll assure
    you
A month's siege will not shake us.

MOROSO Well said, colonel!

MARIA To bed, to bed, Petruchio! Good night,
    gentlemen!
You'll make my father sick with sitting up.
Here you shall find us any time these ten days,
Unless we may march off with our contentment.

PETRUCHIO I'll hang first!

MARIA And I'll quarter, if I do not!
I'll make you know, and fear a wife, Petruchio;
There my cause lies.
You have been famous for a woman-tamer,
And bear the fear'd name of a brave wife-
    breaker:
A woman now shall take those honours off, and
    tame you.
Nay, never look so big! she shall, believe me,
And I am she. What think ye? – Good night to
    all.

Ye shall find sentinels –

BIANCA If ye dare sally.   (*Exeunt above.*)

PETRONIUS The devil's in 'em, even the very
    devil,
The down-right devil!

PETRUCHIO I'll devil 'em; by these ten bones, I
    will!
I'll bring it to th' old proverb, 'No sport, no pie.'
Pox! taken down i' th' top of all my speed?
This is fine dancing! Gentlemen, stick to me:
You see our freehold's touch'd; and, by this light,
We will beleaguer 'em, and either starve 'em
    out,
Or make 'em recreant.

PETRONIUS I'll see all passages stopt, but those
    about 'em.
If the good women of the town dare succour
    'em,
We shall have wars indeed.

SOPHOCLES I'll stand perdue upon 'em.

MOROSO My regiment shall lie before.

JAQUES I think so;
'Tis grown too old to stand.

PETRUCHIO Let's in, and each provide his tackle!
We'll fire 'em out, or make 'em take their
    pardons
(Hear what I say) on their bare knees.
Am I Petruchio, fear'd and spoken of,
And on my wedding-night am I thus jaded?
                                        (*Exeunt.*)

Scene 4

A hall in the same.

(*Enter* ROWLAND *and* PEDRO, *at several doors.*)

ROWLAND Now, Pedro?

PEDRO Very busy, Master Rowland.

ROWLAND What haste, man?

PEDRO I beseech you pardon me,
I am not mine own man.

ROWLAND Thou art not mad?

PEDRO No; but, believe me, as hasty –

ROWLAND The cause, good Pedro?

PEDRO There be a thousand, sir. You are not
    married?

ROWLAND Not yet.

PEDRO Keep yourself quiet then.

ROWLAND Why?

PEDRO You'll find a fiddle
That never will be tuned else: From all women –
                                        (*Exit.*)

ROWLAND What ails the fellow, tro? – Jaques?

(*Enter* JAQUES.)

JAQUES Your friend, sir;
   But very full of business.
ROWLAND Nothing but business?
   Pr'ythee the reason! is there any dying?
JAQUES I would there were, sir!
ROWLAND But thy business?
JAQUES I'll tell you in a word: I am sent to lay
   An imposition upon souse and puddings,
   Pasties, and penny custards, that the women
   May not relieve yon rebels. Fare you well, sir!
ROWLAND How does my mistress?
JAQUES Like a resty jade;
   She's spoil'd for riding.   (*Exit.*)
ROWLAND What a devil ail they?
   Custards, and penny pasties, fools and fiddles!
   What's this to th' purpose? – Oh, well met.

      (*Enter* SOPHOCLES.)

SOPHOCLES Now, Rowland!
   I cannot stay to talk long.
ROWLAND What's the matter?
   Here's stirring, but to what end? Whither go
     you?
SOPHOCLES To view the works.
ROWLAND What works?
SOPHOCLES The women's trenches.
ROWLAND Trenches? Are such to see?
SOPHOCLES I do not jest, sir.
ROWLAND I cannot understand you.
SOPHOCLES Do not you hear
   In what a state of quarrel the new bride
   Stands with her husband?
ROWLAND Let him stand with her
   And there's an end.
SOPHOCLES It should be; but, by'r lady,
   She holds him out at pike's end, and defies him,
   And now is fortified. Such a regiment of rutters
   Never defied men braver: I am sent
   To view their preparation.
ROWLAND This is news,
   Stranger than armies in the air. You saw not
   My gentle mistress?
SOPHOCLES Yes, and meditating
   Upon some secret business; when she had found
     it,
   She leap'd for joy, and laugh'd, and straight
     retired
   To shun Moroso.
ROWLAND This may be for me.
SOPHOCLES Will you along?
ROWLAND No.
SOPHOCLES Farewell.   (*Exit.*)
ROWLAND Farewell, sir! –
   What should her musing mean, and what her joy
     in't

If not for my advantage? Stay you! may not
That bob-tail jade Moroso, with his gold,
His gew-gaudes, and the hope she has to send
   him
Quickly to dust, excite this?

    (*Enter* LIVIA *at one door, and* MOROSO
       at another, hearkening.

Here she comes;
And yonder walks the stallion to discover!
Yet I'll salute her. – Save you, beauteous
   mistress!
LIVIA The fox is kennell'd for me. – Save you, sir!
ROWLAND Why do you look so strange?
LIVIA I use to look, sir,
   Without examination.
MOROSO Twenty spur-royals for that word!
ROWLAND Belike then
   The object discontents you?
LIVIA Yes, it does.
ROWLAND Is't come to this? You know me, do you
   not?
LIVIA Yes, as I may know many, by repentance.
ROWLAND Why do you break your faith?
LIVIA I'll tell you that too:
   You are under age, and no band holds upon you.
MOROSO Excellent wench!
LIVIA Sue out your understanding,
   And get more hair to cover your bare knuckle!
   (For boys were made for nothing but dry kisses)
   And, if you can, more manners!
MOROSO Better still!
LIVIA And then, if I want Spanish gloves, or
    stockings,
   A ten-pound waistcoat, or a nag to hunt on,
   It may be I shall grace you to accept 'em.
ROWLAND Farewell! and when I credit women
    more,
   May I to Smithfield, and there buy a jade
   (And know him to be so) that breaks my neck!
LIVIA Because I have known you, I'll be thus kind
    to you:
   Farewell, and be a man! and I'll provide you,
   Because I see you're desperate, some staid
    chambermaid,
   That may relieve your youth with wholesome
    doctrine.
MOROSO She's mine from all the world! – Ha,
   wench!
LIVIA Ha, chicken!
       (*Gives him a box on the ear, and exit.*)
MOROSO How's this? I do not love these favours. –
   Save you!
ROWLAND The devil take thee!
          (*Wrings him by the nose.*)

MOROSO Oh!

ROWLAND There's a love-token for you! thank me
    now!

MOROSO I'll think on some of ye; and, if I live,
    My nose alone shall not be play'd withal.

                                 (*Exeunt.*)

Act II

Scene 1

A room in the house of PETRONIUS.

        (*Enter* PETRONIUS *and* MOROSO.)

PETRONIUS A box o' th' ear, do you say?

MOROSO Yes, sure, a sound one;
    Beside my nose blown to my hand. If Cupid
    Shoot arrows of that weight, I'll swear devoutly,
    He has sued his livery, and is no more a boy.

PETRONIUS You gave her some ill language?

MOROSO Not a word.

PETRONIUS Or might be you were fumbling!

MOROSO 'Would I had, sir!
    I had been aforehand then; but, to be baffled,
    And have no feeling of the cause –

PETRONIUS Be patient;
    I have a medicine clapp'd to her back will cure
    her.

MOROSO No, sure 't must be afore, sir.

PETRONIUS O' my conscience,
    When I got these two wenches (who till now
    Ne'er shew'd their riding) I was drunk with
      bastard,
    Whose nature is to form things like itself,
    Heady and monstrous. Did she slight him too?

MOROSO That's all my comfort! A mere hobby-
    horse
    She made child Rowland: 'Sfoot, she would not
      know him,
    Not give him a free look, not reckon him
    Among her thoughts; which I held more than
      wonder,
    I having seen her within these three days kiss
      him,
    With such an appetite as though she would eat
      him.

PETRONIUS There is some trick in this. How did
    he take it?

MOROSO Ready to cry, he ran away.

PETRONIUS I fear her:
    And yet I tell you, ever to my anger
    She is as tame as innocency. It may be
    This blow was but a favour.

MOROSO I'll be sworn
    'Twas well tied on then.

PETRONIUS Go to! pray forget it:

I have bespoke a priest, and within these two
    hours
I'll have you married; will that please you?

MOROSO Yes.

PETRONIUS I'll see it done myself, and give the
    lady
    Such a sound exhortation for this knavery,
    I'll warrant you, shall make her smell this
    month on't.

MOROSO Nay, good sir, be not violent.

PETRONIUS Neither –

MOROSO It may be
    Out of her earnest love there grew a longing
    (As you know women have such toys) in
      kindness,
    To give me a box o' th' ear, or so.

PETRONIUS It may be.

MOROSO I reckon for the best still. This night
    then
    I shall enjoy her?

PETRONIUS You shall handsel her.

MOROSO Old as I am, I'll give her one blow for't,
    Shall make her groan this twelvemonth.

PETRONIUS Where's your jointure?

MOROSO I have a jointure for her.

PETRONIUS Have your counsel
    Perused it yet?

MOROSO No counsel but the night, and your
    sweet daughter,
    Shall e'er peruse that jointure.

PETRONIUS Very well, sir.

MOROSO I'll no demurrers on't, nor no rejoinders.
    The other's ready seal'd.

PETRONIUS Come then, let's comfort
    My son Petruchio: He's like little children
    That lose their baubles, crying ripe.

MOROSO Pray tell me,
    Is this stern woman still upon the flaunt
    Of bold defiance?

PETRONIUS Still, and still she shall be,
    Till she be starved out: You shall see such
      justice,
    That women shall be glad after this tempest,
    To tie their husbands' shoes, and walk their
      horses.

MOROSO That were a merry world! – Do you hear
    the rumour?
    They say the women are in insurrection,
    And mean to make a –

PETRONIUS They'll sooner
    Draw upon walls as we do. Let 'em, let 'em!
    We'll ship 'em out in cuck-stools; there they'll
      sail
    As brave Columbus did, till they discover
    The happy islands of obedience.

We stay too long; come!
MOROSO Now, St. George be with us!   (*Exeunt.*)

Scene 2

The court before the house of PETRUCHIO.

(*Enter* LIVIA *alone.*)

LIVIA Now, if I can but get in handsomely,
  Father, I shall deceive you; and this night,
  For all your private plotting, I'll no wedlock:
  I have shifted sail, and find my sister's safety
  A sure retirement. Pray to Heaven that Rowland
  Do not believe too far what I said to him!
  For yon old foxcase forced me; that's my fear.
  Stay, let me see! this quarter fierce Petruchio
  Keeps with his myrmidons: I must be sudden;
  If he seize on me, I can look for nothing
  But martial-law; to this place have I 'scaped him.
  Above there!

(*Enter* MARIA *and* BIANCA *above.*)

MARIA *Qui va là?*
LIVIA A friend.
BIANCA Who are you?
LIVIA Look out and know!
MARIA Alas, poor wench, who sent thee?
  What weak fool made thy tongue his orator?
  I know you come to parley.
LIVIA You're deceived.
  Urged by the goodness of your cause, I come
  To do as you do.
MARIA You're too weak, too foolish,
  To cheat us with your smoothness: Do not we
    know
  Thou hast been kept up tame?
LIVIA Believe me!
MARIA No; pr'ythee, good Livia,
  Utter thy eloquence somewhere else.
BIANCA Good cousin,
  Put up your pipes; we are not for your palate:
  Alas! we know who sent you.
LIVIA O' my word –
BIANCA Stay there; you must not think your
    word,
  Or by your maidenhead, or such Sunday oaths,
  Sworn after even-song, can inveigle us
  To loose our hand-fast: Did their wisdoms think
  That sent you hither, we would be so foolish
  To entertain our gentle sister Sinon,
  And give her credit, while the wooden jade
  Petruchio stole upon us? No, good sister!
  Go home, and tell the merry Greeks that sent
    you,
  Ilium shall burn, and I, as did Æneas,

Will on my back, 'spite of the myrmidons,
  Carry this warlike lady, and through seas
  Unknown, and unbelieved, seek out a land,
  Where, like a race of noble Amazons,
  We'll root ourselves, and to our endless glory
  Live, and despise base men!
LIVIA I'll second you.
BIANCA How long have you been thus?
LIVIA That's all one, cousin;
  I stand for freedom now.
BIANCA Take heed of lying!
  For, by this light, if we do credit you,
  And find you tripping, his infliction
  That killed the prince of Orange, will we sport
  To what we purpose.
LIVIA Let me feel the heaviest!
MARIA Swear by thy sweetheart Rowland, (for by
    your maidenhead
  I fear 'twill be too late to swear) you mean
  Nothing but fair and safe, and honourable
  To us, and to yourself.
LIVIA I swear!
BIANCA Stay yet!
  Swear as you hate Moroso, (that's the surest)
  And as you have a certain fear to find him
  Worse than a poor dried Jack; full of more aches
  Than Autumn has; more knavery, and usury,
  And foolery, and brokery, than Dog's-Ditch;
  As you do constantly believe he's nothing
  But an old empty bag with a grey beard,
  And that beard such a bob-tail, that it looks
  Worse than a mare's tail eaten off with flies;
  As you acknowledge, that young handsome
    wench
  That lies by such a Bilboa blade, that bends
  With ev'ry pass he makes, to th' hilts, most
    miserable,
  A dry-nurse to his coughs, a fewterer
  To such a nasty fellow, a robbed thing
  Of all delights youth looks for; and, to end,
  One cast away on coarse beef, born to brush
  That everlasting cassock that has worn
  As many servants out, as the North-East passage
  Has consumed sailors: If you swear this, and
    truly,
  Without the reservation of a gown,
  Or any meritorious petticoat,
  'Tis like we shall believe you.
LIVIA I do swear it.
MARIA Stay yet a little! Came this wholesome
    motion
  (Deal truly, sister) from your own opinion,
  Or some suggestion of the foe?
LIVIA Ne'er fear me!
  For, by that little faith I have in husbands,

And the great zeal I bear your cause, I come
Full of that liberty you stand for, sister!

MARIA If we believe, and you prove recreant,
Livia
Think what a maim you give the noble cause
We now stand up for! Think what women shall,
An hundred years hence, speak thee, when
examples
Are look'd for, and so great ones, whose rela-
tions,
Spoke, as we do 'em, wench, shall make new
customs!

BIANCA If you be false, repent, go home, and
pray,
And to the serious women of the city
Confess yourself; bring not a sin so heinous
To load thy soul to this place. Mark me, Livia;
If thou be'st double, and betray'st our honours,
And we fail in our purpose, get thee where
There is no women living, nor no hope
There ever shall be!

MARIA If a mother's daughter,
That ever heard the name of stubborn husband,
Find thee, and know thy sin –

BIANCA Nay if old age,
One that has worn away the name of woman,
And no more left to know her by but railing,
No teeth, nor eyes, nor legs, but wooden ones,
Come but i' the windward of thee, for sure she'll
smell thee,
Thou'lt be so rank; she'll ride thee like a
nightmare,
And say her prayers backward to undo thee;
She'll curse thy meat and drink, and, when thou
marriest,
Clap a sound spell for ever on thy pleasures.

MARIA Children of five year old, like little fairies,
Will pinch thee into motley; all that ever
Shall live and hear of thee, I mean all women,
Will (like so many furies) shake their keys,
And toss their flaming distaffs o'er their heads,
Crying, revenge! Take heed; 'tis hideous,
Oh, 'tis a fearful office! If thou hadst
(Though thou be'st perfect now) when thou
camest hither
A false imagination, get thee gone,
And, as my learned cousin said, repent!
This place is sought by soundness.

LIVIA So I seek it,
Or let me be a most despised example!

MARIA I do believe thee; be thou worthy of it!
You come not empty?

LIVIA No, here's cakes and cold meat,
And tripe of proof; behold here's wine and beer!
Be sudden, I shall be surprised else.

MARIA Meet at the low parlour-door; there lies a
close way;
What fond obedience you have living in you,
Or duty to a man, before you enter
Fling it away; 'twill but defile our offerings.

BIANCA Be wary as you come.

LIVIA I warrant you.   (*Exeunt.*)

Scene 3

A street.

(*Enter three* MAIDS.)

1 MAID How goes your business, girls?

2 MAID A-foot, and fair.

3 MAID If fortune favour us. Away to your
strength!
The country forces are arrived. Be gone!
We are discover'd else.

1 MAID Arm, and be valiant!

2 MAID Think of our cause!

3 MAID Our justice!

1 MAID 'Tis sufficient.   (*Exeunt.*)

Scene 4

Another street.

(*Enter* ROWLAND *and* TRANIO, *severally.*)

TRANIO Now, Rowland?

ROWLAND How do you?

TRANIO How dost thou, man?
Thou look'st ill.

ROWLAND Yes. Pray can you tell me, Tranio,
Who knew the devil first?

TRANIO A woman.

ROWLAND So.
Were they not well acquainted?

TRANIO May be so,
For they had certain dialogues together.

ROWLAND He sold her fruit, I take it?

TRANIO Yes, and cheese
That choak'd all mankind after.

ROWLAND Canst thou tell me
Whether that woman ever had a faith,
After she had eaten?

TRANIO That is a school-question.

ROWLAND No, 'tis no question; for believe me,
Tranio,
That cold fruit, after eating, bred nought in her
But windy promises, and cholic vows,
That broke out both ways. Thou hast heard, I
am sure,
Of Esculapius, a far-famed surgeon,
One that could set together quarter'd traitors,

And make 'em honest men.

TRANIO How dost thou, Rowland?

ROWLAND Let him but take (if he dare do a
        cure
    Shall get him fame indeed) a faithless woman,
    (There will be credit for him that will speak
        him)
    A broken woman, Tranio, a base woman,
    And if he can cure such a wreck of honour,
    Let him come here and practise!

TRANIO Now, for honour's sake,
    Why, what ail'st thou, Rowland?

ROWLAND I am ridden, Tranio,
    And spur-gall'd to the life of patience, –
    Heaven keep my wits together! – by a thing
    Our worst thoughts are too noble for, a woman.

TRANIO Your mistress has a little frown'd, it may
        be?

ROWLAND She was my mistress.

TRANIO Is she not?

ROWLAND No, Tranio:
    She has done me such disgrace, so spitefully,
    So like a woman bent to my undoing,
    That henceforth a good horse shall be my
        mistress,
    A good sword, or a book. And if you see her,
    Tell her, I do beseech you, even for love's sake –

TRANIO I will, Rowland.

ROWLAND She may sooner count the good
    I have thought her, our old love and our
        friendship,
    Shed one true tear, mean one hour constantly,
    Be old and honest, married and a maid,
    Than make me see her more, or more believe
        her:
    And now I have met a messenger, farewell, sir!
                                        (*Exit*.)

TRANIO Alas, poor Rowland! I will do it for thee.
    This is that dog Moroso; but I hope
    To see him cold i' th' mouth first, ere he enjoy
        her.
    I'll watch this young man; desperate thoughts
        may seize him,
    And, if my purse or counsel can, I'll ease him.
                                        (*Exit*.)

Scene 5

A room in the house of PETRUCHIO.

    (*Enter* PETRUCHIO, PETRONIUS, MOROSO,
        and SOPHOCLES.)

PETRUCHIO For, look you, gentlemen, say that I
        grant her,
    Out of my free and liberal love, a pardon,

Which you and all men else know, she deserves
    not,
(*Teneatis, amici*) can all the world leave
    laughing?

PETRONIUS I think not.

PETRUCHIO No, by Heaven, they cannot!
    For pray consider, have you ever read,
    Or heard of, or can any man imagine,
    So stiff a Tom-boy, of so set a malice,
    And such a brazen resolution,
    As this young crab-tree? and then answer me!
    And mark but this too, friends, without a cause,
    Not a foul word come cross her, not a fear
    She justly can take hold on; and d'ye think
    I must sleep out my anger, and endure it,
    Sow pillows to her ease, and lull her mischief?
    Give me a spindle first! No, no, my masters,
    Were she as fair as Nell-a-Greece, and housewife
    As good as the wise sailor's wife, and young still,
    Never above fifteen, and these tricks to it,
    She should ride the wild-mare once a-week, she
        should,
    Believe me, friends, she should! I would tabor
        her,
    'Till all the legions that are crept into her,
    Flew out with fire i' th' tails.

SOPHOCLES Methinks you err now;
    For to me seems, a little sufferance
    Were a far surer cure.

PETRUCHIO Yes, I can suffer,
    Where I see promises of peace and amendment.

MOROSO Give her a few conditions.

PETRUCHIO I'll be hang'd first!

PETRONIUS Give her a crab-tree cudgel!

PETRUCHIO So I will;
    And after it a flock-bed for her bones,
    And hard eggs, till they brace her like a drum,
    She shall be pamper'd with;
    She shall not know a stool in ten months,
        gentlemen.

SOPHOCLES This must not be.

    (*Enter* JAQUES.)

JAQUES Arm, arm! out with your weapons!
    For all the women in the kingdom's on ye;
    They swarm like wasps, and nothing can
        destroy 'em,
    But stopping of their hive, and smothering of
        'em.

    (*Enter* PEDRO.)

PEDRO Stand to your guard, sir! all the devils
        extant
    Are broke upon us like a cloud of thunder;
    There are more women marching hitherward.

In rescue of my mistress, than e'er turn'd tail
At Sturbridge-fair, and I believe as fiery.
JAQUES The forlorn-hope's led by a tanner's wife,
(I know her by her hide) a desp'rate woman;
She fled her husband in her youth, and made
Reins of his hide to ride the parish. Take 'em all
together,
They are a genealogy of jennets, gotten
And born thus, by the boisterous breath of
husbands;
They serve sure, and are swift to catch occasion
(I mean their foes or husbands) by the forelocks,
And there they hang like favours: cry they can,
But more for noble spite than fear; and crying
Like the old giants that were foes to Heaven,
They heave ye stool on stool, and fling main pot-
lids
Like massy rocks, dart ladles, tossing irons,
And tongs like thunderbolts, till overlaid,
They fall beneath the weight: yet still aspiring
At those imperious codsheads, that would tame
'em.
There's ne'er a one of these, the worst and
weakest,
(Choose where you will) but dare attempt the
raising,
Against the sovereign peace of Puritans,
A May-pole and a morris, maugre mainly
Their zeal, and dudgeon-daggers; and yet more,
Dares plant a stand of batt'ring ale against 'em,
And drink 'em out o' th' parish.
SOPHOCLES Lo you, fierce
Petruchio! this comes of your impatience.
PEDRO There's one brought in the bears, against
the canons
Of the town, made it good, and fought 'em.
JAQUES Another, to her everlasting fame, erected
Two ale-houses of ease, the quarter sessions
Running against her roundly; in which
business
Two of the disanullers lost their night-caps;
A third stood excommunicate by th' cudgel;
The constable, to her eternal glory,
Drunk hard, and was converted, and she victor.
PEDRO Then are they victualled with pies and
puddings,
(The trappings of good stomachs) noble ale
(The true defender,) sausages, and smoked
ones,
If need be, such as serve for pikes; and pork
(Better the Jews ne'er hated) here and there
A bottle of metheglin, a stout Briton
That will stand to 'em;
What else they want, they war for.
PETRUCHIO Come to council!

SOPHOCLES Now you must grant conditions, or
the kingdom
Will have no other talk but this.
PETRONIUS Away then,
And let's advise the best!
SOPHOCLES Why do you tremble?
MOROSO Have I lived thus long to be knockt o' th'
head
With half a washing beetle? Pray be wise, sir.
PETRUCHIO Come; something I'll do; but what it
is, I know not.
SOPHOCLES To council then, and let's avoid their
follies!
Guard all the doors, or we shall not have a cloak
left.   (*Exeunt.*)

Scene 6

The court before the house.

(*Enter* PETRONIUS, PETRUCHIO, MOROSO,
SOPHOCLES, *and* TRANIO.)

PETRONIUS I am indifferent, though, I must
confess,
I had rather see her carted.
TRANIO No more of that, sir.
SOPHOCLES Are ye resolved to give her fair
conditions?
'Twill be the safest way.
PETRUCHIO I am distracted!
'Would I had run my head into a halter
When I first woo'd her! if I offer peace,
She'll urge her own conditions; that's the devil.
SOPHOCLES Why, say she do?
PETRUCHIO Say, I am made an ass then!
I know her aim: May I with reputation,
(Answer me this) with safety of mine honour,
After the mighty manage of my first wife,
Which was indeed a fury to this filly,
After my twelve strong labours to reclaim her,
Which would have made Don Hercules horn-
mad,
And hid him in his hide, suffer this Cicely,
Ere she have warm'd my sheets, ere grappled
with me,
This pink, this painted foist, this cockle-boat,
To hang her fights out, and defy me, friends,
A well-known man of war? If this be equal,
And I may suffer, say, and I have done.
PETRONIUS I do not think you may.
TRANIO You'll make it worse, sir.
SOPHOCLES Pray hear me, good Petruchio. But
even now,
You were contented to give all conditions,
To try how far she would carry: 'Tis a folly

(And you will find it so) to clap the curb on,
    Ere you be sure it proves a natural wildness,
    And not a forced. Give her conditions;
    For, on my life, this trick is put into her –
PETRONIUS I should believe so too.
SOPHOCLES And not her own.
TRANIO You'll find it so.
SOPHOCLES Then, if she flounder with you,
    Clap spurs on; and in this you'll deal with
        temperance,
    Avoid the hurry of the world –
TRANIO And lose –
MOROSO No honour on my life, sir.
PETRUCHIO I will do it.   (*Music above.*)
PETRONIUS It seems they are very merry.

(*Enter* JAQUES.)

PETRUCHIO Why, God hold it!
MOROSO Now, Jaques?
JAQUES They are i' th' flaunt, sir.
SOPHOCLES Yes we hear 'em.
JAQUES They have got a stick of fiddles, and they
        firk it
    In wond'rous ways: The two grand capitanoes
    (They brought the auxiliary regiments)
    Dance with their coats tuck'd up to their bare
        breeches,
    And bid the kingdom kiss 'em; that's the
        burden.
    They have got metheglin, and audacious ale,
    And talk like tyrants.
PETRONIUS How know'st thou?
JAQUES I peep'd in
    At a loose lansket.
TRANIO Hark!
PETRONIUS A song! Pray silence.

SONG
    A health for all this day,
    To the woman that bears the sway,
            And wear the breeches;
                Let it come, let it come.
    Let this health be a seal,
    For the good of the common-weal,
            The woman shall wear the
                breeches!
    Let's drink then and laugh it,
    And merrily, merrily quaff it,
    And tipple, and tipple a round:
            Here's to thy fool,
            And to my fool;
            Come, to all fools,
    Though it cost us, wench, many a pound.

MOROSO They look out.

(*All the* WOMEN *appear above*, CITIZENS,
    and COUNTRY WOMEN.)

PETRUCHIO Good even, ladies!
MARIA Good you good even, sir!
PETRUCHIO How have you slept to-night?
MARIA Exceeding well, sir.
PETRUCHIO Did you not wish me with you?
MARIA No, believe me,
    I never thought upon you.
COUNTRY WOMAN Is that he?
BIANCA Yes.
COUNTRY WOMAN Sir!
SOPHOCLES She has drank hard: Mark her hood.
COUNTRY WOMAN You are –
SOPHOCLES Learnedly drunk, I'll hang else. Let
        her utter.
COUNTRY WOMAN And I must tell you *viva voce*,
        friend,
    A very foolish fellow.
TRANIO There's an ale-figure.
PETRUCHIO I thank you, Susan Brotes.
CITIZEN Forward, sister.
COUNTRY WOMAN You have espoused here a
        hearty woman,
    A comely, and courageous –
PETRUCHIO Well, I have so.
COUNTRY WOMAN And, to the comfort of
        distressed damsels,
    Women out-worn in wedlock, and such vessels,
    This woman has defied you.
PETRUCHIO It should seem so.
COUNTRY WOMAN And why?
PETRUCHIO Yes, can you tell?
COUNTRY WOMAN For thirteen causes.
PETRUCHIO Pray, by your patience, mistress –
CITIZEN Forward, sister!
PETRUCHIO Do you mean to treat of all these?
CITIZEN Who shall let her?
PETRONIUS Do you hear, velvet-hood? we come
        not now
    To hear your doctrine.
COUNTRY WOMAN For the first, I take it,
    It doth divide itself into seven branches.
PETRUCHIO Hark you, good Maria,
    Have you got a catechiser here?
TRANIO Good zeal!
SOPHOCLES Good three-piled predication, will
        you peace,
    And hear the cause we come for?
COUNTRY WOMAN Yes, bob-tails,
    We know the cause you come for; here's the
        cause: –   (*Pointing to* MARIA.)
    But never hope to carry her, never dream
    Or flatter your opinions with a thought
    Of base repentance in her.

CITIZEN Give me sack!
By this, and next, strong ale –
COUNTRY WOMAN Swear forward, sister!
CITIZEN By all that's cordial, in this place we'll bury
Our bones, fames, tongues, our triumphs, and then all
That ever yet was chronicled of woman,
But this brave wench, this excellent despiser,
This bane of dull obedience, shall inherit
Her liberal will, and march off with conditions
Noble and worth herself.
COUNTRY WOMAN She shall, Tom Tilers,
And brave ones too. My hood shall make a hearse-cloth,
And I'll lie under it like Joan O'Gaunt,
Ere I go less; my distaff stuck up by me,
For the eternal trophy of my conquests,
And loud fame at my head with two main bottles
Shall fill to all the world, the glorious fall
Of old Don Gillian.
CITIZEN Yet a little further.
We have taken arms in rescue of this lady,
Most just and noble: If ye beat us off,
Without conditions, and we recant,
Use us as we deserve; and first degrade us
Of all our ancient chambering, next that
The symbols of our secresy, silk stockings
Hew off our heels; our petticoats of arms
Tear off our bodies, and our bodkins break
Over our coward heads.
COUNTRY WOMAN And ever after,
To make the tainture most notorious,
At all our crests (*videlicet*, our plackets)
Let laces hang, and we return again
Unto our former titles, dairy-maids!
PETRUCHIO No more wars! Puissant ladies, shew conditions,
And freely I accept 'em.
MARIA Call in Livia;
She's in the treaty too.
MOROSO How! Livia?
MARIA Hear you that, sir?
There's the conditions for you; pray peruse 'em.
                              (*Throws down a paper.*)
PETRONIUS Yes, there she is: It had been no right rebellion,
Had she held off. What think you, man?
MOROSO Nay, nothing:
I have enough o' th' prospect. O' my conscience,
The world's end and the goodness of a woman
Will come together.
PETRONIUS Are you there, sweet lady?

LIVIA 'Cry you mercy, sir! I saw you not: Your blessing!
PETRONIUS Yes, when I bless a jade that stumbles with me.
How are the articles?
LIVIA This is for you, sir;
And I shall think upon't.
                          (*Throws a paper to* MOROSO.)
MOROSO You have used me finely!
LIVIA There is no other use of thee now extant,
But to be hung up, cassock, cap, and all,
For some strange monster at Apothecaries.
PETRONIUS I hear you, whore!
LIVIA I must be his then, sir;
For need will then compel me.
CITIZEN Blessing on thee!
LIVIA He will undo me in mere pans of coals,
To make him lusty.
PETRONIUS There is no talking to 'em. –
How are they, sir?
PETRUCHIO As I expected: Liberty and clothes,
                          (*Reads.*)
When, and in what way she will; continual monics,
Company, and all the house at her dispose;
No tongue to say, *why is this:* or, *whither will it?*
New coaches, and some buildings, she appoints here;
Hangings, and hunting-horses; and for plate
And jewels, for her private use, I take it,
Two thousand pound in present; then for music
And women to read French –
PETRONIUS This must not be.
PETRUCHIO And at the latter end a clause put in,
That Livia shall by no man be importuned,
This whole month yet, to marry.
PETRONIUS This is monstrous!
PETRUCHIO This shall be done; I'll humour her awhile:
If nothing but repentance and undoing
Can win her love, I'll make a shift for one.
SOPHOCLES When you are once a-bed, all these conditions
Lie under your own seal.
MARIA Do you like 'em?
PETRUCHIO Yes;
And, by that faith I gave you 'fore the priest,
I'll ratify 'em.
COUNTRY WOMAN Stay! what pledges?
MARIA No, I'll take that oath.
But have a care you keep it!
CITIZEN 'Tis not now
As when Andrea lived.
COUNTRY WOMAN If you do juggle,
Or alter but a letter of these articles

We have set down, the self-same persecution –
MARIA Mistrust him not.
PETRUCHIO By all my honesty –
MARIA Enough; I yield.
PETRONIUS What's this inserted here?
SOPHOCLES That the two valiant women that
    command here
  Shall have a supper made 'em, and a large one,
  And liberal entertainment without grudging,
  And pay for all their soldiers.
PETRUCHIO That shall be too;
  And if a tun of wine will serve to pay 'em,
  They shall have justice. I ordain ye all
  Paymasters, gentlemen.
TRANIO Then we shall have sport, boys!
MARIA We'll meet you in the parlour.
PETRUCHIO Ne'er look sad, sir;
  For I will do it.
SOPHOCLES There's no danger in't.
PETRUCHIO For Livia's article, you shall observe
    it;
  I have tied myself.
PETRONIUS I will.
PETRUCHIO Along then! – Now
  Either I break, or this stiff plant must bow.
                                    (*Exeunt.*)

Act III

Scene 1

A street.

          (*Enter* TRANIO *and* ROWLAND.)

TRANIO Come, you shall take my counsel.
ROWLAND I shall hang first!
  I'll no more love, that's certain; 'tis a bane,
  Next that they poison rats with, the most mortal.
  No, I thank Heaven, I have got my sleep again,
  And now begin to write sense; I can walk ye
  A long hour in my chamber like a man,
  And think of something that may better me,
  Some serious point of learning or my state:
  No more *ah-me*'s, and *misereri*'s, Tranio,
  Come near my brain. I'll tell thee; had the devil
  But any essence in him of a man,
  And could be brought to love, and love a
    woman,
  'Twould make his head ache worser than his
    horns do,
  And firk him with a fire he never felt yet,
  Would make him dance. I tell thee; there is
    nothing
  (It may be thy case, Tranio, therefore hear me)
  Under the sun (reckon the mass of follies

  Crept into th' world with man) so desperate,
  So mad, so senseless, poor and base, so
    wretched,
  Roguy, and scurvy –
TRANIO Whither wilt thou, Rowland?
ROWLAND As 'tis to be in love.
TRANIO And why, for Virtue sake?
ROWLAND And why, for Virtue's sake! Dost thou
    not conceive me?
TRANIO No, by my troth.
ROWLAND Pray then, and heartily.
  For fear thou fall into't. I'll tell thee why too,
  For I have hope to save thee: When thou lovest,
  And first beginn'st to worship the gilt calf,
  Imprimis, thou hast lost thy gentry,
  And, like a 'prentice, flung away thy freedom:
  Forthwith thou art a slave.
TRANIO That's a new doctrine.
ROWLAND Next, thou'rt no more man.
TRANIO What then?
ROWLAND A frippery;
  Nothing but braided hair, and penny ribband,
  Glove, garter, ring, rose, or at best a swabber;
  If thou canst love so near to keep thy making,
  Yet thou wilt lose thy language.
TRANIO Why?
ROWLAND Oh, Tranio!
  Those things in love ne'er talk as we do.
TRANIO No?
ROWLAND No, without doubt; they sigh, and
    shake the head,
  And sometimes whistle dolefully.
TRANIO No tongue?
ROWLAND Yes, Tranio, but no truth in't, nor no
    reason:
  And when they cant (for 'tis a kind of canting)
  You shall hear, if you reach to understand 'em,
  (Which you must be a fool first, or you cannot,)
  Such gibb'rish; such, *believe me – I protest,
  sweet –*
  And, *oh, dear Heavens, in which such
  constellations*
  Reign at the births of lovers – This is too well!
  And, *deign me, lady, deign me, I beseech you.*
  Your poor unworthy lump – and then she licks
    him.
TRANIO A pox on't, this is nothing!
ROWLAND Thou hast hit it.
  Then talks she ten times worse, and wries, and
    wriggles,
  As though she had the itch (and so it may be).
TRANIO Why thou art grown a strange discoverer.
ROWLAND Of mine own follies, Tranio.
TRANIO Wilt thou, Rowland,
  Certain ne'er love again?

ROWLAND I think so, certain;
   And, if I be not dead-drunk, I shall keep it.
TRANIO Tell me but this; what dost thou think of
   women?
ROWLAND Why, as I think of fiddles; they delight
   me,
   Till their strings break.
TRANIO What strings?
ROWLAND Their modesties,
   Faiths, vows, and maidenheads; for they are like
   kits,
   They have but four strings to 'em.
TRANIO What wilt thou
   Give me for ten pounds now, when thou next
   lovest,
   And the same woman still?
ROWLAND Give me the money;
   A hundred, and my bond for't.
TRANIO But pray hear me;
   I'll work all means I can to reconcile ye?
ROWLAND Do, do; give me the money.
TRANIO There!
ROWLAND Work, Tranio.
TRANIO You shall go sometimes where she is.
ROWLAND Yes, straight.
   This is the first good I e'er got by women.
TRANIO You would think it strange now, if
   another beauty
   As good as hers, say better –
ROWLAND Well?
TRANIO (Conceive me,
   This is no point o' th' wager.)
ROWLAND That's all one.
TRANIO Love you as much, or more, than she
   now hates you.
ROWLAND 'Tis a good hearing! Let 'em love: Ten
   pound more,
   I never love that woman.
TRANIO There it is;
   And so an hundred, if you lose.
ROWLAND 'Tis done!
   Have you another to put in?
TRANIO No, no, sir.
ROWLAND I'm very sorry. Now will I erect
   A new game, and go hate for th' bell; I'm sure
   I am in excellent case to win.
TRANIO I must have leave
   To tell you, and tell truth too, what she is,
   And how she suffers for you.
ROWLAND Ten pound more,
   I ne'er believe you.
TRANIO No, sir; I am stinted.
ROWLAND Well, take your best way then.
TRANIO Let's walk. I am glad
   Your sullen fever's off.

ROWLAND 'Shalt see me, Tranio,
   A monstrous merry man now. Let's to the
   wedding;
   And, as we go, tell me the general hurry
   Of these mad wenches, and their works.
TRANIO I will.
ROWLAND And do thy worst.
TRANIO Something I'll do –
ROWLAND Do, Tranio.   (*Exeunt.*)

Scene 2

A room in the house of PETRUCHIO.

(*Enter* PEDRO *and* JAQUES.)

PEDRO A pair of stocks bestride 'em! are they
   gone?
JAQUES Yes, they are gone; and all the pans i' th'
   town
   Beating before 'em. What strange admonitions
   They gave my master, and how fearfully
   They threaten'd, if he broke 'em!
PEDRO O' my conscience,
   He has found his full match now.
JAQUES That I believe too.
PEDRO How did she entertain him?
JAQUES She look'd on him –
PEDRO But scurvily.
JAQUES With no great affection
   That I saw: And I heard some say he kiss'd her,
   But 'twas upon a treaty; and some copies
   Say, but her cheek.
PEDRO Jaques, what wouldst thou give
   For such a wife now?
JAQUES Full as many prayers
   As the most zealous Puritan conceives
   Out of the meditation of fat veal,
   Or birds of prey, cramm'd capons, against
   players,
   And to as good a tune too; but against her,
   'That Heaven would bless me from her!' Mark it,
   Pedro;
   If this house be not turn'd within this fortnight
   With the foundation upward, I'll be carted.
   My comfort is yet, that those Amorites
   That came to back her cause, those heathen
   whores,
   Had their hoods hallowed with sack.
PEDRO How devilish drunk they were!
JAQUES And how they tumbled, Pedro! Didst thou
   mark
   The country cavaliero?
PEDRO Out upon her,
   How she turn'd down the bragget!
JAQUES Ay, that sunk her.

PEDRO That drink was well put to her: What a somersalt,
  When the chair fell, she fetch'd with her heels upward!
JAQUES And what a piece of landskip she discover'd!
PEDRO Didst mark her when her hood fell in the posset?
JAQUES Yes, and there rid, like a Dutch hoy. The tumbrel,
  When she had got her ballast –
PEDRO That I saw too.
JAQUES How fain she would have drawn on Sophocles
  To come aboard, and how she simper'd it –
PEDRO I warrant her, she has been a worthy striker.
JAQUES I' th' heat of summer, there had been some hope on't.
PEDRO Hang her!
JAQUES She offer'd him a Harry-groat, and belch'd out,
  Her stomach being blown with ale, such courtship,
  Upon my life, has given him twenty stools since.
  Believe my calculation, these old women,
  When they are tippled, and a little heated,
  Are like new wheels; they'll roar you all the town o'er
  Till they be greased.
PEDRO The city cinque-pace,
  Dame Toast-and-Butter, had the bob too.
JAQUES Yes:
  But she was sullen drunk, and giv'n to filching;
  I see her offer at a spoon. – My master!
  I do not like his look; I fear he has fasted,
  For all this preparation: Let's steal by him.
                                        (*Exeunt*.)

(*Enter* PETRUCHIO *and* SOPHOCLES.)

SOPHOCLES Not let you touch her all this night?
PETRUCHIO Not touch her.
SOPHOCLES Where was your courage?
PETRUCHIO Where was her obedience?
  Never poor man was shamed so; never rascal
  That keeps a stud of whores was used so basely.
SOPHOCLES Pray you tell me one thing truly; do you love her?
PETRUCHIO I would I did not; upon that condition
  I pass'd thee half my land.
SOPHOCLES It may be then,
  Her modesty required a little violence:
  Some women love to struggle.
PETRUCHIO She had it,
  And so much that I sweat for't, so I did;
  But to no end; I wash'd an Ethiop.
  She swore my force might weary her, but win her
  I never could, nor should, till she consented;
  And I might take her body prisoner,
  But for her mind or appetite –
SOPHOCLES 'Tis strange!
  This woman is the first I ever read of,
  Refused a warranted occasion,
  And standing on so fair terms.
PETRUCHIO I shall quit her.
SOPHOCLES Used you no more art?
PETRUCHIO Yes; I swore to her,
  And by no little ones, if presently,
  Without more disputation on the matter,
  She grew not nearer to me, and dispatch'd me
  Out of the pain I was, (for I was nettled,)
  And willingly, and eagerly, and sweetly,
  I would to her chamber-maid, and in her hearing
  Begin her such a hunts-up –
SOPHOCLES Then she started?
PETRUCHIO No more than I do now: Marry, she answer'd,
  If I were so disposed, she could not help it;
  But there was one call'd Jaques, a poor butler,
  One that might well content a single woman.
SOPHOCLES And he should tilt her?
PETRUCHIO To that sense. And last,
  She bade me yet these six nights look for nothing,
  Nor strive to purchase it, but fair good-night,
  And so good-morrow, and a kiss or two
  To close my stomach; for her vow had seal'd it,
  And she would keep it constant.
SOPHOCLES Stay you, stay you!
  Was she thus when you woo'd her?
PETRUCHIO Nothing, Sophocles,
  More keenly eager: I was oft afraid
  She had been light and easy, she would shower
  Her kisses so upon me.
SOPHOCLES Then I fear
  Another spoke's i' th' wheel.
PETRUCHIO Now thou hast found me!
  There gnaws my devil, Sophocles. Oh, Patience,
  Preserve me! that I make her not example
  By some unworthy way; as flaying her,
  Boiling, or making verjuice, drying her –
SOPHOCLES I hear her.
PETRUCHIO Mark her then, and see the heir
  Of spite and prodigality! She has studied
  A way to beggar us both, and by this hand
  She shall be, if I live, a doxy.

(MARIA *appears at the door, with a* SERVANT *and* WOMAN.)

SOPHOCLES Fy, sir!
MARIA I do not like that dressing; 'tis too poor:
   Let me have six gold laces, broad and massy,
   And betwixt every lace a rich embroidery;
   Line the gown through with plush perfumed,
      and purfle
   All the sleeves down with pearl!
PETRUCHIO What think you, Sophocles?
   In what point stands my state now?
MARIA For those hangings,
   Let 'em be carried where I gave appointment,
   They are too base for my use; and bespeak
   New pieces, of the civil wars of France:
   Let 'em be large and lively, and all silk-work,
   The borders gold.
SOPHOCLES Ay, marry, sir, this cuts it.
MARIA That fourteen yards of satin give my
      woman;
   I do not like the colour, 'tis too civil;
   There's too much silk i' th' lace too. Tell the
      Dutchman,
   That brought the mares, he must with all speed
      send me
   Another suit of horses; and, by all means,
   Ten cast of hawks for th' river: I much care not
   What price they bear, so they be sound, and
      flying;
   For the next winter I am sure for the country,
   And mean to take my pleasure. Where's the
      horseman?
PETRUCHIO She means to ride a great-horse.
SOPHOCLES With a side-saddle?
PETRUCHIO Yes; and she'll run a-tilt within this
      twelvemonth.
MARIA To-morrow I'll begin to learn: But pray sir,
   Have a great care he be an easy doer;
   'Twill spoil a scholar else.
SOPHOCLES An easy doer!
   Did you hear that?
PETRUCHIO Yes; I shall meet her morals
   Ere it be long, I fear not.
MARIA (*Entering*) Oh, good morrow!
SOPHOCLES Good morrow, lady! How is't now?
MARIA 'Faith, sickly;
   This house stands in an ill air –
PETRUCHIO Yet more charges?
MARIA Subject to rots and rheums; out on't! 'tis
      nothing
   But a tiled fog.
PETRUCHIO What think you of the Lodge then?
MARIA I like the seat, but 'tis too little. –
      Sophocles,
   Let me have thy opinion; thou hast judgment.

PETRUCHIO 'Tis very well!
MARIA What if I pluck it down,
   And build a square upon it, with two courts
   Still rising from the entrance?
PETRUCHIO And i' th' midst
   A college for young scolds.
MARIA And to the southward
   Take in a garden of some twenty acres,
   And cast it of the Italian fashion, hanging?
PETRUCHIO An you could cast yourself so too –
      Pray, lady,
   Will not this cost much money?
MARIA Some five thousand;
   Say six. I'll have it battled too –
PETRUCHIO And gilt? – Maria,
   This is a fearful course you take! Pray think on't:
   You are a woman now, a wife, and his
   That must in honesty and justice look for
   Some due obedience from you.
MARIA That bare word
   Shall cost you many a pound more. Build upon't!
   Tell me of due obedience? What's a husband?
   What are we married for? to carry sumpters?
   Are we not one piece with you, and as worthy
   Our own intentions as you yours?
PETRUCHIO Pray hear me!
MARIA Take two small drops of water, equal
      weigh'd,
   Tell me which is the heaviest, and which ought
   First to descend in duty?
PETRUCHIO You mistake me;
   I urge not service from you, nor obedience
   In way of duty, but of love and credit:
   All I expect is but a noble care
   Of what I have brought you, and of what I am,
   And what our name may be.
MARIA That's in my making.
PETRUCHIO 'Tis true, it is so.
MARIA Yes, it is, Petruchio;
   For there was never man without our moulding,
   Without our stamp upon him, and our justice,
   Left anything, three ages after him,
   Good, and his own.
SOPHOCLES Good lady, understand him.
MARIA I do too much, sweet Sophocles: He's one
   Of a most spiteful self-condition,
   Never at peace with anything but age,
   That has no teeth left to return his anger:
   A bravery dwells in his blood yet, of abusing
   His first good wife; he's sooner fire than powder,
   And sooner mischief.
PETRUCHIO If I be so sudden,
   Do not you fear me?
MARIA No, nor yet care for you;
   And, if it may be lawful, I defy you!

PETRUCHIO Does this become you now?

MARIA It shall become me.

PETRUCHIO Thou disobedient, weak, vain-
glorious woman,
Were I but half so wilful as thou spiteful,
I should now drag thee to thy duty.

MARIA Drag me?

PETRUCHIO But I am friends again; take all your
pleasure!

MARIA Now you perceive him, Sophocles.

PETRUCHIO I love thee
Above thy vanity, thou faithless creature!

MARIA (*To* SOPHOCLES.) 'Would I had been so
happy, when I married,
But to have met an honest man like thee,
(For I am sure thou art good, I know thou art
honest)
A handsome hurtless man, a loving man,
Though never a penny with him, and those
eyes,
That face, and that true heart! – Wear this for
my sake,   (*Gives him a ring.*)
And when thou think'st upon me, pity me;
I'm cast away!   (*Exit.*)

SOPHOCLES Why, how now, man?

PETRUCHIO Pray leave me;
And follow your advices.

SOPHOCLES The man's jealous.

PETRUCHIO I shall find a time, ere it be long, to
ask you
One or two foolish questions.

SOPHOCLES I shall answer
As well as I am able, when you call me. –
If she mean true, 'tis but a little killing,
And if I do not venture, it's –
Farewell, sir!   (*Exit.*)

PETRUCHIO Pray, farewell! – Is there no keeping
A wife to one man's use? no wintering
These cattle without straying? 'Tis hard dealing,
Very hard dealing, gentlemen, strange dealing!
Now, in the name of madness, what star reign'd,
What dog-star, bull, or bear-star, when I married
This second wife, this whirlwind that takes all
Within her compass? Was I not well warn'd,
(I thought I had, and I believe I know it,)
And beaten to repentance, in the days
Of my first doting? had I not wife enough
To turn my love too? did I want vexation,
Or any special care to kill my heart?
Had I not every morning a rare breakfast,
Mix'd with a learned lecture of ill language,
Louder than Tom o' Lincoln? and at dinner,
A diet of the same dish? Was there evening
That e'er past over us, without *thou knave*,
Or *thou whore*, for digestion? had I ever

A pull at this same poor sport men run mad for,
But like a cur I was fain to shew my teeth first,
And almost worry her? And did Heaven forgive
me,
And take this serpent from me, and am I
Keeping tame devils now again? My heart aches!
Something I must do speedily: I'll die,
If I can handsomely, for that's the way
To make a rascal of her. I am sick,
And I'll go very near it, but I'll perish.   (*Exit.*)

Scene 3

A room in the house of PETRONIUS.

(*Enter* LIVIA, BIANCA, TRANIO, *and* ROWLAND.)

LIVIA Then I must be content, sir, with my
fortune.

ROWLAND And I with mine.

LIVIA I did not think a look,
Or a poor word or two, could have displanted
Such a fix'd constancy, and for your end too.

ROWLAND Come, come, I know your courses!
There's your gewgaws,
Your rings, and bracelets, and the purse you
gave me:
The money's spent in entertaining you
At plays, and cherry-gardens.

LIVIA There's your chain too.
But, if you'll give me leave, I'll wear the hair
still;
I would yet remember you.

BIANCA Give him his love, wench;
The young man has employment for't.

TRANIO Fy, Rowland!

ROWLAND You cannot *fy* me out a hundred pound
With this poor plot. – Yet, let me ne'er see day
more,
If something do not struggle strangely in me!

BIANCA Young man, let me talk with you.

ROWLAND Well, young woman?

BIANCA This was your mistress once.

ROWLAND Yes.

BIANCA Are you honest?
I see you are young and handsome.

ROWLAND I am honest.

BIANCA Why, that's well said. And there's no
doubt your judgment
Is good enough, and strong enough, to tell you
Who are your foes, and friends: Why did you
leave her?

ROWLAND She made a puppy of me.

BIANCA Be that granted:
She must do so sometimes, and oftentimes;
Love were too serious else.

ROWLAND A witty woman!

BIANCA Had you loved me –

ROWLAND I would I had!

BIANCA And dearly,
And I had loved you so – You may love worse, sir;
But that is not material.

ROWLAND I shall lose!

BIANCA Some time or other, for variety,
I should have call'd you fool, or boy, or bid you
Play with the pages; but have loved you still,
Out of all question, and extremely too:
You are a man made to be loved.

ROWLAND This woman
Either abuses me, or loves me deadly.

BIANCA I'll tell you one thing; if I were to choose
A husband to mine own mind, I should think
One of your mother's making would content me;
For o' my conscience she makes good ones.

ROWLAND Lady,
I'll leave you to your commendations. –
I am in again, the devil take their tongues!

BIANCA You shall not go.

ROWLAND I will. Yet thus far, Livia;
Your sorrow may induce me to forgive you,
But never love again. – If I stay longer,
I have lost two hundred pound.   (*Apart*.)

LIVIA Good sir, but thus much –

TRANIO Turn, if thou be'st a man.

LIVIA But one kiss of you;
One parting kiss, and I am gone too.

ROWLAND Come;   (*Kisses her*.)
I shall kiss fifty pound away at this clap,
We'll have one more, and then farewell.

LIVIA Farewell.

BIANCA Well, go thy ways! thou bear'st a kind
heart with thee.

TRANIO He has made a stand.

BIANCA A noble, brave young fellow,
Worthy a wench indeed!

ROWLAND I will – I will not.   (*Exit*.)

TRANIO He's gone; but shot again. Play you but
your part,
And I will keep my promise; forty angels
In fair gold, lady (wipe your eyes!) he's yours,
If I have any wit.

LIVIA I'll pay the forfeit.

BIANCA Come then; let's see your sister, how she
fares now,
After her skirmish; and be sure Moroso
Be kept in good hand: Then all's perfect, Livia.
                              (*Exeunt*.)

Scene 4

A hall in the house of PETRUCHIO.

(*Enter* JAQUES *and* PEDRO.)

PEDRO Oh, Jaques, Jaques, what becomes of us?
Oh, my sweet master!

JAQUES Run for a physician,
And a whole peck of 'pothecaries, Pedro.
He will die, didle, didle, die, if they come not
Quickly; and bring all people that are skilful
In lungs and livers; raise the neighbours,
And all the *aquavitæ*-bottles extant;
And, oh, the parson, Pedro, oh, the parson!
A little of his comfort, ne'er so little –
Twenty to one you find him at the Bush;
There's the best ale.

PEDRO I fly!   (*Exit*.)

(*Enter* MARIA *and* SERVANTS.)

MARIA Out with the trunks, ho!
Why are you idle? Sirrah, up to th' chamber,
And take the hangings down, and see the linen
Pack'd up, and sent away within this half-hour.
What, are the carts come yet? Some honest body
Help down the chests of plate, and some the
wardrobe;
Alas, we are undone else!

JAQUES Pray, forsooth,
And I beseech you, tell me, is he dead yet?

MARIA No, but he's drawing on. Out with the
armour!

JAQUES Then I'll go see him.

MARIA Thou art undone then, fellow;
No man that has been near him come near me!

(*Enter* SOPHOCLES *and* PETRONIUS.)

SOPHOCLES Why, how now, lady? what means
this?

PETRONIUS Now, daughter!
How does my son?

MARIA Save all you can, for Heaven's sake!

(*Enter* LIVIA, BIANCA, *and* TRANIO.)

LIVIA Be of good comfort, sister.

MARIA Oh, my casket!

PETRONIUS How does thy husband, woman?

MARIA Get you gone,
If you mean to save your lives: The sickness –

PETRONIUS Stand further off, I pr'ythee!

MARIA Is i' th' house, sir. My husband has it now:
Alas, he is infected; and raves extremely:
Give me some counsel, friends.

BIANCA Why, lock the doors up,
And send him in a woman to attend him.

MARIA I have bespoke two women, and the city
Hath sent a watch by this time: Meat nor money
He shall not want, nor prayers.
PETRONIUS How long is't
Since it first took him?
MARIA But within this three hours.

(*Enter* WATCH.)

I am frighted from my wits! – Oh, here's the
watch.
Pray do your office; lock the doors up, friends:
And patience be his angel!
TRANIO This comes unlook'd for.
MARIA I'll to the Lodge: Some that are kind, and
love me,
I know will visit me.
PETRUCHIO (*Within*) Do you hear, my masters?
Ho, you that lock the doors up!
PETRONIUS 'Tis his voice.
TRANIO Hold, and let's hear him.
PETRUCHIO Will ye starve me here?
Am I a traitor, or an heretic?
Or am I grown infectious?
PETRONIUS Pray, sir, pray!
PETRUCHIO I am as well as you are, goodman
puppy.
MARIA Pray have patience!
You shall want nothing, sir.
PETRUCHIO I want a cudgel,
And thee, thou wickedness!
PETRONIUS He speaks well enough.
MARIA He had ever a strong heart, sir.
PETRUCHIO Will ye hear me? First, be pleased
To think I know ye all, and can distinguish
Every man's several voice: You that spoke first,
I know my father-in-law; the other, Tranio;
And I heard Sophocles; the last, pray mark me,
Is my damn'd wife Maria.
If any man misdoubt me for infected,
There is mine arm, let any man look on't!
                    (*Thrusts his arm out of a window*.)

(*Enter* DOCTOR *and* APOTHECARY.)

DOCTOR Save ye, gentlemen!
PETRONIUS Oh, welcome, doctor!
You come in happy time. Pray, your opinion!
What think you of his pulse?
DOCTOR It beats with busiest,   (*Feels his pulse*.)
And shews a general inflammation,
Which is the symptom of a pestilent fever.
Take twenty ounces from him.
PETRUCHIO Take a fool!
Take an ounce from mine arm, and doctor
Deuzace,
I'll make a close-stool of your velvet costard! –

Pox, gentlemen, do you make a May-game on
me?
I tell ye once again, I am as sound,
As well, as wholesome, and as sensible,
As any of ye all. Let me out quickly,
Or, as I am a man, I'll beat the walls down,
And the first thing I light upon shall pay for't.

(*Exeunt* DOCTOR *and* APOTHECARY.)

PETRONIUS Nay, we'll go with you, doctor.
MARIA 'Tis the safest.
I saw the tokens, sir.
PETRONIUS Then there's but one way.
PETRUCHIO Will it please you open?
TRANIO His fit grows stronger still.
MARIA Let's save ourselves, sir:
He's past all worldly cure.
PETRONIUS Friends, do your office!
And what he wants, if money, love, or labour,
Or any way, may win it, let him have it.
Farewell, and pray, my honest friends. (*Exeunt*.)
PETRUCHIO Why, rascals!
Friends! gentlemen! thou beastly wife! Jaques!
None hear me? Who's at the door there?
1 WATCH Think, I pray, sir,
Whither you are going, and prepare yourself.
2 WATCH These idle thoughts disturb you: The
good gentlewoman,
Your wife, has taken care you shall want
nothing.
PETRUCHIO Shall I come out in quiet? Answer
me!
Or shall I charge a fowling-piece, and make
Mine own way? two of ye I cannot miss,
If I miss three. Ye come here to assault me!
I am as excellent well, I thank Heaven for't,
And have as good a stomach at this instant –
2 WATCH That's an ill sign!
1 WATCH He draws on; he's a dead man!
PETRUCHIO And sleep as soundly – Will you look
upon me?
1 WATCH Do you want pen and ink? While you
have sense, sir,
Settle your state.
PETRUCHIO Sirs, I am well as you are,
Or any rascal living.
2 WATCH 'Would you were, sir!
PETRUCHIO Look to yourselves, and, if you love
your lives,
Open the door, and fly me! for I shoot else;
By Heaven, I'll shoot, and presently, chain-
bullets;
And under four I will not kill.
1 WATCH Let's quit him!
It may be 'tis a trick. He's dangerous.

2 WATCH The devil take the hindmost, I cry!
(Exeunt WATCH running.)

PETRUCHIO Have among ye!
    The door shall open too; I'll have a fair shoot.
(Bursts the door open, and enters with a fowling-
piece.)

    Are ye all gone? – Tricks in my old days!
        crackers
    Put now upon me? And by Lady Greensleeves?
    Am I grown so tame after all my triumphs?
    But that I should be thought mad, if I rail'd,
    As much as they deserve, against these women,
    I would now rip up, from the primitive cuckold,
    All their arch-villainies, and all their doubles;
    Which are more than a hunted hare e'er thought
        on.
    When a man has the fairest and the sweetest
    Of all their sex, and as he thinks the noblest,
    What has he then? and I'll speak modestly;
    He has a quartern-ague, that shall shake
    All his estate to nothing, never cured,
    Nor never dying: he has a ship to venture
    His fame and credit in, which if he man not
    With more continual labour than a galley,
    To make her tith, either she grows a tumbrel,
    Not worth the cloth she wears, or springs more
        leaks
    Than all the fame of his posterity
    Can ever stop again. Out on 'em, hedge-hogs!
    He that shall touch 'em has a thousand thorns
    Runs through his fingers: If I were unmarried,
    I would do any thing below repentance,
    Any base dunghill slavery; be a hangman,
    Ere I would be a husband. Oh, the thousand,
    Thousand, ten thousand ways they have to kill
        us!
    Some fall with too much stringing of the fiddles,
    And those are fools; some, that they are not
        suffer'd,
    And those are maudlin-lovers; some, like
        scorpions,
    They poison with their tails, and those are
        martyrs;
    Some die with doing good, those benefactors,
    And leave 'em land to leap away; some few,
    For those are rarest, they are said to kill
    With kindness and fair usage; but what they are
    My catalogue discovers not, only 'tis thought
    They're buried in old walls, with their heels
        upward.
    I could rail twenty days together now!
    I'll seek 'em out; and if I have not reason,
    And very sensible, why this was done,
    I'll go a-birding yet, and some shall smart for't!
(Exit.)

Act IV

Scene 1

A room in the house of PETRONIUS.

(Enter MOROSO and PETRONIUS.)

MOROSO That I do love her is without all
        question,
    And most extremely, dearly, most exactly!
    And that I would even now, this present
        Monday,
    Before all others, maids, wives, women, widows,
    Of what degree, or calling, marry her,
    As certain too; but to be made a whim-wham,
    A jib-crack, and a gentleman o' th' first house,
    For all my kindness to her –
PETRONIUS How you take it!
    Thou get a wench? thou get a dozen night-caps!
    Wouldst have her come and lick thee like a calf,
    And blow thy nose, and buss thee?
MOROSO Not so, neither.
PETRONIUS What wouldst thou have her do?
MOROSO Do as she should do;
    Put on a clean smock, and to church, and marry,
    And then to bed a' God's name! This is fair play,
    And keeps the king's peace. Let her leave her
        bobs
    (I have had too many of them) and her quillets,
    She is as nimble that way as an eel;
    But in the way she ought, to me especially,
    A sow of lead is swifter.
PETRONIUS Quote your griefs down.
MOROSO Give fair quarter: I am old and crazy,
    And subject to much fumbling, I confess it;
    Yet something I would have that's warm, to
        hatch me:
    But understand me, I would have it so,
    I buy not more repentance in the bargain
    Than the ware's worth I have. If you allow me
    Worthy your son-in-law and your allowance,
    Do it a way of credit, let me shew so;
    And not be troubled in my visitations
    With blows, and bitterness, and downright
        railings,
    As if we were to couple like two cats,
    With clawing and loud clamour.
PETRONIUS Thou fond man,
    Hast thou forgot the ballad, 'Crabbed Age?'
    Can May and January match together,
    And never a storm between 'em? Say she abuse
        thee,
    Put case she do!
MOROSO Well?
PETRONIUS Nay, believe she does.

MOROSO I do believe she does.

PETRONIUS And devilishly:
Art thou a whit the worse?

MOROSO That's not the matter;
I know, being old, 'tis fit I am abused;
I know 'tis handsome, and I know moreover
I am to love her for't.

PETRONIUS Now you come to me.

MOROSO Nay, more than this; I find too, and find certain,
What gold I have, pearl, bracelets, rings, or ouches,
Or what she can desire, gowns, petticoats,
Waistcoats, embroider'd stockings, scarfs, cawls, feathers,
Hats, five-pound garters, muffs, masks, ruffs, and ribbands,
I am to give her for't.

PETRONIUS 'Tis right, you are so.

MOROSO But when I have done all this, and think it duty,
Is't requisite another bore my nostrils?
Riddle me that!

PETRONIUS Go, get you gone, and dream
She's thine within these two days, for she is so.
The boy's beside the saddle! Get warm broths,
And feed apace! think not of worldly business,
It cools the blood; leave off your tricks, they are hateful,
And mere forerunners of the ancient measures;
Contrive your beard o' th' top cut, like Verdugo's,
It shews you would be wise; and burn your nightcap,
It looks like half a winding sheet, and urges
From a young wench nothing but cold repentance;
You may eat onions, so you'll not be lavish.

MOROSO I am glad of that.

PETRONIUS They purge the blood and quicken;
But after 'em, conceive me, sweep your mouth,
And where there wants a tooth, stick in a clove.

MOROSO Shall I hope once again? say it!

PETRONIUS You shall, sir;
And you shall have your hope.

MOROSO Why, there's a match then!

(*Enter* BIANCA *and* TRANIO.)

BIANCA You shall not find me wanting; get you gone!
Here's the old man; he'll think you are plotting else
Something against his new son.   (*Exit* TRANIO.)

MOROSO Fare you well, sir!   (*Exit.*)

BIANCA An' ev'ry buck had his doe,
And ev'ry cuckold a bell at his toe;
Oh, what sport should we have then, boys, then,
Oh, what sport should we have then!

PETRONIUS This is the spirit that inspires 'em all.

BIANCA Give you good even!

PETRONIUS A word with you, sweet lady!

BIANCA I am very hasty, sir.

PETRONIUS So you were ever.

BIANCA Well, what's your will?

PETRONIUS Was not your skilful hand
In this last stratagem? Were not your mischiefs
Eking the matter on?

BIANCA In his shutting up?
Is that it?

PETRONIUS Yes.

BIANCA I'll tell you.

PETRONIUS Do.

BIANCA And truly.
Good old man, I do grieve exceeding much
I fear too much.

PETRONIUS I am sorry for your heaviness.
Belike you can repent then?

BIANCA There you are wide too:
Not that the thing was done (conceive me rightly)
Does any way molest me.

PETRONIUS What then, lady?

BIANCA But that I was not in it, there's my sorrow,
There; now you understand me! for I'll tell you,
It was so sound a piece, and so well carried,
And if you mark the way, so handsomely,
Of such a height, and excellence, and art,
I have not known a braver; for, conceive me,
When the gross fool her husband would be sick –

PETRONIUS Pray stay!

BIANCA Nay, good, your patience! – And no sense for't,
Then stept your daughter in –

PETRONIUS By your appointment?

BIANCA I would it had, on that condition
I had but one half-smock, I like it so well! –
And, like an excellent cunning woman, cured me
One madness with another; which was rare,
And to our weak beliefs, a 'wonder.

PETRONIUS Hang you!
For surely, if your husband look not to you,
I know what will.

BIANCA I humbly thank your worship!
And so I take my leave.

PETRONIUS You have a hand I hear too –

BIANCA I have two, sir.

PETRONIUS In my young daughter's business.

BIANCA You will find there

A fitter hand than mine, to reach her frets,
And play *down-diddle* to her.

PETRONIUS I shall watch you.

BIANCA Do.

PETRONIUS And I shall have justice.

BIANCA Where?

PETRONIUS That's all one;
I shall be with you at a turn henceforward.

BIANCA Get you a posset too; and so good even,
sir!   (*Exeunt.*)

Scene 2

An apartment in the house of PETRUCHIO.

(*Enter* PETRUCHIO, JAQUES, *and* PEDRO.)

JAQUES And, as I told your worship, all the
hangings,
Brass, pewter, plate, even to the very looking-
glasses.

PEDRO And that, that hung for our defence, the
armour.
And the March-beer was going too: Oh, Jaques,
What a sad sight was that!

JAQUES Even the two rundlets,
The two that was our hope, of muskadel,
Better ne'er tongue tript over, these two
cannons,
To batter brawn withal at Christmas, sir,
Even those two lovely twins, the enemy
Had almost cut off clean.

PETRUCHIO Go trim the house up.
And put the things in order as they were!
(*Exeunt* PEDRO *and* JAQUES.)
I shall find time for all this! – Could I find her
But constant any way, I had done my business:
Were she a whore directly, or a scold,
An unthrift, or a woman made to hate me,
I had my wish, and knew which way to reign
her;
But while she shews all these, and all their
losses,
A kind of linsey-wolsey, mingled mischief
Not to be guess'd at, and whether true or
borrow'd
Not certain neither – What a hap had I,
And what a tidy fortune, when my fate
Flung me upon this bear-whelp! Here she
comes.

(*Enter* MARIA.)

Now, if she have a colour, (for the fault is
A cleanly one) upon my conscience
I shall forgive her yet, and find a something
Certain I married for, her wit: I'll mark her.

MARIA Not let his wife come near him in his
sickness?
Not come to comfort him? she that all laws
Of Heaven, and nations, have ordain'd his
second,
Is she refused? and two old paradoxes,
Pieces of five and fifty, without faith,
Clapt in upon him? Has a little pet,
That all young wives must follow necessary,
Having their maidenheads –

PETRUCHIO This is an axiom
I never heard before.

MARIA Or say rebellion,
If we durst be so foul, (which two fair words,
Alas, win us from in an hour, an instant,
We are so easy) make him so forgetful
Both of his reason, honesty, and credit,
As to deny his wife a visitation?
His wife, that, though she was a little foolish,
Loved him, oh, Heaven, forgive her for't! nay
doted,
Nay, had run mad, had she not married
him?

PETRUCHIO Though I do know this falser than
the devil,
I cannot choose but love it.

MARIA What do I know
But those that came to keep him, might have
kill'd him?
In what a case had I been then! I dare not
Believe him such a base debosh'd companion,
That one refusal of a tender maid
Would make him feign this sickness out of need,
And take a keeper to him of fourscore
To play at billiards; one that mew'd content
And all her teeth together. Not come near him?

PETRUCHIO This woman would have made a
most rare Jesuit;
She can prevaricate on any thing;
There was not to be thought a way to save her,
In all imagination, beside this.

MARIA His unkind dealing, which was worst of
all,
In sending, who knows whither, all the plate,
And all the household-stuff, had I not cross'd it,
By a great providence, and my friends'
assistance,
Which he will one day thank me for – Alas,
I could have watch'd as well as they, have
served him
In any use, better, and willinger:
The law commands me to do it, Love commands
me,
And my own duty charges me.

PETRUCHIO Heaven bless me!

And, now I have said my prayers, I'll go to her. –
Are you a wife for any man?
MARIA For you, sir,
    If I were worse, I were better: That you are well,
    At least that you appear so, I thank Heaven,
    Long may it hold! and that you are here, I am
       glad too:
    But that you have abused me wretchedly,
    And such a way that shames the name of
       husband,
    Such a malicious mangy way, so mingled –
    Never look strangely on me; I dare tell you –
    With breach of honesty, care, kindness,
       manners –
PETRUCHIO Holla! you kick too fast.
MARIA Was I a stranger?
    Or had I vow'd perdition to your person?
    Am I not married to you? Tell me that!
PETRUCHIO I would I could not tell you!
MARIA Is my presence,
    The stock I come of, which is worshipful –
    If I should say right worshipful I lied not,
    My grandsire was a knight –
PETRUCHIO O' the shire?
MARIA A soldier,
    Which none of all thy family e'er heard of,
    But one conductor of thy name, a grazier
    That ran away with pay! – Or am I grown,
    Because I have been a little peevish to you,
    Only to try your temper, such a dog-leech,
    I could not be admitted to your presence?
PETRUCHIO If I endure this, hang me!
MARIA And two death's heads,
    Two Harry-groats that had their faces worn,
    Almost their names away too –
PETRUCHIO Now hear me!
    For I will stay no longer.
MARIA This you shall!
    However you shall think to flatter me
    For this offence, (which no submission
    Can ever mediate for, you'll find it so)
    Whatever you shall do by intercession,
    What you can offer, what your land can
      purchase,
    What all your friends or families can win,
    Shall be but this, not to forswear your
      knowledge,
    But ever to forbear it. Now your will, sir!
PETRUCHIO Thou art the subtlest woman I think
    living,
    I am sure the lewdest! Now be still, and mark
    me!
    Were I but any way addicted to the devil,
    I should now think I had met a play-fellow
    To profit by, and that way the most learned

That ever taught to murmur. Tell me, thou,
    Thou most poor, paltry, spiteful whore – Do you
      cry?
    I'll make you roar, before I leave.
MARIA Your pleasure!
PETRUCHIO Was it not sin enough, thou fruiterer,
    Full of the fall thou eat'st, thou devil's broker,
    Thou seminary of all sedition,
    Thou sword of vengeance with a thread hung
      o'er us,
    Was it not sin enough, and wickedness
    In full abundance, was it not vexation
    At all points, *cap-a-piè* – Nay, I shall pinch you! –
    Thus like a rotten rascal to abuse
    The name of Heaven, the tie of marriage,
    The honour of thy friends, the expectation
    Of all that thought thee virtuous, with rebellion,
    Childish and base rebellion? but, continuing
    After forgiveness too, and worse, your mischief?
    And against him, setting the hope of Heaven by,
    And the dear reservation of his honour,
    Nothing above-ground could have won to hate
      thee?
    Well, go thy ways!
MARIA Yes.
PETRUCHIO You shall hear me out first:
    What punishment mayst thou deserve, thou
      thing,
    Thou idle thing of nothing, thou pull'd primrose,
    That two hours after art a weed, and wither'd,
    For this last flourish on me? Am I one
    Selected out of all the husbands living,
    To be so ridden by a tit of ten-pence?
    Am I so blind, and bed-rid? I was mad,
    And had the plague, and no man must come
      near me!
    I must be shut up, and my substance 'bezzled,
    And an old woman watch me!
MARIA Well, sir, well;
    You may well glory in't.
PETRUCHIO And when it comes to opening, 'tis
    my plot,
    I must undo myself, forsooth! Doth hear me?
    If I should beat thee now, as much may be,
    Dost thou not well deserve it? O' thy conscience,
    Dost thou not cry, *Come beat me?*
MARIA I defy you?
    And, my last loving tears, farewell! The first
      stroke,
    The very first you give me, if you dare strike,
    (Try me, and you shall find it so) for ever,
    Never to be recall'd, (I know you love me,
    Mad till you have enjoy'd me,) I do turn
    Utterly from you; and what man I meet first,
    That has but spirit to deserve a favour,

Let him bear any shape, the worse the better,
Shall kill you, and enjoy me. What I have said
About your foolish sickness, ere you have me
As you would have me, you shall swear is
   certain,
And challenge any man that dares deny it;
And in all companies approve my actions.
And so, farewell for this time!   (*Exit.*)
PETRUCHIO Grief go with thee!
If there be any witchcrafts, herbs, or potions,
Saying my prayers backward, fiends, or fairies,
That can again unlove me, I am made.   (*Exit.*)

Scene 3

A room in the house of BIANCA.

     (*Enter* BIANCA *and* TRANIO.)

TRANIO Mistress, you must do't.
BIANCA Are the writings ready
I told you of?
TRANIO Yes, they are ready;
But to what use I know not.
BIANCA You are an ass,
You must have all things construed.
TRANIO Yes, and pierced too,
Or I find little pleasure.
BIANCA Now you are knavish;
Go to! Fetch Rowland hither presently;
Your twenty pound lies bleeding else; she's
   married
Within these twelve hours, if we cross it not.
And see the papers of one size!
TRANIO I have you,
BIANCA And for disposing of 'em –
TRANIO If I fail you,
Now I have found the way, use martial law,
And cut my head off with a hand-saw!
BIANCA Well, sir!
Petronius and Moroso I'll see sent for.
About your business; go!
TRANIO I am gone.   (*Exit.*)
BIANCA Ho, Livia!

     (*Enter* LIVIA.)

LIVIA Who's that?
BIANCA A friend of yours. Lord, how you look
   now,
As if you had lost a carrack!
LIVIA Oh, Bianca!
I am the most undone, unhappy woman –
BIANCA Be quiet, wench! thou shalt be done, and
   done,
And done, and double done, or all shall split
   for't.

No more of these minced passions! they are
   mangy,
And ease thee of nothing, but a little wind:
An apple will do more. Thou fear'st Moroso?
LIVIA Even as I fear the gallows.
BIANCA Keep thee there still!
And you love Rowland? say.
LIVIA If I say not,
I am sure I lie.
BIANCA What wouldst thou give that woman,
In spite of all his anger, and thy fear,
And all thy father's policy, that could
Clap ye within these two nights quietly
Into a bed together.
LIVIA How?
BIANCA Why, fairly,
At half-sword, man and wife: – Now the red
   blood comes!
Ay, marry, now the matter's changed.
LIVIA Bianca,
Methinks you should not mock me.
BIANCA Mock a pudding!
I speak good honest English, and good meaning.
LIVIA I should not be ungrateful to that woman.
BIANCA I know thou wouldst not: Follow but my
   counsel,
And if thou hast him not, despite of fortune,
Let me never know a good night more! You
   must
Be very sick o' th' instant.
LIVIA Well, what follows?
BIANCA And in that sickness send for all your
   friends,
Your father and your fever, old Moroso;
And Rowland shall be there too.
LIVIA What of these?
BIANCA Do you not twitter yet? Of this shall
   follow
That which shall make thy heart leap, and thy
   lips
Venture as many kisses as the merchants
Do dollars to the East-Indies: You shall know all;
But first walk in and practise; pray be sick.
LIVIA I do believe you, and I am sick.
BIANCA Do.
To bed then; come! – I'll send away your
   servants
Post for your fool, and father. And, good
   Fortune,
As we mean honesty, now strike an up-shot!
         (*Exeunt.*)

Scene 4

A street.

(*Enter* TRANIO *and* ROWLAND.)

TRANIO Nay, on my conscience, I have lost my money;
But that's all one: I'll never more persuade you;
I see you are resolute, and I commend you.

ROWLAND But did she send for me?

TRANIO You dare believe me?

ROWLAND I cannot tell; you have your ways for profit
Allow'd you, Tranio, as well as I
Have to avoid 'em fear.

TRANIO No, on my word, sir,
I deal directly with you.

(*Enter* SERVANT *hastily.*)

ROWLAND How now, fellow?
Whither post you so fast?

SERVANT Oh, sir, my master!
Pray did you see my master?

ROWLAND Why your master?

SERVANT Sir, his jewel –

ROWLAND With the gilded button?

SERVANT My pretty mistress Livia –

ROWLAND What of her?

SERVANT Is fallen sick o' the sudden –

ROWLAND How, o' th' sullens?

SERVANT O' th' sudden, sir, I say; very sick.

ROWLAND It seems she hath got the tooth-ache
with raw apples.

SERVANT It seems you have got the head-ache:
Fare you well, sir!
You did not see my master?

ROWLAND Who told you so?

TRANIO No, no; he did not see him.

ROWLAND Farewell, blue-bottle. – (*Exit* SERVANT.)
What should her sickness be?

TRANIO For you, it may be.

ROWLAND Yes, when my brains are out, I may
believe it;
Never before, I am sure. Yet I may see her;
'Twill be a point of honesty.

TRANIO It will so.

ROWLAND It may be not too; you would fain be
fingering
This old sin-offering of two hundred, Tranio:
How daintily and cunningly you drive me
Up like a deer to th' toil! yet I may leap it;
And what's the woodman then?

TRANIO A loser by you.
Speak, will you go or not? To me 'tis equal.

ROWLAND Come, what goes less?

TRANIO Nay, not a penny, Rowland.

ROWLAND Shall I have liberty of conscience,
Which, by interpretation, is ten kisses?
Hang me, if I affect her; yet, it may be,
This whoreson manners will require a struggling,
Of two and twenty, or, by'r Lady, thirty.

TRANIO By'r Lady, I'll require my wager then.
For if you kiss so often, and no kindness,
I have lost my speculation: – I'll allow you –

ROWLAND Speak like a gamester now.

TRANIO It may be two.

ROWLAND Under a dozen, Tranio, there's no setting:
You shall have forty shillings, wink at small
faults.
Say I take twenty, come, by all that's honest,
I do it but to vex her.

TRANIO I'll no by-blows.
If you can love her, do; if you can hate her,
Or any else that loves you –

ROWLAND Pr'ythee, Tranio!

TRANIO Why, farewell, twenty pound! 'twill not
undo me;
You have my resolution.

ROWLAND And your money:
Which, since you are so stubborn, if I forfeit,
Make me a Jack o' Lent, and break my shins
For untagg'd points and counters! I'll go with
you;
But if thou gett'st a penny by the bargain –
A parting kiss is lawful?

TRANIO I allow it.

ROWLAND Knock out my brains with apples. Yet,
a bargain?

TRANIO I tell you, I'll no bargains; win and
wear it.

ROWLAND Thou art the strangest fellow!

TRANIO That's all one.

ROWLAND Along then! Twenty pound more, if
thou darest,
I give her not a good word!

TRANIO Not a penny.   (*Exeunt.*)

Scene 5

A room in the house of PETRUCHIO.

(*Enter* PETRUCHIO, JAQUES, *and* PEDRO.)

PETRUCHIO Pr'ythee, entreat her come; I will not
trouble her
Above a word or two.   (*Exit* PEDRO.)
Ere I endure
This life, and with a woman, and a vow'd one
To all the mischiefs she can lay upon me,

I'll go to plough again, and eat leek-porridge!
(Begging's a pleasure to't, not to be number'd.)
No, there be other countries, Jaques, for me,
And other people; yea, and other women:
If I have need, 'here's money,' 'there's your
 ware,'
Which is fair dealing; and the sun, they say,
Shines as warm there as here; and till I have lost
Either myself or her – I care not whether,
Nor which first –

JAQUES Will your worship hear me?
PETRUCHIO And utterly outworn the memory
 Of such a curse as this, none of my nation
 Shall ever know me more.
JAQUES Out, alas, sir,
 What a strange way do you run!
PETRUCHIO Any way,
 So I out-run this rascal.
JAQUES Methinks now,
 If your good worship could but have the
  patience –
PETRUCHIO The patience? why the patience?
JAQUES Why, I'll tell you;
 Could you but have the patience –
PETRUCHIO Well, the patience.
JAQUES To laugh at all she does, or, when she
  rails,
 To have a drum beaten o' the top o' th' house,
 To give the neighbours warning of her larum,
 As I do when my wife rebels –
PETRUCHIO Thy wife?
 Thy wife's a pigeon to her, a mere slumber;
 The dead of night's not stiller –
JAQUES Nor an iron-mill.
PETRUCHIO But thy wife is certain –
JAQUES That's false doctrine;
 You never read of a certain woman.
PETRUCHIO Thou know'st her way.
JAQUES I should do, I am sure;
 I have ridden it night and day, this twenty year.
PETRUCHIO But mine is such a drench of
  balderdash,
 Such a strange carded cunningness, the rainbow,
 When she hangs bent in Heaven, sheds not her
  colours
 Quicker, and more, than this deceitful woman
 Weaves in her dyes of wickedness.

        (*Enter* PEDRO.)

What says she?
PEDRO Nay, not a word, sir; but she pointed to
 me,
 As though she meant to follow. Pray, sir, bear it
 Even as you may: I need not teach your worship
 The best men have their crosses, we are all
  mortal –

PETRUCHIO What ails the fellow?
PEDRO And no doubt she may, sir –
PETRUCHIO What may she? or what does she? or
  what is she?
 Speak and be hang'd!
PEDRO She's mad, sir.
PETRUCHIO Heaven continue it!
PEDRO Amen, if't be his pleasure.
PETRUCHIO How mad is she?
PEDRO As mad as heart can wish, sir: She has
  dress'd herself
 (Saving your worship's reverence) just i' th' cut
 Of one of those that multiply i' th' suburbs
 For single money, and as dirtily:
 If any speak to her, first she whistles,
 And then begins her compass with her fingers,
 And points to what she would have.
PETRUCHIO What new way's this?
PEDRO There came in master Sophocles –
PETRUCHIO And what
 Did master Sophocles, when he came in?
 Get my trunks ready, sirrah! I'll be gone straight.
PEDRO He's here to tell you. –
 She's horn mad, Jaques.

       (*Enter* SOPHOCLES.)

SOPHOCLES Call you this a woman?
PETRUCHIO Yes, sir, she is a woman.
SOPHOCLES Sir, I doubt it.
PETRUCHIO I had thought you had made
  experience.
SOPHOCLES Yes, I did so,
 And almost with my life.
PETRUCHIO You rid too fast, sir.
SOPHOCLES Pray, be not mistaken: By this
  band,
 Your wife's as chaste and honest as a virgin,
 For anything I know! 'Tis true, she gave me
 A ring –
PETRUCHIO For rutting.
SOPHOCLES You are much deceived still:
 Believe me, I ne'er kiss'd her since; and now
 Coming in visitation like a friend,
 (I think she's mad, sir) suddenly she started,
 And snatch'd the ring away, and drew her knife
  out,
 To what intent I know not.
PETRUCHIO Is this certain?
SOPHOCLES As I am here, sir.
PETRUCHIO I believe you honest;
 And pray continue so.

       (*Enter* MARIA.)

SOPHOCLES She comes.
PETRUCHIO Now, damsel,

What will your beauty do, if I forsake you?
                                        (*She makes signs.*)
Do you deal by signs and tokens? As I guess
      then,
You'll walk abroad this summer, and catch
      captains;
Or hire a piece of holy ground i' th' suburbs,
And keep a nest of nuns?
SOPHOCLES Oh, do not stir her!
      You see in what a case she is.
PETRUCHIO She's dogged,
      And in a beastly case, I am sure. – I'll make her,
      If she have any tongue, yet tattle. – Sophocles,
      Pr'ythee observe this woman seriously,
      And eye her well; and when thou hast done, but
            tell me
      (For thou hast understanding) in what case
      My sense was, when I chose this thing.
SOPHOCLES I'll tell you,
      I have seen a sweeter –
PETRUCHIO An hundred times, cry oysters.
      There's a poor beggar-wench about Black-Friars,
      Runs on her breech, may be an empress to her.
SOPHOCLES Nay, now you are too bitter.
PETRUCHIO Never a whit, sir. –
      I'll tell thee, woman, for now I have day to see
            thee,
      And all my wits about me, and I speak
      Not out of passion neither (leave your
            mumping;
      I know you are well enough.) – Now would
            I give   (*Apart.*)
      A million but to vex her! – When I chose thee
      To make a bedfellow, I took more trouble
      Than twenty terms can come to; such a cause,
      Of such a title and so everlasting,
      That Adam's genealogy may be ended
      Ere any law find thee: I took a leprosy,
      Nay worse, the plague, nay worse yet, a
            possession,
      And had the devil with thee, if not more;
      And yet worse, was a beast, and like a beast
      Had my reward, a jade to fling my fortunes:
      For who that had but reason to distinguish
      The light from darkness, wine from water,
            hunger
      From full satiety, and fox from fern-bush,
      That would have married thee?
SOPHOCLES She's not so ill.
PETRUCHIO She's worse than I dare think of;
            she's so lewd
      No court is strong enough to bear her cause;
      She hath neither manners, honesty, behaviour,
      Wifehood, nor womanhood; nor any mortal
      Can force me think she had a mother: No,

I do believe her stedfastly, and know her,
To be a woman-wolf by transmigration:
Her first form was a ferret's under-ground;
She kills the memories of men. – Not yet?
SOPHOCLES Do you think she's sensible of this?
PETRUCHIO I care not!
      Be what she will, the pleasure I take in her,
      Thus I blow off; the care I took to love her,
      Like this point, I untie, and thus I loose it;
      The husband I am to her, thus I sever:
      My vanity, farewell! Yet, for you have been
      So near me, as to bear the name of wife,
      My unquench'd charity shall tell you thus
            much,
      Though you deserve it well, you shall not beg:
      What I ordain'd your jointure, honestly
      You shall have settled on you, and half my
            house;
      The other half shall be employ'd in prayers,
      (That meritorious charge I'll be at also)
      Yet to confirm you christian; your apparel,
      And what belongs to build up such a folly,
      Keep, I beseech you, it infects our uses:
      And now I am for travel.
MARIA Now I love you;
      And now I see you are a man, I'll talk to you;
      And I forget your bitterness.
SOPHOCLES How now, man?
PETRUCHIO Oh, Pliny, if thou wilt be ever
            famous,
      Make but this woman all thy wonders!
MARIA Sure, sir,
      You have hit upon a happy course, a blessed,
      And what will make you virtuous.
PETRUCHIO She'll ship me.
MARIA A way of understanding I long wish'd for;
      And now 'tis come, take heed you fly not back,
            sir!
      Methinks you look a new man to me now,
      A man of excellence; and now I see
      Some great design set in you. You may think
            now
      (And so may most that know me) 'twere my part
      Weakly to weep your loss, and to resist you;
      Nay, hang about your neck, and, like a dotard,
      Urge my strong tie upon you: But I love you,
      And all the world shall know it, beyond woman;
      And more prefer the honour of your country,
      Which chiefly you are born for, and may perfect
      The uses you may make of other nations,
      The ripening of your knowledge, conversation,
      The full ability and strength of judgment,
      Than any private love, or wanton kisses.
      Go, worthy man, and bring home
            understanding.

SOPHOCLES This were an excellent woman to
  breed schoolmen.
MARIA For if the merchant through unknown seas
    plough
  To get his wealth, then, dear sir what must you
  To gather wisdom? Go, and go alone,
  Only your noble mind for your companion;
  And if a woman may win credit with you,
  Go far, too far you cannot, still the farther
  The more experience finds you: And go sparing;
  One meal a-week will serve you, and one suit,
  Through all your travels; for you'll find it
    certain,
  The poorer and the baser you appear,
  The more you look through still.
PETRUCHIO Dost hear her?
SOPHOCLES Yes.
PETRUCHIO What would this woman do, if she
    were suffer'd
  Upon a new religion?
SOPHOCLES Make us Pagans.
  I wonder that she writes not.
MARIA Then when time,
  And fulness of occasion, have new-made you,
  And squared you from a sot into a signor,
  Or nearer, from a jade into a courser;
  Come home an aged man, as did Ulysses,
  And I, your glad Penelope –
PETRUCHIO That must have
  As many lovers as I languages:
  And what she does with one i' th' day, i' th' night
  Undo it with another.
MARIA Much that way, sir;
  For in your absence it must be my honour,
  That, that must make me spoken of hereafter,
  To have temptations, and not little ones,
  Daily and hourly offer'd me, and strongly,
  Almost believed against me, to set off
  The faith and loyalty of her that loves you.
PETRUCHIO What should I do?
SOPHOCLES Why, by my soul, I would travel;
  Did not you mean so?
PETRUCHIO Alas, no; nothing less, man;
  I did it but to try, sir. She's the devil!
  And now I find it, (for she drives me) I must go. –
  Are my trunks down there, and my horses
    ready?
MARIA Sir, for your house, and, if you please to
    trust me
  With that you leave behind –
PETRUCHIO Bring down the money!
MARIA As I am able, and to my poor fortunes
  I'll govern as a widow. I shall long
  To hear of your well-doing, and your profit;
  And when I hear not from you once a quarter,

  I'll wish you in the Indies, or Cataya,
  Those are the climes must make you.
PETRUCHIO How's the wind? –
  She'll wish me out o' th' world anon!
MARIA For France
  'Tis very fair: Get you aboard to-night, sir,
  And lose no time; you know the tide stays no
    man.
  I have cold meats ready for you.
PETRUCHIO Fare thee well!
  Thou hast fool'd me out o' th' kingdom with a
    vengeance!
  And thou canst fool me in again.
MARIA Not I, sir;
  I love you better; take your time, and pleasure.
  I'll see you horsed.
PETRUCHIO I think thou would'st see me hang'd
    too,
  Were I but half as willing.
MARIA Anything
  That you think well of, I dare look upon.
PETRUCHIO You'll bear me to the land's end,
    Sophocles?
  And other of my friends, I hope.
MARIA Ne'er doubt, sir;
  You cannot want companions for your good.
  I am sure you'll kiss me ere I go; I have
    business,
  And stay long here I must not.
PETRUCHIO Get thee going!
  For if thou tarriest but another dialogue,
  I'll kick thee to thy chamber.
MARIA Fare you well, sir!
  And bear yourself, I do beseech you once more,
  Since you have undertaken doing wisely,
  Manly and worthily; 'tis for my credit.
  And for those flying fames here of your follies,
  Your gambols, and ill-breeding of your youth,
  For which I understand you take this travel,
  (Nothing should make me leave you else) I'll
    deal
  So like a wife that loves your reputation,
  And the most large addition of your credit,
  That those shall die. If you want limon-waters,
  Or any thing to take the edge o' th' sea off,
  Pray speak, and be provided.
PETRUCHIO Now the devil,
  That was your first good master, shower his
    blessing
  Upon ye all! into whose custody –
MARIA I do commit your reformation;
  And so I leave you to your *stilo novo*.   (*Exit.*)
PETRUCHIO I will go! – Yet I will not! – Once
    more, Sophocles,
  I'll put her to the test.

SOPHOCLES You had better go.

PETRUCHIO I will go then! – Let's seek my father out,
And all my friends to see me fair aboard:
Then, women, if there be a storm at sea
Worse than your tongues can make, and waves more broken
Than your dissembling faiths are, let me feel
Nothing but tempests till they crack my keel!

(*Exeunt.*)

Act V

Scene 1

A room in the house of PETRONIUS. *A table set out with ink and paper.*

(*Enter* PETRONIUS *and* BIANCA.)

BIANCA Now whether I deserve that blame you gave me,
Let all the world discern, sir.

PETRONIUS If this motion,
I mean this fair repentance of my daughter,
Spring from your good persuasion, as it seems so,
I must confess I have spoke too boldly of you,
And I repent.

BIANCA The first touch was her own,
Taken no doubt from disobeying you;
The second I put to her, when I told her
How good and gentle yet, with free contrition,
Again you might be purchased: Loving woman!
She heard me, and, I thank her, thought me worthy
Observing in this point. Yet all my counsel
And comfort in this case could not so heal her,
But that grief got his share too, and she sicken'd.

PETRONIUS I am sorry she's so ill; yet glad her sickness
Has got so good a ground.

(*Enter* MOROSO.)

BIANCA Here comes Moroso.

PETRONIUS Oh, you are very welcome;
Now you shall know your happiness.

MOROSO I am glad on't.
What makes this lady here?

BIANCA A dish for you, sir,
You'll thank me for hereafter.

PETRONIUS True, Moroso:
Go, get you in, and see your mistress.

BIANCA She is sick, sir;
But you may kiss her whole.

MOROSO How?

BIANCA Comfort her.

MOROSO Why am I sent for, sir?

PETRONIUS Will you in and see?

BIANCA May be she needs confession.

MOROSO By Saint Mary,
She shall have absolution then and penance;
But not above her carriage.

PETRONIUS Get you in, fool! (*Exit* MOROSO.)

BIANCA Here comes the other too.

(*Enter* ROWLAND *and* TRANIO.)

PETRONIUS Now, Tranio! –
Good even to you too! and you are welcome.

ROWLAND Thank you.

PETRONIUS I have a certain daughter –

ROWLAND 'Would you had, sir!

PETRONIUS No doubt you know her well.

ROWLAND Nor never shall, sir:
She is a woman; and the ways unto her
Are like the finding of a certain path
After a deep-fall'n snow.

PETRONIUS Well, that's by th' bye still.
This daughter that I tell you of is fall'n
A little crop-sick, with the dangerous surfeit
She took of your affection.

ROWLAND Mine, sir?

PETRONIUS Yes, sir:
Or rather, as it seems, repenting. And there
She lies within, debating on it.

ROWLAND Well, sir?

PETRONIUS I think 'twere well you would see her.

ROWLAND If you please, sir;
I am not squeamish of my visitation.

PETRONIUS But this I'll tell you, she is alter'd much;
You'll find her now another Livia.

ROWLAND I have enough o' th' old, sir.

PETRONIUS No more fool,
To look gay babies in your eyes, young Rowland,
And hang about your pretty neck –

ROWLAND I am glad on't,
And thank my fates I have 'scaped such execution.

PETRONIUS And buss you till you blush again.

ROWLAND That's hard, sir;
She must kiss shamefully ere I blush at it;
I never was so boyish. Well, what follows?

PETRONIUS She's mine now, as I please to settle her.
At my command, and where I please to plant her:
Only she would take a kind farewell of you,
And give you back a wand'ring vow or two,
You left in pawn; and two or three slight oaths
She lent you too, she looks for.

ROWLAND She shall have 'em,
　With all my heart, sir; and, if you like it better,
　A free release in writing.
PETRONIUS That's the matter;
　And you from her shall have another, Rowland,
　And then turn tail to tail, and peace be with you!
ROWLAND So be't. – Your twenty pound sweats,
　　Tranio.
TRANIO 'Twill not undo me, Rowland; do your
　　worst!
ROWLAND Come, shall we see her, sir?
BIANCA Whate'er she says
　You must bear manly, Rowland; for her sickness
　Has made her somewhat teatish.
ROWLAND Let her talk
　'Till her tongue ache, I care not. By this hand,
　Thou hast a handsome face, wench, and a body
　Daintily mounted! – Now do I feel an hundred
　Running directly from me, as I piss'd it.

(LIVIA *brought in on a bed;* MOROSO *by her.*)

BIANCA Pray draw her softly! the least hurry, sir,
　Puts her to much impatience.
PETRONIUS How is't, daughter?
LIVIA Oh, very sick, very sick; yet somewhat
　Better, I hope, a little lightsomer,
　Because this good man has forgiven me.
　Pray set me higher: Oh, my head!
BIANCA Well done, wench!
LIVIA Father, and all good people that shall hear
　　me,
　I have abused this man perniciously;
　Was never old man humbled so: I have scorn'd
　　him,
　And call'd him nasty names; I have spit at him,
　Flung candles' ends in his beard, and call'd him
　　Harrow,
　That must be drawn to all he does; contemn'd
　　him,
　For methought then he was a beastly fellow, –
　Oh, God, my side! – a very beastly fellow;
　And gave it out his cassock was a barge-cloth,
　Pawn'd to his predecessor by a sculler,
　The man yet living; I gave him purging comfits
　At a great christning once,
　That spoil'd his camblet breeches; and one night
　I strew'd the stairs with pease, as he pass'd
　　down;
　And the good gentleman, (woe worth me for't!)
　Even with his reverend head, this head of
　　wisdom,
　Told two and twenty stairs, good and true,
　Miss'd not a step, and, as we say, *verbatim*
　Fell to the bottom, broke his casting bottle,
　Lost a fair toad-stone of some eighteen shillings,

Jumbled his joints together, had two stools,
　And was translated. All this villainy
　Did I: I, Livia: I alone, untaught.
MOROSO And I, unask'd, forgive it.
LIVIA Where's Bianca?
BIANCA Here, cousin.
LIVIA Give me drink.
BIANCA There.
LIVIA Who's that?
MOROSO Rowland.
LIVIA Oh, my dissembler, you and I must part.
　Come nearer, sir.
ROWLAND I am sorry for your sickness.
LIVIA Be sorry for yourself, sir: You have wrong'd
　　me;
　But I forgive you. – Are the papers ready?
BIANCA I have 'em here: – Will't please you view
　　'em?
PETRONIUS Yes.
LIVIA Shew 'em the young man too; I know he's
　　willing.
　To shift his sails too; 'tis for his more advance-
　　ment:
　Alas, we might have beggar'd one another;
　We are young both, and a world of children
　Might have been left behind to curse our follies;
　We had been undone, Bianca, had we married,
　Undone for ever. I confess I loved him
　(I care not who shall know it) most entirely;
　And once, upon my conscience, he loved me:
　But farewell that! we must be wiser, cousin;
　Love must not leave us to the world. Have you
　　done?
ROWLAND Yes, and am ready to subscribe.
LIVIA Pray stay then.
　Give me the papers, (and let me peruse them,)
　And so much time as may afford a tear
　At our last parting.
BIANCA Pray retire, and leave her;
　I'll call ye presently.
PETRONIUS Come, gentlemen;
　The shower must fall.
ROWLAND 'Would I had never seen her! (*Exeunt.*)
BIANCA Thou hast done bravely, wench.
LIVIA Pray Heaven, it prove so!
BIANCA There are the other papers: When they
　　come,
　Begin you first, and let the rest subscribe
　Hard by your side; give 'em as little light
　As drapers do their wares.
LIVIA Didst mark Moroso,
　In what an agony he was? and how he cried
　　most
　When I abused him most?
BIANCA That was but reason.

LIVIA Oh, what a stinking thief is this!
   Though I was but to counterfeit, he made me
   Directly sick indeed; Thames-street to him
   Is a mere pomander.
BIANCA Let him be hang'd!
LIVIA Amen!
BIANCA And lie you still;
   And once more to your business!
LIVIA Call 'em in. –
   Now, if there be a power that pities lovers,
   Help now, and hear my prayers!

     (*Enter* PETRONIUS, ROWLAND, TRANIO,
      and MOROSO.)

PETRONIUS Is she ready?
BIANCA She has done her lamentations: Pray go
   to her.
LIVIA Rowland, come near me; and, before you
   seal,
   Give me your hand: Take it again; now kiss me!
   This is the last acquaintance we must have!
   I wish you ever happy! There's the paper.
ROWLAND Pray stay a little!
PETRONIUS Let me never live more,
   But I do begin to pity this young fellow;
   How heartily he weeps!
BIANCA There's pen and ink, sir.
LIVIA Even here, I pray you: 'Tis a little emblem
   How near you have been to me.
ROWLAND (*Signs.*) There.
BIANCA Your hands too,
   As witnesses.
PETRONIUS By any means; to the book, son.
MOROSO With all my heart.   (*Signs.*)
BIANCA You must deliver it.
ROWLAND There, Livia; and a better love light on
   thee!
   I can no more.
BIANCA To this you must be witness too.
PETRONIUS We will.   (*They sign.*)
BIANCA Do you deliver it now.
LIVIA Pray set me up.
   There, Rowland, all thy old love back; and may
   A new to come exceed mine, and be happy!
   I must no more.
ROWLAND Farewell!
LIVIA A long farewell!   (*Exit* Rowland.)
BIANCA Leave her by any means, till this wild
   passion
   Be off her head. Draw all the curtains close.
   A day hence you may see her; 'twill be better:
   She's now for little company.
PETRONIUS Pray tend her.
   I must to horse straight; you must needs along
   too,

To see my son aboard: Were but his wife
As fit for pity as this wench, I were happy.
BIANCA Time must do that too. Fare ye well!
   To-morrow
You shall receive a wife to quit your sorrow,
                 (*Exeunt.*)

Scene 2

A room in PETRUCHIO'S *house.*

   (*Enter* JAQUES, PEDRO, *and* PORTERS, *with*
     a chest and hampers.)

JAQUES Bring 'em away, sirs!
PEDRO Must the great trunks go too?
JAQUES Yes, and the hampers. Nay, be speedy,
   masters!
   He'll be at sea before us else.
PEDRO Oh, Jaques!
   What a most blessed turn hast thou –
JAQUES I hope so.
PEDRO To have the sea between thee and this
   woman!
   Nothing can drown her tongue but a storm.
JAQUES By your leave,
   We'll get us up to Paris with all speed;
   For, on my soul, as far as Amiens
   She'll carry blank. Away to Lyon-key,
   And ship 'em presently! we'll follow ye.
PEDRO Now could I wish her in that trunk.
JAQUES God shield, man!
   I had rather have a bear in't.
PEDRO Yes, I'll tell you.
   For in the passage, if a tempest take you,
   As many do, and you lie beating for it,
   Then, if it pleased the fates, I would have the
     master,
   Out of a powerful providence, to cry,
   'Lighten the ship of all hands, or we perish;'
   Then this for one, as best spared, should by all
     means
   Over-board presently.
JAQUES O' that condition,
   So we were certain to be rid of her,
   I would wish her with us. But, believe me,
     Pedro,
   She would spoil the fishing on this coast for
     ever;
   For none would keep her company but dog-fish,
   As currish as herself, or porpoises,
   Made to all fatal uses: The two Fish-Streets,
   Were she but once arrived among the
     whitings,
   Would sing a woful *misereri*, Pedro,
   And mourn in Poor-John, till her memory

Were cast o' shore again, with a strong sea-
    breach;
She would make god Neptune, and his fire-fork,
And all his demi-gods and goddesses,
As weary of the Flemish channel, Pedro,
As ever boy was of the school; 'tis certain,
If she but meet him fair, and were well
    anger'd,
She would break his god-head.

PEDRO Oh, her tongue, her tongue!

JAQUES Rather her many tongues!

PEDRO Or rather strange tongues!

JAQUES Her lying tongue!

PEDRO Her lisping tongue!

JAQUES Her long tongue!

PEDRO Her lawless tongue!

JAQUES Her loud tongue!

PEDRO And her liquorish –

JAQUES Many other tongues, and many stranger
    tongues
Than ever Babel had to tell his ruins,
Were women raised withal; but never a true
    one.

(Enter SOPHOCLES.*)*

SOPHOCLES Home with your stuff again! the
    journey's ended.

JAQUES What does your worship mean?

SOPHOCLES Your master – Oh, Petruchio! Oh,
    poor fellows!

PEDRO Oh, Jaques, Jaques!

SOPHOCLES Oh, your master's dead,
  His body coming back! His wife, his devil,
  The grief of her –

JAQUES Has kill'd him?

SOPHOCLES Kill'd him, kill'd him!

PEDRO Is there no law to hang her?

SOPHOCLES Get ye in,
  And let her know her misery: I dare not,
  For fear impatience seize me, see her more;
  I must away again. Bid her for wife-hood,
  For honesty, if she have any in her,
  Even to avoid the shame that follows her,
  Cry if she can. Your weeping cannot mend it.
  The body will be here within this hour, (so tell
    her,)
  And all his friends to curse her. Farewell,
    fellows!   *(Exit.)*

PEDRO Oh, Jaques, Jaques!

JAQUES Oh, my worthy master!

PEDRO Oh, my most beastly mistress! Hang her –

JAQUES Split her –

PEDRO Drown her directly –

JAQUES Starve her –

PEDRO Stink upon her –

JAQUES Stone her to death! May all she eat be
    eggs.
'Till she run kicking-mad for men!

PEDRO And he,
  That man that gives her remedy, pray Heaven
  He may even *ipso facto* lose his longings!

JAQUES Let's go discharge ourselves; and he that
    serves her,
  Or speaks a good word of her from this hour,
  A Sedgly curse light on him; which is, Pedro,
  'The fiend ride through him booted and spurr'd,
    with a scythe at his back!'   *(Exeunt.)*

Scene 3

A street.

(Enter ROWLAND *with a deed, and* TRANIO
stealing behind him.)

ROWLAND What a dull ass was I to let her go thus!
  Upon my life, she loves me still. Well, paper,
  Thou only monument of what I have had,
  Thou all the love now left me, and now lost,
  Let me yet kiss her hand, yet take my leave
  Of what I must leave ever. Farewell, Livia!
  Oh, bitter words, I'll read you once again,
  And then for ever study to forget ye. – *(Reads.)*
  How's this? let me look better on't! A contract?
  By Heaven, a contract, seal'd and ratified,
  Her father's hand set to it, and Moroso's!
  I do not dream sure! Let me read again;
  The same still; 'tis a contract!

TRANIO 'Tis so, Rowland;
  And, by the virtue of the same, you pay me
  An hundred pound to-morrow.

ROWLAND Art sure, Tranio,
  We are both alive now?

TRANIO Wonder not; you have lost.

ROWLAND If this be true, I grant it.

TRANIO 'Tis most certain!
  There's a ring for you too; you know it?

ROWLAND Yes.

TRANIO When shall I have my money?

ROWLAND Stay you, stay you!
  When shall I marry her?

TRANIO To-night.

ROWLAND Take heed now
  You do not trifle with me: If you do,
  You'll find more payment than your money
    comes to!
  Come, swear, (I know I am a man, and find
  I may deceive myself,) swear faithfully,
  Swear me directly, am I Rowland?

TRANIO Yes.

ROWLAND Am I awake?

TRANIO You are.

ROWLAND Am I in health?

TRANIO As far as I conceive.

ROWLAND Was I with Livia?

TRANIO You were, and had this contract.

ROWLAND And shall I enjoy her?

TRANIO Yes, if you dare.

ROWLAND Swear to all these.

TRANIO I will.

ROWLAND As thou art honest; as thou hast a
   conscience,
  As that may wring thee if thou liest; all these
  To be no vision, but a truth, and serious!

TRANIO Then, by my honesty, and faith, and
   conscience,
  All this is certain.

ROWLAND Let's remove our places.
  Swear it again.

TRANIO By Heaven, it is true.

ROWLAND I have lost then, and Heaven knows I
   am glad on't.
  Let's go; and tell me all, and tell me how,
  For yet I am a pagan in it.

TRANIO I have a priest too;
  And all shall come as even as two testers.

                            (*Exeunt.*)

Scene 4

An apartment in PETRUCHIO'S *house.*

(*Enter* PETRONIUS, SOPHOCLES, MOROSO, *and*
  PETRUCHIO *borne in a coffin.*)

PETRONIUS Set down the body, and one call her
   out!

   (*Enter* MARIA *in black, weeping, and* JAQUES.)

  You are welcome to the last cast of your
   fortunes!
  There lies your husband; there, your loving
   husband;
  There he that was Petruchio, too good for you!
  Your stubborn and unworthy way has killed
   him,
  Ere he could reach the sea: If you can weep,
  Now you have cause, begin, and after death
  Do something yet to the world, to think you
   honest.
  So many tears had saved him, shed in time;
  And as they are (so a good mind go with
   'em)
  Yet they may move compassion.

MARIA Pray ye all hear me.
  And judge me as I am, not as you covet,
  For that would make me yet more miserable:

'Tis true, I have cause to grieve, and mighty
   cause;
  And truly and unfeignedly I weep it.

SOPHOCLES I see there's some good nature yet
   left in her.

MARIA But what's the cause? Mistake me not; not
   this man,
  As he is dead, I weep for; Heaven defend it!
  I never was so childish: But his life,
  His poor, unmanly, wretched, foolish life,
  Is that my full eyes pity; there's my mourning.

PETRONIUS Dost thou not shame?

MARIA I do, and even to water,
  To think what this man was; to think how
   simple
  How far below a man, how far from reason,
  From common understanding, and all gentry,
  While he was living here, he walked amongst
   us.
  He had a happy turn, he died! I'll tell ye,
  These are the wants I weep for, not his person;
  The memory of this man, had he lived
  But two years longer, had begot more follies,
  Than wealthy Autumn flies. But let him rest,
  He was a fool, and farewell he! not pitied,
  I mean in way of life, or action,
  By any understanding man that's honest,
  But only in his posterity, which I,
  Out of the fear his ruins might out-live him
  In some bad issue, like a careful woman,
  Like one indeed born only to preserve him,
  Denied him means to raise.

PETRUCHIO (*Rising*) Unbutton me!
  By Heaven, I die indeed else! – Oh, Maria,
  Oh, my unhappiness, my misery!

PETRONIUS Go to him, whore! By Heaven, if he
   perish,
  I'll see thee hang'd myself!

PETRUCHIO Why, why, Maria –

MARIA I have done my worst, and have my end:
   Forgive me!
  From this hour make me what you please: I
   have tamed you,
  And am now vow'd your servant. Look not
   strangely,
  Nor fear what I say to you. Dare you kiss me?
  Thus I begin my new love.   (*They kiss.*)

PETRUCHIO Once again!

MARIA With all my heart.

PETRUCHIO Once again, Maria! –
  Oh, gentlemen, I know not where I am.

SOPHOCLES Get ye to bed then; there you'll
   quickly know, sir.

PETRUCHIO Never no more your old tricks?

MARIA Never, sir.

PETRUCHIO You shall not need; for, as I have a
     faith,
No cause shall give occasion.
MARIA As I am honest,
   And as I am a maid yet, all my life
   From this hour, since you make so free
      profession,
   I dedicate in service to your pleasure.
SOPHOCLES Ay, marry, this goes roundly off!
PETRUCHIO Go, Jaques,
   Get all the best meat may be bought for money,
   And let the hogsheads blood: I am born again!
   Well, little England, when I see a husband
   Of any other nation, stern or jealous,
   I'll wish him but a woman of thy breeding;
   And if he have not butter to his bread
   Till his teeth bleed, I'll never trust my travel.

(*Enter* ROWLAND, LIVIA, BIANCA, *and* TRANIO.)

PETRONIUS What have we here?
ROWLAND Another morris, sir,
   That you must pipe to.
TRANIO A poor married couple
   Desire an offering, sir.
BIANCA Never frown at it;
   You cannot mend it now: There's your own
      hand,
   And yours, Moroso, to confirm the bargain.
PETRONIUS My hand?
MOROSO Or mine?
BIANCA You'll find it so.
PETRONIUS A trick,
   By Heaven, a trick!
BIANCA Yes, sir, we trick'd you.
LIVIA Father –
PETRONIUS Hast thou lain with him? Speak!
LIVIA Yes, truly, sir.
PETRONIUS And hast thou done the deed, boy?
ROWLAND I have done, sir,
   That that will serve the turn, I think.

PETRUCHIO A match then!
   I'll be the maker-up of this. – Moroso,
   There's now no remedy, you see: Be willing;
   For be, or be not, he must have the wench.
MOROSO Since I am over-reach'd, let's in to
      dinner;
   And, if I can, I'll drink't away.
TRANIO That's well said!
PETRONIUS Well, sirrah, you have play'd a trick:
      Look to't,
   And let me be a grandsire within this twelve-
      month,
   Or, by this hand, I'll curtail half your fortunes!
ROWLAND There shall not want my labour, sir.
      Your money
   Here's one has undertaken.
TRANIO Well, I'll trust her;
   And glad I have so good a pawn.
ROWLAND I'll watch you.
PETRUCHIO Let's in, and drink of all hands, and
      be jovial!
   I have my colt again, and now she carries:
   And, gentlemen, whoever marries next,
   Let him be sure he keep him to his text.
                              (*Exeunt.*)

Epilogue

THE Tamer's Tamed; but so, as nor the men
Can find one just cause to complain of, when
They fitly do consider, in their lives
They should not reign as tyrants o'er their wives:
Nor can the women, from this precedent,
Insult, or triumph; it being aptly meant,
To teach both sexes due equality,
And, as they stand bound, to love mutually.
If this effect, arising from a cause
Well laid and grounded, may deserve applause,
We something more than hope, our honest ends
Will keep the men, and women too, our friends.

Glossary

Andrea a character in Thomas Kyd's *The Spanish Tragedy*

angels gold coins

Babylon a murderous outlaw

balderdash a mixture of liquors

bastard a sweet wine

Bilboa blade an exceptional sword

bobs tricks, deceptions

bob-tail one who is contemptible

bore my nostrils take my place

bragget a drink of honey and ale

bugs-words the words of a ghost or goblin

buss kiss

cætera quis nescit? who doesn't know the rest?

cals caul; a woman's cap

camblet a costly Eastern fabric

cant beg

cap-a-piè from head to foot

capon a castrated rooster

carrack a cargo ship

Cataya China

cinque-pace a dance based on five paces

close-stool a chamber-pot

cockle-boat a small fishing boat

colstave a stick used to carry things

compters counter tokens; false coins

costard a cap; term of contempt

crackers fireworks

cracus tobacco

cuckold adulterous

cuck-stoole restraint chair that allows bystanders to jeer at scolds and other offenders

cudgel a club; weapon

Curtius Marcus Curtius (362 BCE), in the name of arms and valour, leapt into a chasm to save Rome

daw a small bird

devest undress

diall a clock

disanullers to take away one's title

dissembler a deceiver

ditcher a ditch digger

Doctor Deuzace a person of bad luck; contemptible person

dotard one who dotes fondly on another; imbecile

doxy a prostitute

dried Jack dried fish

Dutch hoy a small ship

empyrick a quack; early scientist

Esculapius god of medicine

exordium beginning

eyasses young hawks removed from the nest to be trained; those still being trained

fain shirk; be reluctant

fewterer an attendant

firk to dance about; to beat

flock-bed a cloth-stuffed bed

foist a barge

gew-gaws gaudy trifles; baubles

groats coins

haggard an untamed hawk

handsel initiate

hap fortune; chance

Harry-groat coin (Henry VIII)

hinmost last in line

imputation attribution of fault

inveigle deceive

ipso facto by that very fact

Jack o'Lent a puppet; contemptible person

jade an old horse

jennets small Spanish horses

jib-crack trifle; knick-knack

jointure a widow's estate

kite scavenger bird; rogue

kits small fiddles

Lady Greensleeves a ballad of an inconstant
  woman
larme alarm
linsey-wolsey a woven cotton wool fabric;
  confusion
list to lust; desire
Lucina goddess of childbirth
lusty Laurence a lecher; philanderer

Maudlin Mary Magdalene
maugre in spite of
metheglin a spiced mead
Morris a dance
mountebank a charlatan; quack
mumping mumbling
muskadel a strong sweet wine
myrmidon soldier; faithful follower

Nell-a-Greece Helen of Troy

Ostend place of a great siege that lasted from
  1601 to 1604
ouches brooches

Paphos revels sexual revelries
perdue to stand as a sentinel
pewter cannons chamber pots
pinck a small boat
plackets openings in garments
Pliny Pliny the Elder, a Roman statesman and
  scholar who created one of the first
  encyclopedias of the natural and human worlds
pomander a mixture of sweet smelling
  substances used to protect against illness
poor John salted fish
posset drink of milk and liquor
prevaricate transgress; deviate
prince of Orange Balthazar Gerard, who
  murdered the Prince of Orange, was subjected
  to exemplary torture
puissant powerful
puling whining
purfle an embroidered border

quartern-ague a fever that persists but does not
  kill
quillets quibbles
Qui va là? Who goes there?

ramping rage with violence

recreant false; unfaithful to duty
resty lazy
rhubarb a purgative
rundlets small casks

sack white wine
St Dunstan archbishop of Canterbury 960–988.
  Dunstan siezed the devil, disguised as a woman,
  by the nose with a pair of smith's tongs
St George patron saint of England
Sedgly a town in Staffordshire
simperd to smile; smirk
Sinon the Greek who convinced the Trojans
  to bring the wooden horse into Troy;
  a deceiver
sot a fool
souse pickled preserves
Spinola Marques de Espinola; a Spanish general
  who captured Ostend in 1604
spur-gall'd to be injured or galled by spurs while
  riding
spur-royals gold coins (James I)
stilo novo new style
sumpters a pack horse
swabber a mop

tabor to thrash; beat
tantara fanfare from a trumpet or drum
teatish peevish; irritable
tith tight
toil a trap
Tom o'Lincoln a cathedral bell
Tom Tilers a henpecked husband
tro faith; trust
troth word; truth; betrothed
tumbrel a cart that tips easily to dump its load; a
  flat-bottomed boat or barge
Tyrone Hugh O'Neill the 2nd Earl of Tyrone, an
  Ulster chief who led a Catholic revolt against
  England between 1595 and 1601

Verdugo a hangman
verjuce sour juice
victual'd furnished with supplies
viva voce orally; oral examination

washing beetle a weighted staff used to wash
  clothes
whim-wham a trifle

The History of King Lear

Nahum Tate

Introduction

Nahum Tate was born into a family of Puritan ministers in Ireland, most likely in 1652. He graduated from Trinity College, Dublin, in 1672, and eventually moved to London. There he became acquainted and collaborated with John Dryden, around the time Dryden was working on his Shakespearean adaptations, *All for Love* and *Troilus and Cressida*. From 1680 to 1681 Tate produced three adaptations of Shakespeare: *The History of King Richard the Second*, also called *The Sicilian Usurper* (in order to disguise its content from politically sensitive censors); *The History of King Lear*; and *The Ingratitude of a Common-Wealth*, an adaptation of *Coriolanus*. His other works for the theatre include adaptations of works by Shakespeare's contemporaries, Chapman and Marston, Beaumont and Fletcher, and John Webster. Tate also wrote the libretto for Henry Purcell's opera *Dido and Aeneas*. In 1692 Tate was appointed Poet Laureate. He died in 1715.

Despite his attempt to disguise its content (the play deals with the deposition of a king) at a time of political crisis and insecurity brought on by opposition to the Catholic heir apparent, the future James II, Tate's adaptation of *Richard III* was banned from the stage after only two performances. His adaptation of *Coriolanus* had little success as well. His version of King Lear, however, was effectively to replace Shakespeare's original on the English stage well into the nineteenth century. For 150 years, in the theatre, Tate's version, with some modifications, was the only *King Lear* to be had. Laura Rosenthal notes, however, that printed editions of Shakespeare's play remained faithful to the text even as liberties were taken on the stage (331). Since the nineteenth century, Tate's version has been the subject of much critical derision, and 'Tatefication' was coined as a word for the debasement of great literary works (Spencer: 14). In the last 100 years, Tate's version has been rarely staged. There were, for instance, productions in London in 1949 and 1966 (Black: xxxvii) and Berkeley in 1967 (see Sharkey).

In his dedication to the play, Tate calls his work a 'revival . . . with alterations,' thus capturing both Tate's esteem for Shakespeare and his need to improve upon the original. Tate writes of his 'zeal for all the remains of Shakespeare' and that Shakespeare's *King Lear* appeared to him 'a heap of jewels, unstrung and unpolished, yet so dazzling in their disorder that I soon perceived I had seized a treasure.' To this treasure Tate wishes to bring 'regularity and probability.' Regularity is brought to the play by restringing the jewels in a new order, one which calls for fewer scene changes, which were more trouble in the new Restoration theatre, rich with scenery and scenic effects, than on the bare Shakespearean stage. Tate also avoids 'quaintness of expression,' both in the lines and speeches he adds and in the alterations he makes to language from Shakespeare. In the very first scene of the new play, for instance, based on Edmund's speech in Shakespeare 'Thou, Nature, art my goddess,' Tate avoids the gnarled syntax and strange but powerful diction of the original (see Spencer: 72–74). The language of *King Lear* is thus made to suit the new Restoration aesthetic of regularity and fitness. Tate omits Shakespeare's Fool and his extravagant language probably for the same reason.

Not only regularity but probability, Tate argues, is achieved by one of his two main alterations to the plot: a love interest between Edgar and Cordelia, which gives new motivation to Cordelia's reluctance in the division of the kingdom and Edgar's lingering in hiding as Poor Tom. Moreover, Cordelia's role is expanded, allowing the play to take advantage of the new prominence and popularity of actresses on the Restoration stage.

The love interest also necessitates and effects the other major change in the story: in Tate's play there is a happy ending, in which Lear and Gloucester live and Edgar and Cordelia are betrothed. With this development, the story of Lear becomes something very different from what it was in Shakespeare – what Sandra Clark calls 'romantic melodrama' (lxix) – although editions of Tate's play continued to call it a tragedy. Tate is, therefore, an early example of adapting Shakespeare by changing genre – although Shakespeare, of course, had made equally drastic, if opposite, modifications to the source material for his play, especially by darkening the ending.

Clark notes that Shakespeare's ending appears to highlight extreme contingency and bad luck (lxx). Since the Second World War, the Holocaust, and nuclear destruction, audiences have found the bleakness of Shakespeare's ending not only probable but compellingly apocalyptic. Many, however, in the Restoration and eighteenth century – including Samuel Johnson – found Shakespeare's ending unduly harsh, improbable, and lacking in 'poetic justice' (Clark: lxv). As Johnson said: 'In the present case the publick has decided' (quoted in Clark: lxv). We might add that the public continues to decide, and not always in the same way.

Despite this difference, Restoration and twentieth-century adapters share – if for different reasons – an ethic and aesthetic which gives them licence to modify Shakespeare. Christopher Spencer writes, 'In Tate's age writers regarded the Elizabethan style as inferior to their own in sophistication and regularity' (72). He explains of writers of the Neoclassic age: 'if they admired an author . . . they imitated him, trying to write as they thought he would have written had he been their contemporary. If the author was an English playwright, this practice often meant fitting his work to the stage conditions of the day and adjusting his plot, characters, and language to contemporary taste.' In this way, Tate practiced 'the sincere form of flattery of keeping the works of the dead polished and up to date' (67). And so, as James Black puts it, 'The reasons for the popular success of Tate's version lie in his transformation of Shakespeare's play into typical Restoration drama' (xvi).

A different understanding of Tate's concerns in adapting Shakespeare, however, informs the work of Wikander and Maguire. For Wikander, Tate's adaptations and others of the period 'draw specific analogies between the unrest they depict, contemporary events in the 1680s, and the events of the 1640s that led to the outbreak of civil war' (342), and Maguire writes: 'Tate probably chose, in part, to adapt Lear because Shakespeare's play resonated with the Restoration audience's experience: the mid-century division of the king's two bodies, for instance, and misplaced succession, the dangers of power unwisely delegated, and, of course, civil war' (33). For Maguire, these resonances explain in large part the play's immediate success (39), while Wikander sees in the imposition of 'divine justice' (355) at the end of the play an example of 'regularizing Shakespeare to find a coherent conservative political vision' (342).

Select bibliography

Entries marked * are particularly accessible.

Adler, D. (1985) 'The Half-Life of Tate in *King Lear*,' *Kenyon Review* 7,3: 52–56.
*Black, J. (ed.) (1975) *The History of King Lear*, N. Tate, Lincoln: University of Nebraska Press.
Branam, G. C. (1956) *Eighteenth-Century Adaptations of Shakespearean Tragedy*, Berkeley: University of California Press.
Clark, S. (ed.) (1997) *Shakespeare Made Fit: Restoration Adaptations of Shakespeare*, London: J. M. Dent.
Maguire, N. K. (1991) 'Nahum Tate's *King Lear*: "The King's Blest Restoration,"' in J. I. Marsden (ed.) *The Appropriation of Shakespeare: Post-Renaissance Reconstructions of the Works and the Myth*, New York: St. Martin's Press: 29–43.
Nameri, D. E. (1976) *Three Versions of the Story of King Lear*, 2 vols, Salzburg: Institut für Englische Sprache und Literatur.
Pericord, H. W. (1982) 'Shakespeare, Tate, and Garrick: New Light on Alterations of *King Lear*,' *Theatre Notebook* 36,1: 14–21.
Rosenthal, L. J. (1996) '(Re)Writing Lear: Literary Property and Dramatic Authorship,' in J. Brewer and S. Staves (eds) *Early Modern Conceptions of Property*, London: Routledge.
Sharkey, P. L. (1968) 'Performing Nahum Tate's *King Lear*: Coming Hither by Going Hence,' *Quarterly Journal of Speech* 56: 398–403.
Solomon, J.F. (1984) 'King in Lear: A Semiotic for Communal Adaptation,' *American Journal of Semiotics* 3,2: 56–76.
*Spencer, C. (1972) *Nahum Tate*, New York: Twayne.
*Wikander, M. H. (1986) 'The Spitted Infant: Scenic Emblem and Exclusionist Politics in Restoration Adaptations of Shakespeare,' *Shakespeare Quarterly* 37: 340–358.
Zimbardo, R. A. (1990) 'The King and the Fool: *King Lear* as Self-Destructing Text,' *Criticism* 32,1: 1–29.

The History of King Lear

Nahum Tate

Prologue

Since by Mistakes your best Delights are made,
(For ev'n your Wives can please in Masquerade)
'Twere worth our While t' have drawn you in this
    day
By a new Name to our old honest Play;
But he that did this Evenings Treat prepare
Bluntly resolv'd before-hand to declare
Your Entertainment should be most old Fare.
Yet hopes, since in rich Shakespear's soil it grew,
'Twill relish yet with those whose Tasts are True,
And his Ambition is to please a Few.
If then this Heap of Flow'rs-shall chance to wear
Fresh Beauty in the Order they now bear,
Ev'n this Shakespear's Praise; each Rustick knows
'Mongst plenteous Flow'rs a Garland to Compose,
Which strung by his course Hand may fairer Show,
But 'twas a Pow'r: Divine first made 'em Grow.
Why shou'd these Scenes lie hid, in which we find
What may at Once divert and teach the Mind?
Morals were alwaies proper for the Stage,
But are ev'n necessary in this Age.
Poets must take the Churches Teaching Trade,
Since Priests their Province of Intrigue invade;
But We the worst in this Exchange have got,
In vain our Poets Preach, whilst Church-men Plot.

Act I

(*Enter* BASTARD *solus.*)

BASTARD Thou Nature art my Goddess, to thy
  Law
  My Services are bound, why am I then
  Depriv'd of a Son's Right because I came not
  In the dull Road that custom has prescrib'd?
  Why Bastard, wherefore Base, when I can boast
  A Mind as gen'rous and a Shape as true
  As honest Madam's Issue? why are we
  Held Base, who in the lusty stealth of Nature

Take fiercer Qualities than what compound
The scanted Births of the stale Marriage-bed?
Well then, legitimate *Edgar*, to thy right
Of Law I will oppose a Bastard's Cunning.
Our Father's Love is to the Bastard *Edmund*
As to Legitimate *Edgar*: with success
I've practis'd yet on both their easie Natures:
Here comes the old Man chas't with th'
  Information
Which last I forg'd against my Brother *Edgar*,
A Tale so plausible, so boldly utter'd
And heightned by such lucky Accidents,
That now the slightest circumstance confirms
  him,
And Base-born *Edmund* spight of Law inherits.

(*Enter* KENT *and* GLOSTER.)

GLOSTER Nay, good my Lord, your Charity
  O'reshoots it self to plead in his behalf;
  You are your self a Father, and may feel
  The sting of disobedience from a Son
  First-born and best Belov'd: Oh Villain *Edgar!*
KENT Be not too rash, all may be forgery,
  And time yet clear the Duty of your Son.
GLOSTER Plead with the Seas, and reason down
  the Winds,
  Yet shalt thou ne're convince me, I have seen
  His foul Designs through all a Father's fondness:
  But be this Light and Thou my Witnesses
  That I discard him here from my Possessions,
  Divorce him from my Heart, my Blood and
  Name.
BASTARD It works as I cou'd wish; I'll shew my
  self.
GLOSTER Ha *Edmund!* welcome Boy; O *Kent* see
  here
  Inverted Nature, *Gloster*'s Shame and Glory,
  This By-born, the wild sally of my Youth,
  Pursues me with all filial Offices,
  Whilst *Edgar*, begg'd of Heaven and born in
  Honour,

Draws plagues on my white head that urge me
   still
To curse in Age the pleasure of my Youth.
Nay weep not, *Edmund*, for thy Brother's crimes;
O gen'rous Boy, thou shar'st but half his blood,
Yet lov'st beyond the kindness of a Brother.
But I'll reward thy Vertue. Follow me.
My Lord, you wait the King who comes resolv'd
To quit the Toils of Empire, and divide
His Realms amongst his Daughters, Heaven
   succeed it,
But much I fear the Change.

KENT I grieve to see him
With such wild starts of passion hourly seiz'd,
As renders Majesty beneath it self.

GLOSTER Alas! 'tis the Infirmity of his Age,
Yet has his Temper ever been unfixt,
Chol'rick and suddain; hark, They approach.
               (*Exeunt* GLOSTER *and* BASTARD.)

(*Flourish. Enter* LEAR, CORNWALL, ALBANY,
BURGUNDY, EDGAR, GONERILL, REGAN,
CORDELIA, EDGAR, *speaking to* CORDELIA *at
Entrance.*)

EDGAR *Cordelia*, royal Fair, turn yet once more,
An e're successful *Burgundy* receive
The treasure of thy Beauties from the King,
E're happy *Burgundy* for ever fold Thee,
Cast back one pitying Look on wretched *Edgar*.

CORDELIA Alas what wou'd the wretched *Edgar*
   with
The more Unfortunate *Cordelia*;
Who in obedience to a Father's will
Flys from her *Edgar*'s Arms to *Burgundy*'s?

LEAR Attend my Lords of *Albany* and *Cornwall*
With Princely *Burgundy*.

ALBANY We do, my Liege.

LEAR Give me the Mapp – know, Lords, We have
   divided
In Three our Kingdom, having now resolved
To disengage from Our long Toil of State,
Conferring All upon your younger years;
You, *Burgundy*, *Cornwall* and *Albany*
Long in Our Court have made your amorous
   sojourn
And now are to be answer'd – tell me my
   Daughters
Which of you Loves Us most, that We may place
Our largest Bounty with the largest Merit.
Gonerill, Our Eldest-born, speak first.

GONERILL Sir, I do love You more than words can
   utter,
Beyond what can be valu'd, Rich or Rare,
Nor Liberty, nor Sight, Health, Fame, or Beauty
Are half so dear, my Life for you were vile,

As much as Child can love the best of Fathers.

LEAR Of all these Bounds, ev'n from this Line to
   this
With shady Forests and wide-skirted Meads,
We make Thee Lady, to thine and *Albany*'s Issue
Be this perpetual – What says Our Second
   Daughter?

REGAN My Sister, Sir, in part exprest my Love,
For such as Hers, is mine, though more
   extended;
Sense has no other Joy that I can relish,
I have my All in my dear Lieges Love!

LEAR Therefore to thee and thine Hereditary
Remain this ample Third of our fair Kingdom.

CORDELIA Now comes my Trial, how   (*Aside.*)
   am I distrest,
That must with cold speech tempt the chol'rick
   King
Rather to leave me Dowerless, than condemn
   me
To loath'd Embraces!

LEAR Speak now Our last, not least in Our dear
   Love,
So ends my Task of State, – *Cordelia* speak,
What canst Thou say to win a richer Third
Than what thy Sisters gain'd?

CORDELIA Now must my Love in words fall short
   of theirs
As much as it exceeds in Truth – Nothing my
   Lord.

LEAR Nothing can come of Nothing, speak agen.

CORDELIA Unhappy am I that I can't dissemble,
Sir, as I ought, I love your Majesty,
No more nor less.

LEAR Take heed *Cordelia*,
Thy Fortunes are at stake, think better on't
And mend thy Speech a little.

CORDELIA O my Liege,
You gave me Being, Bred me, dearly Love me,
And I return my Duty as I ought,
Obey you, Love you, and most Honour you!
Why have my Sisters Husbands, if they love you
   All?
Happ'ly when I shall Wed, the Lord whose Hand
Shall take my Plight, will carry half my Love,
For I shall never marry, like my Sisters,
To Love my Father All.

LEAR And goes thy Heart with this?
'Tis said that I am Chol'rick, judge me Gods,
Is there not cause? now Minion I perceive
The Truth of what has been suggested to Us,
Thy Fondness for the Rebel Son of *Gloster*,
False to his Father, as Thou art to my Hopes:
And oh take heed, rash Girl, lest We comply
With thy fond wishes, which thou wilt too late

Repent, for know Our nature cannot brook
A Child so young and so Ungentle.

CORDELIA So young my Lord and True.

LEAR Thy Truth then be thy Dow'r,
For by the sacred Sun and solemn Night
I here disclaim all my paternal Care,
And from this minute hold thee as a Stranger
Both to my Blood and Favour.

KENT This is Frenzy.
Consider, good my Liege –

LEAR Peace Kent.
Come not between a Dragon and his Rage.
I lov'd her most, and in her tender Trust
Design'd to have bestow'd my Age at Ease!
So be my Grave my Peace as here I give
My Heart from her, and with it all my Wealth:
My Lords of Cornwall and of Albany,
I do invest you jointly with full Right
In this fair Third, Cordelia's forfeit Dow'r.
Mark me, My Lords, observe Our last Resolve,
Our Self attended with an hundred Knights
Will make Aboad with you in monthly Course,
The Name alone of King remain with me,
Yours be the Execution and Revenues,
This is Our final Will, and to confirm it
This Coronet part between you.

KENT Royal Lear,
Whom I have ever honour'd as my King,
Lov'd as my Father, as my Master follow'd,
And as my Patron thought on in my Pray'rs –

LEAR Away, the Bow is bent, make from the
Shaft.

KENT No, let it fall and drench within my Heart,
Be Kent unmannerly when Lear is mad:
Thy youngest Daughter –

LEAR On thy Life no more.

KENT What wilt thou doe, old Man?

LEAR Out of my sight!

KENT See better first.

LEAR Now by the gods –

KENT Now by the gods, rash King, thou swear'st
in vain.

LEAR Ha Traytour –

KENT Do, kill thy Physician, Lear,
Strike through my Throat, yet with my latest
Breath
I'll Thunder in thine Ear my just Complaint,
And tell Thee to thy Face that Thou dost ill.

LEAR Hear me rash Man, on thy Allegiance hear
me;
Since thou hast striv'n to make Us break our
Vow
And prest between our Sentence and our Pow'r,
Which nor Our Nature nor our Place can bear,
We banish thee for ever from Our Sight

And Kingdom; if when Three days are expir'd
Thy hated Trunk be found in our Dominions
That moment is thy Death; Away.

KENT Why fare thee well, King, since thou art
resolv'd,
I take thee at thy word, and will not stay
To see thy Fall: the gods protect the Maid
That truly thinks, and has most justly said.
Thus to new Climates my old Truth I bear,
Friendship lives Hence, and Banishment is
Here.   (Exit.)

LEAR Now Burgundy, you see her Price is faln,
Yet if the fondness of your Passion still
Affects her as she stands, Dow'rless, and lost
In our Esteem, she's yours, take her or leave
her.

BURGUNDY Pardon me, Royal Lear, I but demand
The Dow'r your Self propos'd, and here I take
Cordelia by the Hand Dutchess of Burgundy.

LEAR Then leave her Sir, for by a Father's rage
I tell you all her Wealth. Away.

BURGUNDY Then Sir be pleas'd to charge the
breach
Of our Alliance on your own Will
Not my Inconstancy.

          (Exeunt. Manent EDGAR and CORDELIA.)

EDGAR Has Heaven then weigh'd the merit of my
Love,
Or is't the raving of my sickly Thought?
Cou'd Burgundy forgoe so rich a Prize
And leave her to despairing Edgar's Arms?
Have I thy Hand Cordelia, do I clasp it,
The Hand that was this minute to have join'd
My hated Rivals? do I kneel before thee
And offer at thy feet my panting Heart?
Smile, Princess, and convince me, for as yet
I doubt, and dare not trust the dazling Joy.

CORDELIA Some Comfort yet that 'twas no vicious
Blot
That has depriv'd me of a Father's Grace,
But meerly want of that that makes me rich
In Wanting it, a smooth professing Tongue:
O Sisters, I am loth to call your fault
As it deserves; but use our Father well,
And wrong'd Cordelia never shall repine.

EDGAR O heav'nly Maid that art thy self thy
Dow'r,
Richer in Vertue than the Stars in Light,
If Edgar's humble fortunes may be grac't
With thy Acceptance, at thy feet he lays 'em.
Ha my Cordelia! dost thou turn away?
What have I done t'offend Thee?

CORDELIA Talk't of Love.

EDGAR Then I've offended oft, Cordelia too
Has oft permitted me so to offend.

CORDELIA When, *Edgar*, I permitted your
 Addresses,
  I was the darling Daughter of a King,
  Nor can I now forget my royal Birth,
  And live dependent on my Lover's Fortune.
  I cannot to so low a fate submit,
  And therefore study to forget your Passion,
  And trouble me upon this Theam no more.
EDGAR Thus Majesty takes most State in
 Distress!
  How are we tost on Fortune's fickle flood!
  The Wave that with surprising kindness brought
  The dear Wreck to my Arms, has snatcht it back,
  And left me mourning on the barren Shore.
CORDELIA This Baseness of th' ignoble   (*Aside.*)
 Burgundy
  Draws just suspicion on the Race of Men,
  His Love was Int'rest, so may *Edgar*'s be
  And He but with more Complement dissemble;
  If so, I shall oblige him by Denying:
  But if his Love be fixt, such Constant flame
  As warms our Breasts, if such I find his Passion,
  My Heart as gratefull to his Truth shall be,
  And Cold *Cordelia* prove as Kind as He. (*Exit.*)

        (*Enter* BASTARD *hastily.*)

BASTARD Brother, I've found you in a lucky
 minute,
  Fly and be safe, some Villain has incens'd
  Our Father against your Life.
EDGAR Distrest *Cordelia!* but oh! more Cruel!
BASTARD Hear me Sir, your Life, your Life's in
 Danger.
EDGAR A Resolve so sudden
  And of such black Importance!
BASTARD 'Twas not sudden,
  Some Villain has of long time laid the Train.
EDGAR And yet perhaps 'twas but pretended
 Coldness,
  To try how far my passion would pursue.
BASTARD He hears me not; wake, wake Sir.
EDGAR Say ye Brother? – .
  No Tears good *Edmund*, if thou bringst me
 tidings
  To strike me dead, for Charity delay not,
  That present will befit so kind a Hand.
BASTARD Your danger Sir comes on so fast
  That I want time t'inform you, but retire
  Whilst I take care to turn the pressing Stream.
  O gods! for Heav'ns sake Sir.
EDGAR Pardon me Sir, a serious Thought
  Had seiz'd me, but I think you talkt of danger
  And wisht me to Retire; must all our Vows
  End thus! – Friend I obey you – O *Cordelia!*
                                    (*Exit.*)

BASTARD Ha! ha! fond Man, such credulous
 Honesty
  Lessens the Glory of my Artifice,
  His Nature is so far from doing wrongs
  That he suspects none: if this Letter speed
  And pass for *Edgar*'s, as himself wou'd own
  The Counterfeit but for the foul Contents,
  Then my designs are perfect – here comes
  Gloster.   (*Enter* GLOSTER.)
GLOSTER Stay *Edmund*, turn, what paper were
 you reading?
BASTARD A Trifle Sir.
GLOSTER What needed then that terrible dispatch
 of it
  Into your Pocket, come produce it Sir.
BASTARD A Letter from my Brother Sir, I had
  Just broke the Seal but knew not the Contents,
  Yet fearing they might prove to blame
  Endeavoured to conceal it from your sight.
GLOSTER 'Tis *Edgar*'s Character.   (*Reads.*)

*This Policy of Fathers is intollerable that keeps our
Fortunes from us till Age will not suffer us to enjoy
'em; I am weary of the Tyranny: Come to me that of
this I may speak more: if our Father would sleep till
I wak't him, you shou'd enjoy half his Possessions,
and live beloved of your Brother*
                                    Edgar.

  Slept till I wake him, you shou'd enjoy
  Half his possessions – *Edgar* to write this
  'Gainst his indulgent Father! Death and Hell!
  Fly, *Edmund*, seek him out, wind me into him
  That I may bite the Traytor's heart, and fold
  His bleeding Entrals on my vengefull Arm.
BASTARD Perhaps 'twas writ, my Lord, to prove
 my Vertue.
GLOSTER These late Eclipses of the Sun and
 Moon
  Can bode no less; Love cools, and friendship
 fails,
  In Cities mutiny, in Countrys discord,
  The bond of Nature crack't 'twixt Son and
 Father:
  Find out the Villain, do it carefully
  And it shall lose thee nothing.   (*Exit.*)
BASTARD So, now my project's firm, but to make
 sure
  I'll throw in one proof more and that a bold one;
  I'll place old *Gloster* where he shall o're-hear us
  Confer of this design, whilst to his thinking,
  Deluded *Edgar* shall accuse himself.
  Be Honesty my Int'rest and I can
  Be honest too, and what Saint so Divine
  That will successfull Villany decline! (*Exit.*)

(*Enter* KENT *disguis'd.*)

KENT Now banisht *Kent*, if thou canst pay thy
    duty
  In this disguise where thou dost stand
    condemn'd,
  Thy Master *Lear* shall find thee full of Labours.

(*Enter* LEAR *attended.*)

LEAR In there, and tell our Daughter we are here
  Now; What art Thou?
KENT A Man, Sir.
LEAR What dost thou profess, or wou'dst with us?
KENT I do profess to be no less then I seem, to
  serve him truly that puts me in Trust, to love
  him that's Honest, to converse with him that's
  wise and speaks little, to fight when I can't
  choose; and to eat no Fish.
LEAR I say, what art Thou?
KENT A very honest-hearted fellow, and as poor
  as the King.
LEAR Then art thou poor indeed – What can'st
  thou do?
KENT I can keep honest Counsel, marr a curious
  Tale in the telling, deliver a plain Message
  bluntly, that which ordinary Men are fit for I am
  qualify'd in, and the best of me is Diligence.
LEAR Follow me, thou shalt serve me.

(*Enter one of* GONERILL's *Gentlemen.*)

  Now Sir?
GENTLEMAN Sir –   (*Exit;* KENT *runs after him.*)
LEAR What says the fellow? Call the Clatpole
  back.
ATTENDANT My Lord, I know not, but methinks
  your Highness is entertain'd with slender
  Ceremony.
SERVANT He says, my Lord, your Daughter is not
  well.
LEAR Why came not the Slave back when I call'd
  him?
SERVANT My Lord, he answer'd me i'th' surliest
  manner,
  That he wou'd not.

(*Re-enter* GENTLEMAN *brought in by* KENT.)

LEAR I hope our Daughter did not so instruct him:
  Now, who am I Sir?
GENTLEMAN My Ladies Father.
LEAR My Lord's Knave – (*Strikes him.*)
               (GONERILL *at the Entrance.*)
GENTLEMAN I'll not be struck my Lord.
KENT Nor tript neither, thou vile Civet-box.
                        (*Strikes up his heels.*)
GONERILL By Day and Night this is insufferable,
  I will not bear it.

LEAR Now, Daughter, why that frontlet on?
  Speak, do's that Frown become our Presence?
GONERILL Sir, this licentious Insolence of your
  Servants
  Is most unseemly, hourly they break out
  In quarrels bred by their unbounded Riots,
  I had fair hope by making this known to you
  T'have had a quick Redress, but find too late
  That you protect and countenance their out-
  rage;
  And therefore, Sir, I take this freedom, which
  Necessity makes Discreet.
LEAR Are you our Daughter?
GONERILL Come, Sir, let me entreat you to make
  use
  Of your discretion, and put off betimes
  This Disposition that of late transforms you
  From what you rightly are.
LEAR Do's any here know me? why this is not
    Lear.
  Do's *Lear* walk thus? speak thus? where are his
    Eyes?
  Who is it that can tell me who I am?
GONERILL Come, Sir, this Admiration's much o'th'
  savour
  Of other your new humours, I beseech you
  To understand my purposes aright;
  As you are old, you shou'd be staid and wise,
  Here do you keep an hundred Knights and
    Squires,
  Men so debaucht and bold that this our Palace
  Shews like a riotous Inn, a Tavern, Brothel;
  Be then advised by her that else will take
  The thing she beggs, to lessen your Attendance,
  Take half a way, and see that the remainder
  Be such as may befit your Age, and know
  Themselves and you.
LEAR Darkness and Devils!
  Saddle my Horses, call my Train together,
  Degenerate Viper, I'll not stay with Thee;
  I yet have left a Daughter – Serpent, Monster,
  Lessen my Train, and call 'em riotous?
  All men approv'd of choice and rarest Parts,
  That each particular of duty know –
  How small, *Cordelia*, was thy Fault? O *Lear*,
  Beat at this Gate that let thy Folly in,
  And thy dear Judgment out; Go, go, my People.
               (*Going off meets* ALBANY *entring.*)
  Ingratefull Duke, was this your will?
ALBANY What Sir?
LEAR Death! fifty of my Followers at a clap!
ALBANY The matter Madam?
GONERILL Never afflict your self to know the
  Cause,
  But give his Dotage way.

LEAR Blasts upon thee,
   Th' untented woundings of a Father's Curse
   Pierce ev'ry Sense about Thee; old fond Eyes
   Lament this Cause again, I'll pluck ye out
   And cast ye with the Waters that ye lose
   To temper Clay – No, *Gorgon*, thou shalt find
   That I'll resume the Shape which thou dost think
   I have cast off for ever.
GONERILL Mark ye that.
LEAR Hear Nature!
   Dear Goddess hear, and if thou dost intend
   To make that Creature fruitfull, change thy purpose;
   Pronounce upon her Womb the barren Curse,
   That from her blasted Body never spring
   A Babe to honour her – but if she must bring forth,
   Defeat her Joy with same distorted Birth,
   Or monstrous Form, the Prodigy o'th' Time,
   And so perverse of spirit, that it may Live
   Her Torment as 'twas Born, to fret her Cheeks
   With constant Tears, and wrinkle her young Brow.
   Turn all her Mother's Pains to Shame and Scorn,
   That she may curse her Crime too late, and feel
   How sharper than a Serpent's Tooth it is
   To have a Thankless Child! Away, away.
                     (*Exit cum suis.*)
GONERILL Presuming thus upon his numerous Train
   He thinks to play the Tyrant here, and hold
   Our lives at will.
ALBANY Well, you may bear too far.   (*Exeunt.*)

Act II

Scene: GLOSTER'S *house.*

(*Enter* BASTARD.)

BASTARD The Duke comes here to night, I'll take advantage
   Of his Arrival to compleat my project,
   Brother a Word, come forth, 'tis I your Friend,
                     (*Enter* EDGAR.)
   My Father watches for you, fly this place,
   Intelligence is giv'n where you are hid,
   Take the advantage of the Night, bethink ye
   Have not spoke against the Duke of *Cornwall*
   Something might shew you a favourer of
   Duke *Albany*'s Party?
EDGAR Nothing, why ask you?
BASTARD Because he's coming here to Night in haste

And *Regan* with him – heark! the Guards, Away.
EDGAR Let 'em come on, I'll stay and clear my self.
BASTARD Your Innocence at Leisure may be heard,
   But *Gloster*'s storming Rage as yet is deaf,
   And you may perish e're allow'd the hearing.
                   (*Exit* EDGAR.)
   Gloster comes yonder: now to my feign'd scuffle –
   Yield, come before my Father! Lights here, Lights!
   Some Blood drawn on me wou'd beget opinion
                  (*Stabs his Arm.*)
   Of our more fierce Encounter – I have seen
   Drunkards do more than this in sport.

(*Enter* GLOSTER *and* SERVANTS.)

GLOSTER Now, *Edmund*, where's the Traytour?
BASTARD That Name, Sir,
   Strikes Horrour through me, but my Brother, Sir,
   Stood here i'th' Dark.
GLOSTER Thou bleed'st, pursue the Villain
   And bring him piece-meal to me.
BASTARD Sir, he's fled.
GLOSTER Let him fly far, this Kingdom shall not hide him:
   The noble Duke, my Patron, comes to Night,
   By his Authority I will proclaim
   Rewards for him that brings him to the Stake,
   And Death for the Concealer.
   Then of my Lands, loyal and natural Boy,
   I'll work the means to make thee capable.
                   (*Exeunt.*)

(*Enter* KENT, *disguis'd still, and* GONERILL'S
GENTLEMAN, *severally.*)

GENTLEMAN Good morrow Friend, belong'st thou to this House?
KENT Ask them will answer thee.
GENTLEMAN Where may we set our Horses?
KENT I'th' Mire.
GENTLEMAN I am in haste, prethee an' thou lov'st me, tell me.
KENT I love thee not.
GENTLEMAN Why then I care not for Thee.
KENT An' I had thee in *Lipsbury* Pinfold, I'd make thee care for me.
GENTLEMAN What dost thou mean? I know thee not.
KENT But, Minion, I know Thee.
GENTLEMAN What dost thou know me for?
KENT For a base, proud, beggarly, white-liver'd, Glass-gazing, superserviceable finical Rogue;

one that wou'd be a Pimp in way of good
Service, and art nothing but a composition of
Knave, Beggar, Coward, Pandar –

GENTLEMAN What a monstrous Fellow art thou to
rail at one that is neither known of thee nor
knows thee?

KENT Impudent Slave, not know me, who but two
days since tript up thy heels before the King:
draw, Miscreant, or I'll make the Moon shine
through thee.

GENTLEMAN What means the Fellow? – Why
prethee, prethee; I tell thee I have nothing to do
with thee.

KENT I know your Rogueship's Office, you come
with Letters against the King, taking my young
Lady *Vanity*'s part against her royal Father; draw
Rascal.

GENTLEMAN Murther, murther, help Ho!

KENT Dost thou scream Peacock, strike Puppet,
stand dappar Slave.

GENTLEMAN Help Hea'! Murther, help.

(*Exit.* KENT *after him.*)

(*Flourish. Enter* DUKE OF CORNWALL, REGAN,
attended, GLOSTER, BASTARD.)

GLOSTER All Welcome to your Graces, you do me
honour.

DUKE *Gloster* w'ave heard with sorrow that your
Life
Has been attempted by your impious Son,
But *Edmund* here has paid you strictest Duty.

GLOSTER He did betray his Practice, and receiv'd
The Hurt you see, striving to apprehend him.

DUKE Is He pursu'd?

GLOSTER He is, my Lord.

REGAN Use our Authority to apprehend
The Traytour and do Justice on his Head;
For you, *Edmund*, that have so signaliz'd
Your Vertue, you from henceforth shall be ours;
Natures of such firm Trust we much shall need.
A charming Youth and worth my further
Thought.   (*Aside.*)

DUKE Lay comforts, noble *Gloster*, to your Breast,
As we to ours, This Night be spent in Revels,
We choose you, *Gloster*, for our Host to Night,
A troublesome expression of our Love.
On, to the Sports before us – who are These?

(*Enter the Gentleman pursu'd by* KENT.)

GLOSTER Now, what's the matter?

DUKE Keep peace upon your Lives, he dies that
strikes.
Whence and what are ye?

ATTENDANT Sir, they are Messengers, the one
from your Sister,

The other from the King.

DUKE Your Difference? speak.

GENTLEMAN I'm scarce in breath, my Lord.

KENT No marvel, you have so bestirr'd your
Valour,
Nature disclaims the Dastard, a Taylor made
him.

DUKE Speak yet, how grew your Quarrel?

GENTLEMAN Sir this old Ruffian here, whose Life
I spar'd
In pity to his Beard –

KENT Thou Essence Bottle!
In pity to my Beard? – Your leave, my Lord,
And I will tread the Muss cat into Mortar.

DUKE Know'st thou our Presence?

KENT Yes, Sir, but Anger has a Privilege.

DUKE Why art thou angry?

KENT That such a Slave as this shou'd wear a
Sword
And have no Courage, Office and no Honesty.
Not Frost and Fire hold more Antipathy
Than I and such a Knave.

GLOSTER Why dost thou call him Knave?

KENT His Countenance likes me not.

DUKE No more perhaps does Mine, nor His or
Hers.

KENT Plain-dealing is my Trade, and to be plain,
Sir,
I have seen better Faces in my time
Than stands on any Shoulders now before me.

REGAN This is some Fellow that having once been
prais'd,
For bluntness, since affects a sawcy Rudeness,
But I have known one of these surly Knaves
That in his Plainness harbour'd more Design
Than twenty cringing complementing Minions.

DUKE What's the offence you gave him?

GENTLEMAN Never any, Sir.
It pleas'd the King his Master lately
To strike me on a slender misconstruction,
Whilst watching his Advantage this old Lurcher
Tript me behind, for which the King extold him;
And, flusht with th' honour of this bold exploit,
Drew on me here agen.

DUKE Bring forth the Stocks, we'll teach you.

KENT Sir I'm too old to learn;
Call not the Stocks for me, I serve the King,
On whose Employment I was sent to you,
You'll shew too small Respect, and too bold
Malice
Against the Person of my royal Master,
Stocking his Messenger.

DUKE Bring forth the Stocks, as I have Life and
Honour,
There shall he sit till Noon.

REGAN Till Noon, my Lord? till Night, and all
  Night too.
KENT Why, Madam, if I were your Father's Dog
  You wou'd not use me so.
REGAN Sir, being his Knave I will.
GLOSTER Let me beseech your Graces to forbear
  him,
  His fault is much, and the good King his Master
  Will check him for't, but needs must take it ill
  To be thus slighted in his Messenger.
DUKE Wee'l answer that;
  Our Sister may receive it worse to have
  Her Gentleman assaulted: to our business lead.
  (*Exit.*)
GLOSTER I am sorry for thee, Friend, 'tis the
  Duke's pleasure
  Whose Disposition will not be controll'd,
  But I'll entreat for thee.
KENT Pray do not, Sir –
  I have watcht and travell'd hard,
  Some time I shall sleep out, the rest I'll whistle:
  Fare-well t'ye, Sir.   (*Exit* GLOSTER.)
  All weary and o're-watcht,
  I feel the drowzy Guest steal on me; take
  Advantage heavy Eyes of this kind Slumber,
  Not to behold this vile and shamefull Lodging.
  (*Sleeps.*)

(*Enter* EDGAR.)

EDGAR I heard my self proclaim'd,
  And by the friendly Hollow of a Tree
  Escapt the Hunt, no Port is free, no place
  Where Guards and most unusual Vigilance
  Do not attend to take me – how easie now
  'Twere to defeat the malice of my Trale,
  And leave my Griefs on my Sword's reeking
  point;
  But Love detains me from Death's peaceful Cell,
  Still whispering me *Cordelia*'s in distress;
  Unkinde as she is I cannot see her wretched,
  But must be neer to wait upon her Fortune.
  Who knows but the white minute yet may come
  When *Edgar* may do service to *Cordelia*,
  That charming Hope still ties me to the Oar
  Of painfull Life, and makes me too, submit
  To th' humblest shifts to keep that Life a foot;
  My Face I will besmear and knit my Locks,
  The Country gives me proof and president
  Of Bedlam Beggars, who with roaring Voices
  Strike in their numm'd and mortify'd bare
  Arms
  Pins, Iron-spikes, Thorns, sprigs of Rosemary,
  And thus from Sheep-coats Villages and Mills,
  Sometimes with Prayers, sometimes with
  Lunatick Banns

Enforce their Charity, poor *Tyrligod*, poor *Tom*
That's something yet, *Edgar* I am no more.
  (*Exit.*)

(KENT *in the Stocks still; Enter* LEAR *attended.*)

LEAR 'Tis strange that they shou'd so depart from
  home
  And not send back our Messenger.
KENT Hail, noble Master.
LEAR How? mak'st thou this Shame thy Pastime?
  What's he that has so much mistook thy Place
  To set thee here?
KENT It is both He and She, Sir, your Son and
  Daughter.
LEAR No.
KENT Yes.
LEAR No I say.
KENT I say yea.
LEAR By *Jupiter* I swear no.
KENT By *Juno* I swear, I swear I.
LEAR They durst not do't
  They cou'd not, wou'd not do't, 'tis worse then
  Murder
  To doe upon Respect such violent out-rage.
  Resolve me with all modest haste which way
  Thou mayst deserve, or they impose this usage?
KENT My Lord, when at their Home
  I did commend your Highness Letters to them,
  E'er I was Ris'n, arriv'd another Post
  Steer'd in his haste, breathless and panting forth
  From *Gonerill* his Mistress Salutations,
  Whose Message being deliver'd, they took
  Horse,
  Commanding me to follow and attend
  The leisure of their Answer; which I did,
  But meeting that other Messenger
  Whose welcome I perceiv'd had poison'd mine,
  Being the very Fellow that of late
  Had shew'n such rudeness to your Highness, I
  Having more Man than Wit about me, Drew,
  On which he rais'd the House with Coward
  cries:
  This was the Trespass which your Son and
  Daughter
  Thought worth the shame you see it suffer here.
LEAR Oh! how this Spleen swells upward to my
  Heart
  And heaves for passage – down thou climing
  Rage
  Thy Element's below; where is this Daughter?
KENT Within, Sir, at a Masque.

(*Enter* GLOSTER.)

LEAR Now *Gloster*? – ha!
  Deny to speak with me? th'are sick, th'are weary,

They have travell'd hard to Night – meer
    fetches;
  Bring me a better Answer.
GLOSTER My dear Lord,
  You know the fiery Quality of the Duke –
LEAR Vengeance! Death, Plague, Confusion,
  Fiery? what Quality – why *Gloster*, *Gloster*,
  I'd speak with the Duke of *Cornwal* and his Wife.
GLOSTER I have inform'd 'em so.
LEAR Inform'd 'em! dost thou understand me,
    Man,
  I tell thee *Gloster* –
GLOSTER I, my good Lord.
LEAR The King wou'd speak with *Cornwal*, the
    dear Father
  Wou'd with his Daughter speak, commands her
    Service.
  Are they inform'd of this? my Breath and
    Blood!
  Fiery! the fiery Duke! tell the hot Duke –
  No, but not yet, may be he is not well:
  Infirmity do's still neglect all Office;
  I beg his Pardon, and I'll chide my Rashness
  That took the indispos'd and sickly Fit
  For the sound Man – but wherefore sits he
    there?
  Death on my State, this Act convinces me
  That this Retiredness of the Duke and her
  Is plain Contempt; give me my Servant forth,
  Go tell the Duke and's Wife I'd speak with 'em.
  Now, instantly, bid 'em come forth and hear me,
  Or at their Chamber door I'll beat the Drum
  Till it cry sleep to Death –

        (*Enter* CORNWALL *and* REGAN.)

  Oh! are ye come?
DUKE Health to the King.
REGAN I am glad to see your Highness.
LEAR *Regan*, I think you are, I know what cause
  I have to think so; shoud'st thou not be glad
  I wou'd divorce me from thy Mother's Tomb?
  Beloved *Regan*, thou wilt shake to hear
  What I shall utter: Thou coud'st ne'r ha' thought
    it,
  Thy Sister's naught, O *Regan*, she has ty'd
                (KENT *here set at liberty.*)
  Ingratitude like a keen Vulture here,
  I scarce can speak to thee.
REGAN I pray you, Sir, take patience; I have hope
  That you know less to value her Desert,
  Then she to slack her Duty.
LEAR Ha! how's that?
REGAN I cannot think my Sister in the least
  Would fail in her respects, but if perchance
  She has restrain'd the Riots of your Followers

'Tis on such Grounds, and to such wholsome
    Ends
  As clears her from all Blame.
LEAR My Curses on her.
REGAN O Sir, you are old
  And shou'd content you to be rul'd and led
  By some discretion that discerns your State
  Better than you yourself, therefore, Sir,
  Return to our Sister, and say you have wrong'd
    her.
LEAR Ha! ask her Forgiveness?
  No, no, 'twas my mistake thou didst not mean
    so,
  Dear Daughter, I confess that I am old;
  Age is unnecessary, but thou art good,
  And wilt dispense with my Infirmity.
REGAN Good Sir, no more of these unsightly
    passions,
  Return back to our Sister.
LEAR Never, *Regan*,
  She has abated me of half of my Train,
  Lookt black upon me, stabb'd me with her
    Tongue;
  All the stor'd Vengeances of Heav'n fall
  On her Ingratefull Head; strike her young Bones
  Ye taking Ayrs with Lameness.
REGAN O the blest Gods! Thus will you wish on
    me
  When the rash mood –
LEAR No, *Regan*, Thou shalt never have my
    Curse,
  Thy tender Nature cannot give thee o're
  To such Impiety; Thou better know'st
  The Offices of Nature, bond of Child-hood,
  And dues of Gratitude: Thou bear'st in mind
  The half o'th' Kingdom which our love conferr'd
  On thee and thine.
REGAN Good Sir, toth' purpose.
LEAR Who put my Man i'th' Stocks?
DUKE What Trumpet's that?
REGAN I know't, my Sister's, this confirms her
    Letters.
  Sir, is your Lady come?

        (*Enter* GONERILL'*s Gentleman.*)

LEAR More Torture still?
  This is a Slave whose easie borrow'd pride
  Dwells in the fickle Grace of her he follows;
  A Fashion-fop that spends the day in
    Dressing,
  And all to bear his Ladie's flatt'ring Message,
  That can deliver with a Grace her Lie,
  And with as bold a face bring back a greater.
  Out Varlet from my sight.
DUKE What means your Grace?

LEAR Who stockt my servant? *Regan*, I have hope
Thou didst not know it.

(*Enter* GONERILL.)

Who comes here! oh Heavens!
If you do love Old men, if your sweet sway
Allow Obedience; if your selves are Old,
Make it your Cause, send down and take my
   part;
Why, *Gorgon*, dost thou come to haunt me here?
Art not asham'd to look upon this Beard?
Darkness upon my Eyes they play me false,
O *Regan*, wilt thou take her by the Hand?

GONERILL Why not by th' Hand, Sir, how have I
   offended?
All's not Offence that indiscretion finds,
And Dotage terms so.

LEAR Heart thou art too tough.

REGAN I pray you, Sir, being old confess you are
   so,
If till the expiration of your Month
You will return and sojourn with your Sister,
Dismissing half your Train, come then to me,
I am now from Home, and out of that Provision
That shall be needfull for your Entertainment.

LEAR Return with her and fifty Knights dismist?
No, rather I'll forswear all Roofs, and chuse
To be Companion to the Midnight Wolf,
My naked Head expos'd to th' merciless Air
Then have my smallest wants suppli'd by her.

GONERILL At your choice, Sir.

LEAR Now I prithee Daughter do not make me
   mad;
I will not trouble thee, my Child, farewell,
Wee'l meet no more, no more see one another;
Let shame come when it will, I do not call it,
I do not bid the Thunder-bearer strike,
Nor tell Tales of thee to avenging Heav'n;
Mend when thou canst, be better at thy
   leisure,
I can be patient, I can stay with *Regan*,
I, and my hundred Knights.

REGAN Your Pardon, Sir.
I lookt not for you yet, nor am provided
For your fit welcome.

LEAR Is this well spoken now?

REGAN My Sister treats you fair; what fifty
   Followers
Is it not well? what shou'd you need of more?

GONERILL Why might not you, my Lord, receive
   Attendance
From those whom she calls Servants, or from
   mine?

REGAN Why not, my Lord? if then they chance to
   slack you

We cou'd controll 'em – if you come to me,
For now I see the Danger, I entreat you
To bring but Five and Twenty; to no more
Will I give place.

LEAR Hold now my Temper, stand this bolt
   unmov'd
And I am Thunder-proof;
The wicked when compar'd with the more
   wicked
Seem beautifull, and not to be the worst,
Stands in some rank of Praise; now, *Gonerill*,
Thou art innocent agen, I'll go with thee;
Thy Fifty yet, do's double Five and Twenty,
And thou art twice her Love.

GONERILL Hear me, my Lord,
What need you Five and Twenty, Ten, or Five,
To follow in a House where twice so many
Have a Command t'attend you?

REGAN What need one?

LEAR Blood, Fire! hear – Leaprosies and bluest
   Plagues!
Room, room for Hell to belch her Horrors up
And drench the *Circes* in a stream of Fire;
Hark how th' Infernals eccho to my Rage
Their Whips and Snakes –

REGAN How lewd a thing is Passion!

GONERILL So old and stomachfull.

(*Lightning and Thunder*.)

LEAR Heav'ns drop your Patience down;
You see me here, ye Gods, a poor old Man
As full of Griefs as Age, wretched in both –
I'll bear no more: no, you unnatural Haggs,
l will have such Revenges on you both,
That all the world shall – I will do such things
What they are yet I know not, but they shall be
The Terrors of the Earth; you think I'll weep,

(*Thunder again*.)

This Heart shall break into a thousand pieces
Before I'll weep – O Gods! I shall go mad. (*Exit*.)

DUKE 'Tis a wild Night, come out o'th' Storm.

(*Exeunt*.)

Act III

Scene: a desert heath.

(*Enter* LEAR *and* KENT *in the Storm*.)

LEAR Blow Winds and burst your Cheeks, rage
   louder yet,
Fantastick Lightning singe, singe my white
   Head;
Spout Cataracts, and Hurricanos fall
Till you have drown'd the Towns and Palaces
Of proud ingratefull Man.

KENT Not all my best intreaties can perswade him
　　Into some needfull shelter, or to 'bide
　　This poor slight Cov'ring on his aged Head
　　Expos'd to this wild war of Earth and Heav'n.
LEAR Rumble thy fill, fight Whirlwind, Rain and
　　Fire:
　　Not Fire, Wind, Rain or Thunder are my
　　Daughters:
　　I tax not you ye Elements with unkindness;
　　I never gave you Kingdoms, call'd you Children,
　　You owe me no Obedience, then let fall
　　Your horrible pleasure, here I stand your Slave,
　　A poor, infirm, weak and despis'd old man;
　　Yet I will call you servile Ministers,
　　That have with two pernicious Daughters join'd
　　Their high-engendred Battle against a Head
　　So Old and White as mine, Oh! oh! 'tis Foul.
KENT Hard by, Sir, is a Hovel that will lend
　　Some shelter from this Tempest.
LEAR I will forget my Nature, what? so kind a
　　Father,
　　I, there's the point.
KENT Consider, good my Liege, Things that love
　　Night
　　Love not such Nights as this; these wrathfull
　　Skies
　　Frighten the very wanderers o'th' Dark,
　　And make 'em keep their Caves; such drenching
　　Rain,
　　Such Sheets of Fire, such Claps of horrid
　　Thunder,
　　Such Groans of roaring Winds have ne're been
　　known.
LEAR Let the Great Gods,
　　That keep this dreadfull pudder o're our Heads
　　Find out their Enemies now, tremble thou
　　Wretch
　　That hast within thee undiscover'd Crimes.
　　Hide, thou bloody Hand,
　　Thou perjur'd Villain, holy, holy Hypocrite,
　　That drinkst the Widows Tears, sigh now and
　　cry
　　These dreadfull Summoners Grace, I am a Man
　　More sin'd against than sinning.
KENT Good Sir, to th' Hovell.
LEAR My wit begins to burn,
　　Come on my Boy, how dost my Boy? art Cold?
　　I'm cold my Self; shew me this Straw, my
　　Fellow,
　　The Art of our Necessity is strange,
　　And can make vile things precious; my poor
　　Knave,
　　Cold as I am at Heart, I've one place There
　　　　　　　　　　　　　　　　(*Loud Storm.*)
　　That's sorry yet for Thee.　　　　　　(*Exit.*)

(GLOSTER's *Palace. Enter* BASTARD.)

BASTARD The Storm is in our louder Rev'lings
　　drown'd.
　　Thus wou'd I Reign cou'd I but mount a Throne.
　　The Riots of these proud imperial sisters
　　Already have impos'd the galling Yoke
　　Of Taxes, and hard Impositions on
　　The drudging Peasants Neck, who bellow out
　　Their loud Complaints in Vain – Triumphant
　　Queens!
　　With what Assurance do they tread the Crowd.
　　O for a Tast of such Majestick Beauty,
　　Which none but my hot Veins are fit t' engage;
　　Nor are my Wishes desp'rate, for ev'n now
　　During the Banquet I observed their Glances
　　Shot thick at me, and as they left the Room
　　Each cast by stealth a kind inviting Smile,
　　The happy Earnest – ha!
(*Two Servants from several Entrances deliver him
　　each a Letter, and Exit.*)
　　'Where merit is so Transparent, not to behold it
　　　　　　　　　　　　　　　　(*Reads.*)
　　Were Blindness, and not to reward it
　　Ingratitude.
　　　　　　　　　　　　　　　　Gonerill.'
　　Enough! Blind, and Ingratefull should I be
　　Not to Obey the Summons of This Oracle.
　　Now for a Second Letter.　　　(*Opens the other.*)
　　'If Modesty be not your Enemy, doubt not to
　　Find me your Friend
　　　　　　　　　　　　　　　　Regan.'
　　Excellent *Sybill!* O my glowing Blood!
　　I am already sick of expectation,
　　And pant for the Possession – here *Gloster*
　　comes
　　With Bus'ness on his Brow; be husht my Joys.
GLOSTER I come to seek thee, *Edmund*, to impart
　　a business of Importance; I knew thy loyal
　　Heart is toucht to see the Cruelty of these
　　ingratefull Daughters against our royal Master.
BASTARD Most Savage and Unnatural.
GLOSTER This change in the State sits uneasie.
　　The Commons repine aloud at their female
　　Tyrants, already they Cry out for the re-
　　installment of their good old King, whose
　　Injuries I fear will inflame 'em into Mutiny.
BASTARD 'Tis to be hopt, not fear'd.
GLOSTER Thou hast it Boy, 'tis to be hopt indeed,
　　On me they cast their Eyes, and hourly Court
　　me
　　To lead 'em on, and whilst this Head is Mine
　　I am Theirs, a little covert Craft, my Boy,
　　And then for open Action, 'twill be Employment
　　Worthy such honest daring Souls as Thine.

Thou, *Edmund*, art my trusty Emissary,
Haste on the Spur at the first break of day
                                    (*Gives him Letters.*)
With these Dispatches to the Duke of *Combray*;
You know what mortal Feuds have alwaies
    flam'd
Between this Duke of *Cornwall*'s Family, and his
Full Twenty thousand Mountaners
Th' invetrate Prince will send to our Assistance.
Dispatch; Commend us to his Grace, and
    Prosper.

BASTARD Yes, credulous old Man,   (*Aside.*)
I will commend you to his Grace,
His Grace the Duke of *Cornwall* – instantly
To shew him these Contents in thy own
    Character,
And Seal'd with thy own Signet; then forthwith
The Chol'rick Duke gives Sentence on thy
    Life;
And to my hand thy vast Revenues fall
To glut my Pleasure that till now has starv'd.

(GLOSTER *going off is met by* CORDELIA *entring,*
    BASTARD *observing at a Distance.*)

CORDELIA Turn, *Gloster*, Turn, by all the sacred
    Pow'rs
I do conjure you give my Griefs a Hearing,
You must, you shall, nay I am sure you will,
For you were always stil'd the Just and Good.

GLOSTER What wou'dst thou, Princess? rise and
    speak thy Griefs.

CORDELIA Nay, you shall promise to redress 'em
    too,
Or here I'll kneel for ever; I intreat
Thy succour for a Father and a King,
An injur'd Father and an injur'd King.

BASTARD O charming Sorrow! how her Tears
    adorn her
Like Dew on Flow'rs, but she is Virtuous,
And I must quench this hopeless Fire i'th'
    Kindling.

GLOSTER Consider, Princess,
For whom thou begg'st, 'tis for the King that
    wrong'd Thee.

CORDELIA O name not that; he did not, cou'd not
    wrong me.
Nay muse not, *Gloster*, for it is too likely
This injur'd King e're this is past your Aid,
And gone Distracted with his savage Wrongs.

BASTARD I'll gaze no more. – and yet my Eyes are
    Charm'd.

CORDELIA Or what if it be Worse? can there be
    Worse?
As 'tis too probable this furious Night
Has pierc'd his tender Body, the bleak Winds

And cold Rain chill'd, or Lightning struck him
    Dead;
If it be so your Promise is discharg'd,
And I have only one poor Boon to beg,
That you'd Convey me to his breathless Trunk,
With my torn Robes to wrap his hoary Head,
With my torn Hair to bind his Hands and Feet,
Then with a show'r of Tears
To wash his Clay-smear'd Cheeks, and Die
    beside him.

GLOSTER Rise, fair *Cordelia*, thou hast Piety
Enough t' attone for both thy Sisters Crimes.
I have already plotted to restore
My injur'd Master, and thy Vertue tells me
We shall succeed, and suddenly.   (*Exit.*)

CORDELIA Dispatch, *Arante*,
Provide me a Disguise, we'll instantly
Go seek the King, and bring him some Relief.

ARANTE (*A Servant.*) How, Madam? are you
    Ignorant
Of what your impious Sisters have decreed?
Immediate Death for any that relieve him.

CORDELIA I cannot dread the Furies in this case.

ARANTE In such a Night as This? Consider,
    Madam,
For many Miles about there's scarce a Bush
To shelter in.

CORDELIA Therefore no shelter for the King,
And more our Charity to find him out:
What have not Women dar'd for vicious Love,
And we'll be shining Proofs that they can dare
For Piety as much; blow Winds, and Lightnings
    fall,
Bold in my Virgin Innocence, I'll flie
My Royal Father to Relieve, or Die.   (*Exit.*)

BASTARD Provide me a Disguise, we'll instantly
Go seek the King: – ha! ha! a lucky change,
That Vertue which I fear'd would be my
    hindrance
Has prov'd the Bond to my Design;
I'll bribe two Ruffians that shall at a distance
    follow,
And seise 'em in some desert Place, and there
Whilst one retains her t' other shall return
T' inform me where she's Lodg'd; I'll be disguis'd
    too.
Whilst they are poching for me I'll to the
    Duke
With these Dispatches, then to th' Field
Where like the vig'rous *Jove* I will enjoy
This Semele in a Storm, 'twill deaf her Cries
Like Drums in Battle, lest her Groans shou'd
    pierce
My pittying Ear, and make the amorous Fight
    less fierce.   (*Exit.*)

(*Storm still. The Field Scene. Enter* LEAR *and* KENT.)

LEAR Here is the place, my Lord; good my Lord
        enter;
    The Tyranny of this open Night's too rough
    For Nature to endure.
LEAR Let me alone.
KENT Good my Lord, enter.
LEAR Wilt break my Heart ?
KENT Beseech you, Sir.
LEAR Thou think'st 'tis much that this contentious
        Storm
    Invades us to the Skin so, 'tis to thee
    But where the greater Malady is fixt
    The lesser is scarce felt: the Tempest in my
        Mind
    Do's from my Senses take all feeling else
    Save what beats there. Filial Ingratitude!
    Is it not as this Mouth shou'd tear this Hand
    For lifting Food to't? – but I'll punish home.
    No, I will weep no more; in such a Night
    To shut me out – pour on, I will endure
    In such a Night as this: O *Regan, Gonerill*,
    Your old kind Father whose frank heart gave All,
    O that way madness lies, let me shun that,
    No more of that.
KENT See, my Lord, here's the Entrance.
LEAR Well, I'll go in
    And pass it all, I'll pray and then I'll sleep:
    Poor naked Wretches wheresoe're you are,
    That 'bide the pelting of this pittiless Storm,
    How shall your houseless Heads and unfed
        Sides
    Sustain this Shock? your raggedness defend you
    From Seasons such as These.
    O I have ta'ne too little Care of this,
    Take Physick, Pomp,
    Expose thy self to feel what Wretches feel,
    That thou may'st cast the superflux to them,
    And shew the Heav'ns more Just.

EDGAR (*In the Hovell.*) Five Fathom and a half,
        poor *Tom*.
KENT What art thou that dost grumble there i'th'
        Straw?
    Come forth.
EDGAR Away! The foul Fiend follows me –
    through the sharp Haw-thorn blows the cold
    Wind – Mum, Go to thy Bed and warm Thee. –
    ha! what do I see? by all my Griefs the poor old
    King beheaded,   (*Aside.*)
    And drencht in this fow Storm, professing *Syren*,
    Are all your Protestations come to this?
LEAR Tell me, Fellow, dist thou give all to thy
        Daughters?
EDGAR Who gives any thing to poor *Tom*, whom
the foul Fiend has led through Fire and through
Flame, through Bushes and Boggs, that has laid
Knives under his Pillow, and Halters in his Pue,
that has made him proud of Heart to ride on a
Bay-trotting Horse over four inch'd Bridges, to
course his own Shadow for a Traytor. – bless thy
five Wits, *Tom*'s a cold (*Shivers.*) bless thee from
Whirlwinds, Star-blasting and Taking: do poor
Tom some Charity, whom the foul Fiend vexes –
Sa, sa, there I could have him now, and there,
and there agen.
LEAR Have his Daughters brought him to this
        pass?
    Cou'dst thou save Nothing? didst thou give 'em
        All?
KENT He has no Daughters, Sir.
LEAR Death, Traytor, nothing cou'd have subdu'd
        Nature
    To such a Lowness but his unkind Daughters.
EDGAR Pillicock sat upon Pillicock Hill; Hallo,
hallo, hallo.
LEAR Is it the fashion that discarded Fathers
    Should have such little Mercy on their Flesh?
    Judicious punishment, 'twas this Flesh begot
    Those Pelican Daughters.
EDGAR Take heed of the fow Fiend, obey thy
    Parents, keep thy Word justly, Swear not,
    commit not with Man's sworn Spouse, set not
    thy sweet Heart on proud Array: *Tom*'s a Cold.
LEAR What hast thou been?
EDGAR A Serving-man proud of Heart, that curl'd
    my Hair, us'd Perfume and Washes, that serv'd
    the Lust of my Mistresses Heart, and did the Act
    of Darkness with her. Swore as many Oaths as I
    spoke Words, and broke 'em all in the sweet
    Face of Heaven: Let not the Paint, nor the Patch,
    nor the rushing of Silks betray thy poor Heart to
    Woman, keep thy Foot out of Brothels, thy Hand
    out of Plackets, thy Pen from Creditors Books,
    and defie the foul Fiend – still through the
    Haw-thorn blows the cold Wind – Sess, Suum,
    Mun, Nonny, Dolphin my Boy – hist! the Boy,
    Sesey! soft let him Trot by.
LEAR Death, thou wert better in thy Grave, than
    thus to answer with thy uncover'd Body this
    Extremity of the Sky. And yet consider him well,
    and Man's no more than This; Thou art indebted
    to the Worm for no Silk, to the Beast for no
    Hide, to the Cat for no Perfume – ha! here's Two
    of us are Sophisticated; Thou art the Thing it
    self, unaccommated Man is no more than such a
    poor bare forkt Animal as thou art.
    Off, Off, ye vain Disguises, empty Lendings,
    I'll be my Original Self, quick, quick, Uncase
        me.

KENT Defend his Wits, good Heaven!

LEAR One point I had forgot; what's your Name?

EDGAR Poor *Tom* that eats the swimming Frog, the Wall-nut, and the Water-nut; that in the fury of his Heart when the foul Fiend rages eats Cow dung for Sallets, swallows the old Rat and the Ditch-dog, that drinks the green Mantle of the standing Pool that's whipt from Tithing to Tithing; that has Three Suits to his Back, Six Shirts to his Body,

> Horse to Ride, and Weapon to wear,
> But Rats and Mice, and such small Deer
> Have been *Tom*'s Food for Seven long Year.

Beware, my Follower; Peace, Smulkin; Peace, thou foul Fiend.

LEAR One word more, but be sure true Councel; tell me, is a Madman a Gentleman, or a Yeoman?

KENT I fear'd 't wou'd come to This, his Wits are gone.

EDGAR *Fraterreto* calls me, and tells me, *Nero* is an Angler in the Lake of Darkness. Pray, Innocent, and beware the foul Fiend.

LEAR Right, ha! ha! was it not pleasant to have a Thousand with red hot Spits come hizzing in upon 'em?

EDGAR My Tears begin to take his part so much They marr my Counterfeiting.

LEAR The little Dogs and all, Trey, Blanch and Sweet-heart, see they Bark at me.

EDGAR *Tom* will throw his Head at 'em; Avaunt ye Curs.

> Be thy Mouth or black or white,
> Tooth that poysons if it bite,
> Mastiff, Grey-hound, Mungrill, Grim,
> Hound or Spanniel, Brach or Hym,
> Bob-tail, Tight, or Trundle-tail,
> *Tom* will make 'em weep and wail,
> For with throwing thus my Head
> Dogs leap the Hatch, and All are fled.

Ud, de, de, de. Se, se, se. Come march to Wakes, and Fairs, and Market-Towns, – poor *Tom*, thy Horn is dry.

LEAR You Sir, I entertain you for One of my Hundred, only I do not like the fashion of your Garments, you'll say they're *Persian*, but no matter, let 'em be chang'd.

(Enter GLOSTER.)

EDGAR This is the foul *Flibertigibet*, he begins at Curfew and walks at first Cock, he gives the Web and the Pin, knits the Elflock, squints the Eye, and makes the Hair-lip, mildews the white Wheat, and hurts the poor Creature of the Earth;

> *Swithin* footed Thrice the Cold,
> He met the Night-mare and her Nine-fold,
> 'Twas there he did appoint her;
> He bid her alight and her Troth plight,
> And arroynt the Witch arroynt her.

GLOSTER What, has your Grace no better Company?

EDGAR The Prince of Darkness is a Gentleman; *Modo* he is call'd, and *Mahu*.

GLOSTER Go with me, Sir, hard by I have a Tenant. My Duty cannot suffer me to obey in all your Daughters hard Commands, who have enjoyn'd me to make fast my Doors, and let this Tyrannous Night take hold upon you. Yet have I ventur'd to come seek you out, and bring you where both Fire and Food is ready.

KENT Good my Lord, take his offer.

LEAR First let me talk with this Philosopher, Say, *Stagirite*, what is the Cause of Thunder.

GLOSTER Beseech you, Sir, go with me.

LEAR I'll talk a Word with this same Learned *Theban*.
What is your Study?

EDGAR How to prevent the Fiend, and to kill Vermin.

LEAR Let me ask you a Word in private.

KENT His Wits are quite unsetled; Good Sir, let's force him hence.

GLOSTER Canst blame him? his Daughters seek his Death; This Bedlam but disturbs him the more. Fellow, be gone.

EDGAR Child *Rowland* to the dark Tow'r came, His Word was still Fie, Fo, and Fum, I smell the Bloud of a British Man. – Oh Torture!
(Exit.)

GLOSTER Now, I prethee Friend, let's take him in our Arms, and carry him where he shall meet both Welcome, and Protection.
Good Sir, along with us.

LEAR You say right, let 'em Anatomize *Regan*, see what breeds about her Heart; is there any Cause in Nature for these hard Hearts?

KENT Beseech your Grace.

LEAR Hist! – Make no Noise, make no Noise – so so; we'll to Supper i'th' Morning.　　*(Exeunt.)*

(Enter CORDELIA and ARANTE.)

ARANTE Dear Madam, rest ye here, our search is Vain,
Look here's a shed, beseech ye, enter here.

CORDELIA Prethee go in thy self, seek thy own Ease,
Where the Mind's free, the Body's Delicate:
This Tempest but diverts me from the Thought
Of what wou'd hurt me more.

(*Enter Two* RUFFIANS.)

1 RUFFIAN We have dog'd 'em far enough, this
   Place is private,
   I'll keep 'em Prisoners here within this Hovell,
   Whilst you return and bring Lord *Edmund*
   Hither;
   But help me first to House 'em.
2 RUFFIAN Nothing but this dear Devil
                              (*Shows Gold.*)
   Shou'd have drawn me through all this Tempest;
   But to our Work.   (*They seize* CORDELIA *and*
                              ARANTE, *who Shriek out.*)
   Soft, Madam, we are Friends, dispatch, I say.
CORDELIA Help, Murder, help! Gods! some kind
   Thunderbolt.
   To strike me Dead.

(*Enter* EDGAR.)

EDGAR What Cry was That? – ha, Women seiz'd
   by Ruffians?
   Is this a Place and Time for Villany?
   Avaunt ye Bloud-hounds.
                  (*Drives 'em with his Quarter-staff.*)
BOTH The Devil, the Devil!   (*Run off.*)
EDGAR O speak, what are ye that appear to be
   O'th' tender Sex, and yet unguarded Wander
   Through the dead Mazes of this dreadfull Night,
   Where (tho' at full) the Clouded Moon scarce
      darts
   Imperfect Glimmerings.
CORDELIA First say what art thou
   Our Guardian Angel, that wer't pleas'd t' assume
   That horrid shape to fright the Ravishers?
   We'll kneel to Thee.
EDGAR O my tumultuous Bloud!
   By all my trembling Veins *Cordelia*'s Voice!
   'Tis she her self! – My Senses sure conform
   To my wild Garb, and I am Mad indeed.
CORDELIA Whate're thou art, befriend a wretched
   Virgin,
   And if thou canst direct our weary search.
EDGAR Who relieves poor *Tom*, that sleeps on the
   Nettle, with the Hedge-pig for his Pillow.

      Whilst Smug ply'd the Bellows
      She truckt with her Fellows,
         The Freckle-fac't Mab
         Was a Blouze and a Drab,

   Yet *Swithin* made *Oberon* jealous – Oh! Torture.
ARANTE Alack, Madam, a poor wandring
   Lunatick.
CORDELIA And yet his Language seem'd but now
   well temper'd.
   Speak, Friend, to one more wretched than thy
   self,

And if thou hast one Interval of sense,
Inform us if thou canst where we may find
A poor old Man, who through this Heath has
   stray'd
The tedious Night – Speak, sawest thou such a
   One?
EDGAR The King, her Father, whom she's come to
   seek   (*Aside.*)
Through all the Terrors of this Night. O Gods!
That such amazing Piety, such Tenderness
Shou'd yet to me be Cruel –
Yes, Fair One, such a One was lately here,
And is convey'd by some that came to seek him,
T' a Neighb'ring Cottage; but distinctly where,
I know not.
CORDELIA Blessings on 'em,
   Let's find him out, *Arante*, for thou seest
   We are in Heavens Protection.   (*Going off.*)
EDGAR O *Cordelia!*
CORDELIA Ha! – Thou knowst my Name.
EDGAR As you did once know *Edgar*'s.
CORDELIA *Edgar!*
EDGAR The poor Remains of *Edgar*, what your
   Scorn
   Has left him.
CORDELIA Do we wake, *Arante?*
EDGAR My Father seeks my Life, which I
   preserv'd
In hopes of some blest Minute to oblidge
Distrest *Cordelia*, and the Gods have giv'n it;
That Thought alone prevail'd with me to take
This Frantick Dress, to make the Earth my Bed,
With these bare Limbs all change of Seasons
   bide,
Noons scorching Heat, and Midnights piercing
   Cold,
To feed on Offals, and to drink with Herds,
To Combat with the Winds, and be the Sport
Of Clowns, or what's more wretched yet, their
   Pity.
ARANTE Was ever Tale so full of Misery!
EDGAR But such a Fall as this I grant was due
To my aspiring Love, for 'twas presumptuous,
Though not presumptuously persu'd;
For well you know I wore my Flames conceal'd,
And silent as the Lamps that Burn in Tombs,
'Till you perceiv'd my Grief, with modest Grace
Drew forth the Secret, and then seal'd my
   Pardon.
CORDELIA You had your Pardon, nor can you
   Challenge more.
EDGAR What do I Challenge more?
Such Vanity agrees not with these Rags;
When in my prosp'rous State rich *Gloster*'s Heir,
You silenc'd my Pretences, and enjoyn'd me

To trouble you upon that Theam no more;
Then what Reception must Love's Language find
From these bare Limbs and Beggers humble
    Weeds?
CORDELIA Such as the Voice of Pardon to a
    Wretch Condemn'd;
Such as the Shouts
Of succ'ring Forces to a Town besieg'd.
EDGAR Ah! what new Method now of Cruelty?
CORDELIA Come to my Arms, thou dearest, best
    of Men,
And take the kindest Vows that e're were spoke
By a protesting Maid.
EDGAR Is 't possible?
CORDELIA By the dear Vital Stream that baths my
    Heart,
These hallow'd Rags of Thine, and naked
    Vertue,
These abject Tassels, these fantastick Shreds,
(Ridiculous ev'n to the meanest Clown)
To me are dearer than the richest Pomp
Of purple Monarchs.
EDGAR Generous charming Maid,
The Gods alone that made, can rate thy Worth!
This most amazing Excellence shall be
Fame's Triumph, in succeeding Ages, when
Thy bright Example shall adorn the Scene,
And teach the World Perfection.
CORDELIA Cold and weary,
We'll rest a while, *Arante*, on that Straw,
Then forward to find out the poor Old King.
EDGAR Look I have Flint and Steel, the
    Implements
Of wandring Lunaticks, I'll strike a Light,
And make a Fire beneath this Shed, to dry
Thy Storm-drencht Garments, e're thou Lie to
    rest thee;
Then Fierce and Wakefull as th' *Hesperian*
    Dragon,
I'll watch beside thee to protect thy Sleep;
Mean while, the Stars shall dart their kindest
    Beams,
And Angels Visit my *Cordelia*'s Dreams.
                                    (*Exeunt.*)

Scene: the palace.

(*Enter* CORNWALL, REGAN, BASTARD, SERVANTS.
    CORNWALL *with* GLOSTER'*s Letters.*)

DUKE I will have my Revenge e're I depart his
    house.
Regan, see here, a Plot upon our State,
'Tis *Gloster*'s Character, that has betray'd
His double Trust of Subject, and of Oft.

REGAN Then double be our Vengeance, this
    confirms
Th' Intelligence that we but now receiv'd,
That he has been this Night to seek the King;
But who, Sir, was the kind Discoverer?
DUKE Our Eagle, quick to spy, and fierce to seize,
Our trusty *Edmund*.
REGAN 'Twas a noble Service;
O *Cornwall*, take him to thy deepest Trust,
And wear him as a Jewel at thy Heart.
BASTARD Think, Sir, how hard a Fortune I
    sustain,
That makes me thus repent of serving you!
                                    (*Weeps.*)
O that this Treason had not been, or I
Not the Discoverer.
DUKE *Edmund*, Thou shalt find
A Father in our Love, and from this Minute
We call thee Earl of *Gloster*; but there yet
Remains another Justice to be done,
And that's to punish this discarded Traytor;
But least thy tender Nature shou'd relent
At his just Sufferings, nor brooke the Sight,
We wish thee to withdraw.
REGAN The *Grotto*, Sir,   (*To* EDMUND *Aside.*)
    within the lower Grove,
Has Privacy to suit a Mourner's Thought.
BASTARD And there I may expect a Comforter,
Ha, Madam?
REGAN What may happen, Sir, I know not,
But 'twas a Friends Advice.   (*Exit* BASTARD.)
DUKE Bring in the Traytour.

(GLOSTER *brought in.*)

Bind fast his Arms.
GLOSTER What mean your Graces?
You are my Guests, pray do me no foul Play.
DUKE Bind him, I say, hard, harder yet.
REGAN Now, Traytor, thou shalt find –
DUKE Speak, Rebel, where hast thou sent the
    King?
Whom spight of our Decree thou saw'st last
    Night.
GLOSTER I'm tide to th' Stake, and I must stand
    the Course.
REGAN Say where, and why thou hast conceal'd
    him.
GLOSTER Because I wou'd not see thy cruel
    Hands
Tear out his poor old Eyes, nor thy fierce Sister
Carve his anointed Flesh; but I shall see
The swift wing'd Vengeance overtake such
    Children.
DUKE See't shalt thou never, Slaves perform your
    Work,

Out with those treacherous Eyes, dispatch, I say,
If thou seest Vengeance –
GLOSTER He that will think to live 'till he be old,
  Give me some help – O cruel! oh! ye Gods.
                            (*They put out his Eyes.*)
SERVANT Hold, hold, my Lord, I bar your Cruelty,
  I cannot love your safety and give way
  To such a barbarous Practise.
DUKE Ha, my Villain.
SERVANT I have been your Servant from my
    Infancy,
  But better Service have I never done you
  Then with this Boldness –
DUKE Take thy Death, Slave.
SERVANT Nay, then Revenge whilst yet my Bloud
    is Warm.   (*Fight.*)
REGAN Help here – are you not hurt, my Lord?
GLOSTER *Edmund*, enkindle all the sparks of
    Nature
  To quit this horrid Act.
REGAN Out, treacherous Villain,
  Thou call'st on him that Hates thee, it was He
  That broacht thy Treason, shew'd us thy
    Dispatches;
  There – read, and save the *Cambrian* Prince a
    Labour,
  If thy Eyes fail thee call for Spectacles.
GLOSTER O my Folly!
  Then *Edgar* was abus'd, kind Gods forgive me
    that.
REGAN How is't, my Lord?
DUKE Turn out that Eye-less Villain, let him smell
  His way to *Cambray*, throw this Slave upon a
    Dunghill.
  Regan, I Bleed apace, give me your Arm.
                            (*Exeunt.*)

GLOSTER All Dark and Comfortless!
  Where are those various Objects that but now
  Employ'd my busie Eyes? where those Eyes?
  Dead are their piercing Rays that lately shot
  O're flowry Vales to distant Sunny Hills,
  And drew with Joy the vast Horizon in.
  These groping Hands are now my only Guids,
  And Feeling all my Sight.
    O Misery! what words can sound my Grief?
  Shut from the Living whilst among the Living;
  Dark as the Grave amidst the bustling World.
  At once from Business and from Pleasure bar'd;
  No more to view the Beauty of the Spring,
  Nor see the Face of Kindred, or of Friend:
  Yet still one way th' extreamest Fate affords,
  And ev'n the Blind can find the Way to Death,
  Must I then tamely Die, and unreveng'd?
  So *Lear* may fall: No, with these bleeding
    Rings

I will present me to the pittying Crowd,
And with the Rhetorick of these dropping Veins
Enflame 'em to Revenge their King and me;
Then when the Glorious Mischief is on Wing,
This Lumber from some Precipice I'll throw,
And dash it on the ragged Flint below;
Whence my freed Soul to her bright Sphear shall
    fly,
Through boundless Orbs, eternal Regions spy,
And like the Sun, be All one glorious Eye. (*Exit.*)

Act IV

A Grotto.

> (EDMUND *and* REGAN *amorously Seated,*
>   *Listning to Musick.*)

BASTARD Why were those Beauties made
    Another's Right
  Which None can prize like Me? charming Queen
  Take all my blooming Youth, for ever fold me
  In those soft Arms, Lull me in endless Sleep
  That I may dream of pleasures too transporting
  For Life to bear.
REGAN Live, live, my *Gloster*,
  And feel no Death but that of swooning joy,
  I yield thee Blisses on no harder Terms
  Than that thou continue to be Happy.
BASTARD This Jealousie is yet more kind, is't
    possible
  That I should wander from a Paradise
  To feed on sickly Weeds? such Sweets live here
  That Constancy will be no Vertue in me,
  And yet must I forthwith go meet   (*Aside.*)
    her Sister,
  To whom I must protest as much –
  Suppose it be the same; why best of all,
  And I have then my Lesson ready conn'd.
REGAN Wear this Remembrance of me – I dare
    now   (*Gives him a Ring.*)
  Absent my self no longer from the Duke
  Whose Wound grows Dangerous – I hope Mortal.
BASTARD And let this happy Image of your
    Gloster,   (*Pulling out a Picture drops a Note.*)
  Lodge in that Breast where all his Treasure lies.
                            (*Exit.*)
REGAN To this brave Youth a Womans blooming
    beauties
  Are due: my Fool usurps my Bed – What's here?
  Confusion on my Eyes.   (*Reads.*)

Where Merit is so Transparent, not to behold it
were Blindness, and not to reward it, Ingratitude.
                            Gonerill.

Vexatious Accident! yet Fortunate too,

My Jealousie's confirm'd, and I am taught
To cast for my Defence –   (*Enter an Officer.*)
Now, what mean those Shouts? and what thy
   hasty Entrance?

OFFICER A most surprizing and a sudden Change,
The Peasants are all up in Mutiny,
And only want a Chief to lead 'em on
To Storm your Palace.

REGAN On what Provocation?

OFFICER At last day's publick Festival, to which
The Yeomen from all Quarters had repair'd,
Old *Gloster*, whom you late depriv'd of Sight
(His Veins yet Streaming fresh) presents
   himself,
Proclaims your Cruelty, and their Oppression,
With the King's Injuries; which so enrag'd 'em,
That now that Mutiny which long had crept
Takes Wing, and threatens your Best Pow'rs.

REGAN White-liver'd Slave!
Our Forces rais'd and led by Valiant *Edmund*,
Shall drive this Monster of Rebellion back
To her dark Cell; young *Gloster*'s Arm allays
The Storm, his Father's feeble Breath did Raise.
                                        (*Exit.*)

The Field Scene. (*Enter* EDGAR.)

EDGAR The lowest and most abject Thing of
   Fortune
Stands still in Hope, and is secure from Fear,
The lamentable Change is from the Best,
The Worst returns to Better – who comes here
         (*Enter* GLOSTER, *led by an old Man*)
My Father poorly led? depriv'd of Sight,
The precious Stones torn from their bleeding
   Rings!
Some-thing I heard of this inhumane Deed
But disbeliev'd it, as an Act too horrid
For the hot Hell of a curst Woman's fury,
When will the measure of my woes be full?

GLOSTER Revenge, thou art afoot, Success attend
   Thee.
Well have I sold my Eyes, if the Event
Prove happy for the injur'd King.

OLD MAN O, my good Lord, I have been your
Tenant, and your Father's Tenant these
Fourscore years.

GLOSTER Away, get thee Away, good Friend, be
   gone,
Thy Comforts can do me no good at All,
Thee they may hurt.

OLD MAN You cannot see your Way.

GLOSTER I have no Way, and therefore want no
   Eyes,
I stumbled when I saw: O dear Son *Edgar*,
The Food of thy abused Father's Wrath,

Might I but live to see thee in my Touch
I'd say, I had Eyes agen.

EDGAR Alas, he's sensible that I was wrong'd,
And shou'd I own my Self, his tender Heart
Would break betwixt th' extreams of Grief and
   Joy.

OLD MAN How now, who's There?

EDGAR A Charity for poor *Tom*. Play fair, and
defie the foul Fiend.
O Gods! and must I still persue this   (*Aside.*)
   Trade,
Trifling beneath such Loads of Misery?

OLD MAN 'Tis poor mad *Tom*.

GLOSTER In the late Storm I such a Fellow saw,
Which made me think a Man a Worm,
Where is the Lunatick?

OLD MAN Here, my Lord.

GLOSTER Get thee now away, if for my sake
Thou wilt o're-take us hence a Mile or Two
I' th' way tow'rd *Dover*, do't for ancient Love,
And bring some cov'ring for this naked Wretch
Whom I'll intreat to lead me.

OLD MAN Alack, my Lord, He's Mad.

GLOSTER 'Tis the Time's Plague when Mad-men
   lead the Blind.
Do as I bid thee.

OLD MAN I'll bring him the best 'Parrel that I have
Come on't what will.   (*Exit.*)

GLOSTER Sirrah, naked Fellow.

EDGAR Poor *Tom*'s a cold; – I cannot fool it
   longer,
And yet I must – bless thy sweet Eyes they
   Bleed,
Believe't poor *Tom* ev'n weeps his Blind to see
   'em.

GLOSTER Know'st thou the way to *Dover*?

EDGAR Both Stile and Gate, Horse-way and Foot-
path, poor *Tom* has been scar'd out of his good
Wits; bless every true Man's Son from the foul
Fiend.

GLOSTER Here, take this Purse, that I am
   wretched
Makes thee the Happier, Heav'n deal so still.
Thus let the griping Userers Hoard be Scatter'd,
So Distribution shall undo Excess,
And each Man have enough. Dost thou know
   Dover?

EDGAR I, Master.

GLOSTER There is a Cliff, whose high and bending
   Head
Looks dreadfully down on the roaring Deep.
Bring me but to the very Brink of it,
And I'll repair the Poverty thou bearst
With something Rich about me, from that Place
I shall no leading need.

EDGAR Give me thy Arm: poor *Tom* shall guid thee.

GLOSTER Soft, for I hear the Tread of Passengers.

(*Enter* KENT *and* CORDELIA.)

CORDELIA Ah me! your Fear's too true, it was the King;

I spoke but now with some that met him
As Mad as the vext Sea, Singing aloud,
Crown'd with rank Femiter and furrow Weeds,
With Berries, Burdocks, Violets, Dazies, Poppies,
And all the idle Flow'rs that grow
In our sustaining Corn, conduct me to him
To prove my last Endeavours to restore him,
And Heav'n so prosper thee.

KENT I will, good Lady.

Ha, *Gloster* here! – turn, poor dark Man, and hear
A Friend's Condolement, who at Sight of thine
Forgets his own Distress, thy old true *Kent*.

GLOSTER How, *Kent?* from whence return'd?

KENT I have not since my Banishment been absent,
But in Disguise follow'd the abandon'd King;
'Twas me thou saw'st with him in the late Storm.

GLOSTER Let me embrace thee, had I Eyes I now
Should weep for Joy, but let this trickling Blood
Suffice instead of Tears.

CORDELIA O misery!

To whom shall I complain, or in what Language?
Forgive, O wretched Man, the Piety
That brought thee to this pass, 'twas I that caus'd it,
I cast me at thy Feet, and beg of thee
To crush these weeping Eyes to equal Darkness,
If that will give thee any Recompence.

EDGAR Was ever Season so distrest as This?

(*Aside.*)

GLOSTER I think *Cordelia*'s Voice! rise, pious Princess,
And take a dark Man's Blessing.

CORDELIA O, my *Edgar*,

My Vertue's now grown Guilty, works the Bane
Of those that do befriend me, Heav'n forsakes me,
And when you look that Way, it is but Just
That you shou'd hate me too.

EDGAR O wave this cutting Speech, and spare to wound
A Heart that's on the Rack.

GLOSTER No longer cloud thee, *Kent*, in that Disguise,

There's business for thee and of noblest weight;
Our injur'd Country is at length in Arms,
Urg'd by the King's inhumane Wrongs and Mine,
And only want a Chief to lead 'em on.
That Task be Thine.

EDGAR Brave *Britains* then there's Life in 't yet.

(*Aside.*)

KENT Then have we one cast for our Fortune yet.

Come, Princess, I'll bestow you with the King,
Then on the Spur to Head these Forces.
Farewell, good *Gloster*, to our Conduct trust.

GLOSTER And be your Cause as Prosp'rous as tis Just.

(*Exeunt.*)

GONERILL's *Palace.* (*Enter* GONERILL, ATTENDANTS.)

GONERILL It was great Ignorance *Gloster*'s Eyes being out
To let him live, where he arrives he moves
All Hearts against us, *Edmund* I think is gone
In pity to his Misery to dispatch him.

GENTELEMAN No, Madam, he's return'd on speedy Summons.
Back to your Sister.

GONERILL Ha! I like not That,
Such speed must have the Wings of Love;
where's *Albany*.

GENTLEMAN Madam, within, but never Man so chang'd;
I told him of the uproar of the Peasants,
He smil'd at it, when I inform'd him
Of *Gloster*'s Treason –

GONERILL Trouble him no further,
It is his coward Spirit, back to our Sister,
Hasten her Musters, and let her know
I have giv'n the Distaff into my Husband's Hands.
That done, with special Care deliver these Dispatches
In private to young *Gloster*.

(*Enter a* MESSENGER.)

MESSENGER O Madam, most unreasonable News,
The Duke of *Cornwall*'s Dead of his late Wound,
Whose loss your Sister has in part supply'd,
Making brave *Edmund* General of her Forces.

GONERILL One way I like this well;
But being Widow and my *Gloster* with her
May blast the promis'd Harvest of our Love.
A word more, Sir, – add Speed to your Journey,
And if you chance to meet with that blind Traytor,
Preferment, falls on him that cuts him off.

(*Exeunt.*)

Field Scene. (GLOSTER *and* EDGAR.)

GLOSTER When shall we come to th' Top of that
  same Hill?

EDGAR We climb it now, mark how we Labour.

GLOSTER Methinks the Ground is even.

EDGAR Horrible Steep; heark, do you hear the
  Sea?

GLOSTER No truly.

EDGAR Why then your other Senses grow
  imperfect,
  By your Eyes Anguish.

GLOSTER So may it be indeed.
  Methinks thy Voice is alter'd, and thou speak'st
  In better Phrase and Matter than thou did'st.

EDGAR You are much deceiv'd, in nothing am I
  Alter'd
  But in my Garments.

GLOSTER Methinks y'are better Spoken.

EDGAR Come on, Sir, here's the Place, how
  fearfull
  And dizy 'tis to cast one's Eyes so Low.
  The Crows and Choughs that wing the Mid-way
  Air
  Shew scarce so big as Beetles, halfway down
  Hangs one that gathers Sampire, dreadfull
  Trade!
  The Fisher-men that walk upon the Beach
  Appear like Mice, and yon tall Anch'ring Barque
  Seems lessen'd to her Cock, her Cock a Buoy
  Almost too small for Sight; the murmuring Surge
  Cannot be heard so high, I'll look no more
  Lest my Brain turn, and the disorder make me
  Tumble down head long.

GLOSTER Set me where you stand.

EDGAR You are now within a Foot of th' extream
  Verge.
  For all beneath the Moon I wou'd not now
  Leap forward.

GLOSTER Let go my Hand,
  Here, Friend, is another Purse, in it a Jewel
  Well worth a poor Man's taking; get thee further,
  Bid me Farewell, and let me hear thee going.

EDGAR Fare you well, Sir, – that I do Trifle thus
  With this his Despair is with Design to cure it.

GLOSTER Thus, mighty Gods, this World I do
  renounce,
  And in your Sight shake my Afflictions off;
  If I cou'd bear 'em longer and not fall
  To quarrel with your great opposeless Wills,
  My Snuff and feebler Part of Nature shou'd
  Burn it self out; if *Edgar* Live, O Bless him.
  Now, Fellow, fare thee well.

EDGAR Gone, Sir! Farewell.
  And yet I know not how Conceit may rob

The Treasury of Life, had he been where he
  thought,
  By this had Thought been past – Alive, or Dead?
  Hoa Sir, Friend; hear you, Sir, speak –
  Thus might he pass indeed – yet he revives.
  What are you, Sir?

GLOSTER Away, and let me Die.

EDGAR Hadst thou been ought but Gosmore,
  Feathers, Air,
  Falling so many Fathom down
  Thou hadst Shiver'd like an Egg; but thou dost
  breath
  Hast heavy Substance, bleedst not, speak'st, art
  sound;
  Thy Life's a Miracle.

GLOSTER But have I faln or no?

EDGAR From the dread Summet of this chalky
  Bourn:
  Look up an Height, the Shrill-tun'd Lark so high
  Cannot be seen, or heard; do but look up.

GLOSTER Alack, I have no Eyes.
  Is wretchedness depriv'd that Benefit
  To End it self by Death?

EDGAR Give me your Arm.
  Up, so, how is't? feel you your Legs? you stand.

GLOSTER Too well, too well.

EDGAR Upon the Crown o'th' Cliff; what Thing
  was that
  Which parted from you?

GLOSTER A poor unfortunate Begger.

EDGAR As I stood here below, me-thought his
  Eyes
  Were two Full Moons, wide Nostrils breathing
  Fire.
  It was some Fiend, therefore thou happy Father,
  Think that th'all-powerfull Gods who make them
  Honours
  Of Mens Impossibilities have preserv'd thee.

GLOSTER 'Tis wonderfull; henceforth I'll bear
  Affliction
  Till it expire; the Goblin which you speak of,
  I took it for a Man: oft-times 'twould say,
  The Fiend, the Fiend: He led me to that Place.

EDGAR Bear free and patient Thoughts: but who
  comes here?

(*Enter* LEAR, *a Coronet of Flowers on his Head.
  Wreaths and Garlands about him.*)

LEAR No, no, they cannot touch me for Coyning, I
  am the King Himself.

EDGAR O piercing Sight.

LEAR Nature's above Art in that Respect; There's
  your Press-money: that Fellow handles his Bow
  like a Cow-keeper, – draw me a Clothier's yard.
  A Mouse, a Mouse; peace hoa: there's my

Gauntlet, I'll prove it on a Giant: bring up the brown Bills: O well flown Bird; i'th' White, i'th' White – Hewgh! give the Word.

EDGAR Sweet *Marjorum*.

LEAR Pass.

GLOSTER I know that Voice.

LEAR Ha! *Gonerill* with a white Beard! they flatter'd me like a Dog, and told me I had white Hairs on my Chin, before the Black ones were there; to say I and No to every thing that I said, I and No too was no good Divinity. When the Rain came once to wet me and the Winds to make me Chatter; when the Thunder wou'd not Peace at my Bidding. There I found 'em, there I smelt 'em out; go too, they are not men of their words, They told me I was a King, 'tis a Lie, I am not Ague proof.

GLOSTER That Voice I well remember, is't not the King's?

LEAR I, every Inch a King, when I do Stare See how the Subject quakes.
I pardon that Man's Life, what was the Cause? Adultery? Thou shalt not Die. Die for Adultery! The Wren goes to 't, and the small gilded Flie Engenders in my Sight: Let Copulation thrive, For *Gloster*'s Bastard Son was kinder to his Father
Than were my Daughters got i'th' lawfull Bed.
To 't Luxury, pell mell, for I lack Souldiers.

GLOSTER Not all my Sorrows past so deep have toucht me,
As the sad Accents: Sight were now a Torment –

LEAR Behold that simp'ring Lady, she that starts At Pleasure's Name, and thinks her Ear profan'd With the least wanton Word, wou'd you believe it, The Fitcher nor the pamper'd Steed goes to 't With such a riotous Appetite: down from the Wast they are Centaurs, tho Women all Above; but to the Girdle do the Gods inherit, beneath is all the Fiends; There's Hell, there's Darkness, the Sulphurous unfathom'd – Fie! fie! pah! – an Ounce of Civet, good Apothecary, to sweeten my Imagination – There's Money for thee.

GLOSTER Let me kiss that Hand.

LEAR Let me wipe it first; it smells of Mortality.

GLOSTER Speak, Sir; do you know me?

LEAR I remember thy Eyes well enough: Nay, do thy worst, blind *Cupid*, I'll not Love – read me this Challenge, mark but the penning of it.

GLOSTER Were all the Letters Suns I cou'd not see.

EDGAR I wou'd not take this from Report: wretched *Cordelia*,
What will thy Vertue do when thou shalt find

This fresh Affliction added to the Tale Of thy unparrallel'd Griefs.

LEAR Read.

GLOSTER What with this Case of Eyes?

LEAR O ho! are you there with me? no Eyes in your Head, and no money in your Purse? yet you see how this World goes.

GLOSTER I see it Feelingly.

LEAR What? art Mad? a Man may see how this World goes with no Eyes. Look with thy Ears, see how yon Justice rails on that simple Thief; shake 'em together, and the first that drops, be it Thief or Justice, is a Villain. – Thou hast seen a Farmer's Dog bark at a Beggar.

GLOSTER I, Sir.

LEAR And the Man ran from the Curr; there thou mightst behold the great Image of Authority, a Dog's obey'd in Office. Thou Rascal, Beadle, hold thy bloody Hand, why dost thou Lash that Strumpet? thou hotly Lust'st to enjoy her in that kind for which thou whipst her, do, do, the Judge that sentenc'd her has been before-hand with thee.

GLOSTER How stiff is my vile Sense that yields not yet?

LEAR I tell thee the Usurer hangs the Couz'ner, through tatter'd Robes small Vices do appear, Robes and Fur-gowns hide All: Place Sins with Gold, why there 'tis for thee, my Friend, make much of it, it has the Pow'r to seal the Accuser's Lips. Get thee glass Eyes, and like a scurvy Politician, seem to see the Things thou dost not. Pull, pull off my Boots, hard, harder, so, so.

GLOSTER O Matter and Impertinency mixt Reason in Madness.

LEAR If thou wilt weep my Fortunes take my Eyes,
I know thee well enough, thy Name is *Gloster*. Thou must be patient, we came Crying hither Thou knowst, the first time that We tast the Air We Wail and Cry – I'll preach to thee, Mark.

EDGAR Break lab'ring Heart.

LEAR When we are Born we Cry that we are come To this great Stage of Fools. –

(Enter Two or Three GENTLEMEN.*)*

GENTLEMAN O here he is, lay hand upon him, Sir,
Your dearest Daughter sends –

LEAR No Rescue? what, a Prisoner? I am even the natural Fool of Fortune: Use me well, you shall have Ransome – let me have Surgeons, Oh I am cut to th' Brains.

GENTLEMAN You shall have any Thing.

LEAR No Second's? all my Self? I will Die bravely
like a smug Bridegroom, flusht and pamper'd as
a Priest's Whore. I am a King, my Masters, know
ye that?

GENTLEMAN You are a Royal one, and we Obey
you.

LEAR It were an excellent Stratagem to Shoe a
Troop of Horse with Felt, I'll put in proof – no
Noise, no Noise – now will we steal upon these
Sons in Law, and then – Kill, kill, kill, kill?

(*Exit Running.*)

GLOSTER A Sight most moving in the meanest
Wretch,

Past speaking in a King. Now, good Sir, what are
you?

EDGAR A most poor Man made tame to Fortune's
strokes,

And prone to Pity by experienc'd Sorrows; give
me your Hand.

GLOSTER You ever gentle Gods take my Breath
from me,

And let not my ill Genius tempt me more
To Die before you please.

(*Enter* GONERILL's *Gentleman Usher.*)

GENTLEMAN A proclaim'd Prize, O most happily
met,

That Eye-less Head of thine was first fram'd
Flesh

To raise my Fortunes; Thou old unhappy
Traytor,

The Sword is out that must Destroy thee.

GLOSTER Now let thy friendly Hand put Strength
enough to 't.

GENTLEMAN Wherefore, bold Peasant,
Darst thou support a publisht Traytor, hence,
Lest I destroy Thee too. Let go his Arm.

EDGAR 'Chill not Let go Zir, without 'vurther
'Casion.

GENTLEMAN Let go Slave, or thou Dyest.

EDGAR Good Gentleman go your Gate, and let
poor Volk pass, and 'Chu'd ha' bin Zwagger'd
out of my Life it wou'd not a bin zo long as
'tis by a Vort-night – Nay, an' thou com'st near
th' old Man, I'ce try whether your Costard or
my Ballow be th' harder.

GENTLEMAN Out, Dunghill.

EDGAR 'Chill pick your Teeth, Zir; Come, no
matter vor your Voines.

GENTLEMAN Slave, thou hast Slain me; oh
untimely Death.

EDGAR I know thee well, a serviceable Villain,
As duteous to the Vices of thy Mistress
As Lust cou'd wish.

GLOSTER What, is he Dead?

EDGAR Sit you, Sir, and rest you.
This is a Letter Carrier, and may have
Some Papers of Intelligence that may stand
Our Party in good stead, to know – what's
here?

(*Takes a Letter out of his Pocket, opens, and
reads.*)

To *Edmund* Earl of *Gloster.*
*Let our Mutual Loves be remembred, you have many
opportunities to Cut him off, if he return the Conqueror
then I am still a Prisoner, and his Bed my Gaol, from
the loath'd Warmth of which deliver me, and supply the
Place for your Labour.*

Gonerill.

A Plot upon her Husband's Life,
And the Exchange my Brother – here i'th' Sands.
I'll rake thee up thou Messenger of Lust,
Griev'd only that thou hadst no other Deaths-
man.
In Time and Place convenient I'll produce
These Letters to the Sight of th' injur'd Duke
As best shall serve our Purpose; Come, your
Hand.
Far off methinks I hear the beaten Drum,
Come, Sir, I will bestow you with a Friend.

(*Exeunt.*)

A Chamber. (LEAR *a Sleep on a Couch;* CORDELIA,
and ATTENDANTS *standing by him.*)

CORDELIA His Sleep is sound, and may have good
Effect

To Cure his jarring Senses, and repair
This Breach of Nature.

PHYSICIAN We have employ'd the utmost Pow'r
of Art,

And this deep Rest will perfect our Design.

CORDELIA O *Regan, Gonerill*, inhumane Sisters,
Had he not been your Father, these white Hairs
Had challeng'd sure some pity, was this a Face
To be expos'd against the jarring Winds?
My Enemy's Dog though he had bit me shou'd
Have stood that Night against my Fire – he
wakes, speak to him.

GENTLEMAN Madam, do you, 'tis fittest.

CORDELIA How do's my royal Lord? how fares
your Majesty?

LEAR You do me wrong to take me out o'th'
Grave.

Ha! is this too a World of Cruelty?
I know my Priviledge, think not that I will
Be us'd still like a wretched Mortal, no,
No more of That.

CORDELIA Speak to me, Sir, who am I?

LEAR You are a Soul in Bliss, but I am bound
  Upon a wheel of Fire, which my own Tears
  Do scald like Molten Lead.
CORDELIA Sir, do you know me?
LEAR You are a Spirit, I know, where did you Die?
CORDELIA Still, still, far wide.
PHYSICIAN Madam, he's scarce awake; he'll soon
  grow more compos'd.
LEAR Where have I been? where am I? fair Day-
  light!
  I am mightily abus'd, I shou'd ev'n Die with pity
  To see Another thus, I will not swear
  These are my Hands.
CORDELIA O look upon me, Sir,
  And hold your Hands in Blessing o're me, nay,
  You must not kneel.
LEAR Pray do not mock me.
  I am a very foolish fond Old Man,
  Fourscore and upward, and to deal plainly with
    you,
  I fear I am not in my perfect Mind.
CORDELIA Nay, then farewell to patience; witness
  for me
  Ye mighty Pow'rs, I ne're complain'd till now!
LEAR Methinks I shou'd know you, and know this
  Man,
  Yet I am Doubtfull, for I am mainly Ignorant
  What Place this is, and all the skill I have
  Remembers not these Garments, nor do I know
  Where I did Sleep last Night – pray do not mock
    me –
  For, as I am a Man, I think that Lady
  To be my Child *Cordelia*.
CORDELIA O my dear, dear Father!
LEAR Be your Tears wet? yes faith; pray do not
  weep,
  I know I have giv'n thee Cause, and am so
    humbled
  With Crosses since, that I cou'd ask
  Forgiveness of thee were it possible
  That thou cou'dst grant it, but I'm well assur'd
  Thou canst not; therefore I do stand thy
    Justice,
  If thou hast Poyson for me I will Drink it,
  Bless thee and Die.
CORDELIA O pity, Sir, a bleeding Heart, and cease
  This killing Language.
LEAR Tell me, Friends, where am I?
GENTLEMAN In your own Kingdom, Sir.
LEAR Do not Abuse me.
GENTLEMAN Be comforted, good Madam, for the
  Violence
  Of his Distemper's past; we'll lead him in
  Nor trouble him, till he is better Setled.
  Wilt please you, Sir, walk into freer Air.

LEAR You must bear with me, I am Old and
  Foolish.   (*They lead him off.*)
CORDELIA The Gods restore you – heark, I hear
  afar
  The beaten Drum, Old *Kent*'s a Man of's Word.
  O for an Arm
  Like the fierce Thunderer's, when th' earth-born
    Sons
  Storm'd Heav'n, to fight this injur'd Father's
    Battle.
  That I cou'd shift my Sex, and die me deep
  In his Opposer's Blood, but as I may
  With Womens Weapons, Piety and Pray'rs,
  I'll aid his Cause – You never-erring Gods
  Fight on his side, and Thunder on his Foes
  Such Tempest as his poor ag'd Head sustain'd;
  Your Image suffers when a Monarch bleeds.
  'Tis your own Cause, for that your Succours
    bring,
  Revenge your Selves, and right an injur'd King.

Act V

Scene: A Camp.

(*Enter* GONERILL *and* ATTENDANTS.)

GONERILL Our Sisters Pow'rs already are arriv'd,
  And She her self has promis'd to prevent
  The Night with her Approach: have you
    provided
  The Banquet I bespoke for her Reception
  At my Tent?
ATTENDANTS So, please your Grace, we have.
GONERILL But thou, my Poysner, must prepare
  the Bowl
  That Crowns this Banquet, when our Mirth is
    high,
  The Trumpets sounding and the Flutes
    replying,
  Then is the Time to give this fatal Draught
  To this imperious Sister; if then our Arms
    succeed,
  Edmund more dear than Victory is mine.
  But if Defeat or Death it self attend me,
  'Twill charm my Ghost to think I've left behind
    me   (*Trumpet.*)
  No happy Rival: heark, she comes.   (*Exeunt.*)

(*Enter* BASTARD *in his Tent.*)

BASTARD To both these Sisters have I sworn my
  Love,
  Each jealous of the other, as the Stung
  Are of the Adder; neither can be held
  If both remain Alive; where shall I fix?

Cornwall is Dead, and *Regan*'s empty Bed
Seems cast by Fortune for me, but already
I have enjoy'd her, and bright *Gonerill*
With equal Charms brings dear variety,
And yet untasted Beauty: I will use
Her Husband's Countenance for the Battail, then
Usurp at once his Bed and Throne.

                     (Enter Officers.)

My trusty Scouts y' are well return'd, have ye
   descry'd
The Strength and Posture of the Enemy?

OFFICER We have, and were surpriz'd to find
  The banisht *Kent* return'd, and at their Head;
  Your Brother *Edgar* on the Rear; Old *Gloster*
  (a moving Spectacle) led through their Ranks,
  Whose pow'rfull Tongue, and more prevailing
    Wrongs,
  Have so enrag'd their rustick Spirits, that with
  Th' approaching Dawn we must expect their
    Battle.

BASTARD You bring a welcome Hearing; Each to
  his Charge.
  Line well your Ranks and stand on your Award,
  To Night repose you, and i'th' Morn we'll give
  The Sun a Sight that shall be worth his Rising.

                     (Exeunt.)

Scene: *A Valley near the Camp.*

         (Enter EDGAR *and* GLOSTER.*)*

EDGAR Here, Sir, take you the shadow of this
  Tree
  For your good Host, pray that the Right may
  thrive:
  If ever I return to you again
  I'll bring you Comfort.   *(Exit.)*
GLOSTER Thanks, friendly Sir;
  The Fortune your good Cause deserves betide
  you.

  (An Alarum, after which GLOSTER *speaks.)*

The Fight grows hot; the whole War's now at
  Work,
And the goar'd Battle bleeds in every Vein,
Whilst Drums and Trumpets drown loud
  Slaughter's Roar:
Where's *Gloster* now that us'd to head the Fray,
And scour the Ranks where deadliest Danger
  lay?
Here like a Shepherd in a lonely Shade,
Idle, unarm'd, and listning to the Fight.
Yet the disabled Courser, Maim'd and Blind,
When to his Stall he hears the ratling War,
Foaming with Rage tears up the batter'd Ground,

And tugs for Liberty.
No more of Shelter, thou blind Worm, but forth
To th' open Field; the War may come this way
And crush thee into Rest. – Here lay thee down
And tear the Earth, that work befits a Mole.
O dark Despair! when, *Edgar*, wilt thou come
To pardon and dismiss me to the Grave!

               (A Retreat sounded.)

Heark! a retreat, the King has Lost or Won.

        (Re-enter EDGAR, *bloody.)*

EDGAR Away, old Man, give me your Hand, away!
  King *Lear* has lost, He and his Daughter tane,
  And this, ye Gods, is all that I can save
  Of this most precious Wreck: give me your Hand.
GLOSTER No farther, Sir, a Man may Rot even
  here.
EDGAR What? in ill Thoughts again? Men must
  endure
  Their going hence ev'n as their coming hither.
GLOSTER And that's true too.   *(Exeunt.)*

(Flourish. Enter in Conquest, ALBANY, GONERILL,
   REGAN, BASTARD. – LEAR, KENT,
     CORDELIA *Prisoners.)*

ALBANY It is enough to have Conquer'd, Cruelty
  Shou'd ne're survive the Fight, Captain o'th'
    Guards
  Treat well your royal Prisoners till you have
  Our further Orders, as you hold our Pleasure.
GONERILL Heark, Sir, not as you hold our
    Husbands pleasure :   *(To the Captain aside.)*
  But as you hold your Life, dispatch your
  Pris'ners.
  Our Empire can have no sure Settlement
  But in their Death, the Earth that covers them
  Binds fast our Throne. Let me hear they are
  Dead.
CAPTAIN I shall obey your Orders.
BASTARD Sir, I approve it saftest to pronounce
  Sentence of Death upon this wretched King,
  Whose Age has Charms in it, his Title more,
  To draw the Commons once more to his Side,
  'Twere best prevent –
ALBANY Sir, by your Favour,
  I hold you but a Subject of this War,
  Not as a Brother.
REGAN That's as we list to Grace him.
  Have you forgot that He did lead our Pow'rs?
  Bore the Commission of our Place and Person?
  And that Authority may well stand up
  And call it self your Brother.
GONERILL Not so hot,
  In his own Merits he exalts himself
  More than in your Addition.

(*Enter* EDGAR, *disguised.*)

ALBANY What art Thou?

EDGAR Pardon me, Sir, that I presume to stop
　　A Prince and Conquerour, yet e'er you Triumph,
　　Give Ear to what a Stranger can deliver
　　Of what concerns you more than Triumph can.
　　I do impeach your General there of Treason,
　　Lord *Edmund*, that usurps the Name of *Gloster*,
　　Of fowlest Practice 'gainst your Life and
　　　Honour;
　　This Charge is True, and wretched though I
　　　seem
　　I can produce a Champion that will prove
　　In single Combat what I do avouch;
　　If *Edmund* dares but trust his Cause and Sword.

BASTARD What will not *Edmund* dare, my Lord, I
　　beg
　　The favour that you'd instantly appoint
　　The Place where I may meet this Challenger,
　　Whom I will sacrifice to my wrong'd Fame,
　　Remember, Sir, that injur'd Honour's nice
　　And cannot brook delay.

ALBANY Anon, before our Tent, i'th' Army's view,
　　There let the Herald cry.

EDGAR I thank your Highness in my Champion's
　　Name,
　　He'll wait your Trumpet's call.

ALBANY Lead.　　　　　　　　　　　　(*Exeunt.*)

　　(*Manent,* LEAR, KENT, CORDELIA, *guarded.*)

LEAR O *Kent, Cordelia!*
　　You are the onely Pair that I e'er wrong'd,
　　And the just Gods have made you Witnesses
　　Of my Disgrace, the very shame of Fortune,
　　To see me chain'd and shackled at these years!
　　Yet were you but Spectatours of my Woes,
　　Not fellow-sufferers, all were well!

CORDELIA This language, Sir, adds yet to our
　　Affliction.

LEAR Thou, *Kent*, didst head the Troops that
　　fought my Battel,
　　Expos'd thy Life and Fortunes for a Master
　　That had (as I remember) banisht Thee.

KENT Pardon me, Sir, that once I broke your
　　Orders,
　　Banisht by you, I kept me here disguis'd
　　To watch your Fortunes, and protect your
　　Person,
　　You know you entertain'd a rough blunt
　　Fellow,
　　One *Cajus*, and you thought he did you Service.

LEAR My trusty *Cajus*, I have lost him too!
　　　　　　　　　　　　　　　　(*Weeps.*)
　　'Twas a rough Honesty.

KENT I was that *Cajus*,
　　Disguis'd in that course Dress to follow you.

LEAR My *Cajus* too! wer't thou my trusty *Cajus*,
　　Enough, enough –

CORDELIA Ah me, he faints! his Blood forsakes
　　his Cheek,
　　Help, Kent –

LEAR No, no, they shall not see us weep,
　　We'll see them rot first, – Guards lead away to
　　　Prison,
　　Come, *Kent, Cordelia* come,
　　We Two will sit alone, like Birds i'th' Cage,
　　When Thou dost ask me Blessing, I'll kneel
　　　down
　　And ask of Thee Forgiveness; Thus we'll live,
　　And Pray, and Sing, and tell old Tales, and
　　　Laugh
　　At gilded Butter-flies, hear Sycophants
　　Talk of Court News, and we'll talk with them
　　　too,
　　Who loses, and who wins, who's in, who's out,
　　And take upon us the Mystery of Things
　　As if we were Heav'ns Spies.

CORDELIA Upon such Sacrifices
　　The Gods themselves throw Incense.

LEAR Have I caught ye?
　　He that parts us must bring a Brand from
　　　Heav'n.
　　Together we'll out-toil the spight of Hell,
　　And Die the Wonders of the World; Away.
　　　　　　　　　　　　　(*Exeunt, guarded.*)

　　(*Flourish: Enter before the Tents,* ALBANY,
　GONERILL, REGAN, GUARDS *and* ATTENDANTS;
　　GONERILL *speaking apart to the* CAPTAIN OF
　　　　　THE GUARDS *entring.*)

GONERILL Here's Gold for Thee, Thou knowst our
　　late Command
　　Upon your Pris'ners Lives, about it streight, and
　　at
　　Our Ev'ning Banquet let it raise our Mirth
　　To hear that They are Dead.

CAPTAIN I shall not fail your Orders.　　(*Exit.*)

　　(ALBANY, GONERILL, REGAN *take their Seats.*)

ALBANY Now, *Gloster*, trust to thy single Vertue,
　　for thy Souldiers,
　　All levied in my Name, have in my Name
　　Took their Discharge; now let our Trumpets
　　speak,
　　And Herald read out This.　　(*Herald Reads.*)

If any Man of Quality, within the Lists of the Army,
will maintain upon EDMUND, *suppos'd Earl of*
GLOSTER, *that he is a manifold Traytour, let him*

appear by the third sound of the Trumpet; He is
bold in his Defence. – Agen, Agen.

(*Trumpet Answers from within.*)

(*Enter* EDGAR, *Arm'd.*)

ALBANY Lord *Edgar*!
BASTARD Ha! my Brother!
  This is the onely Combatant that I cou'd fear;
  For in my Breast Guilt Duels on his side,
  But, Conscience, what have I to do with Thee?
  Awe Thou thy dull Legitimate Slaves, but I
  Was born a Libertine, and so I keep me.
EDGAR My noble Prince, a word – e'er we engage
  Into your Highness's Hands I give this Paper,
  It will the truth of my Impeachment prove
  Whatever be my fortune in the Fight.
ALBANY We shall peruse it.
EDGAR Now, *Edmund*, draw thy Sword,
  That if my Speech has wrong'd a noble Heart,
  Thy Arm may doe thee Justice: here i'th'
    presence
  Of this high Prince, these Queens, and this
    crown'd List,
  I brand thee with the spotted name of Traytour,
  False to thy Gods, thy Father and thy Brother,
  And what is more, thy Friend; false to this
    Prince:
  If then Thou shar'st a spark of *Gloster*'s Vertue,
  Acquit thy self, or if Thou shar'st his Courage,
  Meet this Defiance bravely.
BASTARD And dares *Edgar*,
  The beaten routed *Edgar*, brave his Conquerour?
  From all thy Troops and Thee, I forc't the Field,
  Thou hast lost the gen'ral Stake, and art Thou
    now
  Come with thy petty single Stock to play
  This after-Game?
EDGAR Half-blooded Man,
  Thy Father's Sin first, then his Punishment,
  The dark and vicious Place where he begot
    thee
  Cost him his Eyes: from thy licentious Mother
  Thou draw'st thy Villany; but for thy part
  Of *Gloster*'s Blood, I hold thee worth my Sword.
BASTARD Thou bear'st thee on thy Mother's Piety,
  Which I despise; thy Mother being chaste
  Thou art assur'd Thou art but *Gloster*'s Son,
  But mine, disdaining Constancy, leaves me
  To hope that I am sprung from nobler Blood,
  And possibly a King might be my Sire:
  But be my Birth's uncertain Chance as 'twill,
  Who 'twas that had the hit to Father me
  I know not; 'tis enough that I am I:
  Of this one thing I'm certain – that I have

  A daring Soul, and so have at thy Heart.
  Sound Trumpet.   (*Fight,* BASTARD *falls.*)
GONERILL and REGAN Save him, save him.
GONERILL This was Practice, *Gloster*,
  Thou won'st the Field, and wast not bound to
    Fight
  A vanquisht Enemy, Thou art not Conquer'd
  But couz'ned and betray'd.
ALBANY Shut your Mouth, Lady,
  Or with this Paper I shall stop it – hold, Sir,
  Thou worse than any Name, reade thy own evil,
  No Tearing, Lady, I perceive you know it.
GONERILL Say if I do, who shall arraign me for't?
  The Laws are Mine, not Thine.
ALBANY Most monstrous! ha, Thou know'st it too.
BASTARD Ask me not what I know,
  I have not Breath to Answer idle Questions.
ALBANY I have resolv'd – your Right, brave Sir,
    has conquer'd,   (*To* EDGAR.)
  Along with me, I must consult your Father.
            (*Exeunt* ALBANY *and* EDGAR.)
REGAN Help every Hand to save a noble Life;
  My half o'th' Kingdom for a Man of Skill
  To stop this precious stream.
BASTARD Away ye Empericks,
  Torment me not with your vain Offices:
  The Sword has pierc't too far; *Legitimacy*
  At last has got it.
REGAN The Pride of Nature Dies.
GONERILL Away, the minutes are too precious,
  Disturb us not with thy impertinent Sorrow.
REGAN Art Thou my Rival then profest?
GONERILL Why, was our Love a Secret? cou'd
    there be
  Beauty like Mine, and Gallantry like His
  And not a mutual Love? just Nature then
  Had err'd: behold that Copy of Perfection,
  That Youth whose Story will have no foul Page
  But where it says he stoopt to *Regan*'s Arms:
  Which yet was but Compliance, not Affection;
  A Charity to begging, ruin'd Beauty!
REGAN Who begg'd when *Gonerill* writ That?
    expose it   (*Throws her a Letter.*)
  And let it be your Army's mirth, as 'twas
  This charming Youth's and mine, when in the
    Bow'r
  He breath'd the warmest ecstasies of Love,
  Then panting on my Breast, cry'd matchless
    Regan
  That *Gonerill* and Thou shou'd e'er be Kin!
GONERILL Die, *Circe*, for thy Charms are at an
    End,
  Expire before my Face, and let me see
  How well that boasted Beauty will become
  Congealing Blood and Death's convulsive Pangs.

Die and be husht, for at my Tent last Night
Thou drank'st thy Bane, amidst thy rev'ling
    Bowls:
Ha! dost thou Smile? is then thy Death thy Sport
Or has the trusty Potion made thee Mad?

REGAN Thou com'st as short of me in thy
    Revenge
As in my *Gloster*'s Love, my Jealousie
Inspir'd me to prevent thy feeble Malice
And Poison Thee at thy own Banquet.

GONERILL Ha!

BASTARD No more, my Queens, of this untimely
    Strife,
You both deserv'd my Love and both possest it.
Come, Souldiers, bear me in; and let
Your royal Presence grace my last minutes:
Now, *Edgar*, thy proud Conquest I forgive;
Who wou'd not choose, like me, to yield his
    Breath
T' have Rival Queens contend for him in Death?
(*Exeunt.*)

Scene: A Prison

(LEAR *asleep, with his Head on* CORDELIA's *Lap.*)

CORDELIA What Toils, thou wretched King, hast
    Thou endur'd
To make thee draw, in Chains, a Sleep so sound?
Thy better Angel charm thy ravisht Mind
With fancy'd Freedom; Peace is us'd to lodge
On Cottage Straw, Thou hast the Begger's Bed
Therefore shou'dst have the Begger's careless
    Thought.
And now, my *Edgar*, I remember Thee,
What Fate has seiz'd Thee in this general
    Wreck
I know not, but I know thou must be wretched
Because *Cordelia* holds Thee Dear.
O Gods! a suddain Gloom o'er-whelms me, and
    the Image
Of Death o'er-spreads the Place. – ha! who are
    These?

(*Enter* CAPTAIN *and* OFFICERS *with Cords.*)

CAPTAIN Now, Sirs, dispatch, already you are
    paid
In part, the best of your Reward's to come.

LEAR Charge, charge upon their Flank, their last
    Wing haults;
Push, push the Battel, and the Day's our own.
Their Ranks are broke, down, down with
    Albany.
Who holds my Hands? – O thou deceiving Sleep,
I was this very Minute on the Chace;

And now a Prisoner here – What mean the
    Slaves?
You will not Murder me?

CORDELIA Help Earth and Heaven!
For your Souls sake's, dear Sirs, and for the
    Gods.

OFFICER No Tears, good Lady, no pleading
    against Gold and Preferment;
Come, Sirs, make ready your Cords.

CORDELIA You, Sir, I'll seize,
You have a humane Form, and if no Pray'rs
Can touch your Soul to spare a poor King's
    Life,
If there be any Thing that you hold dear,
By That I beg you to dispatch me First.

CAPTAIN Comply with her Request, dispatch her
    First.

LEAR Off Hell-hounds, by the Gods I charge you
    spare her;
'Tis my *Cordelia*, my true pious Daughter:
No Pity? – Nay then take an old Man's
    Vengeance.

(*Snatches a Partizan, and strikes down two of them;
    the rest quit* CORDELIA, *and turn upon him.*
        Enter EDGAR *and* ALBANY.)

EDGAR Death! Hell! Ye Vultures hold your
    impious Hands,
Or take a speedier Death than you wou'd give.

CAPTAIN By whose Command?

EDGAR Behold the Duke your Lord.

ALBANY Guards, seize those Instruments of
    Cruelty.

CORDELIA My *Edgar*, Oh!

EDGAR My dear *Cordelia*, Lucky was the Minute
Of our Approach, the Gods have weigh'd our
    Suffrings;
W' are past the Fire, and now must shine to
    Ages.

GENTLEMAN Look here, my Lord, see where the
    generous King
Has slain Two of 'em.

LEAR Did I not, Fellow?
I've seen the Day, with my good biting
    Faulchion
I cou'd have made 'em skip; I am Old now,
And these vile Crosses spoil me; Out of Breath!
Fie, Oh! quite out of Breath and spent.

ALBANY Bring in old *Kent*, and, *Edgar*, guide you
    hither
Your Father, whom you said was near,
(*Exit* EDGAR.)
He may be an Ear-witness at the least
Of our Proceedings.   (KENT *brought in here.*)

LEAR Who are you?

My Eyes are none o' th' best, I'll tell you
   streight;
Oh *Albany*! Well, Sir, we are your Captives,
And you are come to see Death pass upon us.
Why this Delay? – or is 't your Highness
   pleasure
To give us first the Torture? Say ye so?
Why here's old *Kent* and I, as tough a Pair
As e'er bore Tyrant's Stroke: – but my *Cordelia*,
My poor *Cordelia* here, O pitty! –

ALBANY Take off their Chains – Thou injur'd
   Majesty,
The Wheel of Fortune now has made her Circle,
And Blessings yet stand 'twixt thy Grave and
   Thee.

LEAR Com'st Thou, inhumane Lord, to sooth us
   back
To a Fool's Paradise of Hope, to make
Our Doom more wretched? go too, we are too
   well
Acquainted with Misfortune to be gull'd
With Lying Hope; No, we will hope no more.

ALBANY I have a Tale t' unfold so full of Wonder
As cannot meet an easy Faith;
But by that Royal injur'd Head 'tis True.

KENT What wou'd your Highness?

ALBANY Know the noble *Edgar*
Impeacht Lord *Edmund* since the Fight, of
   Treason,
And dar'd him for the Proof to single Combat,
In which the Gods confirm'd his Charge by
   Conquest;
I left ev'n now the Traytor wounded Mortally.

LEAR And whither tends this Story?

ALBANY E'er they fought
Lord *Edgar* gave into my Hands this Paper,
A blacker Scrowl of Treason, and of Lust
Than can be found in the Records of Hell;
There, Sacred Sir, behold the Character
Of *Gonerill* the worst of Daughters, but
More Vicious Wife.

CORDELIA Cou'd there be yet Addition to their
   Guilt?
What will not They that wrong a Father doe?

ALBANY Since then my Injuries, *Lear*, fall in with
   Thine:
I have resolv'd the same Redress for Both.

KENT What says my Lord?

CORDELIA Speak, for me thought I heard
The charming Voice of a descending God.

ALBANY The Troops by *Edmund* rais'd, I have
   disbanded;
Those that remain are under my Command.
What Comfort may be brought to cheer your Age
And heal your savage Wrongs, shall be apply'd;

For to your Majesty we do Resign
Your Kingdom, save what Part your Self
   conferr'd
On Us in Marriage.

KENT Hear you that, my Liege?

CORDELIA Then there are Gods, and Vertue is
   their Care.

LEAR Is't Possible?
Let the Spheres stop their Course, the Sun make
   Hault,
The Winds be husht, the Seas and Fountains
   Rest;
All Nature pause, and listen to the Change.
Where is my *Kent*, my *Cajus*?

KENT Here, my Liege.

LEAR Why I have News that will recall thy Youth;
Ha! Didst Thou hear 't, or did th' inspiring
   Gods
Whisper to me Alone? Old *Lear* shall be
A King again.

KENT The Prince, that like a God has Pow'r, has
   said it.

LEAR *Cordelia* then shall be a Queen, mark that:
Cordelia shall be Queen; Winds catch the Sound
And bear it on your rosie Wings to Heav'n.
Cordelia is a Queen.

(*Re-enter* EDGAR *with* GLOSTER.)

ALBANY Look, Sir, where pious *Edgar* comes
Leading his Eye-less Father: O my Liege!
His wondrous Story will deserve your Leisure:
What He has done and suffer'd for your Sake,
What for the Fair *Cordelia*'s.

GLOSTER Where is my Liege? Conduct me to his
   Knees to hail
His second Birth of Empire; my dear *Edgar*
Has, with himself, reveal'd the King's blest
   Restauration.

LEAR My poor dark *Gloster*.

GLOSTER O let me kiss that once more sceptred
   Hand!

LEAR Hold, Thou mistak'st the Majesty, kneel
   here;
Cordelia has our Pow'r, *Cordelia*'s Queen.
Speak, is not that the noble Suffring *Edgar*?

GLOSTER My pious Son, more dear than my lost
   Eyes.

LEAR I wrong'd Him too, but here's the fair
   Amends.

EDGAR Your leave, my Liege, for an unwelcome
   Message.
Edmund (but that's a Trifle) is expir'd;
What more will touch you, your imperious
   Daughters
Gonerill and haughty *Regan*, both are Dead,

Each by the other poison'd at a Banquet;
This, Dying, they confest.

CORDELIA O fatal Period of ill-govern'd Life!

LEAR Ingratefull as they were, my Heart feels
    yet
A Pang of Nature for their wretched Fall; –
But, *Edgar*, I defer thy Joys too long:
Thou serv'dst distrest *Cordelia*; take her
    Crown'd:
Th' imperial Grace fresh Blooming on her Brow;
Nay, *Gloster*, Thou hast here a Father's Right;
Thy helping Hand t' heap Blessings on their
    Head.

KENT Old *Kent* throws in his hearty Wishes too.

EDGAR The Gods and You too largely recompence
What I have done; the Gift strikes Merit Dumb.

CORDELIA Nor do I blush to own my Self o'er-paid
For all my Suffrings past.

GLOSTER Now, gentle Gods, give *Gloster* his
    Discharge.

LEAR No, *Gloster*, Thou hast Business yet for Life;
Thou *Kent* and I, retir'd to some cool Cell
Will gently pass our short reserves of Time
In calm Reflections on our Fortunes past,
Cheer'd with relation of the prosperous Reign
Of this celestial Pair; Thus our Remains
Shall in an even Course of Thought be past,
Enjoy the present Hour, nor fear the Last.

EDGAR Our drooping Country now erects her
    Head,
Peace spreads her balmy Wings, and Plenty
    Blooms.
Divine *Cordelia*, all the Gods can witness
How much thy Love to Empire I prefer!
Thy bright Example shall convince the World
(Whatever Storms of Fortune are decreed)
That Truth and Vertue shall at last succeed.

                                   (*Exeunt Omnes.*)

Epilogue

(*Spoken by Mrs. Barry, who played* CORDELIA.)

Inconstancy, the reigning Sin o' th' Age,
Will scarce endure true Lovers on the Stage;
You hardly ev'n in Plays with such dispense,
And Poëts kill 'em in their own Defence.
Yet One bold Proof I was resolv'd to give,
That I cou'd three Hours Constancy Out-live.
You fear, perhaps, whilst on the Stage w' are made
Such Saints, we shall indeed take up the Trade;
Sometimes we Threaten – but our Vertue may
For Truth I fear with your Pit-Valour weigh:
For (not to flatter either) I much doubt
When We are off the Stage, and You are out,
We are not quite so Coy, nor You so Stout.
We talk of Nunn'ries – but to be sincere
Whoever lives to see us Cloyster'd There,
May hope to meet our Critiques at Tangier.
For shame give over this inglorious Trade
Of worrying Poëts, and go maule th' Alcade.
Well – since y' are All for blustring in the Pit,
This Play's Reviver humbly do's admit
Your abs'lute Pow'r to damn his Part of it;
But still so many Master-Touches shine
Of that vast Hand that first laid this Design,
That in great Shakespear's Right, He's bold to say
If you like nothing you have seen to Day
The Play your Judgment damns, not you the Play.

King Stephen: A Dramatic Fragment

John Keats

Introduction

John Keats was born in 1795, son to a manager of livery stables in Moorfields Pavement, London. His earliest literary work involved attempting a translation of the *Aeneid* as a schoolboy before he went on to apprentice as an apothecary-surgeon. Profoundly influenced by Elizabethan writers such as Edmund Spenser and Shakespeare, Keats 'acknowledged Shakespeare not only as one of the greatest literary models but as his "good genius" guiding him in his own poetic enterprise' (White: 7). This affinity for Shakespeare has been noted by John Middleton Murry, who argues, in the mode of Matthew Arnold's 'Essay on Keats,' that Keats 'was potentially, at least, our next greatest poet after Shakespeare and the only poet who is *like* Shakespeare' (4). Keats abandoned his apprenticeship in 1815 to study at Guy's Hospital, while also working on early poems. In 1816 he was licensed to work as an apothecary but left the profession to pursue his literary career.

One of the key figures in the Romantic movement, Keats published his first book of poems in March 1817. Despite poor health, in 1818 Keats began what is sometimes called the *annus mirabilis* or Great Year, a period during which he wrote some of his best-known poems, including the first version of *Hyperion*, 'The Eve of St. Agnes,' 'La Belle Dame Sans Merci,' 'Ode on a Grecian Urn,' both parts of *Lamia*, and *The Fall of Hyperion*. Keats 'was writing his own greatest poetry which is often called "Shakespearean",' the result of a 'saturation' in Shakespearean texts, and, as R. S. White argues, 'he had absorbed the influence so deeply that the word "sources" is inadequate to describe [in Keats's writing] the omnipresent but transformed ghost of Shakespeare's poetry and language' (15). During this time Keats also attempted dramatic works, including the unfinished play *King Stephen* (1819),

which 'involved Stephen's seizure of the English crown in 1135, and his eventual defeat by the Empress Maud at Lincoln in 1141' (Motion: 428). Keats was persistently beset by financial problems and his health worsened after his second volume of poems was published in 1820. He died of consumption in Rome in February 1821.

At once a fragmentary tragedy and an attempt at a history play in the style of Shakespeare (what Claude Lee Finney calls a 'chronicle play' [vol. 2: 727]), Keats's *King Stephen* is worth noting for a number of reasons. First, it shows a certain kind of writing potential in relation to an obvious series of influences on Keats's style. Robert Gittings argues that

> The few scenes he wrote have a tremendous sense of physical action; he was seeing the actor in the part . . . The verse too was not merely Shakespearean, but had the rough vigour he had learnt from Dryden and Massinger, and assimilated so well into the first part of *Lamia*. Above all he was writing with confidence and gusto . . .
>
> (1968: 335)

Though Andrew Motion argues that *King Stephen* is 'too frankly derivative, too quick in its narration, and too stiffly theatrical. . . . Abandoning *Stephen* meant that [Keats] could deploy ideas and energies which were already well rehearsed' (429).

Second, the play demonstrates how Keats as a writer in a crucial period of life linked his writing practice with that of Shakespeare. Keats, as Gittings notes, 'wanted to write in unfettered style the play he felt was in him, designed expressly for [Edmund] Kean, and based on the actor's great Richard the Third' (335). Keats quit writing the play because it was rumoured that Kean intended an American tour. In order to complete a book of poetry that would alleviate his financial difficulties, Keats wrote the final 300 lines of *Lamia* after discontinuing *King Stephen*. Gittings notes that as a result 'all the tension and conflict prepared for that play went into *Lamia*' (336), which Gittings characterizes as the 'most consciously artistic of all Keats's productions' (337). *Lamia* opens with a pre-Shakespearean allusion, setting itself in a mythical time 'Before King Oberon's bright diadem, / Sceptre, and mantle, clasp'd with dewy gem, / Frighted away the Dryads and the Fauns' (Cook: 305). The invocation of a time before Oberon, which is to say before the time of the Shakespearean character Oberon from *A Midsummer Night's Dream* (based on a character in turn derived from Huon of Bordeaux), underlines the Shakepearean intertext Keats establishes for the poem. Thus the literary failure of *King Stephen*, a work profoundly associated with Shakespearean adaptation, was part of the context that produced a remarkable narrative poem, whose subject matter not only retained a Shakespearean connection but was also taken from an episode in another early modern text, Robert Burton's *The Anatomy of Melancholy* (1621).

Third, the play is a remarkable example of the power of Shakespeare as a model for imitation. In 1819 Keats was forcefully influenced by his study of Elizabethan literature and its sources, telling his brother in a letter that he was reading Ariosto, going on in that same period to read Holinshed's *Chronicles of England, Scotland, and Ireland* (the source text for many Shakespearean histories and tragedies), attending Hazlitt's *Lectures on the Dramatic Literature of the Age of Elizabeth* at the Surrey Institution, before beginning the composition of *King Stephen*. The idea of working on the historical figure of King Stephen seems to have been in the air, for Coleridge, in his *Lectures on Shakespeare*, had planned a historical drama based on Stephen's story and had even conceived the project of dramatizing the lives of all the kings not written about by Shakespeare through to Henry VII (Finney, vol. 2: 727). Miriam Allott notes that,

> the narrative details in the fragment, which deals with Stephen's defeat at Lincoln in 1141, indicate that [Keats and Brown] were using material based for the most part on Henry of Huntingdon's *Historia Anglorum*, which contains a circumstantial account of the battle, and William of Malmesbury's *Historia Novella* (both first printed 1596).
>
> (1970: 690)

Finney argues that Keats 'derived or intended to derive the matter of *King Stephen* from Holinshed's *Chronicles*, Selden's *Titles of Honor* . . . and Shakespeare's chronicle plays' (vol. 2: 728). The play begins with 'the defeat and capture of King Stephen by Queen Maud in the Battle of Lincoln,' and Keats follows 'closely Holinshed's story of the battle.' Critics have primarily tended to note the play's relationship to Shakespeare, through its use of blank verse and figurative diction, its characterization (fragmentary as it is), and the vigour of its scenes. Amy Lowell states, for instance, that 'Keats was plainly imitating Shakespeare in his historical plays' (vol. 2: 362). R. S. White discusses the indebtedness of 1.2 in *King Stephen* to 1.2 in *Macbeth*, suggesting that:

> Both plays begin at the height of a battle (an opening paralleled in Shakespeare in only *III Henry VI*), and in both a superior figure is brought news of the action . . . there is a clear similarity between the effect which Keats wishes to build up of breathlessly reported action, and the impression of the Sergeant's speeches in *Macbeth*.
>
> (1987: 131)

King Stephen's standing as an unfinished work in the style of Shakespeare marks a particular form of adaptation. The closeness of imitative style and the literary sympathies of the belated writer produce a form of what Keats famously called negative capability, 'which Shakespeare possessed so enormously . . . that is, when man is capable of being in uncertainties, Mysteries, doubts, without any irritable reaching after fact & reason' (Cook: 370). *King Stephen*'s negative capability resides in its lack of closure, the mystery surrounding what might have been had Keats completed the work instead of leaving it a sad fragment in the shadows of a greater work like *Lamia*. That his attempt at rendering Shakespeare ended in the 'uncertainty' of incompletion shows that adaptation in the mode of intense imitation is not always possible, even by the most skilled of epigones, and ultimately, as Keats put it, that 'I am very near Agreeing with Hazlit that Shakespeare is enough for us' (Cook: 356). *King Stephen* is an eloquent memorial to a mode of adaptation that marks the limits of the adapter, even as the works that followed from it show a great poet exploiting the potential inherent in failure.

Select bibliography

Entries marked * are particularly accessible.

Allott, M. (ed.) (1970) *The Poems of John Keats*, London: Longman.

Bate, J. (1997) *The Romantics on Shakespeare*, Harmondsworth: Penguin.

Bate, W. J. (1963) *John Keats*, Cambridge, Massachusetts: Harvard University Press.

Cook, E. (ed.) (1990) *John Keats*, Oxford: Oxford University Press.

*Finney, C. L. (1963) *The Evolution of Keats's Poetry*, 2 vols, New York: Russell & Russell.

Gittings, R. (1968) *John Keats*, London: Heinemann.

Keats, J. (1978) *The Poems of John Keats*, Jack Stillinger (ed.), Cambridge, Massachusetts: Belknap Press of Harvard University Press.

Lowell, A. (1929) *John Keats*, 2 vols, Boston: Houghton Mifflin.

*Motion, A. (1997) *Keats*, London: Faber & Faber.

Murry, J. M. (1968) *Keats and Shakespeare: A Study of Keats' Poetic Life From 1816 to 1820*, London: Oxford University Press.

Spurgeon, C. F. (1966) *Keats's Shakespeare: A Descriptive Study*, Oxford: Clarendon Press.

*White, R. S. (1987) *Keats as a Reader of Shakespeare*, London: Athlone Press.

King Stephen: A Dramatic Fragment

John Keats

Act I

Scene 1

Field of Battle.

> (*Alarum. Enter King* STEPHEN, *Knights,*
> *and Soldiers.*)

STEPHEN If shame can on a soldier's vein-swoll'n
    front
  Spread deeper crimson than the battle's toil,
  Blush in your casing helmets! for see, see!
  Yonder my chivalry, my pride of war,
  Wrench'd with an iron hand from firm array,
  Are routed loose about the plashy meads,
  Of honour forfeit. O that my known voice
  Could reach your dastard ears, and fright you
    more!
  Fly, cowards, fly! Glocester is at your backs!
  Throw your slack bridles o'er the flurried
    manes,
  Ply well the rowel with faint trembling heels,
  Scampering to death at last!
FIRST KNIGHT   The enemy
  Bears his flaunt standard close upon their rear.
SECOND KNIGHT Sure of a bloody prey, seeing the
    fens
  Will swamp them girth-deep.
STEPHEN   Over head and ears,
  No matter! 'Tis a gallant enemy;
  How like a comet he goes streaming on.
  But we must plague him in the flank, – hey,
    friends?
  We are well breathed, – follow!

> (*Enter Earl* BALDWIN *and Soldiers, as defeated.*)

STEPHEN   De Redvers!
  What is the monstrous bugbear that can fright
    Baldwin?
BALDWIN   No scare-crow, but the fortunate star
  Of boisterous Chester, whose fell truncheon
    now

Points level to the goal of victory.
  This way he comes, and if you would maintain
  Your person unaffronted by vile odds,
  Take horse, my Lord.
STEPHEN   And which way spur for life?
  Now I thank Heaven I am in the toils,
  That soldiers may bear witness how my arm
  Can burst the meshes. Not the eagle more
  Loves to beat up against a tyrannous blast,
  Than I to meet the torrent of my foes.
  This is a brag, – be't so, – but if I fall,
  Carve it upon my 'scutcheon'd sepulchre.
  On, fellow soldiers! Earl of Redvers, back!
  Not twenty Earls of Chester shall brow-beat
  The diadem.   (*Exeunt. Alarum.*)

Scene 2

Another part of the Field.

> (*Trumpets sounding a Victory. Enter*
> GLOCESTER [*Queen* MAUD's *half brother*],
> *Knights, and Forces.*)

GLOCESTER Now may we lift our bruised vizors
    up,
  And take the flattering freshness of the air,
  While the wide din of battle dies away
  Into times past, yet to be echoed sure
  In the silent pages of our chroniclers.
FIRST KNIGHT Will Stephen's death be mark'd
    there, my good Lord,
  Or that we gave him lodging in yon towers?
GLOCESTER Fain would I know the great
    usurper's fate.

> (*Enter two Captains severally.*)

FIRST CAPTAIN My Lord!
SECOND CAPTAIN   Most noble Earl!
FIRST CAPTAIN   The King –
SECOND CAPTAIN   The Empress greets –
GLOCESTER What of the King?

FIRST CAPTAIN   He sole and lone maintains
A hopeless bustle 'mid our swarming arms,
And with a nimble savageness attacks,
Escapes, makes fiercer onset, then anew
Eludes death, giving death to most that dare
Trespass within the circuit of his sword!
He must by this have fallen. Baldwin is taken;
And for the Duke of Bretagne, like a stag
He flies, for the Welsh beagles to hunt down.
God save the Empress!
GLOCESTER   Now our dreaded Queen:
What message from her Highness?
SECOND CAPTAIN   Royal Maud
From the throng'd towers of Lincoln hath look'd
    down,
Like Pallas from the walls of Ilion,
And seen her enemies havock'd at her feet.
She greets most noble Glocester from her heart,
Intreating him, his captains, and brave
    knights,
To grace a banquet. The high city gates
Are envious which shall see your triumph pass;
The streets are full of music.

(*Enter Second Knight.*)

GLOCESTER   Whence come you?
SECOND KNIGHT From Stephen, my good Prince,
    – Stephen! Stephen!
GLOCESTER Why do you make such echoing of
    his name?
SECOND KNIGHT Because I think, my lord, he is
    no man,
But a fierce demon, 'nointed safe from wounds,
And misbaptized with a Christian name.
GLOCESTER A mighty soldier ! – Does he still hold
    out?
SECOND KNIGHT He shames our victory. His
    valour still
Keeps elbow-room amid our eager swords,
And holds our bladed falchions all aloof –
His gleaming battle-axe being slaughter-sick,
Smote on the morion of a Flemish knight,
Broke short in his hand; upon the which he
    flung
The heft away with such a vengeful force,
It paunch'd the Earl of Chester's horse, who
    then
Spleen-hearted came in full career at him.
GLOCESTER Did no one take him at a vantage
    then?
SECOND KNIGHT Three then with tiger leap upon
    him flew,
Whom, with his sword swift-drawn and nimbly
    held,
He stung away again, and stood to breathe,

Smiling. Anon upon him rush'd once more
A throng of foes, and in this renew'd strife,
My sword met his and snapp'd off at the hilt.
GLOCESTER Come, lead me to this man – and let
    us move
In silence, not insulting his sad doom
With clamorous trumpets. To the Empress bear
My salutation as befits the time.

(*Exeunt* GLOCESTER *and Forces.*)

Scene 3

The Field of Battle.

(*Enter* STEPHEN *unarmed.*)

STEPHEN Another sword! And what if I could
    seize
One from Bellona's gleaming armoury,
Or choose the fairest of her sheaved spears!
Where are my enemies? Here, close at hand,
Here come the testy brood. O for a sword!
I'm faint – a biting sword! A noble sword!
A hedge-stake – or a ponderous stone to hurl
With brawny vengeance, like the labourer Cain.
Come on! Farewell my kingdom, and all hail
Thou superb, plum'd, and helmeted renown,
All hail – I would not truck this brilliant day
To rule in Pylos with a Nestor's beard –
Come on!

(*Enter* DE KAIMS *and Knights, &c.*)

DE KAIMS   Is't madness, or a hunger after death,
That makes thee thus unarm'd throw taunts at
    us?
Yield, Stephen, or my sword's point dips in
The gloomy current of a traitor's heart.
STEPHEN Do it, De Kaims, I will not budge an
    inch.
DE KAIMS Yes, of thy madness thou shalt take the
    meed.
STEPHEN Darest thou?
DE KAIMS   How dare, against a man disarm'd?
STEPHEN What weapons has the lion but
    himself?
Come not near me, De Kaims, for by the price
Of all the glory I have won this day,
Being a king, I will not yield alive
To any but the second man of the realm,
Robert of Glocester.
DE KAIMS   Thou shalt vail to me.
STEPHEN Shall I, when I have sworn against it,
    sir?
Thou think'st it brave to take a breathing king,
That, on a court-day bow'd to haughty Maud,

The awed presence-chamber may be bold
To whisper, there's the man who took alive
Stephen – me – prisoner. Certes, De Kaims,
The ambition is a noble one.

DE KAIMS   'Tis true,
And, Stephen, I must compasss it.

STEPHEN   No, no,
Do not tempt me to throttle you on the gorge,
Or with my gauntlet crush your hollow breast,
Just when your knighthood is grown ripe and
     full
For lordship.

A SOLDIER   Is an honest yeoman's spear
Of no use at a need? Take that.

STEPHEN   Ah, dastard!

DE KAIMS What, you are vulnerable! my prisoner!

STEPHEN No, not yet. I disclaim it, and demand
Death as a sovereign right unto a king
Who 'sdains to yield to any but his peer,
If not in title, yet in noble deeds,
The Earl of Glocester. Stab to the hilt, De Kaims,
For I will never by mean hands be led
From this so famous field. Do you hear! Be
     quick!

(Trumpets. Enter the Earl of CHESTER
and Knights.)

Scene 4

(A Presence Chamber. Queen MAUD *in a Chair of
State, the Earls of* GLOCESTER *and* CHESTER, *Lords,
Attendants.)*

MAUD Glocester, no more: I will behold that
     Boulogne:
Set him before me. Not for the poor sake
Of regal pomp and a vain-glorious hour,
As thou with wary speech, yet near enough,
Hast hinted.

GLOCESTER   Faithful counsel have I given;
If wary, for your Highness' benefit.

MAUD The Heavens forbid that I should not think
     so
For by thy valour have I won this realm,
Which by thy wisdom I will ever keep.
To sage advisers let me ever bend
A meek attentive ear, so that they treat
Of the wide kingdom's rule and government,
Not trenching on our actions personal.
Advis'd, not school'd, I would be; and henceforth
Spoken to in clear, plain, and open terms,
Not side-ways sermon'd at.

GLOCESTER   Then, in plain terms,
Once more for the fallen king –

MAUD   Your pardon, Brother,
I would no more of that; for, as I said,
'Tis not for worldly pomp I wish to see
The rebel, but as dooming judge to give
A sentence something worthy of his guilt.

GLOCESTER If't must be so, I'll bring him to your
     presence.

(Exit GLOCESTER.*)*

MAUD A meaner summoner might do as well –
My Lord of Chester, is 't true what I hear
Of Stephen of Boulogne, our prisoner,
That he, as a fit penance for his crimes,
Eats wholesome, sweet, and palatable food
Off Glocester's golden dishes – drinks pure
     wine,
Lodges soft?

CHESTER   More than that, my gracious Queen,
Has anger'd me. The noble Earl, methinks,
Full soldier as he is, and without peer
In counsel, dreams too much among his
     books.
It may read well, but sure 'tis out of date
To play the Alexander with Darius.

MAUD Truth! I think so. By Heavens it shall not
     last!

CHESTER It would amaze your Highness now to
     mark
How Glocester overstrains his courtesy
To that crime-loving rebel, that Boulogne –

MAUD That ingrate!

CHESTER   For whose vast ingratitude
To our late sovereign lord, your noble sire,
The generous Earl condoles in his mishaps,
And with a sort of lackeying friendliness,
Talks off the mighty frowning from his brow,
Woos him to hold a duet in a smile,
Or, if it please him, play an hour at chess –

MAUD A perjured slave!

CHESTER   And for his perjury,
Glocester has fit rewards – nay, I believe,
He sets his bustling household's wits at work
For flatteries to ease this Stephen's hours,
And make a heaven of his purgatory;
Adorning bondage with the pleasant gloss
Of feasts and music, and all idle shows
Of indoor pageantry; while syren whispers,
Predestin'd for his ear, 'scape as half-check'd
From lips the courtliest and the rubiest
Of all the realm, admiring of his deeds.

MAUD A frost upon his summer!

CHESTER   A queen's nod
Can make his June December. Here he
     comes . . .

The Public (El público)

Federico García Lorca

Introduction

Federico García Lorca (1898–1936), the Spanish poet, dramatist, painter, and musician, was assassinated by Fascist anti-Republicans at the onset of the Spanish Civil War. One of the men who shot him, Juan Luis Trecastro, 'boasted later that morning in Granada that he had just helped to shoot Lorca, firing, for good measure, "two bullets into his arse for being a queer" ' (Gibson: 468). Born in Andalusia, educated at the universities of Granada and Madrid, García Lorca was precociously talented as a poet and dramatist, eventually leaving, in addition to a substantial body of poetry, a range of theatre pieces in different genres. García Lorca's *The Public* seems to have been conceived in New York in 1929–1930, then written primarily in Cuba in 1930, near the end of an extended trip through the Americas, and completed in Spain in the summer of 1930 (Edwards 1994: xxiv). A major figure in the Spanish cultural scene who was associated with such luminaries as the filmmaker Luis Buñuel, the composer Manuel de Falla, and the painter Salvador Dalí, García Lorca's literary legacy makes him, as Gwynne Edwards puts it, 'the most famous name in Spanish literature' excluding Cervantes (1980: 1).

Critics such as Paul Julian Smith, Edwards, and Andrew Anderson have judged *The Public* to be 'the most hermetic and allusive of García Lorca's plays' (Smith: 122), 'one of the most original and experimental plays in twentieth-century European history' (Edwards 1980: 1), and 'Lorca's most adventurous, daring, exploratory, disconcerting, edgy, and forward-looking play, one that dramatizes the superiority of pure, direct, first-hand (literary or poetic) experience over mediated, second-hand (critical) cognition' (Anderson 1997: 84). Smith avers that García Lorca 'had repeatedly insisted that *El público* and the

other "unplayable" plays constituted his real, true theater' (4). Both Edwards and Anderson note the play's anticipation of and indebtedness to a number of writers, including Shakespeare, Pirandello, Beckett, Genet, and Ionesco, to mention only a few. García Lorca never lived to see the *The Public* staged and the play, other than two scenes, remained unpublished until 1978 and unperformed professionally until 1986–87, in a co-production between the Piccolo Teatro di Milano and the Centro Dramático Nacional in Madrid (under the direction of Lluís Pasqual). García Lorca apparently requested that the play be burned about a month before his death, a request ignored by Martínez Nadal, the friend who received the manuscript. The surreal content of the play, the abstract and highly symbolic action of the plot, the treatment of sexual difference, and the critique of conservative theatre, not to mention the extraordinarily free transmutation of Shakespearean materials, all make the play a highly charged and challenging theatrical experience. Anderson calls it, borrowing from lines spoken by the Director in the play, a 'dificilísimo juego poético,' an exceedingly difficult poetic play (in the many senses of the latter term), and this is confirmed by the maze of shifting characters, often played by the same actors, the highly allusive language, the 'episodic, not to say fragmented, dramatic structure,' and the 'generically named figures and allegorical overtones' (1992: 331).

The play centres on the Director, who mounts an 'experimental and taboo-breaking production of Shakespeare's *Romeo and Juliet*' (Anderson 1992: 331). Paul Binding, in referring to the play's metatheatrical content – it is emphatically a play about the making of theatre – states that 'we are occupied with a performance of *Romeo and Juliet*, an apotheosised scene from which we witness and the entirety of which haunts the play with all its

Plate 1 Photo: Ros Ribas. Co-production of *The Public* by Piccolo Teatro di Milano and the Centro Dramático Nacional, Madrid, 1986–7

complex symbolic overtones' (151). Edwards writes:

> In the action of *The Public* the characters of Romeo and Juliet figure prominently, and . . . *Romeo and Juliet* was one of Lorca's favourite plays. In Lorca's drama there are many echoes of Shakespeare's text and also indications that Lorca, knowing the work well, was writing without the Shakespearean work in hand. And yet, Raphael Nadal argues convincingly that, despite the frequent references to *Romeo and Juliet*, 'the theme of *The Public*, the accidental nature of love, is more closely connected with another Shakespeare play which had always haunted Lorca: *A Midsummer Night's Dream*.' Lorca, in a discussion of the play with Nadal, and especially of the love scenes involving Titania and the ass, had observed that love, which is independent of the free will of the individuals concerned, exists at all levels and with the same intensity, be it between man and woman, man and man, creature and creature. What in Shakespeare's play was happening in a forest near Athens happens everywhere in the real world. This is precisely the theme of *The Public*, the revelation of love in its different forms and the revelation of the characters both as facets of each other and, beyond that, of ourselves.
>
> (1980: 65)

Though it is perhaps overly simplistic to ascribe any singular theme to a play as complex as *The Public*, it is clear that García Lorca radically transforms the gender expectations of his audience by producing a transformation of the male–female love rendered in *Romeo and Juliet* via the ambiguities about sexual difference that crop up in *A Midsummer Night's Dream*. In effect, García Lorca 'queers' texts that already have that potential inscribed in them. Juliet, in Shakespeare's own time, would have been played by a boy, thus staging for an audience the spectacle of male–male desire, masked as male–female desire (something that Shakespeare famously parodies in the Pyramus and Thisby episode of *A Midsummer Night's Dream*). Moreover, *A Midsummer Night's Dream*'s plot is riven by at least three ambiguous instances of desire, figured as either homoerotic or bestial, both alternatives explored by García Lorca in *The Public*: Titania's invocation of the votaress from whom she receives the changeling child, couched in highly eroticized, perhaps even Sapphic language (2.1.122–137); Helena's even more eroticized description of her friendship with Hermia ('So we grew together, / Like to a double cherry, seeming parted, / But yet an union in partition, / Two lovely berries moulded on one stem' 3.2.207–211); and Titania's excursion with

Bottom, transformed into an ass, a bestial figure of liminal sexuality (4.1.1–45).

García Lorca explores these forms of difference in *The Public*, but, typically, underlying such differences is the more radical difference of death. The theatre, for instance, is imagined as 'Tombs with gas spotlights and advertisements and long rows of orchestra seats,' and Man 1 explicitly points to the ultimate form of theatre achieved in death in scene 1: 'I'll have to shoot myself in order to inaugurate the true theater, the theater beneath the sand.' The thematic concerns with death tie in to a crucial element in the Lorcan aesthetic, namely the notion of *duende* (usually meaning a goblin or magic), which Lorca defines enigmatically as a 'power not a work . . . a struggle, not a thought' (García Lorca: 49), and also as 'the spirit of the earth' (49) and the 'constant baptism of newly created things' (62). For García Lorca the 'duende's arrival always means a radical change in forms. It brings to old planes unknown feelings of freshness, with the quality of something newly created, like a miracle, and it produces an almost religious enthusiasm' (53). As a crucial determinant of artistry, the *duende* 'does not come at all unless he sees that death is possible' (58), precipitating a struggle that ends with the *duende* wounding the artist. García Lorca paradoxically states, 'In the healing of that wound, which never closes, lie the strange, invented qualities of a man's work' (58).

The version of *The Public* presented here dramatically exemplifies the degree to which adaptation (and, in this case, translation) can produce a startling new reading of a so-called source text. The very act of radically transforming Shakespearean materials, whether critical or theatrical, frees *The Public* from any simplistic understanding of it as either a text with a singular source or as a text that can easily be separated from the accretions that give it shape. At the same time, *The Public* forcefully demonstrates the complexity with which the adaptive process produces historical and literary convergences that unsettle the orthodoxies of interpretative and theatrical practice.

Select bibliography

Entries marked * are particularly accessible.

*Anderson, A. A. (1985) 'Some Shakespearean Reminiscences in García Lorca's Drama,' *Comparative Literature Studies* 22: 187–210.
— (1992) 'Un dificilísimo juego poético': Theme and Symbol in Lorca's *El público*,' *Romance Quarterly* 39,3: 331–346.
— (1997) 'Una Desorientación Absoluta': Juliet and the Shifting Sands of García Lorca's *El público*,' *Revista Hispánica Moderna*: 67–85.
Binding, P. (1985) *Lorca: The Gay Imagination*, London: GMP Publishers.
*Delgado, M., and Edwards, G. (1990) 'From Madrid to Stratford East: *The Public* in Performance,' *Estreno: Cuadernos del Teatro Espanol Contemporaneo* 16,2: 11–17.
DeLong-Tonelli, B. J. (1981) 'The Trials and Tribulations of Lorca's *El público*,' *García Lorca Review* 9: 153–168.
Edwards, G. (1980) *Lorca: The Theatre Beneath the Sand*, London: Marion Boyars.
— (1988) 'Lorca on the English Stage: Problems of Production and Translation,' *New Theatre Quarterly* 4: 344–355.
— (1994) (trans.) *Lorca. Plays: Three*, London: Methuen.
Figure, P. (1983) 'The Mystification of Love and Lorca's Female Image in *El público*,' *Cincinnati Romance Review* 2: 26–32.
Gibson, I. (1989) *Federico García Lorca*, New York: Pantheon Books.
Londre, F. H. (1983) 'Lorca in Metamorphosis: His Posthumous Plays,' *Theatre Journal* 35,1: 102–108.
Lorca, F. G. (1998) 'Play and Theory of the Duende,' in Christopher Maurer (ed.) *In Search of Duende*, New York: New Directions: 48–62.
Monegal, A. (1994) 'Un-masking the Maskuline: Transvestism and Tragedy in García Lorca's *El público*,' *Modern Language Notes* 109: 204–216.
*Nadal, R. M. (1974) *Lorca's 'The Public': A Study of his Unfinished Play ('El público') and of Love and Death in the Work of Federico García Lorca*, London: Calder & Boyars.
Newton, C. (1995) *Understanding Federico García Lorca*, Columbia: University of South Carolina Press.
Smith, P. J. (1998) *The Theatre of García Lorca: Text, Performance, Psychoanalysis*, Cambridge: Cambridge University Press.

The Public (El público)

Federico García Lorca

Characters

DIRECTOR

MANSERVANT

FOUR WHITE HORSES

FIRST MAN

SECOND MAN

THIRD MAN

FOURTH MAN

HELEN

VINE LEAVES

BELLS

FIRST BOY

CENTURION

EMPEROR

JULIET

BLACK HORSE

PIERROT COSTUME

BALLERINA COSTUME

PYJAMA COSTUME

MALE NURSE

NAKED MAN

FIVE STUDENTS

THREE LADIES

SECOND BOY

TWO THIEVES

PROMPTER

IDIOT SHEPHERD

MAGICIAN

HARLEQUIN

LADY IN BLACK

GONZALO'S MOTHER

ENRIQUE

GONZALO

Scene 1

(Director's room. The Director seated. He is wearing a morning coat. Blue set. A large imprinted hand on the wall. The windows are X-rays.)

SERVANT Sir.

DIRECTOR What?

SERVANT There is the public.

DIRECTOR Show them in.

(Four WHITE HORSES *enter.)*

DIRECTOR What can I do for you? *(The* HORSES *blow their trumpets.)* That might do if I were a man capable of sighing. My theater will always be in the open air! But I've lost my whole fortune. If not, I'd poison the open air. A little syringe, which can pull off the scab over the wound, is all I need. Out of here! Out of my house, horses! *(Aside)* The bed for sleeping with horses has already been invented. *(Weeping)* My little horses.

THE HORSES *(weeping)* For three hundred pesetas, for two hundred pesetas, for a bowl of soup, for an empty perfume bottle, for your saliva, for some of your fingernail clippings.

DIRECTOR Out! Out! Out! *(He rings a buzzer.)*

THE HORSES For nothing! Before, your feet smelled and we were three years old. We waited for you in the toilet, we waited for you behind the doors, and then we filled your bed with tears.

(The SERVANT *enters.)*

DIRECTOR Give me a whip.

THE HORSES And your shoes were baked in sweat, but we were able to understand that the moon had the same type of relationship with rotten apples in the grass.

DIRECTOR (*to the* SERVANT) Open the door!*

THE HORSES No, no, no. Abominable! You're covered with hair and you eat the lime, which isn't yours, off the walls.

SERVANT I don't open the door. I don't want to go into the theater.

DIRECTOR (*hitting him*) Open it!

(*The* HORSES *pull out long golden trumpets and slowly dance to the sound of their tune.*)

WHITE HORSE 1 Abominable!

THE OTHER HORSES Blenamiboá!

WHITE HORSE 1 Abominable!

THE OTHER HORSES Blenamiboá!

(*The* SERVANT *opens the door.*)

DIRECTOR Theater in the open air! Out! Let's go! Theater in the open air! Out of here!

(*The* HORSES *exit.*)

DIRECTOR (*to the* SERVANT) Continue. (*The* DIRECTOR *sits down behind the table.*)

SERVANT Sir.

DIRECTOR What?

SERVANT The public.

DIRECTOR Show them in.

(*The* DIRECTOR *changes his blond wig for a black one. Three* MEN *dressed exactly alike, in tails, enter. They are wearing dark beards.*)

MAN 1 Mr. Director of the Open Air Theater?

DIRECTOR At your service.

MAN 1 We've come to congratulate you on your last play.

DIRECTOR Thank you.

MAN 3 So very original.

MAN 1 And such a pretty title! *Romeo and Juliet*.

DIRECTOR A man and a woman who fall in love.

MAN 1 Romeo could be a bird and Juliet could be a stone. Romeo could be a grain of salt and Juliet could be a map.

DIRECTOR But they'll never stop being Romeo and Juliet.

MAN 1 And in love. Do you believe they were in love?

DIRECTOR Well . . . I'm not inside . . .

MAN 1 Enough, enough! You're giving yourself away.

MAN 2 (*to* MAN 1) Be prudent. It's your fault. Why do you hang around stage doors? You could knock at a forest and it's probable that it would

open up the noise of its sap for your ears. But at a theater!

MAN 1 It's at theaters where one must knock, it's at theaters so . . .

MAN 3 So the truth about tombs be known.

MAN 2 Tombs with gas spotlights and advertisements and long rows of orchestra seats.

DIRECTOR (*trembling*) Gentlemen . . .

MAN 1 Yes. Yes. Director of the Open Air Theater, author of *Romeo and Juliet*.

MAN 2 How did Romeo urinate, Mr. Director? Isn't it nice seeing Romeo urinate? How many times did he pretend to throw himself off the tower in order to be caught in the drama of his sufferings? What was happening, Mr. Director . . . when it wasn't happening? And the tomb? Why, at the end, didn't you go down the steps into the tomb? You could've seen an angel carrying off Romeo's sex while leaving another, his own, the one belonging to him. And if I tell you that the most important character of all was a poisonous flower, what would you think? Answer!

DIRECTOR Gentlemen, that isn't the problem.

MAN 1 (*interrupting*) There isn't any other. We'll have to bury the theater because of everyone's cowardice. And I'll have to shoot myself.

MAN 2 Gonzalo!

MAN 1 (*slowly*) I'll have to shoot myself in order to inaugurate the true theater, the theater beneath the sand.

DIRECTOR Gonzalo . . .

MAN 1 How's that? (*He pauses.*)

DIRECTOR (*reacting*) But I can't. Everything would come crashing down. It would be like leaving my children blind and then . . . what would I do with the audience? What would I do with the audience if I removed the handrails from the bridge? The mask would come and devour me. I once saw a man devoured by the mask. The strongest youths in the city rammed large balls of thrown-away newspapers up his rear with bloodied pickaxes; and once in America there was a boy whom the mask hung by his own intestines.

MAN 1 Magnificent!

MAN 2 Why didn't you say that in the theater?

MAN 3 That's the beginning of a plot.

DIRECTOR In any case, an ending.

MAN 3 An ending caused by fear.

DIRECTOR That's obvious, sir. But don't ever

---

* Here and elsewhere we have followed Lorca's manuscript, deciding not to incorporate the editorial changes and additions made by Rafael Martínez Nadal in the Spanish edition of the work. – Trans.

assume I'm capable of bringing the mask out on stage.

MAN 1 Why not?

DIRECTOR But what about morals? And the spectators' stomachs?

MAN 1 There are people who vomit when an octopus is turned inside out, and others who turn pale if they hear the word cancer pronounced with the right intonation; but you know that against this there exist, as expressive mediums, tin and plaster and the adorable mica and, as a last resort, cardboard, which is well within anyone's means. (*He stands up.*) But what you want to do is deceive us. Deceive us so that everything will go on just the same and make it impossible to help the dead. It's your fault flies fell into the four thousand orange juices I'd made. And once again I'll have to start breaking the roots.

DIRECTOR (*standing up*) I won't argue, sir. But, what do you want from me? Did you bring a new play?

MAN 1 Do you think there could be any newer play than us with our beards . . . and you?

DIRECTOR And me . . . ?

MAN 1 Yes . . . you.

MAN 2 Gonzalo!

MAN 1 (*to* MAN 2 *but looking at the* DIRECTOR) I still recognize him and it seems as if I'm seeing him that morning when he locked up a hare, which was a marvel of quickness, inside a small carrying-case for books. And another time when he put two roses behind his ears, the day when he first discovered the hairstyle with the part in the middle. (*To the* DIRECTOR) And you, do you recognize me?

DIRECTOR This isn't the plot. For the love of God! (*Shouting*) Helen! Helen! (*He runs to the door.*)

MAN 1 But I've got to take you to the stage, whether you want to or not. You've made me suffer too much. Quick! The screen! The screen!

(MAN 3 *brings out a folding screen and places it in the middle of the stage.*)

DIRECTOR (*weeping*) The audience is going to see me. My theater will come crashing down . . . I've done the best dramas of the season, but now . . . !

(THE HORSES' *trumpets sound.* MAN 1 *goes to the back of the stage and opens the door.*)

MAN 1 Come in here, with us. You've got a place in this drama. All of you. (*To the* DIRECTOR) And you, pass behind the screen.

(MEN 2 *and* 3 *push the* DIRECTOR. *He passes behind the folding screen and appearing on the other side is a boy dressed in white satin with a white ruff. He should be played by an actress. She is carrying a little black guitar.*)

MAN 1 Enrique! Enrique! (*He covers his face with his hands.*)

MAN 2 Don't make me pass in back of the screen. Let me be for once, Gonzalo!

DIRECTOR (*coldly and strumming the guitar*) Gonzalo, I've got to spit on you a lot. I want to spit on you and cut your tails up with some nice little scissors. Get me a needle and some silken thread. I want to embroider. I don't like tattoos, but I want to embroider you with silken threads.

MAN 2 (*to* THE HORSES) Take a seat wherever you wish.

MAN 1 (*weeping*) Enrique! Enrique!

DIRECTOR I'll embroider your flesh, and I'd be so pleased to see you sleeping on the roof. How much money have you got in your pocket? Burn it! (MAN 1 *lights a match and burns up the bills.*) I can never really see clearly how the illustrations disappear in the flame. Haven't you got any more money? How poor you are, Gonzalo! And my lipstick? Don't you have any rouge? How irritating.

MAN 2 (*timidly*) I've got some. (*He pulls the lipstick out from under his beard and offers it to him.*)

DIRECTOR Thank you. But . . . but you're here, too! To the screen! You, also . . . to the screen! And you still put up with him, Gonzalo?

(*The Director roughly pushes* MAN 2 *and appearing on the other side of the folding screen is a woman dressed in black pajama pants with a crown of poppies on her head. In her hand she is carrying a lorgnette covered with a blond moustache, which she will put to use by placing it over her mouth at some moments of the drama.*)

MAN 2 (*dryly*) Give me the lipstick.

DIRECTOR Ha, ha, ha! Oh, Maximiliana, Empress of Bavaria! Oh, wanton woman!

MAN 2 (*placing the moustache over his lips*) I would recommend that you be silent for a while.

DIRECTOR Helen! Helen!

MAN 1 (*loudly*) Don't call Helen!

DIRECTOR And why not? She loved me greatly when my theater was in the open air. Helen!

(HELEN *enters from the left. She is dressed as a Grecian. Her eyebrows are blue, her hair white and her feet plaster. Her dress, completely open in front, lets one see her thighs which are covered by tight-fitting pink tights.* MAN 2 *raises the moustache to his lips.*)

HELEN The same thing again?

DIRECTOR Yes, again.

MAN 3 Why have you come out here, Helen? Why have you come out if you're not going to love me anymore?

HELEN Who told you that? But, why do you love me so much? I'd kiss your feet if you were to punish me and go off with other women. But *you* adore me excessively, and only me. We'll have to end this once and for all.

DIRECTOR (*to* MAN 3) And me? Don't you remember me? Don't you remember my torn-out fingernails? How could I have known other women and not you? Why did I call you, Helen? Why did I call you, torment of mine?

HELEN (*to* MAN 3) Go with him! And now confess the truth you're keeping from me. I don't care if you were drunk and now wish to justify it, but you've kissed him and slept in the same bed.

MAN 3 Helen!

(*He passes rapidly behind the folding screen and reappears beardless, with the palest of faces and a whip in his hand. He is wearing leather wrist bands with golden studs.*)

MAN 3 (*whipping the* DIRECTOR) You're always talking, you're always lying. . . and now I must finish you off without the least bit of mercy.

THE HORSES Mercy! Mercy!

HELEN You could keep on beating a whole century and I wouldn't believe in you. (MAN 3 *goes over to* HELEN *and squeezes her wrists.*) You could keep on mutilating my fingers for a whole century and you wouldn't succeed in making even one moan escape my lips.

MAN 3 We'll see who's stronger.

HELEN It'll be me, and always me.

(*The* SERVANT *appears.*)

HELEN (*to the* SERVANT) Take me away from here, fast! Take me away! (*The* SERVANT *passes behind the folding screen and comes out unchanged*) Take me away! Faraway! (*The* SERVANT *takes her in his arms*)

DIRECTOR We can begin.

MAN 1 Whenever you wish.

THE HORSES Mercy! Mercy!

(THE HORSES *sound their trumpets. The characters stand rigid in their places.*)

SLOW CURTAIN

Scene 2

Roman ruin

(*One character, totally covered with red vine leaves, plays a flute while seated upon a capital. Another character, covered with little golden bells, dances in the center of the stage.*)

CHARACTER IN BELLS If I turned into a cloud?

CHARACTER IN VINE LEAVES I'd turn into an eye.

CHARACTER IN BELLS If I turned into caca?

CHARACTER IN VINE LEAVES I'd turn into a fly.

CHARACTER IN BELLS If I turned into an apple?

CHARACTER IN VINE LEAVES I'd turn into a kiss.

CHARACTER IN BELLS If I turned into a breast?

CHARACTER IN VINE LEAVES I'd turn into a white sheet.

VOICE (*sarcastically*) Bravo!

CHARACTER IN BELLS And if I turned into a moon-fish?

CHARACTER IN VINE LEAVES I'd turn into a knife.

CHARACTER IN BELLS (*stopping his dancing*) But why? Why are you tormenting me? Why won't you come along with me, if you love me, to wherever *I* take you? If I turned into a moon-fish, you'd turn into a wave upon the sea, or into seaweed; and if you desire something very far away, because you don't want to kiss me, you'd turn into a full moon . . . but into a knife! You delight in interrupting my dance, and dancing is the only way I have of loving you.

CHARACTER IN VINE LEAVES When you prowl around the bed and other objects in the house I follow you, but I never follow you to those places where you so cleverly pretend to take me. If you turned into a moon-fish, I'd cut you open with a knife, because I'm a man, because I'm nothing else than that, a man . . . more of a man than Adam, and I wish *you'd* be more of a man than I. So much a man that there wouldn't even be a sound in the branches when you pass. But *you* are not a man. If I didn't have this flute, you'd try to escape to the moon, to that moon covered with little lace handkerchiefs and drops of female blood.

CHARACTER IN BELLS (*timidly*) And if I turned into an ant?

CHARACTER IN VINE LEAVES (*energetically*) I'd turn into earth.

CHARACTER IN BELLS (*louder*) And if I turned into earth?

CHARACTER IN VINE LEAVES (*softer*) I'd turn into water.

CHARACTER IN BELLS (*vibrantly*) And if I turned into water?

CHARACTER IN VINE LEAVES (*disheartened*) I'd turn into a moon-fish.

CHARACTER IN BELLS (*shaking*) And if I turned into a moon-fish?

CHARACTER IN VINE LEAVES (*standing up*) I'd turn into a knife. Into a knife sharpened during four long springtimes.

CHARACTER IN BELLS Carry me to the bathtub and drown me. That's the only way you'll ever be able to see me naked. Do you imagine I'm afraid of blood? I know how to dominate you. Do you think I don't know you? To dominate you so completely that if I were to say, 'If I turned into a moon-fish?' you'd answer, 'I'd turn into a sack of little fish eggs.'

CHARACTER IN VINE LEAVES Get an axe and chop off my legs. Let the insects from the ruin come . . . and then get out of here. Because I despise you. I wish you'd get to the bottom of the matter. I spit on you.

CHARACTER IN BELLS Do you want that? Goodbye. I'm not worried. If I go down to the ruin, I'll find love and ever more love all the time.

CHARACTER IN VINE LEAVES (*distressed*) Where are you going? Where are you going?

CHARACTER IN BELLS Don't you want me to go?

CHARACTER IN VINE LEAVES (*in a weak voice*) No, don't go. And if I turned into a tiny grain of sand?

CHARACTER IN BELLS I'd turn into a whip.

CHARACTER IN VINE LEAVES And if I turned into a sack of little fish eggs?

CHARACTER IN BELLS I'd turn into another whip. A whip made of guitar strings.

CHARACTER IN VINE LEAVES Don't whip me!

CHARACTER IN BELLS A whip made of ship's cables.

CHARACTER IN VINE LEAVES Don't whip me on the belly!

CHARACTER IN BELLS A whip made from the stamens of an orchid.

CHARACTER IN VINE LEAVES You'll wind up blinding me!

CHARACTER IN BELLS Blinding you because you're not a man. I am indeed a man. A man who's so much of a man that I faint when hunters awake. A man who's so much of a man that I feel a sharp pain in my teeth when somebody breaks a stem, however tiny it might be. A giant. A giant who's so much of a giant that I can embroider a rose on the fingernail of a newborn child.

CHARACTER IN VINE LEAVES I'm waiting for night, anguished by the whiteness of the ruin, so I can grovel at your feet.

CHARACTER IN BELLS No, don't. Why are you saying that to me? It's you who should force *me* to do it. Aren't *you* a man? A man who's more of a man than even Adam?

CHARACTER IN VINE LEAVES (*falling to the ground*) Oh! Oh!

CHARACTER IN BELLS (*drawing close and in a low voice*) If I turned into a capital?

CHARACTER IN VINE LEAVES Poor me!

CHARACTER IN BELLS You'd turn into the shadow of a capital and nothing more. And then Helen would come to my bed. Helen, dear heart! While you, there underneath the cushions, would be stretched out and dripping with sweat, a sweat that wouldn't be yours, it'd be the sweat of coachmen, of stokers and of doctors who operate on cancer. Then I'd turn into a moon-fish and you'd be nothing more than a little powder box that's passed from hand to hand.

CHARACTER IN VINE LEAVES Oh!

CHARACTER IN BELLS Again? Are you crying again? I'll need to faint for the peasants to come. I'll need to call the Blackmen, those enormous Blacks wounded by yucca knives who day and night battle the muck of the rivers. Get up off the ground, coward! Yesterday I was at the smelter's house and ordered a chain. Don't you dare move away from me! A chain. And I cried the whole night long because my wrists and ankles were hurting me despite not even having it on. (*The* CHARACTER IN VINE LEAVES *blows a silver whistle.*) What are you doing? (*The whistle sounds again.*) Now I know what you want, but I've got time to flee.

CHARACTER IN VINE LEAVES (*standing up*) Flee if you want.

CHARACTER IN BELLS I'll defend myself with grass.

CHARACTER IN VINE LEAVES Try and defend yourself.

(*The whistle sounds. A* YOUNG BOY *dressed in red tights falls from the ceiling.*)

YOUNG BOY The Emperor! The Emperor! The Emperor!

CHARACTER IN VINE LEAVES The Emperor . . .

CHARACTER IN BELLS I'll play your part. Don't reveal yourself. That would cost me my life.

YOUNG BOY The Emperor! The Emperor! The Emperor!

CHARACTER IN BELLS Everything between us was a game. We were playing. And now *I'll* serve the Emperor by feigning your voice. You can stretch out behind that big capital. I've never told you about it. Over there there's a cow that cooks the soldiers' food.

CHARACTER IN VINE LEAVES The Emperor! Now it can't be helped. *You* have broken the spider's thread, and now I feel my large feet becoming so tiny and repugnant.

CHARACTER IN BELLS Do you want some tea? Where could I find a hot drink in this ruin?

YOUNG BOY (*on the ground*) The Emperor! The Emperor! The Emperor!

(*A trumpet sounds and the* EMPEROR *of the Romans appears. With him enters a* CENTURION *with a yellow tunic and grey skin. Behind them come the four* HORSES *with their trumpets. The* YOUNG BOY *goes over to the* EMPEROR. *The* EMPEROR *takes him in his arms and they lose themselves among the capitals.*)

CENTURION The Emperor is searching for one.
CHARACTER IN VINE LEAVES I'm one.
CHARACTER IN BELLS I'm one.
CENTURION Which one of the two of you?
CHARACTER IN VINE LEAVES Me.
CHARACTER IN BELLS Me.
CENTURION The Emperor will guess which one of the two of you is one. With a knife or a gob of spit. May all of your kind be damned! It's your fault I'm roaming the roads and sleeping on the sand. My wife is beautiful, like a mountain. She gives birth out of four or five places at a time and snores beneath the trees at midday. I've got two hundred children. And I'll still have many more. May your kind be damned!

(*The* CENTURION *spits and sings. A long and sustained shout is heard from behind the columns. The* EMPEROR *appears wiping his forehead. He pulls off his black gloves, then some red gloves, and his hands, of a classic whiteness, come into view.*)

EMPEROR (*indifferently*) Which one of the two of you is one?
CHARACTER IN BELLS I am, Lord.
EMPEROR One is one and always one. I've beheaded more than forty boys who didn't want to say it.
CENTURION (*spitting*) One is one and nothing more than one.
EMPEROR And there aren't two.
CENTURION Because if there were two, the Emperor wouldn't be scouring the roads.
EMPEROR (*to the* CENTURION) Undress them!
CHARACTER IN BELLS I'm one, Lord. He's the beggar of the ruins. He lives on roots.

EMPEROR Step aside.
CHARACTER IN VINE LEAVES *You* know me. *You* know who I am. (*He strips off the vine leaves, and a plaster white nude appears.*)
EMPEROR (*embracing him*) One is one.
CHARACTER IN VINE LEAVES And always one. If you kiss me I'll open my mouth so you can drive your sword into my neck afterwards.
EMPEROR That's how I'll do it.
CHARACTER IN VINE LEAVES And leave my head of love in the ruins, the head of one who was always one.
EMPEROR (*sighing*) One.
CENTURION (*to the* EMPEROR) Difficult to believe, but there you have him.
CHARACTER IN VINE LEAVES He's got him because he'll never be able to have him.
CHARACTER IN BELLS Treason! Treason!
CENTURION Shut up, you old rat, you son of a mop!
CHARACTER IN BELLS Gonzalo! Help me, Gonzalo!

(*The* CHARACTER IN BELLS *tugs on a column and it unfolds into the white folding screen of the first scene. From behind it enter the three bearded* MEN *and the* STAGE DIRECTOR.)

MAN 1 Treason!
CHARACTER IN BELLS He's betrayed us!
DIRECTOR Treason!

(*The Emperor is embracing the Character in Vine Leaves.*)

CURTAIN

Scene 3

(*Wall of sand. On the left, and painted on the wall, a transparent moon, almost like gelatin. In the center, an immense green, lanceolate leaf.*)

MAN 1 (*entering*) This is not what's needed. After what's happened, it wouldn't be fair to go back and talk to the children and observe the sky's happiness.
MAN 2 A bad place this is.
DIRECTOR You both witnessed the fight?
MAN 3 (*entering*) Both should've died. I've never witnessed such a bloody feast.
MAN 1 Two lions. Two demigods.
MAN 2 Two demigods, if they didn't have an anus.
MAN 1 But the anus is man's curse. The anus is man's failure, it's his shame and his death. Both

had an anus and neither one of them could battle with the pure beauty of the statues that were shining, preserving intimate desires defended by a flawless surface.

MAN 3   When the moon comes up the farm children get together to defecate.

MAN 1   And behind the bulrushes, along the cool banks of still waters, we've found the footprint of the man who makes the nudes' freedom so horrid.

MAN 3   Both should've died.

MAN 1   (*energetically*) They should've been victorious.

MAN 3   How?

MAN 1   By both being men and not letting themselves be carried away by false desires. By being men entirely. Is it possible that a man could ever cease being a man?

MAN 2   Gonzalo!

MAN 1   They've been beaten, and now everything will only serve for the mocking and jeering of the people.

MAN 3   Neither one of them was a man. Just as the two of you aren't either. I'm disgusted by your company.

MAN 1   There in back, at the far end of the banquet, is the Emperor. Why don't you go out there and strangle him? I recognize your courage as much as I justify your beauty. Why don't you hurry and devour his neck with your very own teeth?

DIRECTOR   Why don't *you* do it?

MAN 1   Because I can't, because I don't want to, because I'm weak.

DIRECTOR   But *he* can, *he* wants to, *he's* strong. (*In a loud voice*) The Emperor is in the ruin!

MAN 3   Let anyone go who wants to inhale his breath.

MAN 1   You.

MAN 3   I could only convince you two if I had my whip.

MAN 1   You know I can't resist you, but I despise you for being a coward.

MAN 2   For being a coward!

DIRECTOR   (*loudly and looking at* MAN 3) The Emperor who drinks our blood is in the ruin!

(MAN 3 *covers his face with his hands.*)

MAN 1   (*to the* DIRECTOR) That's him, do you know him now? He's that brave one who, in the café and in books, winds our veins around long fish spines. He's the man who loves the Emperor in solitude and seeks him out in the taverns of the ports. Enrique, look deeply into his eyes. Look how little bunches of grapes go

down his shoulders. Me he doesn't deceive. But now I'm going to kill the Emperor. Without a knife, just with these frail hands that all women envy.

DIRECTOR   No, he'll go! Wait a little!

(MAN 3 *sits down in a chair and weeps.*)

MAN 3   I wouldn't be able to try on my cloud pajamas! Oh! You didn't know I discovered a marvelous drink that only a few Blacks from Honduras know about.

DIRECTOR   In a putrid swamp is where we should be, under the slime where dead frogs decompose, and not here.

MAN 2   (*embracing* MAN 1) Gonzalo, why do you love me so much?

MAN 1   (*to the* DIRECTOR) I'll bring you the Emperor's head!

DIRECTOR   That'll be the best gift for Helen.

MAN 2   Stay here, Gonzalo, and permit me to wash your feet.

MAN 1   The Emperor's head burns the body of all women.

DIRECTOR   (*to* MAN 1) But you don't realize that Helen can polish her nails in phosphorous and quicklime. Get going with the knife! Helen, Helen, my sweetheart!

MAN 3   My sweetheart for all times! Nobody mention Helen's name here.

DIRECTOR   (*trembling*) Nobody mention her. It'll be much better if we all calm down. By forgetting the theater it'll be possible. Nobody mention her.

MAN 1   Helen.

DIRECTOR   (*to* MAN 1) Shut up! Later I'll be waiting behind the walls of the big warehouse. Hush.

MAN 1   I'd prefer to put an end to this once and for all. Helen! (*He starts to exit.*)

DIRECTOR   (*stopping him*) Listen: and if I turned into a tiny dwarf of jasmines?

MAN 2   (*to* MAN 1) Let's go. Don't be deceived! I'll go to the ruin with you.

DIRECTOR   (*embracing* MAN 1) I'd turn into a pellet of anise, a pellet in which the bulrushes of all the rivers would be squeezed out, and you'd be a great Chinese mountain covered with lively little harps.

MAN 1   (*half closing his eyes*) No, no. Then I wouldn't be a Chinese mountain. I'd be a skin of ancient wine that fills the throat with leeches. (*They fight.*)

MAN 3   We'll have to separate them.

MAN 2   So they don't devour each other.

MAN 3   Even though I'd gain my freedom!

(*The* DIRECTOR *and* MAN 1 *fight silently.*)

MAN 2 But I'd meet my death.

MAN 3 If I've got a slave . . .

MAN 2 It's because I am a slave.

MAN 3 But the two of us being slaves, we can break the chains in a different way.

MAN 1 I'll call Helen!

DIRECTOR I'll call Helen!

MAN 1 NO, please!

DIRECTOR NO, don't call her. I'll turn into whatever *you* desire.

(*Fighting, they disappear to the right.*)

MAN 3 We can push them and they'll fall into the well. Then you and I will be free.

MAN 2 You'll be free. Me, more enslaved than ever.

MAN 3 That doesn't matter. I'll push them. I'm longing to live in my green land, to be a shepherd, to drink water of the rock.

MAN 2 You forget that I'm strong when I want to be. When I was only a child I already yoked my father's oxen. Though my bones are covered with tiny little orchids, I've got a layer of muscles I can put to use whenever I want to.

MAN 3 (*softly*) It'll be much better for them, and for us. Let's go! The well is deep.

MAN 2 1 won't let you!

(*They fight.* MAN 2 *pushes* MAN 3 *and they disappear on the other side of the stage. The wall opens up and Juliet's tomb in Verona appears. Realistic scenery. Rose trees and ivy. Moonlight.* JULIET *is laid out in the tomb. She is wearing a white opera dress. Her two breasts of rose-colored celluloid are uncovered.*)

JULIET (*jumping out of the tomb*) Please. I haven't run into a girlfriend the whole time I've been banished, despite having passed through more than three thousand empty arches. Please. A little help. A little help and oceans of dreaminess. (*She sings.*)
  Oceans of dreaminess,
  a sea of white earth
  and empty arches in the sky.
  My train through ships, through seaweed,
  my train through time.
  Oceans of time.
  Seashore of woodcutter maggots
  and crystal dolphin through cherry trees.
  Oh, pure asbestos of termination! Oh, ruin!
  Oh, archless solitude! Sea of dreams!

(*A commotion of swords and voices breaks out at the back of the stage.*)

JULIET More people all the time. They'll wind up invading my tomb and occupying my very own bed. Me, I don't care about their arguments concerning love or the theater. What I want is to love.

WHITE HORSE 1 (*appearing*) To love. (*The* HORSE *has a sword in his hand.*)

JULIET Yes. With a love that lasts only a moment.

WHITE HORSE 1 I've waited for you in the garden.

JULIET You mean in the tomb.

WHITE HORSE 1 You're still as crazy as ever. Juliet, when will you ever realize the perfection of one day? One day, with a morning and an afternoon.

JULIET And with a night.

WHITE HORSE 1 The night's not the day. And in one day you'll succeed in freeing yourself of anguish, and scare away the impassive walls of marble.

JULIET How?

WHITE HORSE 1 Mount my rump.

JULIET Why?

WHITE HORSE 1 (*moving close to her*) To take you away.

JULIET Where?

WHITE HORSE 1 To the darkness. In the darkness there are soft branches. The cemetery for wings is a thousand surfaces thick.

JULIET (*trembling*) And there, what will you give me?

WHITE HORSE 1 I'll give you the quietest part of the darkness.

JULIET The day?

WHITE HORSE 1 Moss without light. The touch that devours tiny worlds with the tips of the fingers.

JULIET Was it you who were going to show me the perfection of one day?

WHITE HORSE 1 In order to make you pass into the night.

JULIET (*furiously*) And what've I got to do with the night, stupid horse? What've I got to learn from its stars or from its drunks? I'll be forced to use rat poison to free myself of annoying people. But *I* don't want to kill rats. They bring me tiny pianos and little lacquer brushes.

WHITE HORSE 1 Juliet, night isn't a moment, but one moment can last the whole night long.

JULIET (*weeping*) Enough. I don't want to listen to you anymore. Why do you want to take me away? It's a trick, love's word, a broken mirror, footsteps in the water. Then you'd leave me in the tomb again, just as everyone does when trying to convince those listening to them that true love is impossible. Now I'm tired, so I'll stand up and ask for help in throwing out of my tomb all those who theorize about my heart and all those who open my mouth with little marble tweezers.

WHITE HORSE 1 The day's a ghost that sits down.

JULIET But I've known women killed by the sun.

WHITE HORSE 1 Understand one single day fully, so you can love every night.

JULIET Just like everyone! Just like everyone! Just like men, just like trees, just like horses. Everything you're trying to show me, I know perfectly. The moon pushes uninhabited houses gently along, causes the fall of columns, and offers tiny torches to worms, so they can get into the interior of cherries. The moon carries the masks of meningitis into bedrooms, fills the wombs of pregnant women with cold water and, as soon as I'm not careful, throws handfuls of grass on my shoulders. Don't look at me, horse, with that desire I know so well. When I was very small I used to look at the beautiful cows grazing in the meadows of Verona. Later I saw them painted in my books, yet I always remembered them while passing butcher shops.

WHITE HORSE 1 Love that only lasts a moment.

JULIET Yes, a minute; and Juliet, so alive, so joyous, free of the piercing swarm of magnifying glasses. Juliet in the beginning, Juliet at the edge of the city.

(*The commotion of swords and voices breaks out again at the back of the stage.*)

WHITE HORSE 1
    Love. To love. Love.
    Love of the snail, nail, nail, nail,
    sticking out its horns in the sun so pale.
    To love. Love. To love.
    Of the horse that's licking
    the salt in the dell. (*Dances*)

JULIET Yesterday they were forty and I was asleep. The spiders came, then came the little girls, and the young woman raped by the dog, who covered her face with geraniums, and yet I still kept calm. When nymphs talk about cheese it could be that of siren's milk or that of clover. But now they are four, they are four boys who wanted to fit me with a little clay phallus, and they were determined to paint an ink moustache on me.

WHITE HORSE 1
    Love. To love. Love.
    Love of Gnido with the he-goat,
    and the mule with the snail, nail, nail, nail,
    sticking out its horns in the sun so pale.

Of Jupiter with the peacock in the stable
and the horse neighing in the cathedral.

JULIET Four boys, horse. For quite some time I sensed the racket of their play but didn't awake until their knives flashed.

(*The* BLACK HORSE *appears. He has a tuft of feathers of the same color and a wheel in his hand.*)

BLACK HORSE Four boys? The whole world. One land of asphodels and another land of seeds. The dead go on arguing and the living use the scalpel. The whole world.

WHITE HORSE 1 On the shores of the Dead Sea grow some lovely apples composed of ash, but the ash is good.

BLACK HORSE Oh, freshness! Oh, pulp! Oh, dewdrops! I eat ash.

JULIET No, no, ash is good. Who's talking about ash?

WHITE HORSE 1 I'm not talking about ash. I'm talking about ash that has the shape of an apple.

BLACK HORSE Shape! Shape! Blood's anguished desire!

JULIET Riot!

BLACK HORSE The blood's anguished desire and the wheel's boredom!

(THE THREE WHITE HORSES *appear. They have long walking sticks of black lacquer.*)

THE THREE WHITE HORSES Shape and ash. Ash and shape. Mirror. And the one who can finish, let him put on the gold leaf.

JULIET (*wringing her hands*) Shape and ash.

BLACK HORSE Yes. You already know how well I behead doves. When 'rock' is said I comprehend 'air.' When 'air' is said I comprehend 'emptiness.' When 'emptiness' is said I comprehend 'beheaded dove.'

WHITE HORSE 1
    Love. To love. Love.
    Of the moon with the eggshell,
    of the egg yolk with the moon
    and the cloud with the eggshell.

THE THREE WHITE HORSES (*pounding on the floor with their walking sticks*)
    Love. To love. Love.
    Of the cow dung with the sun,
    of the sun with the dead cow
    and the beetle with the sun.

BLACK HORSE No matter how much you shake your walking sticks, things'll happen only as they must. You're damned! You rowdies! It's your fault I've got to make the rounds through the forest several times a week, searching for resin to stop up my ears and restore the silence that belongs to me. (*To* JULIET, *persuasively*) Get going Juliet. I've put out linen sheets for you. Now a fine rain crowned with ivy will begin to fall, one that will soak the heavens and the walls.

THE THREE WHITE HORSES We've got three black walking sticks.

WHITE HORSE 1 And a sword.

THE THREE WHITE HORSES (*to* JULIET) We've got to pass through your womb to find the resurrection of the horses.

BLACK HORSE Juliet, it's three in the morning; if you're not careful, the people will lock the door and you won't be able to get in.

THE THREE WHITE HORSES She'll still have the meadow and the mountain horizon.

BLACK HORSE Juliet, don't pay any attention. In the meadow is the peasant who eats his own snot, and the enormous foot that crushes the tiny mouse, and the army of earthworms that soaks the depraved grass with its slime.

WHITE HORSE 1 She'll still have her hard little breasts and besides, the bed for sleeping with horses has already been invented.

THE THREE WHITE HORSES (*waving their walking sticks*) And we want to go to bed.

WHITE HORSE 1 With Juliet. I was in the tomb that last night, and I know everything that happened.

THE THREE WHITE HORSES (*furiously*) We want to go to bed!

WHITE HORSE 1 Because we're real horses, carriage horses that've broken the wooden stalls and stable windows with our penises.

THE THREE WHITE HORSES Get undressed, Juliet, and leave your rump uncovered for the lash of our tails. We want to be resurrected!

(*Juliet takes refuge with the* BLACK HORSE.)

BLACK HORSE She's crazy, more than crazy.

JULIET (*pulling herself together*) I'm not afraid of any of you. You want to go to bed with me? Right? Well now I'm the one who wants to go to bed with all of you, but I'll give the orders, I'll direct, I'll mount you, I'll cut off your manes with my scissors.

BLACK HORSE Who's going to pass through whom? Oh, love, my love, you need to pass your light through those obscure fevers! Oh, sea resting against the twilight, and flower in the ass of the dead man!

JULIET (*energetically*) I'm not a slave just so they can pierce my breasts with scented punches, nor an oracle for those trembling with love at the edge of the cities. My whole dream had to do with the smell of the fig tree and the waist of the one who cuts the shoots of wheat. Nobody through me! I through all of you!

BLACK HORSE Sleep. Sleep. Sleep.

THE THREE WHITE HORSES (*grab their walking sticks and a jet of water shoots out of the metal caps*) We're urinating on you, we're urinating on you. We're urinating on you the way we urinate on mares, the way the she-goat urinates on the snout of the he-goat and the sky urinates on the magnolias to turn them leathery.

BLACK HORSE (*to* JULIET) To your place. Let nobody pass through you.

JULIET I'm to shut up then? A new-born child is beautiful.

THE THREE WHITE HORSES Beautiful. And he'd drag his shirttail across the whole sky.

(MAN 1 *appears at the right of the stage with the* STAGE DIRECTOR. *The* STAGE DIRECTOR *comes out as in the First Act,* * *transformed into a white Harlequin.*)

MAN 1 Enough, gentlemen!

DIRECTOR Theater in the open air!

WHITE HORSE 1 No. Now we've inaugurated the true theater, the theater beneath the sand.

BLACK HORSE So the truth about tombs be known.

THE THREE WHITE HORSES Tombs with advertisements, gas spotlights, and long rows of orchestra seats.

MAN 1 Yes! We've already taken the first step. But I know positively that three of you are hiding, that three of you are still swimming on the surface. (THE THREE WHITE HORSES *nervously crowd together.*) While accustomed to the coachman's whip and the blacksmith's tongs, you're still afraid of the truth.

BLACK HORSE When they've taken off the last suit of blood, truth will be a nettle, a devoured crab, a bit of leather behind the windowpanes.

MAN 1 They should disappear immediately from this place. They're afraid of the audience. I know the truth, I know they're not looking for Juliet and that they're concealing a desire that wounds me, and which I can read in their eyes.

BLACK HORSE Not one desire; all desires. Like you.

---

* An obvious lapse by the author. – Trans.

MAN 1 I don't have any more than one desire.

WHITE HORSE 1 Like horses, nobody forgets his mask.

MAN 1 I don't have a mask.

DIRECTOR There's nothing but masks. I was right, Gonzalo. If we make fun of the mask, it'll hang us from a tree just like that boy in America.

JULIET (*weeping*) Mask!

WHITE HORSE 1 Shape.

DIRECTOR In the middle of the street, the mask buttons us up and lets us avoid that indiscreet blush which sometimes rises to our cheeks. In the bedroom, when we stick our fingers in our nose or delicately explore our rear, the plaster of the mask presses down so heavily on our flesh that we're barely able to lie down on the bed.

MAN 1 (*to the* DIRECTOR) My struggle was with the mask, until I succeeded in seeing you naked. (*He embraces him.*)

WHITE HORSE 1 (*mockingly*) A lake is a surface.

MAN 1 (*irritated*) Or a volume!

WHITE HORSE 1 (*laughing*) A volume is a thousand surfaces.

DIRECTOR (*to* MAN 1) Don't embrace me, Gonzalo. Your love lives only in the presence of witnesses. Didn't you already kiss me enough in the ruin? I despise your elegance and your theater.

(*They fight.*)

MAN 1 I love you in front of others because I abhor the mask, and because now I've succeeded in ripping it off you.

DIRECTOR Why am I so weak?

MAN 1 (*struggling*) I love you.

DIRECTOR (*struggling*) I spit on you.

JULIET They're fighting!

BLACK HORSE They're loving each other.

THE THREE WHITE HORSES
    Love, love, love.
    Love of the one with the two
    and love of the three that's smothered
    by being the one between the two.

MAN 1 I'll undress your skeleton.

DIRECTOR My skeleton has seven lights.

MAN 1 That's easy for my seven hands.

DIRECTOR My skeleton has seven shadows.

THE THREE WHITE HORSES Leave him alone, leave him alone.

WHITE HORSE 1 (*to* MAN 1) I order you to leave him alone.

(*The* HORSES *separate* MAN 1 *and the* DIRECTOR.)

DIRECTOR (*overjoyed and embracing* WHITE HORSE 1) Though a slave of the lion, I can be a friend of the horse.

WHITE HORSE 1(*embracing him*) My love.

DIRECTOR I'll plunge my hands into the big purses and then fling the coins and the sums covered with bread crumbs into the muck.

JULIET (*to the* BLACK HORSE) Please!

BLACK HORSE (*nervously*) Wait.

MAN 1 The hour hasn't arrived yet when the horses carry away a nude that I've turned white by the force of my tears.

(THE THREE WHITE HORSES *detain* MAN 1.)

MAN 1 (*energetically*) Enrique!

DIRECTOR Enrique? There you have Enrique.

(*He quickly takes off his costume and throws it behind a column. Underneath he is wearing a very delicate woman's ballet costume. From behind the column, Enrique's costume appears. This character is the same white Harlequin, now with a pale yellow mask.*)

THE HARLEQUIN COSTUME I'm cold. Electric light. Bread. They were burning rubber. (*Stops in a rigid position.*)

DIRECTOR (*to* MAN 1) Won't you come along with me now, with Guillermina of the Horses?

WHITE HORSE 1 Moon and vixen, and bottle of the little taverns.

DIRECTOR Pass through me yourselves, and boats and regiments, and if the storks want to, they can pass through me also. Such a female am I!

THE THREE WHITE HORSES Guillermina!

DIRECTOR Not Guillermina. I'm not Guillermina, I'm Dominga de los Negritos.

(*He rips off the chiffon costume and emerges dressed in full-length tights completely covered with little bells. He throws the chiffon costume behind the column and disappears, followed by the* HORSES. *Then the woman's* BALLET COSTUME *character enters.*)

THE BALLET COSTUME Gui-guiller-guillermi-guillermina. Na-nami-namiller-namillergui. Let me in or let me out. (*Falls to the ground asleep.*)

MAN 1 Enrique, be careful on the stairs!

DIRECTOR (*offstage*) Moon and vixen of the drunken sailors!

JULIET (*to the* BLACK HORSE) Give me the medicine to make me sleep.

BLACK HORSE Sand.

MAN 1 (*shouting*) Into a moon-fish, I only wish you were a moon-fish! Turn into a moon-fish! (*He exits violently.*)

THE HARLEQUIN COSTUME Enrique. Electric light. Bread. They were burning rubber.

(MAN 2 *and* MAN 3 *enter from the left.* MAN 2 *is now the woman in the black pajamas and poppies of the First Scene.* MAN 3, *not transformed.*)

MAN 2 He loves me so much that if he were to see us together, he'd be capable of murdering us. Let's go. Now I will serve you forever.

MAN 3 Your beauty was so lovely there beneath the columns.

JULIET (*to the couple*) Let's close the door.

MAN 2 The theater door never closes.

JULIET It's raining hard, my dear girl.

(*It begins to rain.* MAN 3 *pulls out a mask with an ardent expression and covers his face with it.*)

MAN 3 (*gallantly*) And couldn't I stay here in this place to sleep?

JULIET Why?

MAN 3 To enjoy you. (*He talks with her*)

MAN 2 (*to the* BLACK HORSE) Did you see a man with a black beard leaving, dark hair, whose patent leather shoes squeaked a bit?

BLACK HORSE I didn't see him.

MAN 3 (*to* JULIET) And who better than I to defend you?

JULIET And who more worthy of love than your girlfriend?

MAN 3 My girlfriend? (*Furious*) It's your fault I always lose! She's not my girlfriend, she's a mask, an old mop, a weak lap dog.

(*He undresses her violently, pulling off her pajamas, her wig, and* MAN 2 *emerges, without a beard, in his costume of the First Scene.*)

MAN 2 For the love of God!

MAN 3 (*to* JULIET) I brought him here disguised in order to protect him from bandits. Kiss my hand, kiss the hand of your protector.

(*The* PAJAMAS COSTUME *with poppies appears. The face of this character is smooth, white and curved like an ostrich egg.* MAN 3 *pushes* MAN 2 *so that he disappears to the right of the stage.*)

MAN 2 For the love of God!

(*The* PAJAMAS COSTUME *sits down on the steps and slowly hits his smooth face with his hands, until the end of the scene.*)

MAN 3 (*pulling a large red cape from his pocket and throwing it over his shoulders, joining himself to* JULIET) 'Look, love, what envious streaks do lace the severing clouds in yonder east.' The wind does break the branches of the cypress tree . . .

JULIET It doesn't go like that!

MAN 3 . . . And visits, there in India, every woman who has hands of water.

BLACK HORSE (*shaking the wheel*) It's going to close!

JULIET It's raining hard!

MAN 3 Wait, wait. Now the nightingale sings.

JULIET (*trembling*) The nightingale, my God! The nightingale . . . !

BLACK HORSE Don't let it take you by surprise! (*He grabs her quickly and lays her out in the tomb.*)

JULIET (*falling asleep*) The nightingale . . . !

BLACK HORSE (*exiting*) Tomorrow I'll return with the sand.

JULIET Tomorrow.

MAN 3 (*next to the tomb*) My love, come back! The wind does break the leaves of the maple tree. What've you done? (*He embraces her.*)

VOICE (*offstage*) Enrique!

THE HARLEQUIN COSTUME Enrique.

THE BALLET COSTUME Guillermina. Put an end to it once and for all! (*Weeps*)

MAN 3 Wait, wait. Now the nightingale sings. (*A ship's horn is heard.* MAN 3 *places his mask over* JULIET's *face and covers her body with the red cape.*) It's raining so heavily. (*He opens up an umbrella and exits on tiptoe.*)

MAN 1 (*entering*) Enrique, how come you've returned?

THE HARLEQUIN COSTUME Enrique, how come you've returned?

MAN 1 Why are you making fun of me?

THE HARLEQUIN COSTUME Why are you making fun of me?

MAN 1 (*embracing* THE HARLEQUIN COSTUME) You had to come back for me, for my inexhaustible love, after having conquered the grass and the horses.

THE HARLEQUIN COSTUME The horses!

MAN 1 Tell me, tell me that you've come back for me!

THE HARLEQUIN COSTUME (*in a weak voice*) I'm cold. Electric light. Bread. They were burning rubber.

MAN 1 (*violently embracing* THE HARLEQUIN COSTUME) Enrique!

THE HARLEQUIN COSTUME (*in an ever weaker voice*) Enrique . . .

THE BALLET COSTUME (*in a tenuous voice*) Guillermina . . .

MAN 1 (*throwing* THE HARLEQUIN COSTUME *to the ground and climbing the steps*) Enriqueee!

THE HARLEQUIN COSTUME (*on the ground*)
Enriqueeeeee . . .

(*The character with the face of an egg beats incessantly on his head with his hands. Above the noise of the rain sings the true nightingale.*)

CURTAIN

*Scene 5

(*In the center of the stage is a bed, facing the audience and perpendicular to the floor, as though painted by a primitive, on which there is a Red Nude crowned with blue thorns. In the background, some arches and stairs leading to the boxes of a large theater. To the right, the facade of a university building. On raising the curtain, a salvo of applause is heard.*)

NUDE When will all of you be finished?

MALE NURSE (*entering rapidly*) When all the commotion ceases.

NUDE What are they asking for?

MALE NURSE They're demanding the death of the stage director.

NUDE And what are they saying about me?

MALE NURSE Nothing.

NUDE And about Gonzalo, has anybody heard anything?

MALE NURSE They're looking for him in the ruin.

NUDE I wish to die. How many glasses of blood have you taken out of me?

MALE NURSE Fifty. Now I'll give you the gall and then, at eight, I'll come back with the scalpel to deepen the wound in your side.

NUDE That's the one that has more vitamins.

MALE NURSE Yes.

NUDE Did they let out the people beneath the sand?

MALE NURSE Just the opposite. The soldiers and engineers are closing off all the exits.

NUDE How long before we reach Jerusalem?

MALE NURSE Three stations, if there's enough coal left.

NUDE Father, take away this cup of bitterness from me.

MALE NURSE Shut up. This is already the third thermometer you've broken.

(*The STUDENTS appear. They are wearing black student gowns and red academic sashes.*)

STUDENT 1 Why don't we file through the irons?

STUDENT 2 The side street's full of armed people and it's difficult to escape that way.

STUDENT 3 And the horses?

STUDENT 1 The horses were able to escape by breaking through the ceiling above the stage.

STUDENT 4 When I was locked up in the tower I saw them going up the hill in a group. They were with the stage director.

STUDENT 1 Doesn't this theater have an orchestra pit?

STUDENT 2 But even the orchestra pits are being packed by the audience. It's better to stay put.

(*A salvo of applause is heard. The MALE NURSE raises the NUDE to a sitting position and arranges his pillows.*)

NUDE I'm thirsty.

MALE NURSE Somebody's already been sent to the theater for water.

STUDENT 4 The first bomb of the revolution blew the Professor of Rhetoric's head off.

STUDENT 2 To the great joy of his wife, who'll now be working so hard she'll have to put a couple of faucets on her tits.

STUDENT 3 They say a horse would go up to the terrace with her.

STUDENT 1 She was precisely the one who saw everything that was happening through the skylight and gave out a shout of alarm.

STUDENT 4 And even though the poets set up a ladder so they could murder her, she kept on shouting and a crowd gathered.

STUDENT 2 What's her name?

STUDENT 3 Her name is Helen.

STUDENT 1 (*aside*) Selene.

STUDENT 2 (*to STUDENT 1*) What's the matter with you?

STUDENT 1 I'm afraid to go out into the air.

(*The two THIEVES come down the stairs. Several LADIES in evening dress leave their boxes in a rush. The STUDENTS argue.*)

LADY 1 Will the coaches still be at the door?

LADY 2 How ghastly!

LADY 3 They found the stage director inside the tomb.

LADY 1 And Romeo?

LADY 4 They were undressing him when we left.

BOY 1 The audience wants the poet to be dragged off by his hair.

LADY 1 But, why? It was a delightful drama, and the revolution doesn't have any right to profane tombs.

---

* The holograph manuscript is missing Scene 4.

LADY 2 Their voices were so alive, and their appearances, too. What need was there for us to lick the skeletons?

BOY 1 She's right. The act in the tomb was prodigiously developed. But I discovered the deception when I saw Juliet's feet. They were so tiny.

LADY 2 And delightful! You'd never ever want to find fault with them.

BOY 1 Yes, but they were too small to be the feet of a man. They were too perfect and too feminine. They were a man's feet, feet invented by a man.

LADY 2 How ghastly!

(*From the theater come murmurs and the clashing of swords.*)

LADY 3 Won't we be able to leave?

BOY 1 At this moment the revolution's reaching the cathedral. Let's go up the stairs.

(*They exit.*)

STUDENT 4 The rioting started when they saw that Romeo and Juliet really loved each other.

STUDENT 2 It happened for precisely the opposite reason. The rioting started when they observed that they didn't love each other, that they could never love each other.

STUDENT 4 The audience has a genius for discovering everything and for that reason they protested.

STUDENT 2 For precisely that reason. The skeletons loved each other and were yellowed by ardent flame, but the costumes didn't love each other and several times the audience saw Juliet's train covered with dirty little toads.

STUDENT 4 People forget about the costumes during performances, and the revolution broke out when they found the true Juliet underneath the seats and covered with cotton balls so she wouldn't scream.

STUDENT 1 There's everyone's big mistake and for that reason the theater's in the throes of death. The audience shouldn't try to penetrate the silk and cardboard that the poet erects in his bedroom. Romeo could be a bird and Juliet could be a stone. Romeo could be a grain of salt and Juliet could be a map. What difference does it make to the audience?

STUDENT 4 None at all. But a bird can't be a cat, nor can a stone be a tidal wave.

STUDENT 2 It's a question of form, of masks. A cat could be a frog and the winter moon could very well be a bundle of firewood covered with terrified maggots. The audience is to fall asleep upon the words and they must not see through the column to the sheep bleating and the clouds traveling across the sky.

STUDENT 4 For that reason revolution has broken out. The stage director opened the traps and the people were able to see how the poison of false veins caused the real death of many little children. It's not disguised shapes that uplift one's life but the barometer hair behind them.

STUDENT 2 In final analysis, do Romeo and Juliet necessarily have to be a man and a woman for the tomb scene to come off in a heart-rending and lifelike way?

STUDENT 1 It isn't necessary, and that was what the stage director brilliantly intended to demonstrate.

STUDENT 4 (*irritated*) It's not necessary? Then let the machines stop . . . and then go throw grains of wheat upon a field of steel.

STUDENT 2 And what would happen? What would happen is that the mushrooms would come and, perhaps, heartbeats would become even more intense and impassioned. What's the matter is that they know how much a grain of wheat nourishes and yet are unaware of how much a mushroom nourishes.

STUDENT 5 (*leaving the boxes*) The judge has arrived, and before murdering them they're going to make them repeat the scene in the tomb.

STUDENT 4 Let's go. You'll see that I'm right.

STUDENT 2 Yes. Let's go and see the last truly feminine Juliet who'll ever be seen in the theater.

(*They exit rapidly.*)

NUDE Father, forgive them; for they know not what they do.

MALE NURSE (*to* THE THIEVES) Why have you come at this late hour?

THE THIEVES The prompter made a mistake.

MALE NURSE They've given you the injections?

THE THIEVES Yes.

(*They sit down at the foot of the bed with some burning candles. The stage is left in semidarkness. The* PROMPTER *appears.*)

MALE NURSE Is this any time to give the call?

PROMPTER I beg you to pardon me, but Joseph of Arimathea's beard was lost.

MALE NURSE Is the operating room ready?

PROMPTER Only the candlesticks; the chalice and the ampoules of camphorated oil are missing.

MALE NURSE Hurry up.

(*The Prompter exits.*)

NUDE Much longer?

MALE NURSE Not much. They've already given the third bell. When the Emperor dresses up as Pontius Pilate.

BOY 1 (*appearing with the* LADIES) Please! Don't be overcome with panic.

LADY 1 It's terrible to get lost in a theater and not find the exit.

LADY 2 What frightened me more than anything were the cardboard wolf and the four snakes in the tin tank.

LADY 3 When we were climbing the mountain over by the ruin we thought we saw the light of dawn, but we stumbled into the curtains and now I've come back here with my lamé shoes all stained with oil.

LADY 4 (*peering out from behind the arches*) They're performing the tomb scene again. Now it's certain the fire'll break through the doors, because when I saw it just a moment ago, the watchmen's hands were scorched and they couldn't contain it.

BOY 1 From the branches of that tree we can reach one of the balconies and from there we'll shout for help.

MALE NURSE (*in a loud voice*) When is the death knell going to start?

(*A bell is heard.*)

THE THIEVES (*raising their candlesticks*) Holy. Holy. Holy.

NUDE Father, into thy hands I commend my spirit.

MALE NURSE You're two minutes ahead of time.

NUDE It's just that the nightingale's already sung.

MALE NURSE That's true. And the pharmacies are open for the mortal agony.

NUDE For the mortal agony of man alone, on the platforms and in the trains.

MALE NURSE (*in a loud voice and looking at his watch*) Bring me the sheet. Be very careful that the wind that's got to blow won't send your wigs flying. Hurry up.

THE THIEVES Holy. Holy. Holy.

NUDE Everything has been consummated.

(*The bed turns on an axis and the* NUDE *disappears. On the other side of the bed* MAN 1, *stretched out, appears, still with his tails and black beard.*)

MAN 1 (*closing his eyes*) Mortal agony!

(*The light takes on the strong silvery tint of a movie screen. The arches and the stairs in the background are tinted by a grainy blue light. The* MALE NURSE *and the* THIEVES *disappear dancing, without turning their backs to the audience. The* STUDENTS *enter from under one of the arches. They are carrying little electric pocket lamps.*)

STUDENT 4 The audience's attitude was detestable.

STUDENT 1 Detestable. A spectator should never be part of the drama. When people go to the aquarium they don't murder the sea snakes or the water rats or the fish covered with leprosy, rather they run their eyes over the glass and learn.

STUDENT 4 Romeo was a man thirty years old and Juliet a boy of fifteen. The audience's censure was effective.

STUDENT 2 The stage director brilliantly prevented the bulk of the spectators from becoming aware of that, but the horses and the revolution have destroyed his plans.

STUDENT 4 What's inadmissible is that they murdered them.

STUDENT 1 And that they also murdered the true Juliet, who was moaning underneath the seats.

STUDENT 4 Out of pure curiosity, just to see what they had inside of them.

STUDENT 3 And what have they brought to light? A cluster of wounds and an absolute disorientation.

STUDENT 4 The repetition of the act was marvelous because they undoubtedly loved each other with an incalculable love, although *I* don't justify it. When the nightingale sang I couldn't contain my tears.

STUDENT 3 Or anyone else. But later they brandished their knives and walking sticks because the words were stronger than they were, and doctrine, when it lets its hair down, can trample without fear even the most innocent of truths.

STUDENT 5 (*overjoyed*) Look, I've succeeded in getting one of Juliet's shoes. The nuns were preparing her for burial and I stole it.

STUDENT 4 (*seriously*) Which Juliet?

STUDENT 5 Which Juliet would it be? The one who was on stage, the one with the most beautiful feet in the world.

STUDENT 4 (*astonished*) But haven't you realized yet that the Juliet who was in the tomb was a disguised youth a trick of the stage director, and that the true Juliet lay gagged underneath the seats?

STUDENT 5 (*breaking into laughter*) Well, I like *her!* She seemed so very beautiful and even if she was a disguised youth, it doesn't matter at all to me; on the other hand, I never would have picked up the shoe of that girl all covered with dust who was moaning like a cat underneath the seats.

STUDENT 3   And yet they murdered her for that.

STUDENT 5   Because they're crazy. But I who climb the mountain twice each day and, when I finish studying, tend an enormous herd of bulls that I've got to struggle with and overpower at every instant, *I* don't have time to think about whether Juliet's a man or a woman or a child, but only to observe that I like her with such a joyous desire.

STUDENT 1   Magnificent! And if I want to fall in love with a crocodile?

STUDENT 5   You fall in love.

STUDENT 1   And if I want to fall in love with you?

STUDENT 5 (*flinging the shoe at him*) You fall in love also. I'd let you, and I'd carry you on my shoulders along the cliffs.

STUDENT 1   And we'd destroy everything.

STUDENT 5   Roofs and families.

STUDENT 1   And wherever love is talked about we'd run in there with our soccer shoes on, flinging mud all over the mirrors.

STUDENT 5   And we'll burn the book the clergymen read their mass from.

STUDENT 1   Let's go! Let's go quickly!

STUDENT 5   I've got four hundred bulls. With the ropes my father wove with esparto, we'll hitch them to the rocks to split them and then a volcano'll erupt.

STUDENT 1   Joy! Joy of the boys, and of the girls, and of the frogs, and of the tiny little wooden pegs!

PROMPTER (*appearing*) Gentlemen, descriptive geometry class.

MAN 1   Mortal agony.

(*The stage falls into semidarkness. The Students turn on their pocket lamps and enter the university building.*)

PROMPTER (*indifferently*) Don't make the windowpanes suffer.

STUDENT 5 (*fleeing through the arches with* STUDENT 1) Joy! Joy! Joy!

MAN 1   Mortal agony. Man's loneliness in a dream filled with elevators and trains, where you travel at unfathomable speeds. Loneliness of buildings, of street corners, of beaches, where now you'll never ever show up again.

LADY 1 (*on the stairs*) The same scenery? It's horrible!

BOY 1   One door'll be the real one!

LADY 2   Please! Don't let go of my hand!

BOY 1   When it starts to get light we'll be guided by the skylights.

LADY 3   I'm beginning to feel cold in this gown.

MAN 1 (*in a weak voice*) Enrique, Enrique!

LADY 1   What was that?

BOY 1   Keep calm.

(*The stage is in darkness. The pocket lamp of* BOY 1 *illuminates the dead face of* MAN 1.)

CURTAIN

Solo of the Silly Shepherd

(*Blue curtain. In the center, a large wardrobe full of white masks with various expressions. Each mask has a little white light in front of it. The* SILLY SHEPHERD *enters from the right. He is dressed in the skins of a barbarian and has a funnel filled with feathers and tiny wheels on his head. He is playing a barrel organ and dancing to a slow rhythm.*)

THE SHEPHERD
　　The silly shepherd tends the disguises,
　　　the disguises
　　of beggars and those who poetize,
　　those who kill the magpies
　　that fly over still waters at sunrise.
　　Disguise
　　of boys who use the fist that satisfies
　　and rot beneath where a mushroom lies.
　　Disguise
　　and crutch for the eagle of the skies.
　　Disguise of the disguise,
　　out of Cretan plaster they did devise
　　and now violet colors might arise
　　in time for Juliet's tragic demise.

　　Riddle, riddle, riddlize,
　　about a theater without seats to utilize
　　and a sky filled with chairs,
　　with the hollow left by the disguise.
　　Baa, baa, baa, disguises!

(*The masks bleat imitating sheep, and one coughs.*)

　　On mushrooms the horses gluttonize
　　and rot below weather vanes at moonrise.
　　The eagles use the fist that satisfies
　　and are stuck in mud below comet's skies.
　　And the comet devours the magpies
　　that scratch the chest of those who poetize.

Baa, baa, baa, disguises!
Europe pulls out her tits and sighs,
Asia has no theater seats to utilize
and America is a crocodile
that does not need a disguise.
Music, music, music-wise,
a jug and wounded barbs to finalize.

(*He pushes the wardrobe, which is mounted on wheels, and disappears. The masks bleat.*)

Scene 6

(*The same set as in the First Scene. To the left, a large horse's head placed on the floor. To the right, a huge eye and a group of trees with clouds leaning against the wall. The* STAGE DIRECTOR *enters with the* PRESTIDIGITATOR, *who is dressed in tails, a white satin cape that reaches down to his feet and has a top hat on. The* STAGE DIRECTOR *has on the same costume as in the First Scene.*)

DIRECTOR A prestidigitator cannot resolve this matter, nor a doctor, nor an astronomer, nor anyone. It's very simple to set the lions free and then rain sulphur down on them. Don't go on any further.

PRESTIDIGITATOR It seems to me that you, man of masks, do not remember that we use the dark curtain.

DIRECTOR When folks are in heaven; but tell me, what curtain can one use in a place where the wind is so violent that it strips people's clothing off them, and even little boys carry tiny knives to rip up the drop curtains?

PRESTIDIGITATOR Naturally, the prestidigitator's curtain presupposes an order within the obscurity of the trick; but for that reason, why did you choose such a stale tragedy and not do an original drama?

DIRECTOR In order to express what happens every day in all the great cities and in the country, by means of an example that's occurred only once but is recognized by everyone in spite of its originality. I could have chosen Oedipus or Othello. On the other hand, if I had raised the curtain with the original truth, they'd have splattered blood all over the seats right from the first scenes.

PRESTIDIGITATOR If you had employed 'Diana's flower,' which Shakespeare's anguish made ironic use of in *A Midsummer Night's Dream*, it's likely that the performance would have turned out to be a success. If love is pure chance and Titania, Queen of the Fairies, fell in love with an

ass, then, by the same reasoning, there wouldn't be anything extraordinary about Gonzalo drinking in the 'music hall' with a boy dressed in white sitting on his lap.

DIRECTOR I beg you, don't go on any further.

PRESTIDIGITATOR Construct an arch out of wire, put up a curtain and a tree of fresh leaves, open and close the curtain on time and nobody'll be surprised that the tree turns into a serpent's egg. What you wanted to do was murder the dove and leave in its place a piece of marble covered with tiny drops of long-winded spittle.

DIRECTOR It wasn't possible to do anything else. My friends and I dug the tunnel under the sand without the people of the city ever noticing it. Many workers and students helped us, who now deny having worked on it despite having their hands full of cuts. When we reached the tomb we raised the curtain.

PRESTIDIGITATOR And what kind of theater can come out of a tomb?

DIRECTOR All theater comes from confined dampness. All true theater has a profound stench of overripe moon. When the costumes speak, the living characters are already buttons of bone on the walls of the calvary. I made the tunnel in order to take possession of the costumes and, through them, show the profile of a hidden force at a moment when the audience, fully animated and subjugated by the action, didn't have any other choice but be attentive.

PRESTIDIGITATOR Without any effort I can turn a bottle of ink into a severed hand full of ancient rings.

DIRECTOR (*irritated*) But that's deception! That's theater! If I spent three days battling the roots and the pounding waves, it was to destroy theater.

PRESTIDIGITATOR That I knew.

DIRECTOR And to demonstrate that if Romeo and Juliet are in mortal agony and die in order to come back to life smiling when the curtain falls, then my characters, on the other hand, burn the curtain and truly die in the presence of the spectators. The horses, the sea, the army of grasses prevented that. But some day, when they burn down all the theaters, they'll find in the sofas, behind the mirrors and inside the goblets of golden cardboard, the gathering of our dead, locked up in there by the audience. One's got to destroy the theater or live in the theater! Hissing from the windows won't work! And if the dogs are whining in a loving way, one's got to raise the curtain without precautions. I knew a man who'd sweep the roof and clean the skylights and railings only out of gallantry towards the sky.

PRESTIDIGITATOR If you advance one step higher, man'll seem like a blade of grass to you.

DIRECTOR Not a blade of grass, but certainly a navigator.

PRESTIDIGITATOR I can turn a navigator into a sewing needle.

DIRECTOR That's precisely what's done in the theater. For that reason I dared to perform an extremely difficult poetic trick in hopes that love would impetuously rip the costumes to shreds and then give them a new form.

PRESTIDIGITATOR When *you* say 'love,' I am astounded.

DIRECTOR You're astounded, by what?

PRESTIDIGITATOR I see a sandy landscape in a cloudy mirror.

DIRECTOR And what else?

PRESTIDIGITATOR That the dawn never ends.

DIRECTOR That's possible.

PRESTIDIGITATOR (*indifferently and tapping his fingers on the horse head*) Love.

DIRECTOR (*sitting down at the table*) When you say 'love,' I am astounded.

PRESTIDIGITATOR You're astounded, by what?

DIRECTOR I see each grain of sand turning into an ant that's overflowing with life.

PRESTIDIGITATOR And what else?

DIRECTOR That night is falling every five minutes.

PRESTIDIGITATOR (*staring at him*) That's possible. (*He pauses.*) But, what can one expect from a person who inaugurates the Theater Beneath the Sand? If you were to open that door, this place would be filled with mastiffs, with madmen, with rain, with monstrous leaves, with sewer rats. Whoever thought all the doors of a drama could be broken down?

DIRECTOR Breaking down all the doors is the only way in which the drama can justify itself, and by seeing, with its own eyes, that law is a wall that dissolves into the tiniest drop of blood. I'm disgusted by the dying man who draws a door on the wall with his finger and peacefully falls asleep. True drama is an arena made up of arches, where wind and moon and creatures enter and exit without ever having a place to rest. Here you are, standing in a theater where authentic dramas have been performed and where a real combat has raged, one that's cost the lives of all the players. (*He weeps.*)

SERVANT (*entering hastily*) Sir.

DIRECTOR What is it?

(*Enter the* HARLEQUIN COSTUME *and a* WOMAN *dressed in black, her face covered by a heavy tulle netting that prevents one from seeing her visage.*)

WOMAN Where is my son?

DIRECTOR What son?

WOMAN My son Gonzalo.

DIRECTOR (*irritated*) When the performance ended he went rushing down into the pit with that boy who's here with you. Then the prompter saw him stretched out on the imperial bed in the wardrobe. You shouldn't ask *me* anything. Today all that is below the ground.

HARLEQUIN COSTUME (*weeping*) Enrique.

WOMAN Where's my son? This morning the fishermen brought me an enormous moon-fish, pale, decomposed, and they shouted at me: 'Here you have your son!' While a thin trickle of blood flowed steadily from the fish's mouth, the children laughed and painted the soles of their boots red. When I closed my door I heard the people from the market dragging him down to the sea.

HARLEQUIN COSTUME Down to the sea.

DIRECTOR The performance ended hours ago and I'm not responsible for what's happened.

WOMAN I'll press charges and plead for justice in front of everyone. (*She starts to exit.*)

PRESTIDIGITATOR Madam, you won't be able to get out that way.

WOMAN You're right. The lobby's totally dark. (*She starts to exit through the door on the right.*)

DIRECTOR Not that way, either. You'll fall through the skylights.

PRESTIDIGITATOR Madam, be so good as to allow me. I'll show you the way.

(*He takes off his cape and covers the* WOMAN *with it. Then he passes his hands over it two or three times, pulls the cape away, and the* WOMAN *has disappeared. The* SERVANT *pushes the* HARLEQUIN COSTUME *and makes it disappear to the left. The* PRESTIDIGITATOR *takes out a large white fan and begins to fan himself while singing softly.*)

DIRECTOR I'm cold.

PRESTIDIGITATOR How's that?

DIRECTOR I'm telling you I'm cold.

PRESTIDIGITATOR (*fanning himself*) It's a pretty word, 'cold.'

DIRECTOR Thank you very much for everything.

PRESTIDIGITATOR You're welcome. Taking things away is easy. What's difficult is putting them back.

DIRECTOR It's much more difficult to replace them with other things.

SERVANT (*entering after having taken the* HARLEQUIN COSTUME *away*) It's a little cool. Would you like me to put some heat on?

DIRECTOR No. One's got to endure everything because we've broken down the doors, we've razed the roof, and now we're left with only the four walls of the drama. (*The* SERVANT *exits through the center door.*) But it doesn't matter. There's still soft grass to sleep on.

PRESTIDIGITATOR To sleep!

DIRECTOR In the final analysis, to sleep is to plant.

SERVANT Sir! I can't endure this cold.

DIRECTOR I told you that we've got to endure it, that we've got to overcome any trick whatsoever. Fulfill your obligations.

(*The* DIRECTOR *puts on some gloves and pulls up the collar of his tails, shivering terribly. The* SERVANT *disappears.*)

PRESTIDIGITATOR (*fanning himself*) But is the cold such a bad thing?

DIRECTOR (*in a weak voice*) The cold is a dramatic element like any other.

SERVANT (*sticking his head out through the door, his hands crossed over his chest*) Sir!

DIRECTOR What?

SERVANT (*falling to his knees*) There is the public.

DIRECTOR (*falling face down across the table*) Show them in!

(*The* PRESTIDIGITATOR, *seated near the head of the horse, whistles very cheerfully and fans himself. The whole left corner of the stage set opens up and a sky of long clouds, vividly illuminated, appears. Then there is a slow shower of rigid white gloves, well spaced apart.*)

VOICE (*offstage*) Sir.

VOICE (*offstage*) What?

VOICE (*offstage*) The public.

VOICE (*offstage*) Show them in.

(*The* PRESTIDIGITATOR *vigorously waves his fan in the air. On stage, flakes of snow begin to fall.*)

SLOW CURTAIN

Saturday, August 22, 1930.

The Resistible Rise of Arturo Ui

Bertolt Brecht

Introduction

Bertolt Brecht was born in Augsburg, Germany, in 1898. He began working in the theatre in the 1920s, eventually in Berlin, and had success most notably with *The Threepenny Opera*, an adaptation of John Gay's *The Beggar's Opera*, in 1928 (the extensive contributions to this work by Elizabeth Hauptmann went unacknowledged). In this period he adapted Marlowe's *Edward II* and Shakespeare's *Macbeth* and *Hamlet*. He also became deeply interested in Marxism. In 1933, after the night of the Reichstag fire, Brecht fled Nazi Germany. He eventually went to Sweden and Finland before arriving in the United States in 1941. Between 1933 and 1941 Brecht wrote, among other works, *Roundheads and Peakheads* (an adaptation of Shakespeare's *Measure for Measure*), *The Good Person of Szechwan*, *Mother Courage and Her Children*, and *The Resistible Rise of Arturo Ui* (1941) (an adaptation of Shakespeare's *Richard III*). Margarete Steffin made uncredited contributions to a number of these works. In the United States, Brecht worked on *The Caucasian Chalk Circle*, *The Life of Galileo*, and an adaptation of Webster's *The Duchess of Malfi*, and tried his hand in Hollywood at screen writing. In 1947, as the cold war took shape, Brecht was questioned by the House UnAmerican Activities Committee ('unamerican' reminding him disgustedly of the Nazis' *undeutsch* – ungerman), and he returned to Europe, first to Switzerland and then to East Germany. In Berlin he helped found the Berliner Ensemble, the renowned theatre company dedicated in large part to the production of Brecht's plays. During this time he also worked on Shakespeare's *Coriolanus*. Brecht died in 1956, one of the most important figures in twentieth-century theatre.

The Resistible Rise of Arturo Ui was not performed for its intended American audience and was first produced in 1960 by the Berliner Ensemble. It has also been mounted by the Royal National Theatre in London in 1991 (see Eddershaw: 140–149).

Much of Brecht's theatre and theatre theory fall under the rubric of what he called 'epic theatre,' which he distinguished from traditional, conservative, 'aristotelian' theatre. Unlike traditional theatre, epic theatre engages the spectator's rational powers of observation rather than playing on the spectator's feelings, proceeding by argument rather than suggestion. Epic theatre argues that social being determines thought (that individuals think the things that society has primed them to think) and that the human being is alterable and able to alter, not fixed and at the mercy of destiny or insurmountable forces (Brecht: 37). It is in the context of epic theatre that Brecht's complex attitudes toward Shakespeare play themselves out. Brecht finds elements of Renaissance theatre that relate to epic theatre. Both expose the theatrical reality behind the representational illusion. Both proceed episodically through a large number of scenes. Both portray a broad swath of society – plays by Shakespeare and Brecht have equally large numbers of characters. Both present events from history and engage with questions of historical causation. Finally, Brecht claims to be interested in Shakespeare's ambiguities; he writes: 'There's nothing more stupid than to perform Shakespeare so that he's clear. He's by his very nature unclear. He's pure material' (quoted in Heinemann: 206). Brecht also writes that 'one has to grapple with Shakespeare as one does with life' (204). The trouble here, as Margot Heinemann points out, is that Brecht's plays are not ambiguous in the same way Shakespeare's are, and she questions whether Brecht is doing what he claims to be doing:

If, as he says, the power of Shakespeare's dramaturgy lies in the contradictions, the doubleness of character and action, and our conflicting response to it which compels us to think, don't the adaptations tend to harmonise and flatten out the effects, much as he convicts the bourgeois theatre of doing?

(1985: 223)

In order to understand what Brecht does with Shakespeare, it is necessary to look at what he doesn't like in Shakespeare's work. First, there is the emotional attachment to so-called great men. Even surpassing villains like Macbeth and Richard III retain some audience sympathy in Shakespeare. As Ernst Shürer writes: 'Brecht despised the romantic view of history that was prevalent in bourgeois society; his intention was to destroy the aura of greatness surrounding dictators, statesmen, politicians, who were often no more than political criminals' (149). As the Shakespearean actor notes in scene 6 of *Arturo Ui*, Shakespearean heroes provide 'A model of demagogy.' Moreover, as Heinemann writes, 'Thus performed, Shakespeare is of little or even negative value to modern spectators, who unlike Lear or Hamlet are small people, whose destinies are controlled not by fate or their own personal characters or actions but by the behaviour of collectives, large masses, social classes' (205). This raises the second major sticking point between Brecht and Shakespeare. Brecht's plays often conclude with an open-ended call to action: an intolerable situation has been presented; the audience is left with the question as to what to do about it. No answers are provided, but the underlying assumption is that concerted effort can help. *Richard III*, on the other hand, seems to end with cosmic inevitability, although the play's relation to that inevitability, and the place of the contrary force of human agency, remains ambiguous. Whereas Shakespeare presents this ambiguous relation to cosmic forces, Brecht presents an unambiguous opening onto the complexities of historical action. In this regard, as Robert Atkins demonstrates, one point of *Arturo Ui* is 'to attack and ridicule the Nazi pseudo-religion which was casting Hitler as Germany's new Messiah' (371).

The first and most obvious connection in *Arturo Ui* is between Nazism and American gangsterism à la Al Capone. The rise of Hitler is, for Brecht and Germany, '*the gangster play we know*' (quoted in Willett and Manheim: viii). The play was originally intended to show an American audience the thuggery of Hitler in terms with which it was familiar. As early as 1934, however, Brecht foresaw a satire 'on Hitler in the style of a Renaissance historian' (quoted in Willett and Manheim: 119) and 'saw something of the same bloodshed and violence in Elizabethan high drama . . . as in Chicago gang warfare or the Nazi street fighting of Hitler's rise to power' (x). There are a number of explicit and implicit references to *Richard III* in *Arturo Ui*. In the Prologue, Ui is introduced with the lines

Doesn't he make you think of Richard the Third?
Has anybody ever heard
Of blood so ghoulishly and lavishly shed
Since wars were fought for roses white and red?

Scene 13 borrows from Richard's seduction of Anne over her husband's coffin in act 1, scene 2, and scene 14 borrows from Richard's ghostly dream the night before the battle of Bosworth Field. Moreover, scene 6 presents the Shakespearean actor who teaches Ui how to present himself effectively to his audience. Finally, *Arturo Ui* is written throughout in a pastiche of Shakespearean blank verse, so as 'To picture [Ui's] spectacularly vile / Manoeuvres in the grandest style.' The incongruity of high style and base action gives rise to what Heinemann calls 'the deadly clowning' in the play (212): the gangsterism is presented as both ridiculous and horrific but not, as in Shakespeare, a thing of vile beauty.

In the most general terms, *Arturo Ui* like *Richard III* depicts the rise of a vicious man to power. In Brecht, this rise is exposed, without glamour, for the brutality it is. Moreover, the rise to power of Ui is presented as governed by very human forces of trickery and force, and consequently inherently 'resistible.' Finally, by eschewing any fated downfall for the villain, Brecht leaves open the question of how we should act to defeat and prevent the success of such men now and in the future.

Brecht drives Shakespeare towards clarity, but does so while moving away from a narrowly Shakespearean focus, so that what Shakespeare has to offer in *Richard III* is incorporated in a different context and narrative.

Select bibliography

Entries marked * are particularly accessible.

Atkins, R. (1990) "Und es ist kein Gott außer Adolf Hitler': The Biblical Motifs in Brecht's *Arturo Ui* and Related Works as Political Counter-Propaganda,' *Modern Language Review* 85, 2: 373–387.

Brecht, B. (1964) *Brecht on Theatre*, New York: Hill & Wang.

Brooker, P. (1988) *Bertolt Brecht: Dialectics, Poetry, Politics,* London: Croom Helm.

Cohn, R. (1976) *Modern Shakespeare Offshoots*, Princeton: Princeton University Press.

Eddershaw, M. (1996) *Performing Brecht: Forty Years of British Performances*, London: Routledge.

Fuegi, J. (1972) 'The Form and the Pressure: Shakespeare's Haunting of Bertolt Brecht,' *Modern Drama* 15: 291–301.

— (1994) *The Life and Lies of Bertolt Brecht*, London: HarperCollins.

*Heinemann, M. (1985) 'How Brecht Read Shakespeare,' in J. Dollimore and A. Sinfield (eds) *Political Shakespeare: New Essays in Cultural Materialism*, Ithaca: Cornell University Press: 202–230.

Mews, S. (ed.) (1997) *A Bertolt Brecht Reference Companion*, Westport, Connecticut: Greenwood Press.

*Rossi, D. (1996) 'Brecht on Shakespeare: A Revaluation,' *Comparative Drama* 30, 2: 158–187.

*Rouse, J. (1983) 'Shakespeare and Brecht: The Perils and Pleasures of Inheritance,' *Comparative Drama* 17, 3: 266–280.

Shürer, E. (1989) 'Revolution from the Right: Bertolt Brecht's American Gangster Play *The Resistible Rise of Arturo Ui*,' in S. Mews (ed.) *Critical Essays on Bertolt Brecht*, Boston: G. K. Hall.

Thomson, P., and Sacks, G. (eds) (1994) *The Cambridge Companion to Brecht*, Cambridge: Cambridge University Press.

Whall, H. M. (1981–1982) 'The Case Is Altered: Brecht's Use of Shakespeare,' *University of Toronto Quarterly* 51, 2: 127–148.

Willett, J. (1959) *The Theatre of Bertolt Brecht: A Study from Eight Aspects*, London: Methuen.

— and Manheim, R. (eds) (1981) *The Resistible Rise of Arturo Ui*, London: Eyre Methuen.

Wright, E. (1989) *Postmodern Brecht: A Re-Presentation*, New York: Routledge.

The Resistible Rise of Arturo Ui

Bertolt Brecht

Reprinted by kind permission of Methuen Publishing Ltd., London.

Characters

THE ANNOUNCER

FLAKE
CARUTHER
BUTCHER
MULBERRY
CLARK
} Businessmen, directors of the Cauliflower Trust

SHEET, shipyard owner

OLD DOGSBOROUGH

YOUNG DOGSBOROUGH

ARTURO UI, gang leader

ERNESTO ROMA, his lieutenant

EMANUELE GIRI, gangster

The florist GIUSEPPE GIVOLA, gangster

TED RAGG, reporter on *The Star*

DOCKDAISY

BOWL, Sheet's chief accountant

GOODWILL and GAFFLES, members of the city
council

O'CASEY, investigator

AN ACTOR

HOOK, wholesale vegetable dealer

DEFENDANT FISH

THE DEFENCE COUNSEL

THE JUDGE

THE DOCTOR

THE PROSECUTOR

A WOMAN

YOUNG INNA, Roma's familiar

A LITTLE MAN

IGNATIUS DULLFEET

BETTY DULLFEET, his wife

Dogsborough's BUTLER

Bodyguards

Gunmen

Vegetable dealers of Chicago and Cicero

Reporters

Prologue

The Announcer steps before the curtain. Large notices are attached to the curtain: 'New developments in dock subsidy scandal' . . . 'The true facts about Dogsborough's will and confession'. . . 'Sensation at warehouse fire trial'. . . 'Friends murder gangster Ernesto Roma'. . . 'Ignatius Dullfeet blackmailed and murdered'. . . 'Cicero taken over by gangsters'. Behind the curtain popular dance music.

THE ANNOUNCER Friends, tonight we're going to
    show –
  Pipe down, you boys in the back row!
  And, lady, your hat is in the way! –
  The great historical gangster play
  Containing, for the first time, as you'll see
  The truth about the scandalous dock subsidy.
  Further we give you, for your betterment
  Dogsborough's confession and testament.
  Arturo Ui's rise while the stock market fell.
  The notorious warehouse fire trial. What a sell!
  The Dullfeet murder! Justice in a coma!
  Gang warfare: the killing of Ernesto Roma!
  All culminating in our stunning last tableau:
  Gangsters take over the town of Cicero!
  Brilliant performers will portray

The most eminent gangsters of our day.
You'll see some dead and some alive
Some by-gone and others that survive
Some born, some made – for instance, here we
    show
The good old honest Dogsborough!

OLD DOGSBOROUGH *steps before the curtain.*

His hair is white, his heart is black.
Corrupt old man, you may step back.

DOGSBOROUGH *bows and steps back.*

The next exhibit on our list
Is Givola –

GIVOLA *has stepped before the curtain.*

            – the horticulturist.
His tongue's so slippery he'd know how
To sell you a billy-goat for a cow!
Short, says the proverb, are the legs of lies.
Look at his legs, just use your eyes.

GIVOLA *steps back limping.*

Now to Emanuele Giri, the super-clown.
Come out, let's look you up and down!

GIRI *steps before the curtain and waves his hand at
the audience.*

One of the greatest killers ever known!
Okay, beat it!

GIRI *steps back with an angry look.*

And lastly Public Enemy Number One
Arturo Ui. Now you'll see
The biggest gangster of all times
Whom heaven sent us for our crimes
Our weakness and stupidity!

ARTURO UI *steps before the curtain and walks out
along the footlights.*

Doesn't he make you think of Richard the
    Third?
Has anybody ever heard
Of blood so ghoulishly and lavishly shed
Since wars were fought for roses white and
    red?
In view of this the management
Has spared no cost in its intent
To picture his spectacularly vile
Manoeuvres in the grandest style.
But everything you'll see tonight is true.
Nothing's invented, nothing's new
Or made to order just for you.
The gangster play that we present
Is known to the whole continent.

*While the music swells and the sound of a
machine-gun mingles with it,* THE ANNOUNCER
retires with an air of bustling self-importance.

1

a

*Financial district. Enter five businessmen, the
directors of the Cauliflower Trust.*

FLAKE The times are bad!
CLARK   It looks as if Chicago
    The dear old girl, while on her way to market
    Had found her pocket torn and now she's
        starting
    To scrabble in the gutter for her pennies.
CARUTHER Last Thursday Jones invited me and
        eighty
    More to a partridge dinner to be held
    This Monday. If we really went, we'd find
    No one to greet us but the auctioneer.
    This awful change from glut to destitution
    Has come more quickly than a maiden's blush.
    Vegetable fleets with produce for this city
    Still ply the lakes, but nowhere will you find
    A buyer.
BUTCHER It's like darkness at high noon.
MULBERRY Robber and Clive are being auctioned
        off.
CLARK Wheeler – importing fruit since Noah's
        ark –
    Is bankrupt
FLAKE   And Dick Havelock's garages
    Are liquidating.
CARUTHER   Where is Sheet?
FLAKE   Too busy
    To come. He's dashing round from bank to
        bank.
CLARK What? Sheet?

Pause.

                            In other words, the cauliflower
    Trade in this town is through.
BUTCHER   Come, gentlemen
    Chin up! We're not dead yet.
MULBERRY   Call this a life?
BUTCHER Why all the gloom? The produce
        business in
    This town is basically sound. Good times
    And bad, a city of four million needs
    Fresh vegetables. Don't worry. We'll pull
        through.
CARUTHER How are the stores and markets
        doing?
MULBERRY   Badly.

The customers buy half a head of cabbage
And that on credit.

CLARK   Our cauliflower's rotting.

FLAKE Say, there's a fellow waiting in the lobby –
I only mention it because it's odd –
The name is Ui . . .

CLARK   The gangster?

FLAKE   Yes, in person.
He's smelled the stink and thinks he sees an
    opening.
Ernesto Roma, his lieutenant, says
They can convince shopkeepers it's not healthy
To handle other people's cauliflower.
He promises our turnover will double
Because, he says, the shopkeepers would rather
Buy cauliflower than coffins.

They laugh dejectedly.

CARUTHER   It's an outrage.

MULBERRY, *laughing uproariously* Bombs and
    machine guns! New conceptions of
Salesmanship! That's the ticket. Fresh young
Blood in the Cauliflower Trust. They heard
We had insomnia, so Mr Ui
Hastens to offer us his services.
Well, fellows, we'll just have to choose. It's him
Or the Salvation Army. Which one's soup
Do you prefer?

CLARK   I tend to think that Ui's
Is hotter.

CARUTHER Throw him out!

MULBERRY   Politely though.
How do we know what straits we'll come to yet?

They laugh.

FLAKE, to BUTCHER What about Dogsborough and
    a city loan?

To the others.

Butcher and I cooked up a little scheme
To help us through our present money troubles.
I'll give it to you in a nutshell. Why
Shouldn't the city that takes in our taxes
Give us a loan, let's say, for docks that we
Would undertake to build, so vegetables
Can be brought in more cheaply? Dogsborough
Is influential. He could put it through.
Have you seen Dogsborough?

BUTCHER   Yes. He refuses
To touch it.

FLAKE   He refuses? Damn it, he's
The ward boss on the waterfront, and he
Won't help us!

CARUTHER   I've contributed for years
To his campaign fund!

MULBERRY   Hell, he used to run
Sheet's lunchroom! Before he took up politics
He got his bread and butter from the Trust.
That's rank ingratitude. It's just like I've been
Telling you, Flake. All loyalty is gone!
Money is short, but loyalty is shorter!
Cursing, they scurry from the sinking ship
Friend turns to foe, employee snubs his boss
And our old lunchroom operator
Who used to be all smiles is one cold shoulder.
Morals go overboard in times of crisis.

CARUTHER I'd never have expected that of
    Dogsborough!

FLAKE What's his excuse?

BUTCHER   He says our proposition
Is fishy.

FLAKE What's fishy about building docks?
Think of the men we'd put to work.

BUTCHER   He says
He has his doubts about our building docks.

FLAKE Outrageous!

BUTCHER   What? Not building?

FLAKE   No. His doubts.

CLARK Then find somebody else to push the loan.

MULBERRY Sure, there are other people.

BUTCHER   True enough.
But none like Dogsborough. No, take it easy.
The man is good.

CLARK   For what?

BUTCHER   He's honest. And
What's more, reputed to be honest.

FLAKE   Rot!

BUTCHER He's got to think about his reputation.
That's obvious.

FLAKE   Who gives a damn? We need
A loan from City Hall. His reputation
Is his affair.

BUTCHER   You think so? I should say
It's ours. It takes an honest man to swing
A loan like this, a man they'd be ashamed
To ask for proofs and guarantees. And such
A man is Dogsborough. Old Dogsborough's
Our loan. All right, I'll tell you why. Because
    they
Believe in him. They may have stopped
    believing
In God, but not in Dogsborough. A hard-boiled
Broker, who takes a lawyer with him to
His lawyer's, wouldn't hesitate to put his
Last cent in Dogsborough's apron for
    safekeeping
If he should see it lying on the bar.
Two hundred pounds of honesty. In eighty
Winters he's shown no weakness. Such a man
Is worth his weight in gold – especially

To people with a scheme for building docks
And building kind of slowly.

FLAKE   Okay, Butcher
He's worth his weight in gold. The deal he
   vouches
For is tied up. The only trouble is:
He doesn't vouch for ours.

CLARK   Oh no, not he!
'The city treasury is not a grab bag!'

MULBERRY And 'All for the city, the city for itself!'

CARUTHER Disgusting! Not an ounce of humour.

MULBERRY   Once
His mind's made up, an earthquake wouldn't
   change it.
To him the city's not a place of wood
And stone, where people live with people
Struggling to feed themselves and pay the rent
But words on paper, something from the Bible.
The man has always gotten on my nerves.

CLARK His heart was never with us. What does he
   care
For cauliflower and the trucking business!
Let every vegetable in the city rot
You think he'd lift a finger? No, for nineteen
   years
Or is it twenty, we've contributed
To his campaign fund. Well, in all that time
The only cauliflower he's ever seen
Was on his plate. What's more, he's never once
Set foot in a garage.

BUTCHER   That's right.

CLARK   The devil
Take him!

BUTCHER Oh no! We'll take him.

FLAKE   But Clark says
It can't be done. The man has turned us down.

BUTCHER That's so. But Clark has also told us
   why!

CLARK The bastard doesn't know which way is
   up.

BUTCHER Exactly. What's his trouble? Ignorance.
He hasn't got the faintest notion what
It's like to be in such a fix. The question
Is therefore how to put him in our skin.
In short, we've got to educate the man.
I've thought it over. Listen, here's my plan.

*A sign appears, recalling certain incidents in the
recent past.**

b

Outside the produce exchange. FLAKE *and* SHEET *in
conversation.*

SHEET I've run from pillar to post. Pillar was out
Of town, and Post was sitting in the bathtub.
Old friends show nothing but their backs. A
   brother
Buys wilted shoes before he meets his brother
For fear his brother will touch him for a loan.
Old partners dread each other so they use
False names when meeting in a public place.
Our citizens are sewing up their pockets.

FLAKE So what about my proposition?

SHEET   No. I
Won't sell. You want a full-course dinner for the
Price of the tip. And to be thanked for the tip
At that. You wouldn't like it if
I told you what I think of you.

FLAKE   Nobody
Will pay you any more.

SHEET   And friends won't be
More generous than anybody else.

FLAKE Money is tight these days.

SHEET   Especially
For those in need. And who can diagnose
A friend's need better than a friend?

FLAKE   You'll lose
Your shipyard either way.

SHEET   And that's not all
I'll lose. I've got a wife who's likely to
Walk out on me.

FLAKE   But if you sell . . .

SHEET . . . she'll last another year. But what I'm
   curious
About is why you want my shipyard.

FLAKE   Hasn't
It crossed your mind that we – I mean the
   Trust –
Might want to help you?

SHEET   No, it never crossed
My mind. How stupid of me to suspect you
Of trying to grab my property, when you
Were only trying to help.

FLAKE   Such bitterness
Dear Sheet, won't save you from the hammer.

SHEET At least, dear Flake, it doesn't help the
   hammer.

Three men saunter past: ARTURO UI, *the gangster,
his lieutenant* ERNESTO ROMA, *and a bodyguard. In
passing,* UI *stares at* FLAKE *as though expecting to be
spoken to, and, in leaving,* ROMA *turns his head and
gives* FLAKE *an angry look.*

SHEET Who's that?

FLAKE   Arturo Ui, the ganster. . . How
About it? Are you selling?

---

* See the Chronological Table at the end of the play.

SHEET   He seemed eager
  To speak to you.
FLAKE, *laughing angrily* And so he is. He's been
  Pursuing us with offers, wants to sell
  Our cauliflower with his tommy guns.
  The town is full of types like that right now
  Corroding it like leprosy, devouring
  A finger, then an arm and shoulder. No one
  Knows where it comes from, but we all suspect
  From deepest hell. Kidnapping, murder, threats
  Extortion, blackmail, massacre:
  'Hands up!' 'Your money or your life!'
    Outrageous!
  It's got to be wiped out.
SHEET, *looking at him sharply* And quickly. It's
    contagious.
FLAKE Well, how about it? Are you selling?
SHEET, *stepping back and looking at him* No doubt
    about it: a resemblance to
  Those three who just passed by. Not too
    pronounced
  But somehow there, one senses more than sees
    it.
  Under the water of a pond sometimes
  You see a branch, all green and slimy. It
  Could be a snake. But no, it's definitely
  A branch. Or is it? That's how you resemble
  Roma. Don't take offence. But when I looked
  At him just now and then at you, it seemed
  To me I'd noticed it before, in you
  And others, without understanding. Say it
  Again, Flake: 'How about it? Are you selling?'
  Even your voice, I think. . . No, better say
  'Hands up!' because that's what you really mean.

He puts up his hands.

  All right, Flake, Take the shipyard!
  Give me a kick or two in payment. Hold it!
  I'll take the higher offer. Make it two.
FLAKE You're crazy!
SHEET   I only wish that that were true!

2

Back room in DOGSBOROUGH's *restaurant.*
DOGSBOROUGH *and his son are washing glasses.*
Enter BUTCHER *and* FLAKE.

DOGSBOROUGH You didn't need to come. The
    answer is no.
  Your proposition stinks of rotten fish.
YOUNG DOGSBOROUGH My father turns it down.
BUTCHER   Forget it, then.
  We ask you. You say no. So no it is.

DOGSBOROUGH It's fishy. I know your kind of
    docks.
  I wouldn't touch it.
YOUNG DOGSBOROUGH My father wouldn't touch
    it.
BUTCHER   Good.
  Forget it.
DOGSBOROUGH You're on the wrong road,
    fellows.
  The city treasury is not a grab bag
  For everyone to dip his fingers into.
  Anyway, damn it all, your business is
  Perfectly sound.
BUTCHER   What did I tell you, Flake?
  You fellows are too pessimistic.
DOGSBOROUGH   Pessimism
  Is treason. You're only making trouble for
  Yourselves. I see it this way: What do you
  Fellows sell? Cauliflower. That's as good
  As meat and bread. Man doesn't live by bread
  And meat alone, he needs his green goods.
  Suppose I served up sirloin without onions
  Or mutton without beans. I'd never see
  My customers again. Some people are
  A little short right now. They hesitate
  To buy a suit. But people have to eat.
  They'll always have a dime for vegetables.
  Chin up! If I were you, I wouldn't worry.
FLAKE It does me good to hear you, Dogsborough.
  It gives a fellow courage to go on.
BUTCHER Dogsborough, it almost makes me
    laugh to find you
  So staunchly confident about the future
  Of cauliflower, because quite frankly we
  Have come here for a purpose. No, don't worry.
  Not what you think, that's dead and buried.
    Something
  Pleasant, or so at least we hope. Old man
  It's come to our attention that it's been
  Exactly twenty three years this June, since
    you –
  Well-known to us for having operated
  The lunchroom in one of our establishments for
  More than three decades – left us to devote
  Your talents to the welfare of this city.
  If not for you our town would not be what
  It is today. Nor, like the city, would
  The Trust have prospered as it has. I'm glad
  To hear you call it sound, for yesterday
  Moved by this festive occasion, we resolved
  In token of our high esteem, and proof
  That in our hearts we somehow still regard you
  As one of us, to offer you the major share
  Of stock in Sheet's shipyard for twenty thousand
  Dollars, or less than half its value.

He lays the packet of stocks on the bar.

DOGSBOROUGH   I
  Don't understand.
BUTCHER   Quite frankly, Dogsborough
  The Cauliflower Trust is not reputed
  For tenderness of heart, but yesterday
  After we'd made our. . . well, our
  Stupid request about the loan, and heard
  Your answer, honest, incorruptible
  Old Dogsborough to a hair, a few of us –
  It's not an easy thing to say – were close
  To tears. Yes, one man said – don't interrupt
  Me, Flake, I won't say who – 'Good God'
  He said, 'the man has saved us from ourselves.'
  For some time none of us could speak. Then this
  Suggestion popped up of its own accord.
DOGSBOROUGH I've heard you, friends. But what
  is there behind it?
BUTCHER What should there be behind it? It's an
  offer.
FLAKE And one that we are really pleased to
  make.
  For here you stand behind your bar, a tower
  Of strength, a sterling name, the model of
  An upright citizen. We find you washing
  Glasses, but you have cleansed our souls as well.
  And yet you're poorer than your poorest guest.
  It wrings our hearts.
DOGSBOROUGH   I don't know what to say.
BUTCHER Don't say a word. Just take this little
  package.
  An honest man can use it, don't you think?
  By golly, it's not often that the gravy train
  Travels the straight and narrow. Take your boy
  here:
  I know a good name's better than a bank
  Account, and yet I'm sure he won't despise it.
  Just take the stuff and let us hope you won't
  Read us the riot act for *this*!
DOGSBOROUGH   Sheet's shipyard!
FLAKE Look, you can see it from right here.
DOGSBOROUGH, *at the window*   I've seen it
  For twenty years.
FLAKE   We thought of that.
DOGSBOROUGH   And what is
  Sheet going to do?
FLAKE   He's moving into beer.
BUTCHER Okay?
DOGSBOROUGH I certainly appreciate
  Your oldtime sentiments, but no one gives
  Away a shipyard for a song.
FLAKE   There's something
  In that. But now the loan has fallen through
  Maybe the twenty thousand will come in handy.

BUTCHER And possibly right now we're not too
  eager
  To throw our stock upon the open market . . .
DOGSBOROUGH That sounds more like it. Not a
  bad deal if
  It's got no strings attached.
FLAKE   None whatsoever.
DOGSBOROUGH The price you say is twenty
  thousand?
FLAKE   Is it
  Too much?
DOGSBOROUGH No. And imagine, it's the
  selfsame shipyard
  Where years ago I opened my first lunchroom.
  As long as there's no nigger in the woodpile . . .
  You've really given up the loan?
FLAKE   Completely.
DOGSBOROUGH I might consider it. Hey, look
  here, son
  It's just the thing for you. I thought you fellows
  Were down on me and here you make this offer.
  You see, my boy, that honesty sometimes
  Pays off. It's like you say: When I pass on
  The youngster won't inherit much more than
  My name, and these old eyes have seen what
  evil
  Can spring from penury.
BUTCHER   We'll feel much better
  If you accept. The ugly aftertaste
  Left by our foolish proposition would be
  Dispelled. In future we could benefit
  By your advice. You'd show us how to tide
  The slump by honest means, because our
  business
  Would be your business, Dogsborough, because
  You too would be a cauliflower man
  And want the Cauliflower Trust to win.

DOGSBOROUGH *takes his hand.*

DOGSBOROUGH Butcher and Flake, I'm in.
YOUNG DOGSBOROUGH   My father's in.

A sign appears.

3

Bookmaker's office on 122nd Street. ARTURO UI *and
his lieutenant* ERNESTO ROMA, *accompanied by
bodyguards, are listening to the racing news on the
radio. Next to* ROMA *is* DOCKDAISY.

ROMA I wish, Arturo, you could cure yourself
  Of this black melancholy, this inactive
  Dreaming. The whole town's talking.
UI, *bitterly*   Talking? Who's talking?

Nobody talks about me any more.
This city's got no memory. Short-lived
Is fame in such a place. Two months without
A murder and a man's forgotten.

He whisks through the newspapers.

When
The rod falls silent, silence strikes the press.
Even when I deliver murders by the
Dozen, I'm never sure they'll print them.
It's not accomplishment that counts; it's
Influence, which in turn depends on my
Bank balance. Things have come to such a pass
I sometimes think of chucking the whole
    business.
ROMA The boys are chafing too from lack of cash.
Morale is low. This inactivity's
No good for them. A man with nothing but
The ace of spades to shoot at goes to seed.
I feel so sorry for those boys, Arturo
I hate to show my face at headquarters. When
They look at me, my 'Tomorrow we'll see
    action'
Sticks in my throat. Your vegetables idea was
So promising. Why don't we start right in?
UI Not now. Not from the bottom. It's too soon.
ROMA 'Too soon' is good. For four months now –
Remember? – since the Cauliflower Trust
Gave you the brush-off, you've been idly
    brooding.
Plans! Plans! Half-hearted feelers! That rebuff
Frizzled your spine. And then that little
    mishap –
Those cops at Harper's Bank – you've never
    gotten
Over it.
UI   But they fired!
ROMA   Only in
The air. That was illegal.
UI   Still too close
For me. I'd be in stir if they had plugged
My only witness. And that judge! Not two
Cents' worth of sympathy.
ROMA   The cops won't shoot
For grocery stores. They shoot for banks. Look
    here
Arturo, we'll start on Eleventh Street
Smash a few windows, wreck the furniture
Pour kerosene on the veg. And then we work
Our way to Seventh. Two or three days later
Giri, a posy in his buttonhole
Drops in and offers our protection for
A suitable percentage on their sales.
UI No. First I need protection for myself
From cops and judges. Then I'll start to think

About protecting other people. We've
Got to start from the top.

Gloomily.

Until I've put the
Judge in my pocket by slipping something
Of mine in his, the law's against me. I
Can't even rob a bank without some two-bit cop
Shooting me dead.
ROMA   You're right. Our only hope is
Givola's plan. He's got a nose for smells
And if he says the Cauliflower Trust
Smells promisingly rotten, I believe
There's something in it. And there *was* some
    talk
When, as they say, on Dogsborough's
    commendation
The city made that loan. Since then I've heard
Rumours about some docks that aren't being
    built
But ought to be. Yet on the other hand
Dogsborough recommended it. Why should
That do-good peg for fishy business? Here
    comes
Ragg of the 'Star'. If anybody knows
About such things, it's him. Hi Ted.
RAGG, *slightly drunk*   Hi, boys!
Hi, Roma! Hi, Arturo! How are things in
Capua?
UI   What's he saying?
RAGG   Oh, nothing much
That was a one-horse town where long ago
An army went to pot from idleness.
UI   Go to hell!
ROMA, *to Ragg*   No fighting.
Tell us about that loan the Cauliflower
Trust wangled.
RAGG   What do you care? Say! Could you
Be going into vegetables? I've got it!
You're angling for a loan yourselves. See
    Dogsborough.
He'll put it through.

Imitating the old man.

'Can we allow a business
Basically sound but momentarily
Threatened with blight, to perish?' Not an eye
At City Hall but fills with tears. Deep feeling
For cauliflower shakes the council members
As though it were a portion of themselves.
Too bad, Arturo, guns call forth no tears.

The other customers laugh.

ROMA Don't bug him, Ted. He's out of sorts.
RAGG   I shouldn't

Wonder. I hear that Givola has been
To see Capone for a job.
DOCKDAISY   You liar!
You leave Giuseppe out of this!
RAGG   Hi, Dockdaisy!
Still got your place in Shorty Givola's harem?

Introducing her.

Fourth super in the harem of the third
Lieutenant of a –

Points to UI.

                              – fast declining star
Of second magnitude! Oh, bitter fate!
DOCKDAISY Somebody shut the rotten bastard up!
RAGG Posterity plaits no laurels for the gangster!
New heroes captivate the fickle crowd.
Yesterday's hero has been long forgotten
His mug-shot gathers dust in ancient files.
'Don't you remember, folks, the wounds I gave
     you?' –
'When?' – 'Once upon a time.' – 'Those wounds
     have turned
To scars long since.' Alas, the finest scars
Get lost with those who bear them. 'Can it be
That in a world where good deeds go unnoticed
No monument remains to evil ones?' –
'Yes, so it is.' – 'Oh, lousy world!'
UI, *bellows*   Shut
Him up!

The bodyguards approach RAGG.

RAGG, *turning pale* Be careful, Ui. Don't insult
The press.

The other customers have risen to their feet in alarm.

ROMA   You'd better beat it, Ted. You've said
Too much already.
RAGG, *backing out, now very much afraid* See you
     later, boys.

The room empties quickly.

ROMA Your nerves are shot, Arturo.
UI   Those bastards
Treat me like dirt.
ROMA   Because of your long silence.
No other reason.
UI, *gloomily*   Say, what's keeping Giri
And that accountant from the Cauliflower
Trust?
ROMA   They were due at three.
UI   And Givola?
What's this I hear about him seeing Capone?
ROMA Nothing at all. He's in his flower shop
Minding his business, and Capone comes in
To buy some wreaths.

UI   Some wreaths? For who?
ROMA   Not us.
UI I'm not so sure.
ROMA   You're seeing things too black.
Nobody's interested in us.
UI   Exactly.
They've more respect for dirt. Take Givola.
One setback and he blows. By God
I'll settle his account when things look up.
ROMA Giri!

Enter EMANUELE GIRI *with a rundown individual,*
BOWL.

GIRI I've got him, boss.
ROMA, *to Bowl*   They tell me you
Are Sheet's accountant at the Cauliflower
Trust.
BOWL   Was. Until last week that bastard . . .
GIRI He hates the very smell of cauliflower.
BOWL Dogsborough . . .
UI, *quickly*   Dogsborough! What about him?
ROMA What have you got to do with
     Dogsborough?
GIRI That's why I brought him.
BOWL   Dogsborough
Fired me.
ROMA   He fired you? From Sheet's shipyard?
BOWL No, from his own. He took it over on
September first.
ROMA   What's that?
GIRI   Sheet's shipyard
Belongs to Dogsborough. Bowl here was present
When Butcher of the Cauliflower Trust
Handed him fifty-one percent of the stock.
UI So what?
BOWL   So what? It's scandalous . . .
GIRI   Don't you
Get it, boss?
BOWL   . . . Dogsborough sponsoring that
Loan to the Cauliflower Trust . . .
GIRI   . . . when he
Himself was secretly a member of
The Cauliflower Trust.
UI, *who is beginning to see the light* Say, that's
     corrupt.
By God the old man hasn't kept his nose
Too clean.
BOWL   The loan was to the Cauliflower
Trust, but they did it through the shipyard.
     Through
Me. And I signed for Dogsborough. Not for Sheet
As people thought.
GIRI   By golly, it's a killer.
Old Dogsborough. The trusty and reliable
Signboard. So honest. So responsible!

Whose handshake was an honour and a pledge!
The staunch and incorruptible old man!
BOWL I'll make the bastard pay. Can you imagine?
    Firing me for embezzlement when he
        himself . . .
ROMA Cool it! You're not the only one whose
        blood
    Boils at such abject villainy. What do
    You say, Arturo?
UI, *referring to Bowl* Will he testify?
GIRI He'll testify.
UI, *grandly getting ready to leave* Keep an eye on
        him, boys. Let's go
    Roma. I smell an opening.

He goes out quickly, followed by ERNESTO ROMA
and the bodyguards.

GIRI, *slaps Bowl on the back* Bowl, I
    Believe you've set a wheel in motion, which . . .
BOWL I hope you'll pay me back for any loss . . .
GIRI Don't worry about that. I know the boss.

A sign appears.

4

DOGSBOROUGH's *country house.* DOGSBOROUGH
and his son.

DOGSBOROUGH I should never have accepted this
        estate.
    Taking that package as a kind of gift was
    Beyond reproach.
YOUNG DOGSBOROUGH Of course it was.
DOGSBOROUGH   And sponsoring
    That loan, when I discovered to my own
    Detriment that a thriving line of business
    Was languishing for lack of funds, was hardly
    Dishonest. But when, confident the shipyard
    Would yield a handsome profit, I accepted
    This house before I moved the loan, so
        secretly
    Acting in my own interest – that was wrong.
YOUNG DOGSBOROUGH Yes father.
DOGSBOROUGH   That was faulty judgment
    Or might be so regarded. Yes, my boy
    I should never have accepted this estate.
YOUNG DOGSBOROUGH   No.
DOGSBOROUGH We've stepped into a trap.
YOUNG DOGSBOROUGH   Yes, father.
DOGSBOROUGH   That
    Package of stocks was like the salty tidbit
    They serve free gratis at the bar to make
    The customer, appeasing his cheap hunger
    Work up a raging thirst.

Pause.

                            That inquiry
    At City Hall about the docks, has got
    Me down. The loan's used up. Clark helped
    Himself; so did Caruther, Flake and Butcher
    And so, I'm sad to say, did I. And no
    Cement's been bought yet, not a pound! The one
    Good thing is this: at Sheet's request I kept
    The deal a secret; no one knows of my
    Connection with the shipyard.
A BUTLER *enters*   Telephone
    Sir, Mr Butcher of the Cauliflower
    Trust.
DOGSBOROUGH Take it, son.

YOUNG DOGSBOROUGH *goes out with the* BUTLER.
Church bells are heard in the distance.

DOGSBOROUGH   Now what can Butcher want?

Looking out of the window.

    Those poplars are what tempted me to take
    The place. The poplars and the lake down there,
        like
    Silver before it's minted into dollars.
    And air that's free of beer fumes. The fir trees
    Are good to look at too, especially
    The tops. Grey-green and dusty. And the
        trunks –
    Their colour calls to mind the leathers we used
        to wrap around
    The taps when drawing beer. It was the poplars,
        though
    That turned the trick. Ah yes, the poplars.
    It's Sunday. Hm. The bells would sound so
        peaceful
    If the world were not so full of wickedness.
    But what can Butcher want on Sunday?
    I never should have . . .
YOUNG DOGSBOROUGH, *returning* Father, Butcher
        says
    Last night the City Council voted to
    Investigate the Cauliflower Trust's
    Projected docks. Father, what's wrong?
DOGSBOROUGH   My smelling salts!
YOUNG DOGSBOROUGH, *gives them to him* Here.
DOGSBOROUGH What does Butcher want?
YOUNG DOGSBOROUGH   He wants to come here.
DOGSBOROUGH Here? I refuse to see him. I'm not
        well.
    My heart.

He stands up. Grandly

    I haven't anything to do
    With this affair. For sixty years I've trodden

The narrow path, as everybody knows.
They can't involve me in their schemes.
YOUNG DOGSBOROUGH   No, father.
  Do you feel better now?
THE BUTLER *enters*   A Mr Ui
  Desires to see you, sir.
DOGSBOROUGH   The gangster!
THE BUTLER   Yes
  I've seen his picture in the papers. Says he
  Was sent by Mr Clark of the Cauliflower Trust.
DOGSBOROUGH Throw him out! Who sent him?
    Clark? Good God!
  Is he threatening me with gangsters now?
    I'll . . .

Enter ARTURO UI *and* ERNESTO ROMA.

UI   Mr
  Dogsborough.
DOGSBOROUGH Get out!
ROMA   I wouldn't be in such
  A hurry, friend. It's Sunday. Take it easy.
DOGSBOROUGH Get out, I said!
YOUNG DOGSBOROUGH   My father says: Get out!
ROMA Saying it twice won't make it any smarter.
UI, *unruffled* Mr Dogsborough.
DOGSBOROUGH   Where are the servants? Call the
    Police.
ROMA   I wouldn't leave the room if I
  Were you, son. In the hallway you might run
  Into some boys who wouldn't understand.
DOGSBOROUGH Ho! Violence!
ROMA   I wouldn't call it that.
  Only a little emphasis perhaps.
UI Mr Dogsborough. I am well aware that you
  Don't know me, or even worse, you know me
    but
  Only from hearsay. Mr Dogsborough
  I have been very much maligned, my image
  Blackened by envy, my intentions disfigured
  By baseness. When some fourteen years ago
  Yours truly, then a modest, unemployed
  Son of the Bronx, appeared within the gates
  Of this your city to launch a new career
  Which, I may say, has not been utterly
  Inglorious, my only followers
  Were seven youngsters, penniless like myself
  But brave and like myself determined
  To cut their chunk of meat from every cow
  The Lord created. I've got thirty now
  And will have more. But now you're wondering:
    What does
  Arturo Ui want of me? Not much. Just this.
  What irks me is to be misunderstood
  To be regarded as a fly-by-night
  Adventurer and heaven knows what else.

Clears his throat.

  Especially by the police, for I
  Esteem them and I'd welcome their esteem.
  And so I've come to ask you – and believe me
  Asking's not easy for my kind of man –
  To put a word in for me with the precinct
  When necessary.
DOGSBOROUGH, *incredulously* Vouch for you, you
    mean?
UI If necessary. That depends on whether
  We strike a friendly understanding with
  The vegetable dealers.
DOGSBOROUGH   What is your
  Connection with the vegetable trade?
UI That's what I'm coming to. The vegetable
  Trade needs protection. By force if necessary.
  And I'm determined to supply it.
DOGSBOROUGH   No
  One's threatening it as far as I can see.
UI Maybe not. Not yet. But I see further. And
  I ask you: How long with our corrupt police
  Force will the vegetable dealer be allowed
  To sell his vegetables in peace? A ruthless
  Hand may destroy his little shop tomorrow
  And make off with his cash-box. Would he not
  Prefer at little cost to arm himself
  Before the trouble starts, with powerful
    protection?
DOGSBOROUGH I doubt it.
UI   That would mean he doesn't know
  What's good for him. Quite possible. The small
  Vegetable dealer, honest but short-sighted
  Hard-working but too often unaware
  Of his best interest, needs strong leadership.
  Moreover, toward the Cauliflower Trust
  That gave him everything he has, he feels
  No sense of responsibility. That's where I
  Come in again. The Cauliflower Trust
  Must likewise be protected. Down with the
    welchers!
  Pay up, say I, or close your shop! The weak
  Will perish. Let them, that's the law of nature.
  In short, the Trust requires my services.
DOGSBOROUGH But what's the Cauliflower Trust
    to me?
  Why come to me with this amazing plan?
UI We'll get to that. I'll tell you what you
    need.
  The Cauliflower Trust needs muscle, thirty
  Determined men under my leadership.
DOGSBOROUGH Whether the Trust would want to
    change its typewriters
  For tommy-guns I have no way of knowing.
  You see, I'm not connected with the Trust.

UI We'll get to that. You say: With thirty men
Armed to the teeth, at home on our premises
How do we know that we ourselves are safe?
The answer's very simple. He who holds
The purse strings holds the power. And it's you
Who hand out the pay envelopes. How could
I turn against you even if I wanted
Even without the high esteem I bear you?
For what do I amount to? What
Following have I got? A handful. And some
Are dropping out. Right now it's twenty. Or less.
Without your help I'm finished. It's your duty
Your human duty to protect me from
My enemies, and (I may as well be frank)
My followers too! The work of fourteen years
Hangs in the balance! I appeal to you
As man to man.

DOGSBOROUGH As man to man I'll tell
You what I'll do. I'm calling the police.

UI What? The police?

DOGSBOROUGH   Exactly, the police!

UI Am I to understand that you refuse
To help me as a man?

Bellows.

                    Then I demand
It of you as a criminal. Because
That's what you are! I'm going to expose you!
I've got the proofs! There's going to be a scandal
About some docks. And you're mixed up in it!
  Sheet's
Shipyard – that's you. I'm warning you! Don't
Push me too far! They've voted to investigate!

DOGSBOROUGH, *very pale* They never will. They
  can't. My friends . . .

UI You haven't got any. You had some yesterday.
Today you haven't got a single friend
Tomorrow you'll have nothing but enemies.
If anybody can rescue you, it's me
Arturo Ui! Me! Me!

DOGSBOROUGH   Nobody's going to
Investigate. My hair is white.

UI   But nothing else
Is white about you, Dogsborough.

Tries to seize his hand.

Think, man! It's now or never! Let me save you!
One word from you and any bastard who
Touches a hair of yon white head, I'll drill him!
Dogsborough, help me now. I beg you. Once!
Just once! Oh, say the word, or I shall never
Be able to face my boys again.

He weeps.

DOGSBOROUGH   Never!
I'd sooner die than get mixed up with you!

UI I'm washed up and I know it. Forty
And still a nobody. You've got to help me.

DOGSBOROUGH Never.

UI   I'm warning you. I'll crush you.

DOGSBOROUGH   Never
Never while I draw breath will you get away
  with
Your green goods racket!

UI, *with dignity*   Mr Dogsborough
I'm only forty. You are eighty. With God's
Help I'll outlast you. And one thing I know:
I'll break into the green goods business yet!

DOGSBOROUGH Never!

UI Come, Roma. Let's get out of here.

He makes a formal bow and leaves the room with
ERNESTO ROMA.

DOGSBOROUGH Air! Give me air. Oh, what a mug!
Oh, what a mug! I should never have accepted
This house. But they won't dare. I'm sunk
If they investigate, but they won't dare.

THE BUTLER *enters* Goodwill and Gaffles of the
  city council.

Enter GOODWILL *and* GAFFLES.

GOODWILL Hello, Dogsborough!

DOGSBOROUGH   Hello, Goodwill and Gaffles!
Anything new?

GOODWILL Plenty, and not so good, I fear.
But wasn't that Arturo Ui who
Just passed us in the hall?

DOGSBOROUGH, *with a forced laugh* Himself in
  person.
Hardly an ornament to a country home.

GOODWILL   No.
Hardly an ornament. It's no good wind
That brings us. It's that loan we made the Trust
To build their docks with.

DOGSBOROUGH, *stiffly*   What about the loan?

GAFFLES Well, certain council members said –
  don't get
Upset – the thing looked kind of fishy.

DOGSBOROUGH   Fishy.

GOODWILL Don't worry! The majority flew off
The handle. Fishy! We almost came to blows.

GAFFLES Dogsborough's contracts fishy! they
  shouted. What
About the Bible? Is that fishy too?
It almost turned to an ovation for you
Dogsborough. When your friends demanded an
Investigation, some, infected with
Our confidence, withdrew their motion and
Wanted to shelve the whole affair. But the
Majority, resolved to clear your name
Of every vestige of suspicion, shouted:

Dogsborough's more than a name. It stands for
      more than
A man. It's an institution! In an uproar
They voted the investigation.
DOGSBOROUGH   The
    Investigation.
GOODWILL   O'Casey is in charge.
    The cauliflower people merely say
    The loan was made directly to Sheet's shipyard.
    The contracts with the builders were to be
    Negotiated by Sheet's shipyard.
DOGSBOROUGH   By Sheet's shipyard.
GOODWILL The best would be for you to send a
      man
    Of flawless reputation and impartiality
    Someone you trust, to throw some light on this
    Unholy rat's nest.
DOGSBOROUGH   So I will.
GAFFLES   All right
    That settles it. And now suppose you show us
    This famous country house of yours. We'll want
    To tell our friends about it.
DOGSBOROUGH   Very well.
GOODWILL What blessed peace! And church bells!
    All one can
    Wish for.
GAFFLES, *laughing* No docks in sight.
DOGSBOROUGH   I'll send a man.

They go out slowly.

A sign appears.

5

City hall. BUTCHER, FLAKE, CLARK, MULBERRY,
CARUTHER. *Across from them* DOGSBOROUGH,
who is as white as a sheet, O'CASEY, GAFFLES *and*
GOODWILL. REPORTERS.

BUTCHER, *in an undertone* He's late.
MULBERRY He's bringing Sheet. Quite possibly
    They haven't come to an agreement. I
    Believe they've been discussing it all night.
    Sheet *has* to say the shipyard still belongs
    To him.
CARUTHER It's asking quite a lot of Sheet
    To come here just to tell us *he's* the scoundrel.
FLAKE He'll never come.
CLARK   He's got to.
FLAKE   Why should he
    Ask to be sent to prison for five years?
CLARK It's quite a pile of dough. And Mabel Sheet
    Needs luxury. He's still head over heels
    In love with Mabel. He'll play ball all right.
    And anyway he'll never serve his term.
    Old Dogsborough will see to that.

*The shouts of newsboys are heard. A reporter brings
in a paper.*

GAFFLES Sheet's been found dead. In his hotel. A
      ticket
    To San Francisco in his pocket.
BUTCHER   Sheet
    Dead?
O'CASEY, *reading* Murdered.
MULBERRY   My God!
FLAKE, *in an undertone*   He didn't come.
GAFFLES What is it, Dogsborough?
DOGSBOROUGH, *speaking with difficulty* Nothing.
    It'll pass.
O'CASEY Sheet's death . . .
CLARK   Poor Sheet. His unexpected death
    Would seem to puncture your investigation . . .
O'CASEY Of course the unexpected often looks
    As if it were expected. Some indeed
    Expect the unexpected. Such is life.
    This leaves me in a pretty pickle and
    I hope you won't refer me and my questions
    To Sheet; for Sheet, according to this paper
    Has been most silent since last night.
MULBERRY   Your questions?
    You know the loan was given to the shipyard
    Don't you?
O'CASEY   Correct. But there remains a question:
    Who is the shipyard?
FLAKE, *under his breath* Funny question! He's
    Got something up his sleeve.
CLARK, *likewise*   I wonder what.
O'CASEY Something wrong, Dogsborough? Could
    it be the air?

To the others.

    I only mean: some people may be thinking
    That several shovelsful of earth are not
    Enough to load on Sheet, and certain muck
    Might just as well be added. I suspect . . .
CLARK Maybe you'd better not suspect too much
    O'Casey. Ever hear of slander? We've
    Got laws against it.
MULBERRY   What's the point of these
    Insinuations? Dogsborough, they tell me
    Has picked a man to clear this business up.
    Let's wait until he comes.
O'CASEY   He's late. And when
    He comes, I hope Sheet's not the only thing
    He'll talk about.
FLAKE   We hope he'll tell the truth
    No more no less.
O'CASEY   You mean the man is honest?
    That suits me fine. Since Sheet was still alive
    Last night, the whole thing should be clear. I
    only –

To DOGSBOROUGH.

Hope that you've chosen a good man.
CLARK, *cuttingly*   You'll have
To take him as he is. Ah, here he comes.

Enter ARTURO UI *and* ERNESTO ROMA *with bodyguards.*

UI Hi, Clark! Hi, Dogsborough! Hi, everybody!
CLARK Hi, Ui.
UI   Well, it seems you've got some questions.
O'CASEY, *to Dogsborough* Is this your man?
CLARK   That's right. Not good enough?
GOODWILL Dogsborough, can you be . . .?

Commotion among the REPORTERS.

O'CASEY   Quiet over there!
A REPORTER It's Ui!

Laughter. O'CASEY *bangs his gavel for order. Then he musters the bodyguards.*

O'CASEY Who are these men?
UI   Friends.
O'CASEY, *to Roma*   And who
Are you?
UI   Ernesto Roma, my accountant.
GAFFLES Hold it! Can you be serious,
Dogsborough?

DOGSBOROUGH *is silent.*

O'CASEY   Mr
Ui, we gather from Mr Dogsborough's
Eloquent silence that you have his confidence
And desire ours. Well then. Where are the
contracts?
UI What contracts?
CLARK, *seeing that* O'CASEY *is looking at* GOODWILL
The contracts that the shipyard no doubt
Signed with the builders with a view to
enlarging
Its dock facilities.
UI   I never heard
Of any contracts.
O'CASEY   Really?
CLARK   Do you mean
There are no contracts?
O'CASEY, *quickly*   Did you talk with Sheet?
UI, *shaking his head* No.
CLARK Oh. You didn't talk with Sheet?
UI, *angrily*   If any-
One says I talked with Sheet, that man's a liar.
O'CASEY Ui, I thought that Mr Dogsborough
Has asked you to look into this affair?
UI I have looked into it.
O'CASEY   And have your studies
Borne fruit?

UI   They have. It wasn't easy to
Lay bare the truth. And it's not a pleasant truth.
When Mr Dogsborough, in the interest of
This city, asked me to investigate
Where certain city funds, the hard-earned
savings
Of taxpayers like you and me, entrusted
To a certain shipyard in this city, had gone to
I soon discovered to my consternation
That they had been embezzled. That's Point
One.
Point Two is who embezzled them. All right
I'll answer that one too. The guilty party
Much as it pains me is . . .
O'CASEY   Well, who is it?
UI   Sheet.
O'CASEY Oh, Sheet! The silent Sheet you didn't
talk to!
UI Why look at me like that? The guilty party
Is Sheet.
CLARK Sheet's dead. Didn't you know?
UI   What, dead?
I was in Cicero last night. That's why
I haven't heard. And Roma here was with me.

Pause.

ROMA That's mighty funny. Do you think it's
mere
Coincidence that . . .
UI   Gentlemen, it's not
An accident. Sheet's suicide was plainly
The consequence of Sheet's embezzlement.
It's monstrous!
O'CASEY   Except it wasn't suicide.
UI What then? Of course Ernesto here and I
Were in Cicero last night. We wouldn't know.
But this we know beyond a doubt: that Sheet
Apparently an honest businessman
Was just a gangster.
O'CASEY   Ui, I get your drift.
You can't find words too damaging for Sheet
After the damage he incurred last night.
Well, Dogsborough, let's get to you.
DOGSBOROUGH   To me?
BUTCHER, *cuttingly* What about Dogsborough?
O'CASEY   As I understand Mr
Ui – and I believe I understand
Him very well – there was a shipyard which
Borrowed some money which has disappeared.
But now the question rises: Who is this
Shipyard? It's Sheet, you say. But what's a
name?
What interests us right now is not its name
But whom it actually belonged to. Did it
Belong to Sheet? Unquestionably Sheet

Could tell us. But Sheet has buttoned up
About his property since Ui spent
The night in Cicero. But could it be
That when this swindle was put over someone
Else was the owner. What is your opinion
Dogsborough?

DOGSBOROUGH Me?

O'CASEY   Yes, could it be that you
Were sitting in Sheet's office when a contract
Was. . . well, suppose we say, not being drawn
up?

GOODWILL O'Casey!

GAFFLES, *to* O'CASEY Dogsborough? You're crazy!

DOGSBOROUGH   I . . .

O'CASEY And earlier, at City Hall, when you
Told us how hard a time the cauliflower
People were having and how badly they
Needed a loan – could that have been the voice
Of personal involvement?

BUTCHER   Have you no shame?
The man's unwell.

CARUTHER   Consider his great age!

FLAKE His snow-white hair confounds your low
suspicions.

ROMA Where are your proofs?

O'CASEY   The proofs are . . .

UI   Quiet, please!
Let's have a little quiet, friends!

GAFFLES, *in a loud voice*   For God's sake
Say something, Dogsborough!

A BODYGUARD, *suddenly roars* The chief wants
quiet!
Quiet!

Sudden silence.

UI   If I may say what moves me in
This hour and at this shameful sight – a white-
Haired man insulted while his friends look on
In silence – it is this! I trust you, Mr
Dogsborough. And I ask: Is this the face
Of guilt? Is this the eye of one who follows
Devious ways? Can you no longer
Distinguish white from black? A pretty pass
If things have come to such a pass!

CLARK   A man of
Untarnished reputation is accused
Of bribery!

O'CASEY   And more: of fraud. For I
Contend that this unholy shipyard, so
Maligned when Sheet was thought to be the
owner
Belonged to Dogsborough at the time the loan
Went through.

MULBERRY   A filthy lie!

CARUTHER   I'll stake my head

For Dogsborough. Summon the population!
I challenge you to find one man to doubt him.

A REPORTER, *to another who has come in*
Dogsborough's under suspicion!

THE OTHER REPORTER   Dogsborough?
Why not Abe Lincoln?

MULBERRY and FLAKE Witnesses!

O'CASEY   Oh
It's witnesses you want? Hey, Smith, where *is*
Our witness? Is he here? I see he is.

*One of his men has stepped into the doorway and
made a sign. All look toward the door. Short pause.
Then a burst of shots and noise are heard. Tumult.
The REPORTERS run out.*

THE REPORTERS It's outside. A machine-gun. –
What's your witnesses' name, O'Casey? – Bad
business. – Hi, Ui!

O'CASEY, *going to the door* Bowl! *Shouts out the
door.* Come on in!

THE MEN OF THE CAULIFLOWER TRUST What's
going on? – Somebody's been shot – On the
stairs – God damn it!

BUTCHER, *to Ui* More monkey business? Ui, it's all
over
Between us if . . .

UI   Yes?

O'CASEY   Bring him in!

POLICEMEN *carry in a corpse.*

O'CASEY It's Bowl. My witness, gentlemen, I fear
Is not in a fit state for questioning.

*He goes out quickly. The POLICEMEN have set down
BOWL's body in a corner.*

DOGSBOROUGH For God's sake, Gaffles, get me
out of here!

Without answering GAFFLES goes out past him.

UI, *going toward Dogsborough with outstretched
hand* Congratulations, Dogsborough. Don't
doubt
One way or another, I'll get things straightened
out.

A sign appears.

6

Hotel Mammoth. UI's *suite. Two bodyguards lead a
ragged* ACTOR *to* UI. *In the background* GIVOLA.

FIRST BODYGUARD It's an actor, boss. Unarmed.

SECOND BODYGUARD He can't afford a rod. He
was able to get tight because they pay him to

declaim in the saloons when they're tight. But I'm told that he's good. He's one of them classical guys.

UI Okay. Here's the problem. I've been given to understand that my pronunication leaves something to be desired. It looks like I'm going to have to say a word or two on certain occasions, especially when I get into politics, so I've decided to take lessons. The gestures too.

THE ACTOR Very well.

UI Get the mirror.

A BODYGUARD *comes front stage with a large standing mirror.*

UI First the walk. How do you guys walk in the theatre or the opera?

THE ACTOR I see what you mean. The grand style. Julius Caesar, Hamlet, Romeo – that's Shakespeare. Mr Ui, you've come to the right man. Old Mahonney can teach you the classical manner in ten minutes. Gentlemen, you see before you a tragic figure. Ruined by Shakespeare. An English poet. If it weren't for Shakespeare, I could be on Broadway right now. The tragedy of a character. 'Don't play Shakespeare when you're playing Ibsen, Mahonney! Look at the calendar! This is 1912, sir!' – 'Art knows no calendar, sir!' say I. 'And art is my life.' Alas.

GIVOLA I think you've got the wrong guy, boss. He's out of date.

UI We'll see about that. Walk around like they do in this Shakespeare.

The actor walks around.

UI Good!

GIVOLA You can't walk like that in front of cauliflower men. It ain't natural.

UI What do you mean it ain't natural? Nobody's natural in this day and age. When I walk I want people to know I'm walking.

He copies the ACTOR's *gait.*

THE ACTOR Head back. *Ui throws his head back.* The foot touches the ground toe first. *Ui's foot touches the ground toe first.* Good. Excellent. You have a natural gift. Only the arms. They're not quite right. Stiff. Perhaps if you joined your arms in front of your private parts. *Ui joins his arms in front of his private parts.* Not bad. Relaxed but firm. But head back. Good. Just the right gait for your purposes, I believe, Mr Ui. What else do you wish to learn?

UI How to stand. In front of people.

GIVOLA Have two big bruisers right behind you and you'll be standing pretty.

UI That's bunk. When I stand I don't want people looking at the two bozoes behind me. I want them looking at me. Correct me!

He takes a stance, his arms crossed over his chest.

THE ACTOR A possible solution. But common. You don't want to look like a barber, Mr Ui. Fold your arms like this. *He folds his arms in such a way that the backs of his hands remain visible. His palms are resting on his arms not far from the shoulder.* A trifling change, but the difference is incalculable. Draw the comparison in the mirror, Mr Ui.

UI *tries out the new position before the mirror.*

UI Not bad.

GIVOLA What's all this for, boss? Just for those Fancy-pants in the Trust?

UI   Hell, no! It's for
The little people. Why, for instance, do
You think this Clark makes such a show of grandeur?
Not for his peers. His bank account
Takes care of them, the same as my big bruisers
Lend me prestige in certain situations.
Clark makes a show of grandeur to impress
The little man. I mean to do the same.

GIVOLA But some will say it doesn't look inborn. Some people stick at that.

UI   I know they do.
But I'm not trying to convince professors
And smart-Alecks. My object is the little
Man's image of his master.

GIVOLA   Don't overdo
The master, boss. Better the democrat
The friendly, reassuring type in shirtsleeves.

UI I've got old Dogsborough for that.

GIVOLA   His image
Is kind of tarnished, I should say. He's still
An asset on the books, a venerable
Antique. But people aren't as eager as they
Were to exhibit him. They're not so sure
He's genuine. It's like the family Bible
Nobody opens any more since, piously
Turning the yellowed pages with a group
Of friends, they found a dried-out bedbug. But
Maybe he's good enough for Cauliflower.

UI I decide who's respectable.

GIVOLA   Sure thing, boss.
There's nothing wrong with Dogsborough. We can

Still use him. They haven't even dropped him
At City Hall. The crash would be too loud.
UI Sitting.
THE ACTOR Sitting. Sitting is almost the hardest,
Mr Ui. There are men who can walk; there are
men who can stand; but find me a man who can
sit. Take a chair with a backrest, Mr Ui. But
don't lean against it. Hands on thighs, to
abdomen, elbows away from body. How long
can you sit like that, Mr Ui?
UI As long as I please.
THE ACTOR Then everything's perfect, Mr Ui.
GIVOLA You know, boss, when old Dogsborough
passes on
Giri could take his place. He's got the
Popular touch. He plays the funny man
And laughs so loud in season that the plaster
Comes tumbling from the ceiling. Sometimes,
though
He does it out of season, as for instance
When you step forward as the modest son of
The Bronx you really were and talk about
Those seven determined youngsters.
UI   Then he laughs?
GIVOLA The plaster tumbles from the ceiling.
Don't
Tell him I said so or he'll think I've got
It in for him. But maybe you could make
Him stop collecting hats.
UI   What kind of hats?
GIVIOLA The hats of people he's rubbed out. And
running
Around with them in public. It's disgusting.
UI Forget it. I would never think of muzzling
The ox that treads my corn. I overlook
The petty foibles of my underlings.

To the ACTOR.

And now to speaking! Speak a speech for me!
THE ACTOR Shakespeare. Nothing else. Julius
Caesar. The Roman hero. *He draws a little book
from his pocket.* What do you say to Mark
Antony's speech? Over Caesar's body. Against
Brutus. The ringleader of Caesar's assassins. A
model of demagogy. Very famous. I played
Antony in Zenith in 1908. Just what you need,
Mr Ui. *He takes a stance and recites Mark Antony's
speech line for line.*
Friends, Romans, countrymen, lend me your
ears!

Reading from the little book, UI *speaks the lines
after him. Now and then the* ACTOR *corrects him,
but in the main* UI *keeps his rough staccato
delivery.*

THE ACTOR I come to bury Caesar, not to praise
him.
The evil that men do lives after them;
The good is oft interred with their bones;
So let it be with Caesar. The noble Brutus
Hath told you Caesar was ambitious.
If it were so, it was a grievous fault,
And grievously hath Caesar answer'd it.
UI, *continues by himself* Here, under leave of
Brutus and the rest –
For Brutus is an honourable man;
So are they all, all honourable men –
Come I to speak in Caesar's funeral.
He was my friend, faithful and just to me;
But Brutus says he was ambitious;
And Brutus is an honourable man.
He hath brought many captives home to Rome,
Whose ransoms did the general coffers fill;
Did this in Caesar seem ambitious?
When that the poor have cried, Caesar hath
wept;
Ambition should be made of sterner stuff.
Yet Brutus says he was ambitious;
And Brutus is an honourable man.
You all did see that on the Lupercal
I thrice presented him a kingly crown,
Which he did thrice refuse. Was this ambition?
Yet Brutus says he was ambitious;
And sure he is an honourable man.
I speak not to disprove what Brutus spoke,
But here I am to speak what I do know.
You all did love him once, not without cause?
What cause withholds you then, to mourn for
him?

During the last lines the curtain slowly falls.

A sign appears.

7

Offices of the Cauliflower Trust. ARTURO UI,
ERNESTO ROMA, GIUSEPPE GIVOLA, EMANUELE
GIRI *and* BODYGUARDS. *A group of small*
VEGETABLE DEALERS *is listening to* UI. OLD
DOGSBOROUGH, *who is ill, is sitting on the platform
beside* UI. *In the background* CLARK.

UI, *bellowing* Murder! Extortion! Highway robbery!
Machine-guns sputtering on our city streets!
People going about their business, law-abiding
Citizens on their way to City Hall
To make a statement, murdered in broad
daylight!
And what, I ask you, do our town fathers do?
Nothing! These honourable men are much

Too busy planning their shady little deals
And slandering respectable citizens
To think of law enforcement.

GIVOLA   Hear!

UI   In short

Chaos is rampant. Because if everybody
Can do exactly what he pleases, if
Dog can eat dog without a second thought
I call it chaos. Look. Suppose I'm sitting
Peacefully in my vegetable store
For instance, or driving my cauliflower truck
And someone comes barging not so peacefully
Into my store: 'Hands up!' Or with his gun
Punctures my tyres. Under such conditions
Peace is unthinkable. But once I know
The score, once I recognise that men are not
Innocent lambs, then I've got to find a way
To stop these men from smashing up my shop
    and
Making me, when it suits them, put 'em up
And keep 'em up, when I could use my hands
For better things, for instance, counting pickles.
For such is man. He'll never put aside
His hardware of his own free will, say
For love of virtue, or to earn the praises
Of certain silver tongues at City Hall.
If I don't shoot, the other fellow will.
That's logic. Okay. And maybe now you'll ask:
What's to be done? I'll tell you. But first get
This straight: What you've been doing so far is
Disastrous: Sitting idly at your counters
Hoping that everything will be all right
And meanwhile disunited, bickering
Among yourselves, instead of mustering
A strong defence force that would shield you
    from
The gangsters' depredations. No, I say
This can't go on. The first thing that's needed
Is unity. The second is sacrifices.
What sacrifices? you may ask. Are we
To part with thirty cents on every dollar
For mere protection? No, nothing doing.
Our money is too precious. If protection
Were free of charge, then yes, we'd be all for it.
Well, my dear vegetable dealers, things
Are not so simple. Only death is free:
Everything else costs money. And that includes
Protection, peace and quiet. Life is like
That, and because it never will be any
    different
These gentlemen and I (there are more
    outside)
Have resolved to offer you protection.

GIVOLA *and* ROMA *applaud.*

                                                    But
To show you that we mean to operate
On solid business principles, we've asked
Our partner, Mr Clark here, the wholesaler
Whom you all know, to come here and address
    you.

ROMA *pulls* CLARK *forward. A few of the*
VEGETABLE DEALERS *applaud.*

GIVOLA Mr Clark, I bid you welcome in the name
Of this assembly. Mr Ui is honoured
To see the Cauliflower Trust supporting his
Initiative. I thank you, Mr Clark.

CLARK We of the Cauliflower Trust observe
Ladies and gentlemen, with consternation
How hard it's getting for your vegetable
Dealers to sell your wares. 'Because,' I hear
You say, 'they're too expensive.' Yes, but why
Are they expensive? It's because our packers
And teamsters, pushed by outside agitators
Want more and more. And that's what Mr Ui
And Mr Ui's friends will put an end to.

FIRST DEALER But if the little man gets less and
    less
How is he going to buy our vegetables?

UI Your question is a good one. Here's my
    answer:
Like it or not, this modern world of ours
Is inconceivable without the working man
If only as a customer. I've always
Insisted that honest work is no disgrace.
Far from it. It's constructive and conducive
To profits. As an individual
The working man has all my sympathy.
It's only when he bands together, when he
Presumes to meddle in affairs beyond
His understanding, such as profits, wages
Etcetera, that I say: Watch your step
Brother, a worker is somebody who works.
But when you strike, when you stop working,
    then
You're not a worker any more. Then you're
A menace to society. And that's
Where I step in.

CLARK *applauds.*

                            However, to convince you
That everything is open and above
Board, let me call your attention to the presence
Here of a man well-known, I trust, to
Everybody here for his sterling honesty
And incorruptible morality.
His name is Dogsborough.

The VEGETABLE DEALERS *applaud a little louder.*

Mr Dogsborough
I owe you an incomparable debt
Of gratitude. Our meeting was the work
Of Providence. I never will forget –
Not if I live to be a hundred – how
You took me to your arms, an unassuming
Son of the Bronx and chose me for your friend
Nay more, your son.

He seizes DOGSBOROUGH's *limply dangling hand
and shakes it.*

GIVOLA, *in an undertone* How touching! Father
and son!
GIRI, *steps forward* Well, folks, the boss has
spoken for us all.
I see some questions written on your faces.
Ask them! Don't worry. We won't eat you. You
Play square with us and we'll play square with
you.
But get this straight: we haven't got much
patience
With idle talk, especially the kind
That carps and cavils and finds fault
With everything. You'll find us open, though
To any healthy, positive suggestion
On ways and means of doing what must be
done.
So fire away!

The VEGETABLE DEALERS *don't breathe a
word.*

GIVOLA, *unctuously* And no holds barred. I think
You know me and my little flower shop.
A BODYGUARD Hurrah for Givola!
GIVOLA Okay, then. Do
You want protection? Or would you rather have
Murder, extortion and highway robbery?
FIRST DEALER Things have been pretty quiet
lately. I
Haven't had any trouble in my store.
SECOND DEALER Nothing's wrong in my place.
THIRD DEALER Nor in mine.
GIVOLA That's odd!
SECOND DEALER We've heard that recently in
bars
Things have been happening just like Mr Ui
Was telling us, that glasses have been smashed
And gin poured down the drain in places that
Refused to cough up for protection. But
Things have been peaceful in the green goods
business.
So far at least, thank God.
ROMA And what about
Sheet's murder? And Bowl's death? Is that
What you call peaceful?

SECOND DEALER But is that connected
With cauliflower, Mr Roma?
ROMA No. Just a minute.

ROMA *goes over to* UI *who after his big speech has
been sitting there exhausted and listless. After a few
words he motions to* GIRI *to join them.* GIVOLA *also
takes part in a hurried whispered conversation. Then*
GIRI *motions to one of the* BODYGUARDS *and goes
out quickly with him.*

GIVOLA Friends, I've been asked to tell you that a
poor
Unhappy woman wishes to express
Her thanks to Mr Ui in your presence.

*He goes to the rear and leads in a heavily made-up
and flashily dressed woman –* DOCKDAISY *– who is
holding a little girl by the hand. The three stop in
front of* UI, *who has stood up.*

GIVOLA Speak, Mrs Bowl.

To the VEGETABLE DEALERS.

It's Mrs Bowl, the young
Widow of Mr Bowl, the late accountant
Of the Cauliflower Trust, who yesterday
While on his way to City Hall to do
His duty, was struck down by hand unknown.
Mrs Bowl!
DOCKDAISY Mr Ui, in my profound bereavement
over my husband who was foully murdered
while on his way to City Hall in the exercise of
his civic duty, I wish to express my heartfelt
thanks for the flowers you sent me and my little
girl, aged six, who has been robbed of her father.
To the vegetable dealers. Gentlemen, I'm only a
poor widow and all I have to say is that without
Mr Ui I'd be out in the street as I shall gladly
testify at any time. My little girl, aged five, and I
will never forget it, Mr Ui.

UI *gives* DOCKDAISY *his hand and chucks the child
under the chin.*

GIVOLA Bravo!

GIRI *wearing* BOWL's *hat cuts through the crowd,
followed by several gangsters carrying large gasoline
cans. They make their way to the exit.*

UI Mrs Bowl, my sympathies. This lawlessness
This crime wave's got to stop because . . .
GIVOLA, *as the dealers start leaving* Hold it!
The meeting isn't over. The next item
Will be a song in memory of poor Bowl
Sung by our friend James Greenwool, followed
by
A collection for the widow. He's a baritone.

One of the BODYGUARDS *steps forward and sings a sentimental song in which the word 'home' occurs frequently. During the performance the gangsters sit rapt, their heads in their hands, or leaning back with eyes closed, etc. The meagre applause at the end is interrupted by the howling of police and fire sirens. A red glow is seen in a large window in the background.*

ROMA Fire on the waterfront!

A VOICE   Where?

A BODYGUARD *entering*   Is there a vegetable
   Dealer named Hook in the house?

SECOND DEALER   That's me. What's wrong?

THE BODYGUARD Your warehouse is on fire.

HOOK, *the dealer, rushes out. A few follow him Others go to the window.*

ROMA   Hold it!
   Nobody leave the room!

To the BODYGUARD.

         Is it arson?

THE BODYGUARD It must be. They've found
   some gasoline cans.

THIRD DEALER Some gasoline cans were taken
   out of here!

ROMA, *in a rage* What's that? Is somebody
   insinuating
   We did it?

A BODYGUARD, *pokes his automatic into the man's
   ribs* What was being taken out
   Of here? Did you see any gasoline cans?

OTHER BODYGUARDS, *to other dealers* Did you see
   any cans? – Did you?

THE DEALERS   Not I . . .
   Me neither.

ROMA   That's better.

GIVOLA, *quickly*   Ha. The very man
   Who just a while ago was telling us
   That all was quiet on the green goods front
   Now sees his warehouse burning, turned to
      ashes
   By malefactors. Don't you see? Can you
   Be blind? You've got to get together. And quick!

UI, *bellowing* Things in this town are looking very
   sick!
   First murder and now arson! This should show
   You men that no one's safe from the next blow!

A sign appears.

8

The warehouse fire trial. PRESS. JUDGE.
PROSECUTOR. DEFENCE COUNSEL. YOUNG

DOGSBOROUGH. GIRI. GIVOLA. DOCKDAISY.
BODYGUARDS. VEGETABLE DEALERS *and* FISH,
the accused.

a

EMANUELE GIRI *stands in front of the witness's
chair, pointing at* FISH, *the accused, who is sitting in
utter apathy.*

GIRI, *shouting* There sits the criminal who lit the
   fire!
   When I challenged him he was slinking down
      the street
   Clutching a gasoline can to his chest.
   Stand up, you bastard, when I'm talking to you.

FISH *is pulled to his feet. He stands swaying.*

THE JUDGE Defendant, pull yourself together.
   This is a court of law. You are on trial for arson.
   That is a very serious matter, and don't forget it!

FISH, *in a thick voice* Arlarlarl.

THE JUDGE Where did you get that gasoline can?

FISH Arlarl.

At a sign from the JUDGE *an excessively well-dressed,
sinister-looking* DOCTOR *bends down over* FISH *and
exchanges glances with* GIRI.

THE DOCTOR Simulating.

DEFENCE COUNSEL The defence moves that other
   doctors be consulted.

THE JUDGE, *smiling* Denied.

DEFENCE COUNSEL Mr Giri, how did you happen
   to be on the spot when this fire, which reduced
   twenty-two buildings to ashes, broke out in Mr
   Hook's warehouse?

GIRI I was taking a walk for my digestion.

Some of the BODYGUARDS *laugh.* GIRI *joins in the
laughter.*

DEFENCE COUNSEL Are you aware, Mr Giri, that
   Mr Fish, the defendant, is an unemployed
   worker, that he had never been in Chicago
   before and arrived here on foot the day before
   the fire?

GIRI What? When?

DEFENCE COUNSEL Is the registration number of
   your car XXXXXX?

GIRI Yes.

DEFENCE COUNSEL Was this car parked outside
   Dogsborough's restaurant on 87th Street during
   the four hours preceding the fire, and was
   defendant Fish dragged out of that restaurant in
   a state of unconsciousness?

GIRI How should I know? I spent the whole day
   on a little excursion to Cicero, where I met

fifty-two persons who are all ready to testify that they saw me.

The BODYGUARDS *laugh.*

DEFENCE COUNSEL Your previous statement left me with the impression that you were taking a walk for your digestion in the Chicago waterfront area.
GIRI Any objection to my eating in Cicero and digesting in Chicago?

Loud and prolonged laughter in which the JUDGE *joins. Darkness. An organ plays Chopin's* Funeral March *in dance rhythm.*

b

When the lights go on, HOOK, *the vegetable dealer, is sitting in the witness's chair.*

DEFENCE COUNSEL Did you ever quarrel with the defendant, Mr Hook? Did you ever see him before?
HOOK Never.
DEFENCE COUNSEL Have you ever seen Mr Giri?
HOOK Yes. In the office of the Cauliflower Trust on the day of the fire.
DEFENCE COUNSEL Before the fire?
HOOK Just before the fire. He passed through the room with four men carrying gasoline cans.

Commotion on the press bench and among the BODYGUARDS.

THE JUDGE Would the gentlemen of the press please be quiet.
DEFENCE COUNSEL What premises does your warehouse adjoin, Mr Hook?
HOOK The premises of the former Sheet shipyard. There's a passage connecting my warehouse with the shipyard.
DEFENCE COUNSEL Are you aware, Mr Hook, that Mr Giri lives in the former Sheet shipyard and consequently has access to the premises?
HOOK Yes. He's the stockroom superintendent.

Increased commotion on the press bench. The BODYGUARDS *boo and take a menacing attitude toward* HOOK, *the* DEFENCE *and the* PRESS. YOUNG DOGSBOROUGH *rushes up to the* JUDGE *and whispers something in his ear.*

JUDGE Order in the court! The defendant is unwell. The court is adjourned.

Darkness. The organ starts again to play Chopin's Funeral March *in dance rhythm.*

c

When the lights go on, HOOK *is sitting in the witness's chair. He is in a state of collapse, with a cane beside him and bandages over his head and eyes.*

THE PROSECUTOR Is your eyesight poor, Hook?
HOOK, *with difficulty* Yes.
THE PROSECUTOR Would you say you were capable of recognising anyone clearly and definitely?
HOOK No.
THE PROSECUTOR Do you, for instance, recognise this man?

He points at GIRI.

HOOK No.
THE PROSECUTOR You're not prepared to say that you ever saw him before?
HOOK No.
THE PROSECUTOR And now, Hook, a very important question. Think well before you answer. Does your warehouse adjoin the premises of the former Sheet shipyard?
HOOK, *after a pause* No.
THE PROSECUTOR That is all.

Darkness. The organ starts playing again.

d

When the lights go on, DOCKDAISY *is sitting in the witness's chair.*

DOCKDAISY, *mechanically* I recognise the defendant perfectly because of his guilty look and because he is five feet eight inches tall. My sister-in-law has informed me that he was seen outside City Hall on the afternoon my husband was shot while entering City Hall. He was carrying a Webster submachine gun and made a suspicious impression.

Darkness. The organ starts playing again.

e

When the lights go on, GIUSEPPE GIVOLA *is sitting in the witness's chair.* GREENWOOL, *the bodyguard, is standing near him.*

THE PROSECUTOR It has been alleged that certain men were seen carrying gasoline cans out of the offices of the Cauliflower Trust before the fire. What do you know about this?
GIVOLA It couldn't be anybody but Mr Greenwool.
THE PROSECUTOR Is Mr Greenwool in your employ?
GIVOLA Yes.

THE PROSECUTOR What is your profession, Mr Givola?

GIVOLA Florist.

THE PROSECUTOR Do florists use large quantities of gasoline?

GIVOLA, *seriously* No, only for plant lice.

THE PROSECUTOR What was Mr Greenwool doing in the offices of the Cauliflower Trust?

GIVOLA Singing a song.

THE PROSECUTOR Then he can't very well have carried any gasoline cans to Hook's warehouse at the same time.

GIVOLA It's out of the question. It's not in his character to start fires. He's a baritone.

THE PROSECUTOR If it please the court, I should like witness Greenwool to sing the fine song he was singing in the offices of the Cauliflower Trust while the warehouse was being set on fire.

THE JUDGE The court does not consider it necessary.

GIVOLA I protest.

He rises.

The bias in this courtroom is outrageous.
Cleancut young fellows who in broadest daylight
Fire a well-meant shot or two are treated
Like shady characters. It's scandalous.

Laughter. Darkness. The organ starts playing again.

f

When the lights go on, the courtroom shows every indication of utter exhaustion.

THE JUDGE The press has dropped hints that this court might be subject to pressure from certain quarters. The court wishes to state that it has been subjected to no pressure of any kind and is conducting this trial in perfect freedom. I believe this will suffice.

THE PROSECUTOR Your Honour! In view of the fact that defendant Fish persists in simulating dementia, the prosecution holds that he cannot be questioned any further. We therefore move . . .

DEFENCE COUNSEL Your honour. The defendant is coming to!

Commotion.

FISH, *seems to be waking up* Arlarlwaratarlawatrla.

DEFENCE COUNSEL Water! Your Honour! I ask leave to question defendant Fish!

Uproar.

THE PROSECUTOR I object! I see no indication

that Fish is in his right mind. It's all a machination on the part of the defence, cheap sensationalism, demagogy!

FISH Watr.

Supported by the DEFENCE COUNSEL, *he stands up.*

DEFENCE COUNSEL Fish. Can you answer me?

FISH Yarl.

DEFENCE COUNSEL Fish, tell the court: Did you, on the 28th of last month, set fire to a vegetable warehouse on the waterfront? Yes or no?

FISH N-n-no.

DEFENCE COUNSEL When did you arrive in Chicago, Fish?

FISH Water.

DEFENCE COUNSEL Water!

Commotion. YOUNG DOGSBOROUGH *has stepped up to the* JUDGE *and is talking to him emphatically.*

GIRI *stands up square-shouldered and bellows* Frame-up! Lies! Lies!

DEFENCE COUNSEL Did you ever see this man – *He indicates Giri.* – before?

FISH Yes. Water.

DEFENCE COUNSEL Where? Was it in Dogsborough's restaurant on the waterfront?

FISH, *faintly* Yes.

Uproar. The BODYGUARDS *draw their guns and boo. The* DOCTOR *comes running in with a glass. He pours the contents into* FISH's *mouth before the* DEFENCE COUNSEL *can take the glass out of his hand.*

DEFENCE COUNSEL I object. I move that this glass be examined.

THE JUDGE, *exchanging glances with the* PROSECUTOR Motion denied.

DOCKDAISY *screams at* FISH Murderer!

DEFENCE COUNSEL Your Honour!
Because the mouth of truth cannot be stopped with earth
They're trying to stop it with a piece of paper
A sentence to be handed down as though
Your Honour – that's their hope – should properly
Be titled Your Disgrace. They cry to justice:
Hands up! Is this our city, which has aged
A hundred years in seven days beneath
The onslaught of a small but bloody brood
Of monsters, now to see its justice murdered
Nay, worse than murdered, desecrated by
Submission to brute force? Your Honour!
Suspend this trial!

THE PROSECUTOR I object!

GIRI   You dog!
You lying, peculating dog! Yourself
A poisoner! Come on! Let's step outside!
I'll rip your guts out! Gangster!
DEFENCE COUNSEL   The whole
Town knows this man.
GIRI, *fuming*   Shut up!

When the JUDGE *tries to interrupt him.*

                                    You too!
Just keep your trap shut if you want to live!

He runs short of breath and the JUDGE *manages to speak.*

THE JUDGE Order in the court. Defence counsel
will incur charges of contempt of court. Mr
Giri's indignation is quite understandable. *To the*
DEFENCE COUNSEL Continue.
DEFENCE COUNSEL Fish! Did they give you
anything to drink at Dogsborough's restaurant?
Fish! Fish!
GIRI, *bellowing* Go on and shout! Looks like his
tyre's gone down!
We'll see who's running things in this here town!

Uproar. Darkness. The organ starts again to play
Chopin's Funeral March *in dance rhythm.*

g

*As the lights go on for the last time, the judge stands
up and in a toneless voice delivers the sentence. The
defendant is deathly pale.*

THE JUDGE Charles Fish, I find you guilty of
arson and sentence you to fifteen years' hard
labour.

A sign appears.

9

a

Cicero. A WOMAN *climbs out of a shot-up truck and
staggers forward.*

THE WOMAN Help! Help! Don't run away. Who'll
testify?
My husband is in that truck! They got him!
Help!
My arm is smashed. . . And so's the truck. I need
A bandage for my arm. They gun us down
Like rabbits! God! Won't anybody help?
You murderers! My husband! I know who's
Behind it! Ui! *Raging:* Fiend! Monster! Shit!
You'd make an honest piece of shit cry out:
Where can I wash myself? You lousy louse!

And people stand for it! And we go under!
Hey you! It's Ui!

A burst of machine-gun fire nearby. She collapses.

                Ui did this job!
Where's everybody? Help! who'll stop that mob?

b

DOGSBOROUGH's *country house. Night toward
morning.* DOGSBOROUGH *is writing his will and
confession.*

DOGSBOROUGH And so I, honest Dogsborough
acquiesced
In all the machinations of that bloody gang
After full eighty years of uprightness.
I'm told that those who've known me all along
Are saying I don't know what's going on
That if I knew I wouldn't stand for it.
Alas, I know it all. I know who set
Fire to Hook's warehouse. And I know who
dragged
Poor Fish into the restaurant and doped him.
I know that when Sheet died a bloody death
His steamship ticket in his pocket, Roma
Was there. I know that Giri murdered Bowl
That afternoon outside of City Hall
Because he knew too much about myself
Honest old Dogsborough. I know that he
Shot Hook, and saw him with Hook's hat.
I know that Givola committed five
Murders, here itemised. I also know
All about Ui, and I know he knew
All this – the deaths of Sheet and Bowl, Givola's
Murders and all about the fire. All this
Your honest Dogsborough knew. All this
He tolerated out of sordid lust
For gain and fear of forfeiting your trust.

10

Hotel Mammoth. UI's *suite.* UI *is sitting slumped in a
deep chair, staring into space.* GIVOLA *is writing and
two* BODYGUARDS *are looking over his shoulder,
grinning.*

GIVOLA And so I, Dogsborough, bequeath my bar
To good hard-working Givola. My country
House to the brave, though somewhat hot-
headed Giri.
And I bequeath my son to honest Roma.
I furthermore request that you appoint
Roma police chief, Giri judge, and Givola
Commissioner of welfare. For my own
Position I would warmly recommend

Arturo Ui, who, believe your honest
Old Dogsborough, is worthy of it. – That's
Enough, I think, let's hope he kicks it soon.
This testament will do wonders. Now that the
 old
Man's known to be dying and the hope arises
Of laying him to rest with relative
Dignity, in clean earth, it's well to tidy up
His corpse. A pretty epitaph is needed.
Ravens from olden time have battened on
The reputation of the fabulous
White raven that somebody saw sometime
And somewhere. This old codger's their white
 raven.
I guess they couldn't find a whiter one.
And by the way, boss, Giri for my taste
Is too much with him. I don't like it.

UI, *starting up*　　　　　　　　Giri?
What about Giri?

GIVOLA　　　　　　Only that he's spending
A little too much time with Dogsborough.
Don't trust him.

GIRI *comes in wearing a new hat*, HOOK's.

GIVOLA　　　　　　I don't either. Hi, Giri
How's Dogsborough's apoplexy?

GIRI　　　　　　　　　　He refuses
To let the doctor in.

GIVOLA　　　　　　Our brilliant doctor
Who took such loving care of Fish?

GIRI　　　　　　　　　　No other
Will do. The old man talks too much.

UI Maybe somebody's talked too much to him . . .

GIRI What's that? *To Givola* You skunk, have you
been stinking up
The air around here again?

GIVOLA, *alarmed*　　　　　Just read the will
Dear Giri.

GIRI, *snatches it from him* What! Police chief?
 Him? Roma?
You must be crazy.

GIVOLA　　　　　　He demands it. I'm
Against it too. The bastard can't be trusted
Across the street.

ROMA *comes in followed by* BODYGUARDS.

　　　　　　　　　Hi, Roma. Take a look at
This will.

ROMA, *grabbing it out of his hands* Okay, let's see
it. What do you know!
Giri a judge! But where's the old man's scribble?

GIRI Under his pillow. He's been trying to
Smuggle it out. Five times I've caught his son.

ROMA *holds out his hand* Let's have it, Giri.

GIRI　　　　　　　What? I haven't got it.

ROMA Oh yes, you have!

They glare at each other furiously.

　　　　　　　　　I know what's on your mind.
There's something about Sheet. That concerns
 me.

GIRI Bowl figures in it too. That concerns *me*.

ROMA Okay, but you're both jerks, and I'm a man.
I know you, Giri, and you too, Givola.
I'd even say your crippled leg was phony.
Why do I always find you bastards here?
What are you cooking up? What lies have they
Been telling you about me, Arturo? Watch
Your step, you pipsqueaks. If I catch you trying
To cross me up, I'll rub you out like blood spots!

GIRI Roma, you'd better watch your tongue! I'm
 not
One of your two-bit gunmen.

ROMA, *to his bodyguards*　　　That means you!
That's what they're calling you at headquarters!
They hobnob with the Cauliflower Trust –

Pointing to GIRI.

That shirt was made to order by Clark's tailor –
You two-bit gunmen do the dirty work –
And you – *To* UI – put up with it.

UI, *as though waking up*　　　Put up with what?

GIVOLA His shooting up Caruther's trucks!
 Caruther's
A member of the Trust!

UI　　　　　　　Did you shoot up
Caruther's trucks?

ROMA　　　　　I gave no orders. Just
Some of the boys. Spontaneous combustion.
They don't see why it's always the small
 grocers
That have to sweat and bleed. Why not the big
 wheels?
Damn it, Arturo, I myself don't get it.

GIVOLA The Trust is good and mad.

GIRI　　　　　　　　　Clark says they're only
Waiting for it to happen one more time.
He's put in a complaint with Dogsborough.

UI, *morosely* Ernesto, these things mustn't
 happen.

GIRI　　　　　　　　　　Crack down, boss!
These guys are getting too big for their breeches!

GIVOLA The Trust is good and mad, boss!

ROMA *pulls his gun. To* GIRI *and* GIVOLA Okay.
 Hands up!

To their BODYGUARDS

　　　　　　　　　You too!
Hands up the lot of you. No monkey business!
Now back up to the wall.

GIVOLA, *his men, and* GIRI *raise their hands and with an air of resignation back up to the wall.*

UI, *indifferently*　　　　What is all this?
　Ernesto, don't make them nervous. What are you guys
　Squabbling about? So some palooka's wasted
　Some bullets on a cauliflower truck!
　Such misunderstandings can be straightened out.
　Everything is running smooth as silk.
　The fire was a big success. The stores
　Are paying for protection. Thirty cents
　On every dollar. Almost half the city
　Has knuckled under in five days. Nobody
　Raises a hand against us. And I've got
　Bigger and better projects.
GIVOLA, *quickly*　　　　Projects? What
　For instance?
GIRI　　　　Fuck your projects. Get this fool
　To let me put my hands down.
ROMA　　　　Safety first, Arturo.
　We'd better leave them up!
GIVOLA　　　　Won't it look sweet
　If Clark comes in and sees us here like this!
UI　Ernesto, put that rod away!
ROMA　　　　No dice!
　Wake up, Arturo. Don't you see their game?
　They're selling you out to the Clarks and
　　Dogsboroughs.
　'If Clark comes in and sees us!' What, I ask you
　Has happened to the shipyard's funds? We haven't
　Seen a red cent. The boys shoot up the stores
　Tote gasoline to warehouses and sigh:
　We made Arturo what he is today
　And he doesn't know us any more. He's playing
　The shipyard owner and tycoon. Wake up
　Arturo!
GIRI　　　　Right. And speak up. Tell us where
　You stand.
UI *jumps up*　Are you boys trying to pressure me
　At gunpoint? Better not, I'm warning you
　You won't get anywhere with me like that.
　You'll only have yourselves to blame for
　The consequences. I'm a quiet man. But
　I won't be threatened. Either trust me blindly
　Or go your way. I owe you no accounting.
　Just do your duty, and do it to the full.
　The recompense is up to me, because
　Duty comes first and then the recompense.
　What I demand of you is trust. You lack
　Faith, and where faith is lacking, all is lost.
　How do you think I got this far? By faith!
　Because of my fanatical, my unflinching

Faith in the cause! With faith and nothing else
I flung a challenge at this city and forced
It to its knees. With faith I made my way
To Dogsborough. With faith I climbed the steps
Of City Hall. With nothing in my naked
Hands but indomitable faith!
ROMA　　　　And
　A tommy gun!
UI　　　　No, other men have them
　But lack firm faith in their predestination
　To leadership! And that is why you too
　Need to have faith in me! Have faith! Believe that
　I know what's best for you and that I'm
　Resolved to put it through. That I will find
　The road to victory. If Dogsborough
　Passes away, then I decide who gets to
　Be what. I say no more, but rest assured:
　You'll all be satisfied.
GIVOLA *puts his hand on his heart*　Arturo!
ROMA, *sullenly*　　　　Scram
　You guys!

GIRI, GIVOLA *and* GIVOLA's BODYGUARD *go out slowly with their hands up.*

GIRI, *leaving, to* ROMA　I like your hat.
GIVOLA, *leaving*　　　Dear Roma . . .
ROMA　　　　Scram!
　Giri, you clown, don't leave your laugh behind.
　And Givola, you crook, be sure to take
　Your clubfoot, though I'm pretty sure you stole it.

When they are gone, UI *relapses into his brooding.*

UI　I want to be alone.
ROMA, *standing still*　　　Arturo, if I
　Hadn't the kind of faith you've just described
　I'd sometimes find it hard to look my
　Men in the face. We've got to act. And quickly!
　Giri is cooking up some dirty work.
UI　Don't worry about Giri. I am planning
　Bigger and better things. And now, Ernesto
　To you, my oldest friend and trusted lieutenant
　I will divulge them.
ROMA, *beaming*　　　Speak, Arturo. Giri
　And what I had to say of him can wait.

He sits down with UI. ROMA's *men stand waiting in the corner.*

UI　We're finished with Chicago. I need more.
ROMA　More?
UI　　　　Vegetables are sold in other cities.
ROMA　But how are you expecting to get in?

UI   Through
   The front door, through the back door, through
     the windows.
   Resisted, sent away, called back again.
   Booed and acclaimed. With threats and
     supplications
   Appeals and insults, gentle force and steel
   Embrace. In short, the same as here.
ROMA   Except
   Conditions aren't the same in other places.
UI I have in mind a kind of dress rehearsal
   In a small town. That way we'll see
   Whether conditions are so different. I
   Doubt it.
ROMA   And where have you resolved to stage
   This dress rehearsal?
UI   In Cicero.
ROMA   But there
   They've got this Dullfeet with his Journal
   For Vegetables and Positive Thinking
   Which every Saturday accuses me
   Of murdering Sheet.
UI   That's got to stop.
ROMA It will. These journalists have enemies.
   Their black and white makes certain people
   See red. Myself, for instance. Yes, Arturo
   I think these accusations can be silenced.
UI I'm sure they can. The Trust is negotiating
   With Cicero right now. For the time being
   We'll just sell cauliflower peacefully.
ROMA Who's doing this negotiating?
UI   Clark.
   But he's been having trouble. On our account.
ROMA I see. So Clark is in it. I wouldn't trust
   That Clark around the corner.
UI   In Cicero
   They say we're following the Cauliflower
   Trust like its shadow. They want cauliflower,
     but
   They don't want us. The shopkeepers don't like
     us.
   A feeling shared by others: Dullfeet's wife
   For instance, who for years now has been
     running
   A greengoods wholesale house. She'd like to join
   The Trust, and would have joined except for us.
ROMA You mean this plan of moving in on Cicero
   Didn't start with you at all, but with the Trust?
   Arturo, now I see it all. I see
   Their rotten game.
UI   Whose game?
ROMA   The Trust's.
   The goings-on at Dogsborough's! His will!
   It's all a machination of the Trust.
   They want the Cicero connection. You're in

The way. But how can they get rid of you?
   You've got them by the balls, because they
     needed
   You for their dirty business and connived at
   Your methods. But now they've found a way:
   Old Dogsborough confesses and repairs
   In ash and sackcloth to his coffin.
   The cauliflower boys with deep emotion
   Retrieve this paper from his hands and sobbing
   Read it to the assembled press: how he repents
   And solemnly adjures them to wipe out
   The plague which he – as he confesses – brought
   In, and restore the cauliflower trade
   To its time-honoured practices.
   That's what they plan, Arturo. They're all in it:
   Giri, who gets Dogsborough to scribble wills
   And who is hand in glove with Clark, who's
     having
   Trouble in Cicero because of us
   And wants pure sunshine when he shovels
     shekels.
   Givola, who smells carrion. – This Dogsborough
   Honest old Dogsborough with his two-timing
     will
   That splatters you with muck has got to be
   Rubbed out, Arturo, or your best-laid plans
   For Cicero are down the drain!
UI   You think
   It's all a plot? It's true. They've kept me out
   Of Cicero. I've noticed that.
ROMA   Arturo
   I beg you: let me handle this affair!
   I tell you what: my boys and I will beat
   It out to Dogsborough's tonight
   And take him with us. To the hospital
   We'll tell him – and deliver him to the
     morgue.
UI But Giri's with him at the villa.
ROMA   He
   Can stay there.

They exchange glances.

               Two birds one stone.
UI   And Givola?
ROMA On the way back I'll drop in at the florist's
   And order handsome wreaths for Dogsborough.
   For Giri too, the clown. And I'll pay cash.

He pats his gun.

UI Ernesto, this contemptible project of
   The Dogsboroughs and Clarks and Dullfeets
   To squeeze me out of Cicero's affairs
   By coldly branding me a criminal
   Must be frustrated with an iron hand.
   I put my trust in you.

ROMA   And well you may.
  But you must meet with us before we start
  And give the boys a talk to make them see
  The matter in its proper light. I'm not
  So good at talking.
UI, *shaking his hand* It's a deal.
ROMA   I knew it
  Arturo! This was how it had to be
  Decided. Say, the two of us! Say, you
  And me! Like in the good old days. *To his men.*

To his men.

                              What did
  I tell you, boys? He gives us the green light.
UI I'll be there.
ROMA   At eleven.
UI   Where?
ROMA   At the garage.
  I'm a new man. At last we'll see some fight!

He goes out quickly with his men. Pacing the floor, UI
prepares the speech he is going to make to ROMA's
men.

UI Friends, much as I regret to say it, word
  Has reached me that behind my back perfidious
  Treason is being planned. Men close to me
  Men whom I trusted implicitly
  Have turned against me. Goaded by ambition
  And crazed by lust for gain, these despicable
  Fiends have conspired with the cauliflower
  Moguls – no, that won't do – with who? I've got
    it!
  With the police, to coldly liquidate you
  And even, so I hear, myself! My patience
  Is at an end. I therefore order you
  Under Ernesto Roma who enjoys
  My fullest confidence, tonight . . .

Enter CLARK, GIRI *and* BETTY DULLFEET.

GIRI, *noticing that* UI *looks frightened* It's only
  Us, boss.
CLARK   Ui, let me introduce
  Mrs Dullfeet of Cicero. The Trust
  Asks you to give her your attention, and hopes
  The two of you will come to terms.
UI, *scowling*   I'm listening.
CLARK A merger, as you know, is being
    considered
  Between Chicago's Cauliflower Trust
  And Cicero's purveyors. In the course
  Of the negotiations, Cicero
  Objected to your presence on the board.
  The Trust was able, after some discussion
  To overcome this opposition. Mrs Dullfeet
  Is here . . .

MRS DULLFEET To clear up the
  misunderstanding.
  Moreover, I should like to point out that
  My husband, Mr Dullfeet's newspaper
  Campaign was not directed against you
  Mr Ui.
UI   Against who was it directed?
CLARK I may as well speak plainly, Ui. Sheet's
  'Suicide' made a very bad impression
  In Cicero. Whatever else Sheet may
  Have been, he was a shipyard owner
  A leading citizen, and not some Tom
  Dick or Harry whose death arouses no
  Comment. And something else. Caruther's
  Garage complains of an attack on one of
  Its trucks. And one of your men, Ui, is
  Involved in both these cases.
MRS DULLFEET   Every child in
  Cicero knows Chicago's cauliflower
  Is stained with blood.
UI   Have you come here to insult me?
MRS DULLFEET No, no. Not you, since Mr Clark
    has vouched
  For you. It's this man Roma.
CLARK, *quickly*   Cool it, Ui!
GIRI Cicero . . .
UI   You can't talk to me like this!
  What do you take me for? I've heard enough!
  Ernesto Roma is my man. I don't
  Let anybody tell me who to pal with.
  This is an outrage.
GIRI   Boss!
MRS DULLFEET   Ignatius Dullfeet
  Will fight the Romas of this world to his
  Last breath.
CLARK, *coldly* And rightly so. In that the Trust
  Is solidly behind him. Think it over.
  Friendship and business are two separate things.
  What do you say?
UI, *likewise coldly*   You heard me, Mr Clark.
CLARK Mrs Dullfeet, I regret profoundly
  The outcome of this interview.

On his way out, to UI.

                              Most unwise, Ui.

Left alone, UI *and* GIRI *do not look at each other.*

GIRI This and the business with Caruther's truck
  Means war. That's plain.
UI   I'm not afraid of war.
GIRI Okay, you're not afraid. You'll only have
  The Trust, the papers, the whole city, plus
  Dogsborough and his crowd against you!
  Just between you and me, boss, I'd think
    twice . . .

UI I know my duty and need no advice.

A sign appears.

11

Garage. Night. The sound of rain. ERNESTO ROMA *and young* INNA. *In the background gunmen.*

INNA It's one o'clock.
ROMA   He must have been delayed.
INNA Could he be hesitating?
ROMA   He could be.
　Arturo's so devoted to his henchmen
　He'd rather sacrifice himself than them.
　Even with rats like Givola and Giri
　He can't make up his mind. And so he
　　dawdles
　And wrestles with himself. It might be two
　Or even three before he gets a move on.
　But never fear, he'll come. Of course he will.
　I know him, Inna.

Pause.

　　　　　　　When I see that Giri
　Flat on the carpet, pouring out his guts
　I'll feel as if I'd taken a good leak.
　Oh well, it won't be long.
INNA   These rainy nights are
　Hard on the nerves.
ROMA   That's what I like about them.
　Of nights the blackest
　Of cars the fastest
　And of friends
　The most resolute.
INNA   How many years have
　You known him?
ROMA   Going on eighteen.
INNA   That's a long time.
A GUNMAN *comes forward* The boys want whisky.
ROMA   No. Tonight I need
　Them sober.

A little man is brought in by the BODYGUARDS.

THE LITTLE MAN, *out of breath* Dirty works at the
　　crossroads!
　Two armoured cars outside police H.Q.
　Jam-packed with cops.
ROMA   Okay, boys, get the
　Bullet-proof shutter down. Those cops have got
　Nothing to do with us, but foresight's better
　Than hindsight.

Slowly an iron shutter falls, blocking the garage door.

　　　　　　Is the passage clear?

INNA *nods* It's a funny thing about tobacco. When
　a man
　Is smoking, he looks calm. And if you imitate
　A calm-looking man and light a cigarette, you
　Get to be calm yourself.
ROMA, *smiling*   Hold out your hand.
INNA *does so* It's trembling. That's no good.
ROMA   Don't worry. It's all
　Right. I don't go for bruisers. They're unfeeling.
　Nothing can hurt them and they won't hurt you.
　Not seriously. Tremble all you like.
　A compass needle is made of steel but trembles
　Before it settles on its course. Your hand
　Is looking for its pole. That's all.
A SHOUT, *from the side*   Police car
　Coming down Church Street!
ROMA, *intently*   Is it stopping?
THE VOICE   No.
A GUNMAN *comes in* Two cars with blacked-out
　　lights have turned the corner.
ROMA They're waiting for Arturo. Givola and
　Giri are laying for him. He'll run straight
　Into their trap! We've got to head him off!
　Let's go!
A GUNMAN It's suicide.
ROMA   If suicide it is
　Let it be suicide! Hell! Eighteen years
　Of friendship!
INNA, *loud and clear* Raise the shutter!
　Machine-gun ready?
A GUNMAN   Ready.
INNA   Up she goes!

The bullet-proof shutter rises slowly. UI *and* GIVOLA *enter briskly, followed by* BODYGUARDS.

ROMA Arturo!
INNA, *under his breath* Yeah, and Givola!
ROMA   What's up?
　Arturo, man, you had us worried. *Laughs loudly.*
　　Hell!
　But everything's okay.
UI, *hoarsely*   Why wouldn't it be okay?
INNA   We thought
　Something was wrong. If I were you I'd give him
　The glad-hand, boss. He was going to lead
　Us all through fire to save you. Weren't you,
　　Roma?

UI *goes up to* ROMA, *holding out his hand.* ROMA *grasps it, laughing. At this moment, when* ROMA *cannot reach for his gun,* GIVOLA *shoots him from the hip.*

UI Into the corner with them!

ROMA's *men stand bewildered.* INNA *in the lead, they*

are driven into the corner. GIVOLA *bends down over* ROMA, *who is lying on the floor.*

GIVOLA He's still breathing.
UI Finish him off.

To the men lined up against the wall.

Your vicious plot against me is exposed.
So are your plans to rub out Dogsborough.
I caught you in the nick of time. Resistance
Is useless. I'll teach you to rebel against me!
You bastards!
GIVOLA Not a single one unarmed!

Speaking of Roma

He's coming to. He's going to wish he hadn't.
UI I'll be at Dogsborough's country house tonight.

He goes out quickly.

INNA You stinking rats! You traitors!
GIVOLA, *excitedly* Let 'em have it!

The men standing against the wall are mowed down by machine-gun fire.

ROMA *comes to* Givola! Christ.

Turns over, his face chalky-white.

What happened over there?
GIVOLA Nothing. Some traitors have been executed.
ROMA You dog! My men! What have you done to them?

GIVOLA *does not answer.*

And where's Arturo? You've murdered him. I knew it!

Looking for him on the floor.

Where is he?
GIVOLA He's just left.
ROMA, *as he is being dragged to the wall* You stinking dogs!
GIVOLA, *coolly* You say my leg is short, I say your brain is small.
Now let your pretty legs convey you to the wall!

A sign appears.

12

GIVOLA's *flower shop.* IGNATIUS DULLFEET, *a very small man, and* BETTY DULLFEET *come in.*

DULLFEET I don't like this at all.
BETTY Why not? They've gotten rid Of Roma.

DULLFEET Yes, they've murdered him.
BETTY That's how
They do it. Anyway, he's gone. Clark says
That Ui's years of storm and stress, which even
The best of men go through, are over. Ui
Has shown he wants to mend his uncouth ways.
But if you persevere in your attacks
You'll only stir his evil instincts up
Again, and you, Ignatius, will be first
To bear the brunt. But if you keep your mouth shut
They'll leave you be.
DULLFEET I'm not so sure my silence
Will help.
BETTY It's sure to. They're not beasts.

GIRI *comes in from one side, wearing* ROMA's *hat.*

GIRI Hi. Here already? Mr Ui's inside.
He'll be delighted. Sorry I can't stay.
I've got to beat it quick before I'm seen.
I've swiped a hat from Givola.

He laughs so hard that plaster falls from the ceiling, and goes out, waving.

DULLFEET Bad when they growl. No better when they laugh.
BETTY Don't say such things, Ignatius. Not here.
DULLFEET, *bitterly* Nor
Anywhere else.
BETTY What can you do? Already
The rumour's going around in Cicero
That Ui's stepping into Dogsborough's shoes.
And worse, the greengoods men of Cicero
Are flirting with the Cauliflower Trust.
DULLFEET And now they've smashed two printing presses on me.
Betty, I've got a dark foreboding.

GIVOLA *and* UI *come in with outstretched hands.*

BETTY Hi, Ui!
UI Welcome. Dullfeet!
DULLFEET Mr Ui
I tell you frankly that I hesitated
To come, because . . .
UI Why hesitate? A man
Like you is welcome everywhere.
GIVOLA So is a
Beautiful woman!
DULLFEET Mr Ui, I've felt
It now and then to be my duty to
Come out against . . .
UI A mere misunderstanding!
If you and I had known each other from
The start, it never would have happened. It
Has always been my fervent wish that what
Had to be done should be done peacefully.

DULLFEET Violence . . .

UI No one hates it more than I do.
  If men were wise, there'd be no need of it.

DULLFEET My aim . . .

UI   Is just the same as mine. We both
  Want trade to thrive. The small shopkeeper
    whose
  Life is no bed of roses nowadays
  Must be permitted to sell his greens in
    peace.
  And find protection when attacked.

DULLFEET, *firmly*   And be
  Free to determine whether he desires
  Protection. I regard that as essential.

UI And so do I. He's *got* to be free to choose.
  Why? Because when he chooses his protector
  Freely, and puts his trust in somebody he
    himself
  Has chosen, then the confidence, which is
  As necessary in the greengoods trade
  As anywhere else, will prevail. That's always
    been
  My stand.

DULLFEET I'm glad to hear it from your lips.
  For, no offence intended, Cicero
  Will never tolerate coercion.

UI   Of course not.
  No one, unless he has to, tolerates
  Coercion.

DULLFEET Frankly, if this merger with the Trust
  Should mean importing the ungodly bloodbath
  That plagues Chicago to our peaceful town
  I never could approve it.

Pause.

UI   Frankness calls
  For frankness, Mr Dullfeet. Certain things
  That might not meet the highest moral
    standards
  May have occurred in the past. Such things
  Occur in battle. Among friends, however
  They cannot happen. Dullfeet, what I want
  Of you is only that in the future you should
  Trust me and look upon me as a friend
  Who never till the seas run dry will forsake
  A friend – and, to be more specific, that
  Your paper should stop printing these horror
    stories
  That only make bad blood. I don't believe
  I'm asking very much.

DULLFEET   It's easy not
  To write about what doesn't happen, sir.

UI Exactly. And if now and then some trifling
  Incident should occur, because the earth
  Is inhabited by men and not by angels

You will abstain, I hope, from printing lurid
Stories about trigger-happy criminals.
I wouldn't go so far as to maintain that
One of our drivers might not on occasion
Utter an uncouth word. That too is human.
And if some vegetable dealer stands
One of our men to a beer for punctual
Delivery of his carrots, let's not rush
Into print with stories of corruption.

BETTY   Mr
  Ui, my husband's human.

GIVOLA   We don't doubt it.
  And now that everything has been so amiably
  Discussed and settled among friends, perhaps
  You'd like to see my flowers . . .

UI, *to Dullfeet*   After you.

They inspect GIVOLA's *flower shop.* UI *leads* BETTY,
GIVOLA *leads* DULLFEET. *In the following they keep
disappearing behind the flower displays.* GIVOLA *and*
DULLFEET *emerge.*

GIVOLA These, my dear Dullfeet, are Malayan
  fronds.

DULLFEET Growing, I see, by little oval ponds.

GIVOLA Stocked with blue carp that stay stock-
  still for hours.

DULLFEET The wicked are insensitive to flowers.

They disappear. UI *and* BETTY *emerge.*

BETTY A strong man needs no force to win his
  suit.

UI Arguments carry better when they shoot.

BETTY Sound reasoning is bound to take effect.

UI Except when one is trying to collect.

BETTY Intimidation, underhanded tricks . . .

UI I prefer to speak of pragmatic politics.

They disappear. GIVOLA *and* DULLFEET *emerge.*

DULLFEET Flowers are free from lust and
  wickedness.

GIVOLA Exactly why I love them, I confess.

DULLFEET They live so quietly. They never
  hurry.

GIVOLA, *mischievously* No problems. No
  newspapers. No worry.

They disappear. UI *and* BETTY *emerge.*

BETTY They tell me you're as abstinent as a vicar.

UI I never smoke and have no use for liquor.

BETTY A saint perhaps when all is said and done.

UI Of carnal inclinations I have none.

They disappear. GIVOLA *and* DULLFEET *emerge.*

DULLFEET Your life with flowers must deeply
  satisfy.

GIVOLA It would, had I not other fish to fry.

They disappear. UI *and* BETTY *emerge.*

BETTY What, Mr Ui, does religion mean to you?
UI I am a Christian. That will have to do.
BETTY Yes. But the Ten Commandments, where do they
Come in?
UI   In daily life they don't, I'd say.
BETTY Forgive me if your patience I abuse
But what exactly are your social views?
UI My social views are balanced, clear and healthy.
What proves it is: I don't neglect the wealthy.

They disappear. GIVOLA *and* DULLFEET *emerge.*

DULLFEET The flowers have their life, their social calls.
GIVOLA I'll say they do. Especially funerals!
DULLFEET Oh, I forgot that flowers were your bread.
GIVOLA Exactly. My best clients are the dead.
DULLFEET I hope that's not your only source of trade.
GIVOLA Some people have the sense to be afraid.
DULLFEET Violence, Givola, brings no lasting glory.
GIVOLA It gets results, though.
DULLFEET   That's another story.
GIVOLA You look so pale.
DULLFEET   The air is damp and close.
GIVOLA The heavy scent affects you, I suppose.

They disappear. UI *and* BETTY *emerge.*

BETTY I am so glad you two have worked things out.
UI Once frankness showed what it was all about . . .
BETTY Foul-weather friends will never disappoint . . .
UI, *putting his arm around her shoulder* I like a woman who can get the point.

GIVOLA *and* DULLFEET, *who is deathly pale, emerge.* DULLFEET *sees the hand on his wife's shoulder.*

DULLFEET Betty, we're leaving.
UI *comes up to him, holding out his hand*
                        Mr Dullfeet, your
Decision honours you. It will redound to
Cicero's welfare. A meeting between such men
As you and I can only be auspicious.
GIVOLA, *giving Betty flowers* Beauty to beauty!
BETTY   Look, how nice, Ignatius!
Oh, I'm so happy. 'Bye, 'bye.

GIVOLA   Now we can
Start going places.
UI, *darkly*   I don't like that man.

A sign appears.

13

Bells. A coffin is being carried into the Cicero funeral chapel, followed by BETTY DULLFEET *in widow's weeds, and by* CLARK, UI, GIRI *and* GIVOLA *bearing enormous wreaths. After handing in their wreaths,* GIRI *and* GIVOLA *remain outside the chapel. The pastor's voice is heard from inside.*

VOICE And so Ignatius Dullfeet's mortal frame
Is laid to rest. A life of charily
Rewarded toil is ended, of toil expended
For others than the toiler who has left us.
The angel at the gates of heaven will set
His hand upon Ignatius Dullfeet's shoulder
Feel that his cloak has been worn thin and say:
This man has borne the burdens of his neighbours.
And in the city council for some time
To come, when everyone has finished speaking
Silence will fall. For so accustomed are
His fellow citizens to listen to
Ignatius Dullfeet's voice that they will wait
To hear him. 'Tis as though the city's conscience
Had died. This man who met with so untimely
An end could walk the narrow path unseeing.
Justice was in his heart. This man of lowly
Stature but lofty mind created in
His newspaper a rostrum whence his voice
Rang out beyond the confines of our city.
Ignatius Dullfeet, rest in peace! Amen.
GIVOLA A tactful man: no word of how he died.
GIRI, *wearing Dullfeet's hat* A tactful man? A man with seven children.

CLARK *and* MULBERRY *come out of the chapel.*

CLARK God damn it! Are you mounting guard for fear
The truth might be divulged beside his coffin?
GIVOLA Why so uncivil, my dear Clark? I'd think
This holy place would curb your temper. And
Besides, the boss is out of sorts. He doesn't
Like the surroundings here.
MULBERRY   You murderers!
Ignatius Dullfeet kept his word – and silence.
GIVOLA Silence is not enough. The kind of men
We need must be prepared not only to
Keep silent for us but to speak – and loudly.

MULBERRY What could he say except to call you
    butchers?
GIVOLA He had to go. That little Dullfeet was
    The pore through which the greengoods dealers
      oozed
    Cold sweat. He stank of it unbearably.
GIRI And what about your cauliflower? Do
    You want it sold in Cicero or don't
    You?
MULBERRY Not by slaughter.
GIRI   Hypocrite, how else?
    Who helps us eat the calf we slaughter, eh?
    You're funny bastards, clamouring for meat
    Then bawling out the cook because he uses
    A cleaver. We expect you guys to smack
    Your lips and all you do is gripe. And now
    Go home!
MULBERRY A sorry day, Clark, when you brought
    These people in!
CLARK   You're telling me?

The two go out, deep in gloom.

GIRI   Boss
    Don't let those stinkers keep you from enjoying
    The funeral!
GIVOLA   Pst! Betty's coming!

Leaning on another woman, BETTY *comes out of the
chapel.* UI *steps up to her. Organ music from the
chapel.*

UI   Mrs
    Dullfeet, my sympathies!

She passes him without a word.

GIRI, *bellowing*   Hey, you!

She stops still and turns around. Her face is white.

UI   I said, my
    Sympathies, Mrs Dullfeet. Dullfeet – God
    Have mercy on his soul – is dead. But
      cauliflower –
    Your cauliflower – is still with us. Maybe you
    Can't see it, because your eyes are still
    Blinded with tears. This tragic incident
    Should not, however, blind you to the fact
    That shots are being fired from craven ambush
    On law-abiding vegetable trucks.
    And kerosene dispensed by ruthless hands
    Is spoiling sorely needed vegetables.
    My men and I stand ready to provide
    Protection. What's your answer?
BETTY, *looking heavenward*   This
    With Dullfeet hardly settled in his grave!
UI Believe me, I deplore the incident:
    The man by ruthless hand extinguished was
    My friend.

BETTY   The hand that felled him was the hand
    That shook his hand in friendship. Yours!
UI   Am I
    Never to hear the last of these foul rumours
    This calumny which poisons at the root
    My noblest aspirations and endeavours
    To live in harmony with my fellow men!
    Oh, why must they refuse to understand me?
    Why will they not requite my trust? What malice
    To speak of threats when I appeal to reason!
    To spurn the hand that I hold out in friendship!
BETTY You hold it out to murder!
UI   No!
    I plead with them and they revile me!
BETTY   You
    Plead like a serpent pleading with a bird!
UI You've heard her. That's how people talk to
      me.
    It was the same with Dullfeet. He mistook
    My warm, my open-hearted offer of friendship
    For calculation and my generosity
    For weakness. How, alas, did he requite
    My friendly words? With stony silence. Silence
    Was his reply when what I hoped for
    Was joyful appreciation. Oh, how I longed to
    Hear him respond to my persistent, my
    Well-nigh humiliating pleas for friendship, or
    At least for a little understanding, with
    Some sign of human warmth. I longed in vain.
    My only reward was grim contempt. And even
    The promise to keep silent that he gave me
    So sullenly and God knows grudgingly
    Was broken on the first occasion. Where
    I ask you is this silence that he promised
    So fervently? New horror stories are being
    Broadcast in all directions. But I warn you:
    Don't go too far, for even my proverbial
    Patience has got its breaking point!
BETTY   Words fail me.
UI Unprompted by the heart, they always fail.
BETTY You call it heart that makes you speak so
    glibly?
UI I speak the way I feel.
BETTY   Can anybody feel
    The way you speak? Perhaps he can. Your
      murders
    Come from the heart. Your blackest crimes are
    As deeply felt as other men's good deeds!
    As we believe in faith, so you believe in
    Betrayal! No good impulse can corrupt you!
    Unwavering in your inconstancy!
    True to disloyalty, staunch in deception!
    Kindled to sacred fire by bestial deeds!
    The sight of blood delights you! Violence
    Exalts your spirit! Sordid actions move you

To tears, and good ones leave you with deep-
seated
Hatred and thirst for vengeance!

UI   Mrs Dullfeet
I always – it's a principle of mine –
Hear out my Opponent, even when
His words are gall. I know that in your circle
I'm not exactly loved. My origins –
Never have I denied that I'm a humble
Son of the Bronx – are held against me.
'He doesn't even know,' they say, 'which fork
To eat his fish with. How then can he hope
To be accepted in big business? When
Tariffs are being discussed, or similar
Financial matters, he's perfectly capable
Of reaching for his knife instead of his pen!
Impossible! We can't use such a man!'
My uncouth tone, my manly way of calling
A spade a spade are used as marks against me.
These barriers of prejudice compel me
To bank exclusively on my own achievement.
You're in the cauliflower business, Mrs
Dullfeet, and so am I. There lies the bridge
Between us.

BETTY   And the chasm to be bridged
Is only foul murder!

UI   Bitter experience
Teaches me not to stress the human angle
But speak to you as a man of influence
Speaks to the owner of a greengoods business.
And so I ask you: How's the cauliflower
Business? For life goes on despite our sorrows.

BETTY Yes, it goes on – and I shall use my life
To warn the people of this pestilence!
I swear to my dead husband that in future
I'll hate my voice if it should say 'Good morning'
Or 'Pass the bread' instead of one thing only:
'Extinguish Ui!'

GIRI, *in a threatening tone* Don't overdo it, kid!

UI Because amid the tombs I dare not hope
For milder feelings, I'd better stick to business
Which knows no dead.

BETTY   Oh Dullfeet, Dullfeet! Now
I truly know that you are dead.

UI   Exactly.
Bear well in mind that Dullfeet's dead. With him
Has died the only voice in Cicero
That would have spoken out in opposition
To crime and terror. You cannot deplore
His loss too deeply! Now you stand
defenceless
In a cold world where, sad to say, the weak
Are always trampled. You've got only one
Protector left. That's me, Arturo Ui.

BETTY And this to me, the widow of the man

You murdered! Monster! Oh, I knew you'd be
here
Because you've always gone back to the scene of
Your crimes to throw the blame on others. 'No
It wasn't me, it was somebody else.'
'I know of nothing.' 'I've been injured'
Cries injury. And murder cries: 'A murder!
Murder must be avenged!'

UI   My plan stands fast.
Protection must be given to Cicero.

BETTY, *feebly* You won't succeed.

UI   I will! That much I know.

BETTY From this protector God protect us!

UI   Give
Me your answer.

He holds out his hand.

                    Is it friendship?

BETTY   Never while I live!

Cringing with horror, she runs out.

A sign appears.

14

UI's *bedroom at the Hotel Mammoth.* UI *tossing in his
bed, plagued by a nightmare. His* BODYGUARDS *are
sitting in chairs, their revolvers on their laps.*

UI, *in his sleep* Out, bloody shades! Have pity!
Get you gone!

*The wall behind him becomes transparent. The ghost
of* ERNESTO ROMA *appears, a bullet-hole in his
forehead.*

ROMA It will avail you nothing. All this murder
This butchery, these threats and slaverings
Are all in vain, Arturo, for the root of
Your crimes is rotten. They will never flower.
Treason is made manure. Murder, lie
Deceive the Clarks and slay the Dullfeets, but
Stop at your own. Conspire against the world
But spare your fellow conspirators.
Trample the city with a hundred feet
But trample not the feet, you treacherous dog!
Cozen them all, but do not hope to cozen
The man whose face you look at in the mirror!
In striking me, you struck yourself, Arturo!
I cast my lot with you when you were hardly
More than a shadow on a bar-room floor.
And now I languish in this drafty
Eternity, while you sit down to table
With sleek and proud directors. Treachery
Made you, and treachery will unmake you.
Just as you betrayed Ernesto Roma, your
Friend and lieutenant, so you will betray

Everyone else, and all, Arturo, will
Betray you in the end. The green earth covers
Ernesto Roma, but not your faithless spirit
Which hovers over tombstones in the wind
Where all can see it, even the grave-diggers.
The day will come when all whom you struck
   down
And all you will strike down will rise, Arturo
And bleeding but made strong by hate, take
   arms
Against you. You will look around for help
As I once looked. Then promise, threaten,
   plead.
No one will help. Who helped me in my need?

UI, *jumping up with a start* Shoot! Kill him! Traitor!
   Get back to the dead!

The BODYGUARDS *shoot at the spot on the wall
indicated by* UI.

ROMA, *fading away* What's left of me is not afraid
   of lead.

15

*Financial District. Meeting of the Chicago vegetable
dealers. They are deathly pale.*

FIRST VEGETABLE DEALER Murder! Extortion!
   Highway robbery!
SECOND VEGETABLE DEALER And worse:
   Submissiveness and cowardice!
THIRD VEGETABLE DEALER What do you mean,
      submissiveness? In January
   When the first two came barging into
   My store and threatened me at gunpoint, I
   Gave them a steely look from top to toe
   And answered firmly: I incline to force.
   I made it plain that I could not approve
   Their conduct or have anything to do
   With them. My countenance was ice.
   It said: So be it, take your cut. But only
   Because you've got those guns.
FOURTH VEGETABLE DEALER Exactly!
   I wash my hands in innocence! That's what
   I told my missus.
FIRST VEGETABLE DEALER, *vehemently* What do
      you mean, cowardice?
   We used our heads. If we kept quiet, gritted
   Our teeth and paid, we thought those bloody
      fiends
   Would put their guns away. But did they? No!
      It's
   Murder! Extortion! Highway robbery!
SECOND VEGETABLE DEALER Nobody else would
   swallow it. No backbone!

FIFTH VEGETABLE DEALER No tommy gun, you
      mean. I'm not a gangster.
   My trade is selling greens.
THIRD VEGETABLE DEALER My only hope
   Is that the bastard some day runs across
   Some guys who show their teeth. Just let him
      try his
   Little game somewhere else!
FOURTH VEGETABLE DEALER In Cicero
   For instance!

The CICERO *vegetable dealers come in. They are
deathly pale.*

THE CICERONIANS Hi, Chicago!
THE CHICAGOANS   Hi, Cicero!
   What brings *you* here?
THE CICERONIANS   We were told to come.
THE CHICAGOANS By who?
THE CICERONIANS   By him.
FIRST CHICAGOAN Who says so? How can he
      command
   You? Throw his weight around in Cicero?
FIRST CICERONIAN   With
   His gun.
SECOND CICERONIAN Brute force. We're helpless.
FIRST CHICAGOAN   Stinking
      cowards!
   Can't you be men? Is there no law in Cicero?
FIRST CICERONIAN No.
SECOND CICERONIAN   No longer.
THIRD CHICAGOAN   Listen, friends. You've got
   To fight. This plague will sweep the country
   If you don't stop it.
FIRST CHICAGOAN First one city, then another.
   Fight to the death! You owe it to your country!
SECOND CICERONIAN Why us? We wash our
      hands in innocence.
FOURTH CHICAGOAN We only hope with God's
      help that the bastard
   Some day comes across some guys that show
   Their teeth.

Fanfares. Enter ARTURO UI *and* BETTY DULLFEET
– in mourning – followed by CLARK, GIRI, GIVOLA
and BODYGUARDS. *Flanked by the others,* UI *passes
through. The* BODYGUARDS *line up in the
background.*

GIRI   Hi, friends! Is everybody here
   From Cicero?
FIRST CICERONIAN All present.
GIRI   And Chicago?
FIRST CHICAGOAN All present.
GIRI, *to* UI   Everybody's here.
GIVOLA Greetings, my friends. The Cauliflower
   Trust

Wishes you all a hearty welcome. Our
First speaker will be Mr Clark. *To* CLARK
  Mr Clark.
CLARK Gentlemen, I bring news. Negotiations
Begun some weeks ago and patiently
Though sometimes stormily pursued – I'm
  telling
Tales out of school – have yielded fruit. The
  wholesale
House of B. Dullfeet, Cicero, has joined
The Cauliflower Trust. In consequence
The Cauliflower Trust will now supply
Your greens. The gain for you is obvious:
Secure delivery. The new prices, slightly
Increased, have already been set. It is
With pleasure, Mrs Dullfeet, that the Trust
Welcomes you as its newest member.

CLARK *and* BETTY DULLFEET *shake hands.*

GIVOLA And now: Arturo Ui.

UI *steps up to the microphone.*

UI   Friends, countrymen!
Chicagoans and Ciceronians! When
A year ago old Dogsborough, God rest
His honest soul, with tearful eyes
Appealed to me to protect Chicago's green-
Goods trade, though moved, I doubted whether
My powers would be able to justify
His smiling confidence. Now Dogsborough
Is dead. He left a will which you're all free
To read. In simple words therein he calls me
His son. And thanks me fervently for all
I've done since I responded to his appeal.
Today the trade in vegetables –
Be they kohlrabi, onions, carrots or what
Have you – is amply protected in Chicago.
Thanks, I make bold to say, to resolute
Action on my part. When another civic
Leader, Ignatius Dullfeet, to my surprise
Approached me with the same request, this
  time
Concerning Cicero, I consented
To take that city under my protection.
But one condition I stipulated, namely:
The dealers had to want me. I would come
Only pursuant to their free decision
Freely arrived at. Cicero, I told
My men, in no uncertain terms, must not be
Subjected to coercion or constraint!
The city has to elect me in full freedom!
I want no grudging 'Why not?', no teeth-
  gnashing
'We might as well'. Half-hearted acquiescence
Is poison in my books. What I demand

Is one unanimous and joyful 'Yes'
Succinct and, men of Cicero, expressive.
And since I want this and everything else I want
To be complete, I turn again to you
Men of Chicago, who, because you know
Me better, hold me, I have reason to believe
In true esteem, and ask you: Who is for me?
And just in passing let me add: If anyone's
Not for me he's against me and has only
Himself to blame for anything that happens.
Now you may vote!
GIVOLA   But first a word from Mrs
Dullfeet, the widow, known to all of you, of
A man beloved by all.
BETTY   Dear friends
Your faithful friend and my beloved husband
Ignatius Dullfeet is no longer with us to . . .
GIVOLA God rest his soul!
BETTY   . . . sustain and help you. I
Advise you all to put your trust in Mr
Ui, as I do now that in these grievous days
I've come to know him better.
GIVOLA   Time to vote!
GIRI All those in favour of Arturo Ui
  Raise your right hands!

Some raise their hands.

A CICERONIAN Is it permissible to leave?
GIVOLA   Each man
Is free to do exactly as he pleases.

Hesitantly the CICERONIAN *goes out. Two*
BODYGUARDS *follow him. A shot is heard.*

GIRI All right, friends, Let's have your free
  decision!

All raise both hands.

GIVOLA They've finished voting, boss. With deep
  emotion
Teeth chattering for joy, the greengoods dealers
Of Cicero and Chicago thank you
For your benevolent protection.
UI   With
Pride I accept your thanks. Some fifteen years
Ago, when I was only a humble, unemployed
Son of the Bronx; when following the call
Of destiny I sallied forth with only
Seven staunch men to brave the Windy City
I was inspired by an iron will
To create peace in the vegetable trade.
We were a handful then, who humbly but
Fanatically strove for this ideal
Of peace! Today we are a multitude.
Peace in Chicago's vegetable trade
Has ceased to be a dream. Today it is

Unvarnished reality. And to secure
This peace I have put in an order
For more machine-guns, rubber truncheons
Etcetera. For Chicago and Cicero
Are not alone in clamouring for protection!
There are other cities: Washington and
    Milwaukee!
Detroit! Toledo! Pittsburgh! Cincinnati!
And other towns where vegetables are traded!
Philadelphia! Columbus! Charleston! And New
    York!
They all demand protection! And no 'Phooey!'
No 'That's not nice!' will stop Arturo Ui!

*Amid drums and fanfares the curtain falls. A sign
appears.*

Epilogue

Therefore learn how to see and not to gape.
To act instead of talking all day long.
The world was almost won by such an ape!
The nations put him where his kind belong.
But don't rejoice too soon at your escape –
The womb he crawled from still is going strong.

Chronological Table

1 1929–1932. Germany is hard hit by the world crisis. At the height of the crisis a number of Prussian Junkers try to obtain government loans, for a long time without success. The big industrialists in the Ruhr dream of expansion.

2 By way of winning President Hindenburg's sympathy for their cause, the Junkers make him a present of a landed estate.

3 In the autumn of 1932, Adolf Hitler's party and private army are threatened with bankruptcy and disintegration. To save the situation Hitler tries desperately to have himself appointed Chancellor, but for a long time Hindenburg refuses to see him.

4 In January 1933 Hindenburg appoints Hitler Chancellor in return for a promise to prevent the exposure of the *Osthilfe* (East Aid) scandal, in which Hindenburg himself is implicated.

5 After coming to power legally, Hitler surprises his high patrons by extremely violent measures, but keeps his promises.

6 The gang leader quickly transforms himself into a statesman. He is believed to have taken lessons in declamation and bearing from one, Basil, a provincial actor.

7 February 1933, the Reichstag fire. Hitler accuses his enemies of instigating the fire and gives the signal for the Night of the Long Knives.

8 The Supreme Court in Leipzig condemns an unemployed worker to death for causing the fire. The real incendiaries get off scot-free.

10 The impending death of the aged Hindenburg provokes bitter struggles in the Nazi camp. The Junkers and industrialists demand Röhm's removal. The occupation of Austria is planned.

11 On the night of 30 June 1934 Hitler over-powers his friend Röhm at an inn where Röhm has been waiting for him. Up to the last moment Röhm thinks that Hitler is coming to arrange for a joint strike against Hindenburg and Göring.

12 Under compulsion the Austrian Chancellor Engelbert Dollfuss agrees to stop the attacks on Hitler that have been appearing in the Austrian press.

13 Dollfuss is murdered at Hitler's instigation, but Hilter goes on negotiating with Austrian rightist circles.

15 On 11 March 1938 Hitler marches into Austria. An election under the Nazi terror results in a 98% vote for Hitler.

uMabatha*

Welcome Msomi

Introduction

Welcome Msomi is a South African playwright, producer, director, and entrepreneur, who founded the IZulu Dance Theatre and Music in 1965 in Durban and has since gone on to become chief executive officer of Sasani Investments, an entertainment, communication, and education multi-media group aimed at marketing 'the richness of [South African] culture both here and overseas, much like Hollywood has marketed America to the rest of the world' (Kobokoane). Msomi spent considerable time in New York, founding a theatre company there based on South African music and dance. In addition to numerous other theatrical works in Zulu, Msomi has written and acted in radio plays, hosted a radio show, and composed and produced songs for all his musicals under his own record label. As the founder of IAM Records he set up IAM performing arts centres aimed at developing young talent in the rural and urban areas of South Africa. When Nelson Mandela was elected president of South Africa, Msomi was responsible for organizing the inauguration ceremonies.

uMabatha, a Zulu adaptation of *Macbeth*, tells the story of Shaka, an early nineteenth-century Zulu chief made legendary by his martial skills, brutality, and autocratic rule. Like Macbeth he is rumoured to have encountered an Isangoma (witch or diviner) who prophesied: 'You are a man. Already I see a chief of chiefs.' Shaka rose from being the illegitimate son of a minor chief during a time when southern Africa was populated by a range of different tribes. Dingiswayo, king of the powerful Mthethwa tribe, mentored Shaka's rise from successful soldier to Zulu chief, and

Shaka gained renown for building a formidable army that supported his imperial ambitions, eventually occupying all of what is now Natal. In 1828, Shaka was murdered while pursuing fleeing clans. In a scene that Msomi likens to the assassination of Julius Caesar, Shaka's half-brothers Dingane and Mhlangana, and Mbopa, an Induna or Chief Councillor of the Royal Kraal, stabbed him with their spears.

Premiered in Natal (South Africa) in an open-air theatre during the apartheid era, then invited to close the Royal Shakespeare Company's World Theatre season in London in 1972, the production was remounted in 1973 at London's Aldwych Theatre, followed by subsequent productions in the US, Europe, and Africa. The play has achieved significant success worldwide and was, notably, one of six shows chosen to open the rebuilt Globe Theatre in London in 1997. It employs a huge cast (some forty to sixty-five members) that includes drummers, singers, dancers, and actors, using music by Welcome Msomi based on traditional songs. Formal scholarship on the play is virtually nonexistent, perhaps because of its success as popular theatre. The most recent full-length treatment of Shakespeare in South Africa, David Johnson's *Shakespeare and South Africa*, despite its critique of Shakespeare as playing a 'deeply compromised role' in 'larger histories of imperial violence' (214), does not mention Msomi or *uMabatha*.

Msomi is candid about the difficulties he initially had with the idea of adapting Shakespeare: 'It has been a long journey since the birth of *uMabatha* in 1969 when I started writing the play. At first it was an idea I hated, employing Shakespeare's work in a Zulu medium (although I

---

* In Zulu a 'u' is placed in front of the first name much in the same way 'Mr' is placed in front of a Westerner's last name; the play's title substitutes Macbeth's name with Mabatha's.

Plate 2 Motlhalefi Mahlabe, 1995. Production of *uMabatha* in The Civic Theatre, Johannesburg. Left to right: S'Thembile Jali, S'Bongile Nqulunga, Busie Mchunu

must admit that my love for Shakespeare started when I was at St. Christopher's High School in Swaziland, where I even performed in *Julius Caesar*, *Macbeth* and the *Merchant of Venice*) since I felt I was borrowing another writer's ideas' (Msomi, 'Preface': n.p.). Mazisi Kunene, in his foreword to the play, states that 'With a single blow . . . [Msomi] brought Shakespeare out of the bejewelled theatres of Europe and New York into the open festivals of all people, for all people' (Msomi: n.p.). As Kunene argues in his discussion of Shakespearean adaptations, 'The truth of the matter is that it is permissible to adapt a work as long as the adapted work introduces a new element.'

Nelson Mandela's blurb on the back of the Via Afrika edition of the play states that '*uMabatha* . . . illustrates vividly the universality of ambition, greed and fear. Moreover, the similarities between Shakespeare's *Macbeth* and our own Shaka become a glaring reminder that the world is, philosophically, a very small place.' Despite being figured as a symbol of the unity of cultural experience 'through art,' as Nadine Gordimer puts it in her blurb on the play, *uMabatha* is an adaptation that addresses important questions of cultural difference. As with *Lear's Daughters*, what an audience sees figured on stage is a striking reminder that Shakespeare has traditionally been

the domain of men (and boys) and of white culture. *uMabatha*, stages ethnic and linguistic difference, even as it shows those are no guarantee against violence and deception. In fact, in 1995, after his release from prison and election as president of South Africa, Nelson Mandela was behind the push to restage *uMabatha* 'as the perfect opportunity to highlight both the problems of, and the vast opportunity for, change from so many years of apartheid in South Africa' ('Canadian Premiere').

In *uMabatha* numerous new elements are introduced that defamiliarize key features of Shakespeare's *Macbeth*, though the play has substantial echoes from the Shakespearean text, as in Kamdonsela (Lady Macbeth) telling Khondo 'Even if my only child was feeding at my breast / I would hurl him on to the rocks / And shatter his skull / Before I become as weak as you are now'. But what makes *uMabatha*'s place in the history of adaptation noteworthy is the degree to which it exposes the uses of adaptation as a complex series of cultural negotiations, appropriations, and mediations that define the relations between colonial and colonized cultures. Importantly, *uMabatha* decolonizes Shakespeare as a vanguard for colonial values, exposing the ways in which power and its abuses are not unique to colonial Western culture. But at the same time, the play's quick appropriation by Western culture, as symbolized by its staging in the reconstructed Globe's opening season and by the spate of reviewers trumpeting its universalist message, shows the degree to which any adaptation risks having its distinctive features subsumed into the dehistoricized contexts of contemporary popular culture.

Moreover, as Msomi himself controversially states about the success of *uMabatha* in Europe and the United States, 'Our culture was more appreciated there than here – perhaps taken for granted because people grew up with it. It dawned on me what we had was something rich and that it needed to be marketed and preserved' (Kobokoane). Msomi's sense that indigenous South African, Zulu culture is attractive to Europeans and Americans and that this attraction provides a significant opportunity to both market and preserve a culture that has been severely marginalized through repressive state policies such as apartheid points to the decolonizing potential inherent in a play that crosses linguistic, ethnic, and national borders. Thuli Dumakude, Msomi's wife and an assistant director and choreographer, notes that when the play was restaged after Mandela's election to the presidency 'the country was in the midst of a furious debate on whether the spear and the shield should be banned . . . as weapons (they weren't) – and there was our cast on stage with spears and shields' (Filichia). The visual aspects of the play's performance, its material representation of cultural and ethnic difference and identity, underline the way in which theatre reflects a certain kind of cultural memory, in this case of an identity profoundly tied to the symbolic aspects of the spear and the shield. At the same time, when seen by a Western audience, those symbols serve to foreground the differences enacted by the play, even as the play appropriates and deforms the canonical centrality of Shakespeare to Western culture via its African context. In addition to its decolonizing work, then, its exposition of how cultural appropriation is enacted, the play's reception history signals the complex ways in which so-called home cultures can be both oblivious to and galvanized by the very differences that make them unique. No easy solutions exist to the problems invoked by both the play and its reception history. Suffice it to say that the invisible boundaries thought to separate different cultures are challenged by the existence of adaptations like *uMabatha*, which dramatically rethink canonical Shakespearean

works while at the same time achieving a wide cultural presence.

And yet the existence of boundaries and geographic divides alerts us to the uncomfortable tensions between *uMabatha*'s supposed universalist content and the cultural specificities and differences to which it also gives voice. Penina Muhando Mlama argues that 'The neo-colonial character of many African countries explains their tendency to perpetuate the entertainment-based theatre imposed on them by their colonial masters' as opposed to exploring 'the potential of theatre as a tool for raising the consciousness of the people' (28–29). Similarly Michael Etherton has argued that 'Translation, transposition and adaptation have been endemic in European drama: they are the means by which play-texts have survived the process of history, and have become part of a "great tradition" (which itself is part and parcel of a particular static view of history). In taking over the European concern to "rework" the great dramatic works of the past, African playwrights have also taken over this particular historical perspective' (102). While *uMabatha* no doubt plays into this sort of appropriative scenario, its very hybridity (not to mention its original performance context for black audiences under the apartheid regime) complicates any reductive scenario that tries to explain how forms of cultural difference go out into the world to perform their work.

Select bibliography

Entries marked * are particularly accessible.

'Canadian Premiere of Umabatha – The Zulu Macbeth' (downloaded: 14 July 1998), Living Arts Centre Mississauga. Canada News Wire (http://www.newswire.ca/releases/August1997/19/c3234.html).

*Etherton, M. (1982) *The Development of African Drama*, New York: Africana Publishing Company.

Filichia, P. (downloaded: 14 July 1998) 'Blood Brothers,' *The Star Ledger: The Newspaper for New Jersey*. New Jersey (http://www.njo.com/features/ledger/stories/5d1dda.html).

*Johnson, D. (1996) *Shakespeare and South Africa*, Oxford: Clarendon Press.

Kobokoane, T. (downloaded: 14 July 1998) 'All the World's A Stage for Welcome Msomi's Business,' *Business Times* (http://www.btimes.co.za/97/0302/newsm/newsm.html).

*Mlama, P. M. (1991) *Culture and Development: The Popular Theatre Approach in Africa*, Uppsala: Nordiska Afrikainstitutet (The Scandinavian Institute of African Studies).

Msomi, W. (1996) *Umabatha*, Pretoria: Via Afrika.

Pacio, N. (downloaded: 14 July 1998) 'African Epic
    Combines Shakespearean Spirit,' *Daily Bruin*, UCLA
    (http://www.dailybruin.ucla.edu/DB/issues/97/10.01
    /ae.Umab atha.html).

'Umabatha Press Release' (downloaded: 14 July 1998) Cal
    Performances, Berkeley (http://www.calperfs.
    berkeley.edu/news/releases/umabatha.html).
'Umabatha Program Notes' (downloaded: 14 July 1998)
    Cal Performances, Berkeley (http://www.calperfs.
    berkeley.edu/news/prgnotes/umabatnotes.html).

uMabatha

Welcome Msomi

Characters

uMABATHA, (Macbeth), the King's cousin

KAMADONSELA, (Lady Macbeth), his wife

DANGANE, (Duncan), King

DONEBANE, (Donalbain), Prince

MAKHIWANE, (Malcolm), Prince

ISANGOMA 1, 2 & 3, (3 Witches), witchdoctors

BHANGANE, (Banquo), the King's Induna

FOLOSE, (Fleance), Bhangane's son

MAFUDU, (Macduff), King's cousin

KAMAKHAWULANA, (Lady Macduff), Mafudu's wife

INDODANA, (Boy), Mafudu's son

IMBONGI, the King's praise singer

HOSHWENI, (Captain)

LINOLO, (Lennox), attendant

ANGANO, (Angus), attendant

INYANGA, (Doctor), herbal doctor

ISALUKAZI, (A Gentlewoman), nurse

MSIMBITHI, (Messenger), a messenger

3 MUDERERS

3 SPIRITS

Act I

Scene 1 – In the veld

Chanting and heavy beating of Sangoma drums.

(Enter SANGOMA I, II *and* III.)

SANGOMA I Where is the place we will smell out
   our prey?
   I ask. I ask you, oh Bangoma.
SANGOMA II We will meet at the feast.
   There where the clash of the shield
   And the spear have ended.
SANGOMA III That is where life ends too,
   And the sun sets, Mngoma.
SANGOMA I But where is this place, Mngoma?
SANGOMA II There where the earth is trodden
   flat
   With stamping and rejoicing.
SANGOMA III There we will meet with
   Mabatha.
SANGOMA I Yes. I will spit my venom there,
   Mngoma.
SANGOMA II I, too, will be there, Mngoma.

(Song.)

Scene 2

War dance and battle of two impis. *

(Enter DANGANE, IMBONGI, MAKHIWANE,
DONEBANE *and* LINOLO.)

IMBONGI (Praise-Singer) Oh Mighty Mdangazeli of
   Noqongo
   You who tread upon the highest and smallest
   clouds.
   You who have conquered the highest and
   smallest clouds

---

* South African Bantu warriors.

And made the whole sky dark.
Oh Mighty King,
You who have trod on the highest mountain
    peaks
Oh Mighty one who has conquered the
    mountains
With your tread
You caused the leaves to rustle and blow away
With your tread
The small streams dried up
And even the deepest rivers of Noqongo.
Grow to be even mightier than you are
Grow to be mightier than the old horn snake
Which lies with its head always erect
And strikes wherever it pleases.
Oh Mighty King Mdangazeli . . .

(*Enter* MAFUDU – *wounded.*)

DANGANE Hawu! Which warrior lies there
    groaning with his wounds?
    Bring him nearer to me.
    He can tell us the state of the battle.
MAKHIWANE Hawu! This is Mafudu, great King!
    This is the warrior of warriors
    Who saved my life in the thunder of the battle.
    If it were not for his help
    I would now be a feast for the ants.
    Brave warrior,
    Tell the King how bravely our men fought in
    the battle.
MAFUDU Oh Mighty Mdangazeli,
    I have never seen such fighting.
    The thunder of the blows made the mountains
    crash down.
    The traitor from Madonela was screaming
    insults
    His forces were swollen with the rabble from
    every kraal.*
    All were fully armed.
DANGANE Speak on, Mafudu. Let me hear more.
MAFUDU In spite of their fearful numbers,
    Mabatha,
    The brave leader of your warriors,
    Cut his path straight through the impi
    To the traitorous rebel.
    Then his anger spoke louder than words.
    With a mighty thrust of his assegai**
    He parted the flesh from the throat to the
    bowels.
    And held up the animal's head on his assegai
    For all to see.

DANGANE Hawu! This is good news indeed,
    Mafudu.
MAFUDU Just as we thought the battle was won
    We were attacked by a fresh impi
    Led by the rebel from Mkhawundeni.
    Oh Mighty King.
    They seemed possessed with the strength
    Of twenty lions and fiercely attacked again and
    again.
    Mighty Mdangazeli
    I am weak and can speak no more.
DANGANE Thank you, Mafudu.
    Take him to the inyanga
    Who will tend to his wounds.

(*Enter* HOSHWENI *and* ANGANO.)

MAKHIWANE Here comes your warrior, Chief
    Hoshweni.
    Hawu! See how his face is flushed with battle.
HOSHWENI Oh Mighty King Mdangazeli.
DANGANE Where do you come from my son?
HOSHWENI From the hillside of Hoshweni where
    the battle was fought.
    As I talk now, there are mounds and mounds
    of dead bodies lying on the battlefield.
    Khondo, the traitor from Mkhawundeni,
    Is held captive by Mabatha's impi.
    So as the dust settled, victory was ours.
DANGANE Your news gives me great pleasure and
    satisfaction.
    The deeds of my great leaders Mabatha and
    Bhangane will be long remembered.
HOSHWENI Yes, Mighty King, they did wonders.
DANGANE Now Hoshweni, I want you to go back
    and tell Mabatha
    It is my wish that he becomes the chief of
    Mkhawundeni since Khondo must die.
HOSHWENI I take my leave, Mdangazeli.
    I shall carry your news to Mabatha
    Swifter than the Impala.
DANGANE Let us go, my sons.
IMBONGI Oh Mighty Mdangazeli of Noqongo.
    You who tread . . . etc.

Scene 3

Thunder and strong winds.

(*Enter* SANGOMA I, II *and* III.)

SANGOMA I Where have you been, Mngoma?
SANGOMA II I have been spitting strange spells.

---

* Enclosed village of huts.
** A slender iron-tipped spear.

SANGOMA III What spells have you been spitting,
  Mngoma?
SANGOMA I I have been spitting my venom
  To the spirits of darkness and misfortune.
SANGOMA II Spit them Mngoma, spit so that we
  can hear.
SANGOMA III Yes, spit Mngoma, spit so that we
  can hear.
SANGOMA I Elele! Elele! Elele!
SANGOMA II & III Spread your venom!
SANGOMA I I spit to the moon.
SANGOMA II & III Spit them!
SANGOMA I I spit to the sun so that the world
  becomes dark.
SANGOMA II & III Spit them!
SANGOMA I I spit to the sun,
  So that the world becomes dark.
SANGOMA II & III Spit! Spit! Spit your venom!
SANGOMA II I! I will spit to the spirits of
  misfortune.
  And spread the shadow of my venom
  Between the sun and the new day.
SANGOMA III I will spit to the wind
  My venom will cloud the clear water with
  blood.

(*Slow drumbeat.*)

SANGOMA I That is the sign
  Mabatha is near.
ALL THREE (*Sing and dance.*)
  We miss the wisdom of the stones
  When we shake and throw our bones.

(*Enter* MABATHA *and* BHANGANE.)

MABATHA This day's battle
  Will beat in my veins
  Until my life runs out.
BHANGANE The night is at our heels
  If we linger
  Its shadow will reach Umfolosi before we do.
  Hawu! Spirit of my father! What are these!
  By the heavens above! What are you doing here?
  Speak! What are you doing?
  You just stare at me, dumb as the stones
  Hissing like angry mambas.
MABATHA Speak! Who are you?
SANGOMA I (*Throwing bones.*)
  Mabatha! Chief of Dlamasi!
SANGOMA II (*Throwing bones.*)
  Mabatha! Chief of Mkhawundeni!
SANGOMA III Mabatha! The bones rattle for a
  mighty chief.
ALL THREE Elele! Elele! Elele!
BHANGANE Hawu my friend! What is it? You
  shake

Like an old tree, struck by lightning
Whose roots have lost their hold.
Why do you let the breath of these Sangomas
Blow through your branches
Like truth?
Listen to me you serpents!
You tell my friend all that will befall him
  hereafter
Hailing him as a chief
But to me you are dumb.
Throw your bones for me, too, if you can
But I want you to know
I do not beg for food like an old hungry dog.
In my eyes you are the beggars
You are less than dirt.
Do you hear what I say?
ALL THREE Oh Great One!
SANGOMA I (*Throwing bones.*)
  You who seem so very small,
  Like an ant in Mabatha's shadow
  You have your own power.
SANGOMA II (*Throwing bones.*)
  Your life is like an empty pool
  But soon the water will overflow.
SANGOMA III (*Throwing bones.*)
  Your seeds will grow to be the tallest trees of the
  forest.
  But your leaves will never see the light.
ALL THREE Mabatha! Bhangane! Mabatha!
  Bhangane!
MABATHA Stay, you serpents, I say, stay!
  After my father's death
  I know that I will be chief of Dlamasi,
  But when you talk of Mkhawundeni
  Your tongues are forked
  Because I know Khondo is still alive.
  No, these Sangomas prick our ears with thorns.
  Tell me,
  From which bad egg did you suck your wisdom?
  Answer me!
ALL THREE Elele! Elele! Elele!

(*The* SANGOMAS *disappear.*)

BHANGANE Hawu! This is something strange and
  puzzling!
  They have vanished
  Just in the wink of an eye.
  Where have they gone?
MABATHA Like mists into the air!
BHANGANE My thoughts are wild
  My mind unsteady, as if
  Fermented too long in the pot.
  It has tangled my reason.
MABATHA They said your sons would be chiefs.
BHANGANE And that you would be chief.

MABATHA Yes, that I will be chief of
    Mkhawundeni
  Is that not so?
BHANGANE Truly, my ears ring with their words.
  Hold! Raise your shield!
  Who are these?

(*Enter* HOSHWENI *and* ANGANO.)

HOSHWENI Mabatha, Prince of warriors.
  Our great chief Mdangazeli glowed like the sun
  When he heard the news of your feats
  And of your warriors' victory.
  When the lions hunt the cowardly jackal
  There is one whose teeth are sharper
  And whose roar is louder.
  This lion, said the mighty Mdangazeli,
  Shall from this time
  Walk ahead of all the others.
  I swear, great Prince,
  There is not one warrior who does not share his
    joy
  And echo his praise.
ANGANO Yes and I, too, Mabatha, I, too
  Sing your praises with Hoshweni.
  We came at our King's bidding
  To tell you of his pleasure.
HOSHWENI Our King Mdangazeli, son of
    Mphephethwa,
  Is raising you to a higher seat.
  From this day on you will be chief of
  Mkhawundeni.
BHANGANE Hawu! Hawu! Spirit of my ancestor!
  The Sangomas were speaking the truth.
MABATHA Khondo is still alive.
  Why do you present me with another man's
    shield?
ANGANO That Khondo is no more.
  Our warriors stained the hillside
  With his traitorous blood.
MABATHA (*Aside*) Chief of Dlamasi!
  And now chief of Mkhawundeni!
  These words are like a rising tide
  That drowns my reason.
  I thank you, my brothers, for bringing me this
    news.
  (*To* BHANGANE) Bhangane do you hear, my
    friend,
  How the Sangomas words become truths?
  Do you now believe your sons
  Will grow, by their spells, to be chiefs?
BHANGANE Friend, I do not know.
  It may be that the small light we see

Is just the moon's reflection
Not the campfire lit to welcome us.
Let me question our warrior friends further.
MABATHA (*Aside*) Truly, I have climbed two hills
  Guided by these Sangomas.
  And now stand before the great mountain.

(*To* HOSHWENI *and* ANGANO)

  Thank you, children of my Father
  For bringing news of these high honours.
  (*Aside*) What has happened
  Fills me with joy and dread,
  Like two stones lying in a rushing river,
  The one washed clean of Mkhawundeni,
  The other dark with slime.
  These poisonous thoughts weigh me down.
  These dark and murky thoughts
  Fight with my deeds and with my honour
  Until I shake like dry reeds on the river bank.
BHANGANE Look friends, do you see
  How my brother's thoughts
  Keep him from our company.
MABATHA (*Aside*) If I climb as high as chief
    Mdangazeli
  Why should I fear the part,
  When I am guided by the power above?
BHANGANE You know, my friends, this man
  Is busy admiring his new bheshu,*
  He keeps asking himself
  Is it really mine!
MABATHA (*Aside*) Think what we will,
  Our wishes are but chaff
  Which the restless wind will blow.
BHANGANE Mabatha, royal Prince, we wait for
    your command.
MABATHA Hawu! Forgive me friends.
  My thoughts are strangers yet
  To your great news.
  Let us return and show our duty
  To our mighty King Mdangazeli.
  Come let us be swift.

(*Exeunt.*)

Scene 4

*Near the kraal at Umfolozi. Sounds of singing and
rejoicing in the background.*

(*Enter* IMBONGI, DANGANE, MAKHIWANE,
DONEBANE, LINOLO *and attendants.*)

IMBONGI Oh Mighty Mdangazeli of Noqongo
  You who swoop, out of the sun

---

* A buttock-covering made of skin worn by men.

Like the great Eagle
And spread your wings
Covering the whole earth with your shadow.
When you swoop
The beasts run for safety
And hide in the thickets,
When you beat your wings
They peer from their dark holes
With frightened eyes.
Oh Mighty Mdangazeli,
Cover us with your mighty wings.

ALL Mdangazeli! Mightiest of the mighty!

DANGANE Has Khondo paid for his treachery?
Have the warriors who were commanded
Done their duty?

MAKHIWANE I have not heard from them, my
King Mdangazeli,
But the word has passed
That Khondo spoke his guilt before he died
And asked for your forgiveness.

DANGANE I have learned that the face of man
Is like the flower of the Umkumbathi tree.
It has sharp thorns underneath.
Khondo was my trusted chief.

(*Enter* MABATHA, BHANGANE, HOSHWENI *and*
ANGANO.)

Mabatha, bravest of my warriors!
See how my joy overflows to see you here so
soon.
No words can tell, no Imbongi
Sings your praises loud enough.

MABATHA The blows I struck, Mdangazeli,
Were with your hand
And your loud praise is my reward.

DANGANE Come nearer, my son.
Your blood is royal
And you will grow through a Father's care
To be as high as the mountains of uKhahlamba.
You, too, Bhangane.
You, too, have earned a Father's praise
And will grow to be a chief.

BHANGANE If I grow
The light that gives me strength is yours,
Mdangazeli.

DANGANE Today I wish to share my tears of joy.
My sons, children of the Royal Kraal,
And you Ndunas, warriors, followers all,
From this day.
Know that I pronounce Makhiwane, my eldest
son,
Chief of Mkhambathini.

Thus all good deeds deserve fresh honours.
And now let us go on to Mvanencane,
Mabatha's kraal

MABATHA Give me leave, Mdangazeli,
To clear the path before your tread
And at Mvanencane shout out the news
The sun that warms the earth
Will light our kraal this day.

DANGANE My brave Khondo!

MABATHA (*Aside*) Chief of Mkhambathini,
I must not fall like a blind mole
Into this open pit,
But find a way to go around
Or cover up the danger in my path.

(*Exit* MABATHA.)

DANGANE Bhangane, this warrior grows before
our eyes.
Lead you the way
Let us follow at his heels.

(*Exeunt.*)

Act II

Scene I – Mvanencane, Mabatha's kraal

(*Enter* KAMADONSELA *with four women bearing
pots on their heads and singing. They busy
themselves with stamping corn and preparing
tshwala.* Distant drumbeat.)

KAMADONSELA (*Listening*) On the day of our
victory
Came three Sangomas out of the earth
And spoke strange truths.
(*Drumbeat*) When we challenged them
With taunts, they became shadows of the night.
(*Drumbeat*) As we stood wrapped in wonder,
Mdangazeli's word was brought,
Hailing me as Chief of Mkhawundeni.
This title, these Sangomas' bones foretold,
And further, greatest of all chiefs.
(*Drumbeat*) Let this drum beat echo in your
heart
Till I return
Chief of Dlamasi, when you went hence.
When you return, I welcome Khondo,
Chief of Mkhawundeni.
And more shall befall as they foretold.
But yet I fear
The gentle dove that nestles in your heart,

---

* Traditional beer.

Where I would have the wind-swift hawk
That falls like lightning on his prey.
What can you grasp
Without the strong claws of the hawk
And what advantage take
Without his sharp eye and his swift flight.
Yes, my Khondo,
The prey that lies in wait was meant for you.
And therefore I have called
On all the spirits of my ancestors
To breathe fire in your heart
And burn away your fears.

(*Enter* MSIMBITHI.)

What has happened?
MSIMBITHI Mother of the Great Kraal!
KAMADONSELA What is it? Speak: What is your
    news?
MSIMBITHI Oh Great One, I bring word
    That King Mdangazeli will visit Mvanencane
    today.
KAMADONSELA What! Do you speak the truth?
MSIMBITHI I swear this is the truth.
    My Prince Mabatha
    Follows close behind me
    To tell the news again.
    O pardon me, I gasp for breath.
    This news gave my feet wings
    For they hardly touched the ground.
KAMADONSELA Drown his thirst with tshwala,
    He has brought good news this day.

(*Exeunt women singing, with* MSIMBITHI.)

This messenger rolls his eyes
And gasps the name of Dangane in our kraal
Even so will Dangane gasp his life away,
The skies crash down on him
I call again
On all the spirits of my ancestors,
Let my heart be like the devil's thorn
My blood of mamba's poison,
That where I strike no life returns,
Dry up my woman's tears
And let my breasts shrivel with serpent's
    milk,
I call on you
To shade my eyes
And fill my ears with earth,
So none can see or hear
Iklwa,
The assegai's clean path.

(*Enter* MABATHA.)

Khondo! Greatest of all warriors!
I heard your message carried on the wind.

Although the sky is red tonight,
Our tomorrow will be clear and bright.
MABATHA Dangane, our Chief, comes here today.
KAMADONSELA And when will he depart?
MABATHA With the rising of the sun.
KAMADONSELA Never will he rise again!
    Khondo, I see your face
    As in a still pool
    Starting from the waters.
    Look and see yourself.
    Walk bravely, laugh
    And welcome our great guest
    While in your hand a hissing mamba waits.
    Dangane comes like a tame bull
    To the slaughter-block.
    Sharpen your spear
    Be ready for the sacrifice.
MABATHA Let us think about this further.
KAMADONSELA Yes, my Khondo,
    The fruit is ripe and must be plucked
    Or else waste on the branch.

(*Exeunt all.*)

Scene 2 – Outside Mabatha's kraal at Mvanencane

There is the sound of singing in the background.

(*Enter* DANGANE, IMBONGI, MAKHIWANE,
DONEBANE, BHANGANE, LINOLO, MAFUDU,
HOSHWENI, ANGANO *and warriors.*)

DANGANE The air is still – even the shrill beetles
    are quiet.
    All is restful and peaceful here at Mvanencane.
BHANGANE Truly, Mdangazeli, it is most restful
    here.

(*Enter* KAMADONSELA.)

See, here comes the great lady of the kraal.
DANGANE Haah! Wife of our great son Khondo.
    I am sorry that our coming will be a burden to
    you.
KAMADONSELA Our lives, our fortunes are yours,
    great King.
    Your coming has brought sunshine to
    Mvanencane.
DANGANE Where is Khondo?
    We have been following him closely.
    Today, our Mother, we are your guests.
KAMADONSELA Mightiest of the Mighty,
    Mdangazeli, we welcome you.

(*Exeunt all.*)

Scene 3 – At Mvanencane

Feasting and rejoicing. Warriors and maidens enter, and perform a dance and 'Nqonqonqo' (Knock, knock, knock.)

(Enter MABATHA.*)*

MABATHA The wise warrior strikes swiftly
  If he waits to smell out the danger
  The moment will pass with this blow
  I kill all my fears and bury them in the dust.
  But out of the dust
  May rise more shadowy impis
  Who will seek to stain the earth with my blood.
  Dangane comes here
  Like a Father honouring his child
  Opening his heart in joyous welcome.
  How then can I spill my father's blood!
  His praises are sung as the wisest councillor
  His words are greeted with the Royal salute.
  Bayethe! Son of Heaven.
  If he falls
  A thousand throats will howl his death
  And fall upon his murderer.
  No, I have no longer the strength or will
  To do this deed.

(Enter KAMADONSELA.*)*

  What is it? What has happened?
KAMADONSELA The fires are low and the feast is
    ending.
  Why did you leave him?
MABATHA Did he call for me?
KAMADONSELA Yes, he called for Khondo, his
    son.
MABATHA No, my wife. We will chase this
    shadow no further.
  You see yourself how I am being honoured.
  I will not touch Mdangazeli.
KAMADONSELA Khondo, you amaze me.
  The great chief Khondo, who could make the
    whole world
  Kneel at his feet,
  Was that just a coward's dream?
  No, my Khondo, now you are awake
  Now must shake off these fears
  That are the children of your dreams.
  Be brave
  And stamp on the scorpion that blocks your
    path.
MABATHA You see, my wife, you ask of me
  What lies beyond the strength of a man.
KAMADONSELA Why, then, did you open your
    heart to me

If you knew you would soon speak with a
    woman's tongue?
  Dangane has been led into our kraal
  What foolishness is it then to set him free.
  Khondo, I tell you
  Even if my only child was feeding at my breast
  I would hurl him on to the rocks
  And shatter his skull
  Before I become as weak as you are now.
MABATHA What if we fail?
KAMADONSELA I swear by my forefathers we will
    not fail.
  Let your heart and mine beat as one.
  Now listen carefully,
  When Dangane is asleep we will set to work . . .
MABATHA How can we touch him
  When he has warriors who guard him?
KAMADONSELA Sssh! Listen, Khondo.
  The two who guard his hut,
  I will tempt with tshwala until their senses
    wander
  And leave Mdangazeli unattended.
  Our path will then be clear.
MABATHA It is only now, my wife, that I awaken.
  We will smear their assegais with blood
  And leave them to answer for the deed.
KAMADONSELA Truly, all will come about as we
    have planned.
MABATHA You have made me firm and given me
    courage.
  The earth will soak up his blood this day.

(The dancers re-enter singing 'Washumlilo'.
MABATHA *and* KAMADONSELA *join them and lead
them off to Mvanencane. Enter* BHANGANE *and*
FOLOSE.*)*

BHANGANE Hai! My son, it is dark.
  The lights of heaven have all died.
  Have been swallowed by the dark.
FOLOSE Yes, father, it is dark.
  The lights of heaven have all died.
BHANGANE The day's fires are burnt out
  Even the lingering sparks in the night sky
  Have been swallowed by the dark.
FOLOSE Truly the darkness has crept into every
    corner.
BHANGANE Hawu! Hold my shield and assegai,
  I have stood on a thorn.

(Enter MABATHA.*)*

  Give me my assegai! Who is that?
MABATHA Do not be so fierce, my friend,
  It is I, Mabatha.
BHANGANE Oh! Are you not resting yet?
  King Mdangazeli is asleep. He asked me

To bring you these gifts, which speak of his joy
At being received like a father into your kraal.
MABATHA In truth, we were unprepared.
Our joy would have had greater scope had we
more time.
BHANGANE All is well. One word, my friend.
I have been troubled by dreams of these
Sangomas.
For you their bones have spoken truth.
MABATHA I have forgotten – their words meant
nothing.
Let us find some other time to speak of them.
BHANGANE Yes, you are right, Khondo, it is late.
MABATHA I will hear from you shortly?
BHANGANE Yes Khondo.
MABATHA Go safely.
BHANGANE Farewell.

(*Exeunt* BHANGANE *and* FOLOSE.)

MABATHA Msimbithi!
MSIMBITHI (*Entering*) Khondo, my father.
MABATHA Run to my hut and tell my wife
To sound the Makhweyana.*
Prepare my pot of tshwala
Then go yourself and rest.
MSIMBITHI Khondo, my chief, it is done.

(*Exit* MSIMBITHI.)

MABATHA (*Takes a pinch of snuff and sneezes
violently.*) My eyes?
Is it my eyes that shape this assegai in the air
Or do I dream?
Wait! Let me pluck it down.
My hand is empty
And yet the spear still hangs
Where I grasped the air.
How can this be?
Does my mind scorn my weakness
By showing me this waiting spear?
I see it there
The shadow of the assegai which now I hold.
Then lead me, guide me to the victim.
As I look now, the blade is smeared with blood.
No! No, my thoughts run wild.
There is nothing!
Now the whole world lies still
Creeping from one ear to another.
Let everything be dumb
The trees, the stones, the earth that I tread
Lest they scream out my guilt.

(*Sound of Makhweyana.*) The Makhweyana
sounds!
Dangane! It sounds a summons for me,
And you.

(*Exeunt.*)

Scene 4

(*Enter* KAMADONSELA.)

KAMADONSELA The guards robbed of their
senses, give me strength.
(*A dog howls.*)
Khondo is busy now. The guards
Are snoring deep in their last sleep.
(*A muffled shout from the hut.*)
KAMADONSELA I am afraid they have awakened
before his work is done.
Then this attempt will mean our death.
I left the assegai where he could not miss it.

(*Enter* MABATHA.)

MABATHA It is done. Did you hear any sound?
KAMADONSELA I heard the dog howl.
MABATHA Did you cry out?
KAMADONSELA When? Now?
MABATHA As I left the hut.
KAMADONSELA Who me?
MABATHA Wait! Who sleeps in the next hut?
KAMADONSELA Donebane.
MABATHA Donebane! These hands smell of death.
KAMADONSELA It is foolish to nurse these
thoughts.
MABATHA I heard the sound of weeping in the
dark,
Then someone cried 'The earth is gaping'.
KAMADONSELA The King's sons are both asleep.
MABATHA They called upon the spirits of their
ancestors for help,
I thought they had seen my hands, stained with
blood.
KAMADONSELA Khondo, pluck this thorn out of
your mind.
MABATHA I, too, wanted to summon the spirits of
my ancestors.
KAMADONSELA When the rains come we cannot
hold back the flood.
If you let this dark stream rush into your
mind
It will lead to madness.

---

* A musical bow made of wood, with a single string
which also holds in position a calabash resonator;
struck by a grass stalk.

MABATHA My eyes were blind
  The blood in my ears drummed out the
    watchman's cry:
  'Awake! Mabatha comes to steal your life away.'
  A warrior's life should not end with this slow
    horror.
KAMADONSELA What do you mean?
MABATHA A voice was singing in my head,
  'All your days, Mabatha,
  Men will hunt you like the cowardly jackal.'
KAMADONSELA What voice did you hear?
  You make me wonder, Khondo, are you not a
    warrior,
  And does a warrior shake when a shadow
    crosses his path?
  Khondo! Khondo, why did you bring the assegai?
  It must lie with the drunken guards.
MABATHA No! The darkness smothers me.
  I cannot go back to that foul place.
KAMADONSELA Give me the assegai!
  The sleeping guards are harmless as their King.
  I will smear them with his blood.

(KAMADONSELA *exits. Calls from within:*
  'Mabatha!'.)

MABATHA What voice is that?
  Why do I shake like a fevered child?
  See how the sun's wound stains the sky,
  Even so this blood will stain my hands forever.

(*Re-enter* KAMADONSELA.)

KAMADONSELA Khondo, my hands are like yours
  But my heart is firm.

(*Calls from within.*)

  There is someone calling at the gate!
  Let us wash this blood from our hands.
KAMADONSELA Come, Khondo, let us return to
  our hut and be found sleeping.

(*Exeunt.*)

MABATHA There is no hole deep enough to hide
  my fear.

(*Calls from within.*)

  All your breath cannot wake Mdangazeli now.

(*Exit.*)

Scene 5

MSIMBITHI *enters, drinking tshwala from a pot.*
The calls continue.

MSIMBITHI Hawu! The work never ends. Haai!

If I were guarding the kraal of the Great One in
  the sky,
I would grow to be an old Khehla*
Opening and closing the gate for all who come.

(*Calls from within.*)

  You call and call and call, until your lungs burst.
  Hey, who are you?
  Who keeps on waking other people's wives?
  I asked you. So you won't answer.
  Hoh! my father, he thinks I will beg to speak.
  This one sounds like a chief who hanged himself
    on a tree, because he hoped his mealie
    harvest would be plentiful, only to find that
    the fields were dry.
  He took off his bheshu and tried to make
    water – enough to wet his fields, but even
    with all the tshwala he had drunk, he could
    only wet his own toes, and so hanged himself.
  I would open the gates above for him.

(*Calls from within.*)

  Who is the next one? Oh, this must be Ngubane,
    the rascal who steals other people's cattle. As
    soon as they knew he was the thief, they
    locked him inside the cattle-kraal and drove
    the cattle back. The cattle trampled him and
    trampled him until he was mixed with the
    cow-dung. That was the end of Ngubane, the
    clever man from Mabomvini.

(*Calls from within* 'Mabatha'.)

  Shout, shout till you are hoarse!
  Mabatha! Who is there now?
  Oh, here comes Mabheshwana with his bheshu
    in rags,
  While he snored the rats nibbled holes in his
    bheshu and now he swears he is bewitched.

(*Enter* MABHESHWANA.)

  Enough! Enough! Now I am tired of opening and
    closing these gates.
  I might even shut myself out. Be patient, I am
    myself now – just a poor servant of Mabatha.

(*Enter* MAFUDU *and* LINOLO.)

MAFUDU Hawu! Did you sleep in the tshwala
    pot?
  We have been calling since the dawn broke.
MSIMBITHI As you say, Royal Prince,
  We made the night into day with our feasting.
MAFUDU Is King Khondo awake yet?

---

* A very old man.

(*Enter* MABATHA.)

Our shouts have aroused him, here he comes.

LINOLO Great Khondo!

MABATHA Welcome, my friends.

MAFUDU Has our King, Mdangazeli, risen yet?

MABATHA No.

MAFUDU He asked me to come with the first
light
But your guard was deaf to our calls.

MABATHA Let us go to him.

MAFUDU I am loath to trouble you
But yet I know it is a joyful duty.

MABATHA Our duties are all pleasures when we
attend Mdangazeli.
Here is his hut.

MAFUDU I would let him sleep longer, but I must
go in.

(*Exit* MAFUDU.)

LINOLO Does the Chief depart today?

MABATHA He said so.

LINOLO We did not sleep well. The jackals
screamed all night.
And the winds of heaven roared.
Some say that many huts were blown down.

MABATHA It was a bad night. The dead have
risen.

LINOLO Since I was a child I never felt such
terror.

(*Re-enter* MAFUDU.)

MAFUDU Haai! Haai! Oh my friends! My Father
above!
What horror!
Since I was born I have not seen such horror.

MABATHA What has happened?

LINOLO Since I was a child I never felt such
horror.

MAFUDU All is destroyed! Our whole land
And life itself is dead.

MABATHA What do you mean, Mafudu?

LINOLO Do you mean the King?

MAFUDU Enter and see with your own eyes.

(*Exeunt* MABATHA *and* LINOLO.)

MAFUDU Awake! Awake! All who sleep.
Shout this terrible news through the land!
Beat the drum!
Bhangane! Makhiwane! Donebane!
Awake and see this horror.
Makhiwane! Bhangane!

(*Enter* KAMADONSELA, BHANGANE, HOSHWENI
and others.)

KAMADONSELA What terrible noise is this?

MAFUDU Great Lady, I cannot speak,
I cannot tell you of the horror that has
happened.

KAMADONSELA Hawu! Here in our kraal?

BHANGANE Mafudu, speak! Let us know.

MAFUDU Our King Mdangazeli is no more.

(*Re-enter* MABATHA *and* LINOLO.)

MABATHA Before, our life was fruitful, now it is
an empty calabash.
The beer that was real beer is no more.

(*Re-enter* MAKHIWANE *and* DONEBANE.)

DONEBANE What is the matter?

MABATHA You are nothing.
The tree which gave you shade and comfort has
been hacked down.

MAFUDU Our great Mdangazeli has been killed.

MAKHIWANE Awu! Awu! Who did the deed?

LINOLO The drunken guards like evil spirits
Painted their hands and faces with his blood.

MABATHA They are now with their ancestors.

MAFUDU Hawu! You killed them? Why?

MABATHA What man could hold back his hand
seeing that insight?
You Mafudu, would also have struck him
down.
When I saw Mdangazeli's gaping wounds
And the two evil ones crawling in his blood,
My assegai tore their throats.

KAMADONSELA Awu! Give me your hand! Help
me!

(*She faints*.)

MAFUDU Linolo! Help her! Hoshweni!

(KAMADONSELA *is carried out*.)

MAKHIWANE (*Aside to* DONEBANE) Why should
we keep silence.
Soon they will lay the blame on us.

DONEBANE (*Aside*) That is true, my brother, let us
not wait,
Let us leave this place now.

MAKHIWANE (*Aside*) We must not stay to think of
this horror.

BHANGANE We must now question all
Who know of this night's happenings.

MAFUDU Yes, let us bring the truth into the light
of day.

ALL We all agree.

MABATHA Call all the councillors. Let us meet
Beneath the great tree that spreads its shade
Before my kraal. Khondo!

(*Exeunt all except* MAKHIWANE *and* DONEBANE.)

MAKHIWANE When the heat is at its height
  The wisest course is to seek the shade.
  I will flee to Swaziland.
DONEBANE And I will go to the East.
  Now that our father's blood has been shed
  Our lives, too, are in danger.
MAKHIWANE Let us now take different paths.
DONEBANE It is the wisest course. Farewell, my
    brother.

(*They leave by different exits.*)

Act III

Scene 1 – Mfolozi

Funeral scene of MDANGAZELI *attended by*
MABATHA, KAMADONSELA, MAFUDU, LINOLO,
Princes, Warriors and Attendants.

BHANGANE Yes Mabatha! It has all come to pass
  As the Sangomas prophesied,
  They rattled their bones and there stands
    Khondo,
  They kissed their venom, and here,
  The Chief Mbathazeli.

(*Enter* IMBONGI *singing* MABATHA'S *praises.*)

  Hush, son of Bhangane! You had best keep
    silent.
IMBONGI Mbathazeli! Mbathazeli!
  You who tread on the ground so that it cracks.
  It gapes and swallows smaller men.
  You grow taller and taller
  Until men's eyes cannot look so high.
  You, Mbathazeli!
  You, who devoured the traitors.
  With your tread you destroyed the cattle of
    Madonela
  And Khondo's beasts.
  Tread before me Chief Mbathazeli!
  Now men turn to each other and ask
  What giant is this who walks with the thunder?
  They searched everywhere
  But in vain
  Down at Umfolozi
  They did not know that the mighty Chief,
  Mbathazeli, had come and were answered.
ALL Mbathazeli!
MABATHA (*Aside to* KAMADONSELA) Is it wise
    that Bhangane
  Should attend our feast?
KAMADONSELA (*Aside*) It would be a great
    mistake
  If he were to be forgotten.

MABATHA Bhangane! Tonight there will be a feast
    of thanks
  To the spirits of our ancestors
  For their protection and our good fortune.
  Your presence would give us joy.
BHANGANE Mbathazeli, your wish is my
    command.
MABATHA Do you hunt this afternoon?
BHANGANE It is so, Mbathazeli.
  My warriors tell me of a lion
  That kills our cattle in the night.
MABATHA We will miss your wisdom
  At the meeting of our councillors.
  Do you hunt from our kraal?
BHANGANE Not far, my Chief. If our eyes be keen
  And our assegais true, we will be back before
    dark.
MABATHA Take care. The hunted beast fights
  With the strength of ten when he is trapped.
BHANGANE I will not fail, my Chief.
MABATHA I have heard whispers that Donebane
    and Makhiwane
  Spread foul words like sickness.
  They pretend their hands are clean.
  Their hands are black, clotted with their father's
    blood.
BHANGANE Truly, men are blind, Mbathazeli.
  I must take my leave, my chief.
MABATHA Hunt well Bhangane,
BHANGANE Mbathazeli!

(*Exit* BHANGANE.)

MABATHA Friends who attend me here
  Go now to your work and return fresh and joyful
  For the feast tonight.
ALL Mbathazeli! Mbathazeli! Mbathazeli!

(*Exeunt all except* MABATHA.)

MABATHA Msimbithi!

(*Enter* MSIMBITHI.)

MSIMBITHI Mbathazeli!
MABATHA Have you seen the warriors I told
    you of?
MSIMBITHI Yes, Mbathazeli, they are waiting
    outside the Kraal.
MABATHA Bring them to me.

(*Exit* MSIMBITHI)

  Many envious eyes look upon the Chief.
  I do not trust Bhangane. He is well liked by all.
  And is too clever. Only he disturbs my sleep.
  When the Sangomas hailed me as a Chief, he
    laughed
  And made them speak to him.

They said his sons would grow to be great
  Chiefs.
That means Mbathazeli is just a name
A game that children play
And Dangane's blood was spilled
To make a place for Bhangane's sons.
The sons of Bhangane, Chiefs!
No! Let all my ancestors rise from the earth
And take my life, before the seeds of Bhangane
Mock me thus. Who is there?

(*Re-enter* MSIMBITHI *with the* MURDERERS.)

It is well, Msimbithi. Keep watch and later
I will summon you.

(*Exit* MSIMBITHI.)

Do you recall what words I spoke the other day?
MURDERER I Yes great Chief.
MABATHA And did these words not kindle a fire
  in you?
I told you this was the very man who called you
  thieves
And said you stole his cattle.
MURDERER I It is all clear, great Chief.
MABATHA Do you let Bhangane point his finger at
  you,
And make you thieves in other men's eyes?
His word has covered you with mud,
And still you spare him?
Are you not brave warriors?
MURDERER I Yes, my Chief, we are.
MABATHA Why do you wait then to be hunted
  like animals?
Kill this coward Bhangane.
MURDERER II My Chief, I have eaten many
  cowards in my life.
Here is my knobkerrie,* Bhangane is nothing.
MURDERER I I burn like fire, my Chief,
My assegai is my only trusted friend.
MABATHA Now you speak like warriors.
MURDERER You have shown us the thorn that
  inflames us,
Now tell us how to pluck it out.
MABATHA I will show you where to lie in wait.
Do not forget his son, Folose,
The father and the son must fall.
You may depart, and later I will tell you more.
MURDERER I & II We hear you, great Chief.
MABATHA Go then, but do not go far.

(*Exeunt the* MURDERERS.)

It is done, Bhangane is no more.

(*Enter* KAMADONSELA *with* MSIMBITHI.)

KAMADONSELA Has Bhangane left?
MSIMBITHI He is alone, Great Lady.
KAMADONSELA Where is the Chief?
MSIMBITHI He is alone, Great Lady.
KAMADONSELA Leave us now.
Khondo, why do you keep your thoughts close,
Like strangers in our kraal?
MABATHA I have been thinking, Kamadonsela.
The serpent has two heads,
Although the one is crushed
The other waits to spit its venom.
Dangane is at peace with his ancestors,
But still a shadow follows me.
KAMADONSELA Khondo! These dark and fearful
  looks
Will make men wonder.
Shine like the bright sun to warm our feast.
MABATHA It shall be as you say, my wife,
You, too, must welcome Bhangane with your
  smiles,
Let laughter hide your true intent.
KAMADONSELA Why do you talk like this?
MABATHA Do you not know that Bhangane
And his son Folose, yet live?
KAMADONSELA What are your plans, Mbathazeli?
MABATHA Be still my wife! You will rejoice
When this day's work is done.
The earth thirsts for the blood of two warriors.

(*Exeunt.*)

Scene 2 – In the veld

(*Enter* MURDERER I, II *and* III.)

MURDERER I Why are you here? Speak!
Who told you of our plan?
MURDERER III Mabatha!
MURDERER II Let him live. He is Mbathazeli's
  shadow.
MURDERER I Hold fast your assegai and stand
  with us.
MURDERER II I hear someone approaching!
It is the voice of Bhangane.
MURDERER I Hide, then, till I give the sign.
BHANGANE We are almost there, my son,
From the next hill you will see the kraal.
FOLOSE Will there be many warriors at the feast
  tonight?
BHANGANE A swarm of locusts will not equal
The numbers gathering for the feast.

---

* A short stick with knobbed head, used as a weapon.

But the heavens are unkind,
There will be rain tonight.
MURDERER I Let the rain fall.

(*They stab* BHANGANE.)

BHANGANE Awu! Awu! Run, my son!
They have wounded me. Murderers!
Awu! I am dying.

(*Exit* FOLOSE.)

MURDERER III Only one is dead. The son has
fled.
MURDERER II We have failed then.
MURDERER I Let us return to Mbathazeli
And tell him what has happened.

(*Exeunt.*)

Scene 3 – Mvanencane, Mabatha's kraal

*Sounds of feasting and rejoicing. Warriors and
maidens perform a dance, and sing the song of
welcome: 'Mbathazeli has come!'*

(*Enter* MABATHA *as the Chief Mbathazeli,*
KAMADONSELA, HOSHWENI, LINOLO *and
attendants.*)

ALL Mbathazeli!
MABATHA Sit now. Let our Chiefs and councillors
be near me.
Let the tshwala flow
Attend to all their needs, my wife.

(MURDERER I *appears.*)

Your face is streaked with blood!
MURDERER I It is Bhangane's
MABATHA You should not then come here
Where every eye can see your deed?
MURDERER I Yes, my Chief, his breath is stopped.
MABATHA That is well. You are indeed brave
warriors.
And Folose lies with his father?
MURDERER I No Mbathazeli, Folose escaped.
MABATHA Hawu! You have failed me. Folose still
lives?
MURDERER I It was not our aim, my Chief,
But the night's dark hand that was at fault.
MABATHA Do you swear that Bhangane is no
more?
MURDERER I As I stand here, my Chief,
The vultures will enjoy his flesh.
MABATHA I thank you for what you have
done.
Go now, we will meet tomorrow.

(*Exit* MURDERER I.)

KAMADONSELA Khondo, the feast is cold
When the Chief does not drink with his guests.
MABATHA I have not forgotten, my wife,
A pressing matter held me back.

(*The* SPIRIT OF BHANGANE *enters.*)

LINOLO Here is your place, Mbathazeli.
MABATHA Where?
LINOLO Here, my Chief. What is it? Why does
Mbathazeli shake?
MABATHA All! Who did this?
ALL What, Mbathazeli?
MABATHA Do not look at me! My hands are clean.
HOSHWENI I think it would be wise to bid the
guests farewell.
Mbathazeli is not well.
KAMADONSELA Stay, friends. This sickness is like
a cloud
That soon will pass and show the sun again.
He is often thus. If you depart
You will do him wrong. Sit and drink.
Khondo! What foolishness is this?
MABATHA You do not know what witchcraft is
practised here!
KAMADONSELA You disappoint me, Khondo.
When all our plans have reached this height,
and all men hail you as their King,
You show your weakness and your fears to
every eye.
What is it now? Why do you stare so wildly?
MABATHA What do you say? Look! Look there!
This is witchcraft when those we know are dead
Appear once more.

(*The* SPIRIT *disappears.*)

KAMADONSELA What do you mean?
MABATHA I saw him sitting there!
KAMADONSELA Khondo, there is no such thing.
MABATHA I have killed many men in battle.
When they fell by my assegai, the earth
swallowed them,
Their bones were food for ants.
Now they rise and follow us.
KAMADONSELA Khondo, you have alarmed our
guests.
MABATHA I do forget, my wife.
Friends and warriors
I ask you all
To pardon me. This is a sickness.
Which means nothing to those that know me.
Come let us drink and enjoy the feast.
Give me some tshwala. There is only one small
cloud

That darkens our feast, my brother
Bhangane's absence.
Drink my friends.
ALL Mbathazeli!

(*Re-enter the* SPIRIT OF BHANGANE.)

MABATHA Keep away! Keep away from me!
Why do you follow me, and glare
With your dead eyes. Keep away evil spirit!
KAMADONSELA Khondo! Khondo, what is the
matter?
Why do you disrupt our feast
With these wild words?
MABATHA This is witchcraft!
The spirits of the dead have risen
And you ask why I stare.
This horror turns my blood to water.
HOSHWENI What horror, Mbathazeli?
KAMADONSELA I beg you do not question him,
His sickness grows. I entreat you now
To leave and return to your homes.
LINOLO Stay in peace, Great Lady.
We hope Mbathazeli soon shakes off this
sickness
And is himself again.

(*Exeunt all except* MABATHA *and* KAMADONSELA.)

KAMADONSELA Khondo, what poisonous beetles
feed on your mind?
MABATHA I swear by my ancestors I saw him
standing there.
KAMADONSELA It is almost day, come Khondo,
Sleep is your only medicine.
MABATHA Tomorrow when the sun sets
I will visit the three Sangomas.
They will make all things known to me,
Uncover all dark secrets with their bones.
I cannot now turn back,
The path behind is washed with blood
And I must climb, whatever dangers lie ahead.
KAMADONSELA Khondo, sleep and rest will cool
the fever of your thoughts.
MABATHA Leave me! Keep away!
You cannot see or feel
This horror that follows me.

(*Exit* MABATHA *followed by* KAMADONSELA.)

Act IV

Scene I – In the veld

(*Enter* SANGOMA I, II *and* III.)

SANGOMA I The jackal howls three times.

SANGOMA II Three times the Tokoloshe
screams.
SANGOMA III The evil bird cries three times.
SANGOMA I Yes, Bangoma, that means it is time
To prepare our medicine in the pot.
ALL THREE (*Dancing and singing.*)
It boils and boils here in the pot,
The fire burns, the juice is hot.
SANGOMA II Into the pot I throw the skin of
An old horned snake, a horse and beetles
Strong medicine to call up the spirits of our
ancestors.
ALL THREE It boils and boils here in the pot
The fire burns, the juice is hot.
SANGOMA III A sheep's ear and the eye of an ox,
Cow-dung mixed with the hoof of a goat,
All boil together in the pot.
ALL THREE It boils and boils here in the pot
The fire burns, the juice is hot.
SANGOMA I And now the blood of an old baboon
Slaughtered when the moon was full

(*The three* SANGOMAS *sneeze. Slow beating of a
drum.*)

I smell out a stranger approaching our circle.
ALL THREE (*Softly*) It boils and boils here in the
pot
The fire burns, the juice is hot.

(*Enter* MABATHA.)

MABATHA Yes, evil ones, what are you doing?
ALL THREE Work we perform in the dark.
MABATHA Where did you learn this wisdom?
Answer me! You may hiss with the serpent
And listen to the whisper of the wind,
But listen now to me.
SANGOMA I Speak!
SANGOMA II Ask!
SANGOMA III We will answer!
SANGOMA I Do not forget, the voices that speak
through us are the spirits of the dead.
MABATHA Let me hear them speak for your
tongues are forked.
SANGOMA I We will call them, they will appear.
ALL THREE Rise! Rise from the earth!
Awake and rise, spirits of the dead.

(*Drumbeats and cries. The* SANGOMAS *perform a
frenzied dance and fall exhausted. The* FIRST SPIRIT
appears.)

FIRST SPIRIT Mabatha! Mabatha! Mabatha!
Beware of someone. I warn you,
Beware of someone
Who is of unnatural birth.
That is all.

(*Exit.*)

MABATHA I thank you for this warning. Wait
  There is more –
SANGOMAS He will not stay. Here is another
  Greater than the first.
SECOND SPIRIT (*Appearing*) Mabatha! Mabatha!
  Be great as the lion who scorns
  The assegai of men.
  No ordinary warrior can match your strength.

(*Exit.*)

MABATHA These are words that gladden my
  heart.

(*Thunder and drumbeats.* THIRD SPIRIT *appears.*)

  What is this that rises like a mighty chief?
SANGOMA Be still! Listen to his words!
THIRD SPIRIT The lionhearted Mbathazeli will be
  the only chief to reign
  Until the leaves of the forest become impis and
  approach his kraal.

(*Exit.*)

MABATHA Hah! These are wonders that only
  children dream of.
  How can the leaves of Mdansane grow legs and
  become impis?
  You have poured cool water on the fire in my
  head.
  But the thorn that pricks me still is this:
  Will the sons of Bhangane
  Ever grow to be chiefs?
SANGOMAS Do not question more!
MABATHA If you disobey
  My warriors will tear out your hearts
  And leave your flesh for jackal meat.
  Tell me what witchcraft this is!
  Which spirits do you summon now?

(*The* SANGOMAS *sway and chant over the pot.*)

SANGOMAS Appear! Appear! Appear!
  Show! Show! Show!
  Shadows of the night, destroy his sight.

(*A row of spirits with identical masks appears. The
last one is the spirit of* BHANGANE.)

MABATHA Who are these that appear
  In number like the fingers of my hands,
  One like the other
  And all like Bhangane?
  Out of my sight! Be gone, evil spirits!
  They all point and stare at me.
  What does this mean?
  And last of all is Bhangane

Who laughs at me and mocks me.
  Are these all the seeds of Bhangane
  Grown to be mighty chiefs?
  Answer me!

(*The* SANGOMAS *dance and then disappear.*)

MABATHA Where are they?
  Their words still echo in my ears.
  Who is there?

(*Enter* LINOLO.)

LINOLO How can I serve you, my King?
MABATHA Did you see the three Sangomas?
LINOLO No, Mbathazeli.
MABATHA Did they not pass near you?
  Let any man who sees them kill them.
  Their breath is like the rotten smell
  That rises from the still, green pool
  And brings a sickness with it.
  Do you bring me any news?
LINOLO Your messengers, my King, came to
  report.
  Mafudu has fled to Swaziland.
MABATHA Swaziland!
LINOLO Yes, great King.
MABATHA Fool, not to listen to the message of my
  blood!
  My thoughts were children, tortoise-slow
  But now I will strike
  Swifter than the crouching lion
  Who smells the terror of his prey.
  I will destroy Mafudu's kraal,
  His wife, his children, all, and waste no time.
  Lead me to these warriors.

(*Exeunt.*)

Scene 2 – Mafudu's kraal

(*Enter* KAMAKHAWULANA *and her son,*
INDODANA. *She is singing and plaiting straw for a
mat.* HOSHWENI *runs in.*)

HOSHWENI Cousin! Cousin!
KAMAKHAWULANA I am here, Hoshweni.
HOSHWENI I have brought bad news. Mafudu has
  fled to Swaziland.
KAMAKHAWULANA To Swaziland!. This cannot be
  true!
  Why would he do such a rash and foolish thing?
HOSHWENI We cannot tell, cousin. Mafudu is a
  wise man.
KAMAKHAWULANA Is he wise to leave his wife,
  his children
  And his kraal unguarded? Where has he gone?

His love for us is like an empty calabash.
When the fox finds the nest unguarded
There will soon be blood upon his lips.
Mafudu is a coward!

HOSHWENI Listen to me cousin, your husband
Like a wise warrior presses his ear to the ground
And hears the thunder when danger
approaches.
His reasons must be sound ones. I must leave
you now.
Soon I will return.

KAMAKHAWULANA It is said by young maidens
and fools,
When a woman is wedded
She finds shelter from the storm.

HOSHWENI If I stay, you will utter words
Which later will give you pain.
Farewell, cousin.

(*Exit.*)

KAMAKHAWULANA My son, your father has
spread his wings
And flown over the mountains.
What will you do now?

INDODANA I will eat anything I find
Like a bird mother.

KAMAKHAWULANA You will eat earthworms and
locusts?

INDODANA Anything I can find, mother.

KAMAKHAWULANA Oh, my little bird, are you not
afraid of traps?

INDODANA Nothing will happen to me
Because I know my father is still alive

KAMAKHAWULANA My little one, what will you
do without a father?

SON What will you do, mother, without a
husband?

KAMAKHAWULANA Oh, I will not weep.
There are many warriors here
That will make good husbands.

INDODANA Only the ox that has had too much
sun
Will smell around the old cow
When there are young heifers grazing.

KAMAKHAWULANA Hosh! You little monkey
You are being disrespectful.

(*Enter a* MESSENGER.)

MESSENGER Great lady, wife of Mafudu!
You do not know me, or where I come from,
But do not doubt I come here for your safety.
I came to warn you
You must leave this place.
There are men approaching,
Evil men who seem to do you harm.

Do not linger here.
I must leave you now.

(*Exit.*)

KAMAKHAWULANA These are wild and fearful
words.
Where can I go? What is happening to me?
What have I done?

(*Enter* MURDERER I, II *and* III.)

INDODANA Mother, look! Who are these?

KAMAKHAWULANA What do you want? I ask you,
What do you seek here?

MURDERER I Where is your husband?

KAMAKHAWULANA Why do you ask? I do not
know you!

MURDERER I He is a traitor.

INDODANA You are lying! My father is no traitor.

MURDERER II What! You tadpole! (*stabbing him*)
Son of a traitor.

INDODANA Awu! Awu! He has killed me, mother.
Run!

(*Exit* KAMAKHAWULANA *followed by the
murderers.*)

Scene 3 – Swaziland

(*Enter* MAKHIWANE *and* MAFUDU.)

MAKHIWANE Can you explain this, Mafudu?

MAFUDU What, my Prince?

MAKHIWANE That a man should flee
From the land of his forefathers,
When the corn is plentiful
And the sour milk overflows the calabashes.

MAFUDU Oh, let me share your sorrow
Son of our mighty Mdangazeli,
All we desired was to live in peace
Under the shadow of our mighty King.

MAKHIWANE Then suddenly the calabash is
broken
The beast is let loose
And there is blood on the gate.

MAFUDU It is time for us to sit down
And consider these things.

(*Enter* HOSHWENI.)

Who is there?

MAKHIWANE Where does he come from?

MAFUDU It looks like my cousin Hoshweni,
Can it really be he?

MAKHIWANE I, too, seem to know him,
It is long time since last we met,
Hoshweni.

HOSHWENI Yes, it is so, my Prince.

MAFUDU What is the news from our beloved
  Zululand?

HOSHWENI I can hardly tell you, friends.
  It is no longer a happy land.
  The mealie fields are parched and wasted,
  The cattle lie bloated and stinking,
  Horror and death wait behind every tree.
  Each man is fearful he will be the next
  Food for the vultures.

MAFUDU You tell us too much suffering.

HOSHWENI It is so.
  Yet there are still more terrible words that choke
  me,
  But they must be spoken.

MAFUDU Are these words meant for my ears?
  Tell me! I must know.

HOSHWENI Truly, they concern you.

MAFUDU If they concern me, speak! Tell me
  now.

HOSHWENI Your whole kraal is destroyed.

MAFUDU My kraal?

HOSHWENI Your wife and children are no more!

MAKHIWANE Hawu! What does Hoshweni say, are
  they dead?

HOSHWENI Yes.

MAFUDU Awu! Awu! My wife! My children!

HOSHWENI Your wife, your children, servants,
  beasts;
  Everything they came across.

MAFUDU And I was not there to defend them!

MAKHIWANE Let this add fire to our purpose!
  Let us return and destroy these murderers.

MAFUDU He has no children!
  Did he really kill all my dear ones?

MAKHIWANE Try to bear this like a man.

MAFUDU I will bear it like a man.
  But I must first feel it like a man.
  My wife, Awu! And my children!
  I see now they died because of me,
  Because of my cowardice.

MAKHIWANE Let this pain in your heart
  Turn to hatred and revenge.

MAFUDU How these words burn like a slow fire
  In my blood. Listen well to what I say.
  I will return to Zululand and face this monster.
  If I die, that is nothing;
  If he dies, there is some justice.
  But this I promise you,
  I will seek him out and one of us
  Will lie bleeding in the dust.

MAKHIWANE Now you speak bravely.
  Hoshweni! Let us go straight to the Swazi King
  And tell him we are on our way home.
  We ask him for warriors to join our cause.

Mabatha will be repaid in full for all his crimes.
I swear this, in the name of my dead father.

(*Exeunt.*)

Act V

Scene I – At Mvanencane

(*Enter* INYANGA *and* ISALUKAZI.)

INYANGA The moon's eye has closed
  Since first you summoned me.
  When did you last – see this madness seize
  her?

ISALUKAZI I have attended her since
  Mbathazeli climbed his high mountain,
  And thrice have I heard her sing so strangely,
  Seen her seize the hide around her loins
  And tear it with hands and teeth
  Like some wild animal.

INYANGA No, old woman,
  My gums are too soft to chew this bone.
  We are like two old dogs
  Shivering as we guard the kraal,
  When we should be sleeping by the fireside.

(*Enter* KAMADONSELA, *singing and playing the
makhweyana.*)

  Hush! Here she comes!
  Hawu, what grief can make her wail
  And sway so wildly?

ISALUKAZI She is sick. It seems
  There is a poison within her
  That she must vomit out.

(KAMADONSELA *kneels and drops the
makhweyana.*)

INYANGA No, this woman is not sick.
  There is some animal caged within her
  That fights to be free.

ISALUKAZI That is true, my son.

KAMADONSELA Here is blood! Here is blood!

INYANGA What is she doing now?
  Why does she rub her hands?

ISALUKAZI She is often seen clasping her hands
  And rubbing them thus.

KAMADONSELA Khondo! It is time.
  Be brave and fearless.
  Why do you shake with fear
  When no eyes can see your deed?
  Mafudu has fled to Swaziland,
  Where is his wife, where is she?
  Khondo! Your weakness is an open pit
  That will swallow us both.

INYANGA Let us go! What she has spoken
　　Should not be uttered or heard.
ISALUKAZI She has opened the sore
　　And we have seen the poison.
INYANGA Her guilt is a load too heavy to bear.
ISALUKAZI It is a sorrowful sight.
INYANGA I have not the skill to cure her sickness.
KAMADONSELA The smell of the blood follows
　　me.

(*She picks up the makhweyana and caresses it.*)

INYANGA What is she doing now?
ISALUKAZI I cannot tell. This madness is like a
　　fever.
KAMADONSELA Go, wash your hands
　　Be not afraid. Bhangane is with his ancestors,
　　He cannot trouble us.

(*She moves off, singing.*)

INYANGA Will she sleep now?
ISALUKAZI Yes, the fit has left her weak.
KAMADONSELA Someone is calling! Someone is
　　calling!

(*Exit.*)

INYANGA Strange things have happened
　　But my old eyes have never seen such sights
　　　before.
　　Go now, old man, go and rest
　　And do not speak what you have seen this night
ISALUKAZI I am a dumb beast. Farewell.
INYANGA No, my father, he must find another
　　Inyanga.
　　I cannot cure her sickness.
　　I must seek some way to leave this evil place.

(*Enter* MABATHA, LINOLO *and attendants.*)

MABATHA I will hear no more!
　　Let them beat their shields and stamp
　　Until they trample the Bhanganoma forest flat,
　　It will not move me.
　　Makhiwane and Mafudu are but men
　　And what ordinary man can touch Mbathazeli?
　　I care not. Let them shout until their lungs
　　　burst.

(*Enter* MSIMBITHI.)

　　What is the matter fool, cow-dung?
MSIMBITHI There are swarms, Mbathazeli,
　　As far as the eye can see!
MABATHA What? Locust? Birds?
MSIMBITHI Warriors, Mbathazeli.
MABATHA Go! I spit on you!

(*Exit* MSIMBITHI.)

　　Sithole!

SITHOLE Mbathazeli!
MABATHA My mind is uneasy Sithole, I stand
　　now
　　At the edge of a cliff, and each wind that blows
　　May hurl me to the rocks below.
　　I carry the great shield,
　　The Imbongi sings my praises,
　　But no man will look into my eyes,
　　No man will smile when I approach.
　　Instead they whisper in the shadows
　　And await their moment.
　　Sithole! What is the news?
SITHOLE It is true, my King, many warriors are
　　approaching.
MABATHA That is nothing. I will fight.
　　Until I have no strength to lift my assegai.
　　Bring me my attire.
SITHOLE It is not yet time, Mbathazeli.
MABATHA I will be ready! Prepare our warriors
　　For the battle. Destroy these cowards!
　　Bring me my attire. How is your patient, old
　　　man?
INYANGA She has a strange sickness, Mbathazeli,
　　A wild animal has entered her.
MABATHA That is your concern. Kill it with your
　　medicine.
　　Cleanse her troubled mind.
INYANGA Only she can do that.
MABATHA You speak like a fool.
　　Sithole! Bind my arms and legs.
　　Give me my shield. Nyanga, do your work.
　　All my warrior friends have deserted me.
　　Old man, you must work day and night
　　To cure my wife. Do not rest until the cure is
　　　found.
　　Come fasten here!
　　Have you heard of the Swazi warriors?
INYANGA The word has spread, Mbathazeli.
MABATHA I can wait no longer! Bring my
　　weapons after me.
　　Come, make haste!

(*Exit* MABATHA, *followed by* LINOLO, SITHOLE *and
the attendants.*)

INYANGA When I recall the kindness of our great
　　Mdangazeli
　　I cannot kneel before this tyrant, Mabatha.
　　If his bones are broken by the Swazi impi
　　It will be a blessing for our land
　　And for our people.

(*The sound of drums and warriors charging.*)

　　The hour has come, I must creep
　　Into my hole and wait.

(*Exit.*)

Scene 2 – Before the kraal at Mvanencane

(*Enter* MAKHIWANE, MAFUDU, HOSHWENI *and the* SWAZI IMPI.)

MAKHIWANE Hoshweni! You lead one group of warriors
  Straight into battle. We will follow
  And surprise them with a fresh attack.
HOSHWENI It shall be so, Royal Prince.
  We will meet this tyrant face to face today.
MAKHIWANE Warriors and friends! Now is the time
  To show your strength. Now is the moment
  To rid this land of a foul tyrant.
  Let your assegais speak for you.
WARRIORS It shall be so, Royal Prince.

(*Exeunt singing.*)

Scene 3 – Outside Mvanencane

Enter a group of men and women wailing. They throw themselves down and beat the ground.

(*Enter* MABATHA.)

MABATHA What is the matter? Why do you wail
  And beat the ground? Linolo! Speak,
  What is the reason for this madness?
  Sithole!
SITHOLE Mbathazeli!
MABATHA Sithole, why do these people wail?
  Why are they dumb when I question them?
SITHOLE Your wife, Mbathazeli,
  Has joined her ancestors.
MABATHA Awu! Awu! Kamadonsela.
  It is a cold wind that blows
  And takes our breath away.
  Kamadonsela! Had you lived
  Until the next bright day,
  You would have seen a great King
  Destroy his enemies.
  Our wishes are but empty calabashes,
  Our lives have withered slowly
  Since Mdangazeli's branch was hacked away.
  It is no matter, let all things
  Turn against me, I will fight
  Until the last drop of blood is shed
  Foolish women! It is not time for weeping,
  Now it is time to fight.
  Warriors! Attack, and take no prisoners.
  Destroy these warriors that invade our land.

(MABATHA *and* WARRIORS *exeunt.*)

Scene 4

Drums and chanting. The warriors at Bhanganoma near Mvanencane perform a war dance. Enter MAKHIWANE, DONEBANE, MAFUDU, HOSHWENI *and the* SWAZI IMPI. *The two* IMPIS *engage in battle, and* MABATHA's *warriors are driven off.* MABATHA *fights* DONEBANE *and slays him.* MAFUDU *enters and challenges* MABATHA.

MAFUDU I have returned! Turn and face me, murdering dog!
MABATHA Mafudu, there is no hatred in my heart
  For you. Come not near
  Lest I be forced to spill your blood.
MAFUDU You talk of spilling blood!
  What about the blood of my children?
  The blood of my wife?
  The blood of all those dear to me.
  You are not a man, Mabatha,
  But a stinking dog.
MABATHA Mafudu, to see you die
  For a cause that is not your own . . .
MAFUDU What do you mean?
MABATHA Even your children died because of your ill thinking,
  Fighting a battle of Mdangazeli.
  Donebane, the son of Mdangazeli,
  Is now food for the vultures
  His death is justified.
  Only the sons of Mdangazeli
  Must fight this battle – not you!
MAFUDU Mabatha, your hands are steeped in blood
  Of thousands of our people of KwaZulu
  That you have sent to our ancestors.
  Your calabash of greed
  Has left thousands without kraals
  Without food, without hope.
MABATHA Stop hiding behind words,
  Fight like a man.
MAFUDU You, Mabatha, have destroyed
  The spirit of tranquillity,
  The bones of the innocent speak to me.
  They say that the vicious dog must die.
  Your time has come, Mabatha!
MABATHA You cannot tell me anything.
  The sangomas prophesied that Bhangane's sons
  Shall be kings, but they are all dead.
  Mafudu, you will bend like a reed
  Before my blows.
  The only warrior I fear in my life
  Is the one who came into this world
  Like a spirit from the dead.

MAFUDU Then turn and fight.
   Mabatha! I am the one who came
   Into this world in a way unnatural.
   Like a spirit from the dead.
MABATHA If that is so I will not fight you,
   Mafudu.

(MABATHA *runs to stage right* – WARRIORS *push
him down to stage right, and he tries to escape
through other exits, finally being surrounded by more
warriors.*)

MAFUDU You have nowhere to go, Mabatha.
MABATHA I know now, the sangoma's words have
   confirmed the truth.
MAFUDU This is your day to meet your ancestors.

(MABATHA *and* MAFUDU *fight until* MABATHA *is
slain.* MAKHIWANE, *who enters with a group of
warriors rejoices at the death of* MABATHA.
MAKHIWANE *congratulates* MAFUDU.)

MAKHIWANE Warriors! Brave warriors!
   What you have done this day
   Will always make you honoured
   In my father's land,
ALL Mntwana!
MAKHIWANE The dog who snarled and showed
   his teeth
   Is dead. And the evil one, his wife,
   Has taken her own life.
ALL Mntwana!
MAKHIWANE All those loyal warriors who fled
   From the tyrant's cruel hand
   Can return and live in peace.
   The spear has broken.

(*He throws the spear into the ground.* MAKHIWANE
is crowned the new king.)

ALL Mntwana!
   Makhiwane, son of Mdangazeli
   Makhiwane, son of Mdangazeli
   Makhiwane, son of Mdangazeli

(*Drums and chanting.* WARRIORS *exeunt, led by*
MAKHIWANE.)

Measure for Measure

Charles Marowitz

Introduction

Charles Marowitz, born in 1934, moved from New York to England in 1956 to study at the London Academy of Music and Dramatic Art. In London he worked with Peter Brook at the Royal Shakespeare Company, staged a number of adaptations of Shakespeare, beginning with *Hamlet* in 1965, and in 1968 founded the Open Space Theatre, where he staged a number of further adaptations, most of which were collected in *The Marowitz Shakespeare* (1978). *Measure for Measure* was first mounted in 1975. In 1981 he relocated to Los Angeles and worked for a time at the Los Angeles Theater Center. A revised *Measure for Measure* was produced in Los Angeles. An adaptation of *Julius Caesar* is included in *Recycling Shakespeare* (1991). Marowitz has also adapted a number of other playwrights, including Marlowe, Ibsen, and Strindberg.

Marowitz asserts that he writes as a director. Unlike academics (for whom Marowitz shows nothing but contempt), who enter into endless and useless speculation, the director has something specific to say (Marowitz 1978b: 24), and his task is to say what he means (Marowitz 1968: 9). The director works with 'playable values' (Marowitz 1991: 9), what makes sense on stage, rather than with stultifying fidelity to a so-called 'classic.' For Marowitz, 'there is nothing so insidious as art that perpetuates the illusion that some kind of eternal truth is enshrined in . . . "a classic"' (Marowitz 1978b: 25). Such art in the theatre has a negative effect on the experiences of the audience: 'We get what we expect and we expect what we have been led to expect,' whereas 'it is only when we don't get what we have been led to expect that we are on the threshold of having an experience.' Therefore, 'Our job is to retrace, rediscover, reconsider, and re-angle the classics – not simply regurgitate them. I *rethink* therefore I am, said

Descartes – or at least he *should* have done' (Marowitz 1987: 472).

Marowitz claims a 'love–hate relationship with certain old plays – mostly those of Shakespeare' (Marowitz 1978b: 11). 'What I love best in Shakespeare,' he writes, 'are the facets of myself and my world that I find there.' What he likes least are the '"commercials" he has inspired over four centuries' (Marowitz 1991: ix), the status-quoism that appeals to the imbecilic and the conservative – for Marowitz, working on Shakespeare is always about politics (Marowitz 1987: 467). Marowitz values the way Shakespeare recycled his source material in order to rethink that material:

> What we most want now from Shakespeare is not the routine repetition of his words and imagery, but the Shakespearean Experience. And today, ironically, that can come only from dissolving the works into a new compound, and creating that sense of vicissitude, variety, and intellectual vigor with which the author himself confronted the seventeenth century.
>
> (Marowitz 1991: 478)

Nevertheless, Shakespeare's plays are both elastic enough to bend in new directions yet, as they stand, irreconcilable with those new directions. Thus, working on Shakespeare involves 'a head-on confrontation with the intellectual substructure of the plays, an attempt to test or challenge, revoke or destroy [their] intellectual foundation' (Marowitz 1978b: 24).

Inspiration for Marowitz's *Measure for Measure* came when, without having done anything wrong, he was arrested in 1974, accused of shoplifting and vagrancy. Marowitz's brush with the law convinced him that 'The Law is more than an ass, it is the deadly mechanism by which favour and prejudice are allowed to trample innocence and dissent' (Marowitz 1978b: 21). For Marowitz, this is a message at work in Shakespeare's play, but it is presented with an 'irritating ambiguity' (Marowitz 1991: 51) that softens the political effect and runs counter to the directorial project of saying what one means.

Marowitz's first adaptations were 'collages,' which chopped Shakespeare's text into pieces and reassembled them with no adherence to the original narrative development. *Measure for Measure*, however, is a 'variation' and follows Shakespeare's development more closely, at least at first. Nor are there any speeches not to be found in the original (although lines are sometimes given to different characters than in Shakespeare). In this way, Marowitz creates a strategic effect on the audience's expectations: 'For *Measure* to achieve its effects, it had to stick as closely as possible to Shakespeare's original story line, veering away at precisely those points where the moral impact would be greatest' (Marowitz 1978b: 21). Not until the audience believes it is seeing a faithful, if truncated, version of Shakespeare's play, do events unfold in a more sinister fashion. What Marowitz calls the 'arbitrary stratagems from the Duke' (20), which allow for Shakespeare's somewhat comforting ending, are nowhere in sight. Injustice is given unchecked development and, as Guido Almansi says, 'Class solidarity triumphs over justice' (100). With no reassurance that right has been done or wrong redressed, the play leads the audience to feel only disappointment and anger, at injustice and 'false seeming.' It is for this purpose that Marowitz excises all of Shakespeare's comic relief: *Measure for Measure* becomes a relentless and pointed political tragedy.

When working on *Hamlet*, Marowitz was interested in getting back to the myth that was older than the play (Marowitz 1987: 469); in *Measure for Measure*, he invokes Shakespeare's darker sources, in which no bed-trick halts the sexual extortion. Yet he goes those sources one better in denying both prevention and retribution. In the revised version staged in Los Angeles, Marowitz emphasizes the misogyny behind the injustice, and places Isabella's nightmare at the conclusion of the play:

> In the final scene, having been stirred by Isabella's vulnerability, more so than by her suit, [the Duke] coolly decides to appropriate her for himself. (Having been 'had' by Angelo, she is already, in his

eyes, damaged goods.) As she flees from his embrace, her exit is barred by Angelo. As she tries to escape in the other direction, she is intercepted by a predatory Lucio. As she tries to avoid him, she runs smack into a reincarnated Claudio, in whose eyes she reads the same lustful intent that she found in the other men. As the regent, the deputy, the rake and the executed fornicator back her into a corner and simultaneously bear down on her, the lights mercifully fade.
>
> (Marowitz 1991: 48)

However it is reconfigured, Marowitz's *Measure for Measure* (like Dryden's adaptations and Brecht's *Arturo Ui*) is driven by the desire to reduce Shakespearean ambiguities and regulate the text into clarity.

Select bibliography

Entries marked * are particularly accessible.

Almansi, G. (1982) 'The Thumb-Screwers and the Tongue-Twisters: On Shakespearian Avatars,' *Poetics Today* 3,3: 87–100.

Cohn, R. (1976) *Modern Shakespeare Offshoots*, Princeton: Princeton University Press.

Fortier, M. (1995) '"Mortality and Mercy in Vienna": *Measure for Measure*, Foucault, and Marowitz,' *English Studies in Canada* 21,4: 375–392.

Kott, J., and Marowitz, C. (1994) 'The Kott–Marowitz Dialogues: "Measure for Measure,"' *New Theatre Quarterly* 10,38: 157–166.

Marowitz, C. (1968) *The Marowitz Hamlet & The Tragical History of Dr. Faustus*, Harmondsworth, Middlesex: Penguin.

— (1974) *An Othello*, in C. Marowitz (ed.) *Open Space Plays*, Harmondsworth, Middlesex: Penguin.

— (1978a) *The Act of Being*, London: Secker & Warburg.

*— (1978b) *The Marowitz Shakespeare*, New York: Drama Book Specialists.

— (1983) *Sex Wars: Free Adaptations of Ibsen and Strindberg*, London: Boyars (Marion) Publishers.

— (1986) *Prospero's Staff: Acting and Directing in the Contemporary Theatre*, Bloomington: Indiana University Press.

— (1987) 'Shakespeare Recycled,' *Shakespeare Quarterly* 38,4: 467–478.

— (1990) *Burnt Bridges*, London: Hodder & Stoughton.

*— (1991) *Recycling Shakespeare*, New York: Applause.

*Sinfield, A. (1988) 'Making Space: Appropriation and Confrontation in Recent British Plays,' in G. Holderness (ed.) *The Shakespeare Myth*, Manchester: Manchester University Press: 128–144.

Measure for Measure ─────────

Charles Marowitz

─────────────────────────

In Blackout. Sound of the DUKE's *trumpet.*

Lights up.

(ESCALUS, *whose back is to the audience, is examining the Duke's medallion-of-state, which rests on the Throne. After a moment, the* BISHOP *arrives, catches* ESCALUS *in the act.* BISHOP *smiles knowingly to* ESCALUS, *suggesting that he knows, as does* ESCALUS, *this authority will soon be vested on him.* ESCALUS *returns the smile, looks off as he hears someone coming, and takes up a formal position beside the Throne – as does the* BISHOP.)

(*The* PROVOST *arrives very smartly and takes up his formal position. He is followed, at once, by the* DUKE *who strides on, nods, takes the medallion and hat from a cushion now held by* ESCALUS, *and then sits.*)

DUKE Escalus.

ESCALUS My lord.

DUKE Of government the properties to unfold
　Would seem in me t'affect speech and discourse,
　Since I am put to know that your own science
　Exceeds, in that, the lists of all advice
　My strength can give you. Then no more
　　remains
　But that, to your sufficiency, as your worth is
　　able,
　You do those worthy faculties engage
　And let them work. The nature of our people,
　Our city's institutions, and the terms
　For common justice, y'are as pregnant in
　As art and practice hath enriched any
　That we remember. There is our commission,
　From which we would not have you warp. Call
　　hither,
　I say, bid come before us Angelo.
　What figure of us think you he will bear?
　For you must know, we have with special soul
　Elected him our absence to supply,
　Lent him our terror, dressed him with our love,
　And given his deputation all the organs

Of our own power. What think you of it?

ESCALUS (*Concealing his disappointment*) If any in
　Vienna be of worth
　To undergo such ample grace and honour,
　It is Lord Angelo.

(*Enter* ANGELO.)

DUKE Look where he comes.

(BISHOP *and* ESCALUS *exchange fretful looks.*)

ANGELO Always obedient to your grace's will,
　I come to know your pleasure.

DUKE Angelo,
　There is a kind of character in thy life
　That to th'observer doth thy history
　Fully unfold. Thyself and thy belongings
　Are not thine own so proper as to waste
　Thyself upon thy virtues, they on thee.
　Heaven doth with us as we with torches do,
　Not light them for themselves: for if our virtues
　Did not go forth of us, 'twere all alike
　As if we had them not. Spirits are not finely
　　touched
　But to fine issues, nor Nature never lends
　The smallest scruple of her excellence
　But, like a thrifty goddess, she determines
　Herself the glory of a creditor,
　Both thanks and use. But I do spend my speech
　To one that can my part in him advertise.
　Hold therefore, Angelo:

(*Removes his Judge's cap and medallion; placing both on velvet cushion held by* ESCALUS.)

In our remove be thou at full ourself.
　Mortality and mercy in Vienna
　Live in thy tongue and heart. Good Escalus,
　Though first in question, is thy secondary.
　Take thy commission.

ANGELO Now, good my lord,
　Let there be some more test made of my metal
　Before so noble and so great a figure

Be stamped upon't.

DUKE No more evasion.
We have with leavened and prepared choice
Proceeded to you; therefore take your honours,
Our haste from hence is of so quick condition
That it prefers itself, and leaves unquestioned
Matters of needful value. We shall write to you,
As time and our concernings shall importune,
How it goes with us, and do look to know
What doth befall you here. So fare you well.
To th'hopeful execution do I leave you
Of your commissions.

ANGELO Yet give leave, my Lord,
That we may bring you something on the way.

DUKE My haste may not admit it;
Nor need you, on mine honour, have to do
With any scruple. Your scope is as mine own,
So to enforce or qualify the laws
As to your soul seems good. Give me your hand.
I'll privily away: I love the people,
But do not like to stage me to their eyes;
Though it do well, I do not relish well
Their loud applause and Aves vehement,
Nor do I think the man of safe discretion
That does affect it. Once more, fare you well.

ANGELO The heavens give safety to your
purposes!

ESCALUS Lead forth and bring you back in
happiness!

DUKE I thank you. Fare you well.

(ANGELO *and* ESCALUS *exit.*)

(BISHOP, *visibly irate, moves angrily to* DUKE.)

BISHOP I shall desire you sir to give me leave
To have free speech with you,
And it concerns me to look into . . .

DUKE No, holy Father, throw away that thought.

(*Taking drink from concealed bar in arm of*
Throne.)

Nor let thy strictures fall upon my head
Until my greater purpose yet be known.

BISHOP May your Grace speak of it?

DUKE My holy Sir, none better knows than you
How I have ever loved the life removed
And held in idle price to haunt assemblies
Where youth and cost a witless bravery keeps.
I have delivered to Lord Angelo,
A man of stricture and firm abstinence,
My absolute power and place here in Vienna,
And he supposes me travelled to Poland,
For so I have strewed it in the common ear,
And so it is received.
Now, you will demand of me why I do this.

BISHOP Gladly, my lord.

DUKE We have strict statutes and most biting
laws,
The needful bits and curbs to headstrong steeds,
Which for this fourteen years we have let slip;
Even like an o'ergrown lion in a cave,
That goes not out to prey. Now, as fond fathers,
Having bound up the threatening twigs of birch
Only to stick it in their children's sight
For terror, not to use, in time the rod
Becomes more mocked than feared, so our
decrees,
Dead to infliction, to themselves are dead,
And liberty plucks justice by the nose;
The baby beats the nurse, and quite athwart
Goes all decorum.

BISHOP It rests in your grace
To unloose this tied-up justice when you please,
And it in you more dreadful would have seemed
Than in Lord Angelo.

DUKE I do fear, too dreadful.
Sith 'twas my fault to give the people scope,
'Twould be my tyranny to strike and gall them
For what I bid them do; for we bid this be done
When evil deeds have their permissive pass
And not the punishment. Therefore, bethinking
this
I have on Angelo imposed the office,
Who may, in th'ambush of my name, strike
home,
And yet my nature never in the sight
To do it slander. Lord Angelo is precise,
Stands at a guard with envy, scarce confesses
That his blood flows, or that his appetite
Is more to bread than stone. Hence shall we see,
If power change purpose, what our seemers be.

(DUKE *offers drink to* BISHOP *who refuses*
disdainfully.)

(*Fade out.*)

(*Enter* PROVOST, CLAUDIO [*Bound*] *and* LUCIO.)

CLAUDIO Fellow, why dost thou show me thus to
th'world?
Bear me to prison, where I am committed.

PROVOST I do it not in evil disposition,
But from Lord Angelo by special charge.

CLAUDIO Thus can the demigod Authority
Make us pay down for our offence by weight
The words of heaven. On whom it will, it will;
On whom it will not, so: Yet still 'tis just.

LUCIO Why, how now, Claudio? Whence comes
this restraint?

CLAUDIO From too much liberty, my Lucio,
liberty.

As surfeit is the father of much fast,
So every scope by the immoderate use
Turns to restraint. Our natures do pursue,
Like rats that ravin down their proper bane,
A thirsty evil, and when we drink we die.

LUCIO If I could speak so wisely under an arrest, I
would send for certain of my creditors. And yet,
to say the truth, I had as lief have the foppery of
freedom as the mortality of imprisonment.
What's thy offence, Claudio?

CLAUDIO What but to speak of would offend
again.

LUCIO What, is't murder?

CLAUDIO No.

LUCIO Lechery?

CLAUDIO Call it so.

PROVOST Away, sir, you must go.

CLAUDIO One word, good friend. Lucio, a word
with you.

LUCIO A hundred, if they'll do you any good.
Is lechery so looked after?

CLAUDIO Thus stands it with me: upon a true
contract
I got possession of Julietta's bed.
You know the lady. She is fast my wife
Save that we do denunciation lack
Of outward order. This we came not to,
Only for propagation of a dower
Remaining in the coffer of her friends
From whom we thought it meet to hide our love
Till time had made them for us. But it chances
The stealth of our most mutual entertainment
With character too gross is writ on Juliet.

LUCIO With child, perhaps?

CLAUDIO Unhappily, even so.
And the new deputy now for the Duke –
Whether it be the fault and glimpse of newness,
Or whether that the body public be
A horse whereon the governor doth ride,
Who, newly in the seat, that it may know
He can command, lets it straight feel the spur;
Whether the tyranny be in his place,
Or in his eminence that fills it up,
I stagger in – but this new governor
Awakes me all the enrolled penalties
Which have, like unscoured armour, hung by
th'wall
So long that fourteen zodiacs have gone round
And none of them been worn, and for a name
Now puts the drowsy and neglected act
Freshly on me. 'Tis surely for a name.

LUCIO I warrant it is, and thy head stands so
tickle on thy shoulders that a milkmaid, if she
be in love, may sigh it off. Send after the Duke
and appeal to him.

CLAUDIO I have done so, but he's not to be found.
I prithee, Lucio, do me this kind service:
This day my sister should the cloister enter,
And there receive her approbation.
Acquaint her with the danger of my state,
Implore her, in my voice, that she makes friends
To the strict deputy, bid herself assay him.
I have great hope in that, for in her youth
There is a prone and speechless dialect,
Such as move men; beside, she hath prosperous
art
When she will play with reason and discourse,
And well she can persuade.

LUCIO I pray she may, as well for the
encouragement of the like, which else would
stand under grievous imposition, as for the
enjoying of thy life, who I would be sorry should
be thus foolishly lost at a game of tick-tack. I'll
to her.

CLAUDIO I thank you, good friend Lucio.

LUCIO Within two hours.

CLAUDIO Come, officer, away.

(*They exit.*)

(*Enter* ANGELO *and* ESCALUS.)

(*During scene,* ANGELO *dons the Duke's garments
of authority: cap and medallion.*)

ANGELO We must not make a scarecrow of the
law,
Setting it up to fear the birds of prey,
And let it keep one shape, till custom make it
Their perch and not their terror.

ESCALUS Ay, but yet
Let us be keen and rather cut a little
Than fall, and bruise to death. Alas this
gentleman,
Whom I would save, had a most noble father.
Let but your honour know,
Whom I believe to be most strait in virtue,
That, in the working of your own affections,
Had time cohered with place or place with
wishing,
Or that the resolute acting of your blood
Could have attained th'effect of your own
purpose,
Whether you had not sometime in your life
Erred in this point which now you censure him,
And pulled the law upon you.

ANGELO 'Tis one thing to be tempted, Escalus,
Another thing to fall. I not deny,
The jury, passing on the prisoner's life,
May in the sworn twelve have a thief or two
Guiltier than him they try; what's open made to
justice,

That justice seizes; what knows the laws
That thieves do pass on thieves? 'Tis very
   pregnant,
The jewel that we find, we stoop and take't
Because we see it; but what we do not see
We tread upon, and never think of it.
You may not so extenuate his offence
For I have had such faults; but rather tell me,
When I, that censure him, do so offend,
Let mine own judgement pattern out my death
And nothing come in partial. Sir, he must die.

(*Enter* PROVOST.)

ESCALUS Be it as your wisdom will.
ANGELO Where is the provost?
PROVOST Here, if it like your honour.
ANGELO See that Claudio
Be executed by tomorrow morning:
Bring his confessor, let him be prepared;
For that's the utmost of his pilgrimage.

(*As* ANGELO *goes to give execution order to*
PROVOST, *he turns to see* PROVOST *looking darkly*
at ESCALUS. ANGELO *notes the smouldering*
atmosphere between PROVOST *and* ESCALUS,
briskly places the order into the PROVOST's *hands*
and exits. The PROVOST *studies the order for a*
moment then looks up at ESCALUS.)

ESCALUS Well, heaven forgive him, and forgive us
   all.
Some rise by sin, and some by virtue fall:
Some run from brakes of office, and answer
   none,
And some condemned for a fault alone.

(ESCALUS *looks back at the order in his hand.*
'Hmphs' *sarcastically.*)

Fade out.

Lights up:

(ISABELLA *with prayer-book.*)

(LUCIO *arrives briskly. Sees nun with back to him,*
sidles up and begins seductively.)

LUCIO Hail, virgin, if you be, as those cheek-roses
Proclaim you are no less. Can you so stead me
As bring me to the sight of Isabella,
A novice of this place, and the fair sister
To her unhappy brother, Claudio?
ISABELLA Why 'her unhappy brother'? Let me ask,
The rather for I now must make you know
I am that Isabella, and his sister.
LUCIO (*Caught, now respectfully doffing his cap.*)
Gentle and fair, your brother kindly greets
   you.

Not to be weary with you, he's in prison.
ISABELLA Woe me, for what?
LUCIO For that which, if myself might be his
   judge,
He should receive his punishment in thanks.
He hath got his friend with child.
ISABELLA Sir, make me not your story.
LUCIO It is true.
I would not, though 'tis my familiar sin
With maids to seem the lapwing and to jest,
Tongue far from heart, play with all virgins so.
I hold you as a thing enskied and sainted,
By your renouncement an immortal spirit
And to be talked with in sincerity,
As with a saint.
ISABELLA You do blaspheme the good in mocking
   me.
LUCIO Do not believe it. Fewness and truth, 'tis
   thus:
Your brother and his lover have embraced.
As those that feed grow full, as blossoming time
That from the seedness the bare fallow brings
To teeming fusion even so her plenteous womb
Expresseth his full tilth and husbandry.
ISABELLA Someone with child by him? My cousin
   Juliet?
LUCIO Is she your cousin?
ISABELLA Adoptedly, as school-maids change
   their names
By vain though apt affection.
LUCIO She it is.
ISABELLA O, let him marry her.
LUCIO This is the point.
The Duke is very strangely gone from hence.
Upon his place.
And with full line of his authority,
Governs Lord Angelo, a man whose blood
Is very snow-broth, one who never feels
The wanton stings and motions of the sense,
But doth rebate and blunt his natural edge
With profits of the mind, study, and fast.
He, to give fear to use and liberty,
Which have for long run by the hideous law,
As mice by lions, hath picked out an act,
Under whose heavy sense your brother's life
Falls into forfeit; he arrests him on it.
And follows close the rigour of the statute
To make him an example. All hope is gone,
Unless you have the grace by your fair prayer
To soften Angelo. And that's my pith of business
'Twixt you and your poor brother.
ISABELLA Doth he so seek his life?
LUCIO Has censured him
Already and, as I hear, the provost hath
A warrant for his execution.

ISABELLA Alas, what poor ability's in me
  To do him good.
LUCIO Assay the power you have.
ISABELLA My power? Alas, I doubt.
LUCIO Our doubts are traitors
  And make us lose the good we oft might win,
  By fearing to attempt. Go to Lord Angelo,
  And let him learn to know,when maidens sue,
  Men give like gods; but when they weep and
    kneel,
  All their petitions are as freely theirs
  As they themselves would owe them.
ISABELLA I'll see what I can do.
LUCIO But speedily.
ISABELLA I will about it straight,
  No longer staying but to give the Mother
  Notice of my affair. I humbly thank you.
  Commend me to my brother. Soon at night
  I'll send him certain word of my success.

(LUCIO and ISABELLA *exit opposite sides on
Blackout.*)

ANGELO's *chamber – high judicial desk.*

PROVOST I'll know
  His pleasure; maybe he'll relent. Alas,
  He hath but as offended in a dream.
  All sects, all ages smack of this vice, and he
  To die for it!

(*Enter* ANGELO.)

ANGELO Now, what's the matter, provost?
PROVOST Is it your will Claudio shall die
    tomorrow?
ANGELO Did not I tell thee, yea? Hadst thou not
    order?
  Why dost thou ask again?
PROVOST Lest I might be too rash.
  Under your good correction, I have seen
  When, after execution, judgement hath
  Repented o'er his doom.
ANGELO Go to; let that be mine.
  Do you your office, or give up your place,
  And you shall well be spared.

(ANGELO *crosses and sits behind desk.*)

PROVOST I crave your honour's pardon.
  What shall be done, sir, with the groaning Juliet?
  She's very near her hour.
ANGELO Dispose of her
  To some more fitter place, and that with speed.
PROVOST Here is the sister of the man
    condemned
  Desires access to you.
ANGELO Hath he a sister?

PROVOST Ay, my good lord, a very virtuous maid,
  And to be shortly of a sisterhood,
  If not already.
ANGELO Well, let her be admitted. And,
  See you the fornicatress be removed;
  Let her have needful, but not lavish, means.
  There shall be order for't.
PROVOST God save your honour.

(*He exits.*)

(*Enter* ISABELLA.)

ANGELO (*to* ISABELLA) Y'are welcome. What's
    your will?
ISABELLA I am a woeful suitor to your honour,
  Please but your honour hear me.
ANGELO Well, what's your suit?
ISABELLA There is a vice that most I do abhor,
  And most desire should meet the blow of justice,
  For which I would not plead, but that I must,
  For which I must not plead, but that I am
  At war 'twixt will and will not.
ANGELO Well: the matter?
ISABELLA I have a brother is condemned to die.
  I do beseech, you, let it be his fault,
  And not my brother.

(ANGELO *looks up for first time. Sees* ISABELLA.
Registers her. Pause.)

ANGELO Condemn the fault, and not the actor
    of it?
  Why, every fault's condemned ere it be done.
  Mine were the very cipher of a function,
  To fine the faults whose fine stands in record,
  And let go by the actor.
ISABELLA O just, but severe law!
  I had a brother then; heaven keep your honour.
  (*Begins to go: stops.*) Must he needs die?
ANGELO Maiden, no remedy.
ISABELLA Yes, I do think that you might pardon
    him,
  And neither heaven nor man grieve at the
    mercy.
ANGELO I will not do't.
ISABELLA But can you if you would?
ANGELO Look what I will not, that I cannot do.
ISABELLA But might you do't, and do the world no
    wrong,
  If so your heart were touched with that remorse
  As mine is to him?
ANGELO He's sentenced: 'tis too late.
ISABELLA Too late? Why, no. I that do speak a
    word
  May call it back again. Well, believe this,
  No ceremony that to great ones longs,

Not the king's crown, nor the deputed sword,
The marshal's truncheon, nor the judge's robe,
Become them with one half so good a grace
As mercy does.
If he had been as you, and you as he,
You would have slipped like him; but he, like
    you
Would not have been so stern.
ANGELO Pray you, be gone.
ISABELLA (*Riled*) I would to heaven I had your
    potency,
And you were Isabel; should it then be thus?
No, I would tell what 'twere to be a judge,
And what a prisoner.
ANGELO Your brother is a forfeit of the law,
And you but waste your words.
ISABELLA Alas, alas;
Why, all the souls that were were forfeit once,
And He that might the vantage best have took
Found out the remedy. How would you be,
If He, which is the top of judgement, should
But judge you as you are? O think on that,
And mercy then will breathe within your lips,
Like man new made.

(*Pause as* ANGELO *eyes* ISABELLA *curiously.*
ISABELLA, *nervous under his scrutiny.*)

ANGELO Be you content, fair maid,
It is the law, not I, condemns your brother;
Were he my kinsman, brother, or my son,
It should be thus with him. He must die
    tomorrow.
ISABELLA Tomorrow? Oh, that's sudden; spare
    him, spare him.
He's not prepared for death. Even for our
    kitchens
We kill the fowl of season. Shall we serve
    heaven
With less respect than we do minister
To our gross selves? Good, good my lord,
    bethink you:
Who is it that hath died for this offence?
There's many have committed it.
Yet show some pity.
ANGELO I show it most of all when I show justice,
For then I pity those I do not know,
Which a dismissed offence would after gall,
And do him right that, answering one foul
    wrong,
Lives not to act another. Be satisfied
Your brother dies tomorrow. Be content.
ISABELLA (*Hot, angry*) So you must be the first
    that gives this sentence
And he, that suffers. O, 'tis excellent
To have a giant's strength, but it is tyrannous

To use it like a giant.
Could great men thunder
As Jove himself does, Jove would ne'er be quiet,
For every pelting, petty officer
Would use his heaven for thunder,
Nothing but thunder. Merciful heaven,
Thou rather with thy sharp and sulphurous bolt
Splits the unwedgeable and gnarled oak
Than the soft myrtle; but man, proud man,
Dressed in a little brief authority,
Most ignorant of what he's most assured,
His glassy essence, like an angry ape
Plays such fantastic tricks before high heaven
As makes the angels weep; who, with our
    spleens,
Would all themselves laugh mortal.
We cannot weigh our brother with ourself,
Great men may jest with saints: 'tis wit in them,
But in the less, foul profanation.
That in the captain's but a choleric word
Which in the soldier is flat blasphemy.
ANGELO Why do you put these sayings upon me?
ISABELLA Because authority, though it err like
    others,
Hath yet a kind of medicine in itself
That skins the vice o'th'top. Go to your bosom,
Knock there, and ask your heart what it doth
    know
That's like my brother's fault; if it confess
A natural guiltiness such as is his,
Let it not sound a thought upon your tongue
Against my brother's life.
ANGELO (*Aside*) She speaks, and 'tis
Such sense that my sense breeds with it.
Fare you well. (*Leaves desk, begins to go.*)
ISABELLA Gentle my lord, turn back.
ANGELO I will bethink me. Come again
    tomorrow.
ISABELLA Hark how I'll bribe you. Good my lord,
    turn back.
ANGELO How? Bribe me?
ISABELLA Ay, with such gifts that heaven shall
    share with you
Not with fond shekels of the tested gold,
Or stones whose rate are either rich or poor
As fancy values them; but with true prayers
That shall be up at heaven and enter there
Ere sunrise: prayers from preserved souls,
From fasting maids whose minds are dedicate
To nothing temporal.
ANGELO Well, come to me tomorrow.
ISABELLA Heaven keep your honour safe.
ANGELO Amen.
ISABELLA At what hour tomorrow
Shall I attend your lordship?

ANGELO At any time 'forenoon.
ISABELLA God save your honour.

(*Exit* ISABELLA: *spot on* ANGELO.)

ANGELO From thee: even from thy virtue.
What's this? What's this? Is this her fault or mine
The tempter, or the tempted, who sins most?
Ha?
Not she, nor doth she tempt; but it is I
That, lying by the violet in the sun,
Do as the carrion does, not as the flower,
Corrupt with virtuous season. Can it be
That modesty may more betray our sense
Than woman's lightness? Having waste ground
    enough
Shall we desire to raze the sanctuary
And pitch our evils there? O fie, fie, fie!
What dost thou? Or what art thou, Angelo?
Dost thou desire her foully for those things
That make her good? O, let her brother live:
Thieves for their robbery have authority
When judges steal themselves. What, do I love
    her,
That I desire to hear her speak again,
And feast upon her eyes? What is't I dream on?
O cunning enemy that, to catch a saint,
With saints dost bait thy hook. Most dangerous
Is that temptation that doth goad us on
To sin in loving virtue. Never could the
    strumpet
With all her double vigour, art and nature,
Once stir my temper; but this virtuous maid
Subdues me quite. Ever till now,
When men were fond, I smiled and wondered
    how.

(*Looks down at execution order in his hand at Fade
out.*)

CLAUDIO'*s cell.*

PROVOST So then you hope of pardon from Lord
    Angelo?
CLAUDIO The miserable have no other medicine
    But only hope;
    I have hope to live, and am prepared to die.

(*Exit* CLAUDIO *and* PROVOST.)

LUCIO Marry, this Claudio is condemned for
untrussing! A little more leniency to lechery
would do no harm, say I. 'Tis a general vice, and
impossible to extirp it quite til eating and
drinking be put down.
    It was a mad fantastical trick of the Duke to
steal from the State, and usurp the beggary he
was never born to. Some say he is with the
Emperor of Russia; other some, he is in Rome.
Lord Angelo dukes it well in his absence. They
say this Angelo was not made by man and
woman after this downright way of creation.
Some report a sea-maid spawned him. Some that
he was begot between two stock-fishes. But it is
certain when he makes water his urine is
congealed ice.
    Why what a ruthless thing is this in him, for
the rebellion of a cod-piece to take away the life
of a man! Would the Duke that is absent have
done this? Ere he would have hanged a man
for the getting of a hundred bastards, he would
have paid for the nursing of a thousand. He had
some feeling of the sport. The Duke had
crotchets in him. He's not past it yet. Why, he
would mouth with a beggar though she smelt
brown bread and garlic. I would the Duke were
returned again.
    This ungenitured agent will unpeople the
province with continency. Sparrows must not
build in his house-eaves because they are
lecherous. The Duke yet would have dark deeds
darkly answered. He would never bring them to
light. Would he were returned.

ANGELO'*s chamber.*

ANGELO O heavens,
Why does my blood thus muster to my heart,
Making both it unable for itself,
And dispossessing all my other parts
Of necessary fitness?
So play the foolish throngs with one that
    swoons,
Come all to help him, and so stop the air
By which he should revive; and even so
The general, subject to a well-wished king,
Quit their own part, and in obsequious fondness
Crowd to his presence, where their untaught
    love
Must needs appear offence.

(*Enter* ISABELLA.)

How now, fair maid!
ISABELLA I am come to know your pleasure.
ANGELO That you might know it, would much
    better please me
Than to demand what 'tis. Your brother cannot
    live.
ISABELLA Even so. Heaven keep your honour.
    (*Begins to go.*)
ANGELO Yet may he live a while; and it may be
As long as you or I, yet he must die.
ISABELLA Under your sentence?
ANGELO Yea.

ISABELLA When, I beseech you? That in his
    reprieve,
  Longer or shorter, he may be so fitted
  That his soul sicken not.
ANGELO Ha! Fie, these filthy vices! (*Coming down
    from behind desk.*) It were as good
  To pardon him that hath from nature stol'n
  A man already made as to remit
  Their saucy sweetness that do coin God's image
  In stamps that are forbid: 'tis all as easy
  Falsely to take away a life true made
  As to put metal in restrained means
  To make a false one.
ISABELLA 'Tis set down so in heaven, but not in
    earth.
ANGELO Say you so? Then I shall pose you
    quickly.
  Which had you rather, that the most just law
  Now took your brother's life, or to redeem him
  Give up your body to such sweet uncleanness
  As she that he hath stained?
ISABELLA Sir, believe this,
  I had rather give my body than my soul.
ANGELO I talk not of your soul. Our compelled
    sins
  Stand more for number than accompt.
ISABELLA How say you?
ANGELO Nay, I'll not warrant that, for I can speak
  Against the thing I say. Answer to this:
  I, now the voice of the recorded law,
  Pronounce a sentence on your brother's life;
  Might there not be a charity in sin
  To save this brother's life?
ISABELLA Please you to do't,
  I'll take it as a peril to my soul;
  It is no sin at all, but charity.
ANGELO Pleased you to do't, at peril of your soul.
  Were equal poise of sin and charity.
ISABELLA That I do beg his life, if it be sin,
  Heaven let me bear it: you granting of my suit,
  If that be sin, I'll make it my morning prayer
  To have it added to the faults of mine
  And nothing of your answer.
ANGELO Nay, but hear me;
  Your sense pursues not mine. Either you are
    ignorant,
  Or seem so craftily; and that's not good.
ISABELLA Let me be ignorant, and in nothing
    good
  But graciously to know I am not better.
ANGELO Thus wisdom wishes to appear most
    bright
  When it doth tax itself, as these black masks
  Proclaim an enshield beauty ten times louder
  Than beauty could, displayed. But mark me;

To be received plain, I'll speak more gross:
  Your brother is to die.
ISABELLA So.
ANGELO And his offence is so, as it appears,
  Accountant to the law upon that pain.
ISABELLA True.
ANGELO Admit no other way to save his life –
  As I subscribe not that, nor any other,
  But in the loss of question – that you, his sister
  Finding yourself desired of such a person
  Whose credit with the judge, or own great place,
  Could fetch your brother from the manacles
  Of the all-binding law; and that there were
  No earthly mean to save him, but that either
  You must lay down the treasures of your body,
  To this supposed, or else to let him suffer,
  What would you do?
ISABELLA As much for my poor brother as
    myself:
  That is, were I under the terms of death,
  Th' impression of keen whips I'd wear as rubies,
  And strip myself to death as to a bed
  That long I have been sick for, ere I'd yield
  My body up to shame.
ANGELO Then must your brother die.
ISABELLA And 'twere the cheaper way.
  Better it were a brother died at once
  Than that a sister, by redeeming him,
  Should die for ever.
ANGELO Were not you then as cruel as the
    sentence
  That you have slandered so?
ISABELLA Ignomy in ransom and free pardon
  Are of two houses: lawful mercy is
  nothing kin to foul redemption.
ANGELO You seemed of late to make the law a
    tyrant,
  And rather proved the sliding of your brother
  A merriment than a vice.
ISABELLA O pardon me, my lord; it oft falls out
  To have what we would have, to speak not what
    we mean,
  I something do excuse the thing I hate
  For his advantage that I dearly love.
ANGELO We are all frail.
ISABELLA Else let my brother die
  If he alone this sin doth owe and none
  Succeed him in that weakness.
ANGELO Nay, women are frail too.
ISABELLA Ay, as the glasses where they view
    themselves,
  Which are as easy broke as they make forms,
  Women, help heaven! Men their creation mar
  In profiting by them. Nay, call us ten times frail,
  For we are soft as our complexions are,

And credulous to false prints.

ANGELO I think it well,
And from this testimony of your own sex –
Since I suppose we are made to be no stronger
Than faults may shake our frames – let me be
    bold
I do arrest your words. Be that you are,
That is, a woman; if you be more, you're none.
If you be one, as you are well expressed
By all external warrants, show it now,
By putting on the destined livery.

ISABELLA I have no tongue but one. Gentle my
    lord,
Let me entreat you speak the former language.

ANGELO Plainly conceive, I love you.

ISABELLA My brother did love Juliet,
And you tell me that he shall die for't.

ANGELO He shall not, Isabel, if you give me love.

(*Takes* ISABELLA's *hand.*)

ISABELLA (*Pulling away*) I know your virtue hath
    a licence in't,
Which seems a little fouler than it is,
To pluck on others.

ANGELO Believe me, on mine honour,
My words express my purpose.

ISABELLA Ha! Little honour to be much believed,
And most pernicious purpose. Seeming,
    seeming!
I will proclaim thee, Angelo, look for't!
Sign me a present pardon for my brother,
Or with an outstretched throat I'll tell the world
What man thou art.

ANGELO Who will believe thee, Isabel?
My unsoiled name, th'austereness of my life,
My vouch against you, and my place i'th'state,
Will so your accusation overweigh
That you shall stifle in your own report
And smell of calumny. I have begun,
And now I give my sensual race the rein.
Fit thy consent to my sharp appetite,
Lay by all nicety and prolixious blushes,
That banish what they sue for. Redeem thy
    brother
By yielding up thy body to my will,
Or else he must not only die the death,
But thy unkindness shall his death draw out
To lingering sufferance. Answer me tomorrow
Or, by the affection that now guides me most,
I'll prove a tyrant to him. As for you,
Say what you can, my false o'erweighs your true.

(ANGELO *takes* ISABELLA's *hand, despite her
resistance, and kisses it fondly in the palm. As she
pulls away from the kiss* ANGELO *exits and
simultaneously a single spot picks up* ISABELLA.)

ISABELLA To whom should I complain. Did I tell
    this,
Who would believe me? O perilous mouths,
That bear in them one and the selfsame tongue,
Either of condemnation or approof,
Bidding the law make curtsy to their will,
Hooking both right and wrong to th'appetite,
To follow as it draws. I'll to my brother.
Though he hath fall'n by prompture of the
    blood,
Yet hath he in him such a mind of honour
That, had he twenty heads to tender down
On twenty bloody blocks, he'd yield them up,
Before his sister should her body stoop
To such abhorred pollution.
Then, Isabel, live chaste, and, brother, die.
More than our brother is our chastity.

(*Blackout.*)

(*Lights up.*)

CLAUDIO Now, sister, what's the comfort?

ISABELLA Why?
As all comforts are: most good, most good
    indeed.
Lord Angelo, having affairs to heaven
Intends you for his swift ambassador,
Where you shall be an everlasting Leiger.
Therefore your best appointment make with
    speed;
Tomorrow you set on.

CLAUDIO Is there no remedy?

ISABELLA None, but such remedy as, to save a
    head,
To cleave a heart in twain.

CLAUDIO But is there any?

ISABELLA Yes, brother, you may live;
There is a devilish mercy in the judge,
If you'll implore it, that will free your life,
But fetter you till death.

CLAUDIO Perpetual durance?

ISABELLA Ay just. Perpetual durance, a restraint,
Though all the world's vastidity you had,
To a determined scope.

CLAUDIO But in what nature?

ISABELLA In such a one as, you consenting to't,
Would bark your honour from that trunk you
    bear,
And leave you naked.

CLAUDIO Let me know the point.

ISABELLA O, I do fear thee, Claudio, and I quake
Lest thou a feverous life shouldst entertain,
And six or seven winters more respect
Than a perpetual honour. Dar'st thou die?
The sense of death is most in apprehension,

And the poor beetle that we tread upon
In corporal sufference finds a pang as great
As when a giant dies.

CLAUDIO Why give you me this shame?
Think you I can a resolution fetch
From flowery tenderness? If I must die,
I will encounter darkness as a bride,
And hug it in mine arms.

ISABELLA There spake my brother. There my
 father's grave
Did utter forth a voice. Yes, thou must die.
Thou art too noble to conserve a life
In base appliances. This outward-sainted
 deputy,
Whose settled visage and deliberate word
Nips youth i'th'head, and follies doth enew
As falcon doth the fowl, is yet a devil
His filth within being cast, he would appear
A pond as deep as hell.

CLAUDIO The precise Angelo?

ISABELLA Oh, tis the cunning livery of hell,
The damned'st body to invest and cover
In precious guards. Dost thou think, Claudio,
If I would yield him my virginity,
Thou might'st be freed?

CLAUDIO O heavens, it cannot be.

ISABELLA Yes, he would give't thee, from this
 rank offence,
So to offend him still. This night's the time
That I should do what I abhor to name,
Or else thou diest tomorrow.

CLAUDIO Thou shalt not do't.

ISABELLA O, were it but my life
I'd throw it down for your deliverance
As frankly as a pin. Be ready, Claudio,
For your death tomorrow.

CLAUDIO Yes. Has he affections in him
That thus can make him bite the law by th'nose
When he would force it? Sure it is no sin,
Or of the deadly seven it is the least.

ISABELLA Which is the least?

CLAUDIO If it were damnable, he being so wise,
Why would he for the momentary trick
Be perdurably fined? O Isabel?

ISABELLA What says my brother?

CLAUDIO Death is a fearful thing.

ISABELLA And shamed life a hateful.

CLAUDIO Ay, but to die, and go we know not
 where,
To lie in cold obstruction and to rot;
This sensible warm motion to become
A kneaded clod; and the delighted spirit
To bathe in fiery floods, or to reside
In thrilling region of thick-ribbed ice,
To be imprisoned in the viewless winds

And blown with restless violence round about
The pendent world; or to be worse than worst
Of those that lawless and incertain thought
Imagine howling, 'tis too horrible.
The weariest and most loathed wordly life
That age, ache, penury, and imprisonment
Can lay on nature is a paradise
To what we fear of death.

ISABELLA Alas, alas.

CLAUDIO Sweet sister, let me live.
What sin you do to save a brother's life,
Nature dispenses with the deed so far
That it becomes a virtue.

ISABELLA Wilt thou be made a man out of my
 vice?
Is't not a kind of incest to take life
From thine own sister's shame? What should I
 think?
Heaven shield my mother played my father fair,
For such a warped slip of wilderness
Ne'er issued from his blood. Take my defiance,
Die, perish. Might but my bending down
Reprieve thee from thy fate, it should proceed.
I'll pray a thousand prayers for thy death,
No word to save thee.

CLAUDIO Nay, hear me, Isabel.

ISABELLA O, fie, fie, fie!
Thy sin's not accidental, but a trade.
Mercy to thee would prove itself a bawd,
'Tis best that thou diest quickly.

CLAUDIO O hear me, Isabella.

(ISABELLA *gone*, CLAUDIO *falls into* LUCIO's
arms, as he enters.)

Let me ask my sister pardon. I am so out of love
with life that I will sue to be rid of it.

(*Lights out.*)

(ANGELO *standing uneasily with order.*)

(PROVOST *enters.*)

ANGELO Whatsoever you may hear to the
 contrary,
Let Claudio be executed by four of the clock.
For my better satisfaction,
Let me have Claudio's head sent me by five.

PROVOST My lord . . .

ANGELO (*Sharply*) Let this be duly performed,
With a thought that more depends on it then we
 must yet deliver.
Thus fail not to do your office,
As you will answer it at your peril.

(PROVOST *exits.*)

(ANGELO *crosses himself; tries to pray, breaks off.*)

ANGELO (*contd*) When I would pray and think, I
    think and pray
  To several subjects: heaven hath my empty
    words,
  Whilst my invention, hearing not my tongue,
  Anchors on Isabel: God in my mouth,
  As if I did but only chew His name,
  And in my heart the strong and swelling evil
  Of my conception. The state, whereon I studied,
  Is like a good thing, being often read,
  Grown seared and tedious; yea, my gravity,
  Wherein, let no man hear me, I take pride,
  Could I, with boot, change for an idle plume
  Which the air beats for vain. O place, O form,
  How often dost thou with thy case, thy habit,
  Wrench awe from fools, and tie the wiser souls
  To thy false seeming! Blood, thou art blood;
  Let's write 'good Angel' on the devil's horn,
  'Tis not the devil's crest.

  (*Blackout.*)

PROVOST, LUCIO, ESCALUS (*As* ESCALUS *enters*
LUCIO *withdraws to listen in.*)

PROVOST What comfort is for Claudio.
ESCALUS (*Hedging*) There's some in hope.
PROVOST It is a bitter Deputy.

  (*Pause.*)

ESCALUS (*acknowledging the inevitable*) Provost,
  my brother Angelo will not be altered;
  Claudio must die tomorrow. Let him be
    furnished
  With divines, and have all charitable preparation
  If my brother wrought by my pity, it should not
    be
  So with him. Let me desire to know how you
    find
  Claudio prepared?
PROVOST (*To himself*) He professes to have
  received no sinister measure
  From his judge, but most willingly humbles
    himself
  To the determination of Justice.
ESCALUS (*To himself*) I have laboured for the poor
  gentleman to the extremest shore of my
  modesty, but my brother – Justice I have found
  so severe that he hath forc'd me to tell him that
  he is indeed Justice.
PROVOST (*To himself, grimly*) If his own life
  answer the straitness of his proceeding, it shall
  become him well; wherein if he chance to fail,
  he hath sentenc'd himself.
ESCALUS (*to* PROVOST) Not so, not so; his life is
  parallel'd

Even with the stroke and line of his great
    justice
He doth with holy abstinence subdue
That in himself which he spurs on his power
To qualify in others, were he meal'd with that
Which he corrects, then were he tyrannous;
But this being so, he's just . . . (PROVOST *looks
  at* ESCALUS, *searching for irony; finds none*)
I am going to visit the prisoner; fare you well.
PROVOST Peace be with you.
ISABELLA (*Off-stage*) Peace, ho, be here.
PROVOST The tongue of Isabel. She's come to
  know
  If yet her brother's pardon be come hither.
ISABELLA Have you no countermand for Claudio
  yet?
PROVOST None, maid, none.
ISABELLA (*With a curious, self-deluding smile*) As
  near the dawning, provost, as it is,
  You shall hear more ere morning.
PROVOST Happily.
  You something know, yet I believe there comes
  No countermand; no such example have we.
  Besides, upon the very siege of justice
  Lord Angelo hath to the public ear
  Professed the contrary.
ISABELLA (*Smile vanishes, forced to acknowledge the
  truth, bursting into tears*) What a merit were it in
  death to take this poor maid from the world!
  What a corruption in this life that it will let this
  man live!
LUCIO (*Embracing her*) O Pretty Isabella, I am
  pale at mine heart to see thine eyes so red. Thou
  must be patient. I am fain to dine and sup with
  water and bran. I dare not for my head fill my
  belly; one fruitful meal would set me to't. By my
  troth, Isabel, I love thy brother. If the old
  fantastical Duke of dark corners had been at
  home, he had lived.
PROVOST It grieves me for the death of Claudio,
  but there is no remedy.

(ISABELLA *forces herself away from* LUCIO *and*
PROVOST *and is suddenly alone. As she stands
listening intently, she [and we] hear a cacophony of
indistinct voices; echoes from* CLAUDIO, ANGELO,
LUCIO *and the* PROVOST.)

(*Voices on tape.*)

ANGELO (*As before*) Your brother is a forfeit of the
  law.
CLAUDIO (*As before*) If I must die I will encounter
  Darkness like a bride.
ISABELLA (*Fierce*) And strip myself to death as to
  a bed.

ANGELO (*As before*) By yielding up thy body to my will.

ISABELLA (*Modest*) God save your honour.

ANGELO (*As before*) Or else he must not only die the death.

ISABELLA (*Modest*) Please but your honour hear me.

ANGELO (*As before*) But thy unkindness shall his death draw out.

ISABELLA (*Scoffing*) Ha! Little honour to be much believed!

PROVOST (*As before*) Yet I believe there comes no countermand.

CLAUDIO (*As before*) Sure it is no sin . . .

ANGELO (*Cynical*) Or of the deadly seven it is the least.

PROVOST (*As before*) There comes no countermand.

CLAUDIO Sweet sister . . .

ANGELO (*As before*) If you give me love

CLAUDIO Let me live!

(*Over the jumble of voices, we hear the* PROVOST's *voice loud and clear. As soon as he speaks, the lighting turns to red and we are clearly in a kind of surreal dream-sequence.*)

PROVOST (*Facing away; as if to hangman*) Come hither sirrah, can you cut off a man's head?

ISABELLA Good Provost, here is Claudio's pardon;
Purchased by such sin
For which the pardoner himself is in.

PROVOST (*Faced away*) I believe there comes no countermand.

ISABELLA By the vow of mine order, I warrant you, here is the pardon.

PROVOST (*Faced away*) Lord Angelo hath to the public ear confessed to the contrary.

ISABELLA. (*Accusingly*) Claudio whom here you have warrant to execute is no greater forfeit to the law than Angelo who hath sentenced him. (*Pleadingly.*) If anything fall to you upon this, more than thanks and good fortune, by the saint whom I profess, I will plead against it with my life.

PROVOST It is against my oath.

ISABELLA Were you sworn to the Duke or the Deputy?

PROVOST To him and to his substitutes.

ISABELLA You will then have made no offence, if the Duke avouch the justice of your dealing?

PROVOST But what likelihood in that?

DUKE (*Suddenly appearing with* ANGELO *behind; back to back*) Not a resemblance but a certainty.

Look you sir, here is the hand and seal of the Duke.
You know the character, I doubt not, and the signet
Is not strange to you.

PROVOST (*Suddenly respectful*) Pardon me, noble lord.

(CLAUDIO *appears and is unmanacled by the* PROVOST. *He goes to the* DUKE *and kneels.*)

DUKE Thou'rt condemned.
But for those earthly faults, I quit them all.
And pray thee take this mercy to provide
For better times to come.

(ISABELLA, *full of gratitude, bows down before* DUKE.)

ISABELLA My noble Lord!

DUKE (*To* ISABELLA) Put yourself not into amazement how these things should be. All difficulties are but easy when they are known. Give me your hand and . . .

ANGELO (*Transformed from the* DUKE) Plainly conceive, I love you.

ISABELLA (*Playfully*) My brother did love Juliet. And you tell me he shall die for't.

ANGELO (*Fondly*) He shall not Isabel, if you give me love.

ISABELLA I know your virtue hath a licence in't
Which seems a little fouler than it is,
To pluck on others.

ANGELO Believe me, on mine honour,
My words express my purpose.

ISABELLA Ha! Little honour to be much believed,
And most pernicious purpose, Seeming, seeming!
I will proclaim thee, Angelo, look for't,
Sign me a present pardon for my brother,
Or with an outstretched throat I'll tell the world
What man thou art.

ANGELO (*Taking her in his arms*) Who will believe thee, Isabel?

(*They kiss fondly.* ANGELO *suddenly vanishes and* ISABELLA *is discovered kneeling before the* BISHOP.)

BISHOP Repent you, fair one, of the sin you carry?

ISABELLA I do, and bear the shame most patiently.

BISHOP I'll teach you how you shall arraign your conscience
And try your penitence, if it be sound,
Or hollowly put on.

ISABELLA I'll gladly learn.

BISHOP Love you the man that wronged you?

ISABELLA (*Pause*) Yes, as I love the woman that wronged him.

BISHOP So then it seems your most offenceful act Was mutually committed?

ISABELLA Mutually.

BISHOP Then was your sin of heavier kind than his.

ISABELLA I do confess it, and repent it, father.

BISHOP 'Tis meet so, daughter, but lest you do repent
As that the sin hath brought you to this shame,
Which sorrow is always towards ourselves, not heaven,
Showing we would not spare heaven as we love it,
But as we stand in fear.

ISABELLA I do repent me as it is an evil,
And take the shame with joy.

BISHOP There rest.

(BISHOP *bends down as if to bless* ISABELLA *but instead, takes her by the scruff of the neck and hurls her forward, away from him.*)

Harlot!

(*The* BISHOP *vanishes.*)

(CLAUDIO *suddenly materialized: smirking seductively.*)

CLAUDIO Sure, it is no sin
Or of the deadly seven it is the least.

ISABELLA Which is the least?

CLAUDIO If it were damnable, he being so wise
Why would he for the momentary trick
Be perdurably fin'd – O Isabel!

ISABELLA (*Fearful*) What says my brother?

CLAUDIO (*Archly*) Death is a fearful thing.

ISABELLA (*Frightened*) Alas, alas.

CLAUDIO (*Close*) Sweet sister, let me live.
What sin you do to save a brother's life,
Nature dispenses with the deed so far
That it becomes a virtue.

(*There is momentary tension between them, then* CLAUDIO *grabs her rudely and tries to close her in a lecherous embrace.* ISABELLA *pushes him off. He laughs obscenely through her next speech.*)

ISABELLA O you beast! O faithless coward.
O dishonest wretch.
Beast. Beast. Beast.

(*Cacophony of sound on tape as follows.*)

(*Voices on tape.*)

ANGELO Sure it is no sin – or of the deadly seven, it is the least.

BISHOP You must lay down the treasures of your body.

CLAUDIO We are all frail.

ANGELO The treasures of your body.

ISABELLA And strip myself to death as to a bed That long I have been sick for.

ANGELO Plainly conceive that I love you.

BISHOP Love you the man that . . .

ANGELO love you . . .

CLAUDIO Let me live . . .

BISHOP wronged you?

(BISHOP, ANGELO *repeat: Love you. Wronged you while* CLAUDIO'S *voice crescendoes above it.*)

CLAUDIO Let me live. Let me live. Let me live!!!

(*All visions and sound disappear suddenly.* ISABELLA *now alone in a single spot.*)

ISABELLA Dissolve my life, let not my sense unsettle
Lest I should drown, or stab, or hang myself.
O state of Nature, fail together in me
Since the best props are warpt. So which way now?
The best way is the next way to a grave.
Each errant step beside is torment. Lo,
The moon is down, the crickets chirp, the screech-owl
Calls in the dawn. All offices are done
Save what I fail in.
An end, and that is all.

(*Lights blend surreally.* CLAUDIO *suddenly appears.* ISABELLA *rushes into his arms. They embrace desperately.* CLAUDIO *takes her by the hand and leads her towards the curtained-bed. There she is presented to* ANGELO *who clasps* CLAUDIO'S *hand as* CLAUDIO *does his.* ANGELO *then motions for* CLAUDIO *to depart.* CLAUDIO *begins to back out of the scene and into the waiting arms of the* PROVOST *who smiles curiously at* CLAUDIO *then, putting his arm around his shoulder in a fraternal manner, leads him out.*)

(ISABELLA *stands mute and still.* ANGELO *approaches her and tenderly undoes her nun's headpiece.* ISABELLA'S *short, cropped hair is revealed underneath. Then he undoes her nun's habit until she stands naked before him. She remains still and devoid of emotion. Then,* ANGELO *bends down, places his arms around her waist and his head in the pit of her stomach.*)

(*Instinctively,* ISABELLA *makes a move as if to embrace* ANGELO's *head, but the gesture is cut short, and she then resumes her neutral position.* ANGELO *lifts her into his arms, draws open the surrounding curtains, and disappears behind them with* ISABELLA.)

(*Downstage, in a gloomy light, the* BISHOP *appears before* CLAUDIO, *who is kneeling before him, and administers the last rites.*)

BISHOP (*As if intoning a prayer*) Be absolute for
    death: either death or life
Shall thereby be the sweeter. Reason thus with
    life
If I do lose thee, I do lose a thing
That none but fools would keep; a breath thou
    art
Servile to all the skyey influences
That does this habitation where thou keep'st
Hourly afflict. Merely, thou art death's fool,
For him thou labour'st by thy flight to shun,
And yet runn'st toward him still. Thou art not
    noble,
For all th'accommodations that thou bear'st
Are nursed by baseness. Thou'rt by no means
    valiant
For thou dost fear the soft and tender fork
Of a poor worm. The best of rest is sleep,
And that thou oft provok'st, yet grossly fear'st
Thy death, which is no more. Thou art not
    thyself,
For thou exists on many a thousand grains
That issue out of dust. Happy thou art not,
For what thou hast not, still thou striv'st to get,
And what thou hast, forget'st. Thou art not
    certain
For thy complexion shifts to strange effects,
After the moon. If thou art rich, thou'rt poor,
For, like an ass, whose back with ingots bows,
Thou bear'st thy heavy riches but a journey,
And death unloads thee. Friend hast thou
    none,
For thine own bowels, which do call thee sire,
The mere effusion of thy proper loins,
Do curse the gout, serpigo, and the rheum
For ending thee no sooner. Thou hast nor youth
    nor age,
But as it were an after-dinner's sleep,
Dreaming on both, for all thy blessed youth
Becomes as aged, and doth beg the alms
Of palsied eld: and when thou art old and rich,
Thou hast neither heat, affection, limb, nor
    beauty
To make thy riches pleasant. What's yet in this
That bears the name of life? Yet in this life

Lie hid more thousand deaths; yet death we
    fear,
That makes these odds all even.

(BISHOP *gives benediction over* CLAUDIO *and both characters fade out.*)

(*Lights up by bed.*)

(ISABELLA *slowly extricates herself from behind the curtains, stumbles upon a desk on which sits a covered object. She trembles for a moment then whips away the cover revealing severed head of* CLAUDIO. *There is an ear-splitting scream.*)

(*Lights up downstage where* BISHOP *is now hearing* ANGELO *in confession.* ANGELO, *on his knees, before him.*)

ANGELO O my dread Lord,
I should be guiltier than my guiltiness
To think I can be undiscernible
When I perceive your grace, like power divine,
Hath looked upon my passes.
BISHOP (*Harshly*) He who the sword of heaven
    will bear
Should be as holy as severe;
Pattern in himself to know
Grace to stand, and virtue, go:
More not less to others paying
Than by self offences weighing.
Shame to him whose cruel striking
Kills for faults of his own liking.
ANGELO No longer session hold upon my shame,
But let my trial be mine own confession.
Immediate sentence then, and sequent death
Is all the grace I beg.

(BISHOP *raises him up sternly; looks him squarely in the face, and then smiles kindly.*)

BISHOP Grace go with you. Benedicte.   (*Exit.*)
ANGELO (*For a moment relieved, then his face
    darkening with memory.*) He should have
    lived,
Save that his riotous youth with dangerous sense
Might in the times to come have ta'en revenge,
By so receiving a dishonoured life
With ransom of such shame. Would yet he had
    lived.
Alack, when once our grace we have forgot,
Nothing goes right. We would, and we would
    not.

(*Exits.*)

LUCIO (*Who has watched* ANGELO's *confession with mock contempt*) Hark how the villain would

close now, after his treasonable abuses. Such a
fellow is not to be talked about withal. Away
with him to prison. Where is the Provost? Away
with him to prison, I say. Lay bolts upon him.
Let him speak no more.
Being criminal, in double violation
Of sacred chastity, and of promise-breach,
The very mercy of the law cries out,
Most audible, even from his proper tongue,
'An Angelo for Claudio, death for death!'
Haste still pays haste, and leisure answers
    leisure,
Like doth quit like and Measure still for
    Measure.
Then, Angelo, thy faults thus manifested,
'We do condemn thee to the very block
Where Claudio stooped to death, and with like
    haste.'
Away with him.
Take him hence.
To th'rack with him.
Touse him joint by joint!

(*Drops his facetiously vengeful mask and confronts
the audience head-on*)

The business of my state
Made me a looker-on here in Vienna,
Where I have seen corruption boil and bubble
Till it o'errun the stew. Laws for all faults,
But faults so countenanced that the strong
    statutes
Stand like the forfeits in a barber's shop,
As much in mock as mark.

(ISABELLA *enters fierce and resolute.*)

ISABELLA O, I will to him and pluck out his eyes!
    Unhappy Claudio! Wretched Isabel!
    Injurious world! Most damned Angelo!

(*Bursts into tears.*)

LUCIO This nor hurts him nor profits you a jot.
    Forbear it therefore; give your cause to heaven.
    Mark what I say which you shall find
    By every syllable a faithful verity.
    The Duke comes home tomorrow – nay, dry
        your eyes –
    Already he hath carried
    Notice to Escalus and Angelo
    Who do prepare to meet him at the gates
    There to give up their power.
    I have found you out a stand most fit
    Where you may have such vantage on the Duke
    He shall not pass you.
    If you can pace your wisdom
    In that good path that I would wish it go,

And you shall have your bosom
On this wretch,
Grace of the Duke, revenges to your heart,
And general honour.

(ISABELLA *stops crying, and grimly tears the
crucifix from round her neck.*)

(*Blackout.*)

(PROVOST *enters carrying* CLAUDIO's *clothes and
an empty sack. During following speech, he stuffs
clothes into sack.*)

PROVOST What a merry world it is, since, of two
    crimes, the merrier was put down and the
    worser allowed, by order of law a furred gown to
    keep him warm; and furred with fox and
    lambskin too, to signify that craft be richer than
    innocence!
        Here's a change indeed in the common
    wealth! Why, there is so great a fever on
    goodness that only its dissolution will cure it.
    Novelty is only in request, and it is as dangerous
    to be aged in any kind of course as it is to
    be virtuous in any undertaking. There is scarce
    truth enough to make societies secure –
    but security enough to make fellowships
    accurst.
        Much upon this riddle runs the wisdom of the
    world. This news is old enough – yet it is every
    day's news.

(*Pulls drawstring tightly around sack for a
moment, hauls it onto his back and exits on fade
out.*)

(*Sound of the* DUKE's *trumpet as at start of play.*)

(*Lights up.*)

(DUKE *enters from one side;* ANGELO, ESCALUS
and BISHOP *from the other.*)

DUKE My very worthy cousin, fairly met.
    Our old and faithful friend, we are glad to see
        you.
ESCALUS Happy return be to your royal grace.
DUKE Many and hearty thankings to you both.
    We have made inquiry of you, and we hear
    Such goodness of your justice that our soul
    Cannot but yield you forth to public thanks,
    Forerunning more requital.
ANGELO You make my bonds still greater.
DUKE O, your desert speaks loud, and I should
        wrong it
    To lock it in the wards of covert bosom,
    When it deserves with characters of brass
    A forted residence 'gainst the tooth of time

and razure of oblivion. Give me your hand,
And let the subjects see, to make them know
that outward courtesies would fain proclaim
Favours that keep within.

LUCIO (*Entering with* ISABELLA *and* PROVOST)
Now is your time. Speak loud and kneel before
him.

DUKE Come Escalus, you must walk by us on our
other hand
And good supporters are you.

ISABELLA Justice, O royal Duke! Vail your regard
Upon a wronged – I would fain have said, a
maid.
O worthy prince, dishonour not your eye
By throwing it on any other object
Till you have heard me in my true complaint
And given me justice, justice, justice, justice!

DUKE Relate your wrongs. In what? By whom? Be
brief.
Here is Lord Angelo shall give you justice.
Reveal yourself to him.

ISABELLA O worthy Duke,
You bid me seek redemption of the devil.
Hear me yourself, for that which I must speak
Must either punish me, not being believed,
Or wring redress from you. Hear me, O hear
me, hear.

ANGELO My lord, her wits, I fear me, are not
firm.
She hath been a suitor to me for her brother,
Cut off by course of justice –

ISABELLA By course of justice!

ANGELO And she will speak most bitterly and
strange.

ISABELLA Most strange, but yet most truly, will I
speak.
That Angelo's foresworn, is it not strange?
That Angelo's a murderer, is't not strange?
That Angelo is an adulterous thief,
An hypocrite, a virgin-violator,
Is it not strange, and strange?

DUKE Nay, it is ten times strange.

ISABELLA Is it not truer he is Angelo
Than this is all as true as it is strange.
Nay, it is ten times true, for truth is truth
To th'end of reck'ning;

(*Pause.* LUCIO *steps forward giving support to*
ISABELLA.)

DUKE Away with her. Poor soul,
She speaks this in th'infirmity of sense.

ISABELLA O prince, I conjure thee, as thou
believ'st
There is another comfort than this world,
That thou neglect me not with that opinion

That I am touched with madness. Make not
impossible
That which but seems unlike. 'Tis not
impossible
But one, the wicked'st caitiff on the ground,
May seem as shy, as grave, as just, as absolute
As Angelo. Even so may Angelo,
In all his dressings, characts, titles, forms,
Be an arch-villain. Believe it, royal prince.
If he be less, he's nothing: but he's more,
Had I more name for badness.

DUKE By mine honesty,
If she be mad, as I believe no other,
Her madness hath the oddest frame of sense,
Such a dependency of thing on thing,
As e'er I heard in madness.

ISABELLA O gracious Duke,
Harp not on that, nor do not banish reason
For inequality, but let your reason serve
To make the truth appear where it seems hid.

DUKE Many that are not mad
Have sure more lack of reason. What would you
say?

ISABELLA I am the sister of one Claudio,
Condemned upon the act of fornication
To lose his head, condemned by Angelo.
I, in probation of a sisterhood,
Was sent to by my brother. One Lucio
As then the messenger –

LUCIO That's I, an't like your grace,
I came to her from Claudio, and desired her
To try her gracious fortune with Lord Angelo
For her poor brother's pardon.

ISABELLA That's he indeed.

DUKE You were not bid to speak.

LUCIO No, my good Lord,
Nor wished to hold my peace.

DUKE I wish you now, then.
Pray you, take note of it, and when you have
A business for yourself, pray heaven you then
Be perfect.

LUCIO I warrant your honour.

DUKE The warrant's for yourself: take heed to't.
Proceed.

ISABELLA I went
To this pernicious caitiff deputy –

DUKE That's somewhat madly spoken.

ISABELLA Pardon it,
The phrase is to the matter.

DUKE The matter then, proceed.

ISABELLA In brief, to set the needless process by,
How I persuaded, how I prayed, and kneeled,
How he refelled me, and how I replied –
For this was of much length – the vile
conclusion

I now begin with grief and shame to utter.
He would not, but by gift of my chaste body
To his concup'scible intemperate lust
Release my brother, and after much debatement
My sisterly remorse confutes mine honour,
And I did yield to him. But the next morn
    betimes,
His purpose surfeiting, he sends a warrant
For my poor brother's head.

(*Long pause.* DUKE *turns slowly and regards the*
BISHOP, *then turns to* ESCALUS, *and finally to*
ANGELO *who, without expression, returns the*
DUKE's *look. After a goodly pause, the* DUKE
begins to speak – still facing ANGELO.)

DUKE By heaven fond wretch (*then turning*
    towards ISABELLA) thou knowest not what
    thou speak'st.
Or else thou art suborned against his honour
In hateful practice. First, his integrity
Stands without blemish. Next, it imports no
    reason
That with such vehemency he should pursue
Faults proper to himself. If he had so offended,
He would have weighed thy brother by himself,
And not have cut him off. Someone hath set you
    on.
Confess the truth, and say by whose advice
Thou cam'st here to complain.

(ISABELLA *dumbstruck, steps back and turns*
slowly from the DUKE *to the* BISHOP *to* ESCALUS
to ANGELO *seeing them all anew.*)

ISABELLA And is this all?
Then, O you blessed ministers above,
Keep me in patience, and with ripened time
Unfold the evil which is here wrapped up
In countenance. Heaven shield your grace from
    woe,
As I thus wronged hence unbelieved go.
DUKE I know you'd fain be gone. Yet stay awhile.
(*Turning to his own.*) Shall we thus permit
A blasting and a scandalous breath to fall
On him so near us?
No might nor greatness in mortality
Can censure 'scape; back-wounding calumny
The whitest virtue strikes. What king so strong
Can tie the gall up in the slanderous tongue?
Do you not smile at this, Lord Angelo?
O heaven, the vanity of wretched fools!
ANGELO I did but smile till now.
Now, good my lord, give me the scope of justice.
My patience here is touched. I do perceive
These poor informal wretches are no more

But instruments of some more mightier member
That sets them on.
DUKE Thou foolish knave, and thou pernicious
    woman,
Think'st thou thy oaths,
Though they would swear down each particular
    saint,
Were testimonies against his worth and credit
That's sealed in approbation?
Thy slanders now shall by our laws be weighed
And by their Justice priz'd. Take her to prison
And see our pleasure herein executed. To prison
with her! (*Turning front.*)
And all about that can hear, now hear this:
The law hath not been dead, though it hath
    slept.
Those many had not dared to do that evil
If that the first that did th'edict infringe
Had answered for his deed. Now 'tis awake,
Take note of what is done, and like a prophet
Looks in a glass that shows what future evils,
Either now, or by remissness new, conceived,
Are now to have no successive degrees,
But, ere they live, to end.

(DUKE *gestures to suggest formal ceremony is*
ended. ISABELLA *is escorted out by* PROVOST
while tables are set up, and formal gowns are laid
to one side. Before she exits, ANGELO *approaches*
ISABELLA *and whispers for her hearing alone.*)

ANGELO (*Taking her arm*) I have a motion much
    imports your good,
Whereto if you'll a willing ear incline,
What's mine is yours, and what is yours is mine.

(ISABELLA *expressionlessly shoves away*
ANGELO's *hand, turns and moves off swiftly,*
conducted by the PROVOST.)

(*The table is now set. The* DUKE, *now in gay*
private attire, in stark contrast to his judicial robes,
sits at one place; ESCALUS *and* ANGELO *beside*
him; they too are now dressed casually. Food and
drink is brought.)

(*The following dialogue is permeated with a gaiety*
and crudity that belies all we know of these
characters.)

DUKE (*Mimicking the lower-classes*) What news
    abroad i' the world?
ANGELO (*Mock guiltily, also with put-on voice*) Sir, I
    have been an unlawful bawd time out of
    mind, but yet I will be content to be a lawful
    hangman. I would be glad to receive some
    instruction from me fellow partner.
ESCALUS (*Laughing at* ANGELO's *imitation; mock-*

astonished) A bawd, sir? (*To* DUKE.) Fie upon him, he will discredit our mystery.

ANGELO 'Faith, my lord, I spoke it but according to the trick. If you will hang me for it, you may. But I had rather it would please you I might be whipped.

(*All fall about with laughter.*)

DUKE Whipped first, sir, and hanged after. (*This tops last joke and all explode with even greater laughter.*) Proclaim it, Provost, round about the city,
If any woman wronged by this lewd fellow,

As I have heard him swear himself there's one
Whom he begot with child – let her appear,
And he shall marry her.

ANGELO (*Acting craven*) I beseech your highness, do not marry me to a whore. Marrying a punk, my Lord, is pressing to death, whipping *and* hanging.

DUKE (*Pouring wine over* ANGELO's *head*)
Slandering a prince deserves it.

(*All laugh uproariously and carry on clowning, eating and drinking through.*)

(*Fade out.*)

Hamletmachine

Heiner Müller

Introduction

Heiner Müller was born in eastern Germany in 1929. In 1945 he was drafted into the German army and after the end of the Second World War returned home to the part of Germany occupied by the USSR. He took up writing in the 1950s and began a checkered relationship with communist officials in the German Democratic Republic: he worked for the League of German Writers in 1954–1955; he wrote for Berlin's Volksbühne Theatre in 1957; he was expelled for political reasons from the writers' league in 1961, so that his plays could not be performed until 1967; he was invited to join the prestigious Berliner Ensemble (founded by Brecht) in 1969; in the 1970s and 1980s he was given unprecedented freedom to travel to and return from Western Europe and North America, although many of his plays remained banned in East Germany. By this time he had become a world-renowned playwright, 'a sort of socialist William Shakespeare' (Hofacker: 335). After the fall of the East Bloc, Müller was forced to rethink his position in the world and the political role of his theatre (see Croyden, Höfele). He died on 30 December 1995.

Müller adapted a number of Western classics over his career: Sophocles' *Oedipus Rex* (1967) and *Philoctetus* (1968); Shakespeare's *Macbeth* (1972); Brecht's *The Measures Taken* (as *Mauser* 1975); Laclos's *Dangerous Liaisons* (as *Quartet* 1982). Often his point in these adaptations is to show the long history and legacy of barbarism and the limitations of this history faced by people in the present: revolution has never been, is not going to be, easy. Müller describes his project in these terms:

> What I try to do in my writings is to strengthen the sense of conflicts, to strengthen confrontations and contradictions. There is no other way. I'm not interested in answers and solutions. I don't have any to offer. I'm interested in problems and conflicts.
>
> (1982: 50)

Hamletmachine is the most celebrated of Müller's adaptations. It developed over many years from a much longer work into the short, dense, allusive, and difficult text printed here. (A good attempt at detailed and extensive explication can be found in Teroaka: 87–121.) The East German authorities did not allow the play to be produced, so it was first staged in Brussels in 1978 and West Germany in 1979. Since then it has been produced many times in many different and striking ways. Robert Wilson, for instance, brought a very studied and coolly stylized approach to the play in New York in 1986 (see Rogoff), while Montreal's Carbone 14 infused the text with Gallic passion – a number of Ophelia's speeches were delivered as torch songs (see Leonard). The text, such as it is, is open to – even demands – such interpretative leaps. Müller himself included *Hamletmachine* in a seven-and-a-half-hour production of *Hamlet* in Berlin in 1990. In the face of the triumph of the West, the play ends as 'Fortinbras, wearing a business suit and a gold mask, a star warrior of capitalism, takes over' (Höfele: 85).

Müller's two most important precursors are Karl Marx and Bertolt Brecht – note the central truncated quotation from Marx's 'Contributions to the Critique of Hegel's Philosophy of Right' in *Hamletmachine*: that the main point (of revolutionary struggle) is '*to overthrow all those conditions* in which man is an abased, enslaved, abandoned, contemptible being.' However, Müller is anything but doctrinaire and uncritical in his approaches to these influences. For instance, an essay he wrote on Brecht is called 'To Use Brecht without Criticizing Him Is to Betray Him.' Here Müller rejects Brecht's 'posthumous petrification

Plate 3 Photo: © Yves Dubé 1987. Production of *Hamletmachine* by Carbone 14, Montreal

into the father figure by socialist cultural policy' (33). As the world changes, the ideas of the past must be submitted to 'permanent revolution' (31). The lack of unquestioned veneration extends, of course, to Shakespeare, and ultimately to the works of Müller himself – as he writes in 'Reflections on Post-Modernism,' 'Work toward the disappearance of the author is resistance against the disappearance of humankind' (57). One way of freeing texts from the authorial dictates of the past is by crossing them with other voices. This explains the multitude and variety of allusions in *Hamletmachine*, which is not Shakespeare's text, nor Müller's alone.

The invocations of Josef Stalin in *Hamletmachine* point to Müller's struggle within and against East Bloc socialism: he sides with the revolutionary, utopian impulse but not with its ossification into dictatorship. The play is no more accepting, however, of Western capitalism, encapsulated in the line 'Hail Coca Cola.' After 1989, Müller spoke of a 'third way' which is 'not communism, not capitalism, but something else – nobody knows what' (Croyden: 106).

Hamletmachine is structured as alternating sections focused on Hamlet and Ophelia. For Müller, Hamlet is 'the man between the ages who knows that the old age is obsolete, yet the new age has barbarian features he simply cannot stomach' (quoted in Weber: 137). He is the man of Enlightenment reason who cannot deal with the harsh call to action: his failure is his intellectual paralysis in the face of the need to act. Hamlet is similarly paralyzed by his own position of privilege: he sees himself both inside the palace and down with the revolutionaries in the street – a position with which Müller, as renowned author, identifies. Finally, Hamlet is privileged and paralyzed by his gender: he wants to be a woman, but clings to his male advantages. In the end, Hamlet gives up, and abandons the future and revolution to others.

One of the most striking aspects of *Hamletmachine* is the prominence given to Ophelia – Rogoff writes that the play might better be called *Opheliamachine* (57). By having Marx, Lenin, and Mao appear as three naked women, Müller asserts that it is not 'man' who has suffered the most egregious enslavement and abasement. The play does not shy away from the litany of horrific victimization to which Ophelia and other women have been subjected. Indeed, at the end (in a hyperbolic echo of Shakespeare's mad and drowned heroine) Ophelia sits bound to a wheelchair at the bottom of the sea. However, she is also fiercely enduring through ongoing millenniums of oppression. She remains dedicated to the struggle against enslavement. Working in a dialectic of harsh opposition rather than easy reconciliation, the play ends with a quotation from Susan Atkins of the Manson Family: 'When she walks through your bedrooms carrying butcher knives you'll know the truth.' Müller's Ophelia is a victim with a vengeance, clear-sighted and highly unsentimental.

The action also ends 'under the sun of torture.' This allusion to Frantz Fanon's *The Wretched of the Earth* aligns women's interests as an oppressed group with those of non-western peoples subjected to western imperialist domination. In 'The Walls of History,' Müller says, 'The Western paradise is based on hell for the Third World' and 'The Third World is like a big waiting-room, waiting for history' (40, 39). In many ways, therefore, *Hamletmachine* points to the giving way (by Hamlet, Müller, Shakespeare, Brecht, Europe, men) to the revolutionary project of presently oppressed groups who hold the future in their hands. Stylistically and politically, *Hamletmachine* submits Shakespeare's play to dismemberment and a radical influx of myriad historical forces and allusions.

Select bibliography

Entries marked * are particularly accessible.

Blau, H. (1987) 'The Audition of Dream and Events,' *Drama Review* 31,3: 59–73.

Case, S.-E. (1983) 'From Bertolt Brecht to Heiner Müller,' *Performing Arts Journal* 19: 94–102.

Croyden, M. (1990) 'After the Revolution,' *Village Voice* (12 June): 97–98, 106.

Dudley, J. M. (1992) 'Being and Non-Being: The Other and Heterotopia in *Hamletmachine*,' *Modern Drama* 35,4: 562–570.

Fehervary, H. (1976) 'Enlightenment and Entanglement: History and Aesthetics in Bertolt Brecht and Heiner Müller,' *New German Critique* 8: 80–109.

Fortier, M. (1996) 'Shakespeare as "Minor Theater": Deleuze and Guattari and the Aims of Adaptation,' *Mosaic* 29,1: 1–18.

Halpern, R. (1997) 'Hamletmachines,' in *Shakespeare Among the Moderns*, Ithaca: Cornell University Press. 227–288.

Hofacker, E. P., Jr (1992) 'Heiner Müller,' in *Dictionary of Literary Biography*, vol. 124, Detroit: Gale Research: 333–346.

Höfele, A. (1992) 'A Theater of Exhaustion? "*Posthistoire*" in Recent German Shakespeare Productions,' *Shakespeare Quarterly* 43,1: 80–86.

Homberg, A. (1988) 'A Conversation with Robert Wilson and Heiner Müller,' *Modern Drama* 31,3: 454–58.

*Klassen, J. (1986) '"The Rebellion of the Body against Ideas": Heiner Müller's Concept of Tragedy,' in K. V. Hartigan (ed.) *Within the Dramatic Spectrum*, Lanham, Maryland: University Press of America.

Leonard, P. (1988) 'Critical Questioning,' *Canadian Theatre Review* 57: 4–10.

Müller, H. (1982) 'The Walls of History,' with S. Lotringer, *Semiotext(e)* 4,2: 36–76.

— (1984) *Hamletmachine and Other Texts for the Stage*, C. Weber (ed.), New York: PAJ Publications.

— (1986) 'To Use Brecht without Criticizing Him Is to Betray Him,' *Theater* 17,2: 31–33.

— (1989a) *The Battle: Plays, Prose, Poems*, C. Weber (ed.), New York: PAJ Publications.

— (1989b) *Explosions of a Memory: Writings*, C. Weber (ed.), New York: PAJ Publications.

Rogoff, G. (1986) Review of *Hamletmachine* by H. Müller, R. Wilson (dir.), *Performing Arts Journal* 28: 54–57.

*'Special Issue on Heiner Müller' (1998) *New German Critique* 73.

*Teraoka, A. A. (1985) *The Silence of Entropy or Universal Discourse: The Postmodern Poetics of Heiner Müller*, New York: Peter Lang.

Weber, C. (1980) 'Heiner Müller: The Despair and the Hope,' *Performing Arts Journal* 4,3: 135–140.

Hamletmachine

Heiner Müller

1

Family Scrapbook

I was Hamlet. I stood at the shore and talked with the surf BLABLA, the ruins of Europe in back of me. The bells tolled the state-funeral, murderer and widow a couple, the councillors goose-stepping behind the highranking carcass' coffin, bawling with badly paid grief WHO IS THE CORPSE IN THE HEARSE/ABOUT WHOM THERE'S SUCH A HUE AND CRY/'TIS THE CORPSE OF A GREAT/GIVER OF ALMS the lane formed by the populace, creation of his statecraft HE WAS A MAN HE TOOK THEM ALL FOR ALL. I stopped the funeral procession, I pried open the coffin with my sword, the blade broke, yet with the blunt reminder I succeeded, and I dispensed my dead procreator FLESH LIKES TO KEEP THE COMPANY OF FLESH among the bums around me. The mourning turned into rejoicing, the rejoicing into lipsmacking, on top of the empty coffin the murderer humped the widow LET ME HELP YOU UP, UNCLE, OPEN YOUR LEGS, MAMA. I laid down on the ground and listened to the world doing its turns in step with the putrefaction.

I'M GOOD HAMLET GI'ME A CAUSE FOR GRIEF*
AH THE WHOLE GLOBE FOR A REAL SORROW*
RICHARD THE THIRD I THE PRINCE-KILLING
   KING*
OH MY PEOPLE WHAT HAVE I DONE UNTO THEE*
I'M LUGGING MY OVERWEIGHT BRAIN LIKE A
   HUNCHBACK
CLOWN NUMBER TWO IN THE SPRING OF
   COMMUNISM
SOMETHING IS ROTTEN IN THIS AGE OF HOPE*
LET'S DELVE IN EARTH AND BLOW HER AT THE
   MOON*

Here comes the ghost who made me, the ax still in his skull. Keep your hat on, I know you've got one hole too many. I would my mother had one less when you were still of flesh: I would have been spared myself. Women should be sewed up – a world without mothers. We could butcher each other in peace and quiet, and with some confidence, if life gets too long for us or our throats too tight for our screams. What do you want of me? Is one state-funeral not enough for you? You old sponger. Is there no blood on your shoes? What's your corpse to me? Be glad the handle is sticking out, maybe you'll go to heaven. What are you waiting for? All the cocks have been butchered. Tomorrow morning has been cancelled.

SHALL I
AS IS THE CUSTOM STICK A PIECE OF IRON INTO
THE NEAREST FLESH OR THE SECOND BEST
TO LATCH UNTO IT SINCE THE WORLD IS
   SPINNING
LORD BREAK MY NECK WHILE I'M FALLING FROM
   AN
ALEHOUSE BENCH

Enters Horatio. Confidant of my thoughts so full of blood since the morning is curtained by the empty sky. YOU'LL BE TOO LATE MY FRIEND FOR YOUR PAYCHECK/NO PART FOR YOU IN THIS MY TRAGEDY. Horatio, do you know me? Are you my friend, Horatio? If you know me how can you be my friend? Do you want to play Polonius who wants to sleep with his daughter, the delightful Ophelia, here she enters right on cue, look how she shakes her ass, a tragic character. HoratioPolonius. I knew you're an actor. I am too, I'm playing Hamlet. Denmark is a prison, a wall is growing between the two of us. Look what's

---

* The lines with an asterisk are in English in the German text.

211

growing from that wall. Exit Polonius. My mother the bride. Her breasts a rosebed, her womb the snakepit. Have you forgotten your lines, Mama. I'll prompt you. WASH THE MURDER OFF YOUR FACE MY PRINCE/AND OFFER THE NEW DENMARK YOUR GLAD EYE. I'll change you back into a virgin mother, so your king will have a bloodwedding. A MOTHER'S WOMB IS NOT A ONE-WAY STREET. Now, I tie your hands on your back with your bridal veil since I'm sick of your embrace. Now, I tear the wedding dress. Now, I smear the shreds of the wedding dress with the dust my father turned into, and with the soiled shreds your face your belly your breasts. Now, I take you, my mother, in his, my father's invisible tracks. I stifle your scream with my lips. Do you recognize the fruit of your womb? Now go to your wedding, whore, in the broad Danish sunlight which shines on the living and the dead. I want to cram the corpse down the latrine so the palace will choke in royal shit. Then let me eat your heart, Ophelia, which weeps my tears.

2

The Europe of women

Enormous room. Ophelia. Her heart is a clock.*

OPHELIA (CHORUS/HAMLET) I am Ophelia. The one the river didn't keep. The woman dangling from the rope. The woman with her arteries cut open. The woman with the overdose. SNOW ON HER LIPS. The woman with her head in the gas stove. Yesterday I stopped killing myself. I'm alone with my breasts my thighs my womb. I smash the tools of my captivity, the chair the table the bed. I destroy the battlefield that was my home. I fling open the doors so the wind gets in and the scream of the world. I smash the window. With my bleeding hands I tear the photos of the men I loved and who used me on the bed on the table on the chair on the ground. I set fire to my prison. I throw my clothes into the fire. I wrench the clock that was my heart out of my breast. I walk into the street clothed in my blood.

3

Scherzo

The university of the dead. Whispering and muttering. From their gravestones (lecterns), the dead philosophers throw their books at Hamlet. Gallery (ballet) of the dead women. The woman dangling from
the rope. The woman with her arteries cut open, etc. . . . . Hamlet views them with the attitude of a visitor in a museum (theatre). The dead women tear his clothes off his body. Out of an up-ended coffin, labeled HAMLET 1, step CLAUDIUS and OPHELIA, the latter dressed and made up like a whore. Striptease by OPHELIA.*

OPHELIA Do you want to eat my heart, Hamlet? (*Laughs.*)
HAMLET (*Face in his hands.*) I want to be a woman.

(*HAMLET dresses in OPHELIA's clothes, OPHELIA puts the make-up of a whore on his face, CLAUDIUS – now HAMLET's father – laughs without uttering a sound, OPHELIA blows HAMLET a kiss and steps with CLAUDIUS/HAMLETFATHER back into the coffin. HAMLET poses as a whore. An angel, his face at the back of his head: HORATIO. He dances with HAMLET.*)

VOICE(S) (*From the coffin.*) What thou killed thou shalt love.

(*The dance grows faster and wilder. Laughter from the coffin. On a swing, the madonna with breast cancer. HORATIO opens an umbrella, embraces HAMLET. They freeze under the umbrella, embracing. The breast cancer radiates like a sun.*)

4

Pest in Buda / Battle for Greenland

Space 2, as destroyed by OPHELIA. An empty armor, an ax stuck in the helmet.

HAMLET The stove is smoking in quarrelsome October
A BAD COLD HE HAD OF IT JUST THE WORST TIME*
JUST THE WORST TIME OF THE YEAR FOR A REVOLUTION*
Cement in bloom walks through the slums
Doctor Zhivago weeps
For his wolves
SOMETIMES IN WINTER THEY CAME INTO THE VILLAGE
AND TORE APART A PEASANT

(*He takes off make-up and costume.*)

THE ACTOR PLAYING HAMLET I'm not Hamlet. I don't take part any more. My words have nothing to tell me anymore. My thoughts suck the blood out of the images. My drama doesn't happen anymore. Behind me the set is put up.

By people who aren't interested in my drama, for people to whom it means nothing. I'm not interested in it anymore either. I won't play along anymore. (*Unnoticed by the actor playing Hamlet, stagehands place a refrigerator and three TV-sets on the stage. Humming of the refrigerator. Three TV-channels without sound.*) The set is a monument. It presents a man who made history, enlarged a hundred times. The petrification of a hope. His name is interchangeable, the hope has not been fulfilled. The monument is toppled into the dust, razed by those who succeeded him in power three years after the state funeral of the hated and most honored leader. The stone is inhabited. In the spacy nostrils and auditory canals, in the creases of skin and uniform of the demolished monument, the poorer inhabitants of the capital are dwelling. After an appropriate period, the uprising follows the toppling of the monument. My drama, if it still would happen, would happen in the time of the uprising. The uprising starts with a stroll. Against the traffic rules, during the working hours. The street belongs to the pedestrians. Here and there, a car is turned over. Nightmare of a knife thrower: Slowly driving down a one-way street towards an irrevocable parking space surrounded by armed pedestrians. Policemen, if in the way, are swept to the curb. When the procession approaches the government district it is stopped by a police line. People form groups, speakers arise from them. On the balcony of a government building, a man in badly fitting mufti appears and begins to speak too. When the first stone hits him, he retreats behind the double doors of bullet-proof glass. The call for more freedom turns into the cry for the overthrow of the government. People begin to disarm the policemen, to storm two, three buildings, a prison a police precinct an office of the secret police, they string up a dozen henchmen of the rulers by their heels, the government brings in troops, tanks. My place, if my drama would still happen, would be on both sides of the front, between the frontlines, over and above them. I stand in the stench of the crowd and hurl stones at policemen soldiers tanks bullet-proof glass. I look through the double doors of bullet-proof glass at the crowd pressing forward and smell the sweat of my fear. Choking with nausea, I shake my fist at myself who stands behind the bulletproof glass. Shaking with fear and contempt, I see myself in the crowd pressing forward, foaming at the mouth, shaking my fist at myself. I string up my uniformed flesh by my own heels. I am the soldier in the gun turret, my head is empty under the helmet, the stifled scream under the tracks. I am the typewriter. I tie the noose when the ringleaders are strung up, I pull the stool from under their feet, I break my own neck. I am my own prisoner. I feed my own data into the computers. My parts are the spittle and the spittoon the knife and the wound the fang and the throat the neck and the rope. I am the data bank. Bleeding in the crowd. Breathing again behind the double doors. Oozing wordslime in my soundproof blurb over and above the battle. My drama didn't happen. The script has been lost. The actors put their faces on the rack in the dressing room. In his box, the prompter is rotting. The stuffed corpses in the house don't stir a hand. I go home and kill the time, at one/with my undivided self.

Television The daily nausea Nausea
Of prefabricated babble Of decreed cheerfulness
How do you spell GEMÜTLICHKEIT
Give us this day our daily murder
Since thine is nothingness Nausea
Of the lies which are believed
By the liars and nobody else
Nausea
Of the lies which are believed Nausea
Of the mugs of the manipulators marked
By their struggle for positions votes bank
   accounts
Nausea A chariot armed with scythes sparkling
   with punchlines
I walk through streets stores Faces
Scarred by the consumers battle Poverty
Without dignity Poverty without the dignity
Of the knife the knuckleduster the clenched fist
The humiliated bodies of women
Hope of generations
Stifled in blood cowardice stupidity
Laughter from dead bellies
Hail Coca Cola
A kingdom
For a murderer
I WAS MACBETH
THE KING HAD OFFERED HIS THIRD MISTRESS
   TO ME
I KNEW EVERY MOLE ON HER HIPS
RASKOLNIKOV CLOSE TO THE
HEART UNDER THE ONLY COAT THE AX FOR
   THE
ONLY
SKULL OF THE PAWNBROKER
In the solitude of airports
I breathe again I am

A privileged person My nausea
Is a privilege
Protected by torture
Barbed wire Prisons

(*Photograph of the author.*)

I don't want to eat drink breathe love a woman a
man a child an animal anymore. I don't want to
die anymore. I don't want to kill anymore.

(*Tearing of the author's photograph.*)

I force open my sealed flesh. I want to dwell in
my veins, in the marrow of my bones, in the
maze of my skull. I retreat into my entrails. I
take my seat in my shit, in my blood.
Somewhere bodies are torn apart so I can dwell
in my shit. Somewhere bodies are opened so I
can be alone with my blood. My thoughts are
lesions in my brain. My brain is a scar. I want to
be a machine. Arms for grabbing Legs to walk
on, no pain no thoughts.

(*TV screens go black. Blood oozes from the
refrigerator. Three naked women:* MARX, LENIN,
MAO. *They speak simultaneously, each one in his
own language, the text.*)

THE MAIN POINT IS TO OVERTHROW ALL
   EXISTING CONDITIONS . . .*

(*The Actor of Hamlet puts on make-up and
costume.*)

HAMLET THE DANE PRINCE AND MAGGOT'S
   FODDER
STUMBLING FROM HOLE TO HOLE TOWARDS THE
   FINAL
HOLE LISTLESS IN HIS BACK THE GHOST THAT
   ONCE

MADE HIM GREEN LIKE OPHELIA'S FLESH IN
   CHILDBED
AND SHORTLY ERE THE THIRD COCK'S CROW A
   CLOWN
WILL TEAR THE FOOL'S CAP OFF THE
   PHILOSOPHER
A BLOATED BLOODHOUND'LL CRAWL INTO THE
   ARMOR

(*He steps into the armor, splits with the ax the heads
of Marx, Lenin, Mao. Snow. Ice Age.*)

5

FIERCELY ENDURING

MILLENIUMS

IN THE FEARFUL ARMOR

The deep sea. OPHELIA *in a wheelchair. Fish, debris,
dead bodies and limbs drift by.*
OPHELIA (*While two men in white smocks wrap
gauze around her and the wheelchair, from bottom
to top.*)

This is Electra speaking. In the heart of
darkness. Under the sun of torture. To the
capitals of the world. In the name of the victims.
I eject all the sperm I have received. I turn the
milk of my breasts into lethal poison. I take back
the world I gave birth to. I choke between my
thighs the world I gave birth to. I bury it in my
womb. Down with the happiness of submission.
Long live hate and contempt, rebellion and
death. When she walks through your bedrooms
carrying butcher knives you'll know the truth.

(*The men exit.* OPHELIA *remains on stage,
motionless in her white wrappings.*)

---

* English-language productions could use the entire quote from Karl Marx: Introduction to *Critique of Hegel's
Philosophy of Law*.

Lear's Daughters

The Women's Theatre Group and Elaine Feinstein

Introduction

Lear's Daughters (1987) is the co-creation of Elaine Feinstein (an English novelist, poet, and translator born in 1930) and the Women's Theatre Group (WTG), 'one of the first and most enduring of Britain's feminist companies' (Bennett: 51). By virtue of its communal genesis the play puts the very idea of authorship to the question and challenges long-entrenched notions circulating around the individuality of the author. Those notions have a great deal to do with who gains a place in the traditional canon and how that place is constructed and sustained. Shakespeare is a singular example of an authoritative writing presence that anchors canonical notions of excellence and cultural value, and it is no accident that WTG undertook the revision of a major Shakespearean tragedy from the perspective of a feminist collective.

Lizbeth Goodman, in a discussion of the work's collaborative origins, summarizes that 'Feinstein worked with the company [Gwenda Hughes, Janys Chambers, Hilary Ellis, Maureen Hibbert, and Hazel Maycock] in devising some ideas, and then went away to write the script independently. The script which she submitted, however, was found to be unsatisfactory by the company. A rushed series of workshops followed, out of which emerged a revised version of the script, which was used in the first touring production of 1987' (1993a: 97). Goodman notes the different ways of attributing authorship to both Feinstein and the WTG in handbills and programmes, not to mention in the first published version of the play, which ascribes the 'idea to Elaine Feinstein' [Griffin and Aston: 19] while stating that the play was 'written by: Adjoa Andoh, Janys Chambers, Gwenda Hughes, Polly Irvin, Hazel Maycock, Lizz Poulter, and Sandra Yaw' (20), a list significantly different from the list Goodman produces in both *Contemporary Feminist Theatres* and 'Women's Alternative Shakespeares.'

The inconsistencies of authorial attribution that are part of the play's cultural presence produced, in Goodman's estimation, 'an underlying discomfort [in audiences and critics] with the notion of the [communally] devised work. This discomfort may be related to the lack of an individual author, a situation which eliminates the identifiable "subject" (or individual) to be criticized in relation to the "object" which is the play' (1993a: 99). The way in which the play troubles traditional notions of authorship reminds us of the theatre as the site of collaborative effort, and of the difficulties that arise when positing the dramatist as the sole and uncomplicated source of the voices that speak from the stage. This situation has long vexed Shakespeare studies, where enormous effort has been expended on addressing so-called corrupt texts. The purpose of this effort has been to restore and identify an uncontaminated, 'authentic' Shakespearean voice to texts that likely came into being as a function of complex collaborations among different playwrights, directors, actors, and editors.

An adaptation that is a prequel to *King Lear*, but also an adaptation in the sense that it reshapes the ways in which a production comes into being, *Lear's Daughters* exemplifies the innovative strategies of the WTG, which emerged in the early 1970s as a women's street theatre 'performing for demonstrations and similar events' but 'did not formalise itself until 1974' (Itzin: 230). The WTG is distinctive for its more radical precepts, including the decision to 'avoid working in the hierarchical, competitive structures which characterise the male-dominated establishment theatre and media' (230), which effectively meant frequent attempts at deploying group writing strategies; the attention to feminist content and methodologies; the extensive use of improvisation; multi-racial casting; the support of younger writers through extensive and open-ended workshops of new work; the virtual exclusion of men; and the use of alternative performance venues. In addition to *Pretty Ugly*, a show for youth about fashion, and *In Our Way*, an 'adult show exploring the effect of sex discrimination on women workers' (Wandor: 65), WTG has staged numerous new productions through the 1970s and 80s, all of which exhibit the kind of social conscience for which WTG is justly famous: *My Mkinga* (1980) deals with drug dumping in the Third World (Wandor: 66); *New Anatomies* (1981), by Timberlake Wertenbaker, focuses on how 'nineteenth-century women adventurers dressed as men' (Wandor: 67); and *Time Pieces* (1982) explores issues relating to women's history-making.

Lear's Daughters 'takes its shape from the "gaps" in Shakespeare's *King Lear*' (Griffin and Aston: 11) and does this, in Susan Bennett's words, to 'challenge the authority of Shakespeare, the cumulative power of mainstream production, and the operation of that authority in the politics of culture' (51). The play has been called a 'landmark in feminist "reinventing" of Shakespeare' (Goodman 1993b: 220) and Goodman suggests that the play questions 'all of history as presented in standard texts . . . [since history] may represent a genealogy of "false fathers"' (220). Shakespeare, in this reading, is aligned with conventional forms of history-making that require disruption, in this case through a discourse that undoes orthodox gender assumptions about the primacy of the male experience. In the play, the 'daughters' stories are re-told by the androgynous fool' (Griffin and Aston: 11), a comment on the way in which the authority of the narrator is traditionally understood. Furthermore, Griffin's and Aston's reading of the fool's function suggests that s/he 'details the fictions, myths, and structures which are deployed by men to imprison women in patriarchal ideology, to separate them from themselves, their bodies and their desires so that they are only ever daughters, wives, or mothers' (11–12).

The father's material absence from this scenario is one of the major ways in which the play rewrites Shakespeare's version of the story. The depth of characterization that Goneril, Regan, and Cordelia receive through the nurse's telling of 'fairy tales' (Griffin and Aston: 24) from their childhood, along with the focus they receive as staged characters, presents a radical alternative to the way in which audiences have come to expect the telling of Lear's story, with his pathetic request for his daughters to show which of them loves him most and its implicit assumption that it is the daughters' fault that Lear is driven to a tragic end.

Furthermore, as Goodman notes, in *Lear's Daughters* the 'princesses are carefully balanced against each other in terms of character and color' (1993b: 222). The first production, for instance, used a white woman for the role of Cordelia and two black women for the roles of Goneril and Regan, and the second used black women to play the roles of all three daughters, and white women to play the roles of the fool and the nanny. As a result of such casting choices, issues of ethnicity and class (servants are white in the latter inverted scheme of things, mistresses are black) complicate the story of the daughters. Moreover, in *Lear's Daughters*, the daughters gain identity not in relation to a particular patriarchal hierarchy, but rather, from the distinctive features with which they are identified: Cordelia with words, Regan with touch; Goneril with colour. Goodman notes that 'In the final image of *Lear's Daughters*, the crown is thrown into the air and caught by all three daughters at once. The shrinking spotlight highlights the black and white of hands on gold just before the final blackout' (1993b: 222–223). The vision of a potential solidarity and the symbolic empowerment associated with grasping the crown radically remake Shakespeare. Here, adaptation, even as it puts to the question the ideology of the Shakespearean source, asks us not to disregard the Shakespearean source text, nor even to judge it as flawed, inferior, or politically incorrect. Rather, *Lear's Daughters* asks us to consider narrative alternatives that disrupt the sedimentation of convention gathered round its source.

Select bibliography

Entries marked * are particularly accessible.

Bennett, S. (1996) *Performing Nostalgia: Shifting Shakespeare and the Contemporary Past*, London: Routledge.
*Goodman, L. (1993a) *Contemporary Feminist Theatres: To Each Her Own*, London: Routledge.
*— (1993b) 'Women's Alternative Shakespeares and Women's Alternatives to Shakespeare in Contemporary British Theater,' in Marianne Novy (ed.) *Cross-Cultural Performances: Difference in Women's Re-Visions of Shakespeare*, Urbana and Chicago: University of Illinois Press: 206–226.
Griffin, G., and Ashton E. (eds) (1991) *Herstory: Plays by Women for Women*, vol. 1, Sheffield: Sheffield Academic Press.
*Itzin, C. (1980) *Stages in the Revolution: Political Theatre in Britain Since 1968*, London: Eyre Methuen.
Wandor, M. (1986) *Carry On, Understudies: Theatre and Sexual Politics*, London: Routledge & Kegan Paul.

Lear's Daughters

The Women's Theatre Group and Elaine Feinstein

By Adjoa Andoh, Janys Chambers, Gwenda Hughes, Polly Irvin, Hazel Maycock, Lizz Poulter and Sandra Yaw (all of The Women's Theatre Group), from an idea by Elaine Feinstein. Reprinted by permission of The Women's Theatre Group and Elaine Feinstein.

Characters

CORDELIA

REGAN

GONERIL

THE FOOL

THE NURSE/NANNY

Scene 1

The beginning

(*Light up on the* FOOL.)

FOOL There was an old man called Lear
  whose daughters, da da da da, fear,
  The Queen was their mum,
  Da da da da son,
  Da da da da da dada here.
  (*she shakes her head.*)
  Knock, knock.
  Who's there?
  Godfrey.
  Godfrey who?
  Godfrey tickets for
  the play tonight.
  (*looks at audience.*)
  Are you ready?
  (*thinks.*)
  The play.
  (*holds up three fingers.*)
  Three princesses.
  (*holds up two fingers.*)
  Two servants.
  (*holds up one finger.*)
  One king offstage.
  (*holds up one finger on other hand.*)
  One Queen dead.
  (*thinks*)
  Or
  (*same finger business.*)
  Three daughters,
  Two mothers,
  One father,
  and the Fool.
  (*points to herself.*)
  Now:
  Six parts.
  Four actors . . .
  (*looks at fingers, thinks.*)
  The Fool.
  (*smiles.*)
  Right.
  One stage,
  One audience,
  One castle,
  (*stands up, moves centre stage, takes out blindfold.*)
  One prop.
  (*puts it on*)
  Watch!
  (*into game of blind man's bluff.*)

ALL One, Two, Three, One, Two, Three,
  One, Two, Three.

FOOL Goneril!

ALL No. One, Two, Three, One, Two, Three,
  One, Two, Three.

FOOL Cordelia!

(CORDELIA *turns to audience.*)

CORDELIA I like words. Words are like stones,
  heavy and solid and every one different, you
  can feel their shape and their weight on your
  tongue. I like their roughness and their
  smoothness, and when I am silent, I am trying
  to get them right. Not just for beautiful things,
  like the feel of old lace, but for the smell of wet
  soil, or the tug of the brush through my hair. I

Note: When speeches are interrupted by another character, the point in the sentence at which the interruption is made is marked /.

learnt to read by myself. The first thing I ever did on my own. And the voices were so rich and strong that now, I read all through the summer in a garden den of raspberry canes and blackberries, and I look up at the sky, and it's full of words.

ALL One, Two, Three, One, Two, Three, One, Two, Three.

FOOL Regan!

(REGAN *turns to audience*.)

REGAN I love the feel of wood, of bark cracked and mutilated by lightning or curves smooth and worn by wind and rain. I love the musty smell of old wood decaying, or of new wood freshly cut. Sometimes when I touch it, I can almost feel the wood breathing still, its breath, my breath. When I carve, it is as if there is a shape lying within the wood already, waiting to be released, moving my knife independent of the hand that holds it. So on some days I carve slowly, carefully, holding my breath, frightened of what I might create, whilst on other days I carve passionately, wanting to release this shape, this being, because I know that one day the shape that appears will be particular – my shape, me.

ALL One, Two, Three, One, Two, Three, One, Two, Three.

FOOL Goneril!

(GONERIL *turns to audience*.)

GONERIL When I look the world breaks into colours. When I was small – finding paints and brushes in the chest, opening tiny pots and setting them out, taking water – I couldn't believe how the colours sharpened under the wet brush! And now I paint all the time, every minute, big canvas, big strokes, getting it right. Self portrait . . . on a throne . . . scarlet, gold, black – it's outside. Trees cracked by lightning, a knot of raspberry canes and blackberries . . . And my sisters, beside me, our faces upward, smiling – sky full of stars. My painting. And one day, I'll get it right.

ALL One, Two, Three, One, Two, Three, One, Two, Three.

(FOOL *turns to audience*.)

FOOL I like money. And myself. And money.

(FOOL *moves down right*. NANNY *moves upstage centre, sits, and sisters gather upstage centre around her*.)

FOOL Three princesses, living in a castle, listening to fairy-tales in the nursery.

Scene 2

Three Sisters, the Nurse together

NURSE (*to* GONERIL) When you were born, the Queen wore nothing but her crown.

CORDELIA What, nothing?

NURSE Lear was not there. He was in the library looking at something. You came out like a dart, head first, then body, all over scarlet, covered in blood. The crown fell off and over you, encircling you, your whole body.

GONERIL What then?

NURSE And then a comet rushed through the sky, leaving a red trail in the black. (*whispers*) And it was twelve o'clock midday.

GONERIL I remember it. I remember it quite clearly. I remember being born quite clearly. I heard music.

REGAN What about me?

NURSE When you were born, the Queen was sitting on her throne. At midnight you dropped out onto the velvet plush like a ruby.

CORDELIA Where was Daddy this time?

NURSE Still in the library.

REGAN And then what happened?

NURSE A volcano erupted.

REGAN A volcano?

NURSE Yes, the lava got everywhere. We were cleaning for days.

REGAN I remember it. I heard music too.

NURSE And was it beautiful?

REGAN Yes, oh yes.

CORDELIA Now me. What happened when I was born?

NURSE When you were born . . .

(NURSE *looks at her. She draws* CORDELIA *to her, whispers in her ear*.)

GONERIL What?

REGAN What?

GONERIL What did she say?

REGAN What did she say?

(CORDELIA *and* NURSE *look at each other*.)

GONERIL Nothing. Nothing happened did it? Nothing.

NURSE And afterwards we had cake. Victoria sponge on a doily in the parlour with the clock ticking. The cake was cut into three.

REGAN A piece for each of us.

NURSE A piece for Lear. A piece for the Queen. And a piece for me.

REGAN Did it taste nice?

NURSE Ask Lear.

(The NURSE *moves away*.)

REGAN What did she say?

GONERIL What did she say?

REGAN Come on, Cordelia!

CORDELIA (*slowly*) She said that the Queen was outdoors. And I grew like a red rose out of her legs. And there was a hurricane.

REGAN It's the same, it's the same.

CORDELIA And Lear was there.

(*Lights down. Light up on* FOOL *down right.*)

FOOL When she came, there was just a note. It said, 'I'm coming soon. Nanny.' So I went about my business. If the note had any significance it was wasted on me. Two weeks later there was another note, pinned under my cereal bowl. 'There's been a set-back, but wait for me there. Nanny.' I was seven or maybe twelve, I can't be certain, but Goneril was definitely two. The Queen, their mother then, had taken to spooning honey over the flowerbeds. She wore a peg on each finger and had ordered the hair to be removed from all over her body. Everyone said there was something wrong. She'd tipped the scales. She needed a friend or a nurse or 'at least something to cheer her up a bit', everyone said. A third note came. 'Sorry it's taken so long, but I shall be with you by midday tomorrow. Can I bring my ducks?' Signed Nanny or Nurse.

By eleven o'clock next day I was at the city walls watching for a new face. At midday she came, riding sideways on a donkey. I knew it must be her.

(NURSE *moves into space as if entering for the first time.*)

NURSE Sorry I'm late.

FOOL She said.

NURSE But these things take time.

FOOL 'Oh, don't worry, no matter', I said and I helped her carry her things to her room. 'Will you be stopping long?' I asked.

NURSE That's not really up to me.

FOOL She said.

NURSE I do as I'm told.

FOOL I don't know if you're expected, that's the trouble.

NURSE I'll make myself indispensable. Soon they'll come to rely. You know how these folks are, always make the same mistakes.

(FOOL *holds out hand for money.* NURSE *places gloves in* FOOL's *hand.* FOOL *throws bag to* NURSE.)

FOOL Three daughters. With two mothers – one buying, one selling. One paying, one paid.

(FOOL *picks up the* QUEEN's *veil.*)

Scene 3

The Fool is the Queen

(FOOL *sits on box upstage. Arranges veil as the* QUEEN. *During this scene* FOOL *speaks as* FOOL *and* QUEEN.)

FOOL (QUEEN) Nurse! Nurse!

NURSE Yes, your majesty.

FOOL (QUEEN) Is it nearly morning?

NURSE The birds are just beginning.

FOOL (QUEEN) Don't talk to me about birds. The doctor was putting live pigeons on my feet all day yesterday.

FOOL To help her conceive.

NURSE What is this? (*picks up cup*)

FOOL (QUEEN) The doctor gave it to me.

NURSE What for?

FOOL (QUEEN) To help me sleep.

NURSE He's a fake. What are you doing with these? (*picks up ledgers*)

FOOL (QUEEN) Keeping the accounts/

FOOL The budget is in chaos. Taxes aren't being paid, and there's no income from the fields.

NURSE You should leave all that business to him.

FOOL (QUEEN) He is very distressed by reading documents like these/

FOOL so by and large he doesn't read them.

NURSE About your children.

FOOL (QUEEN) I want them taken away.

NURSE You don't see them enough.

FOOL (QUEEN) South.

NURSE He won't like that.

FOOL (QUEEN) I could go with them. For a holiday.

BOTH He won't like that.

FOOL (QUEEN) No, he won't, he likes to have me near him.

NURSE I'll bring them in to see you then, shall I?

FOOL (QUEEN) I'm too tired.

NURSE Later on this afternoon.

FOOL (QUEEN) They wear me out.

NURSE That's settled then. I'll go and arrange it. Good.

(NURSE *crosses down left, pauses at exit. Curtsies.* FOOL *dumps* QUEEN *and moves down centre.*)

FOOL Lear's daughters. Three princesses creeping down the stairs, learning about a father, who is also a king.

(*Going downstairs.*)

(GONERIL, REGAN, CORDELIA *centre stage.* FOOL *circles the sisters and as each one speaks mirrors actions and words.* FOOL *first looks at* GONERIL *and turns suddenly and points to* CORDELIA.)

CORDELIA The first time I go downstairs, I run, bare foot cold on the stone steps. Careful I tell myself. Slow down. Don't slip. But I have to run because of the shadows. In my new white shift, satin rustling as I go downstairs. Looking up, there is a huge oak door, with a handle high above my head. I reach up, wanting to be let in, banging my hands on the door until it opens. There are too many lights and too many faces. And then the one face, clear and sharp, stooping right down and swinging me high above the floor, up to the ceiling, up to the rafters. In a giant's arms, my feet are touching the sky, and then . . . down. The smell of a breath, warm and sweet, soft lips wet on my cheek, bristles scratching my chin and neck, and down on to the table, and I turn, holding my skirt, round and round. Look, Daddy, look, Daddy, look, look, look.

(FOOL *touches* REGAN.)

REGAN I'm not scared going downstairs. It's dark and very late. Goneril is asleep, lying across her bed, with one hand and foot hanging over the side, frowning and talking in her sleep, like she always does. Cordelia is sleeping curled up tight in a ball. Sheets and blankets wrapped tight around her. And I am on my own. Downstairs I go, breathing shallow and seeing nobody. The stairs are rough on my feet. Passing a door I hear men's voices shouting and calling. The door is open and looking in, I can see my Father. He is singing, banging his fist on the table, not quite in tune, not quite in time. And his arm is around Mother's neck. I think it's Mother. He has a hand inside her dress, holding her breast. Not tender, he's just holding her. And Mother's face. It is Mother. I'm certain it is. Her face is blank, without expression, like a figure made of wax. I'm scared now. (*turns back to mirror*)

(FOOL *touches* GONERIL.)

GONERIL The first time I go downstairs, I sit on his throne to see what it is like. It has a high back, carved and uncomfortable. He likes that, likes to feel its weight behind his back. It is so big my feet cannot reach the edge. I stay on a long time, sitting quietly, looking about me. When he comes in, I am smiling, and he is angry because he knows what I am thinking and I smile on – because I want him to know.

(FOOL *addresses audience.*)

FOOL The first time I went downstairs I was pushed. And it bloody hurt. I broke my finger (*holds up little finger – it is straight*) and it's never been straight since. Look. (*bends little finger*)

(FOOL *moves downstage. Looks at notes – the running order.*)

The Guided Tour. (FOOL *walks round centre stage*) The nursery. Books, paints, a knife – for carving – and a Nanny. Down the stairs the parlour – lace, cake, a knife – for slicing – medicines, honey, account books – to keep things in order.

NURSE (*interjects*) And the Nurse.

FOOL Down the stairs. The dining room. The kitchen. The storeroom. The Counting House – for the king! A knife – for the guard. And (*points*) the Fool's room. (*moves to its spot*) And underneath, the sewers, full of Rats. Now. (*gets comfy*) The Fool.

When I was born, nothing happened. There was no bright star, no hurricane, no visitors came from afar. Obviously my parents hadn't read the right books so my arrival was completely overlooked.

Scene 4

The Fool and Sisters

(FOOL *moves centre stage and joins sisters and* NANNY. GONERIL *stands at the back looking out of window.* FOOL *is counting its money.*)

CORDELIA What was your father like?
FOOL Don't know.
REGAN What was your mother like?
FOOL (*concentrating*) Don't know.
CORDELIA How long have you been here?
FOOL Not long.
REGAN How old are you?
FOOL Work or pleasure?
REGAN What?
FOOL Is this question work or pleasure?
REGAN Pleasure.
FOOL Don't know.
REGAN Work then.

(FOOL *holds out hand.* REGAN *gives it a coin.*)

FOOL What was the question?
REGAN How old are you?
FOOL Seventeen.
CORDELIA How do you know?
FOOL It's a feeling I've got.
REGAN And what's that feel like?
FOOL Time for a change.
CORDELIA What were you before you came here?

FOOL I was a singer called Somers. Not with a 'U' you understand, as in summer and winter, but with an 'O', as in some and none.

GONERIL You're lying.

FOOL I am not. I was a singer of filthy and wanton songs and I heard voices. For money.

GONERIL I meant it's a lie that you haven't been here long. You were here when I was little.

FOOL That was some other Fool.

GONERIL That Fool looked exactly like you.

FOOL It's the clothes, they come with the job. And the expression. (*it smiles brightly*) It's a tradition, there's always been a Fool.

(GONERIL *is about to speak but returns instead to the window.*)

REGAN What did you mean, you heard voices for money?

FOOL Heard voices, had fits, saw devils, foamed at the mouth. Standard stuff. I did it to frighten the godless into returning to the faith. Sometimes I fell backwards into fires, but that cost extra.

REGAN You did that for money?

FOOL Of course. Skilled work. Did you expect me to do it for the good of my soul and a bowl of soup?

CORDELIA Are you a man or a woman?

FOOL Depends who's asking.

REGAN Well, which?

FOOL Which would you rather? It's all the same to me.

GONERIL How can you? (FOOL *looks at her*) How can you be so . . . accommodating?

FOOL It's what I'm paid for. Time's up.

CORDELIA If you weren't a Fool, what would you be?

FOOL Time's up. (REGAN *hands* FOOL *another coin*) What was the question?

CORDELIA If you weren't a Fool, what would you be?

FOOL A dog with no masters.

Scene 5

Lear returns triumphant from a sporting tournament

(*It starts to rain.* FOOL *mimes getting wet.*)

FOOL Three princesses sitting in a room, listening to the rain fall and hoping for the sun.
Lear returns triumphant from some sporting tournament. At sixty-five he is still the most agile horseman and best archer. The title 'King'

demeans his status – he is a demi-god. He has competed against the best and won. His countrymen weep with pride, and disbelief. Nanny woke Fool at 4 a.m.

NURSE (*interjects*) It's time.

FOOL It practised smiling in the mirror (*mimes smiling in a mirror*) and put on its man's man suit.

(*Lights up on centre stage.* GONERIL *at window,* REGAN *stands on trunk.* CORDELIA *crosses to mirror.*)

GONERIL He's been away for a very long time.

REGAN I am up even before Nurse, watching a watery sun creep up over the fields.

CORDELIA Nanny makes me spit on her apron so she can wipe a piece of dirt from my cheek.

GONERIL I am so excited. I have missed him so much.

REGAN We are going to get out.

(CORDELIA *crosses down to left stage.* GONERIL *moves down stage to centre.* REGAN *stands to right of* GONERIL.)

GONERIL I am going to see him again. Touch him again. Smell him. He always smells lovely.

REGAN It is drizzling.

GONERIL It is November but it is mild. The sky is clear, crisp blue. No rain – all dry.

CORDELIA Goneril and Regan look beautiful.

REGAN Cordelia chatters like some excited lace-covered guinea-fowl.

CORDELIA Nanny holds me high above her head. It makes me laugh.

GONERIL Cordelia isn't very well – sniffy and crying at the slightest thing.

REGAN Goneril sits with her hands, two tight fists balled up in her lap. She doesn't want him home.

GONERIL Regan keeps wriggling at my side.

REGAN There are crowds of people in the streets, mud-spattered and sodden.

GONERIL So many ordinary people have turned out to greet him.

CORDELIA I can see nothing but people's backs as they leap and stretch higher and higher.

REGAN When they see our coach they surge forward.

GONERIL Cheering and singing.

REGAN Something soft and rotten-smelling hits the side of my face.

GONERIL They love him.

REGAN It slides slowly down my jaw and neck. They are still shouting, but their faces have changed.

GONERIL It is a holiday. He has come home.

REGAN The coach begins to rock violently.

CORDELIA The people cheer and cry so I do as well.

GONERIL I can see him in the distance.

CORDELIA The crowd slowly parts and there he is.

GONERIL He is so upright.

CORDELIA I'd forgotten his face.

GONERIL I can see no-one else in this huge crowd – just him.

CORDELIA He reaches towards Mother and kisses her. She lets go of my hand.

GONERIL He smiles, parts his lips, shows his teeth. He puts one hand on my shoulder and pushes me away.

CORDELIA He puts his hand on our heads one at a time as if he is healing us.

GONERIL And then he lifts Cordelia high into the air and kisses her on each cheek.

REGAN We don't even get out of the coach.

CORDELIA He lifts me back into the coach and Father, Mother, my sisters and I are all together again.

REGAN Mother leaves our coach and joins him in his.

GONERIL Throughout the drive back to the castle I look out of the window.

REGAN I want to lay my head on Goneril's lap, but that space is still occupied by her fists.

GONERIL As Nanny takes us away he touches my cheek.

CORDELIA We all love each other.

GONERIL I don't feel it.

CORDELIA I don't remember everything, but when I do, I remember *exactly*.

FOOL There are only three things I can't remember. I can't remember names. I can't remember faces and I've forgotten what the third thing is.

If they'd only been the two instead of three, things might have been different.

'Cos two is nice, it's manageable.

It's more easily understandable.

Two is one – holding hands with another.

First and last,

Bottom and top,

Master and servant,

Mother and child.

Two is what one is, and the other isn't, a pair.

Whereas three. You're asking for trouble.

Bad news travels in threes.

Three splits two into half, leaving piggy in the middle.

Two against one.

'If she isn't with me then she must be with . . .'

Three means a private detective.

Three sisters, playing in the nursery, with the mother who sells, but not the mother who buys.

Three daughters, visiting in the parlour, with the mother

who's paid and the mother who's paying.

Scene 6

The Sisters and their Mother

(FOOL *is* QUEEN. *Stands centre stage with veil. Sisters and* NANNY *enter.* NANNY *stands to side. Sisters stand around* QUEEN. *As they ask their questions, the sisters circle the* QUEEN. NANNY *claps her hands as sisters enter.*)

GONERIL Hello majesty.

REGAN Mother.

CORDELIA Majesty.

NANNY Curtsy to the Queen.

CORDELIA Hello Mother.

REGAN Majesty.

GONERIL Mother.

NANNY Kiss your mother.

(*Sisters kiss* QUEEN. *She flinches.*)

REGAN Do you like my hair?

CORDELIA Daddy likes my hair.

REGAN Do you like it?

FOOL (QUEEN) Do I like it? (*looks at* NANNY) Do I like it?

CORDELIA Do you like my dress?

GONERIL Come and see my painting.

CORDELIA Do you like it?

GONERIL I'm painting heaven.

CORDELIA Do you like the colour of it?

GONERIL Why do we have a sun and a moon?

REGAN Do you like it?

CORDELIA Am I too young to wear black?

NANNY You are tiring the Queen!

REGAN Can I go out?

GONERIL Why are we always shut in?

CORDELIA Do you like it?

GONERIL Can we go out with you?

REGAN Can we go out?

CORDELIA Can I do a handstand?

REGAN Can I go out?

CORDELIA I can stand on my head.

GONERIL Do you ever go out?

NANNY Keep your voice down.

CORDELIA Can you stand on your head?

GONERIL Do you ever go out?

FOOL (QUEEN) He doesn't like shouting.
CORDELIA Do you stand on your head for Daddy?
FOOL (QUEEN) Keep your voice down.
CORDELIA Do you like it?
NANNY He won't like these boys' manners.
CORDELIA Why are you always in bed?
FOOL (QUEEN) I don't like these boys' manners.
REGAN Do you like it?
CORDELIA Does he like you in bed?
FOOL (QUEEN) Stop these boys' manners!
CORDELIA Are you going to have a baby?
NANNY You are not a boy.
GONERIL Why does he want a boy?
FOOL (QUEEN) You are not a boy.
GONERIL Why do you want a boy?
FOOL (QUEEN) You are not a boy.
REGAN Do you want a boy?
FOOL (QUEEN) Do I want a boy? (*looks at* NANNY)
REGAN Are you sick?
CORDELIA Why don't you have a boy?
GONERIL Are you sick?
CORDELIA Will he be cross?
REGAN Is that why you're sick?
CORDELIA Is he cross with you?
GONERIL Is that why you're sick?
CORDELIA Does he like you?
GONERIL He likes Cordelia.
REGAN Is that why you're sick?
CORDELIA Does he love you?
GONERIL Do you love him?
REGAN Are you sick?

(*Sisters stop circling* QUEEN. *Start pulling at veil.*)

CORDELIA Will you die?
REGAN What will happen to us?
GONERIL If you die?
CORDELIA Are you going to die?
REGAN Who will be Queen?
GONERIL If you die?
REGAN Will it be Goneril?
CORDELIA What will happen to us?
GONERIL If you die?
CORDELIA Will Nanny be our mother?
GONERIL If you die?
REGAN Mother?
CORDELIA Mother, will you die?
FOOL (QUEEN) Stop!
NANNY Stop!

(QUEEN *collapses to floor.*)

FOOL Knock, knock, who's there?
(FOOL *shrugs shoulders in answer.*)

(FOOL *picks up veil and carries it carefully, draped over its arms, back to its spot.*)

FOOL Three princesses listening down the stairs with the mother who lives – for the mother who is dying.

Scene 7

The Nurse and the Sisters

(GONERIL *stands looking out of window.* REGAN *is sitting on trunk,* NANNY *brushes* CORDELIA's *hair down stage.*)

REGAN Tell us about when we were little.
GONERIL Cordelia's still little.
NURSE You are all still small.
REGAN Smaller then.
NURSE When Goneril was very small you weren't there. (*looks at* CORDELIA) And neither were you.
REGAN No, do when we were all three there.
NURSE Even Lear?
REGAN (*pause*) Yes.
NURSE Once, Lear had not been there, and then suddenly he was. It rained for forty days and nights before he came home and when he did, the sun came out. The king walked over the water to meet us.
CORDELIA Over the water?
GONERIL (*to* CORDELIA) Over a bridge.
NURSE Yes. That's better. Over a bridge. We had to build a bridge to get to him. The Queen crossed the bridge and everybody had to cheer.
GONERIL Had to?
NURSE Yes. (*smoothly*) Because it was important to see the Queen at Lear's side.
CORDELIA Then did we cross over?
NURSE I think so, yes.
REGAN Who went first?
NURSE I can't remember.
REGAN I bet I did.
GONERIL In order of age.
CORDELIA Youngest first.
REGAN We went across the bridge together. Everybody cheered. Nanny went quite deaf with the cheering.
NURSE Did I?
REGAN Daddy gave you a present.
NURSE (*laughing*) Did he?
CORDELIA It was cake.
NURSE Was it?
REGAN You were there.
NURSE Was I? (*pause*) If you want me there.
GONERIL No. (*slowly, concentrating. She moves to* NANNY) Nanny stayed on this side of the bridge.
NURSE That is my place. (*curtsies to* GONERIL)

(*Silence.*)

GONERIL (*measured*) I stayed with Nanny. (*smiles at* NANNY)

REGAN So did I.

CORDELIA And so did the Queen. So Daddy must have come to us.

NURSE Yes, he must have come to us.

CORDELIA (*satisfied*) One big happy family.

FOOL (QUEEN) (*off centre stage*) Nurse! Nurse!

(*They all look off. Know* QUEEN *has died.* NURSE *goes off.* GONERIL *takes over brushing* CORDELIA'*s hair.* CORDELIA *shows pain.*)

CORDELIA Stop it, Goneril, you're hurting me.

(GONERIL *stops brushing. Pain continues.*)

CORDELIA Goneril, stop it! It's pulling. Goneril, please, stop it, you're hurting me! Stop it, Goneril, stop it!

Scene 8

Funeral preparations

FOOL (*putting veil down in bundle*) The Queen is dead! Long live the Queen! But who will take her place at the King's right hand? Cordelia the favourite, Goneril the eldest, or Regan the outsider?

(CORDELIA *leaves centre stage.* GONERIL *goes to trunk and puts head on hands.* REGAN *picks up hair brush from floor.*)

REGAN We'd better get changed. We can't go downstairs dressed like this. (GONERIL *is shaking.* REGAN *crosses to her*) Don't cry. (REGAN *comforts her*) Don't cry . . . you're laughing! Stop it! Why are you laughing?

(GONERIL *stops. Shakes head.*)

GONERIL He'll be very upset. He'll have to manage on his own now.

(*They both start to laugh.* FOOL *laughs quietly with them offstage. They stop laughing.*)

REGAN How will we manage without her?

GONERIL Don't worry. I'll take care of everything now.

REGAN We should change.

GONERIL No. He'll be down there all in black. Dressed for sorrow. We'll be fine as we are. (*They smile.* REGAN *turns away*) Regan. I feel sick.

(GONERIL *holds her stomach. Cries.*)

REGAN You'll be fine. You'll be fine.

GONERIL Will it take long?

REGAN No, I don't think so.

(CORDELIA *enters.*)

CORDELIA He said I'm his special girl and I've got to look after him. I'm not going with you, I've got to hold his hand. (GONERIL *goes to trunk.* REGAN *slumps on bench*) Nanny! (NURSE *enters*) Daddy says Mummy's gone to live with God and I can wear a long black dress with gloves. Get me ready.

NURSE Turn around.

CORDELIA He said Mummy would be pleased to know she'd left everything in such good hands. Do you think she can see us now?

NURSE Keep your head still.

CORDELIA He said when we come out of the church all the people will cheer when I stand next to him because I will be so brave. Do you think they will?

NURSE There you are. You'll do.

CORDELIA (*turns to look in mirror*) Oh. Look, Nanny, look, I look really grown up. Just like a Queen.

REGAN (*sharply*) Goneril. Look.

(GONERIL *crosses to window. Looks at* NURSE. NURSE *goes to window.*)

CORDELIA What is it?

(GONERIL *indicates to* NANNY *to take* CORDELIA *away quickly.* NANNY *looks out of the window.*)

NURSE Come with me.

(*When* NURSE *and* CORDELIA *have gone,* REGAN *and* GONERIL *look to the window again, after a while* REGAN *turns away.*)

GONERIL How can he? Today.

REGAN He's disgusting.

GONERIL He's got his hand right up her skirt.

REGAN Anyone can see him. Not just us. Doesn't he care?

GONERIL He's unbuttoning himself.

REGAN Come away.

GONERIL He's so . . . How dare he?

REGAN Who is she?

GONERIL I don't know.

REGAN Doesn't she mind him pawing her like that?

(*They turn away from window.*)

GONERIL What will happen now? Do you think he will marry her?

REGAN I don't know.

GONERIL If he does he'll have a son. I know it. He'll try until he does. I'll never be Queen.

(FOOL *enters from left, whistling 'Sing a song of sixpence'. Circles centre stage and then looks out of window over shoulders of* GONERIL *and* REGAN.)

FOOL (*laughing. Sings*) Wasn't that a dainty dish to set before the King? (FOOL *returns to its spot. Whistles*) Time passes. (*whistles*) It rains. And every spring the river outside the castle overflows, flooding the sewers and disturbing the rats. (*pause*) One morning a stone is thrown through the window, breaking the glass and cracking the mirror. It lands in the middle of the floor. (*makes popping sound. Sisters centre stage look at spot and then turn away in boredom*) Lear takes to riding in his carriage with the shutters down and going the long way round to avoid the crowds. And the Fool amuses the Nanny, and the Nanny amuses the Fool, as they wait for the rain to stop.

Scene 9

The Nurse tells the Fool the story of the Pied Piper

(FOOL *crosses to stage right to the* NANNY'S *spot.*)

FOOL (*sings*) Nanny put the kettle on,
Nanny put the kettle on,
Nanny put the kettle on,
We'll all have tea?

(NANNY *is sitting darning veil. Pause.*)

NURSE Who's there?
FOOL Nanny.
NURSE Nanny who?
FOOL Nanny your business.

(NURSE *snorts.* FOOL *laughs.*)

FOOL I'm tired and I'm hungry. (*fed-up*) Is there anything in the pantry?
NURSE Empty.
FOOL Game?
NURSE Out of season.
FOOL No! Word game. Empty.
NURSE Full.
FOOL Stomach.
NURSE Pregnant.
FOOL Queen.
NURSE Princess.
FOOL Goneril.
NURSE (*triumphantly*) Regan.

(FOOL *is astonished. Mouth falls open.*)

Time's up. You lose.
FOOL Not fair. Not fair.
NURSE You lose. You owe me one favour.
FOOL Can't make me.
NURSE True. But you've got an aptitude for servitude.
FOOL Oh! A rhyming game. Snotty.
NURSE Botty.
FOOL (*hooting and laughing*) Potty.
NURSE Clotty.
FOOL Not a word. S' not a word. You lose, I win! Oh, Nanny, Nanny. Can I sleep in your bed tonight? (*leans backwards across* NURSE's *lap*)
NURSE Can I afford it?
FOOL I'll waive the fee.
NURSE (*to audience*) Now that's what I call a joke.
FOOL Would you prefer it if I set a price? It can be arranged.
NURSE Well, at least I could complain then if I wasn't pleased. (FOOL *turns from her, sulking*) Fool feeling hurt? (FOOL *sulks*) I thought Fool was above such things. You're a funny Fool. What are you after?
FOOL I'm after everyone else. I'm an afterthought. Oh, tell me a story, Nanny. Tell me the one about the Fool who becomes rich and famous, inherits the earth and travels the sky on a magic carpet. That's my favourite.
NURSE Oh, that one.
FOOL There's no such tale.
NURSE Please yourself.
FOOL Nanneeey. (*begging*) Nanny, Nanny.
NURSE Alright. A very long way from here there is a land that is very beautiful, but where it is always raining. The land is full of tiny towns and villages. If you look at it from above they are scattered about like crumbs of cake. And in the middle of it all there is a river, and by the river a castle.
FOOL I know the very spot.
NURSE And over the castle the sun always shines. And in the castle there lives a king and all his court. Landowners, merchants, clerics, bankers.
FOOL Yes, yes, what about me?
NURSE And every so often the people look up from their work in the fields and hold their babies up high to see the castle because it looks so beautiful. But each day it gets harder for them to do this because of one thing.
FOOL The debris of a passing swan. (*whistles, mimes splat in eye*)
NURSE Rats.

FOOL Rats?

NURSE Big, hungry rats, scavenging for food, trampling down the meagre crops, scampering in and out of the mean houses. And one day there comes a terrible famine. And then the rats move.

FOOL Move? Move where?

NURSE Into the castle, where food is still plentiful. And by day the king and his men struggle with the poor that batter against their gates, begging for food, and by night with the rats that run through their stores and kitchens, gnaw even at the king's throne.

FOOL Yes, yes, gnaw, gnaw, nibble, nibble, what about me?

NURSE This is you now.

FOOL Good.

NURSE But then one day there comes into the castle a strange figure who is called the

FOOL Fool.

NURSE No-one knows whether this

FOOL Fool

NURSE is a woman or a man, for it has a woman's voice, but walks with the carriage and stature of a man. The

FOOL Fool

NURSE announces itself as a rat-catcher

FOOL (triumphantly) Ha-Ha!

NURSE and offers to rid the place of the vermin. The king and his men agree and ask the

FOOL Fool

NURSE what the

FOOL Fool

NURSE would like in return and the

FOOL Fool

NURSE replies

FOOL money.

NURSE So it is agreed.

FOOL Lots of it.

NURSE Whereupon the

FOOL Fool

NURSE draws out its pipe (FOOL mimes smoking pipe) and begins to play, (FOOL changes to playing a pipe) so that the rats swarm to follow, out of the castle, into the river, into which they all plunge and drown.

FOOL Ha Ha! And now I get paid.

NURSE No sooner has this happened than the king and his court repent of their bargain, refusing to pay the

FOOL Swine!

NURSE Fool its fee, saying 'Why should we pay this creature, neither man nor woman?' and they drive it from the land.

FOOL Never!

NURSE But that evening the

FOOL Fool

NURSE is back

FOOL Good!

NURSE outside the castle, playing a different tune, and out of the wet fields and ditches, out of the mean houses, come the children, mud-splattered and sodden.

FOOL No.

NURSE And as the king and his men look out of the castle windows, they see the shadows fill with this dark army, and, strangest of all in this strange story, as they look at the children's teeth glinting in the moonlight, at the long fingers scratching at the doors, the men see not children but

(FOOL gags NURSE.)

FOOL Rabbits.

NURSE rats. Clambering up the walls, scrabbling through the slits in the windows, chewing their way up through the thick walls and floors, whetting their teeth against the stones.

FOOL No!

NURSE And soon they have gnawed the flesh from the bodies of the king and his men, picking over the bones and leaving every one bare.

FOOL What about my money? You've forgotten about my money. (angrily)

NURSE As dawn breaks over the town, the song of the

FOOL Fool

NURSE changes

FOOL to one of demand

NURSE and, chattering and tumbling, the

FOOL gold coins

NURSE children

FOOL fall into

NURSE run into

FOOL the Fool's lap.

NURSE the fields where the Fool waits for them and they follow across the fields and are never seen again.

FOOL No, no, no.

NURSE But sometimes

FOOL No.

NURSE at night

FOOL No.

NURSE the sound of music

FOOL No.

NURSE and laughter

FOOL No.

NURSE can be heard

FOOL No.

NURSE as though from a

FOOL No!

NURSE (*shouting*) Better World.

FOOL It's stopped. The rain's stopped. Ha, ha, ha. (*triumphantly*)

(FOOL *crosses back to down left*.)

Scene 10

Investment

(FOOL *takes piece of paper. Reads*.)

FOOL Scene One, Fool introduces play. Good. (*reads. Keeps paper*) Scene Two, Nanny and the princesses. Scene Three, Nanny and the Queen, Fool is Queen. Good. (*keeps paper*) Scene Four. (*reads paper*) Princess, princess, princess. Scene Ten. Nanny tells all about her love life? (*spits. Crumbles paper and throws it aside*) Scene Eleven, princess, prin . . . (*reads quickly*) Ah. Scene Thirteen Fool talks about investment. Investment is . . . (*thinks*) Investment is . . . Money, cash, dosh, lolly, crinks, ackers, makes the world go round, doubloons, duckets, crowns, pieces of eight, muck and brass. Money – Investment. (*puts coin down front of skirt. Mimes rubbing tummy*) Nest egg, pension, taken care of, rainy day, looked after, old age. (*smiles, waits, starts to wriggle as if eruption under skirt. Looks under skirt. Gasps with delight. Gasps. Reaches under skirt and pulls out fool doll. Cradles it as child*) Investment. Three princesses all grown older, thinking about their father and counting the cost.

(CORDELIA *centre stage, looking in mirror*. FOOL *stays in its place*. CORDELIA *humming 'Polly put the kettle on'*.)

FOOL (LEAR) Cordelia, where's my Cordelia?

CORDELIA Here Father – here I am.

FOOL (LEAR) Oh, see my pretty chick. Come my pretty, dance for Daddy.

CORDELIA For you, only for you?

FOOL (LEAR) Of course for me.

CORDELIA But everyone is watching.

FOOL (LEAR) Don't be silly.

CORDELIA I'm shy.

FOOL (LEAR) You're not trying.

CORDELIA I'm too big.

FOOL (LEAR) Spin for Daddy.

CORDELIA I can't.

FOOL (LEAR) Spin! (CORDELIA *picks up skirt*) Gather round gentlemen, please. Show them Lear's baby.

CORDELIA I'm not your baby.

FOOL (LEAR) What? Pardon?

CORDELIA I'm . . . (*she going to repeat above*) I'm tired, Daddy. Cordelia tired.

FOOL (LEAR) Spin. Spin. Spin.

CORDELIA Spin for Daddy. (*begins to spin*)

FOOL (LEAR) Don't let me down, darling. There's my peach.

CORDELIA There's my peach.

FOOL (LEAR) Such lovely hair and lips.

CORDELIA And tongues

FOOL (LEAR) Spin.

CORDELIA and bulging eyes,

FOOL (LEAR) Spin.

CORDELIA shouting and cheering.

FOOL (LEAR) Shouting and cheering.

CORDELIA I'm falling. No. I don't want to. Cordelia not want to be Daddy's girl. (CORDELIA *collapses on floor*)

(REGAN *enters up right. Crosses to down centre, then back to window*.)

REGAN Nurse!

(NURSE *enters*.)

What happened the night Mother died?

NURSE I don't understand.

REGAN The night she died. I can't remember. You and us, what happened?

NURSE I put you all to bed, you were over-tired. I sat up watching in case you were disturbed. Cordelia cried out, but you slept soundly.

REGAN What else?

NURSE You wanted a story, so I told you one.

REGAN About what, about Mother?

NURSE About all of you.

REGAN Tell me. (NURSE *does not respond*) Tell me!

(NURSE *crosses to trunk and sits*.)

NURSE I told you of the time your Father came home and you all went to meet him.

REGAN Over the bridge.

NURSE Yes.

REGAN I remember. You brushed our hair.

NURSE I often did.

REGAN You brushed our hair and you were lying.

NURSE No.

REGAN He came to us. It rained for forty days. When he came home the sun came out. It was lies.

NURSE It was a story. You were all upset. It was for comfort.

REGAN Tell me about Mother.

NURSE How?

REGAN What was she like?

NURSE She was a beautiful woman, but delicate. All perfume and lace.

REGAN Yes.

NURSE When she married your father, it was a love-match.

REGAN You're lying again.

NURSE She meant the world to him.

REGAN How did she die?

NURSE She was delicate.

REGAN What did Father do?

NURSE It was a love-match.

REGAN Tell me the truth. Tell me the truth. Tell me the truth!

(REGAN *walks towards* NURSE.)

NURSE Alright. I used to hear him in the room below, whining on at her to let him fuck her. He wouldn't give up on her having a son. She always gave in, that's why she was always tired.

REGAN A love-match.

NURSE She brought a large dowry. Substantial. She was beautiful.

REGAN And when she died?

NURSE Miscarriage. Her third. Cordelia had finished it for her. She died in the night so he was spared a bedside scene. I was not. I had been up all night. I was tired. He came in the morning to look at the Queen, lying in her white dress. I'd cleaned her up and laid her out. He looked at her for a long moment and then he stormed out.

REGAN We saw him, Goneril and I, out of the window. The day of the funeral.

NURSE Yes. She *was* important to him. She organized the budget. Looked after his interests. Night after night when he wasn't with her, adding and subtracting to balance the figures.

REGAN Did she love us?

NURSE Oh yes, when she had the time. She took you all away once. She came in here with his light all around her, like a net. We sat in the shadows and she told me she wanted to leave him and take all of you with her. I said nothing – packed our belongings in the trunk. I should have guessed but I never did until the time came that I wasn't to go as well. I took my cloak from the trunk and came in here and I never moved for three days. But in the end she had to bring you back. And then it was all up with us and no-one ever left again except by his say-so. She didn't have long after that.

REGAN No.

(NURSE *gets up and moves to* REGAN. *Holds her face and examines it.*)

NURSE How long?

REGAN Two months.

(NURSE *puts hand on* REGAN's *stomach. Shakes head.* REGAN *exits.*)

(GONERIL *enters.*)

GONERIL Nurse? Where's Cordelia?

NURSE Downstairs, with your father.

GONERIL Regan?

NURSE Downstairs. (GONERIL *looks*) In the cellars looking for wood. Why don't you paint?

GONERIL It's raining too hard. I can't see the colours. (*silence*) Have you been down there?

NURSE Where?

GONERIL The cellars.

NURSE Of course.

GONERIL I went down there once. When I was very small. Father took me. I couldn't believe it. Rooms and rooms of food, all those cheeses and flour and racks of meat, hanging from the ceiling.

NURSE We're well provided for against the bad weather.

GONERIL He took me down all these corridors, I could hardly keep up and then he stopped and fumbled in his pocket and took out a key. He opened a door and pushed me inside. And the room was full of gold. Everywhere crowns, coins, breastplates, gold bars, all glowing in the candlelight. I never knew that gold had so many colours. He shut the door and bent down to me and whispered, 'When you are Queen, this will be yours. This will be our secret – just you and me – and you mustn't tell.' And then he put his hand (*silence*) on my shoulder. I never did tell anyone. (*she smiles*) Until now. (NURSE *says nothing*) I went looking for that room again, once. The night Father came home and the crowds cheered and he pushed me away to kiss Cordelia. I couldn't find it. I must have taken a wrong turning and I came into this corridor, with a torch shining at the end of it, and set into the floor . . .

NURSE Yes.

GONERIL Bars. As I walked past, these hands came out from them, clawing and scratching. Nanny. There were people in there. Shut in. I don't know how many. By him. He's the king. He must know they're there.

(GONERIL *moves back to the window.*)

NURSE He knows.

GONERIL I can't put it all together. This is our secret. Just you and me. And the cheering crowds and those people. Can you? (*the* NURSE *can't speak*) And now this.

NURSE What?

GONERIL This. (*holds out ledger*) He came in last night and pushed it at me. 'Your mother used to do this so you can now.' It's the accounts. Columns and columns of figures.

NURSE I know.

(*Silence.*)

GONERIL I have to get out of this place soon.

NURSE You will.

GONERIL (*At window*) There he is now. Going out riding. Something must have annoyed him, to go out riding in this weather. How small he looks from up here. A wooden man on a wooden horse.

(NURSE *exits. Curtsies to* GONERIL. *Lights down centre stage. Lights up on* FOOL.)

Scene 11

Fool introduces marriage

FOOL Lear returns triumphant from yet another sporting tournament . . . Grouse-shooting! Lear's countrymen grow thin, his coffers fat. So. Plenty of grouse about. And remember that at seventy-five he is still the most agile horseman and (*mimes flying an arrow*) archer. Nanny! If a trap's caught three rats, can the one in the middle survive? (NURSE *looks coldly at* FOOL) No, because it's dead–centre! The river is rising again. But how to stop the tide of unrest? What did one king say to another when the flood came in? I can't stop it, can ute? Three daughters alone can't plug a dyke. We need a finger. Three fingers! (*holds up three fingers*)

FOOL (LEAR) Not my little Cordelia.

FOOL Well, two then. (*holds up two fingers*) Two fingers to plug the dyke! One called Albany, one called Cornwall.

(*Lights down on* FOOL. *Up on centre stage.*)

Scene 12

Sisters discuss getting married

(GONERIL *and* REGAN *on stage.* GONERIL *is reading ledger.*)

REGAN Are you getting changed?

GONERIL No.

REGAN Aren't you coming down?

GONERIL No.

REGAN Why not?

GONERIL I'm too busy.

REGAN You have to come. It's our celebration.

GONERIL I must finish this.

REGAN Come down with me.

GONERIL No.

(*Silence.*)

REGAN Goneril.

GONERIL What?

REGAN This wedding. (*there is silence*) What do you feel about it?

GONERIL Nothing.

REGAN I don't understand.

GONERIL I feel nothing about it.

REGAN Do you want this marriage?

GONERIL Wanting doesn't come into it.

REGAN When I lie in bed at night, I can feel my heart beating so fast, it's like I'm living at twice the pace. I'm running out of life. How can you feel nothing about it?

GONERIL It's our job. It's what we're here for. To marry and breed.

REGAN Like dogs?

GONERIL Like dogs. Valuable merchandise. I can show you the figures here if you like.

REGAN I'm scared.

GONERIL It's what we're here for.

REGAN I'm going to have a baby. Seven months' time. Nurse says.

GONERIL How could you be so stupid?

REGAN Oh Goneril? I'm not stupid, but I'm not stone, not dead. You, you've always been the first, the cleverest, the best, and Cordelia, she's the, the pretty, the lovable, Lear's darling. Then there's me, in the middle, neither fish nor fowl, do you see? I've had nothing that's, that's for me, just for me. I've been number two, between one and three, but nothing. So I've taken everything, everything that I can feel or touch or smell or do or be, everything to try and find something, to find me, do you see?

GONERIL Come here, Regan. You see these ledgers? What do they say to you?

REGAN Listen to me?

GONERIL You see these figures! (REGAN *turns away, goes to mirror.* GONERIL *pulls her back to trunk. Forces her to look at ledger*)

REGAN Let go of my arm. (*struggling*)

GONERIL They say Regan, Second Daughter of Lear, is worth this much, and these figures here . . . (REGAN *tries to look away*) Look at them? These figures say My Lord Duke of Cornwall, owns this much. These figures say Regan will marry Cornwall and then Cornwall will own more and Lear will get a grandson, a legitimate heir and they will all be contented men. However, Regan, Second Daughter of Lear, with bastard child, is worth *this* much! (GONERIL *rips out page from ledger, crumbles it and throws it on floor.* REGAN *pulls away to mirror, staring hard into it*) Get rid of it!

REGAN (*looking in mirror*) I can't see your features. Your expression in the mirror. Your face is blank.

GONERIL You're imagining things.

REGAN It's him. You've got his face.

(GONERIL *exits. Lighting change.* REGAN *pacing floor.* NURSE *enters carrying cup and cloth.*)

REGAN Will it take long?

NURSE No, I don't think so. It will hurt.

(REGAN *nods. It is hurting already.*)

REGAN What was it?

NURSE Rue and pennyroyal. (*there is pain.* REGAN *groans aloud*) You mustn't scream. Bite on this.

(NURSE *hands* REGAN *cloth. There is pain.* NURSE *goes to* REGAN *and holds her.*)

REGAN I'm going to die. You've poisoned me.

NURSE You're not going to die yet.

REGAN (*in pain*) Please let it be over. (*pain*) Please.

(NURSE *puts rag in* REGAN's *mouth.* REGAN *groans.* NURSE *stands behind* REGAN. *Holds her.*)

NURSE Breathe. Breathe. You have to push.

REGAN Oh, Jesus.

NURSE You have to.

REGAN I'm frightened.

NURSE Push. Push.

(*There is a pause.*)

REGAN What do I look like?

NURSE You look as if you're laughing.

(*There is no more pushing.* REGAN *collapses to floor.* NURSE *looks down.*)

It would have been a boy.

REGAN I'll get out of here soon.

NURSE You will.

(*Lights down. Lights up on* FOOL.)

Scene 13

The weddings

FOOL Two bridegrooms waiting downstairs. Two brides waiting to be swept off their feet.

(FOOL *walks to window, humming the Wedding March.* GONERIL *and* REGAN *kneeling at altar.* FOOL *stands on window seat.* NURSE *and* CORDELIA *watch.*)

FOOL Who gives this woman?

(*When answering questions* REGAN, CORDELIA, GONERIL *and* NURSE *all speak together and take different poses.*)

CORDELIA So beautiful.
GONERIL/REGAN I promise, I do, I will.
NANNY Lear triumphant.
} (*spoken happily with big smiles*)

FOOL To love, honour and obey.
NANNY That is my place. That is my place.
GONERIL/REGAN I promise, I do, I will.
CORDELIA Spin for Daddy.
} (*spoken happily with big smiles*)

FOOL Just cause or impediment?
NANNY And you mustn't tell. And you mustn't tell.
GONERIL/REGAN I promise, I do, I will.
CORDELIA Just the two of us.
} (*spoken as above*)

FOOL Who gives this woman? (*menacing*)

NANNY Lear triumphant. (*loud*)

CORDELIA So beautiful. (*whispered*)

GONERIL/REGAN I swear to. (*whispered*)

FOOL Love, honour and obey?

NANNY That is my place, that is my place. (*whispered*)

GONERIL/REGAN I promise. I do, I will. (*whispered*)

CORDELIA Spin for Daddy. (*loud*)

FOOL Just cause or impediment?

NANNY And you mustn't tell. (*loud*)

CORDELIA Just the two of us. (*whispered*)

GONERIL/REGAN Triumphant. (*whispered*)

FOOL Kiss the bride. (*happily*)

CORDELIA She means the world to him.
NANNY She brings a large dowry.
GONERIL/REGAN To love and cherish.
} (*spoken loud and happy*)

FOOL Catch the flowers.
CORDELIA Daddy's girl.
NANNY Cordelia the favourite.
GONERIL/REGAN To love and cherish.
} (*spoken loud and happy*)

FOOL Cut the cake.
CORDELIA Together again.
NANNY A knife for slicing.
GONERIL/REGAN To love and cherish.
} (*spoken loud and happy*)

GONERIL/REGAN To love and cherish.
FOOL Kiss the bride. (*menacing*)
NANNY She brings a large dowry. (*loud*)
CORDELIA She means the world to him.
    (*whispered*)
GONERIL/REGAN To love and cherish. (*whispered*)
FOOL Catch the flowers.
CORDELIA Daddy's girl. (*loud*)
NANNY Cordelia the favourite. (*whispered*)
GONERIL/REGAN To love and cherish. (*whispered*)
FOOL Cut the cake.
CORDELIA Together again.
NANNY A knife for slicing. (*loud*)
GONERIL/REGAN Cherish.

(GONERIL *goes for* LEAR's [FOOL's] *eyes with knife. Action freezes. All turn to audience, begin to walk down stage. Chattering, repeating sections of above plus.*)

GONERIL Thank you for coming. Yes, he is
    handsome, isn't he?
NANNY With his light shining all around her, like
    a net.
CORDELIA As they came out of the church the
    people cheered and cried so I did as well.
FOOL One day this will all be yours.
    (*pushing way to front*) And the King said, 'I have
    decided I cannot part with you both yet. Live
    here a while longer.'

(*Silence. Then all begin to speak again.* GONERIL
holding knife moves upstage. GONERIL *drops
knife.*)

REGAN Goneril!

(*Chatter starts again.* GONERIL *slowly moves to
window. In the chatter we hear the name
'*GONERIL*' emerging until it turns into a collective
cry.*)

ALL Goneril!
GONERIL (*on window seat, as though to throw
    herself out*) Nanny! I can't see! The lace is
    scoring into my eyes. I can't see anything.
    Nanny! Nanny!

(NANNY *catches* GONERIL. FOOL *runs away.
Lights out.* GONERIL *and* REGAN *move off-centre.*
NANNY *returns to her spot.* FOOL *walks from its
spot across stage to* NANNY.)

Scene 14

The Nurse reveals all

(FOOL *scuttles across to* NURSE's *spot. Has letter
behind its back.*)

FOOL Knock, knock.
NURSE Who's there?
FOOL Letters.
NURSE Letters who?
FOOL Let us in, I've got a note for you.

(*Hands letter to* NURSE. *Hurries back to* FOOL's
spot.)

NURSE (*opening letter, finds money inside*) My
services are no longer required. Who does he
think he is? Who is he to throw me aside when
he no longer wants me to do the job he chose for
me in the first place! Oh no, I didn't choose it; I
was poor. Just like the Queen when she didn't
make the right sort of boy-child for him –
finished. Well, she died, didn't she? (*mimics*)
Yes, but . . . Yes but what? Why did she die?
How? You don't know. I do. I was there. And
now me. How many more? How many more of
us will he throw away when we no longer suit?
Goneril? Regan? Cordelia even? (*mimics*) Oh-no-
not-Cordelia-she'll-always-fit. Will she though? I
could have dropped her on the castle steps and
her head would have cracked open like an egg. I
could have taught them bad things. Have I? I've
nearly bitten my tongue in two. And sometimes
I haven't bothered. Well, they've learnt. From-
me-with-me-without-me. All but her. Cordelia.
Well, we'll see. Money he gives me. Pieces of
silver. What do I want with his gold? I had a
baby once. Did you know? I had to give my baby
away so that I had milk for his. Milk. When his
Queen died I looked at my shrunken breasts in
the bit of mirror I had and then I put it in the
coffin. What to do? Eat farewell cake in the
parlour? Stab it to crumbs! Leave him a note,
'Cordelia's mine – I swapped her at birth for
your son. Love Nanny.' That would rock his
little world. But is it true? You'll never know. I
do. Walk down the stairs, out of the castle,
through the city, out of the city, beyond into the
countryside, back to where I belong, people I
know. Lear! There are rats gnawing at your
throne and I'll not be in it but I'll watch the
spectacle from afar, smiling, knowing it is what
I've always wanted to happen.

(NURSE *gathers her belongings. Takes off apron.
Walks to centre stage.* CORDELIA *is looking
through window.*)

CORDELIA They've gone. I saw Goneril stop on
the skyline and I thought for a moment they
were turning and coming back. But they didn't.
(*walks round room*) She's left her paints behind. I
suppose I can give her them when they visit.

She can get some more. Just us now, Nanny. You and me, and the Fool. You're very quiet.

NURSE I'm leaving.

CORDELIA Leaving?

NURSE They've gone . . . you're to be married soon – when he's decided on your husband. I'm not needed anymore. He says.

(NURSE *goes to exit.*)

CORDELIA Nanny! (NANNY *turns*) You never liked me, did you? (NURSE *doesn't answer*) No. No-one does but him. (NURSE *turns to go*) Nanny, listen. I've got two voices. Ever since going downstairs and Daddy lifting me onto the table, I've talked like a child, used the words of a child. No-one likes it but him. But I do have another voice. In my head I have words I never say to anyone – never have said to anyone. Till now. I can do it, you see. (*goes up to* NANNY) Nanny, don't go. I could go and see him, he listens to me, I'm his little girl . . . (*trails off. Realizes the difficulty. Starts again*) I could speak to him as a woman, as one adult to another, he'd listen, he'd . . . (*stops. Knows*)

NANNY It doesn't matter, Cordelia. (*turns. Whispers something to* CORDELIA. NURSE *exits, walks to* FOOL) Money he gives me! Pieces of silver? What do I want with his gold? Here, Fool. Grovel for it, Fool, for that I shall never do!

(NANNY *tempts* FOOL *with money. Throws it up in the air and hits the* FOOL *around the face with fist, flattening* FOOL *to ground.* NANNY *exits through audience. Banging doors.* FOOL *gets up.*)

CORDELIA Fool!

(FOOL *gathers money. Goes to* CORDELIA *who is sitting at window seat, crying.* FOOL *tosses coin in air. Decides. Sits next to* CORDELIA *and starts to cry, aping it badly. A caricature of* CORDELIA. CORDELIA *looks at* FOOL *and stops crying.*)

(FOOL *moves quickly to front stage. Lights up on* FOOL.)

FOOL That very night the Fool went downstairs, stood on the table and began its turn.
How many kisses does it take to keep a king happy?
103.
One to kiss his tears away.
One to kiss his fevered brow.
One to kiss him deep in passion and 100 to kiss his arse!
(*mimes being hit in face*)
And the King doesn't laugh.
Who's the biggest stinker in the world?

King Pong!
(*laughs again and mimes being hit in face*)
And the King doesn't laugh.
A man goes up to a woman in the street. 'How much?' he says. She is outraged. 'What do you think I am?' and the man says, 'We know what you are, love, we're just discussing the price'. And the King laughs – and he laughs. He laughs as though he would burst. Taking the Fool's ear he twists it to open its mouth. He places a coin on the edge of its tongue and the Fool. (*mimes swallowing coin, gulps*) Three, two, one and the Fool – standing on the table looking after number one. A Father waiting outside. Two mothers, one dead or gone missing, the other leaving. Three daughters, paying the price.

(*Lights up centre stage.* GONERIL, REGAN, CORDELIA *stand in line,* GONERIL *in middle.*)

GONERIL Looking up, I can't see the sky. There's too much red. Red in my eyes. Red on my hands. They touched and felt but I cannot recognize them. My father's daughter, and still he gives me stop and start. Controlling by my hatred, the order of my life. Lear's daughter. Blood in my eyes and lost to heaven.

REGAN I used to carve with my knife, create beauty from distortion, soft curves from the knottiest, most gnarled woods. When life was at its dullest, most suffocating, I would be full of energy, curiosity. And then 'Get rid of it', she said, 'Get rid of it', and that was all. The veil was pulled away from my eyes and I could see what he had done to her, had done to me. And so I shall set my face to a new game which will not be beautiful, but there'll be a passion still and I'll be there with it till the end, my end, carved out at her hands – and I would not have it any other way.

CORDELIA Words are like stones, heavy and solid and every one different. I hold two in my hands, testing their weight. 'Yes', to please, 'no', to please myself, 'yes', I shall and 'no', I will not. 'Yes' for you and 'no' for me. I love words. I like their roughness and their smoothness, and when I'm silent I'm trying to get them right. I shall be silent now, weighing these words, and when I choose to speak, I shall choose the right one.

(*Lights on* FOOL *on its spot. Bows to audience.*)

FOOL An ending. A beginning. (*throws crown into circle, the sisters all reach up and catch it. Freeze.*) Time's up.

(*Holds out hand for money.*)

(*Blackout.*)

Desdemona: A Play About a Handkerchief

Paula Vogel

Introduction

Paula Vogel, an American playwright, was born in 1951 and educated at Bryn Mawr College, Catholic University, and Cornell University. Having worked at a range of jobs (from secretary to packer for a moving company to factory worker), Vogel lectured at Cornell on women's studies and theatre before becoming artistic director of Theater with Teeth in New York. Author of numerous plays, including *Swan Song of Sir Henry* (1974), *The Oldest Profession* (1981), *And Baby Makes Seven* (1986), *The Baltimore Waltz* (1992), and *Hot 'n' Throbbing* (1992), Vogel '[l]ike Brecht, writes from a deeply rooted political sense' (Savran 1996: xi). Since 1985 she has been an associate professor and director of the Graduate Playwriting Program at Brown University. Winner of numerous fellowships and awards, including the Pulitzer Prize in 1998 for *How I Learned To Drive* (a response to Vladimir Nabokov's novel *Lolita*), Vogel articulates a particular brand of feminism described by David Savran as 'the result of contradictions that molded her when she was growing up' (1998: 17). From a mixed religious background – her father was a New York Jew (who left the family when Vogel was eleven), her mother a New Orleans Catholic – and a working-class family, as well as a lesbian who came out when she was seventeen, Vogel eventually gravitated toward both an academic and a theatrical career.

Vogel's work is startling for how it inverts audience expectations and challenges conventional notions of theatricality, especially with regard to simplistic readings of hot-button topics such as AIDS, domestic violence, the feminization of poverty, the non-traditional family, pornography, the sex trade, and child molestation. As Vogel states, 'I worry that there is no longer a place for audiences to come to a civic space – the theatre – to confront the disturbing questions of our time. I remain scared of the dark – scared of our darkness – and I seek a communal light in the darkness of our theatres' (*The Baltimore Waltz*: 231). Vogel's lesbianism, like her gender politics, is devoted, as Savran writes, 'to exposing not just how women are entrapped and oppressed, but to the possibilities that figures like Desdemona or the oldest professionals have to contest, subvert and redefine the roles they have been assigned' (xi). 'I hate categorization,' Vogel affirms. 'At the same time, I think we have to exhaust categorization in order to break through it' (Clay). Despite this position, Vogel avers, 'I don't hate being "a lesbian woman playwright." I think there's no choice. And I'm aware that the thing has kept me out of a lot of theater companies, or has slowed down the progress of the career (and gender and race do that)' (Clay). Moreover, Vogel argues that 'it would be irresponsible of me, as a teacher and mentor to young men and women regardless of their sexuality, not to be out. It would be reprehensible of me to have a brother who died of AIDS but suffered far more from the homophobia that he experienced and not to be out' (Clay). Vogel complicates this position further by stating that 'I do not write lesbian plays. I will not speak for all women, and I will not speak for all lesbians' (Coen: 27).

Vogel's work has been characterized by crosstalk with other literary figures. *Desdemona*, a revisionist account of Shakespeare's *Othello*, in which Desdemona, Emilia, and Bianca unfold their own unwritten counterplot in the back room of the palace while *Othello*'s action is occurring off stage, 'suggests that Shakespeare's women are not quite the innocent victims of masculine desires they appear to be but active makers – and unmakers – of each others' destinies' (Savran 1996: x). Moreover, *Desdemona* places Shakespeare at the margins of its theatrical context, focusing instead on the society of women, which is at best a minor

Plate 4 Photo: © 1993 Gerry Goldstein. Production of *Desdemona* with (left to right) J. Smith-Cameron, Fran Brill, Cherry Jones

element in the Shakespearean original. Given its first staged reading in October 1987 at Cornell University with Vogel herself directing, the play has been restaged by, among others, the Bay Street Theater Festival in Sag Harbor, New York, and in November 1993 at the Circle Repertory Theater in New York City. The play, which has been called 'a rollicking, bawdy, postmodern, feminist reading of Shakespeare's *Othello* with no male characters' (Peterson and Bennett: 341), has also received predictable criticism for being a 'feminist tract' (Turvin).

Vogel calls the play 'a tribute (i.e., "rip-off") to the infamous play, *Shakespeare the Sadist* by Wolfgang Bauer' (*The Baltimore Waltz*: 176). Bauer, an Austrian dramatist, satirizes cultural pretensions associated with Shakespeare by linking Shakespeare's name with what, in the play, turns out to be a Swedish porno film. The play, which is not an adaptation of any recognizable

theatrical work by Shakespeare, stages the porno film's extreme acts of violence against women, which are enacted by Shakespeare in the notorious 'takes' (or scenes) 24 through 40. These 'takes' swing from the slapstick of the actors who are told by the stage directions to speak 'in imitation Swedish' (Bauer: 18) to Shakespeare's narcissistic self-interest as he reads into a megaphone from his own sonnets before torturing and degrading Sonia in a series of brutal scenes culminating in her decapitation.

Vogel's play imitates Bauer's structurally – it too is set as a series of cinematic takes. But Vogel departs from Bauer in her use of an entirely female cast (as opposed to Bauer's use of a predominantly male cast) and in her interrogation of the possibilities that emerge when an adaptation addresses the large silences in Shakespeare with regard to women's society. As Tish Dace points out, *Desdemona* 'provides us with everything which Shakespeare denies us: full portraits of the three women . . . high spirits which do not willingly suffer their men's foolishness, no easy acquiescence to being victimized, even a lusty, frank sexuality' (253), which includes a deliberately provocative homerotic interlude between Desdemona and Bianca. The play stages the difficulties of female solidarity: Emilia torn between loyalty to her mistress and a husband she barely tolerates; Desdemona, standing in for Bianca the hooker on Tuesday nights at a bawdy-house, torn between her own sensuality and her need for female companionship; and Bianca, split between her desire for a conventional family life and the freedom her status in the sex trade gives her.

Several adaptive strategies in *Desdemona* are worth mentioning. First is Vogel's rewrite of Shakespearean characterization, with a worldly Desdemona and a naive Emilia creating a very different stage dynamic from that in *Othello*. Second, Vogel provocatively recasts Emilia as stage-Irish and Bianca as stage-cockney, the servants being more clearly depicted in terms of class and nation than they are in Shakespeare, where Emilia is not classed in terms of speech at all. The play's notable omission of race as a further mode of adapting *Othello* may represent an unfortunate simplification on the part of Vogel, especially in the context of a play such as Djanet Sears's *Harlem Duet*, another *Othello* adaptation, in which race is the central issue. Vogel's decision to focus on class and female sexuality rather than on race, however, do not prohibit a directorial practice that confronts this issue head on, either through casting choices or through the rescripting of key passages. And her adaptation, like any adaptation, invites questions about the shifting paradigms of assumptions about performance. Does, for instance, Emilia's stage-Irishness necessarily prohibit her from being played by a black actor?

Dace argues that Vogel 'shows us we must blame the social system, implicitly responsible for denying the women sisterhood in a common cause, forcing them instead to depend on destructive men who exercise over them the power of life and death' (253). But the play avoids any reductive politics of blame, staging instead the difficulties of achieving autonomy or genuine solidarity (whether female–female, or female–male). Both Shakespeare and Vogel bring Desdemona to the same end. But with Vogel the sentimentality of Othello's murderous rage as an expression of a quintessentially male passion is displaced by a sensibility that frankly acknowledges the everyday pleasures and horrors of domestic life. That the pleasures and horrors figured in *Desdemona* are not easily reduced to a function of either sororal or patriarchal culture makes the play a sophisticated treatment of domestic life and of adaptive practices that too often reduce the complexities of Shakespeare to the simple solution of a happy ending, as in Nahum Tate's infamous rewrite of *King Lear*.

Like all the adaptations included in this anthology, Vogel's text is very much of its period and thus symptomatic of its cultural moment. Like Murray Carlin's *Not Now, Sweet Desdemona* (1968), which makes Desdemona a reactive partner and is in many ways a pre-feminist text, Vogel's *Desdemona*, with its depiction of pre-AIDS, unprotected libertarian sexuality in scene 11, signals a different historical juncture, a different ideological underpinning. Adaptation, in this light, is one of the ways in which historical (not to mention ideological) difference is represented and, ultimately, negotiated.

Select bibliography

Entries marked * are particularly accessible.

Bauer, W. (1977) *Shakespeare the Sadist*, M. and R. Esslin (trans.), London: Eyre Methuen.
Carlin, M. (1969) *Not Now, Sweet Desdemona: A Duologue for Black and White Within the Realm of Shakespeare's Othello*, Nairobi: Oxford University Press.
Clay, C. (downloaded: 15 July 1998) 'Drive, She Said: Paula Vogel Steers her Pulitzer Winner to Trinity Rep,' Phoenix Theater. The Phoenix Media/Communications Group (http://www.providence phoenix.com/archive/theater/98/05/14/VOGEL.html).
*Coen, S. (1993) 'Paula Vogel,' *American Theatre* 10: 26–27.
Dace, T. (1994) 'Vogel, Paula (Anne),' *Contemporary Women Dramatists*, K. A. Berney (ed.), London: St James Press: 250–254.
*Peterson, J. T., and Bennett, S. (eds) (1997) 'Paula Vogel,' in *Women Playwrights of Diversity: A Bio-Bibliographical Sourcebook*, Westport, Connecticut: Greenwood Press: 340–344.
Savran, D. (1996) 'Loose Screws,' in P. Vogel, *The Baltimore Waltz and Other Plays*, New York: Theatre Communications Group: ix–xv.
*— (1998) 'Driving Ms. Vogel: An Interview by David Savran,' *American Theatre* 15: 16–19, 96.
Sova, K. (1997) 'Time to Laugh: Interview with Paula Vogel,' *American Theatre* 14: 24.
Turvin, M. S. P. (downloaded: 21 July 1998) 'Desdemona and Emilia Are Dead,' In Mixed Company Playwright's Theatre, Phoenix (http://www.primenet.com/~mychele/aaro/desdemona.html).
Vogel, P. (1996) *The Baltimore Waltz and Other Plays*, New York: Theatre Communications Group.
Witchel, A. (1999) 'After the Prize Is the Pressure: Now What?' New York *Times* (7 February): 5–6.

Desdemona: A Play About a Handkerchief

Paula Vogel

Note to directors

Desdemona was written in thirty cinematic 'takes.' The director is encouraged to create different pictures to simulate the process of filming: Change invisible camera angles, do jump cuts and repetitions, etc. There should be no blackouts between scenes. Desdemona was written as a tribute (i.e., 'rip-off') to the infamous play, Shakespeare the Sadist by Wolfgang Bauer.

Characters

DESDEMONA, Upperclass. Very

EMILIA, Broad Irish brogue

BIANCA, Stage-cockney

Place

A back room of the palace on Cyprus.

Time

Ages ago.
The prologue takes place one week before Desdemona's last day on Cyprus.

Prologue

A spotlight in the dark, pinpointing a white handkerchief lying on the ground. A second spotlight comes up on EMILIA, *who sees the handkerchief. She pauses, and then cautiously looks about to see if she is observed. Then, quickly,* EMILIA *goes to the handkerchief, picks it up, stuffs the linen in her ample bodice and exits. Blackout.*

1

A mean, sparsely furnished back room with rough, whitewashed walls. Upstage left there is a small, heavy, wooden back entrance. Another door, stage right, leads to the main rooms of the palace. There are a few benches lining the walls, littered with tools, baskets, leather bits, dirty laundry, etc. The walls bear dark wooden racks that neatly display farm and work equipment made of rough woods, leathers and chain.

In the center of the room, there is a crude work table with short benches. As the play begins, Desdemona *is scattering items and clothing in the air, barely controlling a mounting hysteria.* Emilia, *dark, plump and plain, with a thick Irish brogue, watches, amused and disgusted at the mess her lady is making.*

DESDEMONA Are you sure you didn't see it? The last time I remember holding it in my hand was last week in the arbor – you're sure you didn't see it?

EMILIA Aye –

DESDEMONA It looks like –

EMILIA Like anybody's handkerchief, savin' it has those dainty little strawberries on it. I never could be after embroiderin' a piece of linen with fancy work to wipe up the nose –

DESDEMONA It's got to be here somewhere –

EMILIA After you blow your nose in it, an' it's all heavy and wet, who's going to open the damn thing and look at the pretty stitches?

DESDEMONA Emilia – are you sure it didn't get 'mixed up' somehow with your . . . your things?

EMILIA And why should I be needin' your handkerchief when I'm wearing a plain, soft shift which works just as well? And failing that, the good Lord gave me sleeves . . .

DESDEMONA It's got to be here!
    (*Returns to her rampage of the room*) Oh – skunk water!
    (*A man's undergarment is tossed into the air behind* DESDEMONA's *shoulder*) Dog piddle!!

EMILIA I'm after telling you m'lady –

DESDEMONA Nonsense! It's got to be here!

(*There is a crash of overturned chain.* DESDEMONA's *shifts are thrown into the air*) Goddamn horse urine!!!

EMILIA It was dear, once upon a time, when m'lady was toddling about the palace, and all of us servants would be follerin' after, stooping to pick up all the pretty toys you'd be scatterin' –

DESDEMONA Emilia, please! I cannot bear a sermon.

EMILIA There was the day the Senator, your father, gave you your first strand of pearls from the Indies – you were all of five – and your hand just plucked it from your neck. How you laughed to see us – Teresa, Maria and me – scrabbling on all fours like dogs after truffles, scooping up the rollin' pearls – (*There is a ripping noise*)

DESDEMONA Oh, shit.

(*Two halves of a sheet are pitched into the air.*)

EMILIA But you're a married lady now; and when m'lord Othello gives you a thing, and tells you to be mindin' it, it's no longer dear to drop it willy-nilly and expect me to be findin' it –

DESDEMONA Oh, piss and vinegar!! Where is the crappy little snot rag!
(*She turns and sees Emilia sitting*) You're not even helping! You're not looking!!

EMILIA Madam can be sure I've overturned the whole lot, two or three times . . . It's a sight easier hunting for it when the place is tidy; when all is topsy-turvy, you can't tell a mouse dropping from a cow pie!
(DESDEMONA *returns to the hunt;* EMILIA *picks up the torn sheet*) Now see, this sheet here was washed this morning. Your husband, as you know, is fussy about his sheets; and while it was no problem to have them fresh each night in Venice – I could open the window and dunk them in the canal – here on Cyprus it takes two drooling orderlies to march six times down to the cistern and back again.
(*Regards the sheet carefully*) It's beyond repair. And now that your husband commands fresh sheets, my Iago has got it in his head to be the lord as well; he's got to have fresh sheets each night for his unwashed feet.

DESDEMONA Emilia, please – I may puke.

(DESDEMONA, *in frustration, stamps on the clothes she's strewn from the basket.*)

DESDEMONA It's got to be here, it's got to be here, it's got to be here – Emilia – Help me find it!

EMILIA You're wasting your time, m'lady. I know it's not here.

DESDEMONA (*Straightening herself*) Right. And you knew this morning that my husband wasn't mad at me. Just a passing whim, you said.

EMILIA Ah, Miss Desdemona . . . not even a midwife can foretell the perfidiosity of men.

DESDEMONA Give me strength. Perfidy.

EMILIA That, too.

DESDEMONA It can't have walked off on two feet!

EMILIA Mayhap m'lady dropped it.

DESDEMONA Oh, you're hopeless. No help at all. I'll find it by myself. Go back to your washing and put your hands to use.

EMILIA Yes, m'lady.

2

EMILIA *and* DESDEMONA. EMILIA *scrubs sheets.*

DESDEMONA Will it come out?

EMILIA I've scrubbed many a sheet, but this is the worst in my career . . . It's all that Bianca's fault. I paid her well for the blood, too. 'And be sure,' I says, 'it's an old hen – one on its last gasp. Young chick blood's no good for bridal sheets, it's the devil to come out.' 'Madam's sheets,' I says, 'are the finest to be had in Venice, and we don't want them ruined and rotted from the stain.' And Bianca swore, 'I've an old hen on crutches that will wash out clear as a maidenhead or a baby's dropping.'
Ah, but that chick wasn't a week old. And what with it bakin' in the sun for a month now – but if anyone can, Mealy will scrub it virgin white again.

DESDEMONA Oh, hush about it. I can't stand to think on it . . . barbaric custom. And my best sheets. Nobody displays bridal sheets on Cyprus.

EMILIA There aren't any virgins to be had on Cyprus.

DESDEMONA Half the garrison came to see those sheets flapping in the breeze.

EMILIA Why did the other half come?

DESDEMONA To pay their last respects to the chicken!

(*They laugh.*)

3

We hear EMILIA, *in a good humor, humming 'When Irish Eyes Are Smiling.' Another clatter of heavy metal things being tossed onto the floor.*

DESDEMONA JESUS! WHAT IS THIS?!
EMILIA (*In disbelief*) You didn't find it!

(DESDEMONA *crosses to* EMILIA, *holding a long, crooked bit of iron with a wicked point.*)

DESDEMONA No – this!!

EMILIA 'Tis a hoof-pick.

DESDEMONA A hoof-pick? What is it used for?

EMILIA After all your years of trotting m'lady's bum over field and farrow, and you've never laid your eyes on the like? When your mount picks up a stone in its foot, and it's deep, you take the pick and hold on tight to the hoof, and then you dig it in and down to the quick and pry it out –

DESDEMONA You dig *this* in? Good lord –

EMILIA Aye, takes a goodly amount of sweat and grease. It's work for a proper man, it is.

(DESDEMONA, *absorbed in fondling the hoof-pick, stretches out on the table.*)

DESDEMONA Oh me, oh my – if I could find a man with just such a hoof pick – he could pluck out my stone – eh, Emilia?
(*They laugh.*)
   Emilia, does your husband Iago have a hoof-pick to match?

(EMILIA *turns and looks, then snorts.*)

EMILIA What, Iago?

(DESDEMONA *puts her hand on the base and covers it.*)

DESDEMONA Well, then – this much?

EMILIA Please, mum! It's a matter o' faith between man and wife t –

DESDEMONA Ahh – not that much, eh?
   (*Covers more of the pick*) Like this?

EMILIA Miss Desdemona!

DESDEMONA Come now, Emilia, it's just us –

EMILIA Some things are private!!

DESDEMONA It's only fair – I'm sure you know every detail about my lord –

EMILIA (*Shrugging*) When the Master Piddles, a Servant holds the Pot –

DESDEMONA (*Persisting*) This much hoof?

EMILIA Not near as much as that!

DESDEMONA This much?

   (*Pause.*)

EMILIA (*Sour*) Nay.

DESDEMONA Good God, Emilia, I'm running out of –

EMILIA The wee-est pup of th' litter comes a'bornin' in the world with as much.
   (DESDEMONA *laughs.*)
   There. Is m'lady satisfied?

DESDEMONA Your secret's safe with me.

4

EMILIA, *scrubbing.* DESDEMONA *lies on her back on the table, feet propped up, absentmindedly fondling the pick, and staring into space.*

5

We hear the sound of EMILIA, *puffing and blowing. Lights up on* DESDEMONA *getting a pedicure.*

DESDEMONA Where is she? It's getting late. He'll be back soon, and clamoring for me. He's been in a rotten mood lately . . . Headaches, handkerchiefs, accusations – and of all people to accuse – Michael Cassio!

EMILIA The only one you haven't had –

DESDEMONA And I don't want him, either. A prissy Florentine, that one is. Leave it to a cuckold to be jealous of a eunuch –

EMILIA (*Crowing*) Bianca would die!

DESDEMONA Then we won't tell her what I said, will we?
   (EMILIA *becomes quiet.*)
   What Bianca does in her spare time is her business.

(EMILIA's *face clearly indicates that what* BIANCA *does in her spare time is* EMILIA's *business, too.* DESDEMONA *watches* EMILIA *closely.*)

DESDEMONA You don't much like Bianca, do you, Mealy?
   (*No response.* EMILIA *blows on* DESDEMONA's *toes*)
   Come on, now, tell me frankly – why don't you like her?

EMILIA It's not for me to say . . .

DESDEMONA Emilia!

EMILIA It's just that – no disrespect intented, m'lady – but you shouldn't go a'rubbin' elbows with one o' her class . . . Lie down with hussies, get up with crabs . . .

DESDEMONA Her sheets are clean.
   (*Pause.*)
   You've been simmering over Bianca for some time, Mealy, haven't you?

EMILIA (*Rancorously*) I don't much like to see m'lady, in whose em-ploy I am, traipsing about in flopdens, doin' favors for common sloppots – Bianca! Ha! She's so loose, so low, that she's got to ad-ver-tise Wednesday Night Specials, half price for anything in uniform!

DESDEMONA Well, purge it out of your blood; Bianca will soon be here –

EMILIA Here! Why here? What if someone sees

her sneaking up to the back door? What will the women in town say? A tart on a house call! How can I keep my head up hanging out the wash and feedin' the pigs when her sort comes sniffin' around –

DESDEMONA She's coming to pay me for last Tuesday's customers who paid on credit. And to arrange for next Tuesday –

EMILIA (*Horrified*) Not again!. Once was enough – you're not going there again! I thought to myself, she's a young unbridled colt, is Miss Desdemona – let her cool down her blood – but to make it a custom! I couldn't let you go back again – risking disease and putting us all in danger –

DESDEMONA Oh, tush, Mealy –

EMILIA You listen to me, Miss Desdemona: Othello will sooner or later find out that you're laying for Bianca, and his black skin is goin' to blister off with rage!! Holy Jesus Lord, why tempt a Venetian male by waving red capes? My Iago would beat me for lookin' at the wrong end of an ass!

  (*VERY WORKED UP*) Your husband will find out and when he does! When he does!! (*Makes the noise and gesture of throat cutting*) And then! And then!! AIAIaiaiaiahhh!! My lady!! What's to become of me! Your fateful handmaid! Where will I find another position in this pisshole harbor!

DESDEMONA Stop it, Mealy! Don't be . . . silly, nothing will happen to me. I'm the sort that will die in bed.

EMILIA (*Beseechingly*) You won't leave your poor Mealy stranded?

DESDEMONA You'll always have a position in this household . . . Of some sort. (*Mealy's face turns to stone*)

  Oh, come now, Mealy, haven't I just promoted you?

EMILIA Oh, m'lady, I haven't forgot; not only your scullery maid, but now your laundress as well! I am quite sensible of the honor and the increase in pay – of two pence a week . . .

  (*Suddenly turns bright and cheery*) And whiles we are on the subject –

DESDEMONA Oh, Christ, here it comes.

EMILIA But m'lady, last time an opening came up, you promised to speak to your husband about it in Venice. I suppose poor old Iago just slipped your mind –

DESDEMONA Look, I did forget. Anyway, I recommended Cassio for my husband's lieutenant. An unfortunate choice. But that subject is closed.

EMILIA Yes, mum.

  (EMILIA *starts to return to her laundry. There is a knock at the door, and* DESDEMONA *brightens.*)

DESDEMONA There she is! Emilia, let Bianca in – No, no wait – (*To Mealy's annoyance,* DESDEMONA *arranges herself in a casual tableau.*)

  (*The knock repeats.* DESDEMONA *signals* EMILIA *to go answer the door.* EMILIA *exits through the door to the palace, and then quickly returns.*)

EMILIA M'lady, it's your husband. He's waiting for you outside.

DESDEMONA (*Frightened*) Husband? . . . Shhhittt . . .

  (DESDEMONA *pauses, arranges her face into an insipid, fluttering innocence, then girlishly runs to the door. She flings it open, and disappears through the door.*)

DESDEMONA (*Offstage; breathless*) Othello!

  (*And then, we hear the distinct sound of a very loud slap. A pause, and* DESDEMONA *returns, closes the door behind her, holding her cheek. She is on the brink of tears. She and* EMILIA *look at each other, and then* EMILIA *looks away.*)

6

DESDEMONA *and* EMILIA. DESDEMONA *frantically searches.*

DESDEMONA It's got to be somewhere!! – Are you quite sure –

EMILIA Madam can be sure I overlooked the whole lot several times.

DESDEMONA Um, Emilia . . . should, should you have 'accidentally' taken it – not that I'm suggesting theft in the slightest – but should it have by mistake slipped in with some of your things, your return of it will merit a reward, and all of my gratitude.

  (*Tries to appear casual*) Not that the thing itself is worth anything – it's a pittance of musty linen – but still . . .

EMILIA (*With dignity*) I've never taken a thing, acc-idently or not. I don't make no 'acc-idents.' Mum, I've looked everywhere. Everywhere.

  (*Quietly*) Is m'lord clamoring about it much?

  (*They eye each other. Pause.*)

DESDEMONA Which position, Mealy?

EMILIA (*Puzzled*) Which position?

DESDEMONA For your husband.

EMILIA Oh, Miss Desdemona! I won't forget all your –

DESDEMONA Yes, yes, I'm sure. What opening?

EMILIA It's ever so small a promotion, and so quite equal to his merits. He's ensign third-class, but the budget's ensign second-class.

DESDEMONA Very well, the budget office. Can he write and account and do – whatever it is that they do with the budget?

EMILIA Oh, yes – he's clever enough at that.

DESDEMONA I really don't understand your mentality, Emilia. You're forever harping on how much you detest the man. Why do you beg for scraps of promotion for him? Don't you hate him?

EMILIA I – I –
    (*With relish*) I despise him.

DESDEMONA Then?

EMILIA You see, Miss, for us in the bottom ranks, when man and wife hate each other, what is left in a lifetime of marriage but to save and scrimp, plot and plan? The more I'd like to put some nasty rat-ridder in his stew, the more I think of money – and he thinks the same. One of us will drop first, and then, what's left, saved and earned, under the mattress for th' other one? I'd like to rise a bit in the world, and women can only do that through their mates – no matter what class buggers they all are. I says to him each night, 'I long for the day you make me a lieutenant's widow!'

7

EMILIA *and* DESDEMONA. *We hear the sounds of scrubbing between the scenes.*

DESDEMONA Please, my dear Emilia, I can count on you, can't I? As one closest to my confidence?

EMILIA Oh, m'lady, I ask no greater joy than to be close to your ladyship –

DESDEMONA Then tell me – have you heard anything about me? Why does Othello suspect Cassio?

EMILIA Oh, no, m'lady, he surely no longer suspects Cassio. I instructed Iago to talk him out of that bit of fancy, which he did, risking my lord's anger at no little cost to his own career; but all for you, you know!

DESDEMONA You haven't heard of anything else?

EMILIA No Ma'am.

(*But as* DESDEMONA *is to* EMILIA'*s back,* EMILIA *drops a secret smile into the wash bucket.* EMILIA

raises her head again, though, with a sincere, servile face, and turns to DESDEMONA.)

EMILIA But if I did know anything, you can be sure that you're the first to see the parting of my lips about it –

DESDEMONA Yes, I know. You've been an extremely faithful, hardworking servant to me, Emilia, if not a confidante. I've noticed your merits, and when we return to Venice . . . well – you may live to be my *fille de chambre* yet.

EMILIA (*Not quite sure what a* fille de chambre *is*) I'm very grateful, I'm sure.

DESDEMONA Yes, you deserve a little reward, I think. (EMILIA'*s face brightens in expectancy*)
    I'll see if I can wheedle another tuppence out of my husband each week. (EMILIA *droops*)

EMILIA (*Listlessly*) Every little tiny bit under the mattress helps, I always says to myself.

(*A pause.* DESDEMONA *paces, comes to a decision.*)

DESDEMONA Mealy – do you like the dressing gown you've been mending?

EMILIA It's a lovely piece of work, that is, Miss. I've always admired your dresses . . .

DESDEMONA Yesss . . . yes, but isn't it getting a bit dingy? Tattered around the hem?

EMILIA Not that anyone would notice; it's a beautiful gown, m'lady . . .

DESDEMONA Yes, you're right. I was going to give it to you, but maybe I'll hang on to it a bit longer . . .

(EMILIA, *realizing her stupidity, casts an avaricious, yet mournful look at the gown that was almost hers.*)

EMILIA Oh, m'lady . . . It's . . . it's certainly a lovely cloth, and there's a cut to it that would make one of them boy actors shapely . . .

DESDEMONA (*Peeved at the analogy*) Hmmmm – though, come to think of it, it would fit Bianca much neater, I think . . .

EMILIA Bianca! Bianca! She's got the thighs of a milch cow, m'lady!

DESDEMONA (*Amused*) I've never noticed.

(EMILIA, *sulking again, vigorously scrubs.*)

DESDEMONA (*In conciliation*) No, come to think of it, I believe you are right – it's not really Bianca's fashion. It's all yours. After tonight.

EMILIA Oh, Miss Desdemona!!

8

The same. In the darkness we hear EMILIA *singing a hymn: 'La-la-la-la – Jesus; La-la-la – Sword; La-la-la-la – Crucifix; La-la-la-la – Word.'*

Lights come up on DESDEMONA, *lying stretched out on the table, her throat and head arched over its edge, upside down. A pause.*

DESDEMONA You really think his temper today was only some peeve?

EMILIA I'm sure of it; men get itchy heat rash in th' crotch, now and then; they get all snappish, but once they beat us, it's all kisses and presents the next morning – well, for the first year or so.

DESDEMONA My dear mate is much too miserly to give me anything but his manhood. The only gift he's given me was a meager handkerchief with piddling strawberries stitched on it, and look how he's carrying on because I've lost it! He guards his purse strings much dearer than his wife.

EMILIA I'm sure my lord will be waitin' up for you to come to bed. Full o' passion, and embracin' and makin' a fool o' himself – You just see if your Mealy isn't right.

DESDEMONA Yes, of course you're right. Good old Mealy, I don't know what I'd do without your good common sense. Oh, it's the curse of aristocratic blood – I feel full of whims and premonitions –

EMILIA Perhaps it was something m'lady et?

DESDEMONA (*First she smiles; then she laughs*) Yes – that must be it!

(DESDEMONA *laughs again. Mealy can't understand what is so funny.*)

9

EMILIA *and* DESDEMONA.

EMILIA Ambassador Ludovico gave me a message and is wantin' a response.

DESDEMONA What does my cousin want?

(EMILIA *digs into her bodice.*)

EMILIA It's somewhere in here . . . wait . . . (*Searches*)

DESDEMONA Oh, good Lord, Mealy, you could lose it in there!

(DESDEMONA *runs to* EMILIA, *peers in her bosom and starts to tickle her.*)

EMILIA Miss Desde –! Wait, now – no, STOP!! Here it is now –

(EMILIA *finds a folded paper. She hands it to* DESDEMONA, *and then peers over* DESDEMONA's *shoulder.*)

DESDEMONA (*Sighing*) Oh, Ludovico, Ludovico. 'Deeply desiring the favor . . .' etceteras. '. . . Impatient until I can at last see you in private, throwing off the Robes of State to appear as your humble friend.' He's just too tiresome.

EMILIA What response are you wanting me to give?

DESDEMONA Oh, I don't know. Let the old lecher wait. I told him it was entirely past between us, and then he bribes his way into being appointed Ambassador!

(DESDEMONA *in a loquacious mood.* EMILIA *gives her a rubdown.*)

DESDEMONA Ah, Emilia, I should have married Ludovico after all. There's a man who's always known the worth of ladies of good blood! A pearl for a pinch, a broach for a breast, and for a maiden-head . . .
    (*Breaks into laughter*)
    Ah, that was a lover!

EMILIA I don't know how those sainted sisters could let such is-sagnations go on in their convent –

DESDEMONA Assignations. Really, Emilia, you're quite hopeless. However can I, the daughter of a Senator, live with a washer woman as *fille de chambre*? All fashionable Venice will howl. You must shrink your vowels and enlarge your vocabulary.

EMILIA Yes, mum. As-signations, as it were.
    (*Muttering*) If it were one o' my class, I could call it by some names I could pronounce. I've put many a copper in their poor box, in times past, thinkin' them sisters of charity in a godly house. Not no more. They won't get the parings of my potatoes from me, runnin' a society house of ass-ignations!

DESDEMONA Oh, those poor, dear sisters. I really don't think they knew anything about the informal education their convent girls receive. For one thing, I believe myopia is a prerequisite for Holy Orders. Have you ever noticed how nuns squint?
    (*Beat*)
    Each Sunday in convent we were allowed to take visitors to chapel. Under their pious gaze Ludovico and I would kneel, and there I could devote myself to doing him *à la main* (*Gestures*) right in the pew! They never noticed! Sister

Theresa did once remark that he was a man excessively fond of prayer.

10

EMILIA's *credo*.

EMILIA It's not right of you, Miss Desdemona, to be forever cutting up on the matter of my beliefs. I believe in the Blessed Virgin, I do, and the Holy Fathers and the Sacraments of the Church, and I'm not one to be ashamed of admittin' it. It goes against my marrow, it does, to hear of you, a comely lass from a decent home, giving hand jobs in the pew; but I says to myself, Emilia, I says, you just pay it no mind, and I go about my business. And if I take a break on the Sabbath each week, to light a candle and say a bead or two for my em-ployers, who have given me and my husband so much, and who need the Virgin's love and protection, then where's the harm, say I?

(*Breath. Gets carried away*) Our Lady has seen me through four and ten years of matreemony, with my bugger o' a mate, and that's no mean feat. Four and ten years, she's heard poor Mealy's cries, and stopped me from rising from my bed with my pillow in my hand to end his ugly snores 'til Gabriel – (*Stops and composes herself*)

Ah, Miss Desdemona, if you only knew the peace and love Our Lady brings! She'd help you, mum, if you only kneeled real nice and said to her . . . and said . . .

(EMILIA *can't find the words that such a sinner as* DESDEMONA *should say as polite salutation to Our Lady.* DESDEMONA *erupts into laughter.*)

11

EMILIA *eats her lunch.* DESDEMONA *plays in a desultory fashion with a toy.*

DESDEMONA (*Frightened*) Emilia, have you ever deceived your husband Iago?

EMILIA (*With a derisive snort*) That's a good one. Of course not, Miss – I'm an honest woman.

DESDEMONA What does honesty have to do with adultery? Every honest man I know is an adulterer . . .

(*Pause*)

Have you ever thought about it?

EMILIA What is there to be thinkin' about? It's enough trouble once each Saturday night, than

to be lookin' for it. I'd never cheat – never – not for all the world I wouldn't.

DESDEMONA The world's a huge thing for so small a vice.

EMILIA Not my world, thank you. Mine's tidy and neat and I aim to keep it that way.

DESDEMONA Oh, the world! Our world's narrow and small, I'll grant you; but there are other worlds – worlds that we married women never get to see.

EMILIA Amen – and don't need to see, I should add.

DESDEMONA If you've never seen the world, how would you know? Women are clad in purdah, we decent, respectable matrons, from the cradle to the altar to the shroud . . . bridled with linen, blinded with lace . . . These very walls are purdah.

EMILIA I don't know what this thing called 'purr-dah' means, but if it stands for dressing up nice, I'm all for it . . .

DESDEMONA I remember the first time I saw my husband and I caught a glimpse of his skin, and, oh, how I thrilled. I thought – aha! – a man of a different color. From another world and planet. I thought, if I marry this strange dark man, I can leave this narrow little Venice with its whispering piazzas behind – I can escape and see other worlds.

(*Pause*)

But under that exotic façade was a porcelain white Venetian.

EMILIA There's nothing wrong with Venice; I don't understand why madam's all fired up to catch Cyprus Syph and exotic claps.

DESDEMONA Of course you don't understand. But I think Bianca does. She's a free woman – a new woman – who can make her own living in the world, who scorns marriage for the lie that it is.

EMILIA I don't know where madam's getting this new woman hogwash, but no matter how you dress up a cow, she's still got udders.

Bianca's the eldest one of six girls, with teeth so horsey she could clean 'em with a hoof-pick, and so simple she has to ply the trade she does! That's what your Miss Bianca is!

DESDEMONA Bianca is nothing of the sort. She and I share something common in our blood – that desire to know the world. I lie in the blackness of the room at her establishment . . . on sheets that are stained and torn by countless nights. And the men come into that pitch-black room – men of different sizes and smells and shapes, with smooth skin, with rough skin, with scarred skin. And they spill their seed into me,

Emilia – seed from a thousand lands, passed down through generations of ancestors, with genealogies that cover the surface of the globe. And I simply lie still there in the darkness, taking them all into me. I close my eyes and in the dark of my mind – oh, how I travel!

12

EMILIA *and* DESDEMONA. DESDEMONA *is recklessly excited.*

EMILIA You're leaving?!! Your husband?!!

DESDEMONA It's a possibility!

EMILIA Miss Desdemona, you've been taking terrible chances before, but now – if my lord catches you giving him th' back wind, he'll be after murdering both of us for sure –

DESDEMONA Where's my cousin Ludovico? Is he in his room?

EMILIA He said he was turnin' in early to get some rest before th' morning –

DESDEMONA Yes, he'll catch the first tide back. Well, there's no harm in trying.

EMILIA Trying what!

DESDEMONA Trying on the robes of the penitent daughter. Ludovico can surely see how detestable this island, this marriage, this life is for me.
      (*Has worked herself to the point of tears. Then she smiles*)
      Perhaps a few tears would move him to intercede with my father on my behalf. If the disgrace of eloping with a moor is too great for Venetian society, a small annual allowance from Papa, and I promise never to show my face in town; and then . . . who knows . . . Paris! Yes, I'll go write Ludovico a note right away, asking to see him tonight. – Mealy, just in case, could you pack a few things for me?

EMILIA And what if your husband discovers –

DESDEMONA I'll leave first thing in the morning.

EMILIA If I may make so bold to suggest –

DESDEMONA What, what –

EMILIA That you by all means sleep with your husband tonight. So's he won't suspect anything. While you and he lie together, and if your cousin agrees, Mealy could pack up your things quiet-like in your chamber.

DESDEMONA Yes, that's good. My life rests on your absolute discretion, Emilia.

EMILIA No one will hear a peep out o' me. But, my lady –

DESDEMONA Now what is it?

EMILIA What becomes of me?

DESDEMONA Oh, good heavens, Mealy – I can't think of trivia at a time like this.
      (*Smoothly*) I tell you what. Be a good girl, pack my things, and, of course, should I leave tomorrow, I can't very well smuggle you on board, too; but I will send for you within the week. And your services will be remembered in Venice; with freer purse strings – who knows? Eh, my *fille de chambre*?

(*At this sop to her feelings,* EMILIA *becomes fierce.*)

EMILIA That won't do, m'lady. If you leave me behind, I'll not see you again, as your laundress, much less as your '*fee der schomer.*'

(DESDEMONA, *realizing the power that* EMILIA *now has, kneels beside her.*)

DESDEMONA All right. I'll intercede with my cousin on your behalf. I'll plead with him to take you, too. But I can't promise anything. Are you sure it's what you want? (EMILIA *nods*)
      You'd leave your husband behind? (EMILIA *nods vigorously*)
      Then – not a word. (*Rises*)
      (*In turning to go*) Oh, Emilia, since you're just dawdling over that laundry, why not stop and peel some potatoes for Cook. When my husband comes in, he'll want his usual snack of chips before he turns in – just the way he likes them . . . (*Shudders*) Greasy.

EMILIA But, Miss, it's not my place no more to peel potatoes! I'm promoted now! I'm no mere (*With disgust*) SCULLERY MAID!

DESDEMONA Now, Mealy, just this once –

EMILIA You said I wouldn't have to do potatoes anymore!

DESDEMONA (*Harshly*) I can leave you rotting on Cyprus all together, you know. Do as you're told. Peel the potatoes, and then look sharp and have that wash on the line by the time I return. Do I make myself clear?

EMILIA Yes, m'lady.

DESDEMONA (*Sweetly*) And Emilia, dear, if Bianca comes when I'm gone, let me know immediately – I'll be in my chamber.

EMILIA Very good, Miss Desdemona.

(DESDEMONA *exits.* EMILIA *grudgingly gets up, and finds the barrel of potatoes. On the bench there is a paring knife.* EMILIA *brings everything back to the table, sits, and begins paring potatoes – venting her resentment by gouging out eyes, and stripping the skin from a potato as if flaying a certain mistress alive.*)

EMILIA (*Snorts out in contempt*) '*Fee der shomber*!'

(Then she pauses again, and wonders if Desdemona might not be for real in her offer. She questions the empty room) 'Feeyah der schomber?'

(Before EMILIA's *eyes, she visualizes splendid dresses, the command of a household of subservient maids, a husband less existence – all the trappings that go with the title.*
EMILIA *begins energetically, resolutely and obediently to slice the potatoes.)*

13

EMILIA *is hanging up the wash.* BIANCA *knocks several times; then enters.*

BIANCA Gaw Blimey!

EMILIA And where is't you've lost your manners? Lettin' the door ajar and leavin' in drafts and the pigs –

BIANCA Aw'm sorry, Aw'm sure . . .

(BIANCA closes the door. She hesitates, and then with friendly strides, goes toward the clothesline.)

BIANCA 'Ow do, Emilia!

EMILIA I'd be doin' a lot better if ye'd stop your gaddin' and lend a hand with these things.

BIANCA Oh. Right you are, then.

(BIANCA goes briskly to the clothesline, and works. Silence as the women empty the basket. EMILIA *leaves* BIANCA *to finish and starts in on her sewing. Pause.)*

BIANCA Well, it's – it ain't 'arf swank 'ere, eh? *(Indicates the room)*

EMILIA *(Snorts)* Swank? What, this? This is only the *back* room. The palace is through those doors –

BIANCA Oh. Well, it's swank for a back room wotever it 'tis. Aw niver got to see it much; the Guv'nor in the owld days didn't let me near, said Au made the men tomdoodle on their shifts; like as they'd be dis-tracted by me atomy. Aw think it's sweet o' him to gi' me such credit; me atomy ain't that bleedin' jammy – but then, the owld Guy was the first to gi' me the sheep's eye 'imself. Very sweet on me, 'e was. So you see, Aw'd niver got close to the place before. Aw fink it's swank!

EMILIA *(Icily)* I'm sure you do.

BIANCA Yes, it's quite – wot do ye call it – lux-i-o-rious.

EMILIA Lux-i-o-ri-us!! If I was you, I'd large my voc-abulary, an' shrink me vowels.

BIANCA *(Offended)* 'Ere now! Wot bus'ness is me vowels to you?! Leave me vowels alone –

EMILIA I'm after talking about your voc-abulary – your patter – not your reg-ularity.

BIANCA Oh.
(Keeping up a friendly front with difficulty) Right. Well, then, is Desdemona 'ere?

EMILIA *(Sharply)* Who?

BIANCA Uh . . . Des-de-mona –

EMILIA Is it m'lady you're referrin' to as if she were your mess mate?

BIANCA Look 'ere, Aw'm only doin' as Aw was towld. She tells me to call her Desdemona, and she says Aw was to call and settle up accounts for last Tuesday night for those johns who paid on tick – oh, you know, who paid on credit, as yew la-de-da Venetians would say.

EMILIA *(Softly hissing)* You listen to me, lassie: You're riding for a fall the likes of which you never got paid for by your fancy men. The mistress of this house is not at home, nor will be to the likes of you. What m'lady does in the gutter is her own business, same as yours, but what happens here is the common buzz of all.

BIANCA *(Stunned)* Wot! Miss Desdemona herself is callin' us mates – Aw niver –

EMILIA Then she's gullin' you, as sure as 'tis she's gullin' that ass of a husband who's so taken with her; but let me tell you, you'll go the way like all the other fancies she's had in Venice . . . I should know. We all of us servants in her father's house talked on end about Miss Desdemona. – For a time, she wanted to be a saint, yes! A nun with the sisters of mercy. At age twelve, she was washin' the courtyard stones for penance, with us wiping up behind her. Then she was taken with horses, thank Jesus, and left sainthood behind. And then in turn again, she thought she was dyin' – stopped eating, and moped, and talked all dreamy and a little balmylike – until her father finally saw sense and sent her to the convent to be bred out of her boredom. You're nothin' but the latest whim, a small town floozy with small town slang, and if she's lucky, she'll tire of you before the master finds out. *(Significantly)* If she's lucky.

BIANCA *(Somewhat subdued)* So wot am Aw t'do, Emilia? Aw arsks you –

EMILIA Then ask me by 'Miss Emilia' to you – *(With great dignity)* I'll have you know, I've hereby been promoted to 'fee der shimber' and if I was you, I'd keep on my right side.

BIANCA *(Impressed, scared)* Oh – 'fee dar shimber' –

Aw niver met one o' those before – Aw arsks yer pardon, Miss Emilia, Aw'm sure.

EMILIA That's a bit of all right. You just listen to me: I know what side of me bread is buttered; behind this whimsy-cal missus is a power of a master – so you mind yourself; the smell of your sin's goin' to catch m'lord's whiffin' about, and he's as jealous as he's black. If m'lord Othello had a mind to it, he could have that little lollin' tongue of yours cut clean out of your head, with none of the citizens of Cyprus to say him nay. And then what would you do for your customers! If he catched you degineratin' his wife –

BIANCA (*Starting to cry with fear*) Aw swear, Miss Emilia, Aw'm not degineratin' m'lady; we was just mates, that's wot. If Missus Desdemona wants to lark and gull her smug of a husband, that's her business, then, ain't it? Aw done as she towld me, an' that's all. She's a good lady, an' all, and Aw've just been friendly-like to her –

EMILIA Don't be a little fool hussy. There's no such creature, two-, three- or four-legged, as 'friend' betwixt ladies of leisure and ladies of the night. And as long as there be men with one member but two minds, there's no such thin' as friendship between women. An' that's that. So turn yourself around, go out and close the door behind you, and take all traces of the flophouse with you, includin' your tall tales about your 'friendships' with ladies –

BIANCA (*Anger finally conquering fear*) You can call me wot you like, but Aw'm no liar! Aw'm as 'onest a woman as yerself! And wot's more, mebbe you can wipe yer trotters on women who have to crack their crusts by rolling blokes in Venice, but 'ere it's differnt. – Aw have a place 'ere and Aw'm not ashamed t'own it. Aw'm nice to the wives in town, and the wives in town are rather nice to me. Aw'm doin' them favors by puttin' up wif their screwy owld men, and Aw like me job! The only ponk Aw has to clean up is me own.

(*Starts to leave, but*) And wot's more, Aw likes yer lady, whefer you think so or not. She can see me as Aw am, and not arsk for bowin' and scrapin'. She don't have to be nobby, 'cause she's got breedin', and she don't mind liking me for me own self – wifout th' nobby airs of yer Venetian washer-women! Aw'm at home 'ere in my place – you, you Venetian washerdonna, you're the one out o' yer element!

(BIANCA *stalks to the door, but before she can reach it,* DESDEMONA *enters.*)

DESDEMONA Emilia.

14

The same. DESDEMONA, EMILIA *and* BIANCA.

DESDEMONA Emilia. I thought I told you to tell me the instant Miss Bianca arrived. Well?

EMILIA I didn't want to be botherin' m'lady with the Ambassador –

DESDEMONA I want none of your excuses for your rudeness to our guest. My dear Bianca! I've been waiting impatiently – I could have just died of boredom.
    (*Bestows a warm hug on* BIANCA)
    May I kiss you?

(DESDEMONA *'kisses'* BIANCA *by pressing both sides of their cheeks together.*)

BIANCA (*Stammering*) Aw'm not worthy of it, m'lady –

DESDEMONA Oh, Bianca, so stiff and formal! – What have I done that you should be so angry with me?

BIANCA (*Quickly*) Nofing! Your lady's been all kindness to me . . . but mayhap . . . Aw'm not the sort o' mate for one o' your company!

DESDEMONA Nonsense! I'll decide my own friendships . . .

(DESDEMONA *looks meaningfully at* EMILIA.)

DESDEMONA (*To* BIANCA) You must excuse my entertaining you in such a crude barn of a room; my room's much cozier, but I don't know when my . . . my . . . 'smug' – is that right? (BIANCA *nods*) – When he'll return. (*Laughs*)
    Right now Othello's out in the night somewhere playing Roman Orator to his troops.
    (*Desdemona guides* BIANCA *to the table; they sit side by side*) Emilia . . . Ask Miss Bianca if she'd like some wine. (*To* BIANCA) It's really quite good, my dear.

(EMILIA *glumly approaches* BIANCA.)

EMILIA Well, are you wantin' any?

DESDEMONA Emilia! 'Would you care for some wine, Miss Bianca?'

EMILIA (*Deep breath; red*) 'Would you care for some wine, Miss Bianca?'

BIANCA Why thank you – D-Desdemona, Aw could do w' a sneaker –

DESDEMONA (*Laughs*) How I love the way you talk! . . . Emilia, fetch the wine and two goblets. That will be all.

EMILIA Yes, mum.

(EMILIA *exits and* BIANCA *relaxes.*)

DESDEMONA My poor Bianca; has Emilia been berating you?

BIANCA Well, Aw don't know about that, but she's been takin' me down a bit. Aw don't thinks she likes me very much.

DESDEMONA Oh, what does that matter! Why should you want her friendship? You don't have to care what anyone thinks about you – you're a totally free woman, able to snap your fingers in anyone's face!

BIANCA Yea, that's wot all right – but still, Aw likes people to like me.

DESDEMONA Oh, well, you mustn't mind Emilia. She's got a rotten temper because her husband – her 'smug' is such a rotter. Oh, Iago! (*Shudders*) Do you know him?

BIANCA (*Smiling, looking away*) Aw know 'im by sight –

DESDEMONA You know the one, then – the greasy little man. He's been spilling his vinegar into her for fourteen years of marriage, until he's corroded her womb from the inside out. And every day she becomes more and more hollowed out, just – just a vessel of vinegar herself.

BIANCA (*Disturbed*) Wot a funny way of lookin' at it –

(BIANCA *is bewildered.*)

15

BIANCA *and* DESDEMONA.

BIANCA So you don't fancy Iago, then, do you?

DESDEMONA Detest him. But of course, I don't have anything to do with him – I only need suffer his wife's company. Poor old Mealy –

BIANCA 'Mealy?'

(BIANCA *laughs, her fear of* EMILIA *diminishing.*)

DESDEMONA Yes, I've nicknamed her that, because I suspect it annoys her. Still, it fits.

(DESDEMONA *and* BIANCA *giggle.*)

DESDEMONA Alas, when Othello and I eloped it was on such short notice, and my husband's so stingy with salary that the only maid I could bring was my father's scullery maid.

BIANCA Yer scullery maid! Not . . . nor yer – wot-de-ye-call-it – '*Fee dah – Feyah der –*'

DESDEMONA '*Fille de chambre*!' Heavens, no! I keep her in line with the prospect of eventual advancement, but she's much too unsuitable for that – why she doesn't speak a word of French, and she's crabby to boot. Still, she's devoted and that makes up for all the rest.

BIANCA Wot makes you fink she's devoted?

DESDEMONA Ah, a good mistress knows the secret thoughts of her maids. She's devoted.

BIANCA Well, it's a cooshy enough way to crack a crust . . .

DESDEMONA Crack a crust?

BIANCA Oh, beg yer pardon; Aw mean t'earn a livin' –

DESDEMONA (*Enthralled*) 'Crack a crust!' How clever you are, Bianca!

16

DESDEMONA, BIANCA *and* EMILIA. EMILIA *stands before* DESDEMONA, *bearing a pitcher and two mugs on a tray.*

EMILIA Wine, m'lady . . .

DESDEMONA Ah, excellent.

(EMILIA *serves* DESDEMONA *first with all the grace she can muster; then she negligently pushes the wine in the direction of* BIANCA.)

BIANCA Thank you, Mealy.

DESDEMONA (*Toasting Bianca*) Now, then: To our friendship!

BIANCA T' yer 'ealth –

(DESDEMONA *delicately sips her wine, as* BIANCA *belts it down so that the wine trickles from the corner of her mouth.* EMILIA *is aghast. As* BIANCA *wipes her mouth with her hand, she notices* EMILIA's *shock.*)

BIANCA (*Blurts*) 'Scuse me guttlin' it down me gob –

DESDEMONA Oh, tush, Bianca. Mealy, haven't you mending to carry on with?

(EMILIA *silently seats herself apart and picks up the drawers.*)

DESDEMONA I tell you, Bianca, it's a disgrace. My husband refuses to buy new linen for his drawers, so Emilia must constantly mend the old. (*Confidentially*) He's constantly tearing his crotch hole somehow.

BIANCA (*Amused*) And how does that happen?

DESDEMONA (*Demurely*) I have no idea. – More wine, dear?

17

The same. BIANCA *and* DESDEMONA, *drinking.* EMILIA *sews.*

DESDEMONA How about another . . . round?

BIANCA All right, then.

    (DESDEMONA *pours generously*) But not so much! Aw could get lushy easy.

    (BIANCA *sips her wine;* DESDEMONA *knocks it back, and wipes her mouth with her hand. They laugh.*)

18

DESDEMONA *and* BIANCA, *drinking. They are giggling helplessly, spluttering.* EMILIA *sews.* DESDEMONA *starts to choke on her wine from laughing.*

19

The same. DESDEMONA *and* BIANCA *try to control themselves. Then* DESDEMONA *holds up the hoof-pick, and* BIANCA *and* DESDEMONA *explode in raucous laughter.* EMILIA *is furious.*

20

The same.

BIANCA Listen, luvs, where's yer five-minute lodging?

DESDEMONA My . . . what?

BIANCA Yer Drury Lane? Yer – where's yer bleedin' crapper! Yew know – where do yew make water?

EMILIA M'lady makes her water in a hand-painted Limoges pot, a holy sight with angels havin' a grand time – it's not for the like of you!

DESDEMONA There's an outhouse in the back by the shed . . . careful of the muck and the pigs.

BIANCA Ta. Be back in a few . . . Aw've got t' go see a bloke about a horse.

    (BIANCA *exits.*)

EMILIA And you're after havin' yourself a proper time.

DESDEMONA Oh, Mealy, I'm sorry – we were just having fun –

EMILIA At my husband's expense. You finagled that out o' me, and then you went and told it to My Lady of the Public Square . . .

DESDEMONA It . . . It just . . . slipped out. (*Goes into another gale of laughter; then*) Mealy, I'm going to ask her about Cassio!

EMILIA Why must you be knowin' every man's size?!

    (DESDEMONA *laughs again.*)

DESDEMONA No, I mean I'm going to tell her that Othello suspects him.

EMILIA Are you daft from the wine?

DESDEMONA Why not? Maybe we can get to the bottom of this . . .

EMILIA Why is it mattering? Tomorrow morning we're leaving with the Ambassador –

DESDEMONA Yes, yes, but I can find out why –

EMILIA I don't understand why m'lady is in such a rush to havin' her throat slashed our last night on Cyprus –

DESDEMONA Look, I'll just tell her that my husband is under some false impressions and ask her for –

EMILIA And why should she be believin' you?

DESDEMONA She'll believe me! She'll believe me because . . . I'll give her . . . I'll give her . . . my word of honor.

EMILIA And just how much goat cheese does that buy at market? – I know the world! I've seen flesh buckets fightin' for their fancy men in the streets in Venice, and a pretty sight it was!

DESDEMONA Oh, Mealy –

EMILIA You'll be bleedin' on the wrong time of the month! Those trullies, all of them, carry slashers down in their boots –

    (BIANCA *throws open the door and sticks her head in;* EMILIA *and* DESDEMONA *are startled.*)

BIANCA Did-jew miss me?

21

BIANCA, DESDEMONA *and* EMILIA.

BIANCA 'Ere now – let me settle w' you fer Tuesday night. Let's see . . . (*Rummages in a pocket of her dress*) It were six pence a john, at ten johns makes fer . . . five bob, an' tuppence fer tips.

    (EMILIA *gasps.*)

DESDEMONA I can hear what you're thinking Mealy – Holy Mother, I made more in twenty minutes than you do in a week of washing!

EMILIA Five bob . . .

DESDEMONA How large now the world for so small a vice, eh, Mealy?

EMILIA I'm . . . I'm not to be tempted, Miss Desdemona.

DESDEMONA Brave girl!

BIANCA 'Ere's the brass ready. Tuppence for tips is bleedin' well for a Tuesday.

DESDEMONA Really?

BIANCA It so be as how Wednesday is payday 'ere; Tuesday nights are the cooshiest layin', but the stingiest payin' –

EMILIA Aye, 'Men earns their money like Horses and spends it like Asses . . .'

DESDEMONA Never mind Mealy, Bianca; she's over there calculating what price fidelity. Now about next week –

EMILIA You two can cackle with laughter at me if you like, but it's a duty for me to stop your ladyship from gettin' into danger –

BIANCA (*Offended*) Danger! Wot danger! She helped me out on me Adam an' Eve Night – there's no danger. Aw gave her me lambs; the feisty, firkin' lads come on th' other nights, not on Tuesday. It don't take no elbow grease; Tuesday's just lying back and Adam an' Evein' it –

EMILIA I don't understand your 'Adam and Eve' and I don't think I want to . . .

DESDEMONA Oh yes you do, Mealy; 'Adam and Eve' is what you and Iago did on your wedding night . . .

BIANCA She just might fink it means fallin' asleep –

(EMILIA *vigorously stitches the linen.*)

DESDEMONA She's right, though, Bianca, she's only trying to protect me. – How about if we leave next Tuesday night open. If I can sneak away into the darkness of your boudoir, then I'll send word by Emilia –

BIANCA Right, then, but you understand me, Miss Desdemona, there'll be no firsky johns when you comes clan-decently; just the meek ones who are low on pocket-brass, or the stingy-mingy-gits who don't want to pay for nothin' wild. An' there'll be a fresh bed, an' the room so dark that your own husband wouldn't know you –

DESDEMONA Oh, Bianca – what a thought – do you think he'd come? I'd die for sure – (*Laughs*) And wouldn't he be mad if he'd paid for what he got for free at home!!

BIANCA Well, the room's bleedin' black – blacker than he is.

(BIANCA *and* EMILIA *laugh together;* DESDEMONA *is affronted.*)

DESDEMONA I beg your pardon?

BIANCA No, no, all my Tuesday johns are reg'lars – Aw know 'em all. So if you want, let me know – it'll be treacle next to wot Aw had today –

DESDEMONA Do tell, Bianca –

EMILIA Hasn't m'lady had enough –

DESDEMONA Oh, hush, Mealy – just mend your crotches, and don't listen.

BIANCA All right, then. Aw have this one john who comes once a week for an L 'n B –

DESDEMONA 'L and B?'

BIANCA In th' Life, it's known as a lam an' brim – first they lam you, an' mayhap you lam them, then you brim 'em . . .
(DESDEMONA *looks blank*) You know – first they beat you, an' then you beat them, and then you give 'em wotever – an Adam an' Eve, or a Sunny-Side Over –

DESDEMONA (*Dawning*) You mean men actually pay to beat you? And to be beaten?

BIANCA Oh, well, it costs 'em a pretty penny, Aw can tell you; there's nothin' doin' for less than two bob.

DESDEMONA (*Eyes wide*) My. Well, carry on.

BIANCA Well, there's this one john, an owld mate, who's been on tick for some weeks, an' 'e's got quite a bill. But Aw feels sorry for 'im, 'is wife really lams 'im at 'ome, an' Aw figure 'e needs t' get it off 'is chest. So 'e comes in, an' Aw says, 'Tom, you owe me over two quid, now; when's it comin'?'
'Gaw, Bianca,' 'e says, 'Aw just been out o' collar, an' –'

DESDEMONA 'Out of collar?'

BIANCA Wot yew call un-deployed . . .
'Bianca,' 'e says, 'Gawd luv yew, me owld woman an' Aw've had a row, an' Aw'm all done in. Aw'll pay th' soddin' bill, some'ow; but fer now, fer owld times . . .' 'e says.
Well, Gawd's Wounds, wot was Aw t'do? 'Right, then, Tom,' Aw said. An' Aw lays down on the bed – 'cause 'e liked me to go first – an' 'e puts the straps on me.
'Tom,' Aw says, 'listen, luv, th' straps are bleedin' tight!' An' before Aw knew wot, 'e was lammin' me fer real!! 'E did me fer a jacketin' such as Aw thought would be me last L 'n B!!
Aw bite me teeth not to scream, 'cause the bobbies won't put up with no row, no matter how many quid Aw pay 'em . . . Well, Tom finally gets it over wif, an' it's *my* turn.
'Aw'm sorry, Bianca,' 'e says, 'if Aw got a bit rough.'
'Oh, it's nofin', Tom,' Aw says – 'cause Aw'm determined t' get me own back . . . So, Aw tie 'im down on th' bed – 'e's a big strapper o' a bloke – an' then Aw lam th' *pudding* out o' 'im!! An' 'e's 'ollerin' like it's th' Second Coming. Then after Aw gi' 'im a royal pasting, Aw go through 'is togs, an' in the back pocket Aw find a soddin' crown!
'You been 'olding out on me, Tom! Aw've had it wi' yer dodges an' flams – wot kind o' a soup

kitchen do yew fink me?' An' Aw let into 'im again!!

'Bianca – let me go, an' Aw'll niver flam to ye again!'

'BLEEDIN' RIGHT!' Aw says. So Aw copped 'is brass, takes up the belt, an' let 'im loose – straight into the street 'e runs, naked as a blue jay. Aw had to throw 'is togs after 'im.

'Yew Owld Stringer!' Aw yelled. ''Ere's yer togs, an' fer yer change, Take This!' (*Raises her fist and slaps her elbow. Excited, she catches her breath*)

DESDEMONA Jesus. Weren't you scared?

BIANCA Aw'd be lyin' if Aw said nay. Aw thought it was me last trick. You can't be too careful, there's a lot of maggot-brained doodles in me bus'ness. But Aw can take care o' meself.

DESDEMONA Doesn't . . . doesn't it hurt?

BIANCA Naw, not usual. It's stingy-like, but it's all fakement.

(*Looking into* DESDEMONA's *eyes, gets an idea*) Aw c'n show you if you likes . . . C'mon, it won't hurt you none –

DESDEMONA Well . . . yes, all right, Bianca, show me.

22

The beating scene. EMILIA, BIANCA *and* DESDEMONA.

EMILIA Are you out o' your mind? Lettin' a strumpet strap you in your own house like a monk in Holy Week?

DESDEMONA Turn around, Emilia, and mind your own business. Go on, turn around, and say your beads. Pay no attention.

(*To* BIANCA) Sorry – please continue.

(EMILIA *says her beads through the following.*)

EMILIA Hail Mary Full of Grace the Lord is with Thee . . .

BIANCA Get up on the table wi' yer tale end up –

EMILIA Holy Mary, Mother of – (*Turns and sees* DESDEMONA *spread-eagled*) – GOD!!!

BIANCA Right now. Aw'll just take a strap 'ere, an' Aw'll just brush you wi' it – but when Aw let's go, you move yer tail up. All right?

DESDEMONA I . . . I think so; it's rather like rising to the trot on a horse –

BIANCA Right then. One – up. Two – down. All right, now. One. (DESDEMONA *moves up*) Two. (*Lightly straps* DESDEMONA *as she moves down*) One. (DESDEMONA *moves up*) An' Two. (DESDEMONA *moves down; a strap*) Does it hurt?

DESDEMONA No . . . no, it doesn't, really.

BIANCA Right then. Let's have some sound e-ffecks. One. Two.

(*Desdemona, screams,* EMILIA *clutches her rosary*) NO!! – Not that loud! The bobbies would be in on yew so fast yew wouldn't get yer panties up – just a moan enow to get 'im excited . . . Right, then? Now: One – Two; One – Two; One – Two; One – Two; One – Two; One – Two!!

(DESDEMONA *perfects her synchronized moans, building to a crescendo, at which point she breaks into peals of laughter.*)

DESDEMONA It's smashing! – Mealy – you really must try it!

23

As before.

BIANCA Aw want you t'take this in th' right way now – but if you weren't born a lady, you'd a been a bleedin' good blow-zabella. One o' the best. An' – well, no matter what fate holds, there's always room fer you in me shop.

(*Bashful*) Aw means it, too –

EMILIA Holy Mother, if anyone had so much as whispered in Venice that you'd be makin' a bonnie whore, there'd be a blood duel to settle in the streets!

BIANCA Aw'm payin' yer lady me respecks as one pro-fessional t'anofer. You . . . you got as much notion of me craft as a donkey has of Sunday.

EMILIA Why, thank you – at least someone has noted me merit.

DESDEMONA (*Gently*) I'm very complimented, Bianca . . . and I really did enjoy Tuesday night – but I don't think I'd better risk covering for you again –

BIANCA You're . . . you're not brimmin' fer me anymore?

DESDEMONA No – I don't think I'd better.

EMILIA (*To herself*) Heigh-ho! On to the next –

BIANCA (*Trembling*) But . . . but we c'n still be mates, wot?

DESDEMONA Of course we can! I want that very much. I never tire of hearing your stories. They're so lively, so very funny. What else have I got for amusement's sake.

(BIANCA *is disturbed.* EMILIA *smiles.*)

But you haven't told me yet about your evening off with Cassio last Tuesday . . . did you enjoy yourself?

BIANCA You don't want to 'ear about it none, it's not anyfing amusing –

DESDEMONA Now, just tell me all about it, Bianca; you can tell me your secrets, too. Woman to woman. What did you two do?

BIANCA (*Shyly*) We just talked.

EMILIA (*Snorting*) *All* night?

BIANCA Yes! 'E's differnt, you know. 'E's a gen'l'man, 'e is. An' 'e makes the rest o' the blokes round 'ere look like the ninny-hammers they are –

EMILIA Oh, he's diff'rent, all right. You'd think after all week of tomfoolin' with the like of hicks, you'd have more sense than to go prancin' about with some *Nancy* town stallion.

BIANCA Wot! Nancy! Nancy, is it? Who're you callin' 'Nancy'?

DESDEMONA Now, Mealy, don't tease her –

EMILIA The way I see it, it's no acc-i-dent for himself to be an army man –

BIANCA Aw tell you wot, m'lord Cassio 'twill make a smug more obligin' in bed than the one you've got –

DESDEMONA (*Warningly*) Ladies, ladies –

EMILIA Well, you'll never find out what it is to be havin' the like of a proper husband in the bed.

BIANCA Mayhap Aw will, too. Aw'm ready to let my way of life go fer wash the second 'e arsks me.

DESDEMONA What!

BIANCA Aw'm giving 'alfe me brass each week to the priest, Father Donahue, so's 'e c'n pray fer me sins an' t' gi' me apsolution. Aw'm ready t' say yes whenever 'e arsks me an' – an' Aw c'n go to th' altar as unstained as you were on yer weddin' night.

EMILIA (*Seeing* BIANCA *in a new light*) So, you're after goin' to the priest reg-ular?
    (*Impressed*) That's a lot of money.

BIANCA Bleedin' right.

DESDEMONA (*Crestfallen*) Oh, Bianca – oh, surely you're . . . you're not the type that wants to get married?

(*Depressed*. DESDEMONA *goes and pours herself another mug of wine*.)

BIANCA Wot's wrong wif that? Aw'm still young, an' Aw've got a tidy sum all saved up fer a dowry. An' m'lord Cassio's only got t' arsk fer a transfer to th' garrison 'ere. We'd make a bleedin' jolly life of it, Aw c'n tell you. Aw'd get us a cottage by th' sea, wif winder boxes an' all them kinds of fings, an' 'e could go to th' tipple'ouse as much as 'e likes, wifout me sayin'

nay. An' then . . . then Aw'd be bearin' 'im sons so's to make 'im proud –

EMILIA (*Triumphantly*) There! There's your new woman, m'lady! Free! Does for herself!

BIANCA Why, that 'new woman' kind o' fing's all hogwash!
    (EMILIA *nods her head in agreement*.)
    All women want t'get a smug, it's wot we're made for, ain't it? We may pretend differnt, but inside ev'ry born one o' us want smugs an' babies, smugs wot are man enow t' keep us in our place.

DESDEMONA (*Quietly into her wine*) I don't think I can stand it . . .

BIANCA 'Scusin' my cheek, but you're a lucky lady, an' you don't even know it. Your 'ubby might be wot you call a bit doo-lolly-tap-tap up 'ere (*Taps her head*) but th' maritle knot's tied good 'n' strong. Every time Aw 'ear, (*Dreamily*) "Til deaf do us part,' Aw starts t' snurfle. Aw can't 'elp it. If only Cassio would say them words an' make me th' 'appiest o' –

EMILIA And what makes you think m'lord Cassio – who's Venetian born, an' wears silk next to his skin, not none of your Cyprus scum – is goin' to be marryin' a tried-on strumpet?

BIANCA 'Coz a gen'l'man don't lie to a bird – Aw should soddin' well know where ofs Aw speak. Besides, m'lord Cassio gi' me a token o' 'is es-teem –

EMILIA Hmmpf! And I'm after supposin' you gave him the same, as you've given tokens of esteem to all your customers – a scurvy clap – that's your token.

(DESDEMONA *becomes curious*.)

DESDEMONA Hush, Mealy.
    (*To* BIANCA) Never mind her, Bianca – I believe you. What type of token did Cassio give?

BIANCA (*As enthused as a teenage girl*) It's a real flashy bit o' goods. It's a muckenger so swank Aw don't dare blow me beak in it.
    (*Confidentially*) So Aw carry it down in me knockers an' next to me 'eart.

DESDEMONA (*Lost*) A swank . . . muck . . .

BIANCA Wot Aw mean is, it ain't yer typic sneezer.
    (*Gropes into her bodice, and tenderly takes out an embroidered handkerchief; proudly*) 'Ere it is, now.

DESDEMONA (*Starting*) Why . . . (*Looks carefully;*

then in relief) Oh, thank God, Bianca, you've found it. I'm saved.

(*Stops*) But what – whatever are you doing with my handkerchief?

EMILIA (*To herself*) Oh, Jesus, he gave it to Cassio!

BIANCA (*Blank*) *Your* handkerchief? *Yours*?!

(*Dangerously*) What's Cassio doin' wi' your hand-ker-chief?

DESDEMONA That's precisely what I want to find out – Emilia!

BIANCA (*Fierce*) Aw bet. So – you was goin' t' 'elp me out once a week fer Cassio?

(*Advancing*) You cheatin' hussy – Aw'll pop yer peepers out –

(BIANCA *lunges for* DESDEMONA; EMILIA *runs*.)

EMILIA She's got a KNIFE! –

DESDEMONA Listen, Bianca –

BIANCA When Aw'm gulled by a woman, she don't live to do it twice –

DESDEMONA Bianca, I swear! –

(BIANCA *sees the hoof-pick and picks it up, slowly advancing on a clutching* DESDEMONA, *who backs away toward the clothesline.*)

BIANCA Aw'll carve you up into cag-meat an' feed you to the pigs. Aw'll gag yer puddings out yer gob, you'll choke so hard –

DESDEMONA I never! –

(BIANCA *swipes at* DESDEMONA *with the pick; the two clench each other. Breaking away,* DESDEMONA *falls, and picks up a wine bottle in defense.*)

BIANCA Yer gonna snuff it, m'lady – so say yer prayers, yew goggle-eyed scab o' a WHORE!

(DESDEMONA *ducks behind the hanging clothes, with* BIANCA *following. We hear a scuffle, grunts and screams.* EMILIA *runs for the palace door, calling:*)

EMILIA GUARD! GUARD!! –

(EMILIA *flings the door open. Then she realizes she can't call the guard, and quickly closes the door behind her, turning to face the room with grim desperation.*)

EMILIA (*Softly*) Jesus.

BIANCA (*Offstage*) BLOODY! –

DESDEMONA (*Offstage*) MEALY!!

(EMILIA *runs away from the door, taking out her crucifix.*)

EMILIA Oh, Jesus. Oh, Jesus.

(*And then, we hear a scream, a splash and the sound of a bottle breaking. Slowly a dark, wet stain spreads on a cloth drying on the clothesline. For a moment, there is silence.*

BIANCA *looking grim and fierce, strides out from behind the clothes, holding the hoof-pick. She looks at* EMILIA, *who backs away. There is a pause.*

Then, DESDEMONA *steps from behind the hanging clothes, holding a broken wine bottle. The torso of her gown is splashed with dark, indelible burgundy.*)

EMILIA (*Softly*) Oh, thank Jesus –

DESDEMONA Bianca! . . . Bianca, I never did.

BIANCA Leave me alone . . . Aw've lost me chance of a smug!

(*Erupts into weeping, starts to wipe her nose with the handkerchief*) There! Take yer filthy linen! Aw wouldn't blow me nose in it –

DESDEMONA Bianca – I never did. I never did.

BIANCA Aw loved 'im –

DESDEMONA Bianca –

BIANCA An' Aw lost 'im –

DESDEMONA Bianca –

BIANCA An' oh, oh, the cottage by the sea . . .

DESDEMONA If it makes a difference, I didn't.

BIANCA You gulled yer 'usband an' you gulled me! An' Aw thought we was mates!

(BIANCA *starts to leave;* EMILIA *calls after her.*)

EMILIA I told you there's no such thing as friendship with ladies –

BIANCA You!! Washerdonna!! Shut Yer Potato-Trap! Don't you be so 'igh an' mighty smart!!

(*Reaching the door, she opens it, and turns*) And just where was your Iago last Tuesday night!

(*Triumphantly,* BIANCA *slams the door behind her. A very long pause. Then,* DESDEMONA *tries to sound casual.*)

DESDEMONA Um, Emilia, dear, just . . . just where was Iago last Tuesday night?

EMILIA (*Distressed*) He . . . he said . . . he said he was on guard duty . . .

(EMILIA *begins to cry.* DESDEMONA *sits beside her, and tentatively puts her arms about* EMILIA. *Then,* DESDEMONA *rocks her maid.*)

24

Lights up on DESDEMONA *and* EMILIA, *seated at the table, drinking wine, saying nothing.*

25

DESDEMONA *and* EMILIA, *at table, staring ahead into air.* DESDEMONA *wearily looks into her cup, and pours herself and* EMILIA *another cup of wine. They look at each other, nod to each other, and drink together.*

26

DESDEMONA *is drinking.* EMILIA *grasps her mug.*

EMILIA (*In a low voice*) Do you know which one he was?

DESDEMONA No . . . I don't think so. There were so many that night.

EMILIA Aye, you were having a proper time at it. Travelin' around the world!!

(*Pause.*)

DESDEMONA There was one man . . .
(*Hesitating*) It might have been him.

EMILIA (*Laughs harshly*) My husband's a lover of garlic. Was that the man you're remembering?

DESDEMONA No, it's not that – although . . .

EMILIA Well, what is it you remember!

DESDEMONA There was one man who . . . didn't last very long.

EMILIA Aye. That's the one.

27

The same.

EMILIA When I was married in the church, the knot tied beneath the Virgin's nose, I looked forward to the bed with as much joy as any girl after a hard day. And then Iago – well, he was still a lad, with the softness of a boy, and who could tell he'd turn into the man?
(*Pauses to drink.*)
But all that girl nonsense was knocked out of me by the nights. Night followin' night, as sure as the day's work came after. I'd stretch myself out on the bed, you see, waitin' for my good man to come to me and be my mate – as the priest said he could – but then . . . But then I saw it didn't matter what had gone on between us – the fights, my crying, a good meal or a cold one. Days could pass without a word between us, and he'd take his fill of me the same. I could have been the bed itself. And so, you see, I vowed not to be there for him. As he'd be lying on me in the dark, I'd picture up my Rosary, so real I could kiss the silver. And I'd start at the Blessed Cross itself, while he was somewhere doin' his business above, and I'd say the first wooden bead, and then I'd finger the next bead in my mind, and then onto the next – (*Stops*) But I never did make it to the medallion. He'd be all through with me by the time of the third 'Hail Mary.'
(*Pause*)
Does my lady know what I'm saying?

DESDEMONA I'm not sure. I . . . I don't think it's . . . happened to me like that.

EMILIA Ah, well, men are making fools of themselves over you. The Ambassador is traipsing from the mainland just to hold onto your skirt; and your husband – (*Stops herself*) Well, maybe it's all different for the likes of you.
(DESDEMONA *says nothing.*)
And then, maybe not. It's hard to be seeing, when you're young and men watch you when you pass them by, and the talkin' stops between them. But, all in all, in time you'll know. Women just don't figure in their heads – not the one who hangs the wash – not Bianca – and not even you, m'lady. That's the hard truth. Men only see each other in their eyes. Only each other.
(*Beat.*)
And that's why I'm ready to leave the whole pack of them behind and go with you and the Ambassador. Oh, to see my husband's face tomorrow morning! When he finds out that I can get along by myself, with no thanks to his plotting and hatching! But it's leave him now or be countin' my beads through the years, waitin' for his last breath!

DESDEMONA (*Quietly*) Emilia, I'll be honest with you, even if it puts me in risk to do so . . . You're to stay behind tomorrow. I've asked my cousin for my own safe passage. I wish to go alone with Ludovico.
(EMILIA *stands very still.*)
I am in your hands. You can run and tell my husband all – but I don't want to trifle with your feelings and desert you with the first tide. This way, you see, I'm only temporarily leaving you behind. But I promise I'll need your service in Venice as much as tonight. So, you're to follow me when all household matters are in hand, taking with you whatever my husband permits. As a token of my esteem – here – (*Takes off a ring, and gazes at it wistfully*) I want you to have this. It's a memento given me by Ludovico for . . . well, never you mind what for. Little did he think it would wind up 'round the finger of an honest woman.

(DESDEMONA *gives the ring to* EMILIA)

EMILIA This ring is for me? but it's of value, m'lady . . .

(EMILIA *tries to return it;* DESDEMONA *insists.* EMILIA *makes a decision.*)

EMILIA Listen, Miss, you've gone and leveled with me, and I'm after doing the same with you!
  (*Blurts*) M'lady, don't go to your husband's bed tonight. Lie apart – stay in my chamber.

DESDEMONA Why? Whatever for? It would raise suspicion.

EMILIA I'll say you're ill – with woman sickness.

DESDEMONA But why?

EMILIA Because . . . because . . . oh, m'lady, you know how easy it is to be seduced by a husband's soft word, when it's the like of angry words he pours down upon your head –

DESDEMONA (*Very still*) Emilia – what have you done?

EMILIA I took the handkerchief.

DESDEMONA You took the handkerchief . . . I thought you did.

EMILIA It was to be a joke, you see; my husband put me up to it, as a lark, he said, just to see –

DESDEMONA (*Very softly*) Iago – Oh, my sweet Jesus –

EMILIA And he was laughing about it, ye see, and he was as gay as a boy; he said he'd just . . . hide it for a while, all in jest –

DESDEMONA Oh, no – he . . . he must have . . . planted it on Cassio – that's why . . .

EMILIA It was just for a lark!

DESDEMONA Emilia, what has your husband been thinking!

EMILIA I don't know what he thinks.

(DESDEMONA *twists the handkerchief.*)

DESDEMONA What use is this to me now! If I return it, my husband will say that my lover gave it back to me!!

EMILIA Miss Desdemona – oh my lady, I'm sure your husband loves you!

DESDEMONA How do you know that my husband –!

EMILIA More than the world! He won't harm you none, m'lady – I've often seen him –

DESDEMONA What have you seen?!

EMILIA I've seen him, sometimes when you walk in the garden, slip behind the arbor just to watch you, unawares . . . and at night . . . in the corridor . . . outside your room – sometimes he just stands there, Miss, when you're asleep . . . he just stands there –

DESDEMONA (*Frightened*) Oh, Jesus –

EMILIA And once . . . I saw . . . I came upon him unbeknowin', and he didn't see me – I'm sure – he was in your chamber room and he gathered up the sheets from your bed, like a body, and . . . and he held it to his face, like, like a bouquet, all breathin' it in –

(*The two women pause: They both realize* OTHELLO'*s been smelling the sheets for traces of a lover.*)

DESDEMONA That isn't love. It isn't love.
  (*Beat*)
  Why didn't you tell me this before?

EMILIA (*Carefully*) I always thought it was not my place.

(*The two women do not speak for a moment.* EMILIA *looks toward the palace door.*)

EMILIA Well, what are we to be doin' now?

DESDEMONA We have to make it to the morning. You'd better come with me – it's not safe for you, either.
  (EMILIA *says nothing.*)
  We'll have to leave all behind. It's not safe to pack.

(DESDEMONA *thinks.*)

DESDEMONA (*Carefully*) Now listen, carefully, Emilia. I'll go to my own chamber tonight. You're to wait up for my husband's return – tell him I'm ill and I've taken to my own bed. He's not to disturb me, I'm not well. I'll turn in before he comes, and I'll . . . pretend to sleep if he should come to me.
  (*Pause.*)
  Surely he'll not . . . harm a sleeping woman.

EMILIA I'll do it.

DESDEMONA Good. I'd better go to bed.

(DESDEMONA *starts toward the palace door and stops.*)

EMILIA Would you like me to brush your hair tonight? A hundred strokes?

DESDEMONA Oh, yes, please, Emilia . . .

28

EMILIA *brushes* DESDEMONA'*s hair.*
DESDEMONA *leans back, tense, listening to the offstage palace.*

EMILIA Now, then –
  (*Starts*) One, two, three, four, five, six . . .

29

The same.

EMILIA Forty-five, forty-six, forty-seven . . .

30

DESDEMONA *and* EMILIA. EMILIA *reaches the hundredth stroke.*

EMILIA Ninety-seven . . . ninety-eight . . . ninety-nine . . .

(*They freeze. Blackout.*)

This Island's Mine

Philip Osment

Introduction

Philip Osment grew up in Devon, England, and read Modern Languages at Keble College, Oxford (1971–1974). After spending time in Berlin, he joined Gay Sweatshop in London in the late 1970s. He became one of the artistic directors of the company before leaving in the late 1980s. *This Island's Mine* was first performed as a reading which was part of the Gay Sweatshop Times Twelve Festival in 1987 and opened as a Gay Sweatshop production in 1988. Osment has since written plays inspired by his Devon childhood for the Cambridge Theatre Company, now Method & Madness.

Gay Sweatshop began in 1974 in order to 'put the experiences of lesbians and gay men centre-stage' and to play a role in 'changing attitudes towards homosexuality within the world of theatre and within society as a whole' (Osment 1989: vii); it has provided 'a context for gay people to work together and to allow their sexuality to inform their work in a positive way' (ix). With 'a growing awareness that Britain [has] a multi-cultural pluralistic society' (xi), its mandate has been to produce 'work of the highest standard which puts the experience of gay people centre-stage but speaks to everyone' (liv–lv). Among his personal influences, Osment mentions Charles Dickens, with his ability 'to make links between different people's stories and lives which resonate thematically with each other and build up a picture of a whole society' (lxi), and Anton Chekhov, who shows 'what is dramatic in ordinary life' (Osment: 1997: xiii). The result, as Mike Alfreds notes in his introduction to Osment's *Plays: 1*, is that Osment 'creates "ordinary" people who are given the right to be complex and contradictory, whose human variability can elicit our sympathy, dislike and amusement all in the same breath' (xi).

This Island's Mine arrived on the scene just as the Conservative government of Margaret Thatcher was bringing into law Section 28 of the Local Government Act, which sought to prevent 'local councils from funding lesbian and gay organizations' as well as 'any presentation of positive images of homosexuality in schools and any discussion of alternative living' – so-called 'pretended families' (Osment 1989: lxiii). Osment 'was beginning to feel that [he] no longer belonged in a Britain increasingly hostile to everything [he] believed in' (lxi), and *This Island's Mine* became part of the general struggle against Thatcher's oppressive measures (in this regard, one might also look at Derek Jarman's film adaptation of Christopher Marlowe's *Edward II*).

Direct references to Shakespeare's *The Tempest* are limited in the play to the title, the scenes in which Selwyn is involved in a production of Shakespeare's work, and Osment's production note that 'The doubling of Stephen/Prospero and Marianne/Miranda is important'; these explicit references point, however, to a deeper and more wide-ranging relationship to *The Tempest*.

This Island's Mine is a sweeping update of the systemic colonialism and oppression from the time of *The Tempest*, translating early modern conditions into their current analogues. In the late twentieth century, the United States assumes the role of imperial oppressor, and Britain becomes as much an object of this imperialism as it is an oppressor in its own right. It is fitting that Stephen, the foremost Prospero, is now an American. In this light, the island in *This Island's Mine* is now Britain itself, rather than a land off Africa or the New World. Stephen is, however, the primary but not the only Prospero. As Susan Bennett notes, 'England may well have lost its Empire, but, as Osment's play powerfully demonstrates, the Prosperos have not lost their will for imperialism' (Bennett 1996a: 148). Britain's status in the new world order is further complicated by the presence of those whose ancestors came from its former colonies. In keeping with Gay Sweatshop's growing interest in diversity and pluralism, race, gender, and class join sexual orientation as interrelated sites of oppression and struggle. Caliban's 'This island's mine' becomes a political call for oppressed groups to take rightful possession of contemporary Britain against those – homophobic families, racist police, and so forth – who keep them down.

The director of *The Tempest* within the play gives a very traditional and conservative reading of Shakespeare's work:

> Caliban is a primitive,
> He tried to rape Miranda,
> So don't try and give us the noble savage,
> It just won't work,
> It's an oversimplification
> It will destroy the balance of the play.
> Prospero is the hero,
> Not Caliban.

Against this view, *This Island's Mine* joins those many works, imaginative and critical, which take *The Tempest* as a particularly important ground for exploring colonialist oppression – see, for example, Aimé Césaire's *A Tempest* and Ngũgĩ Wa Thiong'o's comment that 'In the story of Prospero and Caliban, Shakespeare had dramatized the practice and psychology of colonization years before it became a global phenomenon' (Cartelli: 106). The play stages the opposition of such post-colonial readings to naive and conservative readings as part of its explicit and implicit content. In this way, *This Island's Mine* is both a creative and a critical text. It rereads *The Tempest* by adapting it and displacing Prospero and his attitudes from its centre. Here Osment's use of juxtaposed multiple inner voices and narratives instead of the topdown and reductive attitudinizing of Prospero is important: no voice is allowed to dominate; each is heard.

The Tempest is a romance, and Shakespeare's romances are about families. Families are Osment's subject too, but his political interest is not only in the problems and strengths of traditional families but in the possibilities that the myriad forms of 'pretended' families have to offer. As *This Island's Mine* takes an expansive view of forms of oppression, so it does as well of forms of human bonding: Britain and the contemporary world should belong to all the kinds of families that inhabit there. Within these families, more regard is also given to women and mother-figures than in the Shakespearean original.

Osment's multiple narratives expand also on the possible outcomes implicit in Shakespearean romance. Romance often begins with some kind of loss or displacement, often because of familial disruption. *This Island's Mine* begins with Luke's alienation and flight from his family, which takes place in a history involving Martin's earlier estrangement from his sister and brother-in-law. Other characters suffer similar disruptions: Miss Rosenblum's broken relationship with Stephen; Marianne and Jody's estrangements from their father. Romance often ends with recovery, forgiveness, and reconciliation: here we have Martin's partial reconciliation with his family, and Selwyn's and Luke's returns, however temporary, to theirs. Reconciliation, however, is not across the board: the reunion of Stephen and Miss Rosenblum is set up only to be pointedly avoided; Marianne's reconciliations with her father and sister are fraught and fragile indeed. Here the play points to another aspect of the narrative of romance: open adventure, as in Ariel free to the elements at the end of *The Tempest*. Luke's return to his family appears to be prologue to his setting out again; indeed, the alternative families and experiences embraced by many of the characters constitute adventures outside of traditional norms. Finally, romance in *The Tempest* faces up to the finality of death, as in Prospero's 'We are such stuff / As dreams are made on, and our little life / Is rounded with a sleep' – thoughts echoed in *This Island's Mine* by Vladimir the cat's musings as he approaches death.

The Tempest is in part a utopian play, both in its ending and in Gonzalo's fantasy of an ideal kingdom (act 2, scene 1), which is echoed here in Stephen's musings on *pax americana*. But just as Gonzalo's ideal is undercut in *The Tempest*, utopianism is displaced in *This Island's Mine* by the recognition of continuing struggle. Nonetheless, Osment writes that Gay Sweatshop is guided by the love which 'springs out of an ideology of compassion': 'Sometimes it is difficult to keep faith with such an ideology. . . . But it is important to remember that ideas do not die and that we cannot always predict how they will affect the future' (Osment 1989: lxvii). It is with a generosity of spirit and a personal and political openness that Osment rewrites and radically reconfigures *The Tempest*.

Select bibliography

Entries marked * are particularly accessible.

*Bennett, S. (1996a) *Performing Nostalgia: Shifting Shakespeare and the Contemporary Past*, London: Routledge.

— (1996b) 'Rehearsing *The Tempest*, Directing the Post-Colonial Body: Disjunctive Identity in Philip Osment's *This Island's Mine*,' *Essays in Theatre* 15,1: 35–44.

Cartelli, T. (1987) 'Prospero in Africa: *The Tempest* as Colonial Text and Pretext,' in J. E. Howard and M. F. O'Connor (eds), *Shakespeare Reproduced: The Text in History and Ideology*, New York: Methuen: 99–115.

Césaire, A. (1992) *A Tempest*, New York: Ubu Repertory Theater Publications.

*Osment, P. (1989) *This Island's Mine*, in P. Osment (ed.) *Gay Sweatshop: Four Plays and a Company*, London: Methuen.

— (1997) *Plays: 1*, London: Methuen.

This Island's Mine

Philip Osment

Reprinted by kind permission of Methuen Publishing Ltd., London.

Author's Note

This play is written in a mixture of narrative and
dialogue and any production has to be flexible
enough to incorporate both these styles. On the
whole the actors narrate in character and the lines
are informed by the character's attitude and state
of mind – sometimes the narration takes on the
flavour of direct speech such that it becomes
almost part of the dialogue. At other times the
actors tell the story in a more neutral way or with
just a hint of characterization which becomes
stronger in the dialogue scenes. In the first
production all the actors were onstage all the time
which helped the flow of the play and which
meant that they were able to become, for instance,
part of the crowd at the airport or the bystanders
on the pavement with ease. Actors not involved in
a scene also played music, sang, or made tableaux
when appropriate. The doubling of Stephen/
Prospero and Marianne/Miranda is important.*
Debbie and Dave were played by black actors even
though this is not specified in the text.

Music

There is an original score and lyrics written by
Sharon Nassauer to accompany the text. The
music and songs are used to heighten certain
moments or to make links between different parts
of the play. Certain characters or situations are
associated with certain pieces of music which in
the first production were played and sung by the
actors. The lyrics of the funeral song which is
included in the text were written by Sharon
Nassauer.

Scene 1

LUKE The bell rings for the end of school.
  Luke packs up his books,
  Decides,
  With nervous resolution that tonight will be the
    night:
  I'll tell me Mam first –
  When I get home –
  Tonight won't be like other nights;
  Sitting at the table,
  Reading out the headlines from the local paper;
  Instead,
  I'll make her a cup of tea
  Talk to her before our Dad gets home –
  Potatoes boiling on the stove,
  Chops sizzling in the oven –
  Say quite simply:
  'I've got something to tell you Mam,
  I owe it you to tell you,
  I don't want to hide from you.'
  Luke strolls across the playground,
SCHOOLBOY Fourth former behind his back,
  Limply flaps his wrist.
LUKE Luke (usually so quick to notice)
  Fails to register the insult,
  Lost in his preoccupation
  Of how that kitchen-table conversation might
    proceed:
MAGGIE 'What's that my dear?
  Oh, just turn on the gas under those peas,
  Or he'll walk in
  And we won't be ready.
  Now, what is it you don't want to hide from me?
  You've not taken up smoking have you?'
LUKE The cycle sheds –
  Luke straps his briefcase on his bike,
  Pedals down the drive,

---

* Doubling was used extensively in the original production; for instance, one actor played Martin, Stephen and
Prospero, and one actor played Jody, Irina, Debbie and Wayne. – Eds.

Waves to Dave
(His best friend)
Staying late for rugby practice,
'Would he be my best friend if he knew?'
Through the gates and up the hill.
He pants his reassurances in the rhythm of the
    ride,
'You didn't do wrong, Mam,
It's nobody's fault,
I'm happy as I am.'
Pause at the top for a view of the city.
'I always stop here on my way back from school,
It makes me feel . . .
Oh, I don't know . . .
Hopeful
The whole city spread out
You can see our house down on the estate,
And further along at Nethercliffe,
The closed-down factories where our
Dad used to work.'
Everyday he has a rest up here,
After the climb,
Breathing in the view,
Looking right across the city to the moors on the
    other side –
'Where our Dad used to take us for Sunday
    picnics
When we still had the car.'
And way beyond the moors where they
disappear in a blue haze,
Like his whole life spread out before him.
Full of possibilities,
Exciting prospects,
Dimly discernible hopes
In the blue, hazy horizon.
'Things you've only got an inkling of,
But you know they're there,
Waiting for you.
Gives me a funny feeling in my stomach
That's almost like an ache.'
One last look,
Then it's on down the hill,
Freewheeling,
Spirits soaring,
Wind in his hair,
Eyes smarting,
Building up speed,
Then slowing down again
To stop outside the newsagents.
Some headlines,
VOICE ONE DON'T TEACH OUR CHILDREN TO
    BE GAY!
LUKE Some front page headlines,
VOICE TWO GOVERNORS TAKE ACTION TO
    PROTECT HEALTH AND MORALS

LUKE And he's down to earth with a sickening
    thud.
It's a different boy who wearily rides the last few
    hundred yards
Between the two rows of terraced houses,
Twin walls of normality
To stem the tide.
How stupid of him to think that he could fight
    that,
Be accepted here.
As he parks his bike in the shed
He blushes with shame
At the idea
Of what
He had planned to say.

Scene 2

FRIEND 1 London,
FRIEND 2 A restaurant
MARTIN And Martin eating out with friends
    Is holding forth,
    Late into the night.
    'Once upon a time I was lonely,
    I thought I was the only one in the world,
    I was filled with self-disgust.
    Then I discovered hope.
    Pride.
    I came to see that my body was mine,
    To do with as I saw fit,
    And guilt belonged to the past.'
VOICE ONE The waiters look on glumly,
VOICE TWO Cough,
VOICE ONE And tap their feet,
VOICE TWO And ask each other,
    'Aren't these people ever going to leave?'
MARTIN 'Then, from somewhere, comes this
    disease
    And they use it to say,
    "Didn't we tell you?
    It's divine retribution.
    Look where your behaviour has got you!"'
FRIEND 1 They sense the manager listening
MANAGER As he counts the evening's takings
FRIEND 2 'Let's just pay the bill and go.'
MARTIN But Martin has to finish;
    'They tell us what we can and cannot do,
    Don't suck –'
TWO The waiters exchange a knowing smirk.
MARTIN 'Don't fuck –'
MANAGER The manager drops his pile of
    coins.
MARTIN 'And if we're not careful
    We'll all be locked up in our bodies again,
    Scared of touching each other.'

MANAGER 'Gentlemen, please,
  We want to go home.'
MARTIN As he pays the bill
  Martin hardly notices the manager's disdainful
    look.
MANAGER 'Goodnight, gentlemen.'
MARTIN Out on the street they kiss goodnight on
    the corner.
  'Is it true you can't catch it from a kiss?'
  Martin walks home alone,
  And decides . . .
  To give the Heath a miss.
  'Early to bed, early to rise . . .'

Scene 3

MANAGER In the café,
  The manager blows out the last candle,
  Stands at the bar,
  Rattles his keys,
  Waits for his staff to leave.
MARK Mark Leigh, assistant chef,
  Proud of his work, glad of the job,
  Passes the man, says goodnight,
  And goes.
  'Am I imagining it?
  Or are they really being funny with me?
  Ever since I mentioned Selwyn,
  Told them I'd got a boyfriend.'
  As he crosses the street he glances back:
  Dimly lit by the light over the bar
  He sees his workmates gather round his boss –
  Like in some mafioso film –
CHEF The chef,
WAITER 1 The waiters,
CASHIER The cashier . . .
MANAGER The manager holding out a
    newspaper,
  Pointing to headline;
WAITER 2 They read.
WAITER 1 Eyes turn
MANAGER Towards the door
MARK Through which Mark has just walked.

Scene 4

MARTIN Martin lives in a run-down house that
    has seen better days,
  Sitting there on the corner of the street,
  Out of keeping with its neighbours
  Who have been converted according to the
    gospel of the new age –
  Their once spacious rooms
  Divided into flats
  Cut down to size

In order that no tenants get more than their fair
    share of space.
MISS ROSENBLUM Not so the house on the corner,
  It still retains its former grandeur
  (In spite of damp patches on the walls
  And cracks in the moulding on the ceiling)
  Built to house a wealthy merchant and his
    family,
  Now just two people live there:
MARTIN Martin
MISS ROSENBLUM And his landlady, Miss
    Rosenblum.
  One morning,
  Miss Rosenblum,
  Seeing Martin in the hall,
  Stops him between stair and door.
MARTIN Martin just popping out to buy some
    milk for his tea.
MISS ROSENBLUM There amongst the potted
    plants and yucca plants
  She warns him:
  'Beware!
  It can happen again.
  I see the signs, Mr Martin,
  They want someone to blame.'
MARTIN Martin, smiling politely,
  Tries to figure out a way
  Of getting through the front door to the shop
  As quickly as possible, without hurting her
    feelings.
MISS ROSENBLUM Miss Rosenblum –
  A retired piano teacher,
  Spends each morning –
  Nine-thirty till twelve –
  In an alcove at the library
  Scanning every newspaper
  Clicking her tongue and sighing,
  Muttering to herself in Viennese German,
  Reading between the lines
  Looking for the signs . . .
  Her afternoons are spent
  In a patisserie on Finchley Road,
  Where she plays the piano
  Every tea-time from three till five.
  Afterwards she eats Strudel with her friends –
  Ilse, Freddi and Hutch
  And talks to them about what's happening in the
    world,
  Mindful of the time,
  When driven out of house and homeland,
  She fled the terror that swept away half her
    family.
  'Last time, Mr Martin,
  We were the pestilence,
  Now you people are spreading a plague.

I see it.
You must watch.
You must be prepared.'
MARTIN Martin, imagining his tea going cold in
the pot,
Tries to reassure her
And moves towards the door.
MISS ROSENBLUM But the old lady halts him,
Pinching his arm in a bony grip:
'Do not think it cannot happen here!'
MARTIN As he closes the door,
He hears her slowly climb the stairs
Talking to her ginger tom,
MISS ROSENBLUM 'Ja, Vladimir, so ist es,
So wird es sein!'

Scene 5

LUKE Saturday mornings,
Luke gets up late,
Has the house to himself.
His Mam and Dad catch the bus to town,
To get the week's groceries.
Luke lies in bed and hears the back door slam,
Remembers a time when his father wouldn't be
seen dead on a bus
Let alone in a supermarket.
But now,
His male pride battered by lack of work,
He looks forward to these weekly outings with
his wife,
The biggest event of his week.
Luke hears the bus stop at the bottom of the
road
Creeps out of bed,
Pulls back the curtain,
Watches them board.
Then its out the door,
Along the passage,
Into their bedroom.
Stealing across to his Mother's dressing-table,
He catches sight of himself in the mirror,
Looking guilty as a thief.
Then continues.
Slowly opening the top right-hand drawer,
There where she keeps her jewellery
(Such as it is)
And face creams
Her lipstick and mascara,
Reminding him of other Saturdays,
When he'd crept in here, lured by the need
To open the box
And let the Pandora trapped in every man
Parade around his parents' bedroom
Decked out in his Mother's finery.

But not this morning.
He passes over the make-up and the necklaces
And reaches right to the back
Where his mother hides her brother's letters
Carefully wrapped up in tissue-paper,
Out of sight and out of mind of the rest of the
family.
Letters from his uncle,
In London.
He opens one and reads the address,
Repeating it to himself several times,
Committing it to memory.
Then returns it to its envelope,
The envelope to the pile
Which he wraps in tissue as before
Placing the package, how he found it, in the
drawer.

Scene 6

MARTIN While at Heathrow,
Martin waits to meet his wife –
MARIANNE Oh yes, he has a wife –
Returning from an extended trip
To visit friends and family in the States.
Marianne, a southern belle,
Escaped to England to become a dyke
Away from the persistent scrutiny of her North
Carolina family.
From a mother whose little girl can do no
right
And a father whose little girl can do no wrong –
Both impossible to live up to.
And so to England.
A marriage of convenience with Martin,
Arranged by a mutual friend,
Dual nationality was hers.
Although she sometimes feels she has no nation
That she's stuck somewhere in the mid-atlantic.
An exile in both countries.
MARTIN Martin, at the barrier, smiles at a man –
Attractive if a little tipsy –
MAN Who smiles back.
MARTIN Is he?
Isn't he?
Martin's radar can't quite decide.
MAN He asks Martin if he's meeting someone off
the New York flight?
MARTIN 'Yes I am.'
MAN 'So am I. I'm meeting my wife.'
MARTIN ('Ah well, you can't win them all.')
'Really? I'm meeting my wife too.'
And there she is –
MARIANNE 'Hi, hon, thanks for meeting me.'
MARTIN 'That's alright. You OK?'

MARIANNE 'Oh, Martin, Berta's dead.'
Mrs Berta Jones,
The Black woman who raised Marianne,
Nursed her through illness,
Consoled her when upset
Had been more of a Mother
Than the brittle doll-like figure who was her
biological parent.
Marianne can still remember those happy hours
Spent in the kitchen with Berta.
Making bread under her all-seeing supervision
Or sitting in her lap
Face pressed to her bosom,
Listening to the words resonating in her chest
As Berta told stories,
The smell of dough mingling with her perfume
and sweat.
Sometimes
In the arms of a lover,
The memory – so sweet –
Returns to choke her with emotion.
JODY Then there was Jody,
MARIANNE Berta's youngest,
JODY Jody Jones,
MARIANNE Marianne's childhood friend,
JODY Jody,
Light brown skin,
Hair plaited and beribboned,
Eyes,
One moment flashing with anger,
The next brimming with tears of tenderness.
MARIANNE Those long hot summer afternoons
Sitting out back on the porch

(*Both try to do headstands.*)

MARIANNE 'I hate you, Jody Jones,
You pushed me over.'
JODY 'Your legs were all bent,
I was trying to put them straight.'
MARIANNE 'I'm never gonna talk to you
again.'
JODY The misery.
MARIANNE Then the making friends again:
JODY 'Marianne? . . .
Marianne? . . .
You can wear my new ribbon if you
wanna . . .'
MARIANNE 'And you can play with my roller
skates.'
BOTH The joy.

(*They hug.*)

MARIANNE Those years of their childhood –
At the time they seemed to last forever,
JODY But all the same they rushed by.

MARIANNE Marianne was sent off to a private
school in Virginia
Where she excelled.
JODY While Jody went to the local state school.
MARIANNE And later,
Marianne's father paid for Jody to go up North
to college
JODY Where *she* excelled.
MARIANNE And so Jody and Marianne
JODY Went their separate ways,
MARIANNE Lost contact –
JODY Until they came face to face over Berta's
grave.
MARIANNE 'My Daddy and I went to the
funeral,
He wanted to pay his last respects.
Of course Mom didn't go –
She said she had a migraine.
There were so many people there,
She had so many friends.'
ALL We too shall come to the Riverside
One by one, one by one,
And lay our garments all aside
One by one, one by one.
The Lord is with us on the tide
One by one, one by one
As one by one he carries us
To home, to home.
We shall be gathered, fording the river
One by one.
MARIANNE 'Then I saw Jody standing amidst the
mourners –
I recognized her at once':
'Hi, Jody.'
JODY The other woman turning away,
As if she had not heard.
Detaching herself from the group at the
graveside
Heading off towards the waiting cars:
MARIANNE 'Jody, don't you recognize me?'
JODY 'Hello, Marianne.'
MARIANNE 'I'm sorry about your Mom, Jody.'
JODY 'Thanks.'
MARIANNE 'She was the kindest woman I ever
met,
I loved her dearly.'
JODY 'You're looking well, Marianne.'
MARIANNE 'You, too.
Are you working?'
JODY 'Yes.'
MARIANNE 'What are you doing nowadays?'
JODY 'I work for Oxfam,
I spend a lot of my time in Africa.'
MARIANNE 'Oh, you've done well, I'm glad.
Did you see Daddy?'

JODY 'Yes I did.'
MARIANNE 'Come over and say hello.'
JODY 'I can't do that, Marianne.'
MARIANNE 'Why not?
   He'd sure like you to.'
JODY 'Your Daddy and I don't get along anymore,
      Marianne.
   I had a big fight with him the last time I was
      home to see Mom.
   She was furious with me,
   She never forgave me.'
MARIANNE 'What did you fight about?'
JODY 'Ask him, Marianne.
   I have to go.'
MARIANNE 'Well, look, here's my address,
   If you ever get to London,
   Look me up.'
JODY 'OK.'
MARIANNE 'And she just left without explaining
      anything.
   I mentioned it to my Dad
   And he said it all came down to a
      misunderstanding.
   My Mom clammed right up when I asked her
      about it.
   It's a mystery.'

(MARTIN *puts his arm around her.*)

MARTIN Martin tries to comfort her,
   Picks up her suitcase
   And they leave.
MARIANNE 'He was always so good to her.
   I can't believe she'd be so ungrateful without
      reason.
   It's weird.'

Scene 7

PROSPERO Awake, dear heart, awake!
   Thou hast slept well.
   Awake!
MIRANDA The strangeness of your story put
   Heaviness in me.
PROSPERO Shake it off. Come on.
   We'll visit Caliban, my slave, who never
   Yields us kind answer.
MIRANDA 'Tis a villain, sir,
   I do not love to look on.
PROSPERO But as 'tis,
   We cannot miss him. He does make our fire,
   Fetch in our wood, and serves in offices
   That profit us. What, ho! Slave! Caliban!
   Thou, earth, thou! Speak!
CALIBAN There's wood enough within.
DIRECTOR 'No, no, no, no, no.'

In a draughty hall in Belsize Park
Rehearsals are not going well:
'Selwyn, darling,
Caliban is a primitive,
He tried to rape Miranda,
So don't try and give us the noble savage,
It just won't work,
It's an oversimplification
It will destroy the balance of the play.
Prospero is the hero,
Not Caliban.'
SELWYN Who is Selwyn to argue with England's
      greatest playwright?
   Anyway,
   He doesn't want to be labelled as a
      troublemaker.
DIRECTOR 'He's raw physicality and sex.
   We'll dress you up in something skimpy
   Give the punters a treat.'
   Under his breath:
   'God why have I got the only black actor
   Who doesn't know how to use his body?'
SELWYN Selwyn,
   Proud of his work, glad of the job,
   Finds it difficult to stand his ground with tinpot
      theatre gods.
   But still explodes that night,
MARK When Mark tells him the latest news from
      the restaurant,
   How the manager took him aside:
MANAGER 'Come into my office, Mr Leigh.
   Now this is a rather delicate situation.
   The rest of the staff have asked me to talk to
      you.
   They have expressed some concern about
      working with you,
   I'm sure you can understand their fears;
   And so to avoid painful situations,
   I've no alternative but to give you your cards,
   And thank you for your hard work here at the
      restaurant.
   There's a month's full pay.'
MARK Mark speechless,
   Unable at first to reply,
   Then a halting. 'Why?'
MANAGER Is assured that it's nothing personal.
   The manager is not at leave to go into details,
   Is unwilling to prolong
   What must be an embarrassing interview for
      both of them.
   Tells Mark he needn't work out his notice –
   'Someone is filling in for you,
   So that's taken care of.'
   Brushes aside Mark's shocked protests
   And ushers him out.

MARK Mark on the street,
    With a bulging pay-packet,
    But no job.

    (SELWYN *takes* MARK *in his arms.*)

SELWYN 'They can't do that to you.
    You should have told that bastard where he
      could stick his job!'

Scene 8

MISS ROSENBLUM 'Mr Martin, Mr Martin,
    There is a young man at the door for you.'
MARTIN Martin stumbling out of bed,
    Bleary-eyed and overhung,
    Kicks over a glass half-full of Marianne's duty-
      free
    Left over from the night before.
    Swears,
    Puts on his dressing gown
    And opens the door.
MISS ROSENBLUM 'I thought I should wake you
    up.'
MARTIN 'Thank you, Miss Rosenblum.'
    Only then becoming aware of the fair-haired boy
      standing behind her.
    An Adidas bag over his shoulder,
    Looking incongruous in the dusty hall,
    There amongst the potted palms and yucca
      plants,
    As if lost on his way to some squash court
    Or swimming pool.
LUKE 'Hello, Uncle Martin.'
MARTIN Martin's brain is not yet in gear.
LUKE 'I'm your nephew, Luke.
    I've run away from home.'
MARTIN Martin peering at him fuzzily,
    Seeing the family likeness –
    ('Great,
    This is all I need.')
MISS ROSENBLUM 'Well, Mr Martin,
    I go to the shop now,
    To buy my Vladimir his breakfast.'
MARTIN 'Right, thank you Miss Rosenblum.'
MISS ROSENBLUM 'Goodbye, Mr Martin.
    Goodbye, junger Mann.'
LUKE 'Goodbye.'
MARTIN 'Well, Luke, you'd better come in.'

(*End of part one.*)

Scene 9

MISS ROSENBLUM So once again the old house
    gives refuge to one in flight
    As it has done many times before.

It serves a purpose
Though falling now into disrepair:
Slates on the roof are missing,
Window frames are beginning to rot,
The cold water tank has sprung a leak,
Electricity needs rewiring.
Miss Rosenblum often thinks of selling up
Buying herself a little box somewhere
But she can never quite bring herself to do it.
VLADIMIR Meanwhile Vladimir wanders freely
    through its decaying rooms
And up the carpeted stairway at its heart.
Pausing now to sit on the window-sill halfway
    up the stairs
Where the dust rises in the shafts of light.
He looks out on the overgrown half acre of
    garden
And the alley which runs along the back
(Once his favourite nocturnal haunt)
He narrows his eyes in the autumn sun
Radar ears twitching and scanning every
    movement –
Each falling leaf might be prey –
Building up a picture of his surroundings with
    all his senses,
For sight and sound and touch are not separated
    out in his cat's brain
Just as the past and present are all one;
He is old now
But still feels like that kitten
Left on the doorstep in a cardboard box
By some well-meaning child
(In those days everyone knew
That the Russian lady who lived here then
Would always take in a stray).
Vladimir becomes bored with falling leaves,
'Too old now to be chasing pigeons.'
He arches his neck to give his ginger chest a
    desultory lick,
Then jumps down with a thud onto the landing
(Limbs have lost their spring)
To continue his leisurely stroll up through the
    house.
At the top are the servants' quarters,
A depository now for bits of junk and discarded
    furniture;
Vladimir squeezes through the half-open door
And sidles up to an old velvet armchair
Rubs himself against the worn and faded
    fabric –
There where his claws were once
Dug in
And sharpened by his youthful self.
He clambers onto the seat,
Curls up,

And sleeps,
And dreams.
Who knows what pictures now flit across his
    mind?
Does the chair fill up with the figure
Whose pointed elbows made the worn patches
    on its arms?
Whose hair stained the headrest?
MME IRINA Does her perfume linger?
VLADIMIR So that Vladimir imagines he is
    sleeping in her lap?
MME IRINA Perhaps for him she is not dead and
    he can feel
A bejewelled and wrinkled hand stroking his fur,
Madame Irina was a White Russian princess
Brought to London by a far-seeing aunt in 1913.
The story goes that she brought with her
The family jewels
Disguised as a box of truffles
Each gem cunningly coated in chocolate.
She lived out the rest of her life here in this
    house
With a string of paid companions and cats,
Waiting for the day that never came,
When Erkaterinburg would be avenged
And she would return to Mother Russia.
So she ended her days
Sitting in this chair
With her cats around her
At her side a bell
To summon Miss Rosenblum,
Popping chocolates between her pampered lips.
VLADIMIR So Vladimir sleeps at the top of the
    house,
Till he hears below
The sound of Miss Rosenblum opening a tin.
The dream forgotten,
Wide awake,
He scampers almost skittishly down the stairs
To his food dish,
Leaving the ghost alone in her chair.

Scene 10

MARTIN 'We've got a spare room upstairs
    A sort of junk room.
    I'm sure Miss Rosenblum won't mind you using
    it for a few days.'
LUKE 'Thanks.'
MARTIN 'I think we should phone your Mum,
    Let her know where you are.'

    (Pause.)

MARTIN 'Do you want me to phone?'
LUKE 'Yeah.'

MARTIN 'Do you want to talk about why you ran
    away?'
LUKE 'I just had to get away for a while . . .
    I need to think.'
MARTIN 'What about?'
LUKE 'About myself . . . about . . .'
MARTIN 'Yes?'
LUKE 'I think I might be . . .'
    And so Luke tells his uncle why he left,
MARTIN And Martin
    Remembers other times
    When he himself arrived in London
    On the brink of self-acceptance,
    With his law degree from a Northern University
    And his long hair
    To the still swinging London of 1969
    With its happenings and its demonstrations
    When everything seemed possible –
    Or nearly everything –
    For though men talked of brotherly love
    It did not include the kind of love
    That Martin felt for other men.
    Then came the rumours from New York
    Of riots in Greenwich Village,
    And a new sort of Pride was born
    Which quickly spread to Europe.
    Remembers the first rallies in Hyde Park
    The excitement of it all,
    The joy.
    The Isle of Wight and Shepton Mallet
    Had never felt as good as this.
    'Where's that photo –
    I've got it somewhere –
    Of me in drag with an ostrich feather in my hair,
    My arms around David and David
    My two lovers?'
    (In those days you had to have at least two,
    Now even one seems excessive to Martin.)
    Remembers the bystanders on the pavements,
VOICE ONE Some faces jeering,
VOICE TWO Some perplexed,
VOICE THREE The angry ones
VOICE FOUR And ones which showed disgust.
VOICE FIVE Faces where the envy turned to hate.
VOICE TWO But scattered in amongst them were
    faces
    Which spoke of a battle going on inside.
MARTIN Remembers the day when in the crowd
    He saw a little nuclear family –
FRANK Husband,
MAGGIE Wife,
LUKE And child,
MARTIN Looking lost and scared.
MAGGIE Suddenly the woman's eyes meet
    Martin's,

Her hand goes to her face.
When she takes it away,

MARTIN Martin recognizes his sister.

FRANK Now the man has seen him too,
He shields the child's face from the sight
And pulls his wife away into the crowd.

MARTIN 'I've still got that letter she wrote –'

MAGGIE It was a surprise visit
We went to your house in Notting Hill
They told us you were at a rally in Hyde Park.
We didn't know what sort of rally it was
But we thought we might be able to find you.
So we stood at Speakers Corner –
For ages we couldn't make out what the banners
    said
And when we did we couldn't believe our
    eyes.
I thought you must be there as some observer.
Then we saw you,
You were with all those queers
I hardly recognized my own brother.
You were marching with them
With your arms around another man.
There was no doubt.
Frank says he doesn't want you in the house,
He's afraid of the effect you might have on
    Luke.

MARTIN (That had stung more than anything,
He'd lavished love and attention on his baby
    nephew
The last time he was home.
Now the child had to be protected from him.)

MAGGIE Frank says he always thought if anything
    were to happen to us
Then you would be the one to look after Luke.
He's taken it very badly.
It was such a shock
Seeing you there
Shouting it on the streets.
I think it's best we don't see each other for a
    while.

MARTIN Martin had never been able to forgive his
    brother-in-law
And felt that now there was some rough justice
    at work
That the boy was taking shelter with him.
And so he phones his sister,
Calming her,
Telling her that Luke is worried about his
    exams.

MAGGIE A few words with her son help to
    reassure her.

MARTIN 'He can stay with me for a few days,
    Maggie,
I'll look after him.'

MAGGIE 'Thank you, Martin,
I'm so relieved,
And Frank will be too,
He couldn't be in better hands.'

Scene 11

MARIANNE On the tube
Marianne takes the badge from her pocket
Looks at it
Then with nervous resolution pins it to her
    lapel.
Rushing wildly up the stairs at Green Park
Risking her life crossing Piccadilly in the rush
    hour
Colliding with the fur-clad lady at the entrance
    to Fortnum and Mason's,
Finding at last the restaurant –

WAITRESS 'A table for one, Madam?'
The waitress eyes her leather jacket with alarm.

MARIANNE 'Uh, no, I'm meeting someone.'
She narrows her eyes trying to bring the scene
    before her
Into focus.
Spies in the corner the man in his mid-sixties –

STEPHEN White hair in stylish cut
Tanned urbane face
Expensive grey suit
Looking half his age
Relaxed and powerful.

MARIANNE She falters,
Regrets her decision to dress down for the
    occasion,
Fingers go nervously to her lapel,
Remembering Debbie's words this morning:

DEBBIE 'What do you want a badge for?
You don't normally wear badges –
And that's an old one – vintage '86.'

MARIANNE Seeing him sitting there,
She wonders herself what she's trying to prove.
'Ah, damn, I said I'd wear it and I will!'
A deep breath
And she's edging between the tables.

STEPHEN As if he senses her presence the man
    looks up from the menu.

(*He rises to meet her and they hug.*)

Installs her in a chair as if she were in full
    evening dress.

MARIANNE 'Sorry I'm late, Dad,
I had to give Debbie's kid his tea
When he got home from school.'
Trying to make this reference to her
English lover seem
Natural and spontaneous.

BOTH Chasms open.
STEPHEN He hands her the menu.
  'I've only just gotten away myself.
  It all took longer than expected.'
MARIANNE 'What exactly are you doing in
    London, Dad?'
STEPHEN 'There's a conference on health in the
    Third World –
  I'm here to talk about what our company can
    offer in equipment and supplies.
  In some countries there's a chronic shortage.'
MARIANNE That look of concern and sadness
  How well Marianne knows it.
  When she did something bad as a child
  She feared that look more than any
  scolding from her Mother.
  'How's Mom?
  Is she . . . well at the moment?'
STEPHEN 'She went through a rocky patch in the
    Spring.
  She seems to have come through that.
  She's given up booze – for the present anyway.
  Shall we order?'
  Every now and again his eyes come to rest on
    her badge,
  Then they're off again
  Uncertain of what they have seen.
  'When I was in England during the war,
  We used to come to London on leave.
  Fortnum and Mason's restaurant became one of
    our regular haunts.'
MARIANNE 'Bit posh.'
STEPHEN 'Well, we were living it up.
  We were based down in Wiltshire
  On some godforsaken hill
  So it was grand to be in the big city.
  Mind you, it wasn't just Soho that brought us up
    here,
  We were interested in art and theatre.
  England had so much culture and history.
  On one of our visits
  My buddy took me to the British Museum
  To see the Egyptian Mummies.'
  But he doesn't mention to Marianne
  The meeting with the young Jewish girl.
MISS ROSENBLUM Coming from the reading
    room
  Where she had been studying the newspapers
  For any scrap of information about the camps.
BUDDY 'I dare you to speak to her.'
STEPHEN 'OK, I will . . .
  Pardon me, ma'am,
  Can you tell me where I can find the Egyptian
    section?'
  Persuading her to accompany them,

'This seems a dull place to spend your
    afternoons.'
MISS ROSENBLUM And she told him that Karl
    Marx came here to write.
  Later she took him to afternoon tea at Fortnum
    and Mason's.
STEPHEN 'You know, Marianne,
  We carved a white horse on that hill
  down there in Wiltshire.
  There's chalk underneath the turf
  You can cut it away and make a picture.
  Some British regiments carved out their
    insignia,
  But we yanks carved a horse.
  It's still there.'
  And he remembers that last afternoon with
    Luise.
  The walk to the top
  To see the newly finished landmark.
  From up close it didn't look like a horse at all.
  Remembers her saying.
MISS ROSENBLUM 'The English people do not
    know how dearly they buy their victory.
  Today they give you a piece of hill,
  Tomorrow they will sell you their souls.'
STEPHEN She was an oddball,
  With oddball ideas.
  And yet he'd nearly married her.
  Back home,
  Later,
  When Senator McCarthy and J. Edgar Hoover
    were out hunting for witches,
  He believed he'd had a lucky escape.
  And yet as he grew older,
  He thought of her more and more.
  'Hell, Marianne,
  What is that button you're wearing?'
DEBBIE 'You must really care about what your
    Dad thinks of you,
  Going to all that effort to provoke him.'
MARIANNE She hands it to her father.
STEPHEN He holds it
  A tiny badge
  In his large paw
  With its raw message:
  US BASES OUT OF BRITAIN.
  He looks at it for several moments
  Then hands it back.
  'Have you ever considered buying a place to live
    over here, Marianne?'

Scene 12

LUKE Luke sits in the velvet armchair
  In that room at the top of the house.

While putting his clothes in a drawer
He found a cardboard box
With old birthday cards and Christmas cards:
IRINA 'To my dear Luise,
    From one old maid to another,
    Yours Irina.
    Christmas 1960.'
LUKE Letters
    And photos –
    One, faded and torn,
STEPHEN Of a soldier
MISS ROSENBLUM And a young girl
STEPHEN Standing under a statue.
LUKE On the back:
MISS ROSENBLUM Piccadilly Circus, 1945.

(STEPHEN *and* MISS ROSENBLUM *pose as in the*
photo.)

LUKE A tap at the door –
    Luke hides the box guilty behind a chair.
MISS ROSENBLUM 'Junger Mann,
    My cat is up the tree,
    He cannot get down.
    I am worried for him.
    Can you help please?'
LUKE Luke follows her outside to the tree at the
    bottom of the garden.
VLADIMIR Where Vladimir sits in the topmost
    branches,
    Blinking at them defiantly.
LUKE Luke runs to get a ladder
    And coaxes the stubborn cat down.

Scene 13

SELWYN After rehearsals Selwyn pays a visit to
    the library,
    Mindful of last night's row with Mark.
MARK Mark,
    Sitting at home all day
    Depressed.
    Watching the clock.
    Playing records,
    Going to the launderette.
    Watching the clock.
    Cleaning the flat,
    Cooking Selwyn's meal . . .
    Watching the clock –
    Potatoes boiling on the stove,
    Chops sizzling in the oven –
    Listening for steps on the stairway
    And watching the clock.
SELWYN Then the tetchiness when he does arrive
    As if Selwyn is somehow at fault,
    For working when Mark is unemployed.

'Look, I'm going to find out about your rights,
He can't just sack you like that.'
And so the trip to the library.
Finding the book he wants:
GAY WORKERS: TRADES UNIONS AND THE
    LAW.
Hesitating at the checkout
Trying to look unconcerned as the librarian
    reads the title.
He puts it in his bag
Under rehearsal clothes
And dog-eared script.
Then takes the short cut home
Along tree-lined streets,
So unlike the streets of his childhood
Lined with council blocks
With wafer-thin walls
And lifts that never worked.
Selwyn feels pleased with himself –
He's made it in a white man's world,
No need to feel victimized.
Now turning up the alley
That runs along the back of spacious gardens.
Half past six,
He starts to run,
Scared of Mark's reproachful look.
Racing out of the alley onto the busy main road
ONE Where a van screeches to a halt beside him
TWO And three policemen jump out:
THREE 'Where do you think you're going in such
    a hurry?'
ONE 'What are you doing in these parts?'
TWO 'What have you got hidden in the bag, then?'
SELWYN Selwyn backing away
    Remembering trips to the West End with his
    brother, Wayne.
WAYNE 'If they stop us, just turn and run.'
SELWYN 'Why, we haven't done nothing?'
WAYNE 'That won't stop them, just run.'
SELWYN So now he has to fight the impulse.
ONE 'Just don't try doing a runner.'
TWO They hustle him into the seclusion of the
    alley.
SELWYN 'I haven't done anything, let me go.'
THREE 'So, you won't mind us looking in your bag
    then, will you?'
ONE 'Fucking Ada – a book,
    That's an interesting title.'
TWO 'He's a poof.
    You a black pansy then?'
ONE 'I thought you only got pink ones.'
SELWYN 'Oh, very funny.'
    Selwyn tries to sound defiant and strong.
ONE 'Watch your lip, poof,
    Unless you want a truncheon up your arse.'

TWO 'No, he'd enjoy that, too much.'
ONE 'Here's something to remember us by, mate.'
      Punch.
TWO 'Try to be a bit more careful what you carry
      around with you.'
      Kick.
THREE 'Come on, you two, let's go.'
ONE They leave him in a heap.
SELWYN Selwyn falls through the gate
      Lips bleeding, ribs bruised,
      Into the back garden,

      (LUKE and MISS ROSENBLUM rush towards him.)

MISS ROSENBLUM Someone's back garden.
LUKE A young boy with a ginger cat in his arms
      Stares at him in amazement.
      Luke remembers that night during the strike,
      When his father returned from the police station
      With swollen lips and bruises down his back.
MISS ROSENBLUM Miss Rosenblum remembers
      that night
      When they took away her father
      Professor at the University
      For questioning.
      And later,
      When they returned to burn his books.

(*End of Part Two.*)

Scene 14

MARK That night, in bed, Mark comforts Selwyn:
      'Selwyn?'
SELWYN 'Mmmmmm?'
MARK 'You OK?'
SELWYN 'Mmm.'
MARK 'You sure?'
SELWYN 'Mmmm.'
MARK 'Good of that bloke Martin to drive you
      home.'
SELWYN 'Yeah, he was nice guy.'
MARK 'Who was the other one, the young one?'
SELWYN 'Dunno.'
MARK 'Do you think they're lovers?'
SELWYN 'I dunno,
      I didn't ask them.
      Why are you so interested anyway?'
MARK 'No reason.'

      (*Pause.*)

MARK 'He's a solicitor, you know.'
SELWYN 'Who?'
MARK 'Martin.'
SELWYN 'Oh.'
MARK 'Perhaps you could lodge a complaint
      through him.'

SELWYN 'Mmm. Ha.'
MARK 'What you laughing at.'
SELWYN 'Who'd believe me? There were no
      witnesses.'
MARK 'But you can't let them get away with it.'
SELWYN 'They do. All the time.'

      (*Pause.*)

SELWYN 'Owww. Mind my ribs.'
MARK 'Sorry.'
SELWYN 'Just leave me alone, will you?'
MARK 'Don't take it out on me, it's not my fault.'
SELWYN 'Who says?'
MARK 'What?'
SELWYN 'Nothing.'

      (*Pause.*)

SELWYN 'Saturday tomorrow, think I'll go over
      and see my Mum.'
MARK 'Oh.'
SELWYN 'Oh what?'
MARK 'I just thought we could spend the day
      together,
      I quite fancy playing nurse.'
SELWYN 'I'm not hurt that bad.'
MARK 'You sure you're up to going out?'
SELWYN 'I wanna see my Mum.'
MARK Mark thinks back to the festival in Victoria
      Park
      When they came face to face
MOTHER With Selwyn's Mum.
SELWYN Selwyn had already told his Mother
      about Mark.
MOTHER But neither side was prepared for this
      chance meeting –
MARK All through the embarrassed conversation
      She avoided looking at Mark.
MOTHER 'Your sister was asking after you last
      week,
      She says she hasn't seen you since Christmas.'
SELWYN 'Yeah, well, I've been busy.'
MOTHER 'It's like you're living in another
      country.'
      Before they parted she told Selwyn to be sure to
      visit her –
      'Don't listen to that brother of yours
      His fists will be his downfall.'
      Then off she went
      Sighing about the ungratefulness of the young.
MARK 'What was that about your brother Wayne?'
SELWYN 'He's threatened to beat me up if I go
      home.
      He shouldn't worry,
      I won't be going back.'
MARK Mark lies there and broods.

SELWYN 'Look, Mark, we don't have to be together
all the time you know.'
MARK 'I know.'
SELWYN 'Stop sulking then.'
MARK 'Why've you suddenly decided that you've
got to go over to Hackney.'
SELWYN 'I just wanna.'
MARK 'Has it got anything to do with what
happened today?'
SELWYN 'Of course it's fucking to do with what
happened today!
I wanna talk to someone about it.'
MARK 'You can talk to me.'
SELWYN 'You understand, do you?'
MARK 'Course I do.'
SELWYN 'How can you?'
MARK 'What, because I'm white?'
SELWYN 'Maybe.'
MARK 'It's never bothered you before.'
SELWYN 'How do you know what's bothered me
before?'
MARK 'What is this?
Suddenly everything's coming down to black
and white.
It's you I love,
The colour of your skin's not important.'
SELWYN 'Are you sure?'
MARK Mark can see it now –
The first time they made love,
The shock he'd felt when their bodies first made
contact;
Fair skin against dark skin,
Their legs intertwined
Looking down at their bellies touching,
The stark contrast.
Taking his head in his hands
Feeling his hair,
At one point,
Catching a glimpse of the two of them in the
mirror –
Not just man with man
But black with white as well.
The rush of excitement at the breaking of
taboos
Long-held by his race.
'No, Selwyn, I'm not sure.'

Scene 15

DEBBIE 'Marianne,
I can't tell you whether you should let your
Daddy buy you a house!'
Debbie is at the end of her tether!
MARIANNE 'Oh, God, it's such a big decision.
What do I do?

If I say yes,
Then I'll feel that they've gotten a hold over me
again.
It'll be like I never left the States.'
DEBBIE 'Then say no.'
MARIANNE 'If I say no,
It just feels like a childish gesture.'
DEBBIE 'Then say yes.'
MARIANNE 'It's not that simple.'
DEBBIE 'Give me strength.'
MARIANNE 'You don't understand.
The first thing to happen will be that my Mom
will want to come over and visit,
She'll start asking questions and criticizing:
"Why aren't you living with that nice husband of
yours Marianne?"
"Because he's gay, Mom,
And I'm a lesbian."
"Oh, Marianne, don't use such words. You know
how it upsets your Daddy!"
I can't go through all that.'
DEBBIE 'Then don't.'
MARIANNE Marianne feels that Debbie isn't being
very sympathetic.
DEBBIE 'She wants sympathy now!
She's got the luxury of being able to torment
herself
About whether she accepts a handout of seventy
thousand quid,
She spends hours bellyaching to me about it,
Till I'm ready to climb up the wall
And on top of that she wants sympathy!
My heart bleeds!'
MARIANNE 'I think you're jealous.'
DEBBIE 'Me jealous?
Never.
I've got this whole stack of people
Just waiting to buy me houses –
My only problem is whether to choose the
mansion in St. John's Wood,
Or the modest maisonette in Hampstead.
Course I'm bloody jealous.'
MARIANNE 'You don't have to be,
You could always come and live with me.'
DEBBIE 'Don't even think it, Marianne.
I've made my choices.
My kid,
My home,
My independence.
It took me five years to get out of my marriage,
Now
I feel great,
I've got my freedom.
I'm never going to give it up again.'
MARIANNE 'But we could have our own spaces.'

DEBBIE 'I've got my own space,
It's this tatty council flat in dear old Peckham,
And I love it.'
DAVE The doorbell interrupts their conversation –
MARIANNE Marianne opens the door to Debbie's
ten year-old son.
'Hiya kid, howya doin.'
DAVE 'Where's my dinner?'
MARIANNE 'Dave, I said Hi.'
DAVE 'Hi, Marianne.
Where's my dinner, Mum?'
DEBBIE 'Oh god, the lord and master returns',
Debbie can see that her son is in one of his
'I'm the man of the house moods'.
'Marianne's cooking tonight.'
DAVE 'Uhhhh.'
MARIANNE 'Well, gee honey,
You know how to make someone feel
appreciated.'
DAVE 'I'm hungry now,
Can't I have sausage and chips?'
DEBBIE 'But Marianne's bought us some lovely
fish.'
DAVE 'Don't like fish.'
DEBBIE 'Dave, what's the matter with you?
What's wrong with you tonight?'
DAVE 'Nothing's wrong with me.'
DEBBIE But Debbie knows her son,
Underneath the macho nonchalance she senses
something else.
'Look at you your coat's all torn.
Have you been in a fight?'
DAVE 'No.'
DEBBIE 'Dave . . . '
DAVE 'I haven't.'
DEBBIE 'Well, what's this scratch on your face?
Who did that?'
DAVE 'It was . . . '
DEBBIE 'What?'
DAVE 'It was just something that happened on the
way home.'
DEBBIE 'What?'
DAVE 'Ian Parker and Derek and that lot,
They were saying things.'
MARIANNE 'What did they do to you kid?
Shall I go and beat them up?'
DAVE 'No!'
DEBBIE 'What sort of things?'
DAVE 'Things about you and Marianne.'
DEBBIE 'Like what?'
DAVE 'They said you were Lesbians,
They kept on shouting it.
And then . . . '
DEBBIE 'Then?'
DAVE 'They said I was a nancy boy,

And started grabbing me.'
MARIANNE 'Are they still out there?'
Marianne rushes out the door and down the
stairs
To find the bullies.
DAVE 'Where's she going?
It's none of her business.'
DEBBIE 'She's angry for you, Dave.
And so am I.
Come on let me give you a cuddle.'
DAVE 'No, leave me alone.'
DEBBIE 'Dave . . . '
DAVE 'Leave me alone,
I hate you
I want to go and live with my Dad.
I don't want to live with you and Marianne.'

(*He cries in her arms.*)

DEBBIE 'Dave, Dave.'

(MARIANNE *returns.*)

MARIANNE 'They've disappeared,
But I'll get them,
Don't worry, Dave.'
DEBBIE That night Debbie tucks him up in bed,
It's the time of day when they have their heart
to hearts,
When David becomes a small boy again
And lets the hardman's image slip
Just a little.
'Dave?'
DAVE 'Yeah?'
DEBBIE 'If you really want to live with your Dad,
We could ask him.'
DAVE 'I know.'
DEBBIE 'Do you want me to ask him?'
DAVE 'No.'
DEBBIE 'You sure?'
DAVE 'Yes,
I didn't mean it really.'
DEBBIE 'That's good,
Because I like having you live with me.
And Dave?'
DAVE 'Yeah?'
DEBBIE 'Do you want me to pick you up from
school tomorrow
And walk home with you?'
DAVE 'No, I'll be all right.'
DEBBIE 'Night, then, love.'
DAVE 'Night.
Mum?'
DEBBIE 'Yes?'
DAVE 'Tell Marianne,
I liked the fish.'
DEBBIE 'OK, I will.'

271

(*She joins* MARIANNE.)

MARIANNE 'You have to admit, hon,
  That living in a council flat in dear old Peckham
  Does have its disadvantages.'
DEBBIE 'OK, I'll think about it.'

Scene 16

MARTIN ('Hate discos,
  Never come to them')
  Thinks Martin
  As he hands over seven quid to the man on the
    desk.
  ('Music too loud,
  Air too smoky,
  People too busy posing to even look at you
  Let alone smile at you
  Or even talk.')
  Looks at Luke –
LUKE Eyes-a-sparkle –
MARTIN And recalls how desperately hopeful he
    felt at that age.
  Going to the bar for drinks
  He catches sight of himself in the mirror,
  Noting the wrinkles around his eyes,
  The grey hair at his temples.
  'A rum and coke and a pint of lager, please.'
  Looks around for Luke,
LUKE Already deep in conversation
  With an attractive young man
MARK In a pair of torn jeans.
MARTIN Martin recognizes Mark from the
    previous evening,
  When they drove Selwyn home.
  ('Wonder if they're lovers?')
  Now edging his way back through the crowd,
  'Excuse me.
  Excuse me.'
  ('God, if that bloke doesn't move,
  I'll pour this pint down his back.')
  'Thank you so much.'
LUKE But Mark and Luke are off to dance.
MARTIN 'Oh, fine,
  I'll hold your drinks.'
  ('Don't mind me,
  I like standing around on my own at discos
  Trying to look casual and self-possessed
  When all the time I'm feeling totally inadequate
  Because these bright young things with their
    careless elegance
  Are making me think that life has passed me by
  And I'm on the junk heap at thirty-eight.')
  Martin chances a smile at a flat-topped youth –
YOUTH Who looks right through him.

MARTIN ('Is that what we fought for all those
    years?
  Where did all that coming together go?')
  When Mark and Luke return
  He's well into his second pint.
LUKE 'Do you want to dance, Uncle Martin?'
MARTIN ('Does he have to call me that?')
  'No thanks, I don't like dancing.'
  ('Not here anyway,
  We used to dance in the streets.')
  And so the evening wears on
  Martin becoming more and more morose
  With each drink.
LUKE 'Have you got a pen and paper, Uncle
    Martin?'
MARK Mark wants to take down Luke's telephone
    number,
LUKE 'We're going to see a film on Monday night.'
MARTIN ('So they're not going home together
    tonight,
  A good old-fashioned courtship, eh?
  Very romantic,
  That's a sign of the times.')

  (MARK *and* LUKE *kiss.*)

  He watches them say a fond farewell
  Fighting back a sentimental sigh:
  ('Ah, young love –
  Let's hope we can go home now.')
LUKE 'That was a really great evening, Uncle,
  Thanks ever so much.'
MARTIN 'That's OK, Luke.
  Do you like him – Mark?'
LUKE 'Yes I do.
  You know he thought at first you were my
    boyfriend.'
MARTIN ('What a preposterous idea!')
LUKE 'But I told him who you were.'
MARTIN ('I should think so too.')
LUKE 'He said he wished he had a sexy uncle like
    you.'
MARTIN ('Pah, humbug,') thinks Martin
  As they run to catch the last tube home.

Scene 17

MOTHER When she saw his bruises
  Her anger knew no bounds.
  But she was pleased to see him,

  (*They embrace.*)

  Welcomed him with open arms,
  Took him out to the High Street to buy
    him a new pair of shoes,
  Cooked him a special meal
  And invited all the family round –

SELWYN His aunt and her new bloke,
His sister and her new baby,
Even Wayne turned up –
WAYNE Very quiet, cool, not giving much away,
SELWYN But Selwyn saw his presence as a sign
That a truce had been called!
MOTHER Then at bedtime their Mother said,
'Selwyn, your sister's using the spare room,
You'll have to share with Wayne tonight.'
SELWYN This was unexpected.
WAYNE Wayne said nothing
Went straight to his room.
SELWYN Later,
When Selwyn climbed into bed,
WAYNE Pretended to be asleep.
SELWYN Both of them lying there,
WAYNE Wide awake,
SELWYN For over an hour.

(*Pause.*)

SELWYN 'Don't worry, Wayne, I'm not gonna
touch you.'
WAYNE 'I never said I was worried.'
SELWYN 'It's not your fault I'm gay, you know.'
WAYNE 'What you say that for?'
SELWYN 'Do you think I don't remember what we
used to do?'
WAYNE Both of them could remember other
nights
When they had shared this bed,
SELWYN When hands reached out
WAYNE Under the bedclothes,
SELWYN Under the cover of night,
WAYNE And they had caressed each other's
bodies –
SELWYN Something secret that happened
after lights were out
WAYNE Never acknowledged or spoken about in
the cold light of day.
SELWYN Then,
Years later,
Selwyn came out;
The unmentionable was mentioned!
WAYNE 'That was just fooling around, guy.'
SELWYN 'So why do you feel so guilty?'
WAYNE 'Who says I feel guilty?'
SELWYN 'Why else would you wanna mash
me up
When I said I was gay?'
WAYNE 'Look, man, I'm not a battyman, if that's
what you're saying.'
SELWYN 'That's not what I'm saying,
But you're scared, man, scared
That I'll blow your cover,
That someone might find out

That Wayne isn't the he-man he's cracked up to
be.'
WAYNE 'Fuck off, will you?
I'm trying to get to sleep.'

(*Pause.*)

'You should never've gone to that drama school
Letting all them white poufs have your arse.'
SELWYN 'Yeah, the first man I slept with was at
that college,
He was the dance teacher,
He was Black.'
WAYNE 'Tttt.'
SELWYN 'That surprise you?
Did me.
Till then I thought I was the only one
Who'd been letting the side down.
He was a really good teacher
In more ways than one –
I had a hard time of it at that college to start
with,
Trying to fit in with all those white kids,
Trying to make myself into a proper actor.
Then he said to me,
"If you don't fit the mould,
Don't start cutting off bits of yourself,
Break the mould."
That's something that applies to all of us,
Wayne.'

(*Pause.*)

WAYNE 'How's your bruises?'
SELWYN 'All right.'
WAYNE 'Hey, man, I didn't mean it, you know,
I wouldn't really've hurt me own brother
though?'
SELWYN 'No.
We should leave that to the filth,
They're good at that sort of thing.'
WAYNE 'Yeah,
Night mate.'
SELWYN 'Night Wayne.'
WAYNE Sleep comes quite easily
SELWYN To both of them.

(*Interval.*)

Scene 18

LUKE Suddenly he's wide awake –
Something has disturbed him.
Lying there frozen
His heart pounding.
MISS ROSENBLUM A low moan.
LUKE He looks towards the chair

Moving his head on the pillow as noiselessly as
     possible,
And sees her,
Sitting in the velvet chair
Silhouetted against the window
Where the dawn light is creeping in.
At first Luke thinks he has seen a ghost.
Then he realizes it is Miss Rosenblum.

MISS ROSENBLUM Her hair unpinned and loose
     around her neck,
Giving her an unfamiliar outline.
She has been walking in her sleep
And is dreaming of the past –
Those early years
When she had just arrived in England,
With her letter of introduction
To a Mrs Goldsack of West End Lane
Who employed her to scrub floors –
This girl from a rich Viennese family.
With the outbreak of war the Goldsacks decided
     to emigrate,
And so the young Fraülein Rosenblum
Was forced to look for other work.
One day, passing a newsagent's on
Finchley Road,
She saw a card in the window.

IRINA FOREIGN LADY REQUIRES GENTEEL
     COMPANION.

MISS ROSENBLUM So it was that the skinny
     eighteen year old orphan
(Though she didn't yet know she was an
     orphan)
Approached the house for the first time.
It loomed up out of the smog
Like a haunted castle,
Laurels almost blocking the path,
A dingy porch with wrought-iron bell-pull
That sent a tinkling sound throughout the house.
A long wait,
Then footsteps,
And a light,

IRINA A figure behind the frosted glass
Who opens the door.
'Yes?'

MISS ROSENBLUM In her mind's eye she can see
     her still,

IRINA Irina Petrova,
Standing in the doorway
In her long black dress,
Ivory brooch at the neck,
Hair piled up on top of her head,
With three cats rubbing themselves against her
     skirts.

MISS ROSENBLUM 'I've come about the
     advertisement.'

IRINA 'Ah, come in.'

MISS ROSENBLUM At first she had been scared of
     her new employer,
But the work was easier than cleaning –

IRINA 'Oh, you play the piano?
Good, I like to listen to music.'

MISS ROSENBLUM And the room at the top of the
     house was cosy,
Felt like home.
So she stayed.
They only ever disagreed when Fraülein
     Rosenblum wanted time off.

IRINA 'So, you are going out again this afternoon,
     Luise?'

MISS ROSENBLUM 'Yes, I'm going to the British
     Museum as usual.'

IRINA 'Ah, yes, to read the newspapers.'
But one day Irina followed her
Keeping well out of sight,
She boarded the bus which took them –
Not to Russell Square,
But to Piccadilly Circus

STEPHEN Where a tall GI awaited his girlfriend
     under the statue of Eros.

(STEPHEN and MISS ROSENBLUM pose as in the
photo again.)

IRINA She followed them down Piccadilly and
     into Fortnum and Mason's
Sitting in the corner of the restaurant
Spying on them.
Then slipped out as discreetly as she could
And hailed a taxi home.

STEPHEN 'What's wrong, Luise?'

MISS ROSENBLUM 'I'm sure that was Irina Petrova
     who just left.'

STEPHEN 'Your Russian Princess?
What would she be doing here?'
And they let the subject drop

MISS ROSENBLUM And talked instead of Stephen's
     imminent return to the States.

STEPHEN 'I can't wait to get back home, Luise,
It's a great country,
With a great future.
You wait,
We're gonna build a better world,
Where there's no more war,
No more hunger,
No more disease.
Everyday new discoveries are being made
To make our life on earth a better one –
We're on the edge of a new age
My country will lead the way forward
And I'm gonna be part of that.'

MISS ROSENBLUM 'Oh, brave new world that has
  such people in't!'
STEPHEN 'Huh?'
MISS ROSENBLUM 'That's Shakespeare,
  The greatest writer in the English language,
  Your language.'
STEPHEN 'I speak American.
  Now,
  You're gonna come down to Wiltshire before I
    leave?'
MISS ROSENBLUM 'Ja, next week,
  I shall take the whole day off, I shall tell Irina
  That I am meeting with Ilse.'
  That evening as she sat with Irina in her room
  As if by chance,
  Their conversation settled on the topic of
    marriage:
IRINA 'Of course I was very popular as a girl,
  There were several young officers after my hand.
  I remember at a ball in Petersburg
  Two young men had a violent argument
  Over me.
  I believe they fought a duel,
  Although I can't remember what the outcome
    was.
  Pass me those chocolates my dear.
  But, of course, I cannot think of marriage at the
    moment
  With my country suffering under the
  Soviet yoke.
  Help yourself, Luise, –
  Oh, please, don't take that one,
  The truffles are my favourites.
  I suppose, soon, you will find some young man
    to marry,
  And you will be coming to me and saying,
  'I am handing in my notice, Irina Petrova.'
  And I shall be left on my own again.
  But please don't throw yourself away on just
    anyone, my dear,
  You have so many talents
  And there are so many charlatans in the world
    nowadays.'
MISS ROSENBLUM And the young girl shuddered
    inwardly
  At the thought that she might end her days
  Sitting in that velvet chair
  Regretting the past,
  Alone.
  Instead she turned her thoughts to her
    rendezvous
  With her shining knight
  On that windy hillside
  Where a white horse is carved in the chalk.
LUKE 'Miss Rosenblum, are you all right?'

(LUKE *gets out of bed and wakes* MISS
ROSENBLUM.)

MISS ROSENBLUM 'Oh, I'm sorry, junger Mann,
  I must have walked in my sleep.
  This happens sometimes.'
LUKE Luke guides her down the stairs.
MISS ROSENBLUM On the landing she grips his
    hand:
  'How old are you, junger Mann?'
LUKE 'Nearly eighteen.'
MISS ROSENBLUM Standing there in the early
    morning light
  She peers into his face
  Long
  And hard
LUKE Until Luke begins to feel quite unnerved.
MISS ROSENBLUM 'Ja, junger Mann,
  We must make of our lives what we can,
  That is most important.'
  And she releases him
  And moves on down the stairs.
LUKE Luke can see her through the bannister
  Looking frail and childlike
  In her long pink nightgown.

(*End of Part Three.*)

Scene 19

MARTIN 'Luke?
  Luke?
  Are you going to be much longer?'
  It's half past seven,
  Martin has been waiting to use the bathroom
    since half past six.
  'I want to have a bath and wash my hair.'
LUKE 'OK, I won't be long.'
MARTIN ('Kids, who'd have 'em?')
  Martin stomps back into the kitchen,
  Picks up a file,
  Reads through the barrister's notes on tomorrow
    morning's case.
  And waits.
  And waits.
LUKE 'Sorry about that –
  I was getting ready to go out.'
MARTIN 'So I gathered.
  I did want to go out myself tonight, you know.
  You're looking smart.'
LUKE 'Thanks.'
MARTIN 'What coat are you wearing?'
LUKE 'I dunno.'
MARTIN 'Well, you can't wear that blue kagool.'
LUKE 'Actually . . . I wondered –'
MARTIN 'Yes?'

LUKE 'If I could wear your denim jacket.'
MARTIN 'OK.
　It's hanging on the stand by the front door.'
LUKE 'Thanks ever so much, Uncle –
　I mean, Martin.'
MARTIN 'What time does the film start?'
LUKE 'Quarter to nine,
　But I'm meeting Mark at half past eight.'
MARTIN 'Well you'd better go or you'll be late.'
LUKE 'Yeah.'
MARTIN 'Nervous?'
LUKE 'A bit.'
MARTIN 'Well there's no need.'
LUKE 'No . . .'
MARTIN 'Come on, what's wrong?'
LUKE 'Nothing really, just . . .
　Do you worry a lot about AIDS?'
MARTIN Suddenly the penny drops
　And Martin understands his nephew's worried
　　look.
　God, it makes me so angry
　He shouldn't have this to fret about
　As if it isn't difficult enough already!
　So he sits him down
　And explains all the ins and outs –
　As it were.
　('I feel like an anxious father explaining the
　　birds and bees!')
　'So just make sure you're safe, that's all.'
LUKE 'Right.'
MARTIN 'OK?'
LUKE 'Yeah.
　I really appreciate it, Martin
　What you've done for me.'
MARTIN 'It's a pleasure, Luke.'
　('Except when you spend two hours in the
　　bathroom.')
　'Right, now, off you go.'
LUKE 'Yeah,
　Bye then.'
MARTIN 'Bye.'
　Martin hears the front door slam.
　(Sings.) 'Everybody's going out and having fun.'
　('Now, eight 'o' clock,
　Let's have that bath,
　Then – well, perhaps I'll go out for a drink.')
　Martin finds the bathroom swimming in
　　water,
　By the time he's cleaned up the mess it's
　　twenty to nine.
　('And he's used up all my shampoo.
　What do I wash my hair with –
　Fairy Liquid?')
　Martin lies in the bath listening to the noise
　　from upstairs.

MISS ROSENBLUM Monday nights are Miss
　Rosenblum's musical evenings.
ILSE And Ilse –
FREDDI And Freddi –
HUTCH And Hutch –
MISS ROSENBLUM Have all come round.

(They gather around her.)

MARTIN Now Martin's dried and dressed and
　ready for action –
　He looks at his watch –
　It's nine forty-five!
　Martin decides it's too late to go out for the
　　evening,
　So feeling sorry for himself he settles down to
　　work.
　Falling asleep over a client's affidavit –
MISS ROSENBLUM There's a knock on the door at
　quarter past ten.
　'Mr Martin,
　I hope we don't bother you with our music,
　I am teaching Ilse a new song.'
MARTIN 'No, I can hardly hear you.'
MISS ROSENBLUM 'Are you on your own tonight?'
MARTIN 'Yes, Luke's gone out on his first date.'
MISS ROSENBLUM 'Oh ho.'
　So the old lady insists
　That Martin must come up and join them.
MARTIN Martin at first reluctant follows her
　upstairs.
ILSE/FREDDI/HUTCH Ahhhhhhhh!

(They welcome him.)

MISS ROSENBLUM And Luise plays the piano till
　way past midnight
ILSE With Ilse singing –
HUTCH And Hutch on violin.
MARTIN 'This has turned out to be a lovely
　evening,'
　Thinks Martin.
FREDDI As Freddi fills his glass with tonic and
　gin.

Scene 20

DEBBIE 'Look, Marianne, she was an old
　schoolfriend.'
MARIANNE 'So I gathered.'
　Marianne and Debbie are having a row in bed.
DEBBIE About a woman called Helen,
　Who Debbie went to school with.
MARIANNE Who rushed up and hugged her,
　When they were going to catch their tube.
DEBBIE 'She always was boisterous.'
MARIANNE 'Boisterous, is that what you call it?'

DEBBIE 'Shhh! You'll wake Dave.'

MARIANNE 'A loudmouth, I think, would be more
accurate.'

DEBBIE 'I was really pleased to see her again after
all these years.

We didn't know about each other at school.'

MARIANNE 'Yes but did she really have to
announce it to everyone on King's Cross
station?

"Debbie, I thought it was you.

You're a lesbian.

How fantastic!"

That ticket collector's eyes were nearly popping
out of her head.'

DEBBIE 'OK, you didn't like her.'

MARIANNE 'But you obviously did.'

DEBBIE 'What I like is to keep up with people
from my past.'

MARIANNE 'Yes I've noticed that.

Melissa, and Sian, and Kate,

And Sian's lover Caroline,

Who you later had a relationship with

And Caroline's ex-lover and flatmate –

The other Caroline –

Who Melissa went off with after you and Melissa
split up.

It's so incestuous,

Half of them have got the same names.

I get so confused.'

DEBBIE 'You get so jealous.'

MARIANNE 'It's not that,

I just get fed up of worrying,

Whether you're going to be able to fit
me in to your busy schedule.

And now, it's not just ex-lovers,

But ex-schoolfriends as well!

When you arranged to meet her

Thursday night,

I couldn't believe it.

That's the night you said you'd come out with
me and my Dad

It's his last night in London.'

DEBBIE 'Your Dad?

What's he got to do with all this?

You want me to plan my week around your
Dad?

I thought I got away from in-laws when I left my
marriage!

You're obsessed with your bloody Dad.

And then you accuse me of having incestuous
relationships!

To hell with your Dad!'

MARIANNE 'And to hell with you!'

(*They turn away from each other.*)

DEBBIE 'Marianne?

Marianne?

Those women are like my family.

They know things about me that no one else can
know.

People from the past are important to me.

Like Jody's important to you.'

Debbie reaches across to the bedside table,

Picks up the postcard that arrived three days ago

From a village somewhere in the Sudan.

'I was glad for you when you got this,

Glad that she got in contact,

That she wants to meet up with you whilst she's
in London.

Because she's someone that you care about.'

MARIANNE 'It's just that sometimes I seem to
come real low-down on your list.'

DEBBIE 'Marianne, I love you.'

MARIANNE 'I know.'

DEBBIE 'Trust me.'

MARIANNE 'It's hard.'

DEBBIE 'Look, if you really want me to come out
with you and your Dad,

I could cancel,

I could always see Helen on another night.'

MARTIN 'No, don't do that.'

DEBBIE 'You sure?'

MARIANNE 'Yeah.'

DEBBIE 'Come on, let's get some sleep.

It's Tuesday tomorrow,

You've got to look your best for Jody Jones.'

(*They kiss.*)

Scene 21

SELWYN On Tuesday morning,

Selwyn sits having coffee with Miss Rosenblum,

And Martin.

'I just wanted to thank you all

For looking after me last week

When I was beaten up.

I was going to come round sooner,

But I've been staying over in Hackney the last
few days with my Mum.'

MISS ROSENBLUM 'I am pleased you have
recovered, junger Mann,

He gave us quite a shock, didn't he, Vladimir?'

The cat answers her with a feeble and throaty
miaow.

'Ohhhh, he's not feeling well.

Willst du dein Frühstück nicht fressen, mein
Liebling?

He has not eaten for two whole days.'

SELWYN 'Well, I must be off.

I haven't been home since Saturday morning,

Mark must be wondering where I am.
I've got to call in there before rehearsals.'
MARTIN Martin almost mentions seeing Mark at
   the disco,
Then decides not to.
MISS ROSENBLUM 'Oh, ja, the play.
When does it start?'
SELWYN 'Thursday.'
MISS ROSENBLUM 'And can we come and see it?'
SELWYN 'Of course you can,
Come on the first night.'
MISS ROSENBLUM 'Mr Martin, will you come with
   me?
The Tempest is my favourite Shakespeare play,
I would love to see it again.'
MARTIN Martin sees Selwyn to the door,
'When Luke gets up,
I'll tell him that you called.'
SELWYN 'Thanks.
Bring him along on Thursday too.'
As he leaves,
Selwyn bends down to pick up
something from the mat,
'The postman's been,
There's a letter for you.'

Scene 22

MARTIN On Tuesday morning,
Martin reads the letter from his sister:
MAGGIE 'Dear Martin,
Thanks for looking after our Luke.
I wish he'd told us he was so worried about his
   exams,
We could have helped.
But I meant it when I said he couldn't be in
   better hands,
I'm sure you'll say all the right things.
Perhaps it will bring us all closer,
And we'll be able to let bygones be bygones –
This rift has gone on far too long.
I know Frank said some hurtful things
But he didn't know any better
Neither of us did.
And you know,
Sometimes I feel you could have helped us
   more, Martin.
That pride of yours makes you so unforgiving,
I remember that from when you were a kid.'
MARTIN The treachery of a sister
Who promised to take him to the fair
Then went with her boyfriend instead!
No peace offerings,
No nougat,
Or coconut

Would ever make him speak to her again!
He kept it up for two whole weeks.
But then came the fall,
Head over heels off his bike.
MAGGIE 'Come on, our kid,
Let's get you indoors and clean you up.'
MARTIN He had to speak to her then, didn't he?
MAGGIE Frank always feels that you think he isn't
   good enough for me –
But I'm not complaining,
He's been a good husband.
He gets his moods of course –
Especially since the strike,
He's very bitter about being out of work
Having to accept redundancy –
But he's changed a lot you know, over the years,
The strike was a big eye-opener for us all.
When we had the big demonstration
There were several banners
From the lesbians and the gays.
There was this group of lads being right daft
Whistling at them
And being limp-wristed –
You know how they can be –
FRANK 'All right lads, that'll do,
Their support group has given us £300 for the
   strike fund.
How many of you have ever been on one of
   their marches?
People have got to stick together
Help each other out,
Not bash each other over the head.
You should have learnt that by now.'
MAGGIE I was right proud of him.
I suppose what I'm saying, Martin,
Is that I hope you'll come and visit us
Next time you're up this way –
It'd be good to see you after all this time.
I'll phone you up in the week,
Take care of our lad,
Tell him we love him,
We always will,
No matter what.
Your sister,
Margaret.
MARTIN And scrawled at the bottom in a different
   hand,
FRANK Hope you're well, Martin,
Come up and see us,
Frank.
MARTIN Martin reads the letter,
Feels suddenly ashamed,
Takes it upstairs to show it to Luke,
Thinks somehow it will help the lad.
But Luke's bed hasn't been slept in . . .

Scene 23

SELWYN On Tuesday morning Selwyn returns to
    the flat,
    Anticipating recriminations,
    Surprised to notice the bedroom door is still
      closed.
    ('Mark can't be up yet.
    Funny,
    He's usually such an early riser,
    Unemployment must be really getting to him.')
    Mark's notebook lies beside the 'phone –
    So easy to pick it up,
    Flick through,
    Find clues,
    See how he's spent his weekend.
    ('Thus coupledom doth make detectives of us
      all!')

MARK Saturday pm: Sainsbury's for food,
    Cut jeans for club tonight –

SELWYN ('Ohhhh!')

MARK Read booklet Selwyn got from library.

SELWYN ('Well, that's good.
    At least he hasn't been sitting around moping.')

MARK Notes from booklet:
    No good,
    Haven't been working there two years
    Can't go to tribunal.
    Should have been member of union.

SELWYN ('Over the page . . . ')

MARK Sunday am: Phone L.

SELWYN ('Who the hell is L?')

MARK Check times for film for tomorrow night –
    Monday cheap night at Cannon . . .

SELWYN ('He's certainly been living it up.')

MARK Ask L if Martin knows anything about
    unfair dismissal.

SELWYN ('Martin? . . . Martin!
    L!
    Luke!')

MARK Meet L outside Cannon 8.30 tomorrow.
    Monday am.
    Buy *Advertiser* to look for a job . . .

SELWYN ('Yeah . . . yeah . . . ')

MARK Look in Newsagent's window on Finchley
    Road.

SELWYN ('Mmmmmm . . . Oh!')

MARK Buy Selwyn card for opening night.

SELWYN ('Well, thanks for remembering my
    existence.')

MARK Monday pm:
    Wash jeans,
    Haircut,
    Have bath,
    Put clean sheets on bed.

SELWYN ('Uh uhh.')
    Selwyn catching sight for first time of a blue
      denim jacket
    Over a kitchen chair,
    ('Well, that's not Mark's.')
    Looking at the closed bedroom door with new
      eyes.
    ('Shit. And I'm supposed to be the fickle one.')
    Selwyn leaves the flat
    Closing the door as silently as possible.

Scene 24

LUKE It's Tuesday morning
    But no Tuesday morning was ever this bright!
    Heart in his mouth,
    Luke lies there
    With Mark curled up at his side,
    Both of them drifting in and out of sleep.
    Savouring again the images of the night.
    'This morning,
    Early,
    I heard the dawn chorus,
    And I knew my life had changed.
    Then,
    People waking in the flats below,
    Somewhere the smell of bacon.
    Even that seemed strange and new.
    Later,
    Car doors slamming
    Outside
    As people went off to work.
    Later still,
    Children calling to each other
    Running off to school.
    School,'
    Luke remembers that other life
    When Tuesday mornings meant double Maths.
    'Is that life still going on out there, somewhere?'
    A moment's fear
    And guilt.
    He can hardly believe the enormity of his crime.
    'I've done it now,
    No going back.'
    He looks again at the man sleeping beside him –
    'Oh, it felt so good.
    But this painful peace
    Is even more intense.
    I'm in love. I've got a lover,
    I'm in love.'
    He whispers it to himself
    Over
    And over
    Again.

(*End of Part Four*.)

Scene 25

MARIANNE 'Oh, Debbie,
  I feel so naive,
  I really thought my Dad could do no wrong.'
DEBBIE Debbie sits Marianne in a chair
  Tries to calm her,
MARIANNE While Marianne tells of her meeting
    with Jody Jones.
  Sitting in a coffee bar in Leicester Square
  Listening to stories
  Of war,
  Hunger
  And disease.
  And then this latest story,
  A story about blood,
  Unscreened,
  Cheap blood.
  (The tests are so expensive.)
  Shipped off to the Third World –
  A cargo of potential disease and death.
  'As if this virus needed any help!
  There was a lot of noise about it in the
    newspapers back home –
  Jody showed me cuttings.
  There was this letter from my Dad,
  Where he admits that a consignment of blood
  Had not been properly tested
  And then goes on to say
  That the risks involved were minimal.
  How could anyone be so irresponsible?
  Of course I knew that sort of thing went on,
  That there were people without scruples
  On the lookout for a fast buck.
  But my Dad?
  All these years he's been making out
  He cares about the world's poor.'

Scene 26

CALIBAN You taught me language, and my profit
    on't
  Is, I know how to curse. The red plague rid you
  For learning me your language.
PROSPERO Hagseed, hence!
  Fetch us in fuel, and be quick, thou'rt best
  To answer other business. Shrugst thou, malice?
  If thou neglect'st or dost unwillingly
  What I command, I'll rack thee with old cramps,
  Fill all thy bones with aches, make thee roar
  That the beasts shall tremble at thy din.
CALIBAN No pray thee.
  (Aside.) I must obey. His art is of such pow'r
  It would control my dam's god, Setebos,
  And make a vassal of him.

PROSPERO So, slave; hence!
DIRECTOR 'OK,
  Let's have a tea-break now.
  Back in fifteen minutes everyone.
  Selwyn, darling,
  Where's the West Indian accent?
  I thought we agreed you were going to do it with
    a strong accent!'

Scene 27

MARIANNE 'But that's not the whole story –
  Later I took Jody through to St James Park
  And we sat there watching the ducks.'
JODY 'I'm sorry, Marianne,
  I thought you'd know,
  I thought you'd have read about it.'
MARIANNE 'Well, I guess the story wasn't taken
    up by the British press.'
JODY 'When I saw you at the funeral
  I felt myself getting real angry.
  "She sits in England publishing books of poetry
  While our father commits murder."
  That's how it struck me then.'
MARIANNE 'What did you say?'
JODY 'Oh, I know that's not fair.
  I've often come across books you've published,
  They're good.'
MARIANNE 'No, I didn't mean that.
  Did you say "our father"?'
JODY 'Yeah, sure.'
MARIANNE 'Our father?'
JODY 'You mean you didn't know?
  Oh Marianne, Marianne,
  I thought everyone knew about that.'
MARIANNE 'You mean father and Berta . . .'
JODY 'Yeah.
  From what I understand he pursued her,
  When she was in the house
  Cleaning or cooking,
  And your Mom was out,
  Suddenly he'd be there
  Watching her,
  Touching her.
  What was she to do?
  He was white,
  A man
  Her boss.
  She was black
  A woman
  His maid.
  And it was 1949.
  Of course it was all hushed up
  And no one was supposed to know –
  It was my aunty May told me all about it.

She said he told Berta he loved her.
Hmmm.'
MARIANNE The past replays itself in Marianne's
    head –
Suddenly everything fell into place,
The missing clue had been found.
JODY 'You know, Marianne,
    As a kid,
I always felt like a freak.
I'd brought shame both on my Mom and Dad.
I just felt I was bad.
And then there was you –
You were everything that I was not –
It was like I was the negative
And you were the positive
The perfect picture.
God, I so wanted to be you.
Then, one day, while I was still at college,
Berta told me about you;
How you'd gone off to England to live with
    another woman
How you had unnatural tastes as she called it.
I felt this immense relief;
It was the best gift you could ever have ever
    given me,
Not because I'm gay,
I'm not –
At least,
Well,
I don't think I am,
At the moment anyway –
But because
You were not normal either.
It was like a weight had been lifted off my
    shoulders.
So when I saw you at the funeral,
With your beloved Daddy,
I felt you'd let me down.
That's why I got mad at you.'
MARIANNE 'Oh, Jody.'
    In St James Park,
Amidst the office workers eating their lunch
And the au pairs out with their infant
    charges
Two sisters sit crying in each other's arms.
JODY 'Welcome home, Marianne.'

Scene 28

MARTIN (*on the phone*) 'Maggie,
    It's Martin.
Luke's coming home.
Yes, he's fine, but he's got a lot to talk to you
    about.
Well, wait, he'll tell you.

He's getting the early train tomorrow,
He should be up there by lunchtime.
Look, I don't know if he's coming home for
    good –
Well, talk to him.
Actually I thought I might come up one
    weekend.
Yes,
Well, I'd like it too.
OK, I'll let you know when – give you lots of
    warning.
Yes.
All right then, bye.
Yeah, bye – oh, Maggie –
Give my regards to Frank.'

Scene 29

SELWYN (*on the phone*) 'Mark?
    It's me.
Hi.
I'm OK.
At rehearsals.
Look, I came to the flat this morning.
Yeah.
I don't mind.
You don't need to apologize.
You weren't to know I was coming back.
Anyway that's not why I'm phoning you –
I've been thinking,
I wanna move back to Hackney.
No, I've been thinking about it all weekend,
I'd already made up my mind before this
    morning.
And I wanted to warn you, see,
So's you'd know,
And you'd have time to think about it.
Of course I still love you
That's why I wanna move,
'Cos if we carry on living together I think we'll
    split up.
That's one reason anyway –
The other one is –
I don't feel at home over this side of town,
There's a flat near me Mum's,
She thinks she can get it for me.
Look, we'll be able to talk about it later,
I gotta go now.
Yeah, I'll be there about seven.'
DIRECTOR 'Selwyn, love, hurry up,
    We're all waiting for you.
Positions for Act Two.'

Scene 30

MARIANNE They sit there in the hotel lobby,
   Marianne pale,
   Nervous,
   Her lip trembling at the audacity of her
      accusations.
STEPHEN Her father quiet,
   Thoughtful,
   Listening to her,
   Allowing her to finish.
   Then –
   'But honey,
   You're talking as if some crime has been
      committed,
   Those governments knew what they were
      getting,
   They knew that blood hadn't been screened.
   If they're so careless about what they do with it,
   Then we can't be blamed, now, can we?'
MARIANNE 'But you must have known they can't
      afford to screen it,
   That they don't have the facilities.'
STEPHEN 'It's their responsibility, Marianne.'
MARIANNE 'Did you really need the money that
      much, Daddy?'
STEPHEN 'Oh, come on now,
   We were providing them with blood they needed
      badly,
   And a helluva lot cheaper than they
   could get it anywhere else.
   Was that a bad thing to do?
   As for Berta and Jody –
   Hell, I'm no saint, Marianne,
   But I'm no devil either.
   I paid for what happened between me and Berta,
   And I think she forgave me.
   It was all so long ago;
   I was desperate,
   You've no idea what it's like
   To be sharing your life with someone
   And to find that there's no love –
   Love was something I only ever found once,
   And that was when I was very young.
   I should have grasped it, kept it,
   But I let it go.
   Losing that love soured my life for many years.
   Do you know who brought the sweetness back?
   You did, Marianne.
   When you came along I couldn't believe my
      good fortune.
   You're not going to turn against your old Dad
      now, are you?'
MARIANNE 'I . . .'
STEPHEN 'And you'll come out with me on
      Thursday night?

It's my last night in London.'
MARIANNE 'I don't know if I can now.'
STEPHEN 'But you promised,
   You told me you were gonna take me to the
      theatre.'
MARIANNE 'I know.'
STEPHEN 'So, can we still go?'
MARIANNE 'Well . . . I guess so.'
STEPHEN 'What's the play? Is it one I know?'
MARIANNE 'I dunno, it's a Shakespeare.
   You remember Martin?
   You met him last time you were over.'
STEPHEN 'Uhhuh.'
MARIANNE 'Well, he's taking his landlady
   And he thought we could make it a foursome.'
STEPHEN 'Who's this landlady?
   Are you trying to get me hitched?'
MARIANNE 'No.'
STEPHEN 'Well, that will be grand,
   I'll look forward to that.'
MARIANNE 'Good.'
STEPHEN 'Do you love your old Dad,
   Marianne?'

Scene 31

MISS ROSENBLUM And so the stage is set
   For wartime lovers to be reunited.
   Actors are preparing
   Audience is gathering
   But one of the principal characters is about to
      miss her entrance.
   Fate intervenes
   In the shape of a ginger cat
   A negative *deus ex machina*
   And a pattern of co-incidence is casually thrown
      awry.
   Vladimir is dying;
   He has not moved from his place in front of the
      gas fire for days,
   Except to stagger to his food dish,
   Sniff at the contents disconsolately
   And return,
   As if exhausted by all this effort,
   Without touching a single morsel.
   Miss Rosenblum stands looking at him,
   In hat and coat,
   Gloves in hand
   Waiting for Martin to come and collect her
   And take her to the play.
   Outside there is a distant rumble of thunder
   Miss Rosenblum looks out of the window at the
      angry dark clouds
   Heightening her sense of foreboding.
   'Na, mein Liebchen,

Ich lasse dich nicht allein.'
And she takes off her hat and her coat,
Kneels down beside him.
MARTIN This is where Martin finds her later,
  When he comes to take her to the play.
MISS ROSENBLUM 'No, Mr Martin,
  I cannot leave my Vladimir.
  I shall stay with him.
  You must go without me.'
MARTIN Martin tries to reassure her
  But leaves eventually –
  Rather late –
  For the theatre.
  The play has already started as he arrives in his
    seat
  Soaking wet from the downpour which caught
    him
  As he ran from the tube.
MIRANDA If by your art, my dearest father, you
    have
  Put the wild waters in this roar, allay them
  The sky it seems, would pour down stinking
    pitch.
MARIANNE Marianne shoots Martin a questioning
    look,
  'You're late.
  Where's your landlady?'
MARTIN 'Couldn't come.'
DIRECTOR 'SHHHHHHHH!'
MARTIN 'I'll explain later.'
MARIANNE And they settle down
MARTIN To watch the play.

Scene 32

MISS ROSENBLUM Miss Rosenblum is out in the
    garden in a thunderstorm,
  Digging,
  Down on her knees,
  Her thin hair plastered to her head.
  The rain,
  Mingling with her tears,
  Drips off her nose,
  As she scrabbles at the earth with an old garden
    trowel.
  Beside her on the ground is a small bundle of
    fur,
  Brownish and sodden –
  Miss Rosenblum is burying her cat.
  Feeling a pain in her chest from all the effort,
  She decides the grave is deep enough.

(She mimes picking up the dead VLADIMIR and
burying him.)

'Ja, Irina,

He was all that was left of you,
And now he has gone too.'

(She stands with some difficulty.)

'I don't know why I'm crying,
He had a good life.
Perhaps I cry for you, Irina,
For your wasted one;
Sitting there in your chair
Eating your chocolates
Complaining right until the end
About this country,
About the riff-raff they were letting in.
You never seemed to realize that we were part
  of the riff-raff.
Waiting for the day when you would return to
  your land of dreams,
Where men in uniform whisked you off to the
  ball.
Poor Irina,
You were so bitter.
And you never understood
That I did not feel like you.
You called yourself an old maid
Who no one wanted
But that was not how I saw myself!'
STEPHEN 'Well, there it is, Luise,
  What do you think?'
MISS ROSENBLUM She had taken the train from
    Paddington station,
  Excited at the prospect of seeing him,
  Knowing that today was to be an important day
    in her life.
  Her spirits had soared when she saw the white
    horse from the train,
  Trotting proudly across the hill.
  Now,
  From up close,
  It was rather disappointing,
  It didn't look like a horse at all
  Just an expanse of dirty chalk –
  Huge
  And drab,
  And uninspiring.
STEPHEN 'This country's dead, Luise,
  Like the ground we're standing on,
  Chalk,
  Calcium,
  Compressed bones.
  Come with me,
  Come to the States.
  I love you,
  I want to take care of you.'
MISS ROSENBLUM He was saying all she had
    hoped he would say,

And more,
And yet it wasn't right.
'I love you, Stephen,
I love you dearly,
But I cannot marry you.'
And she stood on this hill
Looking over the rolling countryside,
And it was like her whole life spread out before
    her
Full of possibilities,
Exciting prospects,
Dimly discernible hopes
On hazy blue horizons.
'This is my home now,
Here's where I must make my life.'
She did not look back that night
As the train pulled out of the station.
She closed her eyes
And only opened them again
When the hill
And its white horse
Were way behind and out of sight.
'Ja!'
Miss Rosenblum picks up the trowel
And goes indoors.
Her shoes squelch on every step
As she climbs the stairs to her room.
There,
She sits in front of the gas-fire,
Drying her hair with a towel
And toasts herself a teacake.

Scene 33

CALIBAN I must eat my dinner!
    This island's mine by Sycorax my mother
    Which thou takst from me. When thou camst
        first,
    Thou strokst me and made much of me; wouldst
        give me
    Water with berries in't; and teach me how
    To name the bigger light, and how the less,
    That burn by day and night. And then I loved
        thee

And showed thee all the qualities of the isle,
The fresh springs, brine pits, barren place and
    fertile.
Cursed be I that did so! All the charms
Of Sycorax – toads, beetles, bats, light on you!
For I am all the subjects that you have,
Which first was mine own king; and here you
    sty me
In this hard rock, while you do keep from me
The rest of the island.

Scene 34

LUKE The first snowflakes of winter are falling
    As Luke pedals up the hill,
    Wrapped up in scarf,
    And hat,
    And gloves.
    Pause at the top for a view of the city –
    Lungs burning from the effort.
    Standing there looking at the unfamiliar view
    And yet not seeing it
    Eyes smarting,
    Heart aching,
    From the pangs of first love,
    Unrequited.
    Unable to imagine that this pain will ever end.
    Taking the letter from his pocket once again –
    He knows it now almost off by heart,
    But reads it all the same.
MARK 'I hope we can still be friends.'
LUKE 'How can he say that?
    It's not fair!
    I love him,
    I want to be with him.'
    And so a new journey starts
    As he stands there wiping his eyes,
    'Just two more terms
    Then I'll be leaving this dump.'
    Snow now falling fast around him.
    Those distant hills
    Already thickly coated in white
    Beckon him, even more distinctly,
    Into that unknown future.

Harlem Duet

Djanet Sears

Introduction

Djanet Sears was born in London, England, and moved while a teenager to Saskatoon, in the Canadian prairies. Influenced by black women playwrights Ntozake Shange (*For Coloured Girls Who Have Considered Suicide When the Rainbow Is Enuf*) and Lorraine Hansberry (*A Raisin in the Sun*), she has worked as a writer, actor, and director and currently lives in Toronto. *Harlem Duet*, a prequel to Shakespeare's Othello, was workshopped at the Joseph Papp Public Theater in New York City, where Sears spent a season as an international playwright in residence. In Canada, the play received its premier at Tarragon Theatre's Extra Space, before being remounted at the Canadian Stage Theatre in 1997 by Nightwood Theatre, Canada's oldest professional feminist theatre company. The play is a sequel to *Afrika Solo* (1990), the first published stage play by a Canadian woman of African descent. As Joanne Tompkins explains, *Afrika Solo* is an 'auto-bio-mythography' in which Sears, an 'African Canadian, explores her search for a place in white-dominated Canada, using as tools the pop culture that surrounds her (particularly its bias against people of African descent) and the re-discovery of her spiritual past on a visit to Africa' (35).

The play stages the process of seeking and reclaiming identity as a function of the historical and cultural imperatives that have shaped Sears's life: 'The identity she arrives at is a hybrid form of Guyanese and Jamaican from her parents, British from her birth, Canadian from her current home country, and the many African heritages that she has "adopted". . . . The refusal of the final or complete articulation of identity mirrors the way that a final performance text is given over to "process"' (Tompkins: 36). *Afrika Solo* effectively uses a metatheatrical frame, its staging of Sears's reflections on performative process, as a way of addressing the processual dynamics of identity, a recurrent theme in *Harlem Duet*. Sears's other stage writing credits include *Who Killed Katie Ross*, *Double Trouble*, and *Shakes*, and she has directed, among others, Diana Brathwaite's *The Wonder of Man* for Nightwood Theatre, co-directed *Dark Diaspora . . . in Dub* by ahdri zhina mandiela for the Toronto Fringe Festival, and served as artistic director of *Negrophilia: An African American Retrospective: 1959-71* for Toronto Theatre Alliance's Loon Café.

Recipient of significant critical acclaim in Canada, including a Chalmers Award, four Dora Mavor Moore Awards, and the 1998 Canada Council for the Arts Governor General's Literary Award for Drama, *Harlem Duet* is notable for both its border-crossing setting in the US and for the way in which it places issues of race at the centre of a theatrical practice that exorcizes the 'whiteness' of theatrical representation generally. As Sears states, 'I have a dream . . . that one day in the city where I live [Toronto], at any given time of the year, I will be able to find at least one play that is filled with people who look like me, telling stories about me, my family, my friends, my community. For most people of European descent, this is a privilege they take for granted' (1998: 14). *Harlem Duet*, like *Afrika Solo*, challenges what Susan Bennett has called the 'default position for any Western audience,' namely, 'a hegemonic whiteness' (19). Sears locates the origins of the play in her first contact with Shakespeare's *Othello* as played by Laurence Olivier in blackface:

> As a veteran theatre practitioner of African Descent, Shakespeare's *Othello* had haunted me since I was first introduced to him . . . Othello is the first African portrayed in the annals of western dramatic literature. In an effort to exorcise this ghost, I have written *Harlem Duet*. *Harlem Duet*, a rhapsodic blues tragedy, explores the effects of race

and sex on the lives of people of African descent. It is a tale of love. A tale of Othello and his first wife, Billie. Set in 1860, 1928 and contemporary Harlem at the corner of Malcolm X and Martin Luther King Boulevards, this is Billie's story.

(1998: 14–15)

Shakespeare's *Othello*, in Dympna Callaghan's words, 'dramatizes the possible consequences of not excluding the racial other from the community and so presents the dazzling spectacle of someone who is, like Caliban, both monster and man. Yet, even as it does so the play reenacts the exclusionary privilege on which such representations were founded. Othello was a white man' (215). By contrast, Sears's play complicates such a critical position: Othello, as a black man played by a black actor and living in a black community, is dealing with the effects of having been 'not exclud[ed]' from the 'community,' where community becomes a highly charged code word for white culture as an arbitrary index against which one is (problematically) measured for inclusion or exclusion. Thus, Sears overturns the

Plate 5 Photo: Cylla Von Tiedemann. © Nightwood Theatre. Nigel Shawn Williams as Othello and Alison Sealy-Smith as Billie in Djanet Sears' *Harlem Duet*. Nightwood Theatre Production at the Canadian Stage Theatre, 1997

white stage tradition of having Othello played by a white person ('Othello was a white man') in blackface. Further, Sears's play asks important questions about how inclusion and exclusion work for people who are part of the black community, something that *Othello*, with its emphasis on Othello's strangeness to white culture, emphatically does not. Othello, for Sears, is to be understood in relation to a black community, a fundamental shift of focus from the Shakespeare original.

Sears radically reshapes how blackness is performed in the context of white culture, placing black experience thoroughly at the heart of the play's visual and literary representations: all the actors are black (Mona, the sole white character, never makes an appearance except for a glimpse of her arm), the setting of the play is in the symbolic heart (Harlem) of American black culture, and the play, in its non-Shakespearean cultural references (the soundscapes that precede many of the scene changes involve recordings of prominent black figures including Malcolm X, Martin Luther King, Langston Hughes, Marcus Garvey, Paul Robeson, Louis Farrakhan, Jesse Jackson, Christopher Darden, and Anita Hill), is explicit in the way in which it constructs itself as a nexus for different forms of black voice. This is in marked distinction from Shakespeare's *Othello*, where Othello's otherness from white culture is a prime feature of the play, and even from Aphra Behn's rewriting of *Othello* in *Oronooko*, in which black protagonists adhere to the basic pattern of the play, in which the 'hero follows Othello's example by killing his (virtuous) wife before colluding in his own death' (Ferguson: 24).

Moreover, *Harlem Duet*'s performance history is unique in a Canadian cultural context because it is so closely tied to an emergent black theatrical aesthetic, one that challenges Eurocentric practices, even as it is implicated in mediating and revising them. As Alison Sealy-Smith, the creator of the role of Billie (Sybil), states, 'what was wonderful about working on *Harlem Duet* is that we [Black actors] never get to have all Black people in a room. It doesn't happen. And we weren't working on Shakespeare, we weren't saying to the world, "let's just see what happens when these words come out of Black mouths instead of White ones"' (Knowles: 28). Sears herself acknowledges that 'In *Harlem Duet* I wanted a *tension* between European culture and African American culture' (ibid.: 29), while noting the historical circumstances that make *Harlem Duet* distinctive:

'Before *Harlem Duet*, Canadian Stage [a major Canadian theatre] had never produced a work by an author of . . . African descent. And the problem with Canadian Stage is that it's called Canadian Stage, so it represents Canada, and I'm thinking, "I'm Canadian, so it must represent me"' (ibid.: 30). Even as it uses contextual markers that link it to Shakespeare's *Othello* (some names, some thematic materials, and some crucial imagery – the handkerchief, for instance, is a crucial prop in both Shakespeare's and Sears's versions of the Othello story), *Harlem Duet* moves to establish its own revisionary agenda in relation to historical circumstances that have traditionally excluded the representation of black culture from the public stage.

To this end, the play's revision of Shakespeare tells the story from Billie's perspective; addresses issues of racial and sexual significance related to black diasporic experience (slavery, racism, segregation), to same-race and cross-racial relationships, and to affirmative action (which Othello opposes); and contemporizes the story in relation to its American setting, while also showing the historical sweep of the motivations and emotions of its characters as they struggle to deal with the twin variables of race and sexuality in three different temporal moments. The decision to incorporate three distinct historical moments into the play's structure was of particular importance to Sears: 'It gave depth that I wanted. It supported many layers of the play, of the language, and of the contradictions around race' (Knowles: 25). Othello, in his present incarnation, is now a professor of English at Columbia University, and the play finds him leaving Billie for Mona, his newfound white love, a love triangle that the play restages in each of its three historical settings.

As such, the play shifts the focus from interracial relations as perceived by white culture to the ways in which miscegenation affects black women. Billie, in a poignant and difficult moment, recalls the first time she imagines seeing Othello with Mona on the subway and states: 'Here, before me – his woman – all blonde hair and blonde legs. Her weight against his chest. His arm around her shoulders, his thumb resting on the gold of her hair. He's proud. You can see he's proud. He isn't just any Negro. He's special. That's why she's with him. And she . . . she . . . she flaunts.' The pain of Othello's sexual infidelity is coupled with the dissonance that affronts Billie's sense of racial solidarity, thus raising difficult questions about what constitutes racist discourse and how black

identity and cultural solidarity are forever under threat because of historical contingencies relating to white culture. The moment also raises difficult questions about the way in which black masculinity is defined in apparent relation to white culture.

The central conundrum of the play contrasts Othello's over-eager desire to 'pass' in white culture with Billie's purist fixation on a black identity (inevitably) contaminated by what she calls 'white roaches.' Billie's struggle to deal with her own anti-white racism even as she seeks to affirm her identity apart from white culture is the crucial contradiction the play highlights in an exchange between Billie and Magi, her landlord:

> MAGI: Is everything about White people with you? Is every moment of your life eaten up with thinking about them. Do you know where you are? Do you know who you are anymore? What about right and wrong. Racism is a disease my friend, and your test just came back positive . . .
>
> BILLIE: No, no, no . . . It's about Black. I love Black. I really do. And it's revolutionary . . . Black is beautiful. This Harlem sanctuary . . . here. This respite . . . Like an ocean in the middle of the desert. And in my mirror, my womb, he has a fast growing infestation of roaches. White roaches.

The complex problem of resisting assimilation in non-racist terms (as well as in the context of a long history of racial oppression) is captured in this exchange as is the toxic nature of racist discourse, which reinforces reductive notions of racial difference. In the end, Shakespeare's text remains a barely visible (but nonetheless significant) backdrop to the dissolution of Othello's and Billie's relationship. They remain trapped in the impossible circumstances of a cyclical history that will not be forgotten or denied even as Sears's adaptation holds forth the promise of a dialogue that begins to break with the historical inevitability of racism by virtue of its revisionary theatrical practices.

Select bibliography

Entries marked * are particularly accessible.

* Bennett, S. (1995) 'Text as Performance: Reading and Viewing Djanet Sears's *Afrika Solo*,' in Per Brask (ed.) *Contemporary Issues in Canadian Drama*, Winnipeg: Blizzard: 15–25.

Callaghan, D. (1996) '"Othello Was a White Man": Properties of Race on Shakespeare's Stage,' in

Terence Hawkes (ed.) *Alternative Shakespeares*, vol. 2, London: Routledge: 192–215.

Ferguson, M. (1993) 'Transmuting Othello: Aphra Behn's *Oronooko*,' in Marianne Novy (ed.) *Cross-Cultural Performances: Differences in Women's Re-Visions of Shakespeare*, Urbana: University of Illinois Press: 15–49.

* Knowles, R. (ed.) (1998) 'The Nike Method: A Wide-Ranging Conversation between Djanet Sears and Alison Sealy Smith,' *Canadian Theatre Review* (Winter): 24–30.

Sears, D. (1990) *Afrika Solo*, Toronto: Sister Vision.

— (1992) 'Naming Names: Black Women Playwrights in Canada,' in Rita Much (ed.) *Women on the Canadian Stage: The Legacy of Hrotsvit*, Winnipeg: Blizzard: 92–103.

— (1998) 'Notes of a Coloured Girl: 32 Short Reasons Why I Write for the Theater,' *Harlem Duet*, Winnipeg: Scirocco Drama: 11–16.

Tompkins, J. (1993) 'Infinitely Rehearsing Performance and Identity: *Africa Solo* and *The Book of Jessica*,' *Canadian Theatre Review* (Spring): 35–39.

Harlem Duet

Djanet Sears

. . . That handkerchief
Did an Egyptian to my mother give.
She was a charmer . . .
There's magic in the web of it.
A sibyl . . . in her prophetic fury sewed the work.
(William Shakespeare, *Othello*, 3.4.57–74)

Characters

BILLIE, a woman of 37, present day

SHE, Billie, 1928

HER, Billie, 1860

OTHELLO, a man of 40, present day

HE, Othello, 1928

HIM, Othello, 1860

MAGI, the landlady, 41

AMAH, Billie's sister-in-law, 33

CANADA, Billie's father, 67

MONA, White, 30s (an off-stage voice)

Setting

Harlem, 1928, a tiny dressing room.

Harlem, the present, an apartment in a renovated brownstone, at the corner of Martin Luther King and Malcolm X boulevards (125th & Lennox).

Harlem, 1860, on the steps to a blacksmith's forge.

Act I

Prologue

(*Harlem, 1928: late summer – night. As the lights fade to black, the cello and the bass call and respond to a heaving melancholic blues. Martin Luther King's voice accompanies them. He seems to sing his dream in a slow polyrhythmic improvisation, as he reaches the climax of that now famous speech given at the March on Washington. Lights up on a couple in a tiny dressing room.* SHE *is holding a large white silk handkerchief, spotted with ripe strawberries.* SHE *looks at* HE *as if searching for something.* HE *has lathered his face and is slowly erasing the day's stubble with a straight razor.* SHE *looks down at the handkerchief.*)

SHE We keep doing this don't we?
HE I love you . . . But –
SHE Remember . . . Remember when you gave this to me? Your mother's handkerchief. There's magic in the web of it. Little strawberries. It's so beautiful – delicate. You kissed my fingers . . . and with each kiss a new promise you made . . . swore yourself to me . . . for all eternity . . . remember?
HE Yes. Yes . . . I remember.

   (*Pause.*)

SHE Harlem's the place to be now. Everyone who's anyone is coming here now. It's our time. In our place. It's what we've always dreamed of . . . isn't it?
HE Yes.

Note: To amplify the blues aesthetic structure of *Harlem Duet*, the entire play is accompanied by a soundscape that must include a live string duet, comprising a cello and a double base singing the blues. In addition, the play refers to excerpts from an assortment of audio recordings by a variety of Black political, religious and cultural leaders. Most of these can easily be found. Nevertheless, appropriate substitutions may be necessary and some excerpts may need to be recreated from scratch. – D.S.

SHE You love her?

HE I . . . I wish –

SHE Have you sung to her at twilight?

HE Yes.

SHE Does your blood call out her name?

HE Yes.

SHE Do you finger feed her berries dipped in dark and luscious sweets?

HE Yes.

SHE Have you built her a crystal palace to refract her image like a thousand mirrors in your veins?

HE Yes.

SHE Do you let her sip nectar kisses from a cup of jade studded bronze from your immortal parts?

HE Yes.

SHE Does she make your thoughts and dreams and sighs, wishes and tears, ache sweet as you can bear?

HE Yes.

SHE You love her.

HE Yes. Yes. Yes.

(HE *wipes the remaining white foam from his face with a towel.* SHE *stares at the handkerchief laying in her bare hand.*)

SHE Is she White?

(*Silence.*)

Othello?

(*Silence.*)

She's White.

(*Silence.*)

Othello . . .

(*She holds the handkerchief out to him. He does not take it. She lets it fall at his feet. After a few moments, he picks it up.*)

Scene 1

(*Harlem, present: late summer – morning. The strings thump out an urban melody blues/jazz riff, accompanied by the voice of Malcolm X, speaking about the nightmare of race in America and the need to build strong Black communities.*

MAGI *is on the fire escape, leaning on the railing, reading a magazine with a large picture of a blonde woman on the cover. As the sound fades, she closes the magazine, surveying the action on the street below.*)

MAGI Sun up in Harlem. (*She spots the postman.*) Morning Mr. P.! Don't bring me no bill now – I

warned ya before. I'm having a baby. Don't need to get myself all worked up, given my condition . . . I'm gonna have me a Virgo baby, makes me due 'bout this time next year . . . I can count. I just haven't chosen the actual father/husband candidate as yet. Gotta find me a man to play his part. I wanna conceive in the middle of December, so I've booked the Convent Avenue Baptist church for this Saturday. The wedding's at three. You sure look to be the marrying kind. What you up to this weekend, yourself sweetness? Oh well then, wish your wife well for me. Package from where? California? Oohh. Yeh, yeh, yeh. I'll be right – Hey, hey, Amah girl . . . Up here . . . Let yourself in . . . (*She throws a set of keys down to* AMAH.) Mr. P., give that young lady the package . . . Yeh, she'll bring it up for me. (*Beat.*) Thank you, sugar. (*Beat.*) You have yourself a nice day now. Alright, sweetness. Mmn, mmn, mmn!

(AMAH *unlocks the door, enters and makes her way to the fire escape.*)

AMAH Magi, look at you, out on the terrace, watching the summer blossoms on the corner of Malcolm X and Martin Luther King Boulevards.

MAGI Nothing but weeds growing in the Soweto of America, honey. (*Shouting out.*) Billie!

AMAH Where is she?

MAGI I didn't want to wake her up 'till you got here. She didn't get to sleep 'till early morning. I could hear her wailing all the way downstairs.

AMAH I can see a week. A couple of weeks at the most. But what is this?

MAGI Two months – it's not like she's certifiable though.

(*Shouting gently to* BILLIE *in the bedroom.*)

Billie! Billie, Amah's here!

AMAH Well, least she sleeps now.

MAGI She's stillness itself. Buried under that ocean of self help books, like it's a tomb. Like a pyramid over her. Over the bed.

(*Calling out once more.*)

Billie!

(BILLIE'*s body moves slightly and an arm listlessly carves its way to the surface, shifting the tomb of books, several dropping to the floor.*

MAGI *and* AMAH *make their way inside. On a large table is a vase filled with blossoming cotton branches. There is also a myriad of bottles and bags, and a Soxhlet extraction apparatus: flask, extractor and thimble, condenser, siphoning hoses, all held up by two metal stands. A Bunsen burner is placed under the flask.*)

I'm just making her some coffee, can I get you a cup?

(AMAH *inspects the table and searches for a space to put the small package.*)

AMAH Thanks Magi. Where d'you want this? It looks like a science lab in here.

MAGI Some healing concoction I've been helping her make – but she's way ahead of me these days. She's got a real talent for herbs, you know. She's been sending away for ingredients – I can't even figure out what most of them are – put the package down anywhere.

AMAH If I can find a space.

MAGI Right there. On top of that alchemy book – right in the middle. Yeh. Thanks for doing this Amah. For coming. It'll make her feel like a million dollars again.

AMAH Please. Billie and me go so far back, way before Andrew. Besides, sisters-in-law are family too, you know. Jenny's been simply begging to come and see her, you know, for their once a week thing. They eat sausages, mashed potatoes, and corn. Some Canadian delicacy I guess –

MAGI Aren't you guys vegetarians?

AMAH Vegan.

MAGI Vegan?

AMAH We don't eat anything that has eyes. The sausages are tofu. You know they eat exactly the same thing every time. I was glad for the break. I guess I was kinda . . . well . . . it bugged me. Jenny's always full of Auntie Billie this, Auntie Billie that. Now I miss our one night a week without her. I mean – our time alone. And I see how it's a kind of security for her.

MAGI Security for who?

AMAH Oh, I can't rent your ground floor. They won't give me any insurance 'cause I don't have a licence. And I can't get a licence until I get a cosmetician's certificate. And I can't get a cosmetician's certificate until I finish this two year course on how to do White people's hair and make-up. I told them ain't no White people in Harlem. I'd learn how to do work with chemical relaxers and Jheri curls. Now, I do dreadlocks. And do they teach that? Oh no. They're just cracking down on people who do hair in private homes – something about lost tax revenues. I don't know . . . I want my own salon so bad I can taste it. 'The Lock Smiths'.

MAGI 'The Lock Smiths'.

AMAH Billie's supposed to be helping me with the business plan. Besides we've started trying for kid number 2. I need the space.

MAGI You're trying?

AMAH I'm 10 days late.

MAGI No!

AMAH It's still early. Don't tell Billie . . . you know. I'll tell her.

MAGI Good for you, girl! Did I tell you I was having a baby?

AMAH Oh yeh. How was he, that new candidate you were telling me about . . . Warren, no Waldo –

MAGI Wendel? Wedded Wendel as I've discovered.

AMAH He didn't tell –

MAGI Oh no. He believes that the nuclear family is the basis for a healthy society. That's why he's married. He keeps his own personal nuclear family at home in the event that he might someday want to spend time with it.

AMAH Why'd you stop seeing George. I liked George.

MAGI Well I liked him too.

AMAH You two looked pretty serious there for a while.

MAGI We'd been seeing each other the better part of . . . . . . what . . . two years. I'm just not getting any younger. I mean, I kept dropping hints I was ready for him to pop the question. Seems like he don't know what question I'm referring to. So I decided to give him some encouragement. See, I've been collecting things for my trousseau, and I have this negligee . . . all white, long, beautiful lacy thing. Looks like a see-through wedding gown. So, I'm out on my balcony – you know, 'cause it's too hot inside, and I still ain't got around to putting in air conditioning. Anyway, I see him coming up the street. So I rush in and put on the wedding dress negligee, thinking, he'll see me in it, all beautiful like – want to pop the question, you know. So I open the door, me in the negligee, and he . . . He stands there. Mouth wide open. And he says, he guess he should go get a bottle of wine, seeing how this was gonna be some kind of special occasion an' all. Now I don't know whether he got lost . . . or drunk . . . But I ain't seen or heard from him since.

AMAH Aahh nooo.

MAGI I should have margarined his butt when I had the chance.

AMAH Margarined his backside?

MAGI If you want to bind a man –

AMAH You don't mean, what I think you mean?

MAGI If you want to keep a man then, you rub his backside with margarine.

AMAH And it works?

MAGI I don't know. When I'd remember, I could never figure out how to get from the bed to the refrigerator.

AMAH Margarine, huh?

MAGI But you've got to be careful. He might be a fool. You don't want to be dragging no damn fool behind you the rest of your days.

AMAH You're a regular charmer, girl.

MAGI Don't get me wrong. I don't cut the heads off chickens, or anything now.

AMAH You know, a Jamaican lady told me about one where you rinse your underwear and use the dirty water to cook the meal.

MAGI Nooo! Really?

AMAH Really.

MAGI Ooh, I like that. Boil down some greens in panty stock. Hmm!

AMAH Once I buried his socks under the blackberry bush by the front door. Sure enough, he always finds his way back home.

MAGI How is True Drew?

AMAH Oh, Andrew's real good. You know him. He was up here 'till late, night before last, even, playing broad shouldered brother.

MAGI Yep, he's a good man. They're rare. And he went all the way down to D.C. for the Million Man March. Yeh, he's one in a million. If you ever think of trading him in . . .

AMAH Don't even think about it!

MAGI Can't blame a girl for trying. (*Calling out again.*) Billie! Billie you up yet?

(MAGI *gets no response. She goes into the bedroom.*)

Billie? Billie, sorry to wake you, but Amah's here. She waiting.

(BILLIE *emerges. We recognize her as the woman in the prologue. She slowly makes her way to the edge of the bed.*)

BILLIE If I could only stop dreaming, I might be able to get some rest.

MAGI You should jot them down. They're messages from other realms, you know.

BILLIE Jenny's in a large white room – the walls start pressing in all around her . . .

MAGI You OK?

BILLIE Mm mm. Yeh. I'm fine. I'm good.

MAGI (*Gently.*) Come on sweetheart, Amah's waiting.

BILLIE Let me just wash my face, and my mouth.

(MAGI *leaves* BILLIE *to join* AMAH, *who is now on the fire escape.*)

MAGI She's coming . . .

(AMAH *hands* MAGI *a cup of coffee.*)

Ooh . . . Thanks.

AMAH How is she?

MAGI Better. Dreaming hard, though. Like she's on some archeological dig of the unconscious mind.

AMAH His words hit her hard, huh.

MAGI Like a baseball bat hits a mango. Like he was trying for a home run or something. The bat breaks through the skin, smashing the amber flesh, propelling her core out of the park, into the clouds. And she lays there, floating.

AMAH Feeling sorry for herself.

MAGI A discarded fruit sitting in a dish, surrounded by its own ripening mould.

AMAH She feels so much.

MAGI Yeh. Each of her emotions sprout new roots, long, tangled things, intersecting each other like strangle weed.

AMAH She should go out though, get some fresh air once in a while.

MAGI She does. Her trips out into the real world are brief, though. The grocer's for tubs of things you add water to, she calls food; the pharmacy for the pills, and the bookstore. All her money goes up in smokes and writings that tell her she really ain't out of her mind. They'd make her feel better, more beautiful, more well, until she'd see some nice chocolate brown-skinned man, dangling his prize in front of her. 'Cause all the rot inside her would begin to boil, threaten to shoot out. So she comes home, takes some pills and sleeps again that fitful sleep 'till she wakes.

AMAH So she knows?

MAGI Ooh she knows. She knows she's still up there in the clouds.

AMAH She never used to be like that, you know, about colour.

MAGI Guess it ain't never been personal before.

AMAH But it seems bigger than that . . .

MAGI Girl, you've been married what . . . six years?

AMAH Seven this February coming . . .

MAGI How'd you feel if Drew just upped and left you?

AMAH I can't even imagine . . .

MAGI They've been together nine.

AMAH She still moving?

MAGI So she say . . . asked me to pick up some boxes.

AMAH (*Quietly.*) Rumour has it he's getting married.

MAGI So soon. He hasn't told her anything. He still hasn't even moved his stuff yet.

AMAH And she sacrificed so much. Gave up her share of the trust from her mother's life insurance to send him through school.

MAGI No!

AMAH So when it's her turn to go . . . All those years.

MAGI And those babies.

AMAH Yeh, thank god they didn't have any babies.

MAGI No, no . . . Twice . . .

AMAH No!

MAGI First time, he told her he believed in a woman's right to choose, but he didn't think that the relationship was ready for –

AMAH We didn't –

MAGI Nobody did. Second time she miscarried.

AMAH When? I don't –

MAGI 'Bout the same time he left – no, it was before that. She was by herself . . . Set down in a pool of blood. She put it in a ziplock bag . . . in the freezer . . . all purple and blue . . .

AMAH Oohh God . . . No . . . Really?

MAGI Yeh.

AMAH Nooo . . . For real. I'm serious . . .

MAGI Yeh!

AMAH Show me.

(MAGI *turns toward the living area and heads for the kitchen;* AMAH *follows closely behind. They approach the fridge and* MAGI *is about to open the freezer door when* BILLIE *enters from the bedroom.* AMAH *and* MAGI *stop abruptly, as if caught in the act.*)

AMAH Billie!

MAGI (*Overlapping.*) Hey girl!

(BILLIE *waves to them as she exits into the bathroom.* MAGI *turns to* AMAH.)

Or maybe I lied. Gotcha!

AMAH You . . . You . . . little heifer –

(MAGI *laughs.* AMAH *gets infected and joins her.*)

Scene 2

(*Harlem, 1860: late summer – twilight. The instruments sing a blues from deep in the Mississippi delta, while a mature northern American voice reads from the Declaration of Independence.* HIM *steeps hot metal into cool water. He places the*

shackles on an anvil and hammers the metal into shape. HER *is making repairs to a shawl with a needle.*)

HER I pray Cleotis is in heaven.

HIM Yeh . . . I . . . um . . . I . . .

HER You think Cleotis went to heaven?

HIM Well, I . . . I don't . . .

HER You think he's in hell?

HIM No. No.

HER Probably somewhere in between, though. Not Hades. Not God's kingdom. He's probably right there in the hardware store. Probably right there watching every time that Mr. Howard proudly hoists the mason jar. Every time they pay their penny to see through the formaldehyde. Cleotis is probably right there watching them gawk at his shriveled, pickled penis . . . You seen it?

HIM No.

HER You know who did the cutting, though?

HIM No . . . Oh no . . .

HER In France they got the vagina of a sister entombed for scientific research.

HIM No!

HER Venus, the Hottentot Venus. I read it in one of Miss Dessy's books. Saartjie – that's her real name, Saartjie Baartman. When Saartjie was alive they paraded her naked on a pay per view basis. Her derrière was amply endowed. People paid to see how big her butt was, and when she died, how big her pussy was.

HIM Wooo!

HER Human beings went and oohed and ahhed and paid money to see an endowment the creator bestowed on all of us.

HIM That's . . . that's . . . so . . . so . . .

HER They probably go to a special place though – Cleotis and Venus, Emmett. Purgatory. Venus and Cleotis fall in love, marry, but have no tools to consummate it. Must be a lot of us there walking around in purgatory without genitals.

(HIM *wipes his hands and retrieves something from his pocket.*)

HIM I've been meaning to . . . I want . . . (*Laughing to himself.*) I would like to . . .

HER Yes . . . ?

HIM Talk. We should talk.

HER Talk-talk?

HIM Talk-talk.

HER About what . . . ? What's wrong?

HIM Why must something be wrong –

HER I . . . I just figured . . . figure . . .

(HIM *takes* HER's *hand and kisses it, then places a white handkerchief into her palm.*)

HIM My heart . . .

(HIM closes HER's *fingers around the handkerchief. He kisses her fingers. Opening her hand, she examines the cloth.*)

HER Little strawberries on a sheet of white. Berries in a field of snow . . . (*Sighing.*) Ah silk. It's beautiful.

HIM It was my mother's. Given her by my father . . . from his mother before that. When she died she gave it me, insisting that when I found . . . chose . . . chose a wife . . . that I give it to her . . . to you heart.

HER Oh . . . It is so beautiful.

HIM There's magic in the web of it.

HER So delicate . . . so old.

HIM A token . . . an antique token of our ancient love.

HER My ancient love . . .

HIM My wife. My wife before I even met you. Let's do it. There's a war already brewing in the south. Canada freedom come.

HER Yes?

HIM Yes.

HER We're really gonna go?

HIM People will come to me and pay me for my work.

HER Yes sir, Mr. Blacksmith, sir.

HIM Can we have us a heap of children?

HER Four boys and four girls.

HIM And a big white house.

HER A big house on an emerald hill.

HIM Yeh . . . a white house, on an emerald hill, in Canada. (*Pause.*) I want to be with you 'till I'm too old to know. You know that.

HER Even when my breasts fall to my toes?

HIM I'll pick them up and carry them around for you.

HER And when I can't remember my own name?

HIM I'll call it out a thousand times a day.

HER Then I'll think you're me.

HIM I am you.

HER And when I get old, and wrinkled, and enormously fat, you'll –

HIM Fat? Naw. If you get fat, I'll have to leave your ass.

(HIM *kisses inside the crook of* HER's *arm.*)

HER Oh-oh. You're prospecting again.

HIM I'm exploring the heightening Alleghenies of Pennsylvania.

(HIM *kisses* HER.)

The curvaceous slopes of California.

(HIM *kisses* HER.)

The red hills of Georgia, the mighty mountains of New York.

(HIM *kisses* HER *again.*)

I'm staking my claim.

HER I don't come cheap, you know.

HIM I know . . . I'm offering more than money can buy.

HER How much more?

HIM This much.

(HIM *kisses* HER.)

HER I could buy that.

HIM Could you buy this?

(HIM *kisses* HER *deeply.*)

HER Beloved . . .

(HER *kisses* HIM.)

Scene 3

(*Harlem, the present: late summer – morning. Strains of a melodious urban blues jazz keeps time with an oral address by Marcus Garvey on the need for African Americans to return to Africa.*)

MAGI No, I hate it.

AMAH Come on. No one hates it.

MAGI I do.

AMAH Bah humbug?

MAGI What?

AMAH Scrooge?

MAGI Oh no, no, no. You know what I hate about Christmas? Seven days to New Year's Eve. And I hate New Year's Eve. And you know what I really hate about New Year's Eve? It's not the being alone at midnight. It's not the being a wallflower at some bash, because you fired your escort, who asked for time and a half, after 10:00 p.m. It's not even because you babysat your friend's kids the previous two. I really hate New Year's Eve, because it's six weeks to Valentine's Day. And what I really really hate about Valentine's Day – well, maybe that's too strong. No. I really hate it. What I really hate about Valentine's Day is . . . it's my birthday. Don't get me wrong, now. I'm glad I was born. But I look at my life – I'm more than halfway through it, and I wonder, what do I have to show for it? Anyway . . .

AMAH Well you come and spend Kwanzaa with us this year.

MAGI I don't know about the seven days, girl?

Look I gotta go. I'm seeing a certain minister about a certain wedding.

AMAH Whose wedding?

MAGI Mine. And don't say a thing – you know, about him getting married, or anything.

(MAGI *indicates the refrigerator*.)

AMAH Sealed.

MAGI I'll drop by later.

AMAH Alright.

MAGI (*Shouting*.) Billie? I'm gonna drop by later with some boxes, OK?

BILLIE (*Offstage*.) Thanks, Magi.

(MAGI *exits.* AMAH *goes to the table and examines the small chemical factory*.)

AMAH Saracen's Compound . . . Woad . . . Hart's tongue . . . Prunella vulgaris . . .

(*She picks up a book lying among the small packages and vials*.)

Egyptian Alchemy: A Chemical Encyclopedia . . .

(*She puts the book back in its place and picks up another vial*.)

Nux Vomica, warning: Extremely poisonous. Can be ingested on contact with skin . . .

(AMAH *quickly replaces the vial, wiping her hand on her clothes. She turns her attention to the kitchen. She cautiously approaches the refrigerator, and is about to open the freezer section when* BILLIE *comes out of the bathroom*.)

BILLIE Hey Amah.

AMAH Oh – hi girl, how you feeling?

BILLIE Thanks for making the house call, Amah.

AMAH Child, you look so thin.

BILLIE Well, I'm trying to lose a little baby fat before I die.

AMAH Coffee?

BILLIE Oh . . . Thanks. (*Pours coffee*.) You didn't have to come. I'm fine you know.

AMAH You're very welcome. Come sit down.

(AMAH *hands her the cup*.)

BILLIE I didn't mean . . . Thank you.

AMAH You washed your hair?

BILLIE Yesterday.

AMAH Good. A package came for you this morning.

BILLIE Where?

AMAH I put it beside the chemistry set. What is all that?

BILLIE Don't touch anything!

AMAH Alright – alright. I –

BILLIE No. No. I – I mean, some of this stuff can be deadly unless mixed . . . or . . . or diluted. Some ancient Egyptian rejuvenation tonic. If it don't kill me, it'll make me brand new – or so it says. How's my baby?

AMAH Jenny's fine. Andrew's taking her to her first African dance class today. You should see her in the little leotard . . .

BILLIE I should be there.

AMAH She's dying to come over for sausages and mashed potatoes.

BILLIE Yeh, yes, soon. Real soon.

(AMAH *prepares to twist* BILLIE*'s hair. She opens a jar of scented hair oil and takes a generous amount of the oil, rubs it onto her hands and gently works it into* BILLIE*'s hair*.)

AMAH She was so cute, today – you know what she did? She overheard me talking to Andrew about you, and I was saying I thought your breakdown was –

BILLIE You told her I had a nervous breakdown?

AMAH Oh – No. No. She overheard me –

BILLIE I am not having a nervous breakdown.

AMAH She didn't really understand. She thinks you've broken your legs and can't walk, you can't dance. She thinks you've broken your throat, and that's why she can't talk to you on the phone, that's why you don't sing to her on the phone anymore.

BILLIE Please don't tell her I'm crazy.

AMAH I never said you were crazy.

BILLIE I've just been . . . tired. Exhausted. I . . . I didn't want her to see this in me. She'd feel it in me. I never want her to feel this . . .

AMAH I know.

BILLIE But I'm fine now. Really, I'll be fine. I registered for school, I'm only taking one course this term, but that's cool. And first thing next week, I'm redoing the business plan for the salon.

AMAH You need to give me some of that tonic too, girl. That's the best kind of revenge, you know – living the good life.

BILLIE I thought I was living that life.

AMAH Maybe you were just dreaming.

(AMAH *takes a new lock of* BILLIE*'s hair. Taking a large dab of oil, she applies it to the lock, rubbing the strand between her palms*.)

BILLIE Remember when we moved in? The day Nelson and Winnie came to Harlem, remember? Winnie and Nelson – our welcoming committee. They'd blocked off the whole of 125th – it took us 45 minutes to convince the cops to let us through. And me and you and Othe and Drew went down to hear them speak. And Drew went off in search of some grits from a street vendor. And you asked me to hold baby Jenny while you went to the restroom, when this man came up to us and took our picture. Asked to take our picture. Jenny in my arms. Othello beside me. 'The perfect Black family'. That's what he called us. 'The perfect Black family'.

(*The phone rings.*)

AMAH   I'll get it.

BILLIE   No. Let it ring. I know who it is. I can still feel him – feel when he's thinking of me. We've spoken . . . Must be three times, in the last two months. Something about $500 on my portion of his American Express card, which they'd cancel if I didn't pay the bill. Seems I did me some consumer therapy. Last time he called – mad – to announce that the card had been cancelled by AMEX, and that he hoped that I was pleased. And I was. (*Pause.*) Is that crazy?

AMAH   Don't sound crazy. Hold the hair oil for me.

BILLIE   I used to pray that he was calling to say he's sorry. To say how he'd discovered a deep confusion in himself. But now . . .

(*The phone stops ringing.*)

I have nothing to say to him. What could I say? Othello, how is the fairer sexed one you love to dangle from your arm the one you love for herself and preferred to the deeper sexed one is she softer does she smell of tea roses and baby powder does she sweat white musk from between her toes do her thighs touch I am not curious just want to know do her breasts fill the cup of your hand the lips of your tongue not too dark you like a little milk with your nipple don't you no I'm not curious just want to know.

AMAH   You tell Jenny colour's only skin deep.

BILLIE   The skin holds everything in. It's the largest organ in the human body. Slash the skin by my belly and my intestines fall out.

AMAH   Hold the hair oil up.

(AMAH *takes a dab of oil from the jar.*)

BILLIE   I thought I saw them once, you know – on the subway. I had to renew my prescription. And I spot them – him and her. My chest is pounding. My legs can't move. From the back, I see the sharp barber's line, separating his tightly coiled hair from the nape of the skin at the back of his neck. His skin is soft there . . . and I have

to kick away the memory nudging its way into my brain. My lips on his neck, gently . . . holding him . . . Here, before me – his woman – all blonde hair and blonde legs. Her weight against his chest. His arm around her shoulders, his thumb resting on the gold of her hair. He's proud. You can see he's proud. He isn't just any Negro. He's special. That's why she's with him. And she . . . she . . . she flaunts. Yes, she flaunts. They are before. I am behind, stuck there on the platform. My tongue is pushing hard against the roof of my mouth . . . trying to hold up my brain, or something. 'Cause my brain threatens to fall. Fall down through the roof of my mouth, and be swallowed up. Slowly, slowly, I press forward, toward them. I'm not aiming for them though. I'm aiming with them in mind. I'm aiming for beyond the yellow line, into the tracks. The tunnel all three of us will fall into can be no worse than the one I'm trapped in now. I walk – no, well hover really. I'm walking on air. I feel sure of myself for the first time in weeks. Only to be cut off by a tall grey man in a grey uniform, who isn't looking where he's going, or maybe I'm not – Maybe he knew my aim. He looks at me. I think he looks at me. He brushes past. Then a sound emanating from . . . from . . . from my uterus, slips out of my mouth, shatters the spell. They turn their heads – the couple. They see me. It isn't even him.

(*The phone rings again.*)

AMAH   It could be your father, you know. He's been trying to get in touch with you. Says he doesn't know if you're dead or alive. He was calling Drew even up to this morning.

BILLIE   My father . . . I wouldn't have anything to say. It's been so long. What would I say?

(*The phone stops ringing.*)

AMAH   He's been in the hospital, you know. Something about his liver.

BILLIE   He hauled us all the way back to Nova Scotia from the Bronx, to be near Granma, when Mama died.

AMAH   I love that Nova Scotia was a haven for slaves way before the underground railroad. I love that . . .

BILLIE   He's a sot. That's academia speak for alcoholic. My Dad, the drunk of Dartmouth.

AMAH   You're still his children.

BILLIE   A detail I'm glad he's recalled.

AMAH   Better late than never.

BILLIE   Too little, too late.

AMAH Forgiveness is a virtue.
BILLIE What?
AMAH Forgiveness is a virtue.
BILLIE Girl, patience is a virtue.
AMAH Well . . . . . . forgiveness is up there . . .
BILLIE Did Drew tell you about the time my father sang to me at my high school graduation dinner?
AMAH Nooo. That's lovely. My father never sang to me at my graduation.
BILLIE We were eating. He was standing on top of the banquet table.
AMAH Nooo!
BILLIE It's the truth!

(*Pause.*)

AMAH Can I get a glass of water?
BILLIE Yeh. Yeh, help yourself.

(AMAH *goes into the kitchen.*)

I've got O.J. in the fridge, if you want.
AMAH Water will do, thanks. Do you have any . . . ice in your freezer?
BILLIE I'll get it.
AMAH I can get it.

(BILLIE *gets up quickly, and heads toward the kitchen.*)

BILLIE It's OK. It's OK. I'll get it for you.

(BILLIE *opens the freezer and gets her the ice, closing the freezer door immediately behind her.*)

AMAH Thanks. (*Beat.*) What's in there?
BILLIE Frozen shit.

(*The phone begins to ring again. Both women look toward it.*)

Scene 4

(*Same day: noontime. Accompanying the sound of rushing water and the polyrhythmic chorus of strings, Martin Luther King continues to assert his dream, its relationship to the American Constitution, and the Declaration of Independence.*)

OTHELLO (*Offstage.*) Billie!

(*Silence. He knocks again.*)

Billie?! (*To* MONA.) I don't think she's there.

(OTHELLO *unlocks the door. He enters. We recognize him as the man in both 1860 and 1928.*)

Billie? Mona and I are here to pick up the rest of my things. Billie?

(*He hears the shower. He goes over to the bathroom door. He knocks.*)

Billie? . . .

(BILLIE *screams. We hear something crash.*)

It's just me . . . I tried to call. You should get that machine fixed.
BILLIE (*Offstage.*) I'll be out in a minute.

(OTHELLO *returns to* MONA *at the entrance. We see nothing of her but brief glimpses of a bare arm and a waft of light brown hair.*)

OTHELLO It's OK Mona, she's in there. Why don't you wait in the car.
MONA (*Offstage.*) She'll have to get used to me sometime.
OTHELLO I'll be down in a flash. It won't take me that long.

(*She doesn't answer.*)

Hey, hey, hey!
MONA (*Offstage.*) Hey yourself. I do have other things to take care of, you know.

(*He kisses her.*)

OK . . . I still haven't found anything blue. I'll scour the stores. I'll be back in a couple of hours.
OTHELLO Alright.
MONA (*Offstage.*) Alright.

(*He brings in several large empty boxes. He closes the door and looks around. He sees a burning cigarette, picks it up, looks at it, then puts it out. He takes off his jacket. Then he takes several albums from a shelf and places them on the floor. He begins to form two piles. He picks up one of the albums and begins to laugh.* BILLIE *enters dressed in a robe.*)

BILLIE What are you doing here?
OTHELLO I came over to pack my things. The movers are coming in the morning. I tried to call . . .
BILLIE You took my pot.
OTHELLO What . . .
BILLIE My pot. The cast iron Dutch pot.
OTHELLO Oh . . . Well, you never use it.
BILLIE I want it back.
OTHELLO You never use it.
BILLIE The one with the yellow handle.
OTHELLO We need it to make gumbo.
BILLIE She uses it?
OTHELLO I need it to make gumbo.
BILLIE She needs my pot? The one with the carrying rings.

OTHELLO It was a gift to both of us.

BILLIE From my father.

OTHELLO I'll bring it back tomorrow.

BILLIE If you don't have it here for me inside of 30 minutes, I will break every jazz recording on that shelf.

OTHELLO You want me to go all the way back for something you don't even use.

BILLIE Let me see . . .

OTHELLO You never used it.

BILLIE Abbey Lincoln . . .

(*She takes the album from the table. Takes the record from the jacket and breaks it in two. She reaches for another album.* OTHELLO *picks up the broken record.*)

Aah. Max Roach.

(*She takes the cover off the Max Roach album.*)

OTHELLO The Abbey Lincoln was yours.

(*She breaks the Max Roach record too.*)

OK. OK, I'll go and get it.

(*He picks up his jacket and proceeds to the door.*)

BILLIE Fine. It's fine.

OTHELLO Excuse me?

BILLIE It's fine. Tomorrow's fine.

(*Pause. He turns toward her.*)

OTHELLO OK.

(*Pause. He puts his jacket down again. Pause.*)

How are you? You look well.

BILLIE I'm fine. And you?

OTHELLO Great . . . Good.

(*Pause.*)

BILLIE Well you know where your stuff is.

OTHELLO Yep . . . Yes.

(*Pause.*)

BILLIE Drink?

OTHELLO What?

BILLIE Would you like something to drink?

OTHELLO Sure . . . Yes . . . What do you –

BILLIE Peppermint, fennel, chamomile . . . No . . . Just peppermint and fennel. Coffee, wine, cognac, water.

OTHELLO What are you having?

BILLIE Cognac.

OTHELLO Oh. Well . . . That'll do.

(BILLIE *goes to the kitchen.*)

Where's my suitcase?

BILLIE Where you left it.

(*Pause.*)

OTHELLO So you're staying on then?

BILLIE No.

OTHELLO Where are you . . . You know . . . I mean, things are tight, money-wise, but I'll still put money in your account . . . When I can . . . I mean, I hope we can keep in touch.

(*She hands him a glass of cognac.*)

Thank you.

BILLIE You're welcome.

(*Pause.*)

OTHELLO You've lost weight. You look great. (*He takes a large gulp.*) Aaahh! Yes!

(OTHELLO *looks at* BILLIE *for a moment. He then takes one of the boxes and places it at his feet. He approaches the bookshelf. He takes down a large book.*)

African Mythology . . . Is this mine or yours?

BILLIE Mine . . . I think . . . I don't know.

OTHELLO This is going to be interesting.

BILLIE Take what you like. I don't care.

(OTHELLO *takes another book.*)

OTHELLO *The Great Chain of Being*?

BILLIE From man to mollusk. The scientific foundation for why we're not human. An African can't really be a woman, you know. My department agreed to let me take only one course this year – I'm taking a reading course.

OTHELLO Yours . . . Yours . . . Mine . . . *Black Psychology*, you keeping this?

BILLIE Yeh. (*She takes the books from him.*) You'd think there was more information on Black people and mental health. You know . . . Christ, we've been here, what, 400 years. No money in it I guess . . .

OTHELLO What's money got to do with it?

BILLIE You know, grants . . . Scholarships . . .

OTHELLO Race is not an obscure idea.

(*He places several books into a box.*)

BILLIE In genetics, or the study of what's wrong with people of African descent – The Heritage Foundation will give you tons of dough to prove the innate inferiority of . . . The Shakespeare's mine, but you can have it.

OTHELLO Sure, if you don't –

BILLIE No. The Heritage Foundation – that's where that guy Murray, et al, got most of their money for Bell Curve – I think . . . There's just no-one out there willing to give you a scholarship to prove that we're all mad.

OTHELLO We're all mad. This is the founding principle of your thesis?

BILLIE Well, not mad . . . I mean . . . Well . . . Psychologically dysfunctional, then. All cultural groups are to some degree ethnocentric: We–they. But not all intercultural relations are of an inferior/superior type.

OTHELLO Thus we're not all mad.

(*He returns to the bookshelf.*)

BILLIE No, no. In America, this race shit is classic behavioural disorder. Obsessions. Phobias. Delusions. Notions of persecution. Delusions of grandeur. Any one or combination of these can produce behaviours which categorize oneself as superior and another as inferior. You see, this kind of dysfunction is systemically supported by the larger society. Psychology only sees clients who can no longer function in society. We're all mad. We just appear to be functional.

OTHELLO And your solution?

BILLIE You'll have to buy my book.

(*Pause. They continue packing.*)

How's the teaching?

OTHELLO Fine . . . Great . . .

BILLIE Good.

(*Pause.*)

OTHELLO I'll be heading the department's courses in Cyprus next summer.

BILLIE I thought you told me Christopher . . . What's his name?

OTHELLO Chris Yago?

BILLIE Yeh, Yago.

OTHELLO Well everyone thought he would get it. I thought he'd get it. So a whole bunch of them are challenging affirmative action.

BILLIE Rednecks in academia.

OTHELLO No, no . . . Well . . . . . I think it's a good thing.

BILLIE Pul-eese.

OTHELLO Using discrimination to cure discrimination is not –

BILLIE We're talking put asides of 5%. 5% of everything available to Whites. They've still got 95.

OTHELLO Billie . . . Injustice against Blacks can't be cured by injustice against Whites . . . you know that.

BILLIE And younger people won't have the same opportunities you had.

OTHELLO Now look who's sounding White.

BILLIE Who said you sounded White?

OTHELLO It's implied . . . No-one at school tells me I don't know how to do my job . . . it's implied. I'll be at a faculty meeting, I'll make a suggestion and it'll be ignored. Not five minutes later, someone else will make the exact same suggestion and everyone will agree to it. Mona noticed it too. They think I'm only there because I'm Black. I've tested it.

BILLIE So let me get this straight, you're against affirmative action in order for White people to respect you.

OTHELLO For my peers . . . . . . my peers to respect me. You know what it's like. Every day I have to prove to them that I can do my job. I feel that any error I make only goes to prove them right.

BILLIE Well you must be perfect. Mona respects you.

OTHELLO Well, she really sees me. She was the only other faculty to support me on the MLK Day assembly. When we played the video –

BILLIE The 'I have a dream' speech?

OTHELLO They understood. For a moment I got them to understand.

(*He picks up several books and places them in a box.*)

BILLIE 'America has defaulted on this promissory note insofar as her . . .

OTHELLO & BILLIE . . . citizens of colour are concerned.

OTHELLO Instead of honoring this sacred obligation, America has given its coloured people a . . .

OTHELLO & BILLIE bad cheque . . .

BILLIE . . . a cheque that has come back marked . . .

OTHELLO & BILLIE . . . "insufficient funds".'

BILLIE The man was a . . . a . . .

OTHELLO Poet . . . Visionary.

BILLIE A prophet.

OTHELLO After all he'd been through in his life, he could still see that at a deeper level we're all the same.

(*Pause.*)

BILLIE I'm not the same.

OTHELLO In the eyes of God. Billie, we're all the same.

BILLIE One day little Black boys and little White girls –

OTHELLO You're delusional.

BILLIE You're the one looking for White respect.

OTHELLO Wrong again! White respect, Black respect, it's all the same to me.

BILLIE Right on brother man!

OTHELLO When I was growing up . . . in a time of Black pride – it was something to say you were Black. Before that, I'd say . . . My family would say we're Cuban . . . It takes a long time to work through some of those things. I am a member of the human race.

BILLIE Oh, that's a switch. What happened to all that J. A. Rogers stuff you were pushing. Blacks created the world, Blacks are the progenitors of European civilization, gloriana . . . Constantly trying to prove you're as good, no, better than White people. White people are always the line for you, aren't they? The rule . . . the margin . . . the variable of control. We are Black. Whatever we do is Black.

OTHELLO I'm so tired of this race shit, Billie. There are alternatives –

BILLIE Like what? Oh yes, White.

OTHELLO Oh, don't be so –

BILLIE Isn't that really what not acting Black, or feeling Black means.

OTHELLO Liberation has no colour.

BILLIE But progress is going to White schools . . . proving we're as good as Whites . . . like some holy grail . . . all that we're taught in those White schools. All that is in us. Our success is Whiteness. We religiously seek to have what they have. Access to the White man's world. The White man's job.

OTHELLO That's economics.

BILLIE White economics.

OTHELLO God! Black women always –

BILLIE No. Don't even go there . . .

OTHELLO I . . . You . . . Forget it!

BILLIE (Quietly at first.) Yes, you can forget it, can't you. I don't have that . . . that luxury. When I go into a store, I always know when I'm being watched. I can feel it. They want to see if I'm gonna slip some of their stuff into my pockets. When someone doesn't serve me, I think it's because I'm Black. When a clerk won't put the change into my held-out hand, I think it's because I'm Black. When I hear about a crime, any crime, I pray to God the person who they think did it isn't Black. I'm even suspicious of the word Black. Who called us Black anyway? It's not a country, it's not a racial category, its not even the colour of my skin. And don't give me this content of one's character B.S. I'm sorry . . . I am sorry . . . I had a dream. A dream that one day a Black man and a Black woman might find . . . Where jumping a broom was a solemn eternal vow that . . . I . . . Let's . . . Can we just get this over with?

(She goes to the window.

Silence.

He moves toward her.)

OTHELLO I know . . . I know. I'm sorry . . .

BILLIE Yeh . . .

OTHELLO I care . . . you know that.

BILLIE I know.

(Silence.)

OTHELLO I never thought I'd miss Harlem.

(Pause.)

BILLIE You still think it's a reservation?

OTHELLO Homeland/reservation.

BILLIE A sea of Black faces.

OTHELLO Africatown, USA.

(Pause.)

BILLIE When we lived in the Village, sometimes, I'd be on the subway and I'd miss my stop. And I'd just sit there, past midtown, past the upper west side, and somehow I'd end up here. And I'd just walk. I love seeing all these brown faces.

OTHELLO Yeh . . .

BILLIE Since they knocked down the old projects, I can see the Schomberg Museum from here. You still can't make out Harlem Hospital. I love that I can see the Apollo from our – from my balcony.

OTHELLO Fire escape.

BILLIE Patio.

OTHELLO You never did find a pair of lawn chairs, and a table to fit in that space.

BILLIE Terrace.

OTHELLO I never saw the beauty in it.

BILLIE Deck. My deck.

OTHELLO I wish . . .

(He looks at her.)

BILLIE That old building across the street? I didn't know this, but that used to be the Hotel Theresa. That's where Castro stayed when he came to New York . . . Must have been the fifties. Ron Brown's father used to run that hotel.

OTHELLO I . . . . . . I . . . . . . I miss you so much sometimes. Nine years . . . it's a long time.

BILLIE I know.

OTHELLO I'm really not trying to hurt you, Billie.

BILLIE I know.

OTHELLO I never meant to hurt you.

(He strokes her face.)

BILLIE I know.
OTHELLO God you're so beautiful.

(*He kisses her. She does not resist.*)

BILLIE I . . . don't . . . I feel . . .

(*He kisses her again.*)

BILLIE What are you doing?
OTHELLO I . . . I'm . . . I'm exploring the heightening Alleghenies of Pennsylvania.

(*He kisses her again.*)

The curvaceous slopes of California.

(*He kisses her again.*)

The red hills of Georgia, the mighty mountains of New York. Such sad eyes.

(*He kisses her again.*)

I'm an equal opportunity employer.

(*Pause.*)

I am an equal opportunity employer.

(*Pause.*)

I say, I'm an equal opportunity employer, then you say, I don't come . . .
BILLIE I don't come cheap, you know.
OTHELLO I'm offering more than money can buy.
BILLIE How much more?
OTHELLO This much.

(*He kisses her.*)

BILLIE I could buy that.
OTHELLO Could you buy this?

(*He kisses her deeply.*)

BILLIE Be . . . Be . . . Beloved.

(*She kisses him.*)

Scene 5

(*Same day: early afternoon. The stringed duet croons gently as Malcolm X speaks about the need for Blacks to turn their gaze away from Whiteness so that they can see each other with new eyes.* OTHELLO *is lying in the bed.* BILLIE *is in the living room, smoking a cigarette.*)

OTHELLO I've missed you.
BILLIE That's nice.
OTHELLO By the looks of things, I miss you even now.
BILLIE I'm coming.

OTHELLO I noticed.
BILLIE Sometimes . . . Sometimes when we make love. Sometimes every moment lines up into one moment. And I'm holding you. And I can't tell where I end, or you begin. I see everything. All my ancestors lined up below me . . . . . . like a Makonde statue, or something. It's like . . . I know. I know I'm supposed to be here. Everything is here.
OTHELLO Sounds crowded to me.
BILLIE It's actually quite empty.
OTHELLO Not as empty as this bed is feeling right about now.
BILLIE I'm coming. I'm coming.

(*She hurriedly stubs the cigarette out, and heads toward the bedroom. The apartment buzzer rings.* BILLIE *goes to the intercom.*)

BILLIE Hi Magi. I . . . er . . . I'm kinda busy right now.
MONA (*Through intercom.*) It's Mona. Could I have a word with Othello.
OTHELLO (*Overlapping.*) Shit!
BILLIE One second please.

(*He rushes to the intercom, while attempting to put his clothes back on.* BILLIE *tries to hold back her laughter. Her laughter begins to infect* OTHELLO. *He puts a finger over his mouth indicating to* BILLIE *to be quiet.*)

OTHELLO Hey Mone . . . Mone, I'm not done yet. There's more here than I imagined. Why don't I call you when I'm done.

(MONA *does not respond.* OTHELLO's *demeanour changes.*)

Mone? Mona? I'm coming, OK? I'll be right . . . Just wait there one second, OK? OK?

(BILLIE *is unable to hide her astonishment.*)

MONA (*Through intercom.*) OK.
OTHELLO OK.

(*He steps away from the intercom to finish putting on his clothes.* BILLIE *stares at him.*)

I'll be back in . . . Uh . . . I just have to go straighten . . . Uh . . . She wants to help . . . help pack. You'll have to get used to her sometime. I mean . . . I . . .

(BILLIE *continues to stare steadily at* OTHELLO *as he struggles with the buttons on his shirt.*)

I'm sorry . . . Well . . . . . . I'll be right . . . I'll be back.

(*He exits.* BILLIE *does not move.*)

Scene 6

(*Harlem, 1860: late summer – night. A whining delta blues slides and blurs while the deeply resonant voice of Paul Robeson talks of his forbears, whose blood is in the American soil.* HIM *is hammering a newly-forged horseshoe.* HER *rushes in holding a large carrying bag.*)

HER Oh . . . let me catch – catch my breath . . . I thought I was seen . . . Oh my . . . I . . . I've packed a change of clothes for both of us, some loaves . . . I liberated the leftover bacon from yesterday's meal, from out the pantry, seeing how it was staring me right in the face when I was cleaning. It won't be missed. I wish I could pack old Betsy in my bag. She'd be sure an' give us some good fresh milk each mornin'. Oh – and I packed a fleece blanket. I hear the nights get good and cold further north you go. And . . . did I forget . . . no . . . Nothing forgotten. Oh yes, I borrowed the big carving knife – for the bacon, a' course. You still working on those shoes for Miss Dessy's stallion . . . Let her send it to town, or get some other slave to do that . . . She's going to be mad as hell you took off in any event . . . May as well not finish the shoes, it won't placate her none . . .

(HIM *picks up the horseshoe with a pair of tongs.* HIM *inspects it carefully.* HIM *puts the shoe to one side and retrieves the shackles.* HIM *takes a chamois and begins to polish the metal.*)

O? O? Othello? The moon'll be rising. We've got to make any headway under cover of dark . . . Othello, why you trying to please her. I'm so tired of pleasing her. I'm so tired of pleasing White folks. Up in Canada, we won't have to please no White folks no how. I hear they got sailing ships leaving for Africa every day. Canada freedom come . . . O? Othello? Are you coming?

HIM I can't.

HER If we make it to the border there's people there'll help us wade that water – help us cross over.

HIM I'm not going.

HER A big white house on an emerald hill . . .

HIM I know.

HER You need more time, O? I can wait for you. Finish her shoes, I'll . . . I can wait –

HIM No. No.

(*Pause.*)

HER You love her.

HIM Her father going to war.

HER You love her?

HIM I love you. It's just . . . She needs me. She respects me. Looks up to me, even. I love you. It's just . . . When I'm with her I feel like . . . a man. I want . . . need to do for her . . .

HER Do you love her?

HIM Yes.

HER Fight with me I would fight with you. Suffer with me, O . . . I would suffer with you . . .

(*Silence.*)

Scene 7

(*Harlem, present: late summer – late afternoon. Dulcet blue tones barely swing as Louis Farrakhan waxes eloquent on African Americans being caught in the gravity of American society.* BILLIE *is carefully wrapping personal items in newspaper. She places them in a large pile on the floor.* MAGI *enters carrying several large cardboard boxes.*)

MAGI And you know what he says, after turning on the baseball game, in the middle of my romantic dinner? Eyes glued to the screen, he says, I bet you've never made love to a man with 26-inch biceps!

BILLIE (*Smiles.*) Oh . . . no . . .

MAGI I'm telling you, girl. Macho Mack, spot him at any locale selling six-packs. Easily recognizable, everything about him is permanently flexed. His favourite pastime? Weekend NFL football, Monday night football, USFL football – even Canadian foot . . . You look like you're feeling better. Amah did a great job with your hair.

BILLIE What's her motto? We lock heads and minds.

MAGI Hey, can I borrow that beautiful African boubou – I got me a date with an African prince. The brother has it going on! Oh . . . you already have boxes.

(BILLIE *begins placing some of the wrapped objects into a box.*)

BILLIE They're his box –

MAGI When . . . He came over?

BILLIE I even spoke to her.

MAGI You saw her?

BILLIE No. Want this mask?

MAGI You met her?

BILLIE No. Want this mask?.

MAGI I'll keep it for you –

BILLIE I . . . er . . . . . . I don't know how long these things will have to stay in storage.

MAGI You don't have to move, you know. It's not rented yet. I mean, I can always lower the –

BILLIE No, no . . . I'm moving on.

MAGI Good. Good. To where? Where are you going? You haven't given me a date or anything. I've got bills to pay too, you know. When d'you plan to leave? Where are you going?

BILLIE I might go . . . . . . stay with Jenny. I could go home.

MAGI I'll keep it for you –

BILLIE I don't want anything that's – that was ours. If you don't want it, that's OK, I'll just trash it.

(BILLIE *throws the mask onto the floor. It breaks into several pieces.*)

MAGI Something happened. What happened?

BILLIE Nothing.

MAGI Did he tell you about . . . What did he say to you?

BILLIE I'm just tired. Tired of sleeping. Tired of night. It lays over me like a ton of white feathers. Swallows me up. The movers are coming in the morning to pick up his things. It's OK. I'm fine. You know . . . I've lived all my life believing in lies.

MAGI Well, getting your Masters isn't a lie.

BILLIE It's about proving, isn't it? Proving I'm as good as . . . I'm as intelligent as . . .

MAGI Nothing wrong with that.

BILLIE I don't want anything . . . Believe in anything. Really. I've gotta get out of here. I don't even believe in Harlem anymore.

MAGI Come on . . .

BILLIE It's all an illusion. All some imagined idealistic . . . I dunno.

MAGI When I go out my door, I see all the beauty of my Blackness reflected in the world around me.

BILLIE Yeh, and all my wretchedness by the time I get to the end of the block.

MAGI Billie, he's the one who wants to White wash his life.

BILLIE Corporeal malediction.

MAGI Corp-o-re-all mal-e . . . Oooh that's good.

BILLIE A Black man afflicted with Negrophobia.

MAGI Girl, you on a roll now!

BILLIE No, no. A crumbled racial epidermal schema . . .

MAGI Who said school ain't doing you no good.

BILLIE . . . causing predilections to coitus denegrification.

MAGI Booker T. Uppermiddleclass III. He can be found in predominantly White neighborhoods. He refers to other Blacks as 'them'. His greatest accomplishment was being invited to the White House by George Bush to discuss the 'Negro problem.'

BILLIE Now, that is frightening.

MAGI No, what's frightening is the fact that I dated him.

BILLIE What does it say . . . about us?

MAGI Who?

BILLIE You and me.

MAGI Girl, I don't know. I can't even want to go there.

BILLIE Ohh . . . Oh well . . . Least he's happy though. What does he say? Now he won't have to worry that a White woman will emotionally mistake him for the father that abandoned her.

MAGI Isn't he worried the White woman might mistake him for the butler?

BILLIE He'd be oh so happy to oblige.

MAGI I see them do things for White women they wouldn't dream of doing for me.

BILLIE It is a disease. We get infected as children, and . . . and the bacteria . . . the virus slowly spreads, disabling the entire system.

MAGI Are we infected too?

(*There is knocking at the apartment door.*)

Speaking of White minds parading around inside of Black bodies – you want me to stay?

BILLIE Don't you have a date?

MAGI Hakim. But I can cancel . . .

(*There is knocking at the door again.*)

BILLIE I'm OK. I'm OK. I'm fine . . . Truly.

(BILLIE *opens the door.* OTHELLO *enters.*)

OTHELLO The pot!

(*He hands the pot to* BILLIE.)

Magi!

MAGI How's Harlumbia?

OTHELLO Columbia?

MAGI Harlumbia – those 10 square blocks of Whitedom, owned by Columbia University, set smack dab in the middle of Harlem.

OTHELLO Harlumbia, as you call it, is dull without you.

MAGI You could steal honey from a bee, couldn't you. Better watch you don't get stung. Well, I'm off to doll myself up. Billie . . .

BILLIE Yeh, I'll get that boubou . . .

(BILLIE *goes into the bedroom. After a few moments of silence.*)

MAGI Why haven't you told her yet?

OTHELLO About? – Oh yes . . . Yeh . . . I wanted to . . .

(BILLIE *returns with a beautiful multicoloured boubou.*)

BILLIE He won't be able to resist you . . .
MAGI Thank you, thank you. Later you two.
OTHELLO I'll be in touch . . .
BILLIE I'm keeping my fingers crossed for you.
MAGI Good, I'm running out of time.

(MAGI *exits.* OTHELLO *enters.* BILLIE *closes the door. There is a long awkward silence.* BILLIE *continues placing wrapped objects into her boxes.* OTHELLO *steps on a piece of the broken mask. He picks it up, looks at it, then places it on the mantel. He goes over to the bookshelf and begins to pack more of his possessions into his boxes.*)

OTHELLO They're coming at nine.
BILLIE Oh . . . Er . . . I'll be out of your way.
OTHELLO You can be here . . .
BILLIE No. No. No. I have an appointment . . . . . . an early appointment.
OTHELLO Either way . . .

(*They continue packing.*)

Ah . . . I've been meaning to tell you . . . . . . things are real . . . . . . money's real tight right now, what with buying the apartment, and moving and everything . . . I won't be able to cover your tuition this semester. I'll try and put money in your account when I can. Maybe –
BILLIE I told you, I'm only taking one course. If you cover that, I won't be taking a full load 'till next –
OTHELLO I know, that's what I'm saying . . . I can't . . . I just can't do it right now.
BILLIE It's one course . . .
OTHELLO It's $5000.
BILLIE You promised . . .
OTHELLO I'm mortgaged up the wazoo. I don't have it. I just don't have $5000, right now.
BILLIE Ooh . . . . . . okay.
OTHELLO I would if I could, you know that.

(*He continues to pack.*)

I think I brought the bookshelf with me when we first –
BILLIE Take it all.
OTHELLO I don't want all of it.
BILLIE I'm keeping the bed.
OTHELLO What about the rest . . .
BILLIE If you don't want it . . . I'm giving it away . . .
OTHELLO OK, if you're throwing it out . . .
BILLIE I'm keeping the bed.

(*They continue packing in silence.*)

OTHELLO We're getting married.

(*Pause.*)

Me and Mona. We're engaged . . . Officially.

(*Very long pause.*)

BILLIE Congratulations.
OTHELLO I wanted to tell you . . . Hear it from the horse's mouth . . . Hear it from me first. You know . . .
BILLIE Yeh . . . Yes. Yes. Congratulations.
OTHELLO Mona wanted me to tell you.
BILLIE Yes. Yes. Being a feminist and everything – A woman's right to know – since we're all in the struggle . . . I thought you hated feminists.
OTHELLO Well . . . I didn't mean that. I mean . . . the White women's movement is different.
BILLIE Just Black feminists.
OTHELLO No, no . . . White men have maintained a firm grasp of the pants. I mean, White men have economic and political pants that White women have been demanding to share.
BILLIE White wisdom from the mouth of the mythical Negro.
OTHELLO Don't you see! That's exactly my point! You . . . The Black feminist position as I experience it in this relationship, leaves me feeling unrecognized as a man. The message is, Black men are poor fathers, poor partners, or both. Black women wear the pants that Black men were prevented from wearing . . . I believe in tradition. You don't support me. Black women are more concerned with their careers than their husbands. There was a time when women felt satisfied, no, honoured being a balance to their spouse, at home, supporting the family, playing her role –
BILLIE Which women? I mean, which women are you referring to? Your mother worked all her life. My mother worked, her mother worked . . . Most Black women have been working like mules since we arrived on this continent. Like mules. When White women were burning their bras, we were hired to hold their tits up. We looked after their homes, their children . . . I don't support you? My mother's death paid your tuition, not mine . . .
OTHELLO Can't we even pretend to be civil? Can't we? I know this isn't easy. It's not easy for me either. Do you ever consider that?
BILLIE You like it easy, don't you.
OTHELLO The truth is, this is too fucking difficult.
BILLIE You wouldn't know the truth if it stood up and knocked you sideways.

OTHELLO You don't want the truth. You want me to tell you what you want to hear. No, no, you want to know the truth? I'll tell you the truth. Yes, I prefer White women. They are easier – before and after sex. They wanted me and I wanted them. They weren't filled with hostility about the unequal treatment they were getting at their jobs. We'd make love and I'd fall asleep not having to beware being mistaken for someone's inattentive father. I'd explain that I wasn't interested in a committed relationship right now, and not be confused with every lousy lover, or husband that had ever left them lying in a gutter of unresolved emotions. That's the truth. To a Black woman, I represent every Black man she has ever been with and with whom there was still so much to work out. The White women I loved saw me – could see me. Look, I'm not a junkie. I don't need more than one lover to prove my manhood. I have no children. I did not leave you, your mother, or your aunt, with six babies and a whole lotta love. I am a very single, very intelligent, very employed Black man. And with White women it's good. It's nice. Anyhow, we're all equal in the eyes of God, aren't we? Aren't we?

(BILLIE *stares at* OTHELLO. *He continues to pack.*)

Scene 8

(*Harlem. 1928: late summer – night. The cello and bass moan, almost dirge-like, in harmonic tension to the sound of Jesse Jackson's oratory.* SHE *holds a straight-edged razor in her bloodied palms.* HE *lies on the floor in front of her, motionless, the handkerchief in his hand.*)

SHE Deadly deadly straw little strawberries it's so beautiful you kissed my fingers you pressed this cloth into my palm buried it there an antique token our ancient all these tiny red dots on a sheet of white my fingernails are white three hairs on my head are white the whites of my eyes are white too the palms of my hands and my feet are white you're all I'd ever and you my my I hate Sssshh. Shhhhh OK. OK. OK. I'm OK alright don't don't don't don't my eyes on the shadow sparrow my sense in my feet my hands my head shine the light there please scream no sing sing (SHE *tries to sing.*) and if I get a notion to jump into the ocean, ain't nobody's business if

I do do do do If I go to church on Sunday then shimmy down on Monday t'ain't nobody's business if I . . .

Scene 9

(*Harlem, present: late summer – early evening. The instruments sound out a deep cerulean blues, while Malcolm X almost scats the question, 'What difference does colour make?'* OTHELLO *continues to pack.* BILLIE *sits on the floor by the bed watching him from the bedroom.*)

OTHELLO I didn't mean – what I said. You know that. I just . . . Sometimes you make me so mad I . . . People change, Billie. That's just human nature. Our experiences, our knowledge transforms us. That's why education is so powerful, so erotic. The transmission of words from mouth to ear. Her mouth to my ear. Knowledge. A desire for that distant thing I know nothing of, but yearn to hold for my very own. My Mama used to say, you have to be three times as good as a White child to get by, to do well. A piece of that pie is mine. I don't want to change the recipe. I am not minor. I am not a minority. I used to be a minority when I was a kid. I mean my culture is not my mother's culture – the culture of my ancestors. My culture is Wordsworth, Shaw, *Leave it to Beaver, Dirty Harry*. I drink the same water, read the same books. You're the problem if you don't see beyond my skin. If you don't hear my educated English, if you don't understand that I am a middle class educated man. I mean, what does Africa have to do with me. We struttin' around professing some imaginary connection to a land we don't know. Never seen. Never gonna see. We lie to ourselves saying, ah yeh, mother Africa, middle passage, suffering, the Whites did it to me, it's the White's fault. Strut around in African cloth pretending we human now. We human now. Some of us are beyond that now. Spiritually beyond this race shit bullshit now. I am an American. The slaves were freed over 130 years ago. In 1967 it was illegal for a Black to marry a White in sixteen states. That was less than thirty years ago . . . in my lifetime. Things change, Billie. I am not my skin. My skin is not me.

Scene 10

(*Harlem. same day: night. A rhapsody of sound keeps time with Christopher Darden as he asks O. J.*

Simpson to approach the jury and try on the bloody glove. The apartment is virtually full of boxes. BILLIE *is by the chemical factory at the table. The book of Egyptian Alchemy sits open upon it. Something is boiling in the flask and steam is coming out of the condenser. With rubber gloved hands she adds several drops of a violet liquid into the flask. She picks up a large white handkerchief with pretty red strawberries embroidered on it.)*

BILLIE I have a plan, my love. My mate . . . throughout eternity. Feel what I feel. Break like I break. No more – no less. You'll judge me harsher. I know. While Susan Smith . . . She blamed some imaginary Black man for the murder of her two boys and that's why authorities didn't suspect her for nearly two weeks. Stopping every Black man with a burgundy sedan from Union, South Carolina, to the Oranges of New Jersey. And you're still wondering what made her do it. What was she going through to make her feel that this was her only way out. Yet I'll be discarded as some kind of unconscionable bitter shadow, or something. Ain't I a woman? This is my face you take for night – the biggest shadow in the world. I . . . I have nothing more to lose. Nothing. Othello? I am preparing something special for you . . . Othe . . . Othello. A gift for you, and your new bride. Once you gave me a handkerchief. An heirloom. This handkerchief, your mother's . . . given by your father. From his mother before that. So far back . . . And now . . . then . . . to me. It is fixed in the emotions of all your ancestors. The one who laid the foundation for the road in Herndon, Virginia, and was lashed for laziness as he stopped to wipe the sweat from his brow with this kerchief. Or, your great great grandmother, who covered her face with it, and then covered it with her hands as she rocked and silently wailed, when told that her girl child, barely thirteen, would be sent 'cross the state for breeding purposes. Or the one who leapt for joy on hearing of the Emancipation Proclamation, fifteen years late mind you, only to watch it fall in slow motion from his hand and onto the ground when told that the only job he could now get, was the same one he'd done for free all those years, and now he's forced to take it, for not enough money to buy the food to fill even one man's belly. And more . . . so much more. What I add to this already fully endowed cloth, will cause you such such . . . Wretchedness. Othe . . . Othello.

(The contents of the flask have been transformed from violet to clear. BILLIE *places the handkerchief onto a large tray. Then with tongs, she takes the hot flask and pours the contents over the handkerchief She retrieves a vial from the table, opens it.)*

My sable warrior . . . Fight with me. I would fight with you . . . Suffer with me . . . I would suffer –

(She starts to pour, but the vial is empty. The buzzer rings. BILLIE *is surprised. The buzzer rings again.* BILLIE *turns off the Bunsen burner. She takes the flask into the kitchen and pours it into the sink. The buzzer rings once more. Going back to the table, she carefully takes the tray and heads toward the bathroom. There is a knock at her door.)*

BILLIE *(From the bathroom.)* You have a key, let yourself in . . . Make yourself right at home, why don't you –
MAGI *(Offstage.)* Billie? Billie, it's me. Magi.
BILLIE Magi?
MAGI *(Offstage.)* Are you OK?
BILLIE Yes. Yes. I'm fine. Let me call you later, OK Magi?

(We hear the sound of liquid being poured. The toilet flushes. MAGI *offstage mumbles something inaudible.)*

BILLIE What?

*(*MAGI *mumbles something inaudible again.)*

BILLIE What? Door's open!

*(*MAGI *enters and stands in the doorway. She is speaking quietly, as if not wanting someone to hear.)*

MAGI Sweetie, you have a visitor. Shall I –
BILLIE *(Entering the living area.)* Look I'm tired. He's been here practically all day already –
MAGI No, no, no. He said his name is Canada. (BILLIE *turns to* MAGI.) He says he's your father. That's what he said. He said he was your father.

(A man in his late sixties, brushes past MAGI. *He wears a hat, and has a small suitcase in his hand.)*

CANADA Sybil? Sybil! There's my girl. Come and give your Daddy a big hug.

Act II

Scene 1

(*Harlem, present: late summer – night. The cello and bass pluck and bow a funky rendition of Aretha Franklin's 'Spanish Harlem' against the audio sound of Michael Jackson and Lisa Marie Presley's interview on ABC's '20/20'.* CANADA *is sitting on one of the chairs, amidst stacks of boxes.*)

CANADA The first time I came to Harlem, I was scared. Must have been '68 or '69. Yeh . . . We we're living in the Bronx, and your mother was still alive. Everything I'd ever learned told me that I wasn't safe in this part of town. The newspapers. Television. My friends. My own family. But I'm curious, see. I says, Canada you can't be in New York City and not see Harlem. So I make my way to 125th. 'A' train. I'm gonna walk past the Apollo, I'm gonna see this place. I'm gonna walk the ten city blocks to Lexington and catch the '6' train back, if it's the last thing I do. So out of the subway, I put on my 'baddest mother in the city' glare. I walk – head straight. All the time trying to make my stride say, 'I'm mean . . . I'm mean. Killed somebody mean.' So I'm doing this for 'bout five, ten minutes, taking short furtive glances at this place I really want to see, when I begin to realize . . . No-one is taking any notice of me . . . Not a soul. Then it dawns on me: I'm the same as them. I look just like them. I look like I live in Harlem. Sounds silly now. But I just had to catch myself and laugh out loud. Canada, where did you get these ideas about Harlem from?

(*The kettle whistles.*)

BILLIE How do you like it?

(BILLIE *heads to the kitchen to make tea.*)

CANADA Brown sugar. No milk.

BILLIE I don't even know why I asked, I don't have any milk anyway.

CANADA You can't take milk. Never could. When your mother stopped feeding you from her milk, that cow's milk just gave you colic. And those diapers . . . Now that's an image I'll never forget.

BILLIE So what brings you to these parts?

CANADA Just passing through. Since I was in the neighbourhood, thought I'd stop on in.

BILLIE Nova Scotia's nearly a thousand miles away.

CANADA Well, I thought I should see my grandchild. Jenny's almost six and I've only talked to her on the phone. And Andrew and his

wife, and you. Nothing wrong with seeing family is there?

BILLIE Strong or weak?

CANADA Like a bear's bottom.

BILLIE Polar or Grizzly?

CANADA Grizzly.

(BILLIE *returns with a tray.*)

Andrew told me what happened.

BILLIE He did, did he?

CANADA Said you were taking it kinda hard.

BILLIE Oh, I'll be fine. I'm a survivor. But then again, you already know that.

CANADA Tea should be ready. Shall I be mother?

BILLIE Go ahead.

(CANADA *pours the tea.*)

BILLIE I hear you were in the hospital.

CANADA My liver ain't too good. Gave out on me. I guess you reap what you sow.

BILLIE Still drinking?

CANADA Been sober going on five years now.

BILLIE Good. Good for you.

CANADA Don't mean I don't feel like it sometimes though . . .

BILLIE Well . . . How long do you plan to be in town?

CANADA Just a few days. See Andrew and his family. See the sights. I'm staying there – at Andrew's. Went by there earlier . . . No one home. Must have given them the wrong time. Left a note though. Told them to find me at Sybil's.

BILLIE Billie. I've always despised that name. Sybil.

CANADA I gave you that name. It's a good name. It was your Grandmother's name. It means prophetess. Sorceress. Seer of the future. I like it. I don't see anything wrong with that name.

BILLIE Sounds like some old woman living in a cave.

(CANADA *reaches for his suitcase.*)

CANADA I brought something for you.

(*He takes out a small red box.*)

Go on . . . Open it. The box is a bit too big, but . . .

(BILLIE *opens the box.*)

It's your mother's ring. I figured she'd want you to have it.

BILLIE I hardly remember her anymore. I get glimpses of this ghostly figure creeping in and out of my dreams.

CANADA When Beryl first passed on, I couldn't get her off my mind, like she'd gone and left us somehow. Left me . . . With two kids, one a young girl ripening to sprout into womanhood. I was sad, but I was good and mad too. One minute I'd be trying to etch her face into my mind, cause I didn't want to forget. Next thing, I'd be downing another shot of rye . . . I couldn't carry the weight. I just couldn't do it by myself. That's when we moved to Dartmouth. What's that them old slaves used to say? 'I can't take it no more, I moving to Nova Scotia.'

BILLIE I'm thinking of heading back there myself . . .

CANADA 'Cause he left you, or 'cause she's White?

BILLIE I remember that White woman . . . That hairdresser you used to go with . . . The one with the mini skirts . . . What was her name?

CANADA That's going way back . . . You remember her?

BILLIE She was boasting about knowing how to do our kind of hair. And she took that hot comb to my head . . . Sounded like she was frying chicken . . . Burnt my ears and half the hair on my head. I hated her stubby little beige legs and those false eyelashes. She taught me how to put on false eyelashes.

CANADA Deborah.

BILLIE Debbie . . . Yes . . . Debbie.

CANADA I wish . . . I wish things between . . .

(*The buzzer rings.*)

BILLIE That must be Drew.

(BILLIE *goes to the console by the door.*)

Drew?

AMAH (*Through intercom.*) It's me. Amah. Is your –

BILLIE He's here. Come on up.

CANADA You know, an old African once told me the story of a man who was struck by an arrow. His attacker was unknown. Instead of tending to his wound, he refused to remove the arrow until the archer was found and punished. In the meantime, the wound festered, until finally the poison infected his entire body, eventually killing him . . . Now, who is responsible for this man's death, the archer for letting go the arrow, or the man for his foolish holding on?

(*There is a knock at the door.* BILLIE *gets up and heads toward it.*)

BILLIE The drunk?

CANADA A drunken man can get sober but a damn fool can't ever get wise.

(BILLIE *opens the door.* AMAH *enters with some rolls of paper in her arms.*)

AMAH (*Kissing* BILLIE*'s cheek.*) Hi sweetie. And you must be Canada.

CANADA Drew's wife . . .

AMAH So very pleased to meet you at last.

CANADA Delighted . . .

AMAH We weren't expecting you until tomorrow. We ate out tonight. We would have come pick you up. Jenny's so excited.

CANADA No, no . . . No need to fuss. I arrived safe and sound. And Sybil – Billie's been taking good care of me.

AMAH Drew would have come himself. Jenny insisted he give her a bath tonight. You know, it's a father-daughter thing.

(*Silence.*)

Anyway, we should get going. (*To* CANADA) You're probably starving. I can rustle something up for you in no time.

(CANADA *reaches for his coat.*)

(*To* BILLIE.) Look, I'm gonna have to bring that child of mine over here. She's driving me crazy asking for you –

BILLIE No. No . . . not yet.

AMAH Well, if I go mad, you and Drew will have to take care of her. I want you to know that. Oh, Jenny asked me to give these to you. She made them specially for you. She wanted to give you some inspiration. You might not be able to tell, but one's of her dancing, and the other's of her singing.

BILLIE Tell her I miss her.

AMAH I will.

BILLIE Tell her I'll see her real soon.

AMAH I will.

BILLIE (*To* AMAH.) I still have a bone to pick with you, though. (*Indicating* CANADA.)

AMAH No, no. You have a bone to pick with Drew.

CANADA I'll drop in again tomorrow, if that's OK with you.

BILLIE Tomorrow might not be so good. He's moving his stuff in the morning. We'd probably be in the way. I won't even be here until sometime in the afternoon.

CANADA Well then . . . We'll see how things go.

(*He kisses* BILLIE *on the forehead.*)

AMAH Come join us over something to eat –

BILLIE No. Thanks. I'm fine.

CANADA Good to see you, Sybil – Billie.

BILLIE Well it certainly was a surprise. Bye y'all.

>   (AMAH *and* CANADA *exit.* BILLIE *closes the door, then leans against it as she studies the pictures Jenny drew.*)

Scene 2

(*Harlem, the present: the next day – late morning. Lyrical strains give way to an undulating rhythm while Malcolm X recounts the tale of how George Washington sold a slave for a gallon of molasses. The apartment looks empty of furniture, save for the bed, several piles of books, and boxes strewn around the living area.* OTHELLO *walks into the bedroom with a large green garbage bag. After a few moments, the door is unlocked and* BILLIE *peers through the doorway. She hears someone in the bedroom. She quietly closes the door behind her and places a small brown paper bag in her pocket. She makes her way into the kitchen area. She waits.* OTHELLO *exits the bedroom, green garbage bag in tow. He walks to the centre of the living room where he stands for a few moments taking it all in.*)

BILLIE Got everything?

OTHELLO (*Startled.*) Ahh! (*Dropping the garbage bag, he turns around.*) Christ . . .

BILLIE Got everything?

OTHELLO God, I didn't hear you come in.

BILLIE My meeting ended earlier than I expected. I was able to get what I needed . . . I didn't see a van. I figured you'd be done by now.

OTHELLO They just left. I was doing a final check. See if I'd forgotten anything.

BILLIE So the move went well.

OTHELLO Yes . . . yeh. It's amazing how much stuff there is.

BILLIE Yeh. It's hard to throw things away.

OTHELLO I know what you mean. We've got a huge place though.

BILLIE Good. Good for you.

>   (*Pause.*)

OTHELLO This place looks pretty huge right now, though. Remember when we first came to look at this place?

BILLIE Yes.

>   (*Pause.*)

OTHELLO Well . . . I guess that's it.

BILLIE I guess . . .

>   (*Pause.*)

OTHELLO Anyway . . . So when do you plan on leaving?

BILLIE Oh, I don't . . . I don't know.

OTHELLO Ah.

BILLIE I haven't decided.

OTHELLO I see . . . Well . . .

BILLIE So when's the big day?

OTHELLO Oh . . . well . . . Er . . . Three weeks.

BILLIE So soon?

OTHELLO Just a small affair.

BILLIE Good. Good for you. Good for you both.

OTHELLO Yeh . . .

BILLIE I . . . I've been meaning . . . Well . . . I've been thinking.

OTHELLO Hmn Hmm . . .

BILLIE I er . . . I . . . um . . . I want to return something you gave me . . . centuries ago.

OTHELLO Oh?

BILLIE The handkerchief?

OTHELLO Oh! Really? Wow . . . No. No. It's not necessary. Really –

BILLIE No, no, let me finish. I've . . . . . . been foolish. I understand that now. You can understand why. And . . . . . . I'm sorry. That's what I wanted to tell you. And the handkerchief . . . it's yours. Held by me for safekeeping really. To be passed on to our children – if we had any. Since we don't, it should be returned to you, to your line . . .

OTHELLO Why are you doing this?

BILLIE I just thought you might . . . I thought you would . . . After all . . . it's the only thing your mother left you . . .

OTHELLO I don't know what to say.

BILLIE I thought you'd be glad.

OTHELLO Oh, I'm more than glad.

BILLIE But I have to find it first.

OTHELLO Are you sure about –

BILLIE I'm sure. Give me a couple of days, to find it . . . clean it up a bit.

OTHELLO I could come by.

BILLIE Yes. You should have it before . . . You know . . . before your . . . big day.

OTHELLO Thank you.

BILLIE Just trying to play my part well.

OTHELLO Thanks.

BILLIE Forgive me . . .

OTHELLO I know it's been hard.

BILLIE Yeh.

OTHELLO OK. Well . . .

>   (*He reaches to touch her face. She retreats.*)

BILLIE I'll see you in a couple of days then.

OTHELLO Alright.

BILLIE Alright.

OTHELLO Alright. And say Hello to Jenny for me. (*Silence.*) Alright.

(OTHELLO *exits.* BILLIE *takes the small package out of her pocket. She unwraps it, revealing a small vial of fluid. She goes into the kitchen, vial in hand, turns toward the fridge, opens the freezer door and stares into it.*)

BILLIE   Look this way and see . . . your death . . . Othe . . . Othe . . .

(*She places the vial into the freezer.*)

Scene 3

(*Harlem, 1862: late summer – night. Indigo blues groan as if through a delta, while echoes of a presidential voice reads from the Emancipation Proclamation. The sound fades.* HER *holds* HIM *in her arms like Mary holds Jesus in Michelangelo's 'The Pietà'. There is a rope around his neck. He does not move.*)

HER   (*Caressing him.*) Once upon a time, there was a man who wanted to find a magic spell in order to become White. After much research and investigation, he came across an ancient ritual from the caverns of knowledge of a psychic. 'The only way to become White,' the psychic said, 'was to enter the Whiteness.' And when he found his ice queen, his alabaster goddess, he fucked her. Her on his dick. He one with her, for a single shivering moment became . . . her. Her and her Whiteness.

Scene 4

(*Harlem, present: late summer – night. A cacophony of strings grooves and collides as sound bites from the Anita Hill and Clarence Thomas hearings, the L.A. riots, the O.J. Simpson trial, Malcolm X, and Martin Luther King, loop and repeat the same distorted bits of sound over and over again.* BILLIE *is alone in the apartment. She goes into the freezer and removes the vial. Wearing rubber gloves, she places several drops of a liquid substance onto the handkerchief. She replaces the cap of the vial.* BILLIE *carefully folds the handkerchief, hesitates for a moment, looks around and spots the red box on the mantle. She puts the handkerchief back down on the tray and, with her hands in the air, like a surgeon scrubbing for surgery, she gets up and goes to the red box. With one hand she takes off one of the gloves. With the ungloved hand, she opens the red box and slips her mother's ring on her finger. She then takes the red box with her to the table. She very carefully replaces the one glove, picks up the handkerchief, and neatly places it in the*

small red box. She works slowly, and is mindful not to touch the sides of the box with the handkerchief itself.

She removes a single rubber glove once more, picks up the cover to the box, and places it on top of the other half. She is still for a few moments, staring at the box.

BILLIE *gets up and crosses the room, as if looking for something, only to stop in her tracks and return to the box. She paces. Her pacing appears more methodical than hysterical. Suddenly she stops. She turns to look at the small red box.*

She shakes her head and takes a seat on a large, full, cardboard box at her feet. Her breathing becomes more apparent as she begins to rock, almost imperceptibly at first. Finally she places her head in her hands.

After several moments, BILLIE*'s face slowly emerges from her hands.*

She glares at the gloved hand incredulously, as she realizes that she has inadvertently transferred some of the potion onto her own skin. She quickly removes the second glove, and proceeds to wipe her face with her own clothes.)

BILLIE   (*To herself.*) Oh god! Oh my god! Shit! Shit! Shit! Shit!

(BILLIE *gets up and rushes to the kitchen sink, turns on the tap and frantically washes her hands and face in the water.*)

Scene 5

(*The following day: early evening. In counterpoint to the cello and bass, the distorted sound loop becomes a grating repetition.* MAGI *and* CANADA *are on either side of a large box, sitting on two smaller ones. The larger box is covered by a scarf to resemble a table cloth, on top of which is a small feast. They are eating.* MAGI *gets up and goes to the door of the bedroom. She peeks in. After a few moments she closes the door and returns to her seat.*)

MAGI   She's in distant realms. I checked in on her when I got back from church. I thought she was speaking in tongues. I couldn't understand a thing she was saying. I don't think she slept a wink all night. Those pills work like a charm, though. (*Beat.*) How is it?

CANADA   Mmn! Those greens . . . She looks like an angel and cooks like one too.

MAGI   Can I get you some more?

CANADA   No, no, I don't want to appear too greedy now.

MAGI Here . . . (*Serving him another helping.*) There you go. And I won't tell a soul. Promise.

CANADA I haven't tasted cooking like this in a long time.

MAGI My Mama would say, some food is good for the mind, some is good for the body, and some food is good for the soul.

CANADA Your Mama taught you how to cook like this?

MAGI Once she even taught me how to cook a soufflé. She used to have a restaurant downstairs from as far back as I can recall. And I guess the boys returning home from the war in Europe kept asking for the Parisian food, and it ended up on her menu. She'd say, now this Parisian food ain't good for nothing. Soufflé ain't nothing more than baked eggs. And eggs is for breakfast. Eggs don't do no one no good past noon.

CANADA So you've lived here all your life?

MAGI And my mother before me, and her mother before her. My great grandmother, worked for the family that lived here, most of her life. She never married, but she had two children by the man she worked for – seems his wife never knew they were his. One brown baby looks just like another to most White folks. And when the wife died, my great grandmother just stayed on. Everybody thinking she's just the maid, but she was living like the queen of the manor – him being her babies' father and everything. And his other children were all grown by then. So when he died, he left everything to his White children, 'cept this house. He left it in my great grandmother's name, and it's been in my family ever since.

CANADA So the White man's children ever find out? About their brown skinned relatives.

MAGI I don't know. The Van Dykes – they were Dutch. We used to watch the Dick Van Dyke show, and my Grandmother used to always say, 'That there's your relative!' But we didn't pay her too much mind. More greens?

CANADA If I eat another thing, I will truly burst. This was wonderful. Thank you. Thank you very much.

MAGI You're more than welcome.

CANADA When I was a boy, I used to love to sop the pot liquor.

MAGI It's nearly the best part.

CANADA You sure know the way to a man's heart.

MAGI Haven't had any luck so far.

CANADA Yet.

(*There is an awkward silence between them, after which they both start speaking at once.*)

MAGI (*Overlapping.*) Well I better get started with these dishes . . .

CANADA (*Overlapping.*) I should go in and check on Sybil . . . Let me give you a hand.

MAGI No, no, it's quite alright. I can handle this.

(BILLIE *enters.*)

CANADA Billie! Marjorie was kind enough to share her dinner with me.

MAGI Billie, come and have something to eat.

BILLIE I'm not hungry. I heard voices. I need to go back and lay down . . . get some reading done.

MAGI You can't have eaten anything for the day, girl.

BILLIE I'm fine.

CANADA What you need is a good meal inside you.

BILLIE I said I was fine.

MAGI I'll just take these things downstairs.

(MAGI *exits.*)

CANADA I'll make you some tea, OK.

BILLIE I don't – don't need any tea. I don't want anything to eat. I'm fine. I'm sorry. I don't – don't – don't mean . . . to be like this . . . But I haven't seen you in God knows how long . . . And you just show up, and expect things to be all hunky dory.

CANADA Well, I'll be off then.

(*He goes for his coat.*)

BILLIE I'm sorry.

CANADA Me too.

(*He heads for the door.*)

BILLIE And I am glad you came . . . Maybe this can be . . . You know . . . like a beginning of something . . . I don't know.

CANADA I nearly came before . . . Two or three times . . . You know, when I heard. I wished your mother was here. I really wished for her . . . Her wisdom. I mean Beryl would know what to do. A girl needs her mother. And I know you didn't have her all those times . . . I mean, I couldn't tell you. What could I tell you? I kept seeing your face. It's your mother's face. You've got my nose. My mouth. But those eyes . . . The shape of your face . . . The way your head tilts to one side when you're thinking, or just listening. It's all her. You've got her moods. I used to call them her moods. Once 'bout every three months, on a Friday, when she'd have the weekend off, she'd come home from that hospital, take off her clothes and lay down in her bed and stay there 'till Sunday afternoon. She'd say she'd done turned the other cheek so many times in the past little while, she didn't have no more smiles for anybody. She'd say, better she just face God and the pillow than shower me and the children with the evil she had bottled up inside her. See, if you spend too much time among White people, you start believing what they think of you. So I'd take you and Drew and we'd go visiting. We'd take the whole weekend and visit all the folks we knew, in a fifteen mile radius . . . When we'd get home, she'd have cleaned the house, washed the clothes and even made a Sunday dinner. And after I'd pluck the guitar . . . And she'd start to sing . . . And you'd dance . . . You remember? You'd dance. You'd stomp on that floor like you were beating out some secret code to God or something . . . I know you – we don't see eye to eye. I know you haven't wanted to see very much anything of me lately. But I've known you all your life. I carried you in my arms and on my back, kissed and spanked you when you needed, and I watched you start to talk, and learn to walk, and read and I just wanted to come . . . I just wanted to come. And I know I can't make everything alright. I know. But I was there when you arrived in this world. And I didn't think there was space for a child, I loved your mother so much. But there you were and I wondered where you'd been all my life, like something I'd been missing and didn't know I'd been missing. And I don't know if you've loved anybody that long. But behind your mother's face you're wearing, I still see the girl who shrieked with laughter, and danced to the heavens sometimes . . .

(CANADA *slowly approaches* BILLIE. *She does not move. He takes her in his arms. He holds her in his arms for a long time.*)

Scene 6

(*Harlem, 1928: late summer – night. The strident movement of the strings is joined by the rising tempo of the distorted sound loop.* HE *and* SHE *are both in a tiny dressing room, as in the prologue. On a counter is a shaving brush, a straight-edged razor, greasepaint and a top hat.* HE *wipes his face with a towel.* SHE *holds the handkerchief out to him.* HE *does not take it.* SHE *lets it fall at his feet. After a few moments,* HE *picks it up.*)

HE (*Referring to the handkerchief at first.*) White, red, black, green, indigo . . . What difference does it make? That makes no sense . . . makes no difference. 'If virtue no delighted beauty lack, Your son-in-law is far more fair than black.' Far more fair than black. I want . . . I need to do this . . . For my soul. I am an actor. I –

SHE (*Kindly.*) A minstrel. A Black minstrel . . .

(HE *places the towel on the counter beside the toiletries.*)

HE It's paid my way.

(SHE *caresses the towel.*)

SHE Stay, my sable warrior . . .

(*Her hand stumbles upon the razor.*)

HE I'll not die in black-face to pay the rent. I am of Ira Aldridge* stock. I am a classical man. I long to play the Scottish king. The prince of Denmark. 'The slings and arrows of outrageous . . .' Or . . . Or . . . 'There's a divinity that shapes our ends, Rough-hew them how we will' . . . Those words . . . I love those words. They give me life. Mona sees my gift. She's cast me as the prince of Tyre. She's breathed new life into a barren dream. She . . . She . . . She has a serene calmness about her. That smile . . . I bet they named her Mona because even at birth, she had that constant half smile, like the Mona Lisa. Skin as smooth as monumental alabaster . . . As warm as snow velvet.

(SHE *exposes the blade.*)

SHE My onyx prince . . .
HE Ooohh . . .

(SHE *approaches him from behind.*)

SHE My tourmaline king . . .

(SHE *leans her head on his back.*)

HE S'alright . . .
SHE My raven knight . . .

(SHE *wraps her arms around him.* HE *turns his head toward her.*)

HE Oh sweet . . .
SHE My umber squire . . .
HE I wish . . . I wish –

---

* Major nineteenth-century black actor.

(Her hand rises, the razor is poised, nearly touching the skin of his neck, just below his ear, within his peripheral vision.)

SHE My Cimmerian lord . . .

(HE turns around, as if to see what SHE's holding, and in that turn, his neck appears to devour the blade. The razor's shaft at once hidden by his flesh, swiftly withdraws, leaving a rushing river of red like a scarf billowing around his neck and her hands. HE yields to gravity.)

Scene 7

(Harlem, the present: late summer night. The plucked strings and the distorted audio loop have become even more dissonant. BILLIE is clutching the small red box.)

MAGI . . . You know, Hakim has seven children, and he's never been married. Brother Hakim. Spot him at any street rally where the subject is prefaced by the words 'Third World'. He's the one with the 'Lumumba Lives' button prominently displayed on his authentic kente cloth dashi – Billie? Billie, what's up? You don't look so good.
Billie?

BILLIE Sybil. I'm Sybil.

MAGI That's what your Daddy calls you.

BILLIE Yes.

MAGI Your Daddy sure is one good-looking gentleman.

BILLIE Trapped in history. A history trapped in me.

MAGI I'm serious. I mean . . . I wanna know if you mind? Really. You were still a little girl when your mama died.

BILLIE I don't remember Beryl's funeral. I see my father dressed in black, sewing a white button, on to his white shirt, with an enormous needle. He attaches the button and knots the thread so many times it's like he's trying to hold onto more than just the button. Like he can't bear for anything else in his life to leave him.

MAGI He's a nice man. Would you mind?

BILLIE Am I nice?

MAGI Billie, I bet you haven't eaten today.

BILLIE Can you keep a secret?

MAGI No, but that's never stopped you before.

BILLIE Then sorry . . .

MAGI OK, OK. I promise.

BILLIE I am about to plunge into very dangerous waters. Give me your word.

MAGI You're not going to do something stupid, now.

BILLIE Your word?

MAGI Yeh, OK.

BILLIE I've drawn a line.

MAGI A line? A line about what?

BILLIE I'm returning the handkerchief – the one his mother give him. The one he gave to me when we first agreed to be together . . .

MAGI I don't understand.

BILLIE I've concocted something . . . A potion . . . A plague of sorts . . . I've soaked the handkerchief . . . Soaked it in certain tinctures . . . Anyone who touches it – the handkerchief, will come to harm.

MAGI Now that is not a line, Billie, that is a trench!

BILLIE I'm supposed to . . .

MAGI Billie, if this kind of stuff truly worked, Africans wouldn't be in the situation we're in now. Imagine all them slaves working magic on their masters – didn't make no difference. If it truly worked, I'd be married to a nice man, with three little ones by now. But if it makes you feel better –

BILLIE He's going to marry her . . . Officially . . .

MAGI I know . . . I know. Remember, what goes around comes around. Karma is a strong and unforgiving force.

BILLIE I haven't seen it affect White people too much.

MAGI Is everything about White people with you? Is every living moment of your life is eaten up with thinking about them. Do you know where you are? Do you know who you are anymore? What about right and wrong. Racism is a disease my friend, and your test just came back positive. You're so busy reacting, you don't even know yourself.

BILLIE No, no, no . . . It's about Black. I love Black. I really do. And it's revolutionary . . . Black is beautiful . . . So beautiful. This Harlem sanctuary . . . here. This respite . . . Like an ocean in the middle of a desert. And in my mirror, my womb, he has a fast growing infestation of roaches. White roaches.

MAGI Billie?

BILLIE Did you ever consider what hundreds of years of slavery did to the African American psyche?

MAGI What? What are you . . . ?

BILLIE Every time someone mentions traditional values or the good old days – who exactly were those days good for?

(*The phone rings.* BILLIE *goes over to it. She sits on the bare floor but does not answer.*)

Jenny . . . Is that you Jenny. My beauty. My little girl. It's Sybil. . . . Auntie Sybil . . . The woman who lives in the cave.

(BILLIE *laughs.*)

MAGI I'll get it for you.

(BILLIE *picks up the receiver.*)

BILLIE Yes, yes, I'm here. Oh, Othe . . . Othello. I didn't recognize your voice. You sound . . . . . . different. No. No, no, you can't pick it up. I mean – I've got it, yes. It's right here. No. No, I won't be in . . . No, no. I haven't changed my mind. But – I mean . . . I have to go . . . Roaches. Yeh, blue roaches. Green roaches. So I have to go now. I – I just have to go.

(BILLIE *replaces the receiver.*)

MAGI He's coming over?

BILLIE I don't want a Mona Lisa smile . . .

MAGI Oh Billie . . . Billie, you're all in bits and pieces.

BILLIE I know. I know. A tumour. Suddenly apparent, but its been there, tiny, growing slowly for a long time. What kind of therapy to take? Chop it out? Radiate it? Let it eat me alive? I see roaches all around me. In me. Blue roaches. Green roaches. Aah! Get off! Get it off. I eat roaches. I pee roaches. Help! I'm losing . . . I don't don't . . . I'm falling . . .

MAGI Billie? Billie?

BILLIE I have a dream today.

MAGI You had a dream?

BILLIE I have a dream that one day every valley shall be engulfed, every hill shall be exalted and every mountain shall be made low . . . oh . . . oh . . . the rough places will be made plains and the crooked places will be made . . .

MAGI (*Overlapping.*) It's gonna be alright, Billie.

(MAGI *goes to the phone and dials.*)

BILLIE (*Overlapping.*) . . . straight and the glory of the Lord shall be revealed and all flesh shall see it together.

MAGI (*Overlapping.*) It's Magi. You all better get over here, now. No, no, no. NOW. Alright. Alright.

(MAGI *puts down the receiver and returns to* BILLIE. *She gently takes the red box from out of* BILLIE's *hands, and places it on the mantel.*)

BILLIE (*Overlapping.*) . . . This is our hope . . .

MAGI (*Overlapping.*) It's gonna be alright. I know . . . I know . . .

BILLIE (*Overlapping.*) . . . With this faith we will be able to hew out of the mountain of despair a stone of hope . . .

MAGI (*Overlapping.*) It's OK. It's OK. Let's start with a little step. Come on. Come with me. (MAGI *helps* BILLIE *up.*) Come on . . . Good. Let's get some soup into you. Warm up that frozen blood of yours. (MAGI *leads her to the door.*) Warm up your insides. Come . . . Come on . . . Chase all the roaches out . . .

(BILLIE *breaks loose of* MAGI *and rushes to the window.*

MAGI *is no longer in the room.* OTHELLO *appears wearing a brightly coloured dashiki. He is inspecting a broom, laying against the fridge. It is now Fall, seven years earlier. Save for the broom, and the fridge, the apartment is empty.*)

BILLIE Look . . . Come, look . . . You can see the Apollo from the window. I love it.

OTHELLO Where?

BILLIE Over there. See.

OTHELLO Oh yeh – If I crane my neck.

BILLIE I could find some lawn chairs and table and we'd have a city terrace.

OTHELLO On the fire escape?

BILLIE We'd have our own little balcony.

OTHELLO Patio.

BILLIE Terrace . . .

OTHELLO We could buy a house up here.

BILLIE We can't afford to buy a house until I finish school. If I'm going to go to school full-time, this fall, like we agreed – you'd go to school, then I'd go to school – how can we afford a down payment on a house?

OTHELLO I know. I know.

(*Pause.*)

BILLIE I love it. Don't you love it?

OTHELLO I love you.

BILLIE I love you and I love it.

OTHELLO Think Chris Yago and Mona and the other faculty will feel uncomfortable coming up here . . . for meetings and the like . . .

BILLIE It's on the subway line.

OTHELLO And boy do they need to take the journey. I'll take them on a cultural field trip – blow their minds.

BILLIE I've longed for this sanctuary.

OTHELLO I know what you mean.

BILLIE Black boutiques.

OTHELLO Black bookstores.

BILLIE Black groceries.

OTHELLO Filled with Black doctors and dentists. Black banks.

BILLIE Black streets teeming with loud Black people listening to loud Jazz and reggae and Aretha . . . (*Singing.*) 'There is a rose in Spanish Harlem. (*He joins her.*) A rose in Black and Spanish Harlem. (*Forgetting the lyrics.*) Da da da, da da da . . ' Maybe later we could buy a place on 'strivers row', that's where all the rich Black folks live.

OTHELLO Strivers row.

BILLIE Owned by Blacks hued from the faintest gold to the bluest bronze. That's my dream.

OTHELLO By then you'd have your Ph.D.

BILLIE And a small lecturer's position at a prestigious Manhattan university. We might even have enough money to get a small house in the country too.

OTHELLO A big house in the country too?

BILLIE A big house with a white picket fence.

OTHELLO On a rolling emerald hill.

BILLIE I want 2.5 kids.

(*He kisses her lightly.*)

OTHELLO You're mad, you know that.

BILLIE That makes you some kinda fool for loving me, baby.

OTHELLO Let's do it. There's an old broom right over there. Wanna jump it with me?

(OTHELLO *retrieves the broom.*)

BILLIE Are you asking me to m –

OTHELLO Yes . . . Yes, I am asking.

BILLIE Yes . . . Then yes.

(OTHELLO *kisses her. He places the broom in the middle of the floor. He takes* BILLIE's *hand. They stand in front of it.*)

What will we use for rings?

OTHELLO Think them old slaves had rings? Slave marriages were illegal, remember. This broom is more than rings. More than any gold. (*He whispers.*) My ancient love.

BILLIE (*She whispers.*) My soul.

(OTHELLO *kisses her hand. The couple gaze at each other, preparing to jump over the broom. They jump. They hold each other. The landlady enters.*)

MAGI Oh – I'm sorry.

BILLIE No, no. We were just . . . just –

(OTHELLO *picks up the broom and places it to one side.*)

OTHELLO I think we'll take it.

MAGI I didn't mean to rush you. I can give you another few minutes if you need to make good and sure?

BILLIE I think we're sure. (*To* OTHELLO.) You sure? (*To* MAGI.) We're sure.

(MAGI *looks gravely at* BILLIE. *They are the only ones in the room. We are back in the present.* MAGI *carefully approaches* BILLIE. BILLIE *stares at where* OTHELLO *stood, only moments ago.*)

MAGI Come on. Come with me. Come on . . . Good. Let's get some soup into you. Warm up that frozen blood of yours. (MAGI *leads her to the door.*) Warm up your insides. Come . . . come on . . . Chase all the roaches out . . . One by one . . . One by one . . .

(*They exit.*)

Scene 8

(*Harlem, present: late summer, afternoon. A lyrical rhapsody swings to the sound of a commentator describing the scene at the Million Man March. The apartment is virtually empty.* CANADA *is cleaning the kitchen, taking tubs and bags from out of the freezer. He gives them a brief once-over and then throws them into the trash.* OTHELLO *enters.*)

OTHELLO Billie? Billie?

CANADA Othello! Othello, good to see you son.

(*They shake hands.*)

Good to see you.

OTHELLO I didn't know . . . When did you get here?

CANADA A few days.

OTHELLO Billie didn't say a word.

CANADA Well, Billie's in . . . she's . . . Billie's not here right now.

OTHELLO (*Scanning the apartment.*) Did she leave anything for me. An envelope . . . A package –

(*He sees the red box on the mantel.*)

Oh. Maybe . . .

(*He goes over to it.*)

CANADA Oh, she said no one was to touch that . . . I'm supposed to throw it out.

OTHELLO Great! (*He opens the red box and takes out the handkerchief.*) It's OK, this is it. It's mine. This is what I was looking for.

CANADA I was just about to throw it in with the trash from the fridge.

OTHELLO Just in time, huh?

CANADA Yeh, some of this stuff's about ready to crawl out by itself.

OTHELLO I can imagine.

CANADA I swear, one thing had actually grown little feet.

OTHELLO Well, Billie wasn't one for cleaning . . . I guess neither of us was.

(*There is an awkward silence between them.*)

Well . . . I should be off.

(*He takes some keys from out of his pocket and places them where the red box was laying.*)

CANADA She tells me you're getting married.

OTHELLO I do confess the vices of my blood.

CANADA I'm real sorry it didn't work out . . . Between you and Billie . . . I mean . . . I was hoping . . .

OTHELLO Yes. I know.

CANADA She's my child, so –

OTHELLO I know, I know.

CANADA You young'uns don't know the sweetness of molasses . . . Rather have granulated sugar, 'stead of a deep clover honey, or cane sugar juice from way into the Demerara. Better watch out for that refined shit. It'll kill ya. A slow kinda killin'. 'Cause it kills your mind first. So you think you living the life, when you been dead a long time.

(*Silence.*)

OTHELLO Well sir . . . I should be somewhere.

CANADA (*Nodding.*) Well, I hope we can catch up sometime . . .

(OTHELLO *goes to the door.*)

OTHELLO That would be great. Tell Billie I came by.

CANADA I'll tell her that. She'll be glad to know.

OTHELLO Good seeing you.

CANADA You too . . . son . . . You too.

(OTHELLO *takes one last look at the apartment, takes out a tiny cellular phone, and exits.* CANADA *is still for a few moments. From the hallway we hear* OTHELLO.)

OTHELLO (*Offstage.*) Chris Yago, please.

(CANADA *returns to the fridge, and continues to clean.*)

Scene 9

(*Harlem, 1928: late summer – night. The music softly underscores the voice of Paul Robeson speaking about not being able to get decent acting roles in the U.S., and how fortunate he feels to be offered a contract to play* OTHELLO *in England.* HE *is alone.* HE *proceeds to cover his face in black grease paint.* HE *begins to speak, as if rehearsing, at first.*)

HE It is most true; true, I have married her.
It is most . . .
It is most true; true, I have married her.
For know, but that I love the gentle Desdemona,
(She) questioned me the story of my life
From year to year – the battles, sieges, fortunes,
That I have passed. These things to hear
Would Desdemona seriously incline;
But still the house affairs would draw her thence,
Which ever as she could with haste dispatch
She'd come again, and with a greedy ear
Devour up my discourse. Which I, observing,
Took once a pliant hour . . .
And often did beguile her of her tears,
When I did speak of some distressful stroke
That my youth suffered . . .

(*In the background we can hear a children's song.* HE *begins to add a white greasepaint to his lips, completing the mask of the minstrel.*)

. . . My story being done,
She gave me for my pains a world of sighs.
She wished she had not heard it, yet she wished
That heaven had made her such a man. She thanked me,
She thanked me . . .
She thanked me . . .
She thanked me . . .

Scene 10

(*Harlem, the present: late summer – night. A beryline blues improvisation of 'Mama's Little Baby' cascades alongside a reading of the Langston Hughes poem 'Harlem'.* AMAH *sits beside* BILLIE *in the visitors lounge of the psychiatric ward.* AMAH *is clearly saddened by* BILLIE'S *state.*)

BILLIE (*Singing.*) Sally, Sally, Sally,
Step back Sal-ly, all night long.
Strut-in' down the al-ley, al-ley, al-ley,
Strut-in' down the al-ley, all night long.

AMAH & BILLIE I looked over there, and what did I see?
A big fat lady from Ten-nes-see.

(BILLIE *gets up and begins to dance.*)

I bet you five dollars I can beat that man,

To the front, to the back, to the side, side, side.
To the front, to the back, to the side, side, side.

(*The two women laugh.*)

BILLIE I haven't done that in . . . in years.

AMAH I never knew that one – I just saw Jenny
do it the other day.

BILLIE I even remember the dance. (*Singing under
her breath.*) . . . Bet you five dollars I can beat
that man . . .

AMAH It's not so bad here.

BILLIE You'd think the doctors at Harlem hospital
would be Black. Especially in psychiatrics. Most
of the nurses are Black.

AMAH But they're nice to you – the doctors?

BILLIE They help. I don't – don't want anymore
pills. And that's OK. They don't really
understand, though. I had this dream. Lucinda –
she's my main doctor. Lucinda was sitting at
the edge of a couch and I asked her a
question. But she couldn't answer because her
eyes kept flashing. Like neon lights. Flash,
flash, flash. That was it. That was the dream. I
knew it was important, but I didn't get it. And I
told her. And she didn't get it either. But it
gnawed away at me . . . For days . . . The
flashing eyes. And that was it! The eyes were
flashing blue. Her eyes were flashing blue. She
could only see my questions through her blue
eyes.

AMAH Something in you really wants to heal.

BILLIE Exorcism.

AMAH Pardon?

BILLIE Repossess.

AMAH Self-possession?

BILLIE I hate. I know I hate. And he loves. How
he loves.

AMAH Billie?

BILLIE Why is that, you think?

AMAH Some of us spend our entire lives making
our own shackles.

BILLIE Canada freedom come.

AMAH And the experienced shackle-wearer
knows the best polish for the gilt.

BILLIE I wanna be free.

AMAH It must be hard, though. I feel for him.

BILLIE I'm not that evolved.

AMAH Forgiveness.

BILLIE Forgiveness . . .

AMAH If I don't forgive my enemy, if I don't

forgive him, he might just set up house, inside
me.

BILLIE I just . . . I – I despise – I know . . . I know
. . . Moment by moment. I forgive him now. I
hate – I love him so – I forgive him now. And
now.

(*She moves as if to speak, but stops herself.*)

And I forgive him now.

AMAH My time's up, sweetie.

BILLIE I have a dream . . .

AMAH Sorry?

BILLIE I had a dream . . .

AMAH Yes . . . I know.

BILLIE Tell Jenny . . . Tell her for me . . . Tell her
that you saw me dancing.

AMAH I will tell her.

BILLIE And tell her . . . Tell her that you heard me
singing.

AMAH I will.

BILLIE And tell her . . . I'll see her real soon.

AMAH I will tell her, Billie. I will tell her.

(AMAH *kisses* BILLIE *on the cheek and begins to
exit.* CANADA *enters.*)

BILLIE (*In the background softly.*)
Betcha five dollars I can beat that man.
To the front, to the back, to the side, side, side.
To the front, to the back, to the side, side, side.

CANADA How's she doing?

AMAH Mmm, so-so.

CANADA Okay. Thanks.

AMAH We'll really miss you when you go – back
to Nova Scotia.

CANADA Oh. I don't think I'm going anywhere
just yet – least if I can help it. Way too much
leaving gone on for more than one lifetime
already.

(BILLIE *stops singing for a moment, then segues
into a version of Aretha Franklin's 'Spanish
Harlem', more hummed than sung.*

CANADA *pats* AMAH *on the back.* AMAH *turns
and exits.* CANADA *approaches* BILLIE *and sits
down beside her.*

*Shortly, he joins her in the song. He rests his
hand on hers.*

After several moments: The lights fade to black.)

Further Adaptations

The suggestions we are making for further reading in *Adaptations of Shakespeare* are meant to be more than preliminary but less than exhaustive. Those beginning a study in this area will find a group of key texts in this anthology; those who wish to go further can follow up on the readings we are suggesting; those who wish to study the field in more depth will need to do work beyond this volume's pointers. References for all the adaptations mentioned in this section can be found in the bibliography.

Those interested in Shakespeare's own period would do well to consult the many adaptations by Shakespeare himself, from Holinshed's *Chronicles* (see Allardyce, Calina, and Holinshed), Greek and Roman History, Roman comedy, English tragedy, and English and Italian novellas. For adaptations in the Restoration and in the eighteenth century one might look at the adaptations collected in Clark's anthology and those of David Garrick, including *Catherine and Petruchio*, which ends with a slightly more companionate marriage than in Shakespeare's *Taming of the Shrew*. In the early nineteenth century one might turn to Goethe's rewriting of *Romeo and Juliet* (see Carlson: 255–258 and Williams: 100–104). From later in the century, a student pursuing further study might seek out Maurice Dowling's *Othello Travestie* of 1834, in which Desdemona survives – in this light one might also look at Stanley Wells's anthology of nineteenth-century burlesques of Shakespeare. Also of importance are the American Charlotte Barnes's *The Forest Princess*, an adaptation of *The Tempest* discussed in the General Introduction, and Ernest Renan's *Caliban*, a French adaptation of the same play. Anyone interested in modernism should also study Alfred Jarry's *Ubu Roi*, an irreverent adaptation of *Macbeth* for marionettes. Also of note in this period are George Bernard Shaw's various theatrical responses to Shakespeare: *Caesar and Cleopatra*, *The Dark Lady of the Sonnets*, and *Shakes versus Shav*, Percy MacKaye's *Caliban by the Yellow Sands*, and Brecht's *Roundheads and Peakheads*, an adaptation

of *Measure for Measure*. Exploring contemporary aesthetic freedoms further would certainly entail looking at the following works: Marowitz's many other adaptations of Shakespeare, each strikingly different in its techniques; Edward Bond's stark *Lear* and *The Sea*, an adaptation of *The Tempest*; Tom Stoppard's reduction of *Hamlet* to *The Fifteen-Minute Hamlet*, as well as his existentialist, self-reflexive comedy, *Rosencrantz and Guildenstern Are Dead*; Nicolas Abraham's *The Phantom of Hamlet*, a sixth act to Shakespeare's play inspired by psychoanalysis; Aimé Césaire's groundbreaking *A Tempest*, which brings Afro-Caribbean politics and theatrical traditions to the adaptation of Shakespeare; similarly, Derek Walcott's *A Branch of the Blue Nile*, which explores what it means to produce *Antony and Cleopatra* in a Caribbean context; Herbert Blau's postmodern and highly theoretical theatrical essays, *Elsinore* (on *Hamlet*) and *Crooked Eclipses* (on the *Sonnets*); the Italian Carmelo Bene's *Richard III*, written in conjunction with the theorizing of Gilles Deleuze (see *Superpositions*); Günter Grass's *The Plebeians Rehearse the Uprising*, an adaptation of *Coriolanus*; similarly, John Osbourne's *A Place Calling Itself Rome*, also an adaptation of *Coriolanus*; Howard Barker's *7 Lears*; Murray Carlin's South African adaptation of *Othello*, *Not Now, Sweet Desdemona*; the Australian David Malouf's *Blood Relations*, an adaptation of *The Tempest*; Ann-Marie MacDonald's *Goodnight Desdemona (Good Morning Juliet)*, which adapts Shakespearean tragedy to comic, feminist ends; the Québecois René-Daniel Dubois's *Pericles, Prince of Tyre, by William Shakespeare* and Normand Chaurette's *The Queens*, an adaptation of *Richard III*; Robert Lepage's one-man *Hamlet, Elsinore*; the plays inspired by the *Sonnets* in *Love's Fire*. Even this very partial list gives a sense of the explosion of recent adaptations of Shakespeare.

What follows is a list of adaptations arranged in terms of the Shakespeare plays they adapt. We hope this will be a useful starting point for students wishing to explore further the idea of one play adapted in different ways in different contexts at different times. The list is far from comprehensive, as it concentrates upon the few plays adapted by the works in this anthology and limits suggestions to a small number of readily available texts. However, an extensive listing of adaptations of all Shakespeare's plays is available on the Routledge website [http://www.routledge.com/routledge/shakespeare/adaptations.html].

Adaptations of Hamlet

1772 David Garrick's *Hamlet, Prince of Denmark*.
1967 Tom Stoppard's *Rosencrantz and Guildenstern are Dead*, an existentialist, self-reflexive comedy.
1976 *The Fifteen-Minute Hamlet*, also by Tom Stoppard.
1979 Tom Stoppard again, with *Dogg's Hamlet*.
1981 *Elsinore: An Analytical Scenario* by American theorist and dramaturge Herbert Blau.
1988 Nicholas Abraham's *The Phantom of Hamlet*, a sixth act to Shakespeare's play.
1992 *Lion in the Streets*, by Judith Thompson.
1995 Ken Gass's *Claudius*.

Adaptations of King Lear

1972 Edward Bond's socialist drama *Lear*.
1990 Howard Barker's *7 Lears*.

Adaptations of Macbeth

1674 William Davenant's *Macbeth*.
1896 Alfred Jarry's *Ubu Roi*, an adaptation for marionettes.
1922 *Gruach*, by Gordon Bottomley.
1972 Eugene Ionesco's *Macbett*.
1978 Charles Marowitz's *A Macbeth*.
1979 *Cahoot's Macbeth*, an adaptation by Tom Stoppard.

Adaptations of Measure for Measure

1673 *The Law Against Lovers*, by William Davenant.
1936 Bertolt Brecht's *Roundheads and Peakheads*.

Adaptations of Othello

1834 Maurice Dowling's *Othello Travestie*, where Desdemona survives.
1969 *Not Now, Sweet Desdemona*, Murray Carlin's South African adaptation of the play.

1977 *Cruel Tears*, by Ken Mitchell.
1990 *Goodnight Desdemona (Good Morning Juliet)*, a feminist adaptation drawing upon both *Romeo and Juliet* and *Othello*, by Canadian Ann-Marie MacDonald.

Adaptations of King Richard the Third

1700 *The Tragical History of King Richard III*, Colley Cibber's Restoration adaptation (in Clark's *Shakespeare Made Fit*).
1979 Italian director Carmelo Bene's radical, avant-garde *Richard III*, coupled with the theorizing of Gilles Deleuze in *Superpositions*.
1992 *The Queens* by Normand Chaurette.

Adaptations of Romeo and Juliet

1812 Johann Wolfgang Goethe's *Romeo and Juliet* (see Carlson: 255–258 and Williams: 100–104).
1990 *Goodnight Desdemona (Good Morning Juliet)*, a feminist adaptation drawing upon both *Romeo and Juliet* and *Othello*, by Canadian Ann-Marie MacDonald.

Adaptations of The Taming of the Shrew

1698 *Sauny the Scot*, by Restoration playwright John Lacy (in Sandra Clark's anthology *Shakespeare Made Fit*).
1756 David Garrick's *Catherine and Petruchio*, which ends with a slightly more companionate marriage.
1978 Charles Marowitz's *A Shrew*.

Adaptations of The Tempest

1670 John Dryden and William Davenant's *The Tempest or the Enchanted Island* (in Clark's *Shakespeare Made Fit*).
1844 Charlotte Barnes's *The Forest Princess*, which adapts the play to an American context.
1916 Percy MacKaye's *Caliban by the Yellow Sands*, first performed to mark the three-hundredth anniversary of Shakespeare's death.
1969 Aimé Césaire's *A Tempest*, a post-colonial adaptation.
1982 *The Sea*, by Edward Bond.
1988 Australian David Malouf's *Blood Relations*.

Bibliography

Abraham, N. (1988) *The Phantom of Hamlet or the Sixth Act: Preceded by the Intermission of 'Truth'*, in *Diacritics* (Winter): 2–19.

Barker, H. (1990) *7 Lears*, London: John Calder.

Barnes, C. (1848) *The Forest Princess*, in *Plays, Prose and Poetry*, Philadelphia: E. H. Butler: 145–270.

Bene, C., and Deleuze, G. (1979) *Superpositions*, Paris: Les Éditions de Minuit.

Blau, H. (1981) *Elsinore: An Analytic Scenario*, *Cream City Review* 6,2: 57–99.

— (n.d.) *Crooked Eclipses*, unpublished play.

Bond, E. (1972) *Lear*, London: Methuen.

— (1982) *The Sea*, London: Methuen.

Bottomley, G. (1980) *Gruach and Britain's Daughter: Two Plays*, Great Neck, NY: Roth Pub.

Brecht, B. (1966) *Roundheads and Peakheads*, in *The Jungle of Cities and Other Plays*, New York: Grove.

Carlin, M. (1969) *Not Now, Sweet Desdemona: A Duologue for Black and White Within the Realm of Shakespeare's* Othello, Nairobi: Oxford University Press.

Carlson, M. (1978) *Goethe and the Weimar Theatre*, Ithaca: Cornell University Press.

Césaire, A. (1992) *A Tempest*, New York: Ubu Repertory Theater Publications.

Chaurette, N. (1992) *The Queens*, Toronto: Coach House Press.

Clark, S. (ed.) (1997) *Shakespeare Made Fit: Restoration Adaptations of Shakespeare*, London: J. M. Dent.

Davenant, W. (1968) *Works of Sir William Davenant*, North Stratford, NH: Ayer Co. Pub. Inc.

Dowling, M. (n.d.) *Othello Travestie, an Operatic Burlesque Burletta*, London: Lacey's Acting Editions.

Dubois, R.-D. *Pericles, Prince of Tyre, by William Shakespeare*, unpublished play.

Garrick, D. (1981) *The Plays of David Garrick*, Carbondale: Southern Illinois University Press.

Gass, K. (1997) *Claudius*, Saint Paul, MN: Consortium Book Sales and Dist.

Grass, G. (1966) *The Plebeians Rehearse the Uprising*, New York: Harcourt, Brace, & World.

Ionesco, E. (1989) *Macbett*, New York: French and European Publications Inc.

Jarry, A. (1968) *Ubu Roi*, in S. M. Taylor (ed.) *The Ubu Plays*, New York: Grove Weidenfeld.

Lepage, R. *Elsinore*, unpublished play.

Love's Fire: Seven New Plays Inspired by Seven Shakespearean Sonnets (1998) New York: William Morrow.

MacDonald, A.-M. (1990) *Goodnight Desdemona (Good Morning Juliet)*, Toronto: Coach House Press.

MacKaye, P. (1916) *Caliban by the Yellow Sands*, Garden City, N.Y.: Doubleday.

Malouf, D. (1988) *Blood Relations*, Sydney: Currency.

Marowitz, C. (1978) *The Marowitz Shakespeare*, London: Marion Boyars.

Mitchell, K. (1977) *Cruel Tears*, Vancouver: Talonbooks Ltd.

Nicoll, A. (ed.), Nicoll, J. (ed.), and Holinshed, R. (1959) *Holinshed's Chronicles As Used in Shakespeare's Plays*, London: Dent.

Osborne, J. (1973) *A Place Calling Itself Rome*, London: Faber & Faber.

Renan, E. (1911) *Caliban*, Queensborough, NY: Marion Press.

Shaw, G.B. (1914) *The Dark Lady of the Sonnets*, London: Constable.

— (1926) *Caesar and Cleopatra*, London: Constable.

— (1950) *Shakes versus Shav*, London: Constable.

Stoppard, T. (1967) *Rosencrantz and Guildenstern Are Dead*, New York: Grove.

— (1976) *The Fifteen-Minute Hamlet*, London: Samuel French.

— (1996) *Tom Stoppard Plays 1: The Real Inspector Hound, Dirty Linen, Dogg's Hamlet, Cahoot's Macbeth*, London: Faber & Faber.

Thompson, J. (1997) *A Lion in the Streets*, Saint Paul, MN: Consortium Book Sales and Dist.

Walcott, D. (1986) *A Branch of the Blue Nile*, in *Three Plays*, NewYork: Farrar.

Wells, S. N. (ed.) (1977) *Nineteenth-Century Shakespeare Burlesques*, London: Diploma Press.

Williams, S. (ed.) (1990) *Shakespeare on the German Stage*, vol. 1, Cambridge: Cambridge University Press.